TEST PREP SERIES

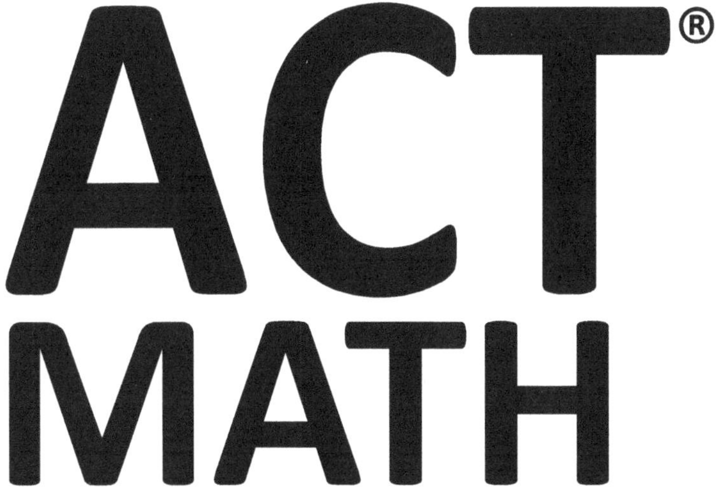

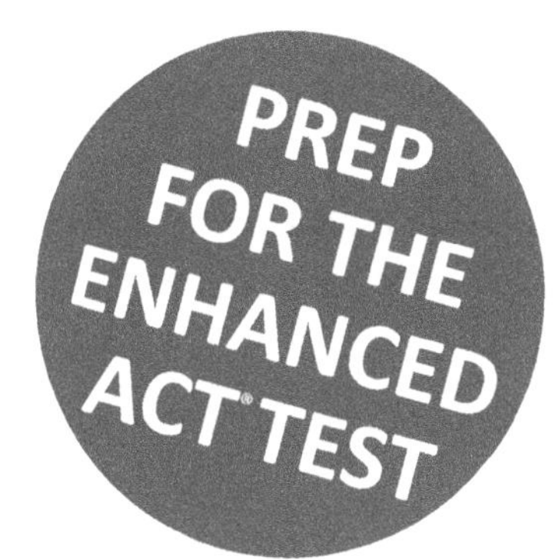

PRACTICE QUESTIONS 2025-2026

- 650+ practice questions
- 2 full-length Math practice tests
- Detailed answer explanations
- Perfect for individual self-study or classroom instruction

Scan the QR Code to access Online Resources
bit.ly/ACT-MPQ

ACT® Math Practice Questions

Published by Vibrant Publishers LLC, USA, **www.vibrantpublishers.com**

Paperback ISBN 13: 978-1-63651-505-2
Ebook ISBN 13: 978-1-63651-566-3

Library of Congress Control Number: 2025939622

Vibrant Publishers' books are available at special quantity discounts for sales promotions, or for use in corporate training programs. For more information, please write to **bulkorders@vibrantpublishers.com**

Please email feedback/corrections (technical, grammatical, or spelling) to **spellerrors@vibrantpublishers.com**

Vibrant publishes in a variety of print and electronic formats and by print-on-demand. Some material included with standard print versions of this book may not be included in e-books or in print-on-demand. To access the complete catalog of Vibrant Publishers, visit **www.vibrantpublishers.com**

This page is intentionally left blank

Table of Contents

How to Use This Book

Welcome to your ultimate resource for conquering the ACT Math section! Whether you are just beginning your preparation or looking to refine your skills, this book is designed to help you improve your mathematical thinking, boost your confidence, and maximize your ACT Math score through targeted and strategic practice.

The ACT Math section can be challenging, but with focused practice and consistent review, you can master the skills it tests. This book offers **650+ high-quality practice questions**, **two full-length math practice tests**, and an **online ACT Math cheat sheet** to support your preparation. It is structured to offer both comprehensive topic-based practice and real-test simulation, so you are fully prepared on exam day.

Let's walk through how to use this book to get the best results.

1. Start with the Basics

Before jumping into practice questions, it's important to understand what you're preparing for. The book begins with two introductory chapters:

- **About the ACT**: This section gives you an overview of the Enhanced ACT as a whole—its structure, timing, scoring, and how the Math section fits into the test.
- **Overview of the ACT Math Section**: Here, you'll find a breakdown of the types of questions, content areas, and skills tested in ACT Math. This chapter outlines key topics like algebra, functions, geometry, and statistics, as well as test-taking strategies specific to math.

Reading these chapters first will help you gain a clear understanding of what the test demands and how to tailor your study plan accordingly.

2. Understand the Book's Structure

The core of this book is divided into **five chapters**, each aligned with the official ACT Math content categories:

1. **Number and Quantity**
2. **Algebra**
3. **Functions**
4. **Geometry**
5. **Statistics and Probability**

Each chapter contains a variety of problems that range from basic to advanced difficulty. The goal is to reinforce conceptual understanding and expose you to the different question formats you'll see on test day.

In addition to these chapters, the book includes:

- **Two full-length ACT Math practice tests**, found at the end of the book. These simulate real exam conditions and allow you to apply what you've learned.
  An online ACT Math cheat sheet, a handy resource that compiles essential formulas, rules, and strategies in a clear and concise format for quick reference.

3. Create a Study Plan

Because this book includes hundreds of practice questions, it's important to create a personalized and realistic study schedule. Your plan will depend on how much time you have before your test date.

- **If you have 3 months**: Spend one to two weeks per chapter, followed by review and timed tests in the final weeks.
- **If you have 6 months or more**: Spread out the chapters over several months, with light, consistent practice followed by deeper review later.

You'll find detailed 3-month and 6-month study plans later in the book to guide you through this process. Both plans balance topic-specific study with full-length practice tests and built-in review time.

Be sure to adjust the schedule to suit your personal strengths and weaknesses. If you know that geometry or functions are weak areas, spend extra time on those topics early in your prep.

4. Practice Actively, Not Passively

To get the most out of each practice session, follow these strategies:

- **Don't rush**: Try each problem before looking at the answer. Give yourself time to think through the question logically.
- **Check your work**: Review not just the correct answer but also *why* it's correct. Even if you got the question right, ask yourself: Was it luck or understanding?
- **Track your mistakes**: Keep a notebook or spreadsheet of every incorrect answer. Note what type of question it was and what went wrong—was it a conceptual misunderstanding, a calculation error, or a misreading of the question?
- **Revisit errors**: After every few study sessions, go back to your mistake log and try those questions again. Reinforcing these areas is essential to improving.

5. Use the Online Math Cheat Sheet

The **online ACT Math cheat sheet** summarizes key formulas and rules for every topic tested on the ACT. It's perfect for quick reference when you forget a concept or need a refresher before a practice session.

How to use it effectively:

- **Before practice**: Glance through the relevant formulas or rules for the topic you're working on.
- **During review**: Use it to identify whether you missed a question because you forgot a formula or misunderstood a concept.
- **Before the test**: Print or save a copy on your device and go over it multiple times in the days leading up to the exam.

This cheat sheet is designed to save you time and keep essential information at your fingertips.

6. Take the Full-Length Practice Tests

At the back of the book, you'll find **two full-length ACT Math practice tests**. These are structured to match the Enhanced ACT in terms of:

- **Number of questions**: 45 questions per test
- **Time limit**: 50 minutes

You can use an approved calculator when appearing for these tests. See Chapter 2 for a list of approved calculators on the ACT.

These practice tests are vital to:

- Build test-taking endurance
- Practice pace and time management
- Apply strategies across a wide mix of topics

Simulate real testing conditions: find a quiet space, use a timer, and complete the test without interruptions. Afterward, thoroughly review every answer—both right and wrong—to refine your strategy.

7. Be Consistent and Flexible

Consistency is the key to success. It's better to study for 30 minutes several days a week than to cram for hours in one sitting. Build a routine you can stick to, and hold yourself accountable by tracking your progress.

At the same time, be flexible. If you're feeling burned out, scale back your sessions. If you're ahead of schedule, challenge yourself with mixed-topic question sets or increase your practice test frequency.

Here are a few flexible study ideas:

- Solve 10–15 questions daily from any topic
- Review the cheat sheet during commutes or breaks
- Focus on a single topic over a weekend (e.g., Geometry Saturday)
- Pair up with a study buddy and quiz each other on formulas or strategies

Final Thoughts

This book is more than just a collection of practice problems—it's a complete toolkit for ACT Math success. When used consistently and strategically, it will help you strengthen your core math skills, overcome common traps, and approach the test with confidence.

Use the content chapters to master one topic at a time. Use the practice tests to measure your progress. Use the online cheat sheet to stay sharp. And most importantly, use your mistakes as learning opportunities.

Stay persistent, stay positive, and trust the process. You've got this!

3-Month ACT Math Study Plan

Ideal for: Students preparing for the ACT within 10–12 weeks. This plan is focused, efficient, and includes weekly review and full-length tests.

This plan is designed based on the format of this book, but you can easily adapt it to suit any other book or resource by customizing it to meet your specific needs.

Overview:

- **Duration**: 12 weeks
- **Weekly Commitment**: 4–5 sessions/week (1 to 1.5 hours each)
- **Goal**: Cover all Math topics + take two practice tests + review effectively

Weeks 1–2: Kickoff & Diagnostic

- Read the *About the ACT* and *Overview of ACT Math Section* chapters.
- Explore the **online cheat sheet** to review essential formulas.
- Take **Practice Test 1** (timed). Use it as a diagnostic to identify weak areas.
- Analyze your results and log your strengths and weaknesses.
- Start with **Number and Quantity** (complete ~60 questions).

Weeks 3–4: Number and Quantity + Algebra

- Finish the remaining **Number and Quantity** questions.
- Begin **Algebra** (~60 questions in Week 4).
- Start reviewing one mistake set per week.
- Use the cheat sheet to reinforce concepts between sessions.

Weeks 5–6: Finish Algebra + Start Functions

- Complete all **Algebra** questions (~125 total).
- Begin **Functions** (first 50 questions).
- Do one **mixed-topic timed set** each week (10–15 questions).
- Update your error log weekly.

Weeks 7–8: Finish Functions + Start Geometry

- Complete the **Functions** chapter.
- Begin **Geometry** (~60 questions).
- Review past errors and revisit weak question types.

Weeks 9–10: Finish Geometry + Start Statistics

- Finish the remaining **Geometry** questions.
- Begin **Statistics and Probability** (~60 questions).
- Skim cheat sheet formulas for geometry and stats during warmups.

Week 11: Review & Mixed Practice

- Complete the remaining **Statistics and Probability** questions.
- Reinforce common ACT traps, formulas, and weak areas.

Week 12: Final Test & Strategy Tune-up

- Take **Practice Test 2** (full timed simulation).
- Thoroughly review all answers—log any recurring errors.
- Revisit the cheat sheet daily.
- In the last few sessions, focus on pacing, calculator strategy, and mental math.

6-Month ACT Math Study Plan

Ideal for: Students with more time to prepare, aiming for a slower pace and deeper review alongside school and other commitments.

This plan is designed based on the format of this book, but you can easily adapt it to suit any other book or resource by customizing it to meet your specific needs

Overview:

- **Duration**: 24 weeks
- **Weekly Commitment**: 2–3 sessions/week (45 mins to 1 hour)
- **Goal**: Strengthen conceptual understanding + reduce test-day anxiety

Month 1: Orientation + Light Practice

- Read *About the ACT* and *Overview of ACT Math Section* chapters.
- Explore the **online cheat sheet**.
- Take **Practice Test 1** as a diagnostic.
- Begin **Number and Quantity** (aim for 25–30 questions per week).

Month 2: Deepen Number and Quantity + Intro to Algebra

- Finish **Number and Quantity**.
- Start **Algebra** (~30–40 questions).
- Create flashcards for rules you often forget.
- Spend one session per week reviewing previous mistakes.

Month 3: Complete Algebra + Start Functions

- Finish all **Algebra** questions (~125 total).
- Begin **Functions** (~20–30 questions).
- Start weekly **timed sets** (10 questions in 10 minutes).
- Use the cheat sheet regularly for quick review.

Month 4: Continue Functions + Begin Geometry

- Finish **Functions**.
- Begin **Geometry** (~50 questions).
- Alternate practice sessions: one day for practice questions, one day for review.

Month 5: Finish Geometry + Statistics and Probability

- Complete remaining **Geometry**.
- Start **Statistics and Probability** (~30–40 questions).
- Create a running error log and categorize your mistakes.
- Review cheat sheet once a week.

Month 6: Final Review + Full-Length Practice

- Finish **Statistics and Probability**.
- Spend two weeks doing **mixed-topic timed sets**.
  Take **Practice Test 2** (timed).
- Analyze your results deeply: pacing, accuracy, error patterns.
- Spend last week reinforcing weak topics, reviewing formulas, and simulating final test-day conditions.

Chapter 1

About the ACT®

College admissions are highly competitive and multi-layered. In addition to your high school GPA, extracurricular involvement, letters of recommendation from teachers and mentors, admission interviews, and personal essays, standardized test scores remain a crucial component of your application. The ACT and SAT are among the most commonly accepted standardized tests for college applications. Both are designed to assess a student's academic readiness for college.

The ACT continues to be available in both online and paper-pencil formats. However, the online test has undergone a few major changes. While the initial rollout of the enhanced ACT began in April 2025 for students in the U.S. who opt for online testing, international students will have access to the updated format starting in September 2025. This includes both online and paper-based versions of the test. The enhanced test is shorter, and you will have the option to skip the science test. This change gives you more control over your test while still helping you meet the essential requirements for college.

NOTE: The 5 sections on the ACT exam are called "tests" (English test, Mathematics test, and so on).

Quick Glance at the ACT Enhancements

- **Test format:** There are now **44 fewer questions** in total.
- **Test duration:** You can now finish the main tests in **125 minutes** instead of 195 and still receive a college-reportable Composite score. Each question now allows for more time, giving you a better pace during the test.
- **Choices:** In the Math test, questions offer **four answer choices** instead of five.
- **Optional science test:** You can now decide whether or not to take the Science test. For state and district testing, the schools or testing programs will decide whether to include the science test.
- **Scoring:** The Composite score will include only English, Math, and Reading. If you choose to take the Science test, that score will be reported separately.
- **Test day:** If you choose to take only the English, Math, and Reading tests, you will be dismissed after the Reading test is complete.

But Wait—What is the ACT?

The ACT is an assessment that evaluates how well you have mastered essential academic subjects that play a key role in college and career success. These include English, mathematics, reading, science, and writing.

It is an achievement test that focuses on what you have learned through regular classroom instruction throughout your school years. The test is designed and developed using inputs from educators, curriculum specialists, and college faculty members by using a variety of tools such as classroom surveys and curriculum standards guides, thus making it a precise and reliable diagnostic tool.

Each part of the ACT is meticulously designed to assess specific skills and knowledge gained over time. Thus, **the ACT is meant to reflect long-term learning, not short-term preparation.**

The ACT comprises the following tests:

- English
- Math
- Reading
- Science (optional)
- Writing (optional)

NOTE: The option to take the ACT with or without science is only available with online testing during the April, June, and July 2025 test dates. When taking a paper test, Science will be included as part of the testing experience.

Who Should Take the ACT?

The ACT is typically taken by students in grades 10 through 12, with most choosing to take it during their junior or senior year, after finishing the majority of their core academic subjects. However, some students opt to take it as early as sophomore year, especially if they're aiming for college credit, advanced placement, or honors-level classes.

Why is the Test Taken?

The ACT may be taken for several important reasons. Largely, it is taken for college admissions, helping universities assess your college readiness. Additionally, many scholarships rely on ACT scores as part of their eligibility criteria. The test is also used for placement purposes, determining which courses a student is best suited for in college. In some states, it is a requirement to meet graduation standards. Sometimes, companies also use the ACT for their placement drives. Overall, the ACT serves as a valuable tool for students pursuing higher education and various other academic opportunities.

ACT vs. SAT—Which is Better?

Test-takers are always left confused about whether to take the ACT or the SAT. While both test your college readiness and are widely recognized assessments for college admissions across the world, the chief differences lie in their format, scoring, and what they emphasize.

Aspect	ACT	SAT
Total Test Time	2 hours 20 minutes + Optional 35 minutes for Science test + Optional 40-minute essay	2 hours 14 minutes
Subject Balance	English, Math, Reading, Science, and Essay writing	Reading, Writing, and Math

Aspect	ACT	SAT
Breaks	Students taking the optional Science or Writing tests will remain in the room after the main test, while others are dismissed. A short break is given before each 40-minute test. Science includes 40 questions (40 min); Writing consists of one prompt. All additional testing is done in the same room, with breaks and material changes between tests.	10-minute break between Reading & Writing and Math sections
Scoring	Scored on a scale of 1-36 for each test, with a Composite score (average of tests)	Scored on a scale of 400-1600. The Reading & Writing and Math sections each use a scale of 200-800 and are combined for a total score.
Mode	Both paper-and-pencil and online tests	Only online testing
Strengths	Ideal for students who excel in a broad range of subjects and prefer a fast-paced test that tests generic academic skills	Best for students who are strong in reading comprehension and critical reasoning, with less emphasis on the science subject, and who prefer a slower-paced test
Question Difficulty	Each test has a fixed length, and question difficulty remains constantly mixed throughout the test	The second module of each section adjusts in difficulty based on performance in the first module

Testing Format

The Old Paper-and-Pencil Format

The traditional paper-and-pencil format of the ACT was the standard testing method for many years. In this format, students received a physical test booklet and answer sheet. They filled in their answers by bubbling in responses with a pencil. This format requires no digital tools or devices, with all calculations and note-taking done manually.

The New Digital Format

The new and enhanced digital format of the ACT offers several features designed for a smooth, accessible, and inclusive testing experience. Some of the features include:

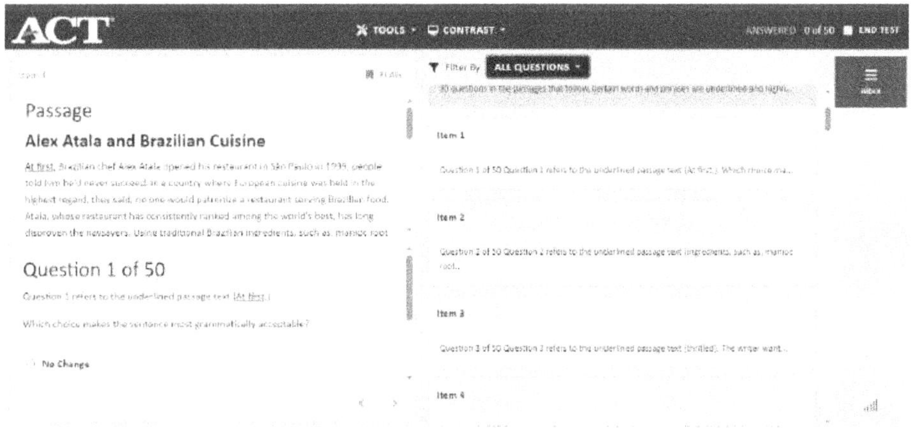

Clear interface with a navigation bar

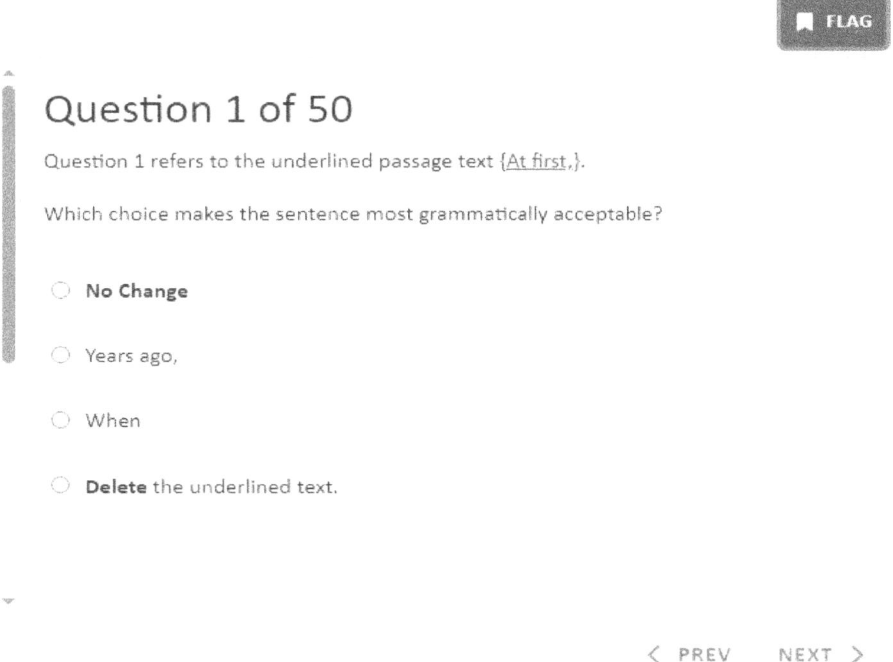

Option for flagging questions to revisit later

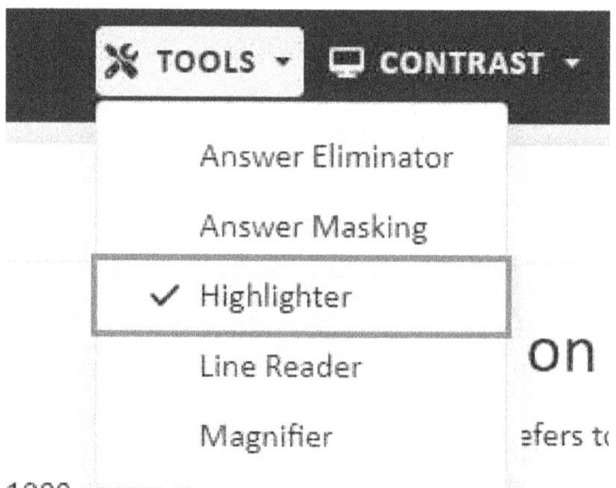

On-screen highlighter to mark important text

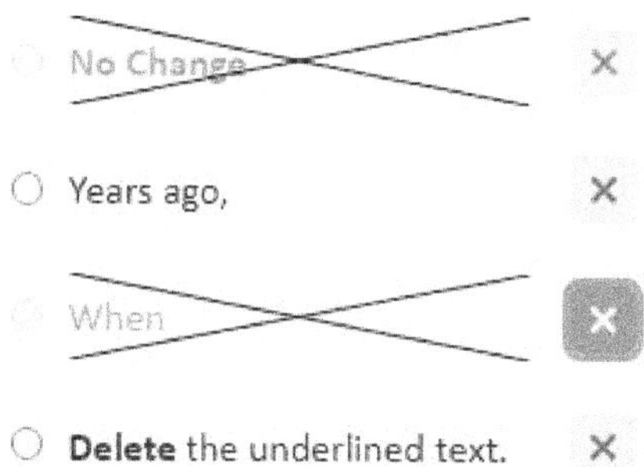

Answer eliminator

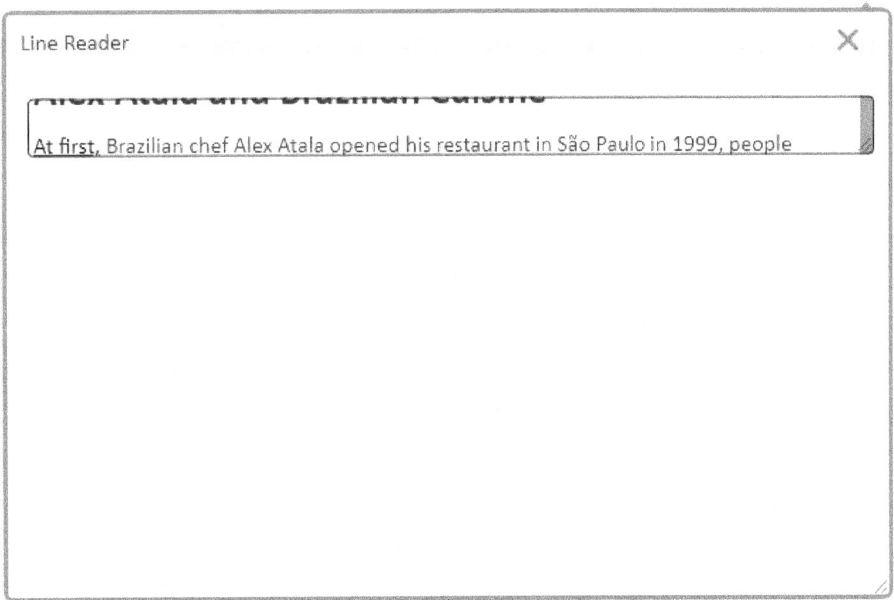

Line reader to isolate text for easier reading

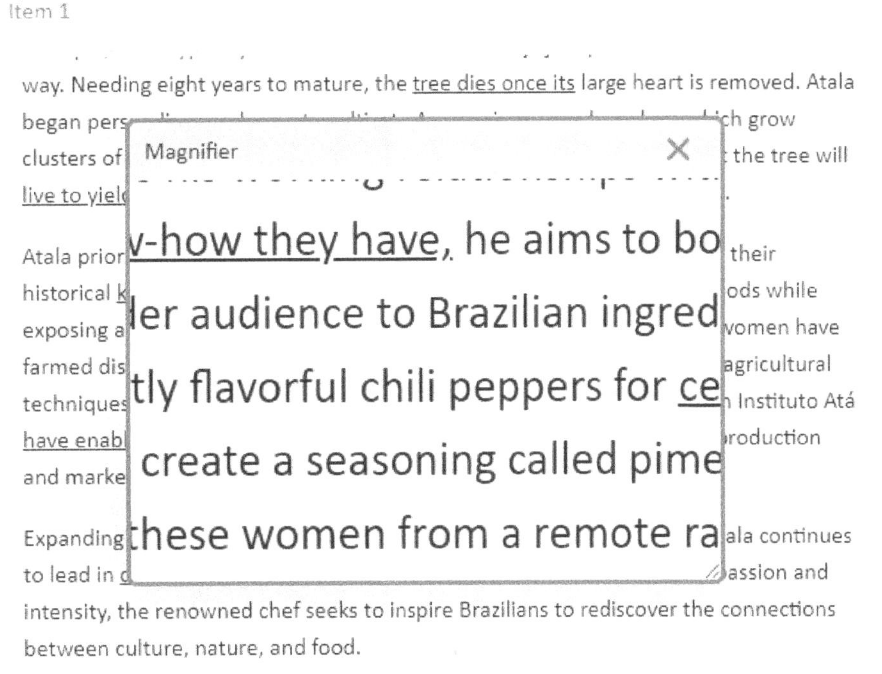

Screen magnifier

Answer masking tool to hide answer choices and focus on the question stem

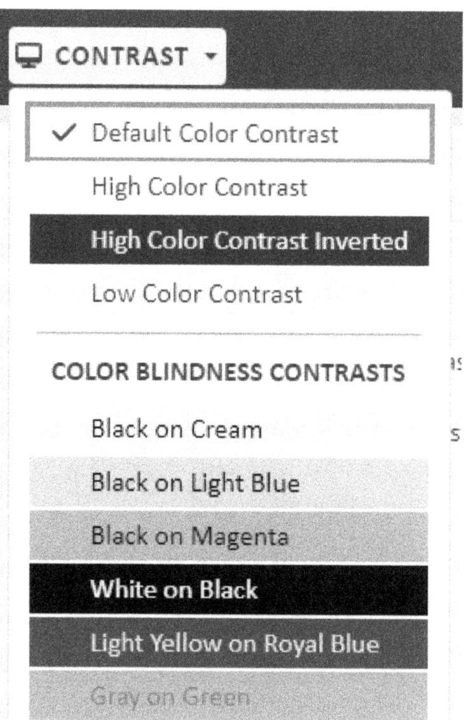

Contrast adjustments for students with visual impairments

Before appearing for the ACT, familiarize yourself with the online test's interface. The ACT offers 1 online full-length test on their website in timed and untimed versions (https://www.act.org/content/act/en/products-and-services/the-act/test-changes/online-testing/sample-questions.html). Take this test in the timed version to simulate the test experience and the untimed version to get familiar with the features and question types.

Why Are These Enhancements Happening?

These enhancements are part of ACT's ongoing commitment to improvement, aligning with industry best practices and fostering innovation to support your academic success more efficiently and further streamline the process of college admissions. The goal is to provide a test-taking experience that aligns with your unique skillset, ensuring that you can perform your best on test day.

When Will the Enhanced ACT Be Applicable Worldwide?

The enhancements will be available for online test-takers worldwide starting with the April 2025 test. The paper version will incorporate these changes beginning in September 2025. Schools and districts in the U.S. will have access to these options starting in the spring of 2026.

What is Staying the Same?

While the ACT continues to evolve, there are some aspects that remain unaffected. Let's take a quick look at what is staying the same.

- The section order will remain the same.

  English → Mathematics → Reading → Science (optional) → Writing (optional)
- The types of skills assessed in the test will not change.
- The overall scoring scale will continue to be 1–36.
- Scores from previous ACTs will not be affected by the introduction of the new Composite score.
- Individual subject scores, along with their corresponding test dates, will still be reported.
- The scoring window will stay the same, with results typically released within two to eight weeks.
- Both paper-and-pencil and online testing formats will still be available.
- The optional Writing test will continue to be offered.
- The ACT's ability to predict success in first-year college credit-bearing courses will remain consistent.

Test Availability, Registration, and Test Dates

You can register for the ACT through the official ACT website (https://www.act.org/), where you'll choose your preferred test date and location after creating an account with a valid email address and a proper photograph. See the photo checklist for more

PHOTO CHECKLIST	
✓	Portrait-oriented
✓	Full face and shoulders visible
✓	Head cover for religious reasons is allowed but it should allow a clear full-face view
✓	Plain background
✗	Edits
✗	Blurred
✗	Filters
✗	Dark glasses
✗	Text or stickers on photo
✗	Too much light, shadows, busy background

The ACT is offered seven times a year in the U.S. (February, April, June, July, September, October, December) and five times internationally (February, April, June, September, October). Test centers are available across various regions, and you can use the ACT Test Center Locator on the website to find one near you. Some schools also offer the ACT on designated school days, but availability may vary by school.

For all the updated information on the test, visit the official website: https://www.act.org/content/act/en/products-and-services/the-act/registration.html

Registration Fees and Fee Waivers

Here is a quick breakdown of the ACT costs:

	Fee	Details
The ACT Test	$65.00	The ACT Test includes the English, Math, and Reading tests.
Writing Add-On Fee	$25.00	Can be added or removed through the late deadline.
Science Add-On Fee	$4.00	Can be added or removed through the late deadline.

[**NOTE:** All fees are non-refundable unless otherwise noted.]

Additional costs

You can add these costs to the test fee (except for the test center change) for the services detailed below:

	Fee	Details
Late registration	$38.00	This is the fee for modifications to registration or test dates completed during the late registration window for a national test date.
Standby testing	$69.00	This fee is refunded if you are denied admission to the test center on test day or if your registration is canceled due to a missing photo.
Change fee	$44.00	This fee includes costs for making changes to the test form, test date, or test center.
Score reports to 5th and 6th college choices	$19.00	This fee is for sending score reports to your 5th and 6th college choices, and you need to request it online before your test date. It is refundable upon written request if you don't test.
Additional score reports	$19.00	This fee is for sending additional score reports after registration. You can request this online anytime after registration.
ACT My Answer Key (TIR)	$32.00	This fee is for ordering the ACT My Answer Key (TIR) prior to the test.
	$40.00	This applies if the order for the ACT My Answer Key (TIR) is placed after testing.
Score verification	$61.00	This fee is for verifying multiple-choice test scores.
	$61.00	This fee is for verifying writing test scores.
	$122.00	This fee is for verifying both multiple-choice and writing test scores.

[**NOTE**: If you make changes to your test registration, certain fees—such as those for sending scores to a 5th or 6th college, requesting additional score reports, or ordering the Test Information Release (TIR)—will be adjusted to match current pricing. The original amount you paid will be automatically refunded, and the updated fee will be charged accordingly.]

Who Can Apply for a Fee Waiver?

To qualify for the ACT fee waiver, you must be a current 11th or 12th grade student enrolled in high school. You should be testing in the U.S., its territories, or Puerto Rico. Fee waiver eligibility in the ACT is based on financial need. Therefore, you must meet at least one of the following criteria:

- Receive free or reduced-price lunch at school (based on US Department of Agriculture [USDA] income levels)
- Participate in a federally funded program for economically disadvantaged students (like GEAR UP or Upward Bound)
- Live in a foster home
- Be a ward of the state or legally homeless
- Receive public assistance

- Live in subsidized housing
- Have a family income that falls within USDA income guidelines

To apply for an ACT fee waiver, start by checking with your school counselor to confirm your eligibility. If you qualify, you can receive up to four fee waivers to take the ACT for free, along with access to free learning resources. When registering for the ACT—either online or by mail—be sure to use your assigned fee waiver code.

Let us deep dive into the test components of the ACT and see what each test comprises:

Test	Number of Questions	Time Per Test	Time Per Question	What's tested
English	50	35	1.42 mins	Demonstrates your ability to revise and edit a variety of short texts and essays across different genres. It reflects your grasp of grammar, punctuation, sentence structure, and rhetorical skills typically taught in high school.
Mathematics	45	50	1.11 min	Assesses the mathematical knowledge and skills commonly acquired through courses up to the beginning of 12th grade. This includes algebra, geometry, functions, statistics, and some elements of trigonometry, emphasizing problem-solving and reasoning abilities.
Reading	36	40	1.11 mins	Measures your ability to read and understand complex texts, reason logically using textual evidence, and synthesize information from multiple passages. It reflects your reading comprehension and critical thinking skills essential for college-level work.
Science (Optional)	40	40	1.14 mins	Evaluates your interpretation, analysis, evaluation, and problem-solving skills within the context of natural sciences, including biology, chemistry, physics, and Earth/space science. It focuses on your ability to work with data, draw conclusions, and apply scientific reasoning rather than recall specific facts.

Test	Number of Questions	Time Per Test	Time Per Question	What's tested
Writing (Optional)	1	40	40 mins	Tests your ability to write a clear, well-organized essay that develops a perspective on a given issue. It mirrors the writing skills emphasized in high school, including ideation, analysis, argument development, organization, and language use according to conventions.

Scoring of the ACT

While ACT strives to deliver scores promptly, within the standard two-to-eight-week window, an exact release date cannot be guaranteed. Your results will be shared with the colleges and high school you selected at registration, and you'll also be able to view them through your official ACT web account.

How ACT Scores are Calculated

First, ACT counts how many questions you answered correctly on each test—there's no deduction for incorrect answers. These raw scores are then converted into scaled scores ranging from 1 (low) to 36 (high), which makes results comparable across different test dates.

Your Composite score is the average of your scores in English, Math, and Reading tests, rounded to the nearest whole number. The Science and the Writing tests, if taken, will be scored separately.

For the calculation of your Writing score, the ACT follows a definite process. First, the ACT provides a sample prompt along with six possible responses, ranging from weak to strong, to give you a clear idea of how to maximize your score. Your writing score will be based on four key domains: Ideas and Analysis, Development and Support, Organization, and Language Use and Conventions. Each of these domains is scored on a scale of 2 to 12. The final domain score is determined by averaging the ratings from two independent readers, each scoring on a scale of 1 to 6.

You'll also see a breakdown of how you performed in different skill areas (called reporting categories), including how many questions you answered correctly and your percentage of correct responses.

Sending Scores to Colleges

You can send ACT scores from test dates dating back to September 2011 (for general tests and till September 2016 for the Writing test), including available superscores, to colleges and scholarship agencies. These scores are delivered to valid college codes provided by the recipients.

Additionally, you can send scores from September 2018 onward to your high school as an additional score report. If your superscore is from these dates, you may also request to send it. All scores are delivered electronically via ACT's online reporting services platform.

Reporting Categories

Test	Test Number of Questions	Reporting Categories
English	50	• Production of Writing (29-32%) • Knowledge of Language (15-17%) • Conventions of Standard English (52-55%)
Mathematics	45	• Preparing for Higher Math (57-60%) • Number & Quantity (7–10%) • Algebra (12–15%) • Functions (12–15%) • Geometry (12–15%) • Statistics & Probability (8–12%) • Essential Skills (40-43%) • Modeling
Reading	36	• Key Ideas and Details (52-60%) • Craft and Structure (25-30%) • Integration of Knowledge and Ideas (13-23%)
Science (Optional)	40	• Interpretation of Data (40-50%) • Scientific Investigation (20-30%) • Evaluation of Models, Inferences, and Experimental Results (25-35%)
Writing (Optional)	1	• Ideas and Analysis (25%) • Development and Support (25%) • Organization (25%) • Language Use (25%)

Superscoring

Your ACT superscore is calculated by averaging your highest scores from each of the four tests—English, Mathematics, Reading, and Science—across all your ACT test attempts. This composite score is rounded to the nearest whole number. ACT superscoring allows you to present your highest possible composite score by combining your top subject scores from multiple test attempts. This method is advantageous for test takers aiming to showcase their strongest performance across all tests. To be eligible for a superscore, you must have taken the ACT at least twice since September 2016.

Automatic Delivery of Your Superscore Reports

While your ACT scores are automatically sent to the colleges and high school you selected during registration, plans can change. You can still send your ACT scores to additional colleges or scholarship agencies even after the test day.

Sending Your Superscore

To send your superscore to colleges or scholarship agencies, log in to your MyACT account. From there, you can request to send your superscore along with scores from the individual test events that comprise it. Once your scores (including Writing, if applicable) are available, requests are automatically processed—usually on the same day—ensuring timely delivery to your chosen recipients.

Considerations for Colleges

Not all colleges accept superscores. While many institutions do, it's important to check each college's admissions policy to understand how they consider ACT scores.

Inside the ACT: What's Tested

After understanding the ACT at a broad level, let us learn more about the finer nuances of each test in the ACT exam.

English Test

The ACT English test features **6-7 passages and 50 multiple-choice questions** to be completed in **35 minutes.** The passages will be of two types: long and short. The longer passages will be around 350 words and will ask 10 questions based on them, while the shorter passages will be around 180-190 words and will have 5 questions. Each passage is carefully chosen for its engaging and relatable content, showcasing a variety of rhetorical styles and genres to showcase different writing contexts. Your overall score is based on your performance across all questions, and you'll also receive three sub-scores that highlight specific skill areas. The skills/domains that are tested in the English test are as follows:

Production of Writing	**Topic development in terms of purpose and focus**	You will be required to assess how relevant certain details are to the overall topic or main idea of a written text. Additionally, you will be required to recognize the intent behind specific words or phrases, such as their role in identifying a person, defining a term, or describing an object. The test will also evaluate whether the passage successfully achieves its intended purpose or goal. Furthermore, you may need to select a word, phrase, or sentence that effectively communicates a particular emotion, attitude, or concept, or helps to clarify a given point or statement.
	Organization, unity, and cohesion	You will need to assess when transition words or phrases are necessary to clarify relationships of time or logic. Additionally, you must determine the best position for sentences within a paragraph or the overall passage, as well as identify appropriate introductions and conclusions for paragraphs. You may also be asked to rearrange sentences or paragraphs to create a more logical flow or to divide a paragraph in the most effective way to meet a specific goal.
Knowledge of Language	This domain assess your ability to communicate in a clear and lucid manner in writing. This includes revising unclear or awkward sentences, eliminating unnecessary words, ensuring consistency in style and tone, identifying logical connections between clauses, and selecting the most fitting words or phrases to convey the sentence's meaning.	
Conventions of Standard English	This domain evaluates your ability to correct sentence structure issues, such as fixing run-on sentences, misplaced modifiers, and verb tense shifts, etc. You will also need to recognize and apply appropriate parts of speech, maintain consistency in verb tense, voice, and pronoun person usage, and ensure proper sentence coordination and clarity.	

Mathematics Test

The ACT Math test includes **45 multiple-choice questions** to be completed in **50 minutes**. It assesses your ability to reason through and solve real-world math problems, focusing on key concepts essential for success in college-level math. While a strong grasp of fundamental math skills and concepts is expected, the test does not require memorization of advanced formulas or lengthy calculations. Some questions may be grouped around the same data set, such as a graph or chart. It is essential to note that the use of an approved calculator is permitted during this test.

In Mathematics, the reporting criteria that make up this test are as follows:

Preparing for Higher Mathematics (PHM)	**Number and Quantity**	The **Number and Quantity** questions, will test you on fundamental operations with whole numbers, decimals, fractions, and rational numbers. You'll need to understand place value, factors, ordering, patterns, and properties of numbers, including exponents, complex numbers, and irrational numbers. The test also includes questions on absolute value, distance on the number line and coordinate plane, matrix operations, vectors, and rational exponents. This section checks your ability to reason numerically and apply core mathematical principles.
	Algebra and Functions	The **Algebra and Functions** questions test your ability to solve equations, work with expressions, and understand functions. You'll solve linear, quadratic, and polynomial equations, factor, use exponents and scientific notation, and interpret graphs. Function-related questions will assess your understanding of patterns, domains, ranges, function notation, and transformations. You'll also evaluate functions and apply them to real-world situations.
	Geometry	**Geometry** questions focus on understanding and applying properties of shapes, figures, and measurements. You'll work with points, lines, angles, triangles, polygons, and 3D objects to solve problems involving length, perimeter, area, surface area, and volume. Key skills include using geometric formulas, angle relationships, symmetry, and coordinate geometry.
	Statistics and Probability	**Statistics and Probability** questions assess your ability to interpret, analyze, and draw conclusions from numerical data. You'll be expected to calculate averages, weighted means, and missing values, as well as convert and interpret data from tables, charts, and graphs. Understanding and applying principles of probability, demonstrating your knowledge of basic counting techniques, and interpreting various statistical charts are necessary. Overall, this section emphasizes critical thinking and precision when working with data.

Integrating Essential Skills	**Modeling**	**Modeling** involves using mathematics to create models that represent real-world situations, helping us predict or understand them better. This category includes questions that require students to produce, interpret, understand, evaluate, and improve models. Each modeling question is also counted in the relevant mathematical categories, making this category a comprehensive measure of a student's ability to apply modeling skills across various mathematical concepts.

Reading Test

The Reading Test consists of **4 passages and 36 questions** (three long passages and one passage split into two to be completed in 40 minutes), which are usually reflective of the type of texts typically found in first-year college courses. Each passage will have **9 questions** based on it. The passages include literary narratives and informational texts from a variety of domains such as the humanities, natural sciences, and social sciences. Of the two, one passage may include a mixed-information format, incorporating visual elements like graphs, diagrams, and tables that provide additional context. The passages are usually asked in the following order:

Literary Narrative → Social Science → Humanities → Natural Science

The Reading test measures your reading comprehension in three general areas:

Key Ideas and Details	**Close reading**	Close-reading skills assess your ability to locate and interpret key details in a passage, draw logical conclusions, and paraphrase statements effectively. You might also be asked to identify the correct sequence of events, understand cause-and-effect relationships, and recognize both stated and implied comparisons within the text.
	Central ideas, themes, and summaries	Questions on central ideas, themes, and summaries test your ability to identify or infer the main idea of a paragraph or passage, its overarching themes, differentiate between key ideas and extraneous details, grasp the core message, and effectively summarize important information.

Craft and Structure	**Word meanings and word choice**	Reading questions in this category test your ability to understand the meaning or impact of specific words and phrases. This includes using context to determine technical, academic, or connotative meanings, understanding the implications of specific words, or interpreting figurative and descriptive language.
	Text structure	Text-structure questions require you to analyze how the structure of a passage serves its purpose. This may involve examining the overall structure, understanding how specific sentences relate to the passage as a whole, identifying the function of paragraphs, and determining the effect of particular words or phrases within the passage.
	Purpose and point of view	Purpose and point of view questions assess your ability to identify or infer the author's or narrator's purpose or intent, understand how this purpose influences the content and style of the passage, and recognize the point of view.
Integration of Knowledge and Ideas	**Arguments**	Questions in this category may test your ability to identify or infer the central claim of the passage, analyze how sentences provide reasons or support for the claim, differentiate between facts and personal opinion, and recognize errors in reasoning or information that could strengthen or weaken the claims.
	Multiple texts	Multiple-text questions require reading two passages and may test your ability to make connections between people, relationships, and ideas across the passages, draw logical conclusions using information from both, and compare the text structure, purpose, and perspective in each passage.
	Mixed-information format	Mixed-information format questions test your visual comprehension skills or your ability to interpret and understand information presented in graphic formats. These questions also assess your ability to draw conclusions and compare information across both the passage and graphic elements.

Science Test (Optional)

The Science test includes **40 questions** to be answered in **40 minutes**. The questions check your scientific aptitude and whether you are capable of logical reasoning, cognitive flexibility, critical thinking, and application of scientific concepts across various fields of science, including life sciences, physical sciences, geoscience, and astronomy. The questions under this test contain multiple sets of scientific data, each accompanied by related multiple-choice questions. The data could be presented in various formats, including written passages, charts, graphs, tables, and illustrations.

There are three reporting categories in this test:

Interpretation of Data	**Interpretation of Data** involves the ability to select, analyze, and compare data from various sources such as graphs, tables, and diagrams. This includes identifying key features, understanding scientific terminology accurately, and determining how variables change in relation to each other. It also requires translating information into different formats, performing interpolation or extrapolation, and using mathematical relationships to analyze and combine data.
Scientific Investigation	**Scientific Investigation** questions assess your ability to understand and analyze experiments and research. These questions test skills such as identifying experimental information, understanding tools and methods, and recognizing the experimental design, including controls. You may need to compare experiments, predict results from trials, and understand precision issues. Additionally, you may be asked to identify hypotheses, suggest alternative testing methods, and predict the impact of design or method modifications on experiment outcomes.
Evaluation of models, inferences, and experimental results	**Evaluation of models, inferences, and experimental results** questions test your ability to assess and interpret scientific models and data. To answer these questions, you must identify key information and assumptions in a model, recognize implications, and compare models for similarities and differences. You might also need to evaluate whether a hypothesis, prediction, or conclusion aligns with data, models, or text information. Additionally, you may need to determine the strengths and weaknesses of models, assess how new information impacts conclusions, and use models to make predictions.

Writing (Optional)

The ACT Writing test asks you to write **1 essay** in **40 minutes.** It evaluates key writing skills taught in high school and early college courses. You'll respond to a prompt about a current issue, which includes three different perspectives. Your task is to develop your own viewpoint, support it with reasoning, and connect it to at least one other perspective by analyzing agreements or conflicts. Trained readers score your essay across four domains explained below:

Ideas and Analysis	Development and Support	Organization	Language Use and Conventions
This evaluates the depth and clarity of your argument. To perform well in this category, you must develop a clear and crisp thesis that delineates your stand. Essays that are scored high on this category carefully analyze how your viewpoint relates to at least one other perspective and demonstrate a clear understanding of the issue by providing a meaningful context. They examine the features that make the issue more nuanced and detailed. This includes connecting the topic to broader real-world situations.	This focuses on how effectively you expand your ideas and support them with clear reasoning and arguments. High-scoring essays not only state arguments but also reinforce them using persuasive examples. They explore strengths, facts, counterarguments, exceptions, and limitations to make their argument compelling and convince the test scorer that they are aware of the complexity of the issue and the strength of their position.	A well-organized essay presents a clear, controlling idea or thesis and ensures all parts of the essay support it. Each paragraph should focus on a specific, related idea, contributing to the overall coherence of the argument. Strong organization also means presenting your ideas in a logical sequence—beginning with an introduction, followed by clearly structured body paragraphs, and ending with a conclusion. Effective transitions, both within and between paragraphs, help maintain the flow and clarity of your essay.	This refers to how effectively you communicate your ideas through word choice, sentence structure, and grammar. Strong writing in this category uses exact language to clearly express ideas, avoiding ambiguous, overly general terms, or repetitions. It also demonstrates your control over various sentence types and constructions. In this category, essays that are scored high usually use a tone or style of writing to suit the purpose of the essay and the needs of the target audience. Additionally, using correct mechanics of writing is essential to maintain lucidity and enhance readability.

✓ Checklist for Test Day

Like all standardized exams, the ACT is a secure, proctored test with specific rules and regulations that must be followed. Keep the checklist below handy to ensure a smooth experience on test day.

Permissible Items	Prohibited Items
✓ Make sure to print a copy of your **admission ticket** before heading to the test center, as it contains important information such as registration match details or your online launch code. After uploading your photo, you can print the ticket through MyACT.	✕ **Textbooks, notes, and scratch paper** are not permitted in a paper-and-pencil test; all responses must be written directly in the provided test booklet or answer sheet.
✓ You will need to present a **valid photo identification document** at the test center for entry. If your ID does not meet the ACT's requirements, you will not be allowed to take the test.	✕ **Dictionaries**, including those for foreign languages, are prohibited.
✓ Remember to bring several **sharpened No. 2 pencils** with good erasers. Mechanical pencils and ink pens are not allowed, and no other writing instruments should be brought into the test room.	✕ **Writing tools** such as colored pens, highlighters, pencils, and correction fluid or tape are not allowed.
✓ You may bring a simple **watch, timer, or stopwatch** to help you manage time during the test, but it should not have an alarm or be a 'smart' device. Keep your timekeeping device on your desk where it is visible to test staff throughout the session. If the alarm goes off, you will be dismissed, and your test will not be scored.	✕ **Tobacco products** are strictly prohibited in the testing area under any circumstances.
✓ A **permitted calculator** can be used during the math portion of the test, but it's your responsibility to ensure the calculator meets ACT guidelines. You are not required to use a calculator, but if you choose to, it must be approved.	✕ **Cell phones, smartwatches, and fitness bands** must be turned off and stored out of sight, even if not in use.
✓ Feel free to bring a **snack and water bottle**, but it must be consumed outside the testing room during the scheduled break.	✕ **Devices with internet, Wi-Fi, or recording capabilities**, including laptops, tablets, and e-readers, are not allowed in the testing area.

The ACT has stringent rules when it comes to identity documents. You will not be allowed to take the ACT if you present an ID that does not meet the official ACT requirements. Many commonly used documents are not acceptable, even if they include your name or photo.

General Test-Taking Strategies

Since the ACT is a high-stakes test to define your academic success and future, it is essential to draw up a basic preparation plan to maximize your chances of achieving a desired score. Some basic pointers to keep in mind are listed below:

- **Solve past papers** to understand and embed the test format, structure, and content domains. While the test has undergone some changes, the key areas tested on it remain the same. Past papers will give you a comprehensive practice of all the tests and familiarize you with the overall structure of the test. So far, ACT has released one free online test in the new enhanced format. You can take the test from here - https://www.act.org/content/act/en/products-and-services/the-act/test-changes/online-testing/sample-questions.html

Focus on the areas that have more weightage to increase your chances of getting a better score.

- **Solve additional questions.** Past papers can familiarize you with the test but additional practice apart from taking tests is always recommended. This practice guide gives you 1100+ practice questions for the English and Reading tests. The chapters are divided as per passage topics and cover all the question types asked on the ACT. Create a study plan or follow the one given in this guide to solve the questions strategically.
- **Pace yourself** while attempting the test and manage your time wisely by approximating how long you'll spend on each test. Divide the remaining time by the number of questions to determine how long to spend per question. Keep some time at the end to review difficult questions.
- **Understand the question requirements** and read each question thoroughly. Some may require multiple steps, while others are simpler and quicker to answer. Also, pay attention to the instructions for each question.
- **Tackle easy questions first.** Start by answering easy questions first and build confidence as you go. You can return to the difficult questions towards the end.
- **Use logic** for difficult questions and eliminate obviously incorrect answers. Use a rationale to make an informed guess from the remaining choices.
- **Answer all questions.** There's no negative marking in the ACT, so answer every question within the allotted time.
- **Analyse the passage carefully**. Before attempting questions in the Reading test, read the entire passage thoroughly. Always consider the text when answering, as some questions will require direct information from the passage, while others may ask you to infer meanings, draw conclusions, or make comparisons.
- **Use the permitted calculator wisely.** While most math problems can be solved without one, some may be quicker with a calculator. Apply discretion for its use to manage your time.
- **Write all the steps**. Some problems require multiple steps. Ensure your final answer reflects the entire process, not just the final or a transitional result.
- **Plan:** While attempting the Writing test, thoroughly read and consider the prompt. Make good use of the optional planning questions to analyze the prompt and organize your ideas. Though this part is not scored, it helps structure an effective essay which ultimately yields a high score.
- **Review your answers** if you finish early. Remember, once time is up for a test, you cannot return to it.
- **Practice:** Prepare by immersing yourself in English. Read articles, advertisements, brochures, and a variety of texts. Watch news, listen to TED talks and podcasts, and speak to an English-speaking friend or colleague to gather perspectives and build fluency. Practice writing for various purposes and audiences, including essays, letters, opinion pieces, and so on. Time

yourself during practice sessions to simulate real test conditions and gauge your test readiness. Even if you don't plan to take the ACT with writing, this practice will improve your writing skills for life.

Test Centre Protocols

Following standard protocols gives you a stress-free test experience. Here is some useful test day information for the ACT:

- **Pre-test planning:** If you are not familiar with the location of your test center, consider doing a trial visit to the center in advance. This will help you figure out the best/shortest possible route and the time it takes to reach there. You should try making the trip on a different day to avoid any surprises on the test day.
- **Appropriate dressing:** Wear comfortable clothing on test day. Dressing in layers is a good idea, as it allows you to easily adjust to varying room temperatures, whether it is too warm or too cold.
- **Arrival time:** Arrive at the test center by 8:00 a.m. to ensure timely check-in and seating. Late arrivals will strictly not be admitted.
- **Check-in process:** Upon arrival, present your admission ticket and acceptable photo ID for verification. The testing staff will assign you to a designated seat in a test room.
- **Test timings:** From April through July 2025, if you take the ACT online (no writing or science), you will finish around 11:15 a.m. If you take the ACT with science or writing, you will typically finish around 12:15 p.m. If you take the ACT with science and writing, you will finish around 1:00 p.m.
- **Post-test procedures:** After the test, retrieve your belongings and exit the testing center promptly.

Test Security and Integrity

The ACT has comprehensive guidelines in order to maintain test security and uphold test integrity. To maintain impartiality, prevent any kind of disruptions, and safeguard the sanctity of the test materials, certain behaviors are strictly prohibited at the test center. If you engage in any of these actions, you will be dismissed, and your test will not be scored.

Here are the prohibited behaviors listed in the ACT Terms and Conditions:

- ✕ **Altering responses:** You cannot modify or fill in answers after time is called for any test, even if it's just a stray mark or accidental keystroke.
- ✕ **Revisiting tests:** You are not allowed to look back at any section once time has been called or look ahead to other tests. This applies to both online and paper-and-pencil tests.
- ✕ **Viewing other test takers' work:** You cannot view another test-taker's test or answers.
- ✕ **Providing or receiving assistance:** Giving or receiving help by any means, whether verbal, written, or through gestures, is forbidden.
- ✕ **Sharing test information:** Discussing or sharing test content, including questions and answers, at any time (during the test, breaks, or afterward) is not allowed. Disclosing anything about the test content, even in part, including on social media, is not allowed.

- ✗ **Photographing or memorizing test content:** You cannot attempt to take photos, copy, or memorize test-related information, or remove any test materials from the room in an unauthorized manner.
- ✗ **Failure to comply with online testing rules:** If you're taking the ACT online, you must comply with all technical requirements and system checks.
- ✗ **Using unapproved calculators:** As mentioned earlier, only permitted calculators are allowed, and that too in the mathematics test. Using a calculator in other tests, sharing calculators, or using one with non-permissible features is prohibited.
- ✗ **Using unsanctioned devices:** Watches or other timing devices with recording, internet, communication, or calculator capabilities (e.g., smartwatches) are not allowed. All other devices, including cell phones and wearables, must be turned off and stored out of sight.
- ✗ **Using prohibited materials:** Highlighter pens, colored pens/pencils, notes, or unauthorized dictionaries are not allowed. Scratch paper is also prohibited.
- ✗ **Unruly behavior:** Exhibiting confrontational, threatening, or any kind of disorderly behavior will result in dismissal from the test.
- ✗ **Violation of laws**: Any suspected criminal activities related to the test may be reported to suitable law enforcement agencies.

Retaking the ACT

There's no limit to how many times you can take the ACT, and most test takers take it 2-3 times to reach their target score. Retaking the test allows you to refine your preparation strategy and improve weaker areas. While you can't resit the test for individual tests, you can create an official Superscore by combining your best scores from different test dates.

Furthermore, if you tested under certain specific conditions, you can purchase an ACT My Answer Key (formerly TIR), which gives you a detailed review of your ACT performance, including a copy of the test questions, answer key, your responses, and performance insights. It becomes an important resource if you're planning to retake the ACT.

Requesting Accommodations for the ACT

Testing accommodations are modifications or supports provided to eligible students with documented disabilities, ensuring equitable access to the ACT. These accommodations may include extended time, alternate test formats, separate or quiet testing environments, or the use of assistive technology. The purpose is to minimize the impact of a student's disability on their test performance, allowing them to demonstrate their true academic abilities under fair conditions. ACT provides accommodations for students who need them, but these must be approved before test day and should reflect the support a student already receives in school. Here are the steps that you must follow if you require any of these accommodations:

Step 1: Register and indicate need for accommodations

This must be done during the registration process itself.

Step 2: Work with your school official

After registering, forward the confirmation email to your school official and submit the Consent to Release Information to ACT form. Your school will then submit the request through ACT's Test

Accessibility and Accommodations (TAA) system before the late registration deadline. Ensure all necessary documentation is included. Processing may take 5–10 business days, so follow up if you don't receive a response.

Step 3: Review the decision

Once the request is processed, your school official will review the decision. If denied, you can appeal before the late registration deadline. If you were previously approved, confirm with your school that the approval is still valid.

Step 4: Special testing arrangements

If approved for special testing, coordinate with your school to schedule testing within the special testing window. If your school cannot administer the test, contact ACT for alternatives. If you are a non-English-speaking test-taker, the ACT offers a variety of accommodations for students with documented disabilities, including but not limited to— extended time (up to one and one-half times the standard duration), access to approved bilingual dictionaries (without definitions), test directions in the student's native language, and testing in a familiar environment or small group.

Final Step: Prepare for Test Day

Upload your photo and print your admission ticket. Review your ticket to confirm your accommodations are listed correctly.

Summary

- The ACT is a standardized college admissions test used to assess a student's readiness for college, measuring skills in English, Math, Reading, Science, and Writing.
- The ACT now has **44 fewer questions** overall and can be completed in **125 minutes** (previously 195 minutes), allowing more time per question.
- The **Math section** now has **4 answer choices** instead of 5. The **Science section** is optional, and if taken, its score will be reported separately from the Composite score, which includes only **English**, **Math**, and **Reading**.
- The ACT covers five sections: English, Math, Reading, Science (optional), and Writing (optional).
- **English**: 50 questions, 35 minutes, 1.42 minutes per question, testing grammar, punctuation, sentence structure, and rhetorical skills.
- **Math**: 45 questions, 50 minutes, 1.11 minutes per question, covering algebra, geometry, functions, statistics, and some trigonometry.
- **Reading**: 36 questions, 40 minutes, 1.11 minutes per question, testing reading comprehension and critical thinking skills.
- **Science** (optional): 40 questions, 35 minutes, 1.14 minutes per question, focusing on scientific reasoning and data interpretation.
- **Writing** (optional): 1 essay, 40 minutes, testing the ability to write a clear, well-organized essay.

Chapter 2

Overview of the ACT Math Test

The ACT Math[1] section is designed to assess your mathematical reasoning and problem-solving skills—abilities that are crucial for success in college-level coursework. Whether you're planning to major in engineering, science, business, or any technical discipline, a solid performance in this section signals readiness for rigorous academic challenges.

This section assesses your grasp of mathematical concepts typically covered through the end of 11th grade. It focuses on the ability to solve problems using numerical operations, algebra, geometry, and data analysis, all to be completed within a limited time frame. **The goal is not just to test rote memorization but to measure critical thinking and practical application of math skills.**

Colleges and universities use ACT scores to evaluate academic preparedness. For institutions that consider standardized test scores as part of their admissions process, the Math score can be a deciding factor for programs with a strong quantitative component. A high Math score can also open doors to merit-based scholarships and honors programs.

While all test-takers should aim for a strong Math score, it's especially important for students aspiring to pursue degrees in STEM (Science, Technology, Engineering, and Mathematics), business, economics, architecture, or any field that involves analytical and quantitative reasoning. Success in this section demonstrates a foundational skill set essential for success in those majors.

The Math test is the second test of the ACT, following the English test.

Quick Glance at the Math Test

- **Number of questions:** 45
- **Time allotted:** 50 minutes
- **Time per question:** 1.11 minutes
- **Question Format:** Multiple-choice Questions only
- **Number of options:** 4
- **Test design:** Some questions may appear straightforward, while others may require interpreting diagrams, graphs, or word problems before calculations can even begin.

Calculator Policy

Calculators are permitted **only** in the Math test. However, you must use approved models. Graphing calculators are permitted, but calculators with Computer Algebra System (CAS) capabilities (which can manipulate symbolic algebra) are prohibited. While calculators are useful for complex arithmetic and graph-based questions, many questions can be solved more quickly by hand. See the section on "Calculator Use" for a list of approved calculators.

1 The ACT "Mathematics" test will be called ACT "Math" test throughout the book.

Content Domains and Skills Tested

The Math test draws from five major areas of mathematics.

- **Number and Quantity:** Understanding real and complex number systems, performing operations, and applying quantitative reasoning.
- **Algebra:** Solving, interpreting, and creating expressions, equations, and inequalities.
- **Functions:** Recognizing, analyzing, and modeling relationships between quantities using linear, quadratic, exponential, and other types of functions.
- **Geometry:** Applying concepts related to shapes, sizes, relative positions, and properties of space, including coordinate geometry.
- **Statistics and Probability:** Analyzing data, understanding distributions, and applying basic principles of probability to solve problems.

The test emphasizes not just mathematical computation, but also understanding of concepts, reasoning, and strategy. Some problems may require multi-step thinking or integration of concepts across different math domains. You are expected to solve problems using different strategies, choose the most efficient method when time is limited, and perform calculations correctly. These abilities show that you not only know math but can use it effectively in real-world situations, which is essential for college-level coursework and professional problem-solving.

What the Math Test Measures

The ACT Math test is carefully designed not just to test rote memorization, but to assess a broad range of critical skills that you will use in college and in real-world problem-solving situations. Understanding what is measured can help you prepare more strategically and approach the test with the right mindset.

Problem-solving and analytical skills: One of the primary goals of the Math test is to evaluate your ability to think critically and logically when faced with a mathematical problem. Test-takers must analyze information, identify relationships, and determine the most effective solution path. Many problems involve multiple steps, requiring careful attention to detail and strong decision-making skills under time pressure.

Mathematical modeling and reasoning: You are expected to translate real-world scenarios into mathematical language through **modeling**. This means creating equations, inequalities, functions, or geometric representations to describe a situation. Success in this area demonstrates the ability to:

- Set up appropriate mathematical models,
- Interpret what the model means in context, and
- Draw conclusions or make predictions based on the model.

Mathematical reasoning is also key—you must logically justify your approaches and conclusions based on mathematical principles.

Understanding and applying mathematical concepts: Beyond simply solving equations, the Math test measures how well you understand underlying mathematical ideas. Test-takers need to apply formulas, properties, and theorems appropriately, often in new or unfamiliar ways. A strong performance shows not only memorization but also flexibility in applying learned concepts to different types of problems.

Topics assessed include, but are not limited to:

- Properties of numbers,
- Algebraic expressions and equations,
- Functions and their behaviors,
- Geometric relationships and measurements, and
- Basic statistics and data interpretation.

Real-world math applications: Finally, the Math test emphasizes real-world relevance. Many questions are framed within practical contexts, such as calculating costs, analyzing graphs, interpreting scientific data, or solving problems related to everyday activities like shopping, traveling, or building.

This reflects the ACT's mission to assess college and career readiness: you must show you can apply math skills beyond the classroom, solving practical problems you are likely to encounter in your academic, personal, and professional lives.

Content Domains Tested

The ACT Math test is structured around three major categories that reflect the kinds of skills you'll need for college-level mathematics and real-world problem solving. These categories are divided further into specific content domains, each with its own focus and set of skills.

Preparing for Higher Math (PHM)

PHM is broken down into five domains:

Number & Quantity

This domain assesses your comfort with different types of numbers, number systems, and the ability to reason quantitatively. The focus is on applying these concepts in both abstract and real-world contexts.

Detailed Skill Breakdown

- **Perform calculations on whole numbers and decimals:** You should be able to confidently add, subtract, multiply, and divide both whole numbers and decimals. This includes understanding decimal placement and performing multi-step calculations.
- **Recognize equivalent fractions and fractions in the lowest terms:** This involves simplifying fractions by identifying common factors and recognizing when two fractions are equal.
- **Locate rational numbers on the number line:** Rational numbers include integers, fractions, decimals, and mixed numbers. You should be able to place them accurately on a number line and compare their values.
- **Recognize single-digit factors of a number:** Know how to identify numbers that divide evenly into another number without leaving a remainder.

- **Identify a digit's place value:** Understand the value of each digit in a number based on its position (ones, tens, hundreds, tenths, etc.).
- **Demonstrate knowledge of elementary number concepts:** This includes rounding decimals or whole numbers (e.g., 4.68 → 5), ordering decimals from least to greatest, identifying patterns in number sequences, understanding prime numbers, and finding greatest common factors (GCF).
- **Write powers of 10 using exponents:** Understand and apply exponential notation, especially powers of 10.
- **Comprehend length on the number line and find distances between points:** Distance is the difference between two numbers, regardless of direction (using absolute value).
- **Understand absolute value in terms of distance:** Absolute value represents the distance between a number and 0 on the number line.
- **Find the distance between two points with the same x- or y-coordinate:** You should understand how to calculate vertical or horizontal distances using subtraction.
- **Add, subtract, and multiply matrices:** You should be able to manipulate small matrices (grids of numbers), typically 2 × 2.
- **Order fractions:** Compare fractions by converting to common denominators or decimals.
- **Find and use the least common multiple (LCM):** Understand how to find the smallest number that two or more numbers divide evenly into.
- **Demonstrate knowledge of complex numbers and multiply two complex numbers:** Use the standard form a+bi and apply algebraic operations like FOIL (remembering that i2 = −1).
- **Comprehend the concept of irrational numbers:** Irrational numbers cannot be written as a simple fraction (e.g., π, 2) and do not terminate or repeat.
- **Apply properties of rational exponents:** Understand how fractional exponents relate to roots.
- **Use vector and matrix operations:** Add, subtract, and perform scalar multiplication on vectors and matrices.
- **Analyze and draw conclusions based on number concepts:** Interpret patterns, properties, and relationships among numbers to make logical inferences.

Solved Example

What is $\frac{3}{5}$ of 32% of 115?

A. 14.72

B. 22.08

C. 37.4

D. 134.2

Answer Explanation:

Choice B is correct. Convert $\frac{3}{5}$ and 32% to numerical values before multiplying the 3 numbers together.

$\frac{3}{5} = 0.6$ and $32\% = 0.32$ then $0.6 \times 0.32 \times 115 = 22.08$.

Choice A is incorrect because 14.72 is the result of $\frac{3}{5}$ of 32% of 76.667.

Choice C is incorrect because 37.4 is the result of $\frac{3}{5}$ of 32% of 194.79.

Choice D is incorrect because 134.2 is the result of $\frac{3}{5}$ of 32% of 698.96.

Algebra

This domain focuses on your ability to understand, manipulate, and solve algebraic expressions, equations, and inequalities. These skills are foundational for higher-level math and real-world problem-solving.

Detailed Skill Breakdown

- **Demonstrate knowledge of basic expressions, such as b + g to identify a total:** This involves interpreting simple algebraic expressions and understanding what they represent in a real-world or abstract context.
- **Solve equations in the form x + a = b (where a and b are whole numbers or decimals):** You must isolate the variable to find its value using inverse operations.
- **Use substitution to evaluate mathematical expressions:** Plug in given values for variables to calculate the expression's value.
- **Combine like terms, such as $2x + 5x$:** Only terms with the same variable and exponent can be combined by adding or subtracting their coefficients.
- **Add and subtract algebraic expressions:** This requires distributing signs and combining like terms properly.
- **Multiply two binomials:** Apply the distributive property (often using the FOIL method).
- **Match inequalities with their graphs on the number line:** Understand inequality symbols and which types of points (open or closed) and shading they represent.
- **Demonstrate knowledge of slope:** Understand slope as "rise over run" and how it appears in equations of the form $y = mx + b$.
- **Solve real-world problems using first-degree equations:** Translate word problems into algebraic equations and solve for the unknown.
- **Solve inequalities:** Use the same steps as solving equations, but remember to reverse the inequality sign when multiplying or dividing by a negative.
- **Match linear or compound inequalities with graphs:** Know how to interpret compound inequalities like $-2 < x \leq 4$ on a number line using appropriate symbols and shading.
- **Add, subtract, and multiply polynomials:** Apply operations to polynomials of various degrees.
- **Solve quadratic equations:** Use methods such as factoring, completing the square, or the quadratic formula.
- **Factor quadratics:** Break down quadratic expressions into binomial factors.
- **Work with squares/square roots and cubes/cube roots of numbers:** Understand inverse operations and simplify radicals.
- **Work with scientific notation:** Convert numbers into or out of scientific notation and perform operations.

- **Solve problems involving positive integer exponents:** Apply the laws of exponents to simplify expressions.
- **Determine the slope of a line from an equation:** Identify the slope directly from equations in slope-intercept form $y = mx + b$ or calculate it from standard form.
- **Solve linear inequalities when the method involves reversing the inequality sign:** When multiplying or dividing both sides by a negative number, reverse the sign.
- **Solve systems of two linear equations:** Use substitution, elimination, or graphing to find the point where two lines intersect.
- **Solve absolute value equations and inequalities:** Split into two cases: one for the positive and one for the negative scenario.
- **Match quadratic inequalities with their graphs:** Understand how parabolas open (up or down), where they are positive or negative, and how to use test points to graph solutions.

Solved Example

Granny bought an old-school TV from a thrift store. It has a square glass screen with an area of 300 square inches. What is the approximate side length of the TV to the nearest inch?

A. 15

B. 17

C. 18

D. 16

Answer Explanation:

Choice B is correct because the side length of the TV is approximately 17 inches.

Use the formula for the area of the square $A = s^2$.

$A = s^2$

$300 = s^2$

$\sqrt{300} = \sqrt{s^2}$

$17.32 = s$

$17 \approx s$

Choice A is incorrect because 15 is less than the obtained value of the side length.

Choice C is incorrect because 18 is greater than the obtained value of the side length.

Choice D is incorrect because 16 is less than the obtained value of the side length.

Functions

It tests understanding of function notation, properties, behaviors, and transformations.

 Detailed Skill Breakdown

- **Understand the concept of a function having a well-defined output value at each valid input value:** A function assigns exactly one output (y-value) to each input (x-value). You must know how to determine whether a relation (like a table, graph, or equation) is a function.
- **Extend a given pattern by a few terms for patterns that have a constant increase or decrease between terms or that have a constant factor between terms:** This involves arithmetic (add/subtract same amount) and geometric (multiply/divide by the same number) sequences.
- **Evaluate linear, quadratic, and polynomial functions expressed in function notation at the integer level:** Plug integer values into functions like $f(x)=2x+1, f(x)=x^2-3x+4$, or $f(x)=x^3-x$, and others. Focus is on proper substitution and simplification.
- **Interpret statements that use function notation in terms of their context:** Understand real-world function notation such as $f(5)=20$ meaning "at time 5, the output is 20" or "when x = 5, y = 20". This is useful in word problems, graphs, and tables.
- **Find the domain of polynomial functions and rational functions:** Domain is all valid input values. For polynomials, the domain is all real numbers. For rational functions, exclude values that make the denominator zero.
- **Find the range of polynomial functions:** Range is all possible output values. Often determined by analyzing the graph, turning points, or limits.
- **Find where a rational function's graph has a vertical asymptote:** A vertical asymptote occurs where the function is undefined due to division by zero. Solve for values of x that make the denominator zero (and not canceled by the numerator).
- **Use function notation for simple functions of two variables:** Recognize and evaluate functions like $f(x,y)=x+2y$. Plug in two input values and compute the result.
- **Relate a graph to a situation described qualitatively in terms of faster change or slower change**
- **Interpret graphs in context: e.g., steep slope = faster change:** You must be able to describe how a quantity is increasing or decreasing over time and relate that to graph shape.
- **Build functions for relations that are inversely proportional or exponential:** Inverse proportion: $y=\frac{k}{x}$

  Exponential: $y=a\cdot b^x$

  You'll be asked to construct these from context or tables.

- **Find a recursive expression for the general term in a sequence described recursively:** Write recursive rules: example $a_n=a_{n-1}+3$ for arithmetic, or $a_n=2a_{n-1}$ for geometric sequences. You must be able to express how one term depends on the previous term.
- **Evaluate composite functions of integer values:** Composite functions: $f(g(x))$. Plug the input into one function, then use that output as input for the next.
- **Compare actual values and the values of a modeling function to judge model fit and compare models:** Given real data and a function model, compare predicted and actual values. Choose which model better fits the data based on closeness of values or graph alignment.

- **Demonstrate knowledge of geometric sequences:** Know the general form: $a_n = a_1 \cdot r^{n-1}$. Be able to find the common ratio, next terms, or n[th] term. Recognize exponential growth/decay in sequence format.
- **Demonstrate knowledge of unit circle trigonometry:** Know sine, cosine, tangent values at key angles: $0°, 30°, 45°, 60°, 90°$. Know the coordinates of points on the unit circle and how they relate to trigonometric functions.
- **Match graphs of basic trigonometric functions with their equations:** Recognize forms of $y = sin(x), y = cos(x), y = tan(x)$, and their transformations. Identify amplitude, period, phase shift, and vertical shift from equations and graphs.
- **Use trigonometric concepts and basic identities to solve problems:** Use identities like $sin^2(x) + cos^2(x) = 1$, $tan(x) = \frac{sin(x)}{cos(x)}$. Solve for unknown angles or sides in right triangles or simple trigonometric equations.
- **Demonstrate knowledge of logarithms:** Understand definitions: $log_b(x) = y \Leftrightarrow b^y = x$. Be familiar with log properties: $log_b(xy) = log_b(x) + log_b(y)$. Convert between exponential and logarithmic form.
- **Write an expression for the composite of two simple functions:** Construct a composite function algebraically: If $f(x) = x + 2, g(x) = 3x$, then $f(g(x)) = 3x + 2$. This builds algebraic reasoning and understanding of input-output behavior.

Solved Example

A banquet hall can extend the length of their tables to add in more chairs. One banquet table can accommodate eight chairs. Adding another banquet table adds six additional seats. How many banquet tables are needed to accommodate 32 people?

A. 5

B. 6

C. 7

D. 8

Answer Explanation:

Choice A is correct because the formula to determine the number of chairs based on n tables would be $6n + 2$. This is found using the arithmetic relationship of $a_n = a_1 + d(n-1)$.

In this case, $a_1 = 8$ and the common difference, d, is 6.

This would make the expression determine the number of seats to be $a_n = 8 + 6(n-1)$.

Distributing and simplifying would result in the expression $a_n = 8 + 6n - 6 = 6n + 2$. Setting this expression equal to 32 would allow you to solve for the number of tables needed for 32 people. This would be $32 = 6n + 2$. Subtract 2 and divide by 6 to yield $n = 5$.

Choice B is incorrect because this is more tables than needed and would result in 38 chairs.

Choice C is incorrect because this is more tables than needed and would result in 44 chairs.

Choice D is incorrect because this is more tables than needed and would result in 50 chairs.

Geometry

Geometry on the ACT assesses spatial reasoning, knowledge of properties of shapes, the ability to apply geometric formulas, and understand how algebra and geometry intersect. You're expected to work with points, lines, planes, and figures in two and three dimensions.

Detailed Skill Breakdown

- **Estimate the length of a line segment based on other lengths in a geometric figure:** Use proportional reasoning and spatial judgment to approximate lengths. Skills tested may include understanding scale and identifying reference lengths.
- **Calculate the length of a line segment based on the lengths of other line segments that go in the same direction:** Focus on collinear segments, adjacent lengths, or sides of polygons with right angles. Often requires adding or subtracting known lengths.
- **Perform common conversions of money and of length, weight, mass, and time within a measurement system:** Know conversion factors like inches to feet, minutes to hours, etc. Apply arithmetic to solve real-world conversion problems.
- **Compute the area and perimeter of triangles, rectangles, and other polygons:** May also require combining multiple shapes.
- **Use properties of parallel lines to find the measure of an angle:** Know angle relationships formed by transversals: corresponding, and alternate interior. Often tested with diagrams requiring angle calculations.
- **Exhibit knowledge of basic angle properties and special sums of angle measures**
- **Use geometric formulas when all necessary information is given:** Direct application of area, perimeter, volume, and surface area formulas. No extra steps or manipulation needed.
- **Locate points in the coordinate plane:** Understand and use coordinates (x, y). Identify quadrant placement or distance from origin.
- **Translate points up, down, left, and right in the coordinate plane:** Know that up/down affects the y-coordinate and left/right affects the x-coordinate.
- **Use several angle properties to find an unknown angle measure:** Combine multiple angle rules, such as supplementary, vertical, and triangle angle sum.
- **Count the number of lines of symmetry of a geometric figure:** Identify all axes over which a figure can be folded and match perfectly. Tested on regular polygons and other symmetrical shapes.
- **Use the symmetry of isosceles triangles to find unknown side lengths or angle measures:** Know that base angles are congruent and the legs are equal. Apply symmetry to divide triangles and solve.
- **Recognize that real-world measurements are typically imprecise and that an appropriate level of precision is related to the measuring device and procedure:** Understand significant figures and rounding based on context. Choose the level of precision that matches measurement tools.
- **Compute the perimeter of composite geometric figures with unknown side lengths:** Combine shapes and infer missing dimensions using given lengths and geometric relationships.

- **Compute the area and circumference of circles:** Use formulas:
  Circumference: $C = 2\pi r$

  Area: $A = \pi r^2$

- **Given the length of two sides of a right triangle, find the length of the third side:**
  Apply the Pythagorean Theorem: $a^2 + b^2 = c^2$

- **Express the sine, cosine, and tangent of an angle in a right triangle as a ratio of given side lengths:** Use SOH-CAH-TOA. No need for calculator-based trigonometry here.
- **Determine the slope of a line from points or a graph:** Use $m = \frac{y_2 - y_1}{x_2 - x_1}$. Recognize slope visually from rise/run in graphs.
- **Find the midpoint of a line segment:** Apply midpoint formula: $\frac{x_1 + x_2}{2}, \frac{y_1 + y_2}{2}$.
- **Find the coordinates of a point rotated 180° around a given center point**
- **Use relationships involving the area, perimeter, and volume of geometric figures to compute another measure:** Interrelate geometric formulas.
- **Use the Pythagorean theorem:** Use to solve for sides of right triangles.
- **Apply properties of 30°–60°–90°, 45°–45°–90°, similar, and congruent triangles**
- **Apply basic trigonometric ratios to solve right-triangle problems:** Use sine, cosine, tangent with side-angle relationships.
- **Use the distance formula**
- **Use properties of parallel and perpendicular lines to determine an equation of a line or coordinates of a point:** Know that parallel lines have the same slope and perpendicular lines have negative reciprocal slopes.
- **Find the coordinates of a point reflected across a vertical or horizontal line or across $y = x$**
- **Find the coordinates of a point rotated 90° across a vertical**
- **Recognize special characteristics of parabolas and circles:** For parabolas: identify vertex, axis of symmetry, direction. For circles: standard form $(x-h)^2 + (y-k)^2 = r^2$, identify **center** and **radius.**
- **Use relationships among angles, arcs, and distances in a circle:** Understand central angles, inscribed angles, arc length, and sector area.
- **Compute the area of composite geometric figures when planning and/or visualization is required:** Break down into known shapes (triangles, rectangles, etc.). May require subtracting one area from another.
- **Use scale factors to determine the magnitude of a size change:** Use scale factors to calculate change in length, area and volume.
- **Analyze and draw conclusions based on a set of conditions:** Deductive reasoning with geometric constraints.
- **Solve multi step geometry problems that involve integrating concepts, planning, and/or visualization:** These problems test deeper understanding and integration of multiple topics. You may need to draw auxiliary lines, translate verbal descriptions to visual diagrams, or combine area, angle, and algebra concepts.

Solved Example

The figure shown below is internally tangent circles which means that the inside circle passes through the center of the large circle. What is the area of the shaded region?

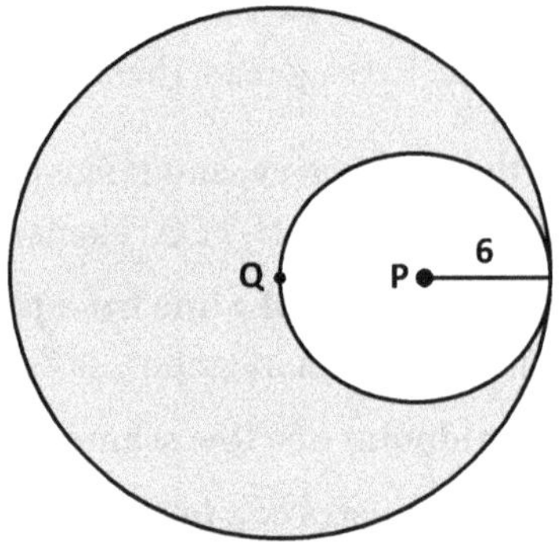

A. 108π

B. 144π

C. 36π

D. 12π

Answer Explanation:

Choice A is correct because the obtained answer is 108π.

Given: Radius of small circle = 6

Radius of big circle = diameter of the small circle = 2(6)=12

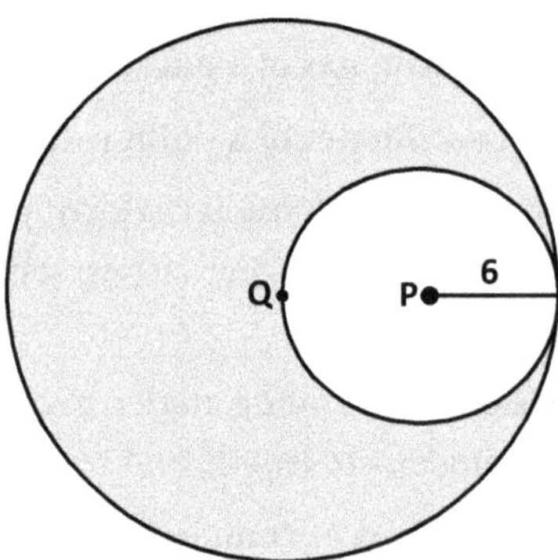

Find the area of shaded region by taking the difference between the area of the bigger circle and the smaller circle.

$$A_{big} = \pi(12)^2 = 144\pi$$

$$A_{small} = \pi(6)^2 = 36\pi$$

$$A_{shaded\ region} = A_{big} - A_{small} = 144\pi - 36\pi = 108\pi$$

Choice B is incorrect because 144π is the area of the big circle.

Choice C is incorrect because 36π is the area of the small circle.

Choice D is incorrect because 12π represents the circumference of the smaller circle.

Statistics & Probability

This domain focuses on understanding data distributions, interpreting statistical results, calculating probabilities, and evaluating models based on data. These skills are especially important for interpreting real-world data accurately and making data-driven decisions.

Detailed Skill Breakdown

- **Calculate averages:** Mean (average) = Sum of all data values ÷ Number of data values. Common in both word problems and straightforward arithmetic.
- **Read and extract relevant data from a basic table or chart and use the data in a computation:** Identify values in tables, bar graphs, or line charts.
- **Use the relationship between the probability of an event and the probability of its complement:** You must understand that $P(Event)+P(Not\ Event)=1$. If given the probability of an event not happening, subtract from 1 to find the event's probability.
- **Calculate the missing data value given the average and all other data values**
- **Translate from one data representation to another (e.g., bar graph to circle graph):** Interpret data and express it in a different visual format. Understand proportions, percentages, and sectors in a pie chart.
- **Compute probabilities:** Use the formula: $P(Event)=\frac{Favorable\,Outcomes}{Total\,Outcomes}$. Could be a single event, multiple independent/dependent events, or compound probabilities.
- **Describe events as combinations of other events (e.g., using AND, OR, NOT):** Use set operations:

  AND (Intersection) → Both must happen

  OR (Union) → Either or both happen

  NOT (Complement) → Opposite event

- **Demonstrate knowledge of and apply counting techniques:** Use fundamental counting principle, permutations, and combinations
- **Calculate the average given the frequency counts of all the data values:** Multiply each data value by its frequency, then divide the total by the total frequency.
- **Manipulate data from tables and charts:** Combine rows/columns, compute totals or differences, or convert values into percentages or ratios.
- **Use Venn diagrams in counting:** Understand overlapping groups using Venn diagrams.
- **Recognize that when data summaries are reported in the real world, results are often rounded and must be interpreted as having appropriate precision:** Understand that reported statistics may not be exact and need rounding tolerance.
- **Recognize that when a statistical model is used, model values typically differ from actual values:** Identify the concept of residuals (actual - predicted). Understand that models are simplifications of real-world data.

- **Calculate or use a weighted average**
- **Interpret and use information from tables and charts, including two-way frequency tables.**
- **Recognize the concepts of conditional and joint probability and of independence expressed in real-world contexts:**

  Joint probability: P(A and B)

  Conditional probability: P(A | B)

- **Distinguish among mean, median, and mode for a list of numbers:**

  Mean: Average

  Median: Middle value when ordered

  Mode: Most frequent value

- **Analyze and draw conclusions based on information from tables and charts, including two-way frequency tables:** Apply reasoning to draw insights, compare categories, and find probabilities.
- **Understand the role of randomization in surveys, experiments, and observational studies:** Recognize why random selection and random assignment reduce bias. Know differences between observational studies, controlled experiments, and surveys.
- **Demonstrate knowledge of conditional and joint probability**
- **Recognize that part of the power of statistical modeling comes from looking at regularity in the differences between actual values and model values:** This refers to the residuals in a model. Patterns in residuals may reveal flaws in the model or suggest better-fitting alternatives.

Solved Example

A problem in mathematics is given to three students A, B and C. If the probability of A solving the problem is $\frac{1}{2}$ and B not solving it is $\frac{1}{4}$. The whole probability of the problem being solved is $\frac{63}{64}$ then What is the probability that student C solves the problem?

A: $\frac{1}{2}$

B: $\frac{1}{8}$

C: $\frac{1}{64}$

D: $\frac{7}{8}$

Answer Explanation: Choice D is correct because the probability of solving the problem is $\frac{7}{8}$.

Given :

Let A be the event of A solving the problem

Let B be the event of B solving the problem

Let C be the event of C solving the problem

Given

$P(a)=\frac{1}{2}$, $P(\sim B)=\frac{1}{4}$ and $P(A\cup B\cup C)=\frac{63}{64}$

We know $P(A\cup B\cup C)=1-P(\overline{A\cup B\cup C})$

$$=1-P(\overline{A})P(\overline{B})P(\overline{C})$$

Let $P(\overline{C})=P$

$$\frac{63}{64}=1-\left(\frac{1}{2}\right)\left(\frac{1}{4}\right)(P)$$

$$\frac{63}{64}=1-\left(\frac{P}{8}\right)$$

$$\frac{63}{64}=\left(\frac{8-P}{8}\right)$$

$$P=\frac{1}{8}$$

$$P(\overline{C})=1-\frac{1}{8}$$

$$P(\overline{C})=\frac{7}{8}$$

Choice A is incorrect because $\frac{1}{2}$ is less than the obtained answer.

Choice B is incorrect because $\frac{1}{8}$ is less than the obtained answer.

Choice C is incorrect because $\frac{1}{64}$ is less than the obtained answer.

Integrating Essential Skills

This category assesses how well students can solve complex, multi-step problems by combining knowledge from different math areas.

Multi-Step Problem Solving

This domain assesses your ability to combine multiple mathematical concepts and carry out sequential steps to solve problems. It reflects how well you apply math to more complex, real-world scenarios—exactly the kind of thinking required in academic and work settings.

Detailed Skill Breakdown

- **Solve problems that require multiple operations:** You may need to use a combination of operations such as addition, subtraction, multiplication, division, or exponents in a logical order. Often involves applying order of operations (PEMDAS) correctly.

- **Apply math concepts in real-world scenarios:** Includes interpreting and solving word problems involving ratios, proportions, percentages, and unit conversions.
- **Work with multiple formulas in a single problem:** You may be required to apply more than one formula to get to the final answer. Common in problems involving **geometry**, **algebra**, or **physics-style applications** (e.g., distance = rate × time)/
- **Understand and manipulate rates, averages, and proportions:** Combine ratios, unit rates, average speed, or weighted averages across different stages of a problem. Requires understanding relationships and being able to convert and apply them step-by-step.
- **Interpret multi-part graphs, charts, and tables:** Some questions involve using data from multiple sources or interpreting more than one element in a chart or graph.
- **Use logic and estimation to guide multi-step decisions:** You may not need an exact answer in early steps but should use estimation to eliminate choices or simplify calculations.
- **Solve problems involving multiple representations:** Switch between equations, graphs, tables, and verbal descriptions. Often seen in problems where you're given a table or graph and asked to build or interpret a corresponding algebraic expression or function.
- **Integrate concepts from different math domains:** These problems combine algebra, geometry, statistics, and number properties in a single scenario.
- **Maintain accuracy over several steps:** Minor calculation errors in early steps can lead to incorrect final answers. Emphasis on careful arithmetic, checking work, and keeping track of units and steps.

Solved Example

There are two circles C_1 and C_2 of radii 3 and 8 units, respectively. The common internal tangent, T touches the circles at points P_1 and P_2 respectively. The line joining the centers of the circles intersects .. at X. The distance of X from the center of the smaller circle is 5 units. What is the length of the line segment P_1P_2?

A: 12

B: 10

C: 15

D: 9

Answer Explanation: Choice C is correct because the obtained answer is 15.

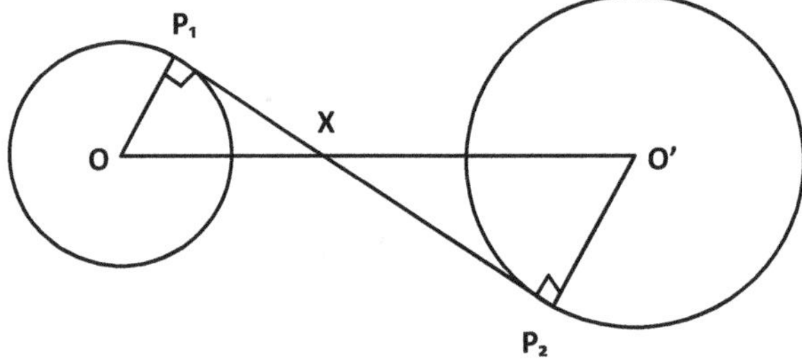

Find P_1X using Pythagorean theorem. Note that $r_{small\ circle} = P_1$ and $OX = 5$.

OX is the hypotenuse, P_1O and P_1X are side lengths.

$$(P_1X)^2 = (OX)^2 - (P_1O)^2$$
$$(P_1X)^2 = (5)^2 - (3)^2 \backslash$$
$$(P_1X)^2 = 25 - 9$$
$$(P_1X)^2 = 16$$
$$P_1X = 4$$

The tangent line is perpendicular to the radius, thus creating a right triangle OXP_1 and $O'XP_2$.

Since the right triangle OXP_1 and $O'XP_2$ share a common vertex X, this would mean they are similar. Use the similar right triangle theorem.

$$\frac{P_1X}{P_2X} = \frac{P_1O}{P_2O'}$$
$$\frac{4}{P_2X} = \frac{3}{8}$$
$$P_2X = \frac{(4 \times 8)}{3} = 10.67$$

The length of line segment P_1P_2 is $P_1X + P_2X = 4 + 10.67 = 14.67 \approx 15$.

Choice A is incorrect because 12 is less than the obtained value.

Choice B is incorrect because 10 is less than the obtained value.

Choice D is incorrect because 9 is less than the obtained value.

Application of Skills to Real-World Situations

This domain measures how well you can apply mathematical concepts to solve problems based on real-world contexts. These questions are designed to test your mathematical reasoning, data interpretation, and problem-solving abilities in practical, everyday scenarios—such as budgeting, measurement, travel planning, and workplace calculations.

Detailed Skill Breakdown

- **Solve word problems involving real-world contexts:** Apply arithmetic, algebra, geometry, and proportions to interpret and solve everyday problems.
- **Use units and unit conversion in context:** Convert between units (e.g., inches to feet, minutes to hours) and interpret answers in terms of real-world meaning.
- **Apply percents, discounts, markups, and taxes:** Use percent increases and decreases in practical situations such as sales, interest rates, and population growth. Understand how to compute totals after applying discounts or taxes.
- **Use averages and weighted averages in practical settings:** Understand and apply formulas for mean and weighted average in contexts like grading systems, financial planning, or scheduling.
- **Interpret graphs, charts, and tables:** Use visuals such as bar graphs, pie charts, and tables to extract, compare, and calculate values. Evaluate trends, make predictions, or compute missing data.

- **Apply geometry to everyday scenarios:** Solve perimeter, area, volume, and angle problems in contexts such as flooring, fencing, packaging, or carpentry.
- **Solve distance, rate, and time problems:** Apply the formula Distance = Rate × Time to scenarios like driving, running, or shipping. May involve working backward (e.g., finding time given distance and rate).
- **Apply algebra to business or consumer scenarios:** Set up and solve equations based on practical contexts, such as profit and loss, break-even analysis, or loan interest.
- **Interpret and work with proportions and ratios:** Used in problems involving scale drawings, maps, recipes, population comparisons, etc. May involve solving for missing values or comparing ratios.
- **Use logic and reasoning in real-world decision-making:** Identify reasonable answers based on estimation, patterns, or logical deduction.

Solved Example

A boat travels east at a speed of 4 miles per hour and north at a speed of 5 miles per hour. What is the boat's resultant speed?

A: 20 mph

B: 9 mph

C: $\sqrt{41}$ mph

D: $\sqrt{36}$ mph

Answer Explanation: Choice C is correct. The resultant speed is the magnitude of the velocity vector $\vec{v} = \left(\sqrt{41}\right)$.

From the given $x = 4$ and $y = 5$.

Substitute the given into the formula $\|\vec{v}\| = \sqrt{x^2 + y^2}$ to get $\|\vec{v}\| = \sqrt{4^2 + 5^2} = \sqrt{16+25} = \sqrt{41}$

Choice A is incorrect. This is the result of xy.

Choice B is incorrect. This is the result of $x + y$.

Choice D is incorrect. This may result from calculation error.

Modeling

Modeling focuses on creating and interpreting mathematical models based on given information.

Interpretation and Building of Mathematical Models

This domain evaluates your ability to translate real-world scenarios into mathematical representations—like equations, graphs, and diagrams—and then use those models to analyze and solve problems. You're expected to both interpret existing models and construct new ones from context.

Detailed Skill Breakdown

- **Identify the type of model that best fits a situation:** Determine whether a linear, quadratic, exponential, or other type of model is appropriate based on a description or a set of data points.
- **Translate real-world scenarios into algebraic or graphical representations:** Given a situation (e.g., pricing a service, population growth, or physical movement), write an equation or inequality that models it.
- **Interpret the meaning of components in a mathematical model:** Understand the real-world meaning of coefficients, variables, and constants in a given expression or equation.
- **Analyze graphs and tables to extract or predict values:** Use a graph or table to find specific values, trends, intercepts, or turning points.
- **Modify a model based on a change in scenario:** Adjust an existing equation or graph to reflect a change in conditions (e.g., increase in rate, new starting point).
- **Use graphs to evaluate or compare different models:** Compare multiple equations or data sets and determine which one best fits a situation or provides the most accurate prediction.
- **Validate or refine models based on context or data:** Use reasonableness, estimation, or comparison with actual data to confirm whether a model makes sense or needs adjustment.
- **Solve real-world problems using models:** Use the model to answer a question, like calculating total cost, finding break-even points, or predicting future values.
- **Represent constraints in real-world problems mathematically:** Identify and include inequalities or domain restrictions that make sense in context (e.g., time can't be negative).
- **Interpret the domain and range in context:** Understand which values of input and output make sense for a particular real-world model.

Solved Example

After arranging the flower bed, Joshua decides to make the flower bed more attractive by setting one of the angles in the triangle as a right angle. He decides to palace the right angle at vertex A and to leave AB and AC as 4 feet and 5 feet respectively. Which figure represents the problem above and the measure of the piece of a lumber that he would need to replace the original 6-foot piece?

A: , 6.1

B: , 6.4

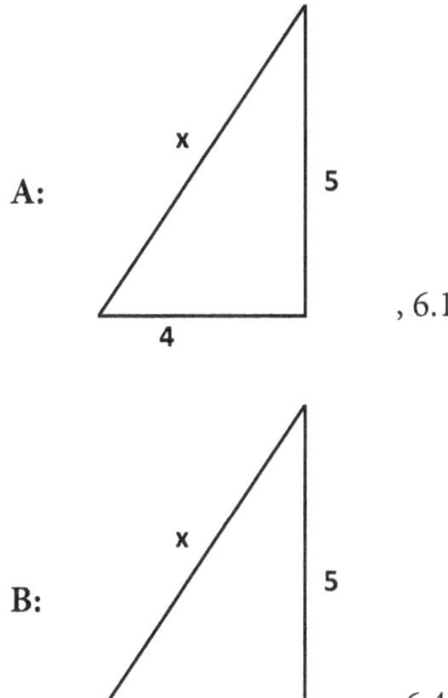

C: 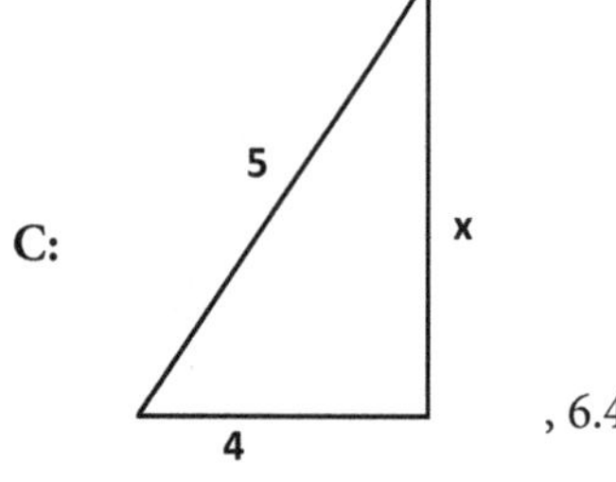

, 6.4

D: 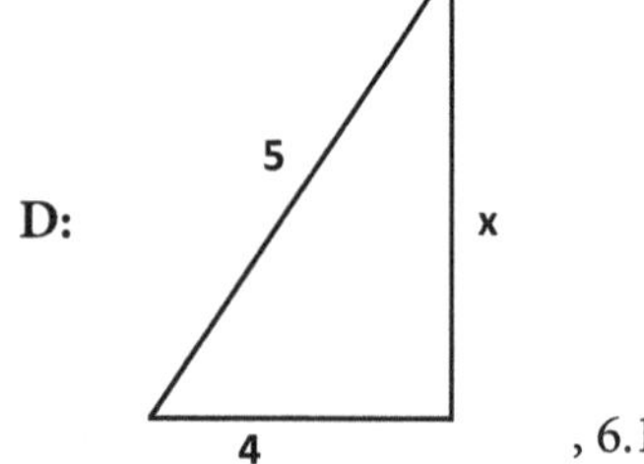

, 6.1

Answer Explanation:

Choice B is correct because the given figure represents the flower bed and the value of the third side is also correct.

Draw the flower bed.

Make a right triangle and label A as the right angle.

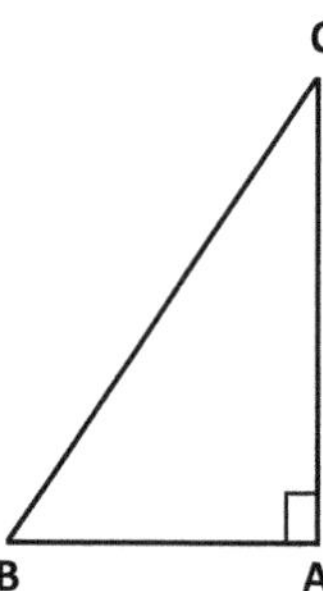

Label AB and AC as 4 feet and 5 feet .

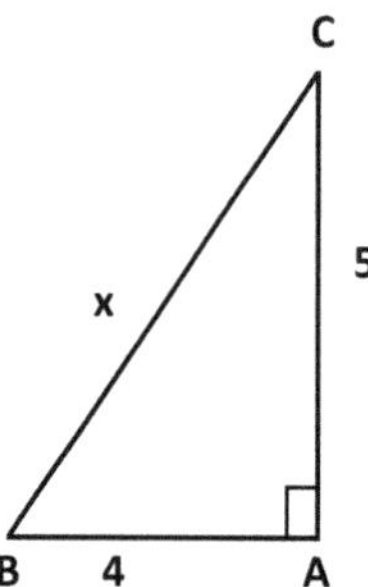

Find the new value x.

$$x^2 = 5^2 + 4^2$$
$$x^2 = 25 + 16$$
$$x^2 = 41$$
$$\sqrt{x^2} = \sqrt{41}$$
$$x = 6.4$$

Hence, Choice B matches the answers.

Choice A is incorrect because the value of the new length of the lumber is incorrect.

Choice C is incorrect because the figure does not represent the given problem.

Choice D is incorrect because both figure and value of the new length is incorrect.

Representing Data and Functions

This domain evaluates your ability to use graphs, tables, and symbolic expressions to visualize, interpret, and analyze mathematical relationships and data. You should be able to connect different representations of a function and understand how changes in one format affect the others.

Detailed Skill Breakdown

- **Interpret graphs of functions and data sets:** Read and analyze various types of graphs, such as line graphs, bar charts, scatterplots, or parabolas. Identify features like intercepts, slope, turning points, and trends.
- **Match equations to their graphs:** Given a function (linear, quadratic, exponential, etc.), recognize or sketch its graph. Conversely, be able to choose the correct equation for a given graph.
- **Translate between representations (tables, graphs, and equations):** Move fluidly between tables of values, algebraic expressions, and graphical representations of the same relationship.
- **Identify key features of functions from different representations**
- **Represent real-world situations with functions:** Use function notation, graphs, or tables to model real-world relationships such as speed vs. time or cost vs. quantity.
- **Use data to create or improve models:** Fit a line or curve to a set of data points, and evaluate whether the model is a good fit.
- **Understand and apply function notation:** Interpret and use function notation (like f(x)) to represent relationships.
- **Model piecewise or multi-part functions:** Understand how functions can behave differently across intervals, and how those behaviors appear in graph or equation form.

Solved Example

Carefully study the graph below and answer the following:

What is the percentage of the car sold in 2004 for company A over the total number of cars sold over the years for company A?

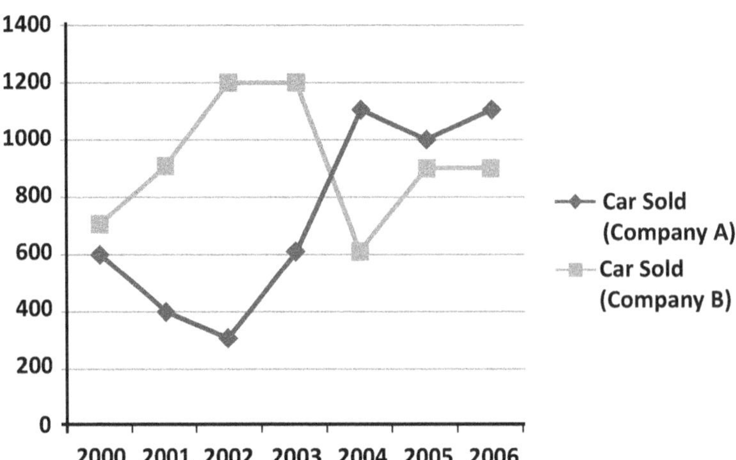

A: 24.46 %

B: 18.30 %

C: 19.64 %

D: 21.57%

Answer Explanation: Choice D is correct because the obtained value is 21.57%.

Find the total number of cars sold for company A.

Total cars sold by company $A = 600 + 400 + 300 + 600 + 1100 + 1000 + 1100 = 5100$

Percentage of the car sold in 2004 for company A over the total number of cars sold over the years for company A $= \frac{1100}{5100} \times 100\% = 21.57\%$.

Choice A is incorrect because 24.46 % is greater than the obtained value.

Choice B is incorrect because 18.30 % is less than the obtained value.

Choice C is incorrect because 19.64 % is less than the obtained value.

Question Types

The Math test consists entirely of multiple-choice questions—there are **no grid-ins or student-produced responses**.

Now, each question offers *four answer* choices instead of five.

Types of Problems in the Math test:

- Equations: Solving linear, quadratic, rational, and radical equations
- Graphs: Interpreting and analyzing data from graphs (line graphs, bar charts, scatterplots).
- Word Problems: Translating real-life scenarios into mathematical models and solving them.

Use of Figures and Diagrams

Many questions include diagrams, such as:

- Geometry Figures (triangles, circles, coordinate planes, rectangles, squares, polygons, 3D figures)

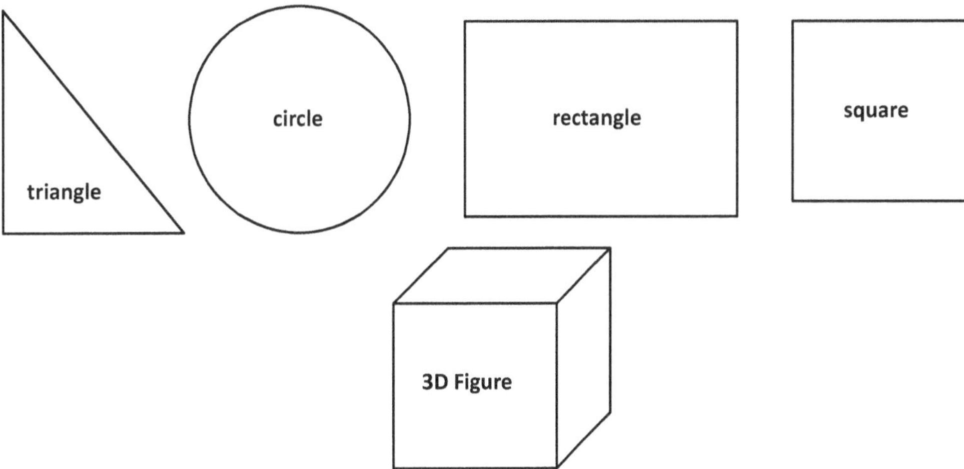

- Function Graphs (parabolas, linear function, exponential)

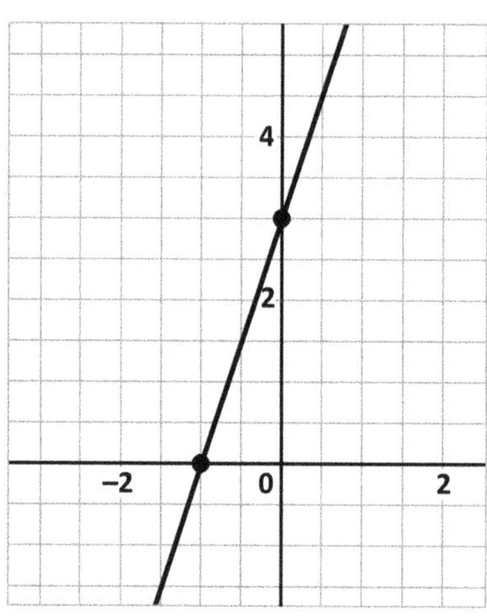

linear

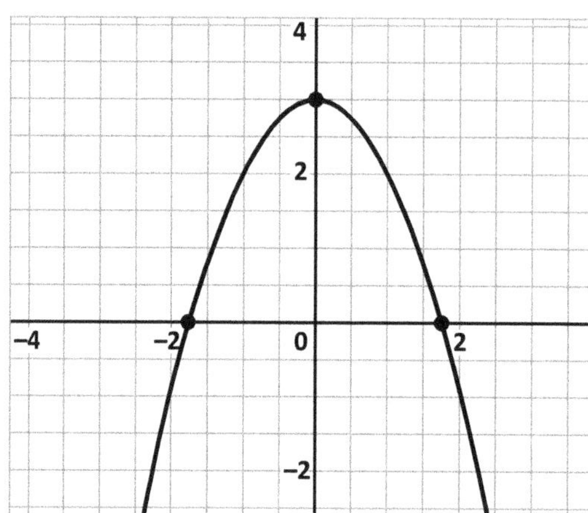

- Data Representations (bar graphs, histograms, scatterplots)

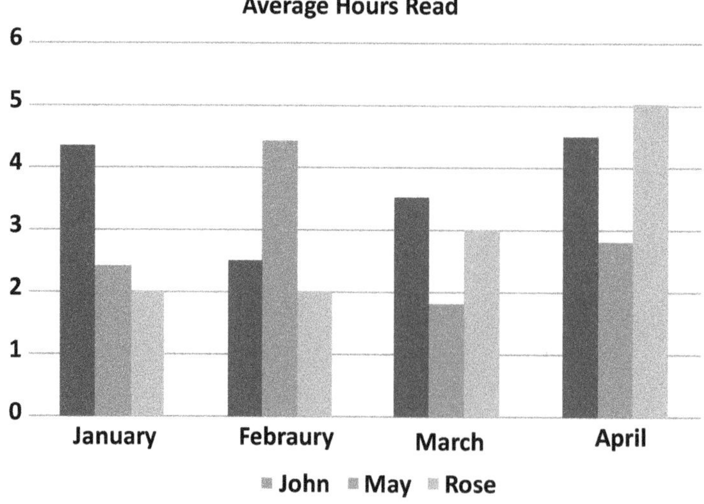

Calculator Use

The ACT permits the use of calculators, but only approved types are allowed.

List of Approved Calculators

✓ **4-Function Calculators**	Four-function, or "basic," calculators are designed with four main functions: addition, subtraction, multiplication, and division. Some basic calculators may include additional functions such as square roots and percentages.
✓ **Graphing Calculators (except those with CAS - Computer Algebra Systems)**	Graphing calculators offer capabilities such as plotting graphs, analyzing data, and performing complex mathematical functions like trigonometry and logarithms.
✓ **Scientific Calculators**	Scientific calculators are equipped with advanced functions necessary for solving high-level math, science, and engineering problems. Some of their features include scientific notation, statistical and probability functions, built-in memory, and much more.
✓ **Built-in Calculator in Digital ACT**	A built-in on-screen calculator is available during the Math section of the digital ACT. However, external calculators must not be connected to the testing computer or device in any form.

✓ WHEN to Use a Calculator

Use a calculator when:

1. **Performing complex arithmetic**
    - e.g., fractions, decimals, or large numbers like: 1234×567 or $7.25 \div 0.15$
2. **Dealing with long equations or formulas**
    - e.g., applying the quadratic formula or the distance formula.
3. **Solving with exponents, square roots, or pi**
    - Especially when estimating or rounding answers.
4. **Checking your final answer**
    - Quickly re-plugging values back into the original equation.

✕ WHEN NOT to Use a Calculator

Avoid the calculator when:

1. **The math is simple and faster by hand**
    - e.g., 6×5, subtracting small numbers, simplifying expressions.
2. **The question tests logic or pattern recognition**
    - e.g., sequence, estimation, or probability questions.

3. **The calculator might slow you down**
    - If you're typing multiple long inputs, it might be faster to simplify first.

HOW to Use a Calculator Effectively

1. **Know your calculator well**
    - Practice using the same calculator before test day (preferably a graphing or scientific calculator allowed by ACT).
2. **Use parentheses for accuracy**
    - For example, to input 3(5 + 2)^2 ÷ (4 – 1), use:
      3 × (5 + 2)^2 ÷ (4 – 1)
3. **Double-check entries**
    - A single typo can cost points — re-read your inputs before pressing =.
4. **Don't rely on it for concepts**
    - You still need to know the math concepts (algebra, geometry, etc.) — the calculator can't solve logic-based problems for you.
5. **Use it to test answer choices**
    - Especially helpful for plug-in or back-solving problems. Try answer choices in the equation to see which one works.

Scoring and Difficulty

The ACT Math section is scored on a scale ranging from 1 to 36. As you move through the section, the questions typically increase in difficulty, meaning that the earlier problems are usually more straightforward while the later ones may require more advanced reasoning or multi-step problem solving. There is no penalty for guessing on the ACT, so it is always in your best interest to select an answer for every question, even if you're unsure. Leaving a question blank only guarantees zero points, whereas guessing gives you a chance to earn credit.

Tips for Success in the Math Test

Succeeding on the ACT Math section requires more than just knowing formulas—it also takes strategic thinking and test-savvy habits. Below are some essential tips to help you maximize your score:

- **Work steadily and pace yourself:** With 45 questions to answer in 50 minutes, time management is crucial. Aim to spend about 1 to 1.5 minutes per question. If a problem seems complex, don't get stuck. Move on and return to it later if time allows. Maintaining a steady pace ensures that you have the opportunity to attempt all questions.
- **Flag difficult questions:** One benefit of the digital ACT is the ability to flag or mark questions you're unsure about. Use this feature wisely: if you find yourself spending too long on a tricky problem, flag it and move on. Come back after tackling the easier questions. This keeps your momentum going and helps you avoid time pressure at the end.

- **Use the calculator wisely:** Don't rely on the calculator for everything—it can slow you down. Use it for computations involving decimals, square roots, or multi-step arithmetic. For simple calculations, mental math or quick scratch work is often faster.
- **Watch out for common traps:** Many wrong answer choices are designed to reflect common mistakes (e.g., misapplying a formula or misunderstanding a graph). Double-check your work, especially on questions you find easy—you might overlook a key detail.
- **Memorize key formulas:** The ACT does not provide formulas on test day. Memorize all essential formulas required on test day. **Download the Free Math Cheat Sheet from the Online Resources of this book to memorize and keep all essential formulas handy.**

3 Key Strategies for ACT Math

Plugging In Answer Choices

The "Plugging In" strategy involves taking each answer choice and testing it directly in the given equation or condition, rather than solving the equation algebraically. It is especially useful when you're short on time, the equation looks complicated or intimidating, and the question has **simple answer choices** and asks for a value that "**could be**" or "**satisfies**" a condition.

Solved Example

The square of the sum of a number and 3 is 16 times the number. Which of the following could be the number?

A: –9

B: –1

C: 9

D: 10

Answer: (Hint : $(x+3)^2 = 16x$)

First, you need to understand the equation.

"The square of the sum of a number and 3" means $(x+3)^2$.

"Is 16 times the number" means $16x$.

So the full equation becomes $(x+3)^2 = 16x$

Now, let's plug in answer choices, but start with the middle choice.

Instead of checking all four options in order, start with the middle choices, B or C. Why?

✓ Because if the **value works**, you're done.

✗ If it's **too big** or **too small**, you can often eliminate two answers at once.

Try Choice C: $x=9$.

Substituting into the equation $(x+3)^2 = 16x$ yields $(9+3)^2 = 16(9)$

$(12)^2 = 144$

$144 = 144$

Both sides match! Therefore, $x = 9$ is the solution.

You've found the correct answer **on the first try** — no need to test A, B, or D.

Tips for using the Plugging In strategy more efficiently:

1. Start with the middle choice (usually B or C).
    - If it's too small or large, you can eliminate more than one option.
    - This avoids checking all four blindly.
2. Look for values that create easy arithmetic.
    - In this example, small integers like 9 or -1 make quick calculations easier.

Back-Solving

Back-solving is a strategy where you start with the answer choices and plug them into the problem to see which one works. But in some cases—especially when the question has variable expressions—you can also plug in a number that fits the condition given, and then test each answer choice with that number.

This is useful when the question gives a **range or condition** like "for $x < 1$", you're **comparing values of expressions**, not solving for an exact value, and **answer choices contain variables** or expressions.

Solved Example

For $x < -1$, which expression has the greatest value?

A: x^2

B: $2x$

C: x^3

D: $-x^2$

To solve using back-solving, pick a test value for x. Since the question says "for $x < -1$", choose a value **less than -1**.

Let's try $x = -2$ (a simple number that fits the condition).

Evaluate each expression at $x = -2$.

Choice A. $x^2 = (-2)^2 = 4$

Choice B. $2x = 2(-2) = -4$

Choice C. $x^3 = (-2)^3 = -8$

Choice D. $-x^2 = -(-2)^2 = -4$

Comparing the values, the greatest value is 4, which is Choice A.

This strategy is different from plugging in answer choices. Plugging in is when you are solving for a specific value by testing each given answer while Back-solving is when you pick your own number to evaluate or compare expressions, especially when answer choices contain variables.

Eliminating Wrong Answers Quickly

The elimination strategy involves ruling out answer choices that are clearly incorrect—even if you don't immediately know the right answer. This narrows your options and increases your odds if you need to guess, and it often leads you toward the correct answer more efficiently.

This technique is especially helpful when you're under time pressure, the question includes a clue that limits the possible answers, and you can test values or check for logic without full calculations

Solved Example

If $p=-7$ is one of the roots for $p^2+np-28=0$, what must be the other root?

A: – 4

B: 0

C: 1

D: 4

To solve, use the property of quadratic roots. When you know one root of a quadratic equation and the constant term (–28), you can use the fact that the product of the roots is equal to the constant term, if the equation is in standard form $p^2+np+c=0$, then the product of the roots is $r_1 \cdot r_2 = c$.

Eliminate wrong answers quickly by multiplying each choices by –7 and the answer should be –28.

Choice A: $-7\times(-4)=28$. Eliminate since it is not -28.

Choice B: $-7\times 0=0$. Eliminate since it is not -28.

Choice C: $-7\times 1=-7$. Eliminate since it is not -28.

Choice D: $-7\times 4=-28$. This is the correct answer.

Instead of solving for n or factoring the quadratic (which takes time), you can use the product of roots rule to test each choice. Within 15–20 seconds, you can eliminate three options and find the correct one without doing any algebraic factoring or rewriting.

Common Pitfalls to Avoid

Misreading Questions

Many ACT Math errors come not from misunderstanding math, but from misinterpreting what the question actually asks.

Common mistakes include ignoring keywords like "positive," "integer," "least," or "greatest", overlooking whether the question asks for *x*, *2x*, or another related value, and missing hidden details in word problems.

For example:

Find the positive difference between 3 and 8.

✗ Incorrect (misread): $3-8=-5$

✓ Correct (carefully read): $|8-3|=5$

Tip: Slow down briefly when you first read each question. Underline or mentally highlight critical words.

Rushing Through Easy Problems

Because the ACT is timed, many students hurry through the early, easier questions to "save time" for harder ones. This can backfire—simple errors can cost easy points.

Common rushing errors include skipping steps in basic arithmetic, failing to distribute correctly in algebra, and making mistakes on unit conversions in word problems.

For example:

Simplify: $5(2+4)$

✗ Quick, careless mistake: $5(2)+4=10+4=14$

✓ Careful step-by-step: $2+4=6$, $5(6)=30$

Tip: Treat *every* question seriously, no matter how easy it looks.

Getting Stuck on Time-Consuming Calculations

Some ACT Math problems are deliberately designed to be calculation-heavy to trap students into wasting time.

Common traps include problems with large numbers or fractions that look messier than they are and Geometry problems requiring tedious area/volume computations.

For example:

Find the area of an irregular polygon with 7 sides.

Instead of spending 5 minutes trying to calculate every part perfectly, it's smarter to flag the question and return to it later if you have time.

Tip: If you're stuck after 20–30 seconds without real progress, move on and come back later.

Misusing the Calculator

Calculators are a helpful tool, but they can cause as many errors as they solve if not used properly.

Common calculator mistakes are typing errors (wrong parentheses, missing negative signs), confusing exponents and multiplication, and using incorrect calculator settings (e.g., radians vs degrees for trigonometry).

For example:

Evaluate 2^3.

✗ Incorrect calculator use: $2\times3=6$ (Incorrect, multiplying instead of exponentiating)

✓ Correct: $2^3=2\times2\times2=8$

Tip:

- Always double-check calculator entries
- Know when mental math is faster and safer.
- Familiarize yourself with your calculator's specific functions *before* test day.

In short, slow down when it matters, be strategic with your time, trust but verify calculator results, and always stay attentive to question wording.

Learning to sidestep these common mistakes will help you pick up "easy points" that many other students miss.

How to Prepare

- **Review Core Concepts Thoroughly**: Start by mastering the foundational math topics most commonly tested on the ACT. Make sure you not only memorize formulas, but also know when and how to apply them.
- Algebra: Understand linear equations, inequalities, systems of equations, and quadratic functions.
- Geometry: Review angles, triangles, circles, coordinate geometry, and basic trigonometry.
- Functions: Get comfortable with interpreting and manipulating function notation, graphs, and translations.
- **Practice Mixed Question Sets**: The ACT Math section doesn't group questions by topic, so you'll need to quickly switch from algebra to geometry to data analysis within a single section. Use official ACT practice tests and questions from this book to simulate this variety.
- Practice sets that include a mix of question types.
- This trains your brain to adapt quickly and recognize the type of math a question requires without being told.
- **Take Timed Practice Tests**: Timing is a key challenge in the ACT Math section — you have 50 minutes for 45 questions. This helps build endurance, speed, and test-day confidence.
- Regularly take full-length, timed practice tests to simulate the real testing environment.
- Pay attention to your pacing: if you're spending more than a minute or so on most problems, work on strategies like skipping and returning to harder ones later.
- **Analyze Your Mistakes**: Improvement comes more from reviewing why you got a question wrong than just doing more practice. After each practice session or test:
- Don't just note what you got wrong — ask why. Was it a concept issue? A careless mistake? Misreading?
- Keep a mistake sheet where you track errors by topic. This will help you spot patterns and focus your review.
- Resolve the problem without looking at the solution—ensure you've actually learned how to solve it correctly.

Summary

- The ACT Math section consists of **45 multiple-choice questions** that must be completed in **50 minutes**, giving students approximately **1.1 minutes** per question.
- Each question has four answer choices, and students are expected to use a combination of mathematical reasoning, calculation, and strategic thinking to arrive at the correct answer.
- The Math test evaluates more than just the ability to perform calculations; it also assesses a student's understanding of mathematical concepts and their ability to solve real-world problems.
- Some questions are straightforward, while others require students to interpret graphs, diagrams, or word problems before beginning the computation.
- The Math section is divided into three major reporting categories:
  - **Preparing for Higher Math (PHM):** This category includes questions from five domains—Number & Quantity, Algebra, Functions, Geometry, and Statistics & Probability.
  - **Integrating Essential Skills (IES):** This category tests the ability to solve complex problems by combining knowledge from different areas of mathematics and applying it to real-life situations.
  - **Modeling:** This involves building and interpreting mathematical models and analyzing the relationships between data and functions.
- Calculators are allowed only during the Math section, but they must meet ACT's guidelines regarding permissible types.
- Acceptable calculators include basic four-function calculators, scientific calculators, and graphing calculators that do not have Computer Algebra System (CAS) functionality.
- In the digital version of the test, a built-in on-screen calculator is provided, but students may also use external calculators that are not connected to the test device.
- The ACT Math section requires more than memorization; it demands flexible strategies, precise execution under time pressure, and the ability to apply math concepts across topics and in real-world contexts.

Chapter 3

Number and Quantity Practice Questions

1.

A quadratic equation $x^2 + 4x + 20 = 0$ models the resonance of a system. The roots are $a + bi$ and $a - bi$, where a and b are real numbers.
What is the value of a and b, the real and imaginary part of the roots?

A. $a = 2$ and $b = 4$
B. $a = 2$ and $b = -4$
C. $a = -2$ and $b = 4$
D. $a = -2$ and $b = -4$

2.

What is the product of $(3+2i)$ and $(1-4i)$?

A. $11 - 10i$
B. $3 - 14i$
C. $11 + 10i$
D. $-5 + 10i$

3.

What is $(2+3i) + (4-5i)$?

A. $-2 + 8i$
B. $6 + 8i$
C. $6 - 2i$
D. $6 - 8i$

4.

An electronics engineer is analyzing a circuit where the current is represented by the complex number $I = 4 + 3i$ amperes, and the voltage across a component is given by $V = 2 - i$ volts. The power P (in volt-amperes) is calculated as $P = I \times V$. What is the power P in terms of real and imaginary parts?

A. $5 + 10i$
B. $8 + 11i$
C. $11 + 2i$
D. $5 - i$

5.

An engineer models a signal as $S = 6 + 8i$. The noise in the signal is represented as $N = 2 - 3i$. What is the resultant signal R when the noise is subtracted from the original signal?

A. $4 + 11i$
B. $8 + 5i$
C. $4 + 5i$
D. $8 + 11i$

6.

Sophia is analyzing a set of circuits. In one circuit, the current is represented as $3 + 2i$, where i is the imaginary unit ($i^2 = -1$). The voltage is represented as $5 - 3i$. To calculate the impedance Z of the circuit, she uses the formula $Z = \frac{voltage}{current}$.

What is the impedance Z, simplified into standard form $a + bi$?

A. $\frac{5}{15} - \frac{19i}{13}$
B. $\frac{9+9i}{13}$
C. $2+i$
D. $\frac{9-19i}{13}$

7.

In an electrical circuit, the resistance (R) is 6 ohms, and the reactance (X) is $4i$ ohms, where i is the imaginary unit. The impedance (Z) of the circuit is calculated using the formula $Z = R + X$.

What is the impedance Z of the circuit?

A. $6 + 4i$
B. $-4i$
C. $4 + 6i$
D. $10 + i$

8.

While driving her car along a highway, Marci counted 5 road signs every 2 minutes. If she travels along the highway for 24 minutes, how many road signs will she count?

A. 48
B. 120
C. 60
D. 72

9.

A Physics student is tasked to analyze the motion of a particle whose graph is shown below. The student is interested in finding the non-real (roots) the particle could theoretically occupy. What are the non-real roots of the particle's motion?

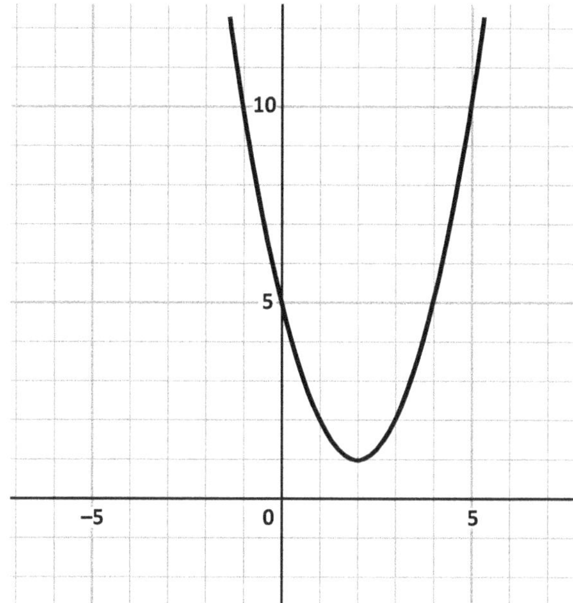

A. $2 \pm 2i$

B. $2 \pm i$

C. $2i \pm$

D. $5 \pm 2i$

10.

If $x = 3 + \sqrt{2}$, what can be said about x?

A. Rational
B. Irrational
C. Whole number
D. Undefined

11.

Which of the following expressions yields a rational number?

A. $\sqrt{-9}$

B. $i\sqrt{-9} \cdot i\sqrt{3}$

C. $(3-i)(3+i)$

D. $(3+i)(3+i)$

12.

A quadratic equation $x^2 - 4x + 8 = 0$ has complex roots. Let the roots of the equation be $a + bi$ and $a - bi$, where a and b are real numbers.
What is the value of a, the real part of the roots?
A. −4
B. 2
C. 4
D. 8

13.

A fabricating machine cuts out an ellipse from a piece of sheet metal to make an emblem for a product. The length of the major axis, k, of the ellipse that is cut out must be within 0.001 inches of the desired length of 8 inches.

Which of the following statements is true about the length of the major axis?

A. $|k-0.001|<8|k-0.001|<8|k-0.001|<8$

B. $|k+0.001|<8|k+0.001|<8|k+0.001|<8$

C. $|k+8|<0.001|k+8|< 0.001|k+8|<0.001$

D. $|k-8|<0.001|k-8|< 0.001|k-8|<0.001$

14.

A physicist is modeling wave interference and multiplies two complex numbers: $z_1 = 2 + 3i$ and $z_2 = 1 - i$. What is the product of z_1 and z_2?

A. $5 + i$
B. $2 + 5i$
C. $5 - i$
D. $5 + 5i$

15.

A scientist models a signal as $z = 2 + 3i$, where i represents the imaginary unit. Another signal is modeled as $w = 1 - 4i$. What is the combined signal $z + w$?

A. 3 − i
B. 1 + i
C. 3 − 7i
D. $3 + i$

16.

What is the standard form of 4/(2+i)?

A. $\frac{48}{25}-\frac{64}{25}i$
B. $\frac{8}{5}-\frac{4}{5}i$
C. $\frac{16}{5}-\frac{8}{5}i$
D. $\frac{13}{5}-\frac{4}{5}i$

17.

Which of the following numbers is both real and complex?

A. 3
B. $2 + 3i$
C. $-i$
D. $4i$

18.

What is the value of $(2 + i)^2$?

A. $3 + 4i$
B. $4 + 4i$
C. $5 + 4i$
D. $3 + 2i$

19.

A wave's displacement is modeled as $z = a + bi$, where a is the real part and b is the imaginary part. If $z = 4 + 3i$, what is the conjugate z?

A. $\overline{z} = 2 + 3i$
B. $\overline{z} = 3 - 4i$
C. $\overline{z} = 4 + 3i$
D. $\overline{z} = 4 - 3i$

20.

Freddy is analyzing a set of circuits. In one circuit, the current is represented as $3 + 2i$, where i is the imaginary unit ($i^2 = -1$). The voltage is represented as $5 - 3i$. To calculate the impedance Z of the circuit, he uses the formula $Z = \frac{voltage}{current}$.

What is the conjugate of the denominator in Freddy's calculation?

A. $3 - 2i$
B. $3 + 2i$
C. $5 - 3i$
D. $5 + 3i$

21.

If $z = 3 + bi$ is a complex number where b is a real number, which value of b makes z a purely real number?

A. -1
B. 0
C. 1
D. 3

22.

Which of the following is a rational number?

A. $\sqrt{2}$
B. $\sqrt{5}$
C. $\sqrt{32}$
D. $\sqrt{49}$

23.

Which of the following is not a real number?

A. $\sqrt{2}$
B. 5–2i
C. $\sqrt{3}$
D. π

24.

Let $z_1 = 3+4i$ and $z_2 = 1-2i$. Simplify $z = \frac{z_1}{z_2}$ into standard form $a+bi$.

A. $-2+i$
B. $-1+2i$
C. $-\frac{7}{5}+\frac{16}{5}i$
D. $-1-2i$

25.

A mechanical system uses a complex number $z = 5 + 12i$ to represent displacement. The phase angle of z is used to calculate the direction of displacement, and the magnitude of z represents the amplitude.

The system multiplies z by $2i$. What is the resulting complex number?

A. $-24 + 10i$
B. $24 - 10i$
C. $-10-24i$
D. 10+24i

26.

Simplify the expression $(3 + 4i) + (-5 - 2i)$.

A. $-2 + 6i$
B. $-2 + 2i$
C. $-8 + 6i$
D. $-8 + 2i$

27.

Two points on the complex plane are represented by the numbers $3 + 4i$ and $-1-2i$. What is the distance between these two points?

A. $\sqrt{29}$
B. 7
C. $\sqrt{52}$
D. 8

28.

In an electrical circuit, the impedance Z (in ohms) is modeled by the equation $Z = R + Xi$, where R is the resistance (in ohms), and X is the reactance (in ohms). If the impedance of the circuit is given as $Z = 5 + 12i$, what is the magnitude of Z?

A. 12
B. 13
C. 17
D. 25

29.

Which of the following is irrational?

A. 2×3
B. $\sqrt{2} \times 4$
C. $\sqrt{25} \times 5$
D. $\frac{1}{2} \times \frac{4}{5}$

30.

If $z = 3 + 4i$ and $w = 2 - 3i$, what is the value of $z + w$?

A. $5 + i$
B. $5 - i$
C. $1 + i$
D. $1 - i$

31.

Solve the inequality $|2x - 5| > 7$. Which of the following values of x satisfies the inequality?

A. $x = -1$
B. $x = 0$
C. $x = 6$
D. $x = 7$

32.

A group of friends decides to meet at a park. Their locations on a straight road are represented by points on a number line:
Anna: $x = -3$
Ben: $x = 5$
Carla: $x = 2$

Who is closer to Carla: Anna or Ben?

A. Anna
B. Ben
C Both are equally close
D. Neither is close

33.

A tennis ball company packages 490 balls per box, but each box may contain up to 6 balls more or less. What range of tennis balls is acceptable in a single box?

A. $444 \leq x \leq 486$
B. $484 \leq x \leq 496$
C. $473 \leq x \leq 490$
D. $490 \leq x \leq 496$

34.

A solution containing water and 5% sugar is added to 2 quarts of a second solution containing water and 8% sugar. How many quarts of the 5% sugar solution should be added to the 8% sugar solution to make a solution that is 7% sugar?

A. 1
B. 2.6
C. 3
D. 5.2

35.

Three cities—City A, City B, and City C—are located along a straight highway.
City A is at $x = -5$
City B is at $x = 2$
City C is at $x = 10$
A delivery truck starts from City A and travels to City B, then to City C.

What is the distance between City A and City B?

A. 3
B. 5
C. 7
D. 10

36.

Zack spends 30% of his day at school. Of the other 70% of his day, Zack spends 20% doing homework. How many hours are left in Zack's day that is not spent in school or doing homework?

A. 3.36
B. 13.44
C. 16.80
D. 5.04

37.

One-half of a number is 54. One-fourth of one-half of another number is 12. What is the sum of the two numbers?

A. 66
B. 30
C. 123
D. 204

38.

The sale price for a laptop computer has been discounted to $485. If the normal sale price for the laptop computer is $550, what is the discount expressed as a percent?

A. 88
B. 13
C. 12
D. 15

39.

If $|x + 4| > 6$, which of the following is correct?

A. $-10 < x < 2$
B. $2 < x < -10$
C. $-6 < x < 6$
D. $6 < x < -6$

40.

On a number line, points A, B, and C are positioned such that $|A - B| = 3$ and $|B - C| = 4$. What is the maximum possible distance between A and C?

A. 1
B. 3
C. 4
D. 7

41.

The sum of two numbers is 6, and their absolute difference is 10. What are the numbers?

A. 8 and −2
B. 7 and −1
C. 9 and −1
D. 6 and 0

42.

On a number line, what is the distance between −4 and 3?

A. 3
B. 4
C. 7
D. 8

43.

Four points, A, B, C, and D, are located on a number line at A = −10, B = −3, C = 5, and D = 12, respectively. Which of the following points is farthest from $x = 2$?

A. A
B. B
C. C
D. D

44.

Which number is closest to 0 on the number line?

A. $-\frac{5}{4}$
B. −0.9
C. $\sqrt{0.7}$
D. $\frac{7}{6}$

45.

Lara, James, and Mia live along the same straight street. Lara lives at $x = -4$, James lives at $x = 5$, and Mia lives at $x = 2$.

What is the distance between Lara and James?

A. 7
B. 8
C. 9
D. 10

46.

Which absolute value function has the same solution set as the number line shown below?

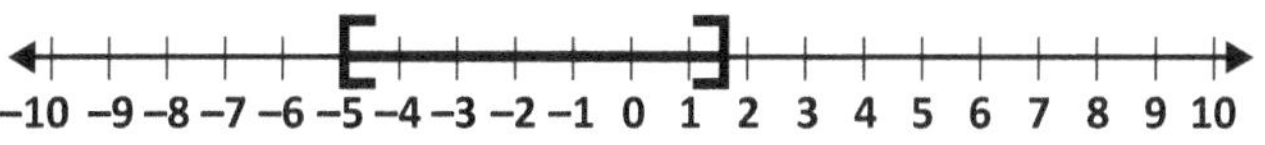

A. $2|5x + 3| - 4 \geq -10$
B. $-3|7x - 2| \leq -13$
C. $-2|3x + 5| + 7 \geq -13$
D. $|3x + 5| + 7 \geq -13$

47.

Solve for x in the equation $|3x - 5| = 7$.

A. $x = 4$ or $x = -\frac{2}{3}$
B. $x = 5$ or $x = -1$
C. $x = 3$ or $x = -1$
D. $x = 4$ or $x = 2$

48.

If $|x| = 6$, what are the possible values of x?

A. 6 only
B. −6 only
C. 6 and −6
D. None of the above

49.

What fraction is represented by the point P on the number line below?

P

|- - - -|- -|- -|- - - -|- - - -|

0 $\frac{1}{4}$ $\frac{1}{2}$ $\frac{3}{4}$ 1

A. $\frac{3}{8}$
B. $\frac{1}{2}$
C. $\frac{5}{8}$
D. $\frac{3}{4}$

50.

Which of the following is the solution to the inequality $|x + 3| \leq 5$?

A. $-2 \leq x \leq 8$
B. $-8 \leq x \leq 8$
C. $-2 \leq x \leq 2$
D. $-8 \leq x \leq 2$

51.

A number line is divided into 8 equal parts between 0 and 4. What fraction does the point at the third mark represent?

A. $\frac{3}{8}$
B. $\frac{1}{2}$
C. $\frac{3}{4}$
D. $\frac{6}{8}$

52.

How many integers lie between $-\frac{15}{3}$ and $\frac{16}{3}$?

A. 9
B. 10
C. 11
D. 12

53.

Four points, A, B, C, and D, are located on a number line at $A = -10$, $B = -3$, $C = 5$, and $D = 12$, respectively. Which of the following points is farthest from $x = 2$?

A. A
B. B
C. C
D. D

54.

Which of the following satisfies $|x| > 3$?

A. −2
B. 0
C. 3
D. 4

55.

Which of the following represents the solution to $|3x-2| \leq 4$?

A. $-\frac{2}{3} \leq x \leq 2$
B. $-\frac{4}{3} < x < 4$
C. $-\frac{2}{3} < x < 2$
D. $-\frac{2}{3} \leq x \leq 1$

56.

On the number line, what is the midpoint between −5 and 1?

A. −3
B. −2
C. −1
D. 0

57.

If $|2x{-}3| = 7$, what are the possible values of x?

A. −2 and 5
B. −2 and 4
C. 2 and 5
D. 2 and −4

58.

A number line shows fractions between −3 and 3, divided into 6 equal intervals. What is the fraction at the second mark to the right of 0?

A. $\frac{1}{6}$
B. $\frac{1}{3}$
C. $\frac{2}{6}$
D. $\frac{2}{3}$

59.

Which of the following inequalities represents the solution set of $|x + 1| \leq 3$?

A. $-2 \leq x \leq 4$
B. $-4 \leq x \leq 2$
C. $x \geq -2$ or $x \leq 4$
D. $x < -4$ or $x > 2$

60.

Two points, P and Q, are located at $x = -18$ and $x = 6$, respectively. If R is the midpoint between P and Q, and S is the midpoint between R and Q, what is the location of S?

A. −6
B. 0
C. 1.5
D. 3

61.

How many integers lie between $\frac{7}{3}$ and 5?

A. 1
B. 2
C. 3
D. 4

62.

Which statement is equivalent to $|2x + 1| \geq 3$?

A. $3 \leq 2x + 1 \leq -3$
B. $-3 < 2x + 1 < 3$
C. $3 \leq 2x \leq -4$
D. $1 \leq x \leq -2$

63.

On a number line, the distance between two points is 10. If one point is −7, what is the other?

A. 3 or −17
B. −3 or −17
C. 7 or 17
D. −7 or 10

64.

On a number line, points A, B, and C are located at $x = -12$, $x = 4$, and $x = 10$, respectively. What is the absolute difference between the distance from A to B and the distance from B to C?

A. 2
B. 6
C. 8
D. 10

65.

Which fraction is represented by T on the number line below?

```
              T
|- - - -|- -|- -|- - - -|- - - - - - -|
-1    -7/8   -3/4    -1/2            0
```

A. $-\frac{7}{8}$
B. $-\frac{3}{4}$
C. $-\frac{5}{8}$
D. $-\frac{1}{2}$

66.

Solve for x: $|3x - 9| > 6$.

A. $x > 5$ or $x < 1$
B. $x > 4$ or $x < 0$
C. $x > 6$ or $x < 1$
D. $x > 6$ or $x < -1$

67.

A delivery truck must deliver items to three houses located at $x = -4$, $x = 1$ and $x = 7$ on a number line. The truck starts at $x = 0$.

What is the distance the truck must travel to reach the house at $x = -4$?

A. 2
B. 4
C. 6
D. 8

68.

C, F, and E lie on the same ray as shown in the diagram below. The ratio of CF to FE is 3:1. Which of the following statements must be true?

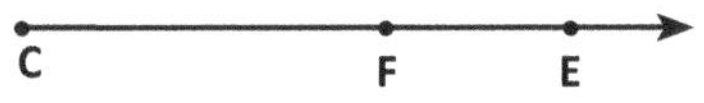

A. FE = 4CE
B. $FE = \frac{1}{3} CE$
C. $FE = \frac{3}{4} CE$
D. $CF = \frac{3}{4} CE$

69.

The temperature of oil in a car is recorded in the table below for the first 5 minutes after the car is turned off.

Time (minutes)	Temperature (°F)
0	275
1	262
2	242
3	202
4	152
5	91

Which of the following statements is true about the temperature?

A. The temperature of the oil is decreasing at an increasing rate.
B. The temperature of the oil is decreasing at a decreasing rate.
C. The temperature of the oil is decreasing at a constant rate.
D. The temperature of the oil is inversely proportional to time.

70.

On the number line, which of the following represents the solution set for $|x| < 4$?

A. $-4 < x < 4$
B. $-4 \leq x \leq 4$
C. $x < -4$ or $x > 4$
D. $x = -4$ or $x = 4$

71.

Let $a = -3$.
If x satisfies $|x - a| = 10$, what are the possible values of x?

A. 7,–13
B. 10,–7
C. 13,–7
D. 3,–7

72.

If $y = |2x - 1|$, what is the smallest possible value of y?

A. –2
B. –1
C. 0
D. 1

73.

Let $a = -3$, $b = 4$, and $c = 7$.
Which of the following is closest to the midpoint between b and c on the number line?

A. 4.5
B. 5
C. 5.5
D. 6

74.

Which point on the number line represents $|-4| + |1|$?

A. -5
B. -3
C. 3
D. 5

75.

Let $a = -3$, $b = 4$, and $c = 7$.
What is the value of $|a - b|$?

A. 1
B. 5
C. 7
D. 10

76.

Simplify $(x^2 y^3)^4 \div x^3 y^5$

A. $x^5 y^{12}$
B. $x^5 y^7$
C. $x^8 y^7$
D. $x^8 y^{12}$

77.

Simplify $\dfrac{(a^2b^{-1})^3}{(a^{-1}b^2)^2}$

A. a^6b^{-3}
B. $a^{-8}b^7$
C. a^8b^{-7}
D. $a^{-2}b^4$

78.

Simplify $\dfrac{(3a^{-1}b^2)^2 \cdot \left(a^3b^{-4}\right)}{(a^2b^{-1})^3}$

A. $\dfrac{9a^3b^{-1}}{a^6b^{-3}}$
B. $9a^{-3}b^7$
C. $9a^{-5}b^3$
D. $9a^{-3}b^7$

79.

A machine can produce 2^k widgets every hour, where k is the number of hours since the machine started operating. How many widgets can the machine produce in total after n hours?

A. 2^{n-1}
B. $n \cdot 2n$
C. $2^{2n} - 1$
D. $2^{n+1} - 2$

80.

Simplify the expression $3^4 \cdot 3^2$

A. 3^6
B. 3^8
C. 9^2
D. 18^3

81.

Simplify $(2x^{-3}y^2)^2 \cdot \dfrac{x^4}{y^{-1}}$

A. $4x^{-2}y^5$
B. $4x^{-2}y^3$
C. $4x^{-6}y^3$
D. $4x^{-6}y^5$

82.

Simplify $\dfrac{2^5 \cdot 2^3}{2^4}$

A. 2^2
B. 2^3
C. 2^4
D. 2^5

83.

If $x = 2^3$ and $y = 2^4$, find the value of $\dfrac{y^2}{x^3}$.

A. 2^{-1}
B. 2^2
C. 2^5
D. 2^8

84.

Simplify the expression $\left(3^2 \cdot 3^4\right) \div 3^3$

A. 3^2
B. 3^3
C. 3^6
D. 3^9

85.

Simplify the expression $\frac{9a^6b^3}{3a^2b^4}$

A. $6a^3b^2$
B. $6a^8b^{-1}$
C. $3a^3b^3$
D. $3a^4b^{-1}$

86.

Two cars exit an airport at the same time, one car traveling due north and the other due south. One car's speed is 4 miles an hour faster than the other car. After 3 hours, the cars are 204 miles apart. How fast, in miles per hour, is the slower car going?

A. 20
B. 25
C. 30
D. 32

87.

Find the distance between $1+2i$ and $-3+4i$.

A. 5
B. $\sqrt{20}$
C. 10
D. $\sqrt{25}$

88.

A ship starts at point $2 + 3i$ on a map and sails to point $6 + 7i$. What is the distance traveled by the ship?

A. 4
B. $\sqrt{16}$
C. $\sqrt{32}$
D. 8

89.

If $z=5-2i$, what is the result of $z\cdot\overline{z}$?

A. 29
B. 25
C. $5 - 2i$
D. $5 + 2i$

90.

Two cities on a grid are located at $-3 + 4i$ and $1 + 6i$. What is the midpoint of the two cities?

A. $-2 + 5i$
B. $0 + 5i$
C. $-1 + 6i$
D. $-1 + 5i$

91.

What is the product of $2 + 3i$ and its complex conjugate?

A. 13
B. $4 + 9i$
C. $4 - 9i$
D. 5

92.

What is the distance between the complex numbers $3 + 4i$ and $0 + 0i$?

A. 3
B. 4
C. 5
D. $\sqrt{29}$

93.

A drone moves from $2 + 3i$ to $-4 + 7i$. Later, it travels to $6 - 5i$. What is the total distance traveled by the drone?

A. $\sqrt{100}+\sqrt{200}$
B. $\sqrt{52}+\sqrt{244}$
C. $\sqrt{40}+\sqrt{180}$
D. 14

94.

What is the midpoint of the complex numbers $6 + 8i$ and $2 + 4i$?

A. $8 + 12i$
B. $4 + 6i$
C. $3 + 7i$
D. $2 + 6i$

95.

Two points in the complex plane are $4+7i$ and $-8-3i$. A third point, $x+yi$, lies exactly halfway between these two points. What is the value of $x+y$?

A. −2
B. −1
C. 0
D. 1

96.

What will be the value of $a < 0$ if the determinant $[ad\text{-}bc]$ of the matrix $\begin{bmatrix} 5 & a \\ a & 3 \end{bmatrix}$ is twice the value of a?

A. −5
B. −3
C. −2
D. −1

97.

Vector $\vec{A}=(5,12)$, and vector $\vec{B}=(-3,4)$. What is the magnitude of $\vec{A}-\vec{B}$?

A. $\sqrt{64}$
B. $\sqrt{128}$
C. 16
D. 64

98.

A ship sails 8 miles east and 6 miles south. How far is the ship from its starting point?

A. 9 miles
B. $\sqrt{91}$ miles
C. 10 miles
D. 12 miles

99.

Vector $\vec{A}=(3,4)$. What is the magnitude of $\vec{A}$?

A. $\sqrt{10}$
B. 5
C. 7
D. 25

100.

A boat travels in a straight line at 30 mph on a bearing of 45° (northeast). Simultaneously, a current pushes the boat at 10 mph directly south. What is the boat's resultant speed?

A. $\sqrt{170}$ mph
B. $\sqrt{200}$ mph
C. 24 mph
D. 35 mph

101.

Vector $\vec{D}=(1,-2)$. If $3\vec{D}$ is the scaled version of $\vec{D}$, what is $3\vec{D}$?

A. (3,−6)
B. (4,−8)
C. (−3,6)
D. (3,6)

102.

A car drives 60 miles south and 80 miles west. What is the magnitude of the car's displacement from its starting point?

A. 90 miles
B. 100 miles
C. $\sqrt{12100}$ miles
D. $\sqrt{14400}$ miles

103.

An airplane moves at 200 mph north and 150 mph west. What is the magnitude of its displacement?

A. $\sqrt{32000}$ mph
B. $\sqrt{50000}$ mph
C. 250 mph
D. 350 mph

104.

Two vectors, $\vec{A}=(3,4)$ and $\vec{B}=(5,-12)$, are added together. What is the magnitude of the resulting vector $\vec{A}+\vec{B}$?

A. −64
B. 8
C. $8\sqrt{2}$
D. $\sqrt{170}$

105.

A vector $\vec{E}$ has components $(x,3)$. If the magnitude of $\vec{E}$ is 5, what is the value of x?

A. −5
B. 3
C. 4
D. 5

106.

A theater has two seating sections. Section A has 3 rows with 4 seats per row, and Section B has 2 rows with 5 seats per row. Represent the seating arrangement as a matrix, where each row represents a section, and each column represents a row in that section.
Which of the following matrices correctly represents this arrangement?

A. $\begin{bmatrix} 3 & 3 & 3 \\ 2 & 2 & \end{bmatrix}$

B. $\begin{bmatrix} 4 & 4 & 4 \\ 5 & 5 & \end{bmatrix}$

C. $\begin{bmatrix} 3 & 4 \\ 2 & 5 \end{bmatrix}$

D. $\begin{bmatrix} 3 & 3 & 3 \\ 5 & 5 & \end{bmatrix}$

107.

A tech company analyzes the number of projects completed by two teams across three quarters using the matrix $M = \begin{bmatrix} 8 & 12 & 10 \\ 15 & 18 & 20 \end{bmatrix}$. Each project earns \$5,000 in Quarter 1, \$6,000 in Quarter 2, and \$7,000 in Quarter 3. Representing these earnings in matrix $E = \begin{bmatrix} 5000 \\ 6000 \\ 7000 \end{bmatrix}$, what is the total revenue generated by both teams combined?

A. \$141,000
B. \$182,000
C. \$323,000
D. \$505,000

108.

A school tracks its students' grades in two subjects: math and science. There are three students, and their grades are represented in the matrix below, where rows represent students and columns represent subjects

$$\begin{bmatrix} 85 & 90 \\ 78 & 88 \\ 92 & 95 \end{bmatrix}.$$

What is the science grade for the second student?

A. 85
B. 88
C. 90
D. 95

109.

A restaurant tracks its daily sales of beverages and desserts in two different weeks using matrices. The sales are represented as $A = \begin{bmatrix} 20 & 15 \\ 25 & 10 \end{bmatrix}$, $B = \begin{bmatrix} 18 & 12 \\ 22 & 8 \end{bmatrix}$.

Here, the rows represent beverages and desserts, and the columns represent Week 1 and Week 2, respectively.

The restaurant owner wants to calculate the total sales for beverages and desserts over both weeks. What is the resulting matrix?

A. $\begin{bmatrix} 38 & 27 \\ 47 & 18 \end{bmatrix}$

B. $\begin{bmatrix} 38 & 27 \\ 50 & 20 \end{bmatrix}$

C. $\begin{bmatrix} 40 & 29 \\ 49 & 20 \end{bmatrix}$

D. $\begin{bmatrix} 20 & 15 \\ 25 & 10 \end{bmatrix}$

110.

Matrix $A=\begin{bmatrix}1 & 2\\ 3 & 4\end{bmatrix}$ and $B=\begin{bmatrix}2 & 0\\ 1 & -1\end{bmatrix}$. Find $A\times B$.

A. $\begin{bmatrix}4 & -2\\ 6 & -5\end{bmatrix}$

B. $\begin{bmatrix}5 & -1\\ 6 & -5\end{bmatrix}$

C. $\begin{bmatrix}4 & -2\\ 10 & -4\end{bmatrix}$

D. $\begin{bmatrix}5 & 2\\ 10 & -4\end{bmatrix}$

111.

What is the value for k if the determinant for the matrix $\begin{bmatrix}6 & k\\ k & 4\end{bmatrix}$ is 5 times k?

A. −8
B. −3
C. 4
D. 8

112.

A company tracks the performance of two teams over three months using the matrix $P=\begin{bmatrix}20 & 30 & 25\\ 15 & 35 & 40\end{bmatrix}$

The rows represent Team A and Team B, and the columns represent months 1, 2, and 3. The matrix $Q=\begin{bmatrix}2\\ 3\\ 1\end{bmatrix}$ represents the revenue multiplier (in thousands of dollars) for each month. What is the total revenue for Team A.

A. \$130,000
B. \$140,000
C. \$145,000
D. \$155,000

113.

A delivery company uses the following matrix to represent the number of packages delivered on weekdays by two delivery teams $A=\begin{bmatrix}10 & 12\\ 15 & 18\end{bmatrix}$.

Each delivery team earns \$5 per package. What is the total earnings for both teams combined?

A. \$250
B. \$270
C. \$275
D. \$290

114.

Given $C=\begin{bmatrix}3 & 5\\ 1 & 4\end{bmatrix}$, find the determinant of C.

A. −7
B. −1
C. 7
D. 17

115.

If the scalar 2 is multiplied with the matrix $\begin{bmatrix}3 & 5\\ 7 & 9\end{bmatrix}$, what is the resulting matrix?

A. $\begin{bmatrix}6 & 10\\ 14 & 27\end{bmatrix}$

B. $\begin{bmatrix}9 & 15\\ 21 & 18\end{bmatrix}$

C. $\begin{bmatrix}6 & 15\\ 21 & 18\end{bmatrix}$

D. $\begin{bmatrix}6 & 10\\ 14 & 18\end{bmatrix}$

Answer Key

Question	Correct	Make your correct answers
1	C	
2	A	
3	C	
4	C	
5	A	
6	D	
7	A	
8	C	
9	B	
10	B	
11	C	
12	B	
13	D	
14	A	
15	A	
16	B	
17	A	
18	A	
19	D	
20	A	
21	B	
22	D	
23	B	
24	B	
25	A	
26	B	
27	C	
28	B	
29	B	
30	A	
31	D	
32	B	

Question	Correct	Make your correct answers
33	B	
34	A	
35	C	
36	B	
37	D	
38	C	
39	B	
40	D	
41	A	
42	C	
43	A	
44	C	
45	C	
46	C	
47	A	
48	C	
49	A	
50	D	
51	A	
52	B	
53	A	
54	D	
55	A	
56	B	
57	A	
58	D	
59	B	
60	B	
61	B	
62	A	
63	A	
64	D	

Question	Correct	Make your correct answers
65	C	
66	A	
67	B	
68	D	
69	A	
70	A	
71	A	
72	C	
73	C	
74	D	
75	C	
76	B	
77	C	
78	C	
79	D	
80	A	
81	A	
82	C	
83	A	
84	B	
85	D	
86	D	
87	B	
88	C	
89	A	
90	D	
91	A	
92	C	
93	B	
94	B	
95	C	
96	A	

Question	Correct	Make your correct answers
97	B	
98	C	
99	B	
100	C	
101	A	
102	B	
103	C	
104	C	
105	C	
106	B	
107	D	
108	B	
109	A	
110	C	
111	A	
112	D	
113	C	
114	C	
115	D	

1.

Category: IES & Modeling
Skill: Real and complex number systems | **Level:** Easy

Choice C is correct. For a quadratic equation $ax^2 + bx + c = 0$, the real part of the root is given by $-\frac{b}{2a}$.
Substituting $a = 1$ and $b = 4$ into the formula yields
$-\frac{4}{2(1)} = -2$.
The imaginary part of the roots is given by

$$b = \sqrt{\left(-\frac{b}{2a}\right)^2 - \frac{c}{a}} = \sqrt{(-2)^2 - \frac{20}{1}} = \sqrt{4-20} = \sqrt{-16} = 4i$$

Choice A is incorrect. It incorrectly makes the real part positive instead of negative. **Choice B** is incorrect. It flips both the real and imaginary parts to the wrong signs. **Choice D** is incorrect. It gives the correct real part but flips the imaginary part's sign.

2.

Category: PHM
Skill: Real and complex number systems | **Level:** Easy

Choice A is correct. Using the distributive property to multiply the given complex numbers $(3 + 2i)$ and $(1 - 4i)$ yields

$$(3 + 2i)(1 - 4i)$$
$$= 3(1)+3(-4i)+2i(1)+2i(-4i)$$
$$= 3 - 12i + 2i - 8i^2$$

Since $i^2 = -1$, thus, $-8i^2 = -8(-1) = 8$
Combining like terms yields $3 + 8 - 12i + 2i = 11 - 10i$

Choice B is incorrect. This may be due to calculation or conceptual error. **Choice C** is incorrect. This may be due to calculation or conceptual error. **Choice D** is incorrect. This may be due to calculation or conceptual error.

3.

Category: PHM
Skill: Real and complex number systems | **Level:** Easy

Choice C is correct. Adding the real parts and imaginary parts of the given complex numbers $(2 + 3i) + (4 - 5i)$ separately yields

$$(2 + 4) + (3i - 5i)$$
$$= 6 - 2i$$

Choice A is incorrect. This may result if the given is $(2 + 3i) - (4 - 5i)$. **Choice B** is incorrect. This may result if the given is $(2 + 3i) + (4 + 5i)$. **Choice D** is incorrect. This may result if the given is $(2 - 3i)+(4 - 5i)$.

4.

Category: PHM
Skill: Real and complex number systems | **Level:** Medium

Choice C is correct. To find P, multiply the two complex numbers I and V using distributive property to get

$$P = I \times V = (4 + 3i)(2 - i)$$
$$= (4 \times 2) + (4(-i))+(3i \times 2)+(3i \times (-i))$$
$$= 8 - 4i + 6i - 3i^2$$
$$= 8 + 2i - 3i^2$$

Since $i^2 = -1$, then substitute -1 for i^2 to get

$$= 8 + 2i - 3(-1)$$
$$= 8 + 2i + 3$$
$$P = 11 + 2i$$

Choice A is incorrect. This may be due to calculation error. **Choice B** is incorrect. This may be due to calculation error. **Choice D** is incorrect. This may be due to calculation error.

5.

Category: IES & Modeling
Skill: Real and complex number systems | **Level:** Easy

Choice A is correct. To find the signal R, subtract N from S to get

$$R = S - N$$
$$R = (6 + 8i) - (2 - 3i)$$
$$R = 4 + 11i$$

Choice B is incorrect. This may be due to calculation error. **Choice C** is incorrect. This may be due to calculation error. **Choice D** is incorrect. This may be due to calculation error.

6.

Category: IES
Skill: Real and complex number systems | **Level:** Medium

Choice D is correct. To find Z, substitute the given voltage, $5 - 3i$ and current, $3 + 2i$ into the formula

$$Z = \frac{voltage}{current} \text{ to get } Z = \frac{5-3i}{3+2i} = \frac{5-3i}{3+2i} \times \frac{3-2i}{3-2i}$$

$$Z = \frac{15-10i-9i+6i^2}{9-6i+6i-4i^2} = \frac{15-19i-6}{9+4} = \frac{9-19i}{13}$$

Choice A is incorrect. This may be due to calculation error. **Choice B** is incorrect. This may result from swapping the sign of the imaginary part to positive. **Choice C** is incorrect. This may be due to calculation error.

7.

Category: PHM
Skill: Real and complex number systems | **Level:** Medium

Choice A is correct. The impedance is calculated as
$Z = R + X$.
It is given that $R = 6$ ohms and $X = 4i$ ohms; thus
$Z = 6 + 4i$.

Choice B is incorrect. This has the wrong sign for the imaginary part. **Choice C** is incorrect. This swaps the real and imaginary part. **Choice D** is incorrect. This may be due to calculation error.

8.

Category: IES
Skill: Real and complex number systems | **Level:** Medium

Choice C is correct because the obtained answer is 60.

Marci sees 5 road signs every 2 minutes.

She drives for 24 minutes.

Determine how many 2-minute intervals are in 24 minutes $= \dfrac{24}{2} = 12$ intervals

Multiply the number of signs per interval by the number of intervals:

$12 \times 5 = 60$ road signs

Hence, the answer is Choice C.

Choice A is incorrect because this assumes only 4 road signs per 2 minutes or a miscalculation in the number of intervals **Choice B** is incorrect because this assumes **5 road signs per minute**, not per 2 minutes — doubling the correct rate. **Choice D** is incorrect because this assumes a slightly higher rate than 5 signs per 2 minutes or a miscalculated number of intervals, possibly using 6 signs per 2 minutes.

9.

Category: PHM and Modeling
Skill: Real and complex number systems | **Level:** Medium

Choice B is correct because the obtained answer is $-2 \pm i$. Find the equation of the given graph.

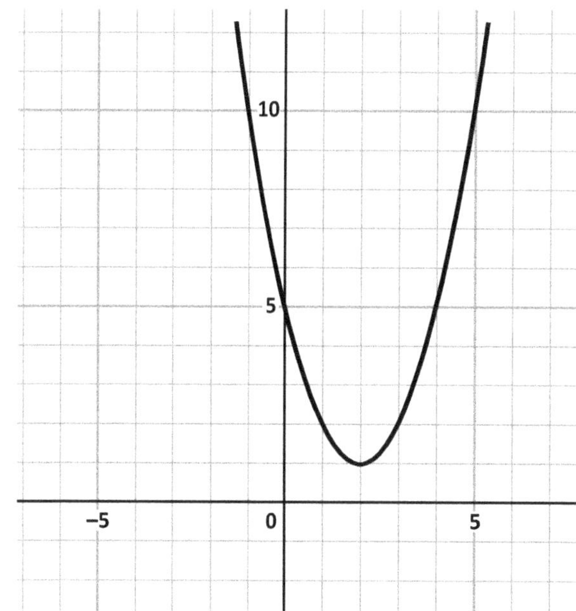

From the graph, take 3 points. Use the points (0, 5),(1, 2),(2, 1). Substitute these values into the equation $y = ax^2 + bx + c$.

$$y = ax^2 + bx + c$$
$$5 = a(0)^2 + b(0) + c$$
$$5 = c$$
$$y = ax^2 + bx + c$$
$$2 = a(1)^2 + b(1) + 5$$
$$2 = a + b + 5$$
$$-3 = a + b \quad \ldots\ldots (1)$$
$$y = ax^2 + bx + c$$
$$1 = a(2)^2 + b(2) + 5$$
$$1 = 4a + 2b + 5$$
$$-4 = 4a + 2b$$
$$-2 = 2a + b \quad \ldots\ldots (2)$$

Find the values of a and b using equation (1) and (2).

$$-3 = a + b$$
$$+2 = -2a - b$$
$$-1 = -a$$
$$1 = a$$

Use the value of a to find b.

$$-3 = a + b$$
$$-3 = 1 + b$$
$$-4 = b$$

Hence, the equation of the graph is $y = x^2 - 4x + 5$.

Use the quadratic equation to find the roots of the equation.

$$x = \frac{-b \pm \sqrt{b^2 - 4ac}}{2a}$$

$$x = \frac{-(-4) \pm \sqrt{(-4)^2 - 4(1)(5)}}{2(1)}$$

$$x = \frac{4 \pm \sqrt{16-20}}{2}$$

$$x = \frac{4 \pm \sqrt{-4}}{2}$$

$$x = 2 \pm i$$

Hence, the answer is Choice B.

Choice A is incorrect because $2 \pm 2i$ is not a non-real root of the given graph. **Choice C** is incorrect because $2i$ is not a non-real root of the given graph. **Choice D** is incorrect because $5 \pm 2i$ is not a non-real root of the given graph.

10.

Category: PHM & Modeling
Skill: Real and complex number systems | **Level:** Easy

Choice B is correct. The sum of a rational number, 3 and an irrational number, $\sqrt{2}$ is always irrational.

Choice A is incorrect. It is not rational because $\sqrt{2}$ is irrational. **Choice C** is incorrect. It is not a whole number because $\sqrt{2}$ is not an integer. **Choice D** is incorrect. $x = 3 + \sqrt{2}$ is well-defined as a number.

11.

Category: PHM
Skill: Real and complex number systems | **Level:** Medium

Choice C is correct because $(3 - i)(3 + i) = 9 - i^2 = 9 - (-1) = 9 + 1 = 10$. This is a rational number, and no imaginary part remains. This is a standard identity: $(a - b)(a + b) = a^2 - b^2$, where $b = i$.

Choice A is incorrect because $\sqrt{-9}$ equals $3i$. This is an imaginary number, and rational numbers must be real. So this expression does not yield a rational number.

Choice B is incorrect because $i\sqrt{9} \cdot i\sqrt{3} = (i \cdot 3)(i \cdot \sqrt{3}) = 3i \cdot i\sqrt{3} = i^2 \cdot 3\sqrt{3} = -1 \cdot 3\sqrt{3} = -3\sqrt{3}$. This result is irrational (because of $\sqrt{3}$), so it does not yield a rational number.

Choice D is incorrect because $(3 + i)(3 + i) = (3 + i)^2 = 9 + 6i + i^2 = 9 + 6i - 1 = 8 + 6i$. The result is a complex number, not a rational number.

12.

Category: PHM
Skill: Real and complex number systems | **Level:** Medium

Choice B is correct. For a quadratic equation $ax^2 + bx + c = 0$, the real part of the root is given by $-\frac{b}{2a}$. Substituting $a = 1$ and $b = -4$ into the formula yields $-\frac{-4}{2(1)} = 2$.

Choice A is incorrect. This has the wrong sign. **Choice C** is incorrect. This is the positive value of b. **Choice D** is incorrect. This is the value of c.

13.

Category: PHM
Skill: Real and complex number systems | **Level:** Medium

Choice D is correct because $|k-8|<0.001|k-8|<0.001|k-8|<0.001$ means that the difference between k and the target value of 8 inches is less than 0.001 inches. This is the correct mathematical expression of the statement "k must be within 0.001 inches of 8.

Choice A is incorrect because $|k-0.001|<8|k - 0.001|< 8|k-0.001|<8$ does not describe a value being close to 8. This inequality simply says that the difference between k and 0.001 is less than 8, which is not the condition we need. **Choice B** is incorrect because $|k+0.001|<8|k+ 0.001|< 8|k+0.001|<8$ again compares the wrong values. It checks how close k is to -0.001 relative to 8, which is irrelevant in this context. **Choice C** is incorrect because $|k+8|<0.001|k+8|<0.001|k+8|<0.001$ implies that k is extremely close to -8, which contradicts the given requirement that k should be close to positive 8 inches.

14.

Category: IES & Modeling
Skill: Real and complex number systems | **Level:** Medium

Choice A is correct. Using distributive property to multiply z_1 and z_2 yields $(2 + 3i)(1 - i)$

$$= 2(1) + 2(-i) + 3i(1) + 3i(-i)$$
$$= 2 - 2i + 3i - 3i^2$$
$$= 2 + i + 3$$
$$= 5 + i$$

Choice B is incorrect. This may be due to calculation error. **Choice C** is incorrect. This may be due to calculation error. **Choice D** is incorrect. This may be due to calculation error.

15.

Category: IES & Modeling
Skill: Real and complex number systems | **Level:** Easy

Choice A is correct. Adding the two complex numbers $z = 2 + 3i$ and $w = 1-4i$ yields

$z + w = (2 + 1) + (3i + (-4i)) = 3-i.$

Therefore, the correct answer is $z + w = 3-i$.

Choice B is incorrect. This may be due to calculation error. **Choice C** is incorrect. This may result if the imaginary part is subtracted $(-4i - 3i)$. **Choice D** is incorrect. This may result if the sign on the imaginary part is swapped to positive.

16.

Category: PHM
Skill: Real and complex number systems | **Level:** Easy

Choice B is correct. To solve the given $\frac{4}{2+i}$, multiply the numerator and denominator by the conjugate of the denominator to get

$$\frac{4}{2+i}\times\frac{2-i}{2-i}=\frac{4(2-i)}{(2+i)(2-i)}$$

$$=\frac{8-4i}{4+1}=\frac{8-4i}{5} \text{ or } \frac{8}{5}-\frac{4}{5}i$$

Choice A is incorrect. This may result if the given was multiplied by itself. **Choice C** is incorrect. This may result if the given was added by $\frac{4}{2+i}$. **Choice D** is incorrect. This may result if the given was added by $\frac{2-i}{2-i}$ instead of multiplied.

17.

Category: IES
Skill: Real and complex number systems | **Level:** Easy

Choice A is correct. All real numbers are also considered complex numbers with an imaginary part of 0. Thus, 3 is a real number because it has no imaginary part and is also complex since it can be written as $3 + 0i$.

Choice B is incorrect. This is a complex number because it has both a real part and imaginary part, but it is not purely real. **Choice C** is incorrect. This is a purely imaginary number, thus it is complex but not real. **Choice D** is incorrect. This is a purely imaginary number, thus it is complex but not real.

18.

Category: PHM
Skill: Real and complex number systems | **Level:** Easy

Choice A is correct. Using the formula $(a + b)^2 = a^2 + 2ab + b^2$ to get the value of the given $(2 + i)^2$ yields

$$\begin{aligned}&(2 + i)^2\\&= 2^2+2(2)(i) + i^2\\&= 4 + 4i + (-1)\\&= 3 + 4i\end{aligned}$$

Choice B is incorrect. This may be due to calculation error. **Choice C** is incorrect. This may be due to calculation error. **Choice D** is incorrect. This may be due to calculation error.

19.

Category: IES & Modeling
Skill: Real and complex number systems | **Level:** Easy

Choice D is correct. The conjugate of a complex number $z = a + bi$ is $\bar{z} = a - bi$.
For the given $z = 4 + 3i$, the conjugate is $\bar{z} = 4 - 3i$.
Therefore, the correct answer is Choice D.

Choice A is incorrect. This may be due to conceptual or calculation error. **Choice B** is incorrect. This may be due to conceptual or calculation error. **Choice C** is incorrect. This may be due to conceptual or calculation error.

20.

Category: IES
Skill: Real and complex number systems | **Level:** Medium

Choice A is correct. To simplify the division of complex numbers $Z = \frac{voltage}{current}$, Freddy multiplies both numerator and denominator by the conjugate of the denominator $3+2i$ to get $3-2i$.

Choice B is incorrect. This is the value of the denominator. **Choice C** is incorrect. This is the value of the numerator. **Choice D** is incorrect. This is the value of the numerator with a positive imaginary part.

21.

Category: IES
Skill: Real and complex number systems | **Level:** Easy

Choice B is correct. For z to be a purely real number, the imaginary part must be zero. Since the imaginary part of z is bi, set $b = 0$ to eliminate the imaginary component. Therefore, the correct answer is Choice B.

Choice A is incorrect. If $b = -1$, then $z = 3 - i$, which is a complex number with a non-zero imaginary part. **Choice C** is incorrect. If $b = 1$, then $z = 3 + i$, which is a complex number with a non-zero imaginary part. **Choice D** is incorrect. If $b = 3$, then $z = 3 + 3i$, which is a complex number with a non-zero imaginary part.

22.

Category: PHM
Skill: Real and complex number systems | **Level:** Easy

Choice D is correct. To determine which is a rational number, identify the option that results in a whole number.
Evaluating **Choice A,** $\sqrt{2} \approx 1.4142$ is irrational because it is a non-repeating decimal.
Evaluating **Choice B,** $\sqrt{5} \approx 2.236$ is irrational because it is a non-repeating decimal.
Evaluating **Choice C,** $\sqrt{32} \approx 5.6569$ is irrational because it is a non-repeating decimal.
Evaluating **Choice D,** $\sqrt{49} = 7$ is rational because it is an integer.
Therefore, the correct answer is Choice D.

Choice A is incorrect. Based on the explanation above, $\sqrt{2}$ is an irrational number. **Choice B** is incorrect. Based on the explanation above, $\sqrt{5}$ is an irrational number. **Choice C** is incorrect. Based on the explanation above, $\sqrt{32}$ is an irrational number.

23.

Category: IES
Skill: Real and complex number systems | **Level:** Easy

Choice B is correct. $5 - 2i$ is a complex number with a real part and a non-zero imaginary part, so it is not a real number.
Therefore, Choice B is correct.

Choice A is incorrect. $\sqrt{2}$ is an irrational number but still a real number. **Choice C** is incorrect. $\sqrt{3}$ is an irrational number but still a real number. **Choice D** is incorrect. π is an irrational number but still a real number.

24.

Category: PHM
Skill: Real and complex number systems | **Level:** Hard

Choice B is correct. To simplify $z = \frac{z_1}{z_2}$, multiply the numerator and denominator by the conjugate of z_2 which is $1+2i$ to get $z = \frac{\overline{z_1}}{z_2} \times \frac{\overline{z_2}}{\overline{z_2}} = \frac{(3+4i)(1+2i)}{(1-2i)(1+2i)}$

$$= \frac{3+6i+4i+8i^2}{1+2i-2i-4i^2} = \frac{3+10i-8}{1+4} = \frac{-5+10i}{5} = -1+2i.$$

Choice A is incorrect. This may be due to calculation error. **Choice C** is incorrect. This may be due to calculation error. **Choice D** is incorrect. This may be due to calculation error.

25.

Category: IES
Skill: Real and complex number systems | **Level:** Hard

Choice A is correct. Multiplying $z = 5 + 12i$ by $2i$ yields $(5 + 12i)(2i) = 10i + 24i^2$
Since $i^2 = -1$, thus $10i - 24 = -24 + 10i$.
Therefore, $z = -24 + 10i$.

Choice B is incorrect. This swaps the sign of the real and imaginary part. **Choice C** is incorrect. This swaps the real and imaginary part. **Choice D** is incorrect. This is due to calculation error.

26.

Category: PHM & Modeling
Skill: Real and Complex number systems | **Level:** Medium

Choice B is correct. Adding the real and imaginary parts separately yields $(3 + 4i) + (-5-2i) = (3-5) + (4i - 2i) = -2 + 2i$.
Therefore, the correct answer is $-2 + 2i$.

Choice A is incorrect. This may be due to calculation error. **Choice C** is incorrect. This may be due to calculation error. **Choice D** is incorrect. This may be due to calculation error.

27.

Category: IES & Modeling
Skill: Real and complex number systems | **Level:** Medium

Choice C is correct. Use the distance formula $\sqrt{(x_2 - x_1)^2 + (y_2 - y_1)^2}$ to find the distance between two points to get $\sqrt{(-1-3)^2 + (-2-4)^2} = \sqrt{(-4)^2 + (-6)^2} = \sqrt{16+36} = \sqrt{52}$.

Choice A is incorrect. This may be due to calculation error. **Choice B** is incorrect. This may be due to calculation error. **Choice D** is incorrect. This may be due to calculation error.

28.

Category: PHM & Modeling
Skill: Real and complex number systems | **Level:** Easy

Choice B is correct. The magnitude of a complex number $Z = a + bi$ is calculated using the formula $|Z| = \sqrt{a^2 + b^2}$. From the given $Z = 5 + 12i$, $a = 5$ and $b = 12$. Substituting the given into the formula yields

$|Z| = \sqrt{5^2 + 12^2} = \sqrt{25 + 144} = \sqrt{169} = 13$.

Therefore, the correct answer is Choice B.

Choice A is incorrect. This represents the reactance *X*, which is the imaginary part of *Z*. **Choice C** is incorrect. This may result from adding *R* and *X* directly. **Choice D** is incorrect. This may result from squaring the resistance *R*.

29.

Category: PHM
Skill: Real and complex number systems | **Level:** Easy

Choice B is correct. To determine which is irrational, evaluate each option that is expressed as a ratio of two integers.
Evaluating **Choice A**, $2 \times 3 = 6$, since 6 is an integer, then it is rational.
Evaluating **Choice B**, $\sqrt{2} \times 4 = 4\sqrt{2}$, since $\sqrt{2}$ is irrational, then $4\sqrt{2}$ is irrational.
Evaluating **Choice C**, $\sqrt{25} \times 5 = 5 \times 5 = 25$; since 25 is an integer, it is rational.
Evaluating **Choice D**, $\frac{1}{2} \times \frac{4}{5} = \frac{4}{10} = \frac{2}{5}$; since $\frac{2}{5}$ is a fraction of two integers, it is rational.
Therefore, the correct answer is Choice B.

Choice A is incorrect. Based on the explanation above, 2×3 is rational. **Choice C** is incorrect. Based on the explanation above, $\sqrt{25} \times 5$ is rational. **Choice D** is incorrect. Based on the explanation above, $\frac{1}{2} \times \frac{4}{5}$ is rational.

30.

Category: PHM
Skill: Real and complex number systems | **Level:** Easy

Choice A is correct. To solve $z + w$, add the real parts and the imaginary parts of the given $z = 3 + 4i$ and $w = 2 - 3i$ to get

$$\begin{aligned} z + w &= (3 + 4i) + (2 - 3i) \\ &= (3 + 2) + (4i - 3i) \\ &= 5 + i \end{aligned}$$

Choice B is incorrect. This may be due to conceptual or calculation error. **Choice C** is incorrect. This may be due to conceptual or calculation error. **Choice D** is incorrect. This may be due to conceptual or calculation error.

31.

Category: PHM & Modeling
Skill: Number line and absolute value | **Level:** Hard

Choice D is correct. Rewrite the given inequality $|2x - 5| > 7$ as two cases $2x - 5 > 7$ and $2x - 5 < -7$.
Adding 5 to both inequalities yields $2x > 12$ and $2x < -2$.
Diving both inequalities by 2 yields $x > 6$ and $x < -1$.
Therefore, the solution is $x > 6$ or $x < -1$.
From the choices, $x = 7$ satisfies $x > 6$

Choice A is incorrect. -1 is on the boundary and does not satisfy $x < -1$. **Choice B** is incorrect. 0 is not in the solution set. **Choice C** is incorrect. 6 is on the boundary and does not satisfy $x > 6$.

32.

Category: PHM
Skill: Number line and absolute value | **Level:** Medium

Choice B is correct. Comparing distances to Carla $x = 2$ yields
From Anna $x = -3$: $|-3-2| = |-5| = 5$
From Ben $x = 5$: $|5 - 2| = |3| = 3$
Therefore, Ben is closer to Carla.

Choice A is incorrect. Anna is farther away than Ben. **Choice C** is incorrect. Their distances differ, thus both are not equally close. **Choice D** is incorrect. Ben is closer to Carla.

33.

Category: PHM
Skill: Number line and absolute value | **Level:** Medium

Choice B is correct because the obtained answers are 484 and 496.

Let *x* be the possible value of the number of tennis balls inside the box.

Write the absolute value inequality.

$$|x - 490| \le 6$$
$$-6 \le x - 490 \le 6$$
$$-6 + 490 \le x - 490 + 490 \le 6 + 490$$
$$-6 + 490 \le x \le 6 + 490$$
$$484 \le x \le 496$$

Hence, the answer is Choice B.

Choice A is incorrect because $444 \le x \le 486$; the minimum value is lower than the acceptable value of the tennis balls. **Choice C** is incorrect because $473 \le x \le 490$; the minimum and the maximum value are lower than the acceptable values of the tennis balls. **Choice D** is incorrect because $490 \le x \le 496$; the minimum value is greater than the acceptable value of the tennis balls.

34.

Category: IES & Modeling
Skill: Number line and absolute value | **Level:** Hard

Choice A is correct. Let x be the number of quarts of the 5% sugar solution to be added. So, $0.05x$ is the number of quarts of sugar in the 5% solution. The 8% sugar solution contains $0.08 \times 2 = 0.16$ quarts of sugar. Mixing the solutions to make a solution that is 7% sugar will have $0.07(x + 2)$ quarts of sugar. Now,

$$0.05x + 0.16 = 0.07(x+2)$$
$$5x + 16 = 7(x+2)$$
$$5x + 16 = 7x + 14$$
$$-2x = -2$$
$$x = 1$$

1 quart of the 5% solution needs to be added.

Choice B is incorrect. This may result from wrong calculation and use of formula. **Choice C** is incorrect. This may result from wrong calculation and use of formula. **Choice D** is incorrect. This may result from wrong calculation and use of formula.

35.

Category: IES
Skill: Number line and absolute value | **Level:** Medium

Choice C is correct. The distance between City A ($x = -5$) and City B ($x = 2$) is given by $|A-B| = |-5-2| = |-7| = 7$.

Choice A is incorrect. This is the result of 5-2. **Choice B** is incorrect. This is the positive point of City A. **Choice D** is incorrect. This is may be due if City B is ($x = 5$).

36.

Category: IES
Skill: Number line and absolute value | **Level:** Medium

Choice B is correct because the obtained answer is 13.44.

Zack spends 30% of his day at school:
$30\%\ of\ 24 = 0.30 \times 24 = 7.2\ hours$

The rest of the day is:
$24 - 7.2 = 16.8\ hours$

Of these remaining 16.8 hours, Zack spends 20% doing homework
$20\%\ of\ 16.8 = 0.20 \times 16.8 = 3.36\ hours$

Time not spent in school or doing homework:
$24 - (7.2 + 3.36) = 24 - 10.56 = 13.44$ hours
So, the number of hours left in Zack's day is 13.44 hours

Hence, the answer is Choice B.

Choice A is incorrect because it represents only the time Zack spends on homework, not what is left. **Choice C** is incorrect because it represents the time left after school, before subtracting homework time. **Choice D** is incorrect as it results from a miscalculation or subtracting homework time from school time instead of the full 24 hours

37.

Category: IES
Skill: Number line and absolute value | **Level:** Medium

Choice D is correct because the obtained answer is 204.

One-half of 108 is 54, so the first number is 108.
Let x be the other number then,

$$\frac{1}{4} * \frac{1}{2}x = 12 \Rightarrow \frac{1}{8}x = 12 \Rightarrow x = 12 \times 8 = 96$$

The sum of the 2 numbers is, 108 + 96 = 204.
Hence, the answer is Choice D.

Choice A is incorrect because it adds 54 and 12, which are just parts of the numbers, not the actual values. **Choice B** incorrect because it likely comes from misusing fractions or subtracting values incorrectly. **Choice C** incorrect because it uses 108 + 15, misinterpreting the second part of the question.

38.

Category: IES
Skill: Number line and absolute value | **Level:** Medium

Choice C is correct because the obtained answer is 12.

The amount of discount received on the laptop is
\$550 – \$485 = \$65
As a percent, the discount is $\frac{65}{550} = 0.118$ or about 12%.

Hence, the answer is Choicec C.

Choice A is incorrect because it is significantly too high, likely resulting from reversing the percentage calculation. **Choice B** is incorrect due to a rounding error or an approximation mistake. **Choice D** is incorrect because it may stem from overestimating the value without performing an actual calculation.

39.

Category: IES & Modeling
Skill: Number line and absolute value| **Level:** Easy

Choice B is correct. The given $|x + 4| > 6$ splits into two inequalities $x + 4 < -6$ and $x + 4 > 6$.
Subtracting 4 yields $x < -10$ and $x > 2$.
Therefore, the correct answer is $2 < x < -10$.

Choice A is incorrect because it combines the inequality into one range. **Choice C** is incorrect. This may be due to conceptual or calculation error. **Choice D** is incorrect. This may be due to conceptual or calculation error.

40.

Category: PHM & Modeling
Skill: Number line and absolute value | **Level:** Easy

Choice D is correct. The two given absolute difference $|A - B| = 3$ means $A = B + 3$ or $A = B - 3$ and $|B - C| = 4$ means $C = B + 4$ or $C = B - 4$.
The distance between A and C is $|A - C|$, thus substituting yields $|(B + 3) - (B - 4)| = 7$ or $|(B - 3) - (B + 4)| = 7$.
Therefore, the correct answer is Choice D.

Choice A is incorrect. This may be due to calculation error. **Choice B** is incorrect. This may be due to calculation error. **Choice C** is incorrect. This may be due to calculation error.

41.

Category: IES
Skill: Number line and absolute value | **Level:** Easy

Choice A is correct. Let the numbers be a and b.
It is given that the sum of two numbers is 6; thus $a + b = 6$ and their absolute difference is 10, thus $|a - b| = 10$.
The absolute difference equation gives two equation which are $(1) a - b = 10$ and $(2) a - b = -10$.
For $(1) a - b = 10$, add the equation for the sum of two numbers to get $(a + b) + (a - b) = 6 + 10$ or $2a = 16$ or $a = 8$.
Substitute 8 for a into $a + b = 6$ to get $8 + b = 6$ or $b = -2$.
For $(2) a - b = -10$, add the equation for the sum of two numbers to get $(a + b) + (a - b) = 6 + (-10)$ or $2a = -4$ or $a = -2$.
Substitute -2 for a into $a + b = 6$ to get $-2 + b = 6$ or $b = 8$.
Therefore, the two numbers are 8 and -2.

Choice B is incorrect. This may be due to conceptual or calculation error. **Choice C** is incorrect. This may be due to conceptual or calculation error. **Choice D** is incorrect. This may be due to conceptual or calculation error.

42.

Category: PHM
Skill: Number line and absolute value | **Level:** Easy

Choice C is correct. The distance between two points is the absolute value of the difference between them which yields $|-4-3| = |-7| = 7$.
Therefore, the correct answer is Choice C.

Choice A is incorrect. This may result from calculation error. **Choice B** is incorrect. This may result from calculation error. **Choice D** is incorrect. This may result from calculation error.

43.

Category: PHM
Skill: Number line and absolute value | **Level:** Hard

Choice A is correct. To find the point farthest from $x = 2$, calculate the absolute value of the difference between each point and $x = 2$ to get

Distance from A: $|-10-2| = |-12| = 12$

Distance from B: $|-3-2| = |-5| = 5$

Distance from C: $|5-2| = |3| = 3$

Distance from D: $|12-2| = |10| = 10$

The farthest point from $x = 2$ is A, with a distance of 12.

Choice B is incorrect. B is 5 units away from $x = 2$, which is closer than A. **Choice C** is incorrect. C is 3 units away from $x = 2$, which is the shortest distance. **Choice D** is incorrect. D is 10 units away from $x = 2$.

44.

Category: PHM
Skill: Number line and absolute value | **Level:** Easy

Choice C is correct. The distance to 0 is determined by the absolute value.
Calculating the absolute values of each option yields

A: $\left|-\frac{5}{4}\right| = \frac{5}{4} = 1.25$

B: $|-0.9| = 0.9$

C: $\left|\sqrt{0.7}\right| = \sqrt{0.7} \approx 0.837$

D: $\left|\frac{7}{6}\right| = \frac{7}{6} \approx 1.167$

Therefore, Choice C is the smallest among the given absolute values.

Choice A is incorrect. $-\frac{5}{4}$ is farther from 0 than $\sqrt{0.7}$.
Choice B is incorrect. -0.9 is farther from 0 than $\sqrt{0.7}$.

Choice D is incorrect. $\frac{7}{6}$ is farther from 0 than $\sqrt{0.7}$.

45.

Category: IES & Modeling
Skill: Number line and absolute value | **Level:** Medium

Choice C is correct. Calculating the distance between Lara and James yields
Distance = |–4-5| = |–9| = 9.

Choice A is incorrect. This may result from adding James and Mia 5+2. **Choice B** is incorrect. This may be due to calculation error. **Choice D** is incorrect. This may be due to calculation error.

46.

Category: IES & Modeling
Skill: Number line and absolute value| **Level:** Medium

Choice C is correct because the obtained answer is $-2|3x+5|+7\geq-13$.

Find the solution set of the given number line.

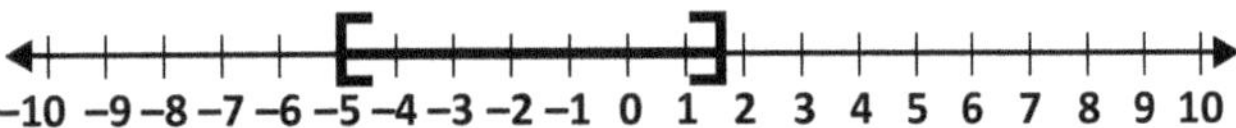

The number line has a solution set of $\left[-5,\frac{5}{3}\right]$ or $-5\leq x\leq\frac{5}{3}$.

Check the choices.

Choice A:

$$2|5x+3|-4\geq-10$$
$$2|5x+3|\geq-10+4$$
$$2|5x+3|\geq-6$$
$$|5x+3|\geq-3$$
$$3\geq5x+3\geq-3$$
$$3-3\geq5x+3-3\geq-3-3$$
$$0\geq5x\geq-6$$
$$0\geq x\geq-\frac{6}{5}$$ not the same as the solution set of the number line

Choice B:

$$-3|7x-2|\leq-13$$
$$|7x-2|\geq\frac{-13}{-3}$$
$$|7x-2|\geq\frac{13}{3}$$
$$-\frac{13}{3}\geq7x-2\geq\frac{13}{3}$$
$$-\frac{13}{3}+2\geq7x-2+2\geq\frac{13}{3}+2$$
$$-\frac{1}{3}\geq x\geq\frac{19}{21}$$ not the same as the solution set of the number line

Choice C:

$$-2|3x+5|+7\geq-13$$
$$-2|3x+5|\geq-13-7$$
$$-2|3x+5|\geq-20$$
$$|3x+5|\leq10$$
$$-10\leq3x+5\leq10$$
$$-10-5\leq3x+5-5\leq10-5$$
$$-15\leq3x\leq5$$
$$-5\leq x\leq\frac{5}{3}$$ the same as the solution set of the number line
$$0\geq x\geq-\frac{6}{5}$$

Choice D:

$$|3x+5|+7\geq-13$$
$$|3x+5|\geq-13-7$$
$$|3x+5|\geq-20$$

The absolute value of any real expression is always ≥ 0. Therefore, $x\in$R"

Hence, the answer is Choice C.

Choice A is incorrect because $2|5x+3|-4\geq-10$ does not result to the solution set given by the number line. **Choice B** is incorrect because $-3|7x-2|\leq-13$ has a solution not equal to the given solution set of the number line. **Choice D** is incorrect because $|3x+5|+7\geq-13$ has a different solution set.

47.

Category: IES & Modeling
Skill: Number line and absolute value | **Level:** Medium
Choice A is correct. Split the given

$|3x-5|=7$ into two cases which are $3x-5=7$ and $3x-5=-7$.

Adding 5 to both yields $3x=12$ and $3x=-2$.

Dividing both by 4 yields $x=5$ and $x=-\frac{2}{3}$.

Therefore, the solutions are $x=4$ or $x=-\frac{2}{3}$

Choice B is incorrect. This may be due to calculation error. **Choice C** is incorrect. This may be due to calculation error. **Choice D** is incorrect. The second solution is the positive value of $3x$.

48.

Category: PHM
Skill: Number line and absolute value| **Level:** Easy

Choice C is correct. The absolute value equation of $|x| = 6$ has two solutions which are $x = 6$ and $x = -6$.
Choice A is incorrect because this omits $x = -6$.
Choice B is incorrect because this omits $x = 6$. **Choice D** is incorrect because solutions exist.

49.

Category: IES & Modeling
Skill: Number line and absolute value| **Level:** Easy

Choice A is correct. The number line is divided into 4 equal parts between 0 and 1.
The fractions are 0, $\frac{1}{4}$, $\frac{1}{2}$, $\frac{3}{4}$, and 1.
Point P lies between $\frac{1}{4}$ and $\frac{1}{2}$, dividing the segment into smaller parts.
The segment between $\frac{1}{4}$ and $\frac{1}{2}$ is

$$\frac{1}{2}-\frac{1}{4}=\frac{2}{4}-\frac{1}{4}=\frac{1}{4}.$$

P divides this segment evenly, thus the value of P is

$$\frac{1}{4}+\frac{1}{8}=\frac{2}{8}+\frac{1}{8}=\frac{3}{8}.$$

Choice B is incorrect. This is the marked point on the number line, to the right of P. **Choice C** is incorrect. This would lie between $\frac{1}{2}$ and $\frac{3}{4}$. **Choice D** is incorrect. This is the marked point on the number line, far to the right of P.

50.

Category: PHM & Modeling
Skill: Number line and absolute value | **Level:** Medium

Choice D is correct. Write the given inequality $|x + 3| \leq 5$ as a compound inequality $-5 \leq x + 3 \leq 5$.
Subtracting 3 from all parts yields $-8 \leq x \leq 2$.
Therefore, the correct answer is $-8 \leq x \leq 2$.

Choice A is incorrect. This miscalculates the range of values. **Choice B** is incorrect. One side of the inequality is miscalculated. **Choice C** is incorrect. One side of the inequality is miscalculated.

51.

Category: IES
Skill: Number line and absolute value | **Level:** Easy

Choice A is correct. The interval from 0 to 4 is divided into 8 equal parts, thus the length of each parts is $\frac{4}{8}=\frac{1}{2}$.
Starting from 0, the value of the third mark is $3\times\frac{1}{2}=\frac{3}{2}$.
To express $\frac{3}{2}$ as a fraction of the total interval which is 4, divide $\frac{3}{2}$ by 4 to get $\frac{3}{2}\div 4=\frac{3}{2}\times\frac{1}{4}=\frac{3}{8}$
Therefore, the correct answer is Choice A.

Choice B is incorrect because this represents the value at the 4th mark on the number line. **Choice C** is incorrect because this corresponds to the 6th mark on the number line. **Choice D** is incorrect because this simplifies to corresponds to $\frac{3}{4}$, which represents the 6th mark on the number line.

52.

Category: IES
Skill: Number line and absolute value | **Level:** Easy

Choice B is correct. Simplifying $-\frac{15}{3}$ yields -5 and $\frac{16}{3}$ yields 5.333.
Thus, the range is between -5 and 5.333.
The integers between them are $-4, -3, -2, -1, 0, 1, 2, 3, 4$, and 5.
Therefore, there are 10 integers between $-\frac{15}{3}$ and $\frac{16}{3}$.

Choice A is incorrect. There are 10 integers instead of just 9. **Choice C** is incorrect. There are 10 integers instead of 11. **Choice D** is incorrect. There are 10 integers instead of 12.

53.

Category: PHM
Skill: Number line and absolute value | **Level:** Hard

Choice A is correct. To find the point farthest from $x = 2$, calculate the absolute value of the difference between each point and $x = 2$ to get
Distance from A: $|-10-2| = |-12| = 12$
Distance from B: $|-3-2| = |-5| = 5$
Distance from C: $|5-2| = |3| = 3$
Distance from D: $|12-2| = |10| = 10$
The farthest point from $x = 2$ is A, with a distance of 12.

Choice B is incorrect. B is 5 units away from $x = 2$, which is closer than A. **Choice C** is incorrect. C is 3 units away from $x = 2$, which is the shortest distance. **Choice D** is incorrect. D is 10 units away from $x = 2$.

54.

Category: PHM
Skill: Number line and absolute value | **Level:** Easy

Choice D is correct. For the given $|x|>3$, x must be greater than 3 or less than −3.
Out of the given options, $x = 4$ satisfies this inequality.

Choice A is incorrect. −2 does not satisfy the inequality as it is greater than −3. **Choice B** is incorrect because 0 is less than 3. **Choice C** is incorrect because the inequality is just greater than 3 and not equal to 3.

55.

Category: PHM & Modeling
Skill: Number line and absolute value | **Level:** Easy

Choice A is correct. The given $|3x-2| \le 4$ means $-4 \le 3x-2 \le 4$.
Adding 2 on both sides yields $-2 \le 3x \le 6$.
Dividing both sides by 3 yields $-\frac{2}{3} \le x \le 2$.
Choice B is incorrect because the inequalities are doubled and the equality symbol is omitted. **Choice C** is incorrect because the equality symbol is omitted. **Choice D** is incorrect because the upper bound is reduced to 1.

56.

Category: PHM
Skill: Number line and absolute value| **Level:** Easy

Choice B is correct. The midpoint is the sum of the endpoints divided by 2.
Midpoint is $\frac{-5+1}{2} = \frac{-4}{2} = -2$.
Choice A is incorrect because −3 is not halfway.
Choice C is incorrect because −1 is closer to 1.
Choice D is incorrect because 0 is further from −5.

57.

Category: PHM
Skill: Number line and absolute value | **Level:** Easy

Choice A is correct. The given $|2x–3| = 7$ gives two equation which are (1)$2x–3 = 7$ and (2)$2x–3 = –7$.

(1)
$$2x-3 = 7$$
$$2x = 7 + 3$$
$$2x = 10$$
$$x = 5$$

(2)
$$2x-3 = -7$$
$$2x = -7 + 3$$
$$2x = -4$$
$$x = -2$$

Therefore, Choice A is correct.

Choice B is incorrect because 4 is included incorrectly instead of 5. **Choice C** is incorrect because 2 is positive instead of negative. **Choice D** is incorrect because of calculation error.

58.

Category: IES
Skill: Number line and absolute value | **Level:** Easy

Choice D is correct. The total range of the number line is $3-(-3)=6$.

Dividing the range into 6 equal intervals yields the interval size which is $\frac{6}{6}=1$.

The second mark to the right of 0 is $1+1=2$.
Therefore, the fraction at the second mark to the right of 0 is $\frac{2}{3}$.
Choice A is incorrect. This may be due to conceptual or calculation error. **Choice B** is incorrect. This may be due to conceptual or calculation error. **Choice C** is incorrect. This may be due to conceptual or calculation error.

59.

Category: PHM
Skill: Number line and absolute value | **Level:** Easy

Choice B is correct. The given inequality $|x + 1| \le 3$ means $-3 \le x + 1 \le 3$.
Subtracting 1 to both sides yields $-4 \le x \le 2$.
Choice A is incorrect because this reverses and misplaces the bounds. **Choice C** is incorrect. This is the result for $x + 1 \ge -1$ or $x + 1 \le 5$. **Choice D** is incorrect. This is the result for $x + 1 > 3$ or $x + 1 < -3$.

60.

Category: IES & Modeling
Skill: Number line and absolute value | **Level:** Hard
Choice B is correct. Finding the midpoint R between $P(-18)$ and $Q(6)$ yields $R = \frac{-18+6}{2} = \frac{-12}{2} = -6$.
Finding the midpoint S between $R(-6)$ and $Q(6)$ yields $R = \frac{-6+6}{2} = \frac{0}{2} = 0$.

Choice A is incorrect. This is the value of midpoint R.
Choice C is incorrect. This may be due to calculation

error. **Choice D** is incorrect. This may be due to calculation error.

61.

Category: IES
Skill: Number line and absolute value | **Level:** Easy

Choice B is correct. Converting $\frac{7}{3}$ into a decimal yields 2.333; thus the range is between 2.333 to 5.
The integers between them are 3 and 4.
Therefore, there are 2 integers between $\frac{7}{3}$ and 5.

Choice A is incorrect. There are 2 integers instead of just 1. **Choice C** is incorrect. There are 2 integers instead of 3. **Choice D** is incorrect. There are 2 integers instead of 4.

62.

Category: PHM & Modeling
Skill: Number line and absolute value | **Level:** Easy

Choice A is correct. The given $|2x + 1| \geq 3$ splits into two inequalities $2x + 1 \geq 3$ or $2x + 1 \leq -3$.
Therefore, the correct answer is $3 \leq 2x + 1 \leq -3$.
Choice B is incorrect. This combines the inequality with incorrect logical operators. **Choice C** is incorrect. This may be due to calculation error. **Choice D** is incorrect. This may be due to calculation error.

63.

Category: PHM
Skill: Number line and absolute value | **Level:** Easy

Choice A is correct. The formula for the distance between two points x_1 and x_2 on the number line is given by $|x_2 - x_1| =$ distance.
It is given that one point is –7, thus $x_1 = -7$ and the distance is 10.
Substituting the given into the formula yields $|x_2-(-7)| = 10$.
Simplifying yields $|x_2 + 7| = 10$ which means $x_2+7 = 10$ or $x_2 + 7 = -10$.
Subtracting 7 yields $x_2 = 3$ or $x_2 = -17$.
Therefore, the two possible values for x_2 are 3 or –17.
Choice B is incorrect because –3 is not a distance of 10 from –7. **Choice C** is incorrect because 7 and 17 does not satisfy the condition. **Choice D** is incorrect because –7 and 10 does not satisfy the condition.

64.

Category: IES
Skill: Number line and absolute value | **Level:** Hard

Choice D is correct. To solve, find the distance from *A* to *B* and the distance from *B* to *C*.
Distance from *A* to *B*: $|-12-4| = |-16| = 16$
Distance from *B* to *C*: $|4-10| = |-6| = 6$
The absolute difference between the distances is $|16-6| = |10| = 10$.
Choice A is incorrect. This may be due to calculation error. **Choice B** is incorrect. This is the distance from B to C. **Choice C** is incorrect. This is the distance from A to B.

65.

Category: IES & Modeling
Skill: Number line and absolute value | **Level:** Easy

Choice C is correct. The number line is divided into 4 equal parts between –1 and 0. The fractions are –1, $-\frac{7}{8}$, $-\frac{3}{4}$, $-\frac{1}{2}$ and 0.
Point *T* lies between $-\frac{3}{4}$ and $-\frac{1}{2}$, dividing the segment into smaller parts.
The segment between $-\frac{3}{4}$ and $-\frac{1}{2}$ is
$-\frac{1}{2}-\left(-\frac{3}{4}\right)=-\frac{2}{4}-\left(-\frac{3}{4}\right)=\frac{1}{4}$.
T is the first mark in this interval and it adds half of the segment to $-\frac{3}{4}$, thus the value of *T* is
$-\frac{3}{4}+\frac{1}{8}=-\frac{6}{8}+\frac{1}{8}=-\frac{5}{8}$.

Choice A is incorrect. This is the marked point on the number line, far to the right of T. **Choice B** is incorrect. This is the marked point on the number line, to the left of T. **Choice D** is incorrect. This is the marked point on the number line, to the right of T.

66.

Category: PHM
Skill: Number line and absolute value | **Level:** Easy

Choice A is correct. The given *x*: $|3x - 9| > 6$ yields two inequalities which are $3x - 9 > 6$ or $3x- 9 < -6$.
Adding 9 to both inequalities yields $3x > 15 \Rightarrow x > 5$ or $3x < 3 \Rightarrow x < 1$.
Therefore, the value of *x* are $x > 5$ or $x < 1$.
Choice B is incorrect. This may be due to calculation error. **Choice C** is incorrect. This may be due to calculation error. **Choice D** is incorrect. This may be due to calculation error.

67.

Category: PHM
Skill: Number line and absolute value | **Level:** Medium

Choice B is correct. It is given that the truck starts at $x = 0$ and travels to the house at $x = -4$.
The distance is $|0-(-4)| = |4| = 4$.
Therefore, the correct answer is 4.
Choice A is incorrect. This is half the distance traveled.
Choice C is incorrect. This adds 2 to the distance traveled.
Choice D is incorrect. This doubles the distance traveled.

68.

Category: PHM
Skill: Number line and absolute value | **Level:** Medium

Choice D is correct. Since CF is 3 parts of CE and FE is 1 part of CF so, CF is three-fourths of CE and FE is one-fourth of CE.
This correlates to option K, CF = $\frac{3}{4}$ CE.

Choice A is incorrect. FE is one-fourth of CE. **Choice B** is incorrect. FE is one-fourth of CE. **Choice C** is incorrect. FE is one-fourth of CE.

69.

Category: PHM
Skill: Number line and absolute value | **Level:** Medium

Choice A is correct. As seen in the table, the oil is decreasing over the 5-minute interval. Since the difference in the temperatures from one minute to the next is getting larger, we say the rate of change in the difference in the temperatures is increasing so, Choices B and C can be eliminated. There is no direct variation in the temperature in terms of time, and the temperature and time are not inversely proportional with each other so, Choice D can be eliminated, leaving A as the correct choice.

Choice B is incorrect. As per the explanation above, the rate of change in the difference in temperatures is increasing and not decreasing. **Choice C** is incorrect. As per the explanation above, the rate of change in the difference in temperatures is increasing and not decreasing. **Choice D** is incorrect. As per the explanation above, the temperature and time are not inversely proportional to each other.

70.

Category: IES & Modeling
Skill: Number line and absolute value | **Level:** Easy

Choice A is correct. The given $|x| < 4$ means $-4 < x < 4$. The absolute value indicates the distance from 0, and the solution lies between −4 and 4.

Choice B is incorrect. This includes the boundaries −4 and 4. **Choice C** is incorrect. This represents greater than inequality, not less than. **Choice D** is incorrect because it includes only the boundary points, not the interval.

71.

Category: PHM
Skill: Number line and absolute value | **Level:** Medium

Choice A is correct. Solving $|x - a| = 10$, substitute the given $a = -3$ to get $|x-(-3)| = 10 = |x + 3| = 10$.
Breaking the equation into two yields
$x + 3 = 10$ and $x + 3 = -10$.
Subtracting 3 from both equations yields
$x = 7$ and $x = -13$.
Therefore, the possible values of x is 7 and −13.

Choice B is incorrect. This may be due to calculation error. **Choice C** is incorrect. This may be due to calculation error. **Choice D** is incorrect. This may be due to calculation error.

72.

Category: PHM
Skill: Number line and absolute value | **Level:** Easy

Choice C is correct. The absolute value of the given $y = |2x-1|$ is minimized when $2x-1 = 0$; thus $x = 0.5$.
Substituting 0.5 for x yields $y = |2(0.5)-1| = 0$.
Choice A is incorrect. This may be due to calculation error. **Choice B** is incorrect. Absolute values are non-negative. **Choice D** is incorrect. Absolute values are non-negative.

73.

Category: PHM
Skill: Number line and absolute value | **Level:** Medium

Choice C is correct. Use the midpoint formula $\frac{b+c}{2}$ to get the midpoint between $b=4$ and $c=7$.
Substituting the given into the formula yields

$$\frac{4+7}{2}=\frac{11}{2}=5.5.$$

Choice A is incorrect. This shifts the midpoint closer to b.
Choice B is incorrect. This rounds down the midpoint.
Choice D is incorrect. This rounds up the midpoint.

74.

Category: PHM
Skill: Number line and absolute value | **Level:** Easy

Choice D is correct. Calculate the absolute value of each term.
The absolute value of $|-4| = 4$ and $|1| = 1$.
Adding them together yields $|-4| + |1| = 4 + 1 = 5$.

Choice A is incorrect. Absolute values cannot be negative.
Choice B is incorrect. Absolute values cannot be negative.
Choice C is incorrect. This may be due to calculation error.

75.

Category: PHM
Skill: Number line and absolute value | **Level:** Medium

Choice C is correct. From the given $a = -3$ and $b = 4$, the value of $|a - b| = |-3-4| = |-7| = 7$.
Therefore, the correct answer is 7.

Choice A is incorrect. This may result if the required is $|b + a|$. **Choice B** is incorrect. This may be due to calculation error. **Choice D** is incorrect. This may result if the required is $|c\text{-}a|$.

76.

Category: PHM
Skill: Exponents | **Level:** Medium

Choice B is correct. Simplifying $(x^2y^3)^4$ by applying the power rule $(a^m)^n = a^{m\cdot n}$ yields $(x^2y^3)^4 = x^{2\cdot4}y^{3\cdot4} = x^8y^{12}$.
Dividing by x^3y^5 using $\frac{a^m}{a^n} = a^{m-n}$ yields

$$\frac{x^8y^{12}}{x^3y^5} = x^{8-3}y^{12-5} = x^5y^7.$$

Choice A is incorrect. This may be due to conceptual or calculation error. **Choice C** is incorrect. This may result if the denominator is y^5. **Choice D** is incorrect. This is the result of simplifying the numerator.

77.

Category: IES
Skill: Exponents | **Level:** Medium

Choice C is correct. Simplifying the numerator $(a^2b^{-1})^3$ yields a^6b^{-3}.
Simplifying the denominator $(a^{-1}b^2)^2$ yields $a^{-2}b^4$.
Dividing the numerator by the denominator yields

$$\frac{a^6b^{-3}}{a^{-2}b^4} = a^{6-(-2)}b^{-3-4} = a^8b^{-7}$$

Choice A is incorrect. This is the result of simplifying the numerator. **Choice B** is incorrect. This results in swapping the positive and negative symbols. **Choice D** is incorrect. This is the result of simplifying the denominator.

78.

Category: PHM
Skill: Exponents | **Level:** Hard

Choice C is correct. Simplifying each part of the given expression $\frac{(3a^{-1}b^2)^2\cdot\left(a^3b^{-4}\right)}{(a^2b^{-1})^3}$ yields

Numerator: $(3a^{-1}b^2)^2 = 3^2a^{-2}b^4 = 9a^{-2}b^4$

Denominator: $(a^2b^{-1})^3 = a^6b^{-3}$
Combining terms in the numerator yields

$$9a^{-2}b^4\left(a^3b^{-4}\right) = 9a^{-2+3}b^{4+(-4)} = 9a^1b^0 = 9a$$

Diving by the denominator a^6b^{-3} yields

$$\frac{9a}{a^6b^{-3}} = 9a^{1-6}b^{0-(-3)} = 9a^{-5}b^3$$

Choice A is incorrect. This may be due to calculation error. **Choice B** is incorrect. This may be due to calculation error. **Choice D** is incorrect. This may be due to calculation error.

79.

Category: IES
Skill: Exponents | **Level:** Hard

Choice D is correct. The production in each hour forms a pattern,
In the first hour $(k=1)$: $2^1 = 2$ widgets
In the second hour $(k=2)$: $2^2 = 4$ widgets
In the *n*-th hour $(k=n)$: 2^n widgets
The total number of widgets produced is the sum of the widgets produced which is $2^1 + 2^2 + ... + 2^n$
This is a geometric series with the first term $(a) = 2^1 = 2$, common ratio $(r) = 2$, and number of terms (n).
Applying the sum formula for a geometric series $S_n = a\cdot\frac{r^n-1}{r-1}$ yields $S_n = 2\cdot\frac{2^n-1}{2-1}$ or $S_n = 2\cdot(2^n-1) = 2^{n+1}-2$.

Therefore, the correct answer is Choice D.
Choice A is incorrect. This may result when omitting the doubling effect over the n hours. **Choice B** is incorrect. This may result if the machine produces 2^n widgets every hour. **Choice C** is incorrect. This may result if the n is squared.

80.

Category: PHM
Skill: Exponents | **Level:** Easy

Choice A is correct. Multiplying expressions with the

same base, add the exponents to get $3^4 \cdot 3^2 = 3^{4+2} = 3^6$. **Choice B** is incorrect. This results if the exponents are multiplied instead of added. **Choice C** is incorrect. This may be due to calculation error. **Choice D** is incorrect. This may be due to calculation error.

81.

Category: IES
Skill: Exponents | **Level:** Medium

Choice A is correct. Simplifying $(2x^{-3}y^2)^2$ using the power rule $(a^m)^n = a^{m \cdot n}$ yields $(2x^{-3}y^2)^2 = 2^2 x^{-3 \cdot 2} y^{2 \cdot 2} = 4x^{-6}y^4$.

Multiplying by $\frac{x^4}{y^{-1}}$ yields

$$4x^{-6}y^4 \cdot \frac{x^4}{y^{-1}} = 4x^{-6+4}y^{4+1} = 4x^{-2}y^5$$

Therefore, the correct answer is $4x^{-2}y^5$.

Choice B is incorrect. This may result if the exponent for y was subtracted $(4-1)$ instead of added. **Choice C** is incorrect. This may result if the first expression is multiplied by y^{-1}. **Choice D** is incorrect. This may result if the first expression is multiplied by $\frac{1}{y^{-1}}$.

82.

Category: IES & Modeling
Skill: Exponents | **Level:** Easy

Choice C is correct. Simplify the numerator using the rule $a^m \cdot a^n = a^{m+n}$; thus $2^5 \cdot 2^3 = 2^{5+3} = 2^8$

Dividing 2^4 using the rule $\frac{a^m}{a^n} = a^{m-n}$ yields

$$\frac{2^8}{2^4} = 2^{8-4} = 2^4.$$

Choice A is incorrect. This may result if the exponent in the numerator is subtracted instead of added. **Choice B** is incorrect. This may result if the denominator is 2^5. **Choice D** is incorrect. This may result if the denominator is 2^3.

83.
Category: PHM
Skill: Exponents | **Level:** Medium

Choice A is correct. Substituting the given $x = 2^3$ and $y = 2^4$ into the expression $\frac{y^2}{x^3}$ yields $\frac{y^2}{x^3} = \frac{(2^4)^2}{(2^3)^3}$.

Using the power rule $\frac{a^m}{a^n} = a^{m-n}$ and $(a^m)^n = a^{m \cdot n}$ yields

$$\frac{(2^4)^2}{(2^3)^3} = 2^8 \cdot 2^{-9} = 2^{8-9} = 2^{-1}.$$

Therefore, the correct answer is 2^{-1}.

Choice B is incorrect. This may be due to conceptual or calculation error. **Choice C** is incorrect. This may be due to conceptual or calculation error. **Choice D** is incorrect. This may be due to conceptual or calculation error.

84.

Category: IES
Skill: Exponents | **Level:** Easy

Choice B is correct. Simplifying the multiplication by adding the exponents yields $3^2 \cdot 3^4 = 3^{2+4} = 3^6$
Dividing by 3^3 by subtracting the exponents yields

$$\frac{3^6}{3^3} = 3^{6-3} = 3^3.$$

Therefore, the correct answer is 3^3.

Choice A is incorrect. This may result if the exponent is subtracted 6 – 4 instead of 6 – 3. **Choice C** is incorrect. This may result if the exponent is stopped at multiplying without dividing. **Choice D** is incorrect. This may result if the exponent is added instead of subtracting.

85.

Category: PHM & Modeling
Skill: Exponents | **Level:** Easy

Choice D is correct. Simplifying the constant yields $\frac{9}{3} = 3$.

For the terms, subtract the exponents with the same base to get $\frac{9a^6b^3}{3a^2b^4} = 3a^{6-2}b^{3-4} = 3a^4b^{-1}$.

Therefore, the correct answer is $3a^4b^{-1}$.

Choice A is incorrect. This may be due to calculation error. **Choice B** is incorrect. This may be due to calculation error. **Choice C** is incorrect. This may be due to calculation error.

86.

Category: IES & Modeling
Skill: Imaginary and complex numbers | **Level:** Hard

Choice D is correct. Let x miles/hour be the speed of the slower car, then $(x + 4)$ miles/hour is the speed of the faster car. The distance the slower car travels in 3 hours is $3x$ miles and the faster cars distance is $3(x + 4)$ miles. Since one car travels due north and the other due south, they are traveling along a vertical line, so the total distance travelled is the sum of their distances travelled. Then,

$$3x+3(x+4)=204$$
$$6x+12=204$$
$$6x=192$$
$$x=32$$

So, the slower car's speed is 32 miles per hour.

Choice A is incorrect. This may result if the cars are 132 miles apart. **Choice B** is incorrect. This may result if the cars are 162 miles apart. **Choice C** is incorrect. This may result if the cars are 192 miles apart.

87.

Category: IES & Modeling
Skill: Imaginary and complex numbers | **Level:** Medium

Choice B is correct. The distance between two complex numbers is given by $\sqrt{(a-c)^2+(b-d)^2}$.

From the given $1+2i$ and $-3+4i$, $a=1$, $b=2$, $c=-3$, and $d=4$.
Substitute the given into the formula to get $\sqrt{(1-(-3))^2+(2-4)^2}=\sqrt{16+4}=\sqrt{20}$.

Choice A is incorrect. This may result if the distance is $\sqrt{25}$ instead of $\sqrt{20}$. **Choice C** is incorrect. This may result if all the numbers are added. **Choice D** is incorrect. This may result if the distance is $\sqrt{25}$ instead of $\sqrt{20}$.

88.

Category: IES
Skill: Imaginary and complex numbers | **Level:** Medium

Choice C is correct. The distance between two complex numbers is given by $\sqrt{(a-c)^2+(b-d)^2}$.
From the given $2+3i$ and $6+7i$, $a=2$, $b=3$, $c=6$, and $d=7$.
Substitute the given into the formula to get
$\sqrt{(2-6)^2+(3-7)^2}=\sqrt{16+16}=\sqrt{32}$.

Choice A is incorrect. This may be due to calculation error. **Choice B** is incorrect. This may result if only the real or imaginary part was solved. **Choice D** is incorrect. This is the result for $\sqrt{16}$.

89.

Category: PHM
Skill: Imaginary and complex numbers | **Level:** Medium

Choice A is correct. The conjugate of $z=5-2i$ is $\overline{z}=5+2i$.
Multiplying the two yields
$(5-2i)(5+2i)=5^2-(2i)^2=25-(-4)=29$.

Choice B is incorrect. This is the value of the real part.
Choice C is incorrect. This is the value of z.
Choice D is incorrect. This is the value of $\overline{z}$.

90.

Category: IES & Modeling
Skill: Imaginary and complex numbers | **Level:** Medium

Choice D is correct. The midpoint formula for two complex numbers $a+bi$ and $c+di$ is

$$midpoint=\left(\frac{a+c}{2}\right)+\left(\frac{b+d}{2}\right)i.$$

From the given $-3+4i$ and $1+6i$, $a=-3$, $b=4$, $c=1$, and $d=6$.
Substitute the given into the formula to get

$$midpoint=\left(\frac{-3+1}{2}\right)+\left(\frac{4+6}{2}\right)i=\frac{-2}{2}+\frac{10}{2}i=-1+5i$$

Choice A is incorrect. This may result if the real part is not divided by 2. **Choice B** is incorrect. This may result if the real part is 0. **Choice C** is incorrect. This may be due to calculation error.

91.

Category: PHM
Skill: Imaginary and complex numbers | **Level:** Easy

Choice A is correct. The complex conjugate of a complex number $a+bi$ is $a-bi$, thus the conjugate of the given $2+3i$ is $2-3i$.
Multiplying the two yields $(2+3i)(2-3i)=2^2-(3i)^2=4-(-9)=13$.
Choice B is incorrect. This may be due to conceptual or calculation error. **Choice C** is incorrect. This may be due to conceptual or calculation error. **Choice D** is incorrect. This may be due to conceptual or calculation error.

92.

Category: PHM & Modeling
Skill: Imaginary and complex numbers | **Level:** Easy

Choice C is correct. The distance between two complex numbers is given by $\sqrt{(a-c)^2+(b-d)^2}$.
From the given $3+4i$ and $0+0i$, $a=3$, $b=4$, $c=0$, and $d=0$.

Substitute the given into the formula to get
$\sqrt{(3-0)^2+(4-0)^2}=\sqrt{9+16}=\sqrt{25}=5.$

Choice A is incorrect. This is the value of the real part. **Choice B** is incorrect. This is the value of the imaginary part. **Choice D** is incorrect. This may be due to calculation error.

93.

Category: PHM
Skill: Imaginary and complex numbers | **Level:** Hard

Choice B is correct. The distance between two complex numbers is given by $\sqrt{(a-c)^2+(b-d)^2}$.
Calculating the distance between $2+3i$ and $-4+7i$ yields
$\sqrt{(2-(-4))^2+(3-7)^2}=\sqrt{6^2+(-4)^2}=\sqrt{36+16}=\sqrt{52}$.

Calculating the distance between $-4+7i$ and $6-5i$ yields
$\sqrt{(-4-6)^2+(7-(-5))^2}=\sqrt{(-10)^2+(12)^2}=\sqrt{100+144}=\sqrt{244}$.

Therefore, the total distance is $\sqrt{52}+\sqrt{244}$.

Choice A is incorrect. This may be due to calculation error. **Choice C** is incorrect. This may be due to calculation error. **Choice D** is incorrect. This may be due to calculation error.

94.

Category: IES & Modeling
Skill: Imaginary and complex numbers | **Level:** Easy

Choice B is correct. The midpoint formula for two complex numbers $a+bi$ and $c+di$ is
$midpoint=\left(\frac{a+c}{2}\right)+\left(\frac{b+d}{2}\right)i$.

From the given $6+8i$ and $2+4i$, $a=6$, $b=8$, $c=2$, and $d=4$.
Substitute the given into the formula to get
$midpoint=\left(\frac{6+2}{2}\right)+\left(\frac{8+4}{2}\right)i=\frac{8}{2}+\frac{12}{2}i=4+6i$

Choice A is incorrect. This may result if the midpoint is not divided by 2. **Choice C** is incorrect. This may be due to calculation error. **Choice D** is incorrect. This may result from miscalculation of the real part.

95.

Category: IES
Skill: Imaginary and complex numbers | **Level:** Hard

Choice C is correct. The midpoint formula for two complex numbers $a+bi$ and $c+di$ is
$midpoint=\left(\frac{a+c}{2}\right)+\left(\frac{b+d}{2}\right)i$.

From the given $4+7i$ and $-8-3i$, $a=4$, $b=7$, $c=-8$, and $d=-3$.

Substitute the given into the formula to get
$midpoint=\left(\frac{4+(-8)}{2}\right)+\left(\frac{7+(-3)}{2}\right)i=\frac{-4}{2}+\frac{4}{2}i=-2+2i$

Thus, $x=-2$ and $y=2$. Therefore, the value of $x+y=-2+2=0$

Choice A is incorrect. This is the value of x.

Choice B is incorrect. This may result of $\frac{x}{y}$.

Choice D is incorrect. This may result of $-\frac{x}{y}$.

96.

Category: PHM
Skill: Vectors | **Level:** Easy

Choice A is correct. For a matrix in the form $\begin{bmatrix} a & b \\ c & d \end{bmatrix}$, the value of the determinant is *ad* – *bc*. So,

$$\begin{aligned} 5\cdot 3-a\cdot a &= 2a \\ 15-a^2 &= 2a \\ a^2+2a-15 &= 0 \\ (a+5)(a-3) &= 0 \\ a=-5 \text{ or } a &= 3 \end{aligned}$$

Since *a* must be negative, *a* = –5.
Choice B is incorrect. This may be due to calculation error. **Choice C** is incorrect. This may be due to calculation error. **Choice D** is incorrect. This may be due to calculation error.

97.

Category: PHM
Skill: Vectors | **Level:** Medium

Choice B is correct. Solving $\vec{A}-\vec{B}$ yields
$\vec{A}-\vec{B}=(5-(-3),12-4)=(8,8)$.
From the solution, $x=8$ and $y=8$.
Substitute the given into the formula $\left\|\vec{A}-\vec{B}\right\|=\sqrt{x^2+y^2}$ to get $\left\|\vec{A}-\vec{B}\right\|=\sqrt{8^2+8^2}=\sqrt{64+64}=\sqrt{128}$.

Choice A is incorrect. This is the square root of one of the components. **Choice C** is incorrect. This may result from *x* + *y*. **Choice D** is incorrect. This may result from *xy*.

98.

Category: IES & Modeling
Skill: Vectors | **Level:** Medium

Choice C is correct. The displacement vector $\vec{d} = (8,-6)$. From the given $x = 8$ and $y = -6$.
Substitute the given into the formula $\|\vec{d}\| = \sqrt{x^2 + y^2}$ to get $\|\vec{d}\| = \sqrt{8^2 + (-6)^2} = \sqrt{64+36} = \sqrt{100} = 10$ miles.

Choice A is incorrect. This is the result if the magnitude calculates $\sqrt{81}$. **Choice B** is incorrect. This may be due to calculation error. **Choice D** is incorrect. This is the result of $x - y$.

99.

Category: PHM
Skill: Vectors | **Level:** Easy

Choice B is correct. The magnitude of a vector $\vec{A} = (x, y)$ is given by $\|\vec{A}\| = \sqrt{x^2 + y^2}$.

From the given $\vec{A} = (3,4)$, $x = 3$ and $y = 4$.
Substitute the given into the formula to get

$\|\vec{A}\| = \sqrt{3^2 + 4^2} = \sqrt{9+16} = \sqrt{25} = 5$.

Choice A is incorrect. This may result from calculation error. **Choice C** is incorrect. This is the result of $x + y$. **Choice D** is incorrect. This is the square of the magnitude.

100.

Category: IES
Skill: Vectors | **Level:** Hard

Choice C is correct. Converting the boat's velocity to components yields

$$(x, y) = (30cos45°, 30sin45°)$$

$$= \left(30 \cdot \frac{\sqrt{2}}{2}, 30 \cdot \frac{\sqrt{2}}{2}\right) = \left(15\sqrt{2}, 15\sqrt{2}\right)$$

The current velocity is $(0,-10)$.

The resultant velocity is $\vec{v} = \left(15\sqrt{2}, 15\sqrt{2} - 10\right)$.

The magnitude of $\vec{v}$ is

$$\|\vec{v}\| = \sqrt{(15\sqrt{2})^2 + (15\sqrt{2} - 10)^2}$$

$$= \sqrt{450 + 450 - 300\sqrt{2} + 100} = \sqrt{1000 - 300\sqrt{2}} \approx 24.$$

Choice A is incorrect. This may be due to conceptual or calculation error. **Choice B** is incorrect. This may be due to conceptual or calculation error. **Choice D** is incorrect. This may be due to conceptual or calculation error.

101.

Category: PHM & Modeling
Skill: Vectors | **Level:** Easy

Choice A is correct. Scaling a vector $\vec{D} = (x, y)$ by a scalar k is done by multiplying both components by k to get $3\vec{D} = ((3 \cdot 1), (3 \cdot -(2))) = (3,-6)$

Therefore, the correct answer is $(3,-6)$.

Choice B is incorrect. This may result if the scalar is 4 instead of 3. **Choice C** is incorrect. This swaps the signs of both components. **Choice D** is incorrect. This changes the sign of y to be positive.

102.

Category: IES
Skill: Vectors | **Level:** Medium

Choice B is correct. The magnitude of the displacement vector $\vec{d} = (-80,-60)$.
From the given $x = -80$ and $y = -60$.
Substitute the given into the formula $\|\vec{d}\| = \sqrt{x^2 + y^2}$ to get

$\|\vec{d}\| = \sqrt{(-80)^2 + (-60)^2} = \sqrt{6400 + 3600} = \sqrt{10000} = 100$ miles.

Choice A is incorrect. This may be due to calculation error. **Choice C** is incorrect. This may be due to calculation error. **Choice D** is incorrect. This may be due to calculation error.

103.

Category: IES & Modeling
Skill: Vectors | **Level:** Easy

Choice C is correct. The magnitude of the displacement vector $\vec{d} = (-150, 200)$.
From the given $x = -150$ and $y = 200$.

Substitute the given into the formula $\|\vec{d}\| = \sqrt{x^2 + y^2}$ to get

$\|\vec{d}\| = \sqrt{(-150)^2 + 200^2} = \sqrt{22500 + 40000} = \sqrt{62500} = 250$ mph.

Choice A is incorrect. This results from calculation error. **Choice B** is incorrect. This results from calculation error. **Choice D** is incorrect. This result from $y - x$.

104.

Category: PHM
Skill: Vectors | **Level:** Hard

Choice C is correct. Solving the resultant vector $\vec{A}+\vec{B}$ yields $\vec{A}+\vec{B}=(3+5),(4+(-12))=(8,-8)$.
From the solution, $x=8$ and $y=-8$.
Substitute the given into the formula $\|\vec{A}-\vec{B}\|=\sqrt{x^2+y^2}$ to get $\|\vec{A}-\vec{B}\|=\sqrt{8^2+(-8)^2}=\sqrt{64+64}=\sqrt{128}=8\sqrt{2}$.

Choice A is incorrect. This is the result of *xy*. **Choice B** is incorrect. This is the value of *x*. **Choice D** is incorrect. This may be due to calculation error.

105.

Category: PHM & Modeling
Skill: Vectors | **Level:** Medium

Choice C is correct. The magnitude of $\vec{E}=(x,3)$ is given by $\|\vec{E}\|=\sqrt{x^2+3^2}=5$.
Squaring both sides yields $x^2+9=25$. Subtracting 9 from both sides yields $x^2=16$ or $x=\pm 4$.
From the choices, the correct answer is 4.

Choice A is incorrect. This may be due to calculation error. **Choice B** is incorrect. This is the *y* component.
Choice D is incorrect. This is the magnitude of $\vec{E}$.

106.

Category: IES
Skill: Matrices | **Level:** Easy

Choice B is correct. Each row of the matrix corresponds to a section which is Section A: 3 rows of 4 seats each [4, 4, 4] and Section B: 2 rows of 5 seats each [5, 5].
Therefore, the correct matrix is $\begin{bmatrix} 4 & 4 & 4 \\ 5 & 5 & \end{bmatrix}$.

Choice A is incorrect. This lists the number of rows in each section instead of seats per row. **Choice C** is incorrect. Combines the number of rows and seats per row incorrectly. **Choice D** is incorrect. Section A lists the number of rows instead of seats per row.

107.

Category: IES
Skill: Matrices | **Level:** Hard

Choice D is correct. To find the total revenue, calculate the product of *M* and *E* to get

$$M\times E=\begin{bmatrix} 8 & 12 & 10 \\ 15 & 18 & 20 \end{bmatrix}\times\begin{bmatrix} 5000 \\ 6000 \\ 7000 \end{bmatrix}.$$

For Team 1: $(8\times 5000)+(12\times 6000)+(10\times 7000)$
$=40{,}000+72{,}000+70{,}000=182{,}000$
For Team 2: $(15\times 5000)+(18\times 6000)+(20\times 7000)$
$=75{,}000+108{,}000+140{,}000=323{,}000$
Adding the total yields $182{,}000+323{,}000=505{,}000$.

Choice A is incorrect. This is the difference between Team 2 and Team 1's revenue. **Choice B** is incorrect. This is Team 1's revenue. **Choice C** is incorrect. This is Team 2's revenue.

108.

Category: IES & Modeling
Skill: Matrices | **Level:** Easy

Choice B is correct. In the matrix, each row represents a student, and each column represents a subject with Column 1: Math grades and Column 2: Science grades. The second student's grades are in row 2: [78, 88].
The science grade (column 2) is 88.

Choice A is incorrect. This is the math grade for the first student. **Choice C** is incorrect. This is the science grade for the first student. **Choice D** is incorrect. This is the science grade for the third student.

109.

Category: IES
Skill: Matrices | **Level:** Medium

Choice A is correct. To calculate the total sales, add corresponding elements of matrices *A* and *B* to get

$$A+B=\begin{bmatrix} 20+18 & 15+12 \\ 25+22 & 10+8 \end{bmatrix}=\begin{bmatrix} 38 & 27 \\ 47 & 18 \end{bmatrix}$$

Choice B is incorrect. This miscalculates desserts as 50 and 20 instead of 47 and 18. **Choice C** is incorrect. This adds 2 units to all elements. **Choice D** is incorrect. This is the original matrix A.

110.

Category: PHM
Skill: Matrices | **Level:** Medium

Choice C is correct. Matrix multiplication follow the rule

$$A\times B=\begin{bmatrix} 1 & 2 \\ 3 & 4 \end{bmatrix}\times\begin{bmatrix} 2 & 0 \\ 1 & -1 \end{bmatrix}=\begin{bmatrix} (1\times 2)+(2\times 1) & (1\times 0)+(2\times(-1)) \\ (3\times 2)+(4\times 1) & (3\times 0)+(4\times(-1)) \end{bmatrix}$$

$$=\begin{bmatrix} 4 & -2 \\ 10 & -4 \end{bmatrix}$$

Choice A is incorrect. This may be due to conceptual or calculation error. **Choice B** is incorrect. This may be due to conceptual or calculation error. **Choice D** is incorrect. This may be due to conceptual or calculation error.

111.

Category: PHM
Skill: Matrices | **Level:** Easy

Choice A is correct. For a matrix in the form $\begin{bmatrix} a & b \\ c & d \end{bmatrix}$, the value of the determinant is $ad - bc$. So,

$$6\cdot 4 - k\cdot k = 5k$$
$$24 - k^2 = 5k$$
$$k^2 + 5k - 24 = 0$$
$$(k+8)(k-3) = 0$$
$$k = -8 \text{ or } k = 3$$

Only –8 is a correct choice to choose, so the correct choice is A.

Choice B is incorrect. This factor $k^2 + 5k - 24$ as $(k - 8)$ and $(k + 3)$. **Choice C** is incorrect. This factor $k^2 + 5k - 24$ as $(k - 4)$ and $(k + 6)$. **Choice D** is incorrect. This factor $k^2 + 5k - 24$ as $(k - 8)$ and $(k + 3)$.

112.

Category: PHM
Skill: Matrices | **Level:** Hard

Choice D is correct. To find the revenue for Team A, perform the matrix multiplication of Team A's row with Q,

thus $R_A = [20\ 30\ 25] \times \begin{bmatrix} 2 \\ 3 \\ 1 \end{bmatrix}$

$= 40 + 90 + 25 = 155.$

Since revenue is in thousands, the total revenue is $155 \times 1000 = 155{,}000$.

Choice A is incorrect. This may be due to conceptual or calculation error. **Choice B** is incorrect. This may be due to conceptual or calculation error. **Choice C** is incorrect. This may be due to conceptual or calculation error.

113.

Category: IES & Modeling
Skill: Matrices | **Level:** Medium

Choice C is correct. To calculate the total earnings, find the total number of packages delivered by summing all elements in $C = 10 + 12 + 15 + 18 = 55$.
Multiplying the total by $5 per package yields
$55 \times 5 = 275$.
Therefore, the total earnings is $275.

Choice A is incorrect. This may result if there are only 50 packages delivered. **Choice B** is incorrect. This may result if there are 54 packages delivered. **Choice D** is incorrect. This may result if there are 58 packages delivered.

114.

Category: PHM & Modeling
Skill: Matrices | **Level:** Medium

Choice C is correct. The determinant of a 2x2 matrix $C = \begin{bmatrix} a & b \\ c & d \end{bmatrix}$ is calculated as $det(C) = ad - bc$

For $C = \begin{bmatrix} 3 & 5 \\ 1 & 4 \end{bmatrix}$, the determinant is

$det(C) = (3)(4) - (5)(1) = 12 - 5 = 7$

Choice A is incorrect. This may result if the formula was swapped to 5–12. **Choice B** is incorrect. This may be due to calculation error. **Choice D** is incorrect. This may result if the determinant is added instead of subtracted.

115.

Category: PHM
Skill: Matrices | **Level:** Easy

Choice D is correct. To solve scalar multiplication, multiply each element in the matrix by the scalar 2 to get

$$\begin{bmatrix} 3 & 5 \\ 7 & 9 \end{bmatrix} \times 2 = \begin{bmatrix} 3\times 2 & 5\times 2 \\ 7\times 2 & 9\times 2 \end{bmatrix} = \begin{bmatrix} 6 & 10 \\ 14 & 18 \end{bmatrix}.$$

Choice A is incorrect. The 4th position is a miscalculation as 9 × 3. **Choice B** is incorrect. The 1st to 3rd position is multiplied by the scalar 3 instead of 2. **Choice C** is incorrect. The 2nd and 3rd position is multiplied by the scalar 3 instead of 2.

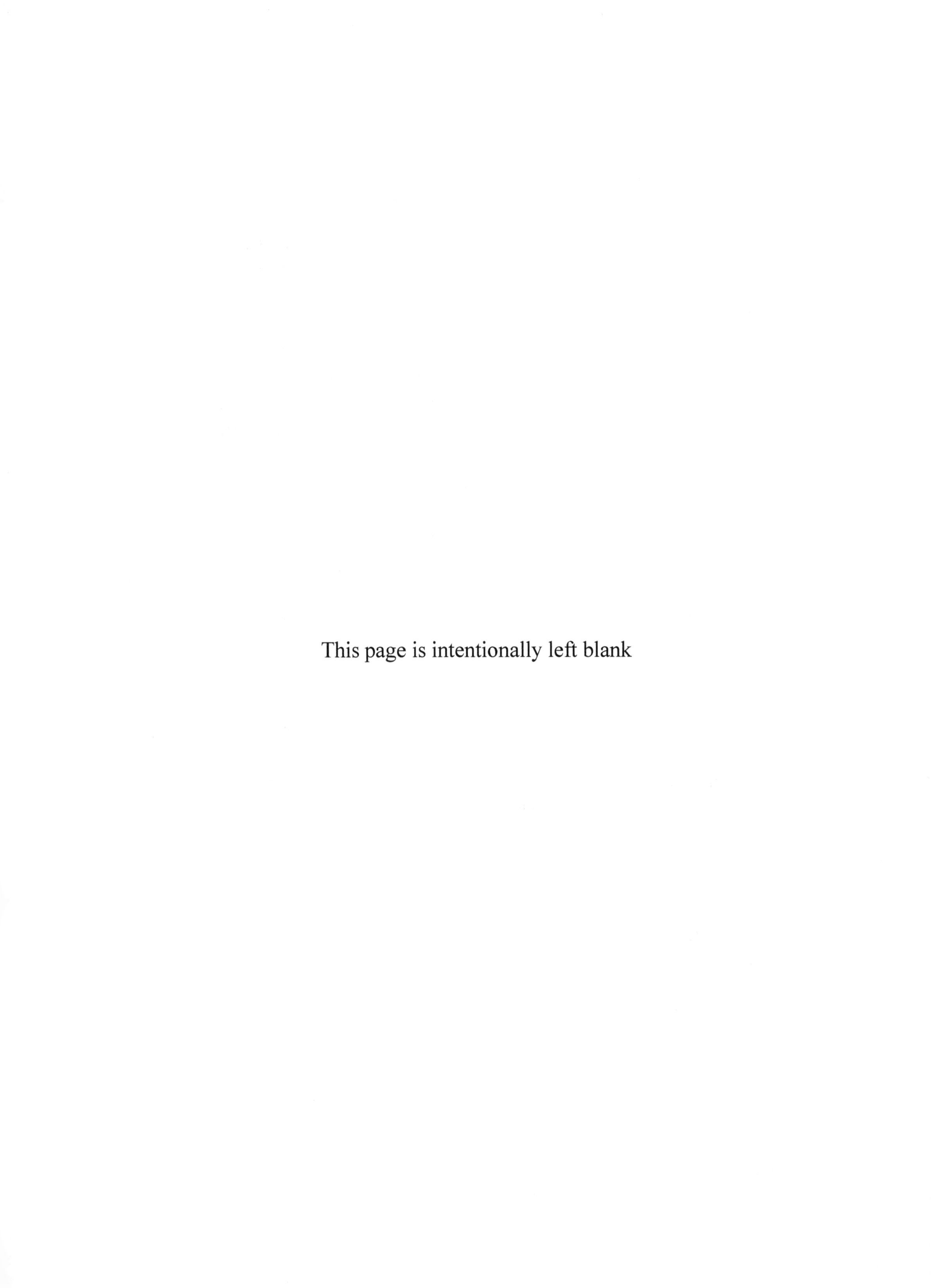

This page is intentionally left blank

Chapter 4
Algebra Practice Questions

1.

An amount is deposited in a bank paying an annual interest rate of 3%, compounded continuously. The balance after 3 years is $860,568.07. Find the principal amount and express it in scientific notation.

A. 78.65×10^6
B. 7.865×10^3
C. 7.865×10^4
D. 78.65×10^4

2.

In a delicate circuit, the microcurrent through the electrode is held constant at 3.6×10^{-8} amperes. The defect in the part of the circuit causes the current to be 1000 times smaller. What was the current, in amperes, caused by this defect?

A. 3.6×10^{-11}
B. 3.6×10^{-24}
C. 3.6×10^{-5}
D. $3.6 \times 10^{-8/3}$

3.

112.1478×10^{-2} is equal to which of the following?

A. 1.121478×10^1
B. 1.121478×10^{-4}
C. 1.121478×10^0
D. 11.21478×10^1

4.

James had a vacation in Paris. He visited the famous art museum, Louvre. He took a 3.5 kilometer cab ride from the Louvre to Eiffel Tower. A tour guide named Shane informed him that it took 2.5 million rivets to build the tower that stands 320 meters tall. Which expression is equivalent to the number of rivets used to build the Eiffel Tower in scientific notation.

A. 2.5×10^6
B. 2.5×10^5
C. 2.5×10^{-6}
D. $2.5 \times 10^{1/6}$

5.

Scientist testing certain atomic reaction expected it to take place in 7.3×10^{-7} seconds. In fact, the reaction usually lasted 100 times longer than they expected. How long did the reaction actually last, in seconds?

A. 7.3×10^{-4}
B. 7.3×10^5
C. 7.3×10^{-9}
D. 7.3×10^{-5}

6.

A certain plant cell has a measurement of 0.000001 meter. Which of the following represents the measurement?

A. 10^{-5} meters
B. 10^{-6} meters
C. 10^6 meters
D. 10^{-4} meters

7.

In scientific notation, 870,000,000 + 3,000,000 = ?

A. 8.10×10^8
B. 8.73×10^{16}
C. 9.00×10^8
D. 8.73×10^8

8.

Students at Arizona Community College pay 1.239×10^4 dollars for tuition. There will be a tuition fee increase of 15% for the next year. Anna has 3.15×10^2 savings. How much does she need to be able to cover the tuition fee?

A. 1.208×10^2
B. 1.208×10^4
C. 1.393×10^4
D. 1.383×10^2

9.

Uranium-238 has a half-life of 4.5×10^9 years. The half-life of carbon-14 is 5.7×10^3 years. How many times greater is the half-life of uranium-238 than that of carbon-14?

A. 7.9×10^5
B. 7.9×10^6
C. 7.9×10^{12}
D. 7.9×10^9

10.

The fastest plane has a cruising speed that is three times the speed of sound. What is the cruising speed in scientific notation of the plane? (speed of sound = 7.6×10^2)

A. 2.28×10^3
B. 22.8×10^3
C. 2.28×10^2
D. 2.28×10^4

11.

Which expression is equivalent to $(4x^3 + 3xy - 5) - x(2x^2 - 7y + 6)$?

A. $2x^3 - 10xy - 11$
B. $2x^3 + 10xy - 11x$
C. $2x^3 - 10xy + 6x - 5$
D. $2x^3 + 10xy - 6x - 5$

12.

In a Physics class, students are studying the motion of a rolling ball at a constant rate along a straight line. The table below gives the distance, d feet. The ball was from a reference point at 1-second intervals from $t = 0$ seconds to $t = 5$ seconds.

t	0	1	2	3	4	5
d	8	16	24	32	40	48

Which of the following relationship between d and t?

A. $d = t + 8$
B. $d = 8t + 8$
C. $d = 8t + 16$
D. $d = 4t + 8$

13.

In the real numbers, what is the solution of the the equation $27^{x-5} = 9^{5-x}$

A. 8
B. 7
C. 5
D. 3

14.

How old is Gina if she is 25 years younger than her father and the sum of their ages is 53?

A. 7
B. 14
C. 25
D. 39

15.

Find the missing step in finding the equivalent expression of $\frac{5}{k} + \frac{k+3}{k+5}$.

Step 1: $\frac{5}{k} + \frac{k+3}{k+5}$

Step 2: ?

Step 3: $\frac{5k + 25 + k^2 + 3k}{k(k+5)}$

Step 4: $\frac{k^2 + 8k + 25}{k(k+5)}$

A. $\frac{(k+5)}{(k+5)} \cdot \frac{k}{k} + \frac{(k+3)}{(k+5)} \cdot \frac{5}{k}$
B. $\frac{(k+5)}{(k+5)} + \frac{(k+3)}{(k+5)} + \frac{k}{k}$
C. $\frac{(k+5)}{(k+5)} + \frac{5}{k} + \frac{(k+3)}{(k+5)} + \frac{k}{k}$
D. $\frac{(k+5)}{(k+5)} \cdot \frac{5}{k} + \frac{(k+3)}{(k+5)} \cdot \frac{k}{k}$

16.

If $y = x + 3$, find $(x - y)^3$.

A. -27
B. -9
C. 9
D. 27

17.

If $y = 7x + 5$ *and* $g = 2x + 9$, then $yg = ?$

A. $(7x+5)(2x-9)$
B. $(7x+5)(2x+9)$
C. $14x^2 + 63x + 45$
D. $14x^2 + 73x + 35$

18.

A dance club was preparing for a fitness program. They were asked to check the trapezoid-shaped stage to make necessary planning for their steps. The formula for the area of a trapezoid is $A=\frac{1}{2}h(b_1+b_2)$, where b_1 and b_2 are the lengths of the to parallel sides and h is the height. Which of the following is an expression for b_2?

A. $\frac{2A}{h}+b_1$

B. $\frac{2A}{h+b_1}$

C. $\frac{2h}{A-b_1}$

D. $\frac{2A}{h}-b_1$

19.

A box has a length 3 inches less than twice its width, in inches. Which of the following equations for length l, in inches, in terms of the width, w inches, of the box?

A. $l=\frac{1}{2}w+3$

B. $l=2w-3$

C. $l=3-2w$

D. $l=w-3$

20.

Find x when $2x + 4 = 3x - 3$.

A. 1

B. 2

C. 4

D. 7

21.

The equation $|3x - 4| + 2 = 6$ has 2 solutions. Those solutions are equal to the solutions to which of the following pair of equations?

A. $3x-4=8;\ -(3x-4)=8$

B. $3x-4=4;\ -(3x-4)=4$

C. $3x-4=8;\ -3x-4=8$

D. $3x+4=4;\ -3x+4=4$

22.

A cat is stuck in a tree. A fireman needs to use a ladder of 25 feet in length to rescue the cat. The tree is 50 feet high, and the cat is 15 feet off the ground straight up in the trunk of the tree. How far from the bottom of the tree will the ladder have to be in order to reach the point at which the cat is?

A. 18

B. 20

C. 21

D. 22

23.

Cici owns 6 different dress blouses, 3 different skirts, and 5 different headbands. How many distinct outfits, each consisting of a blouse, a skirt, and a headband, can Cici make?

A. 14

B. 85

C. 90

D. 120

24.

If $x = 2t + 5$ and $y = 4 - 8t$, which of the following properly expresses y in terms of x?

A. $y=-4x+1$

B. $y=8x+5$

C. $y=-(8x+1)$

D. $y=-4(x-6)$

25.

Charise is able to read 800 words of text in only one minute because she is skilled reader. Joshua reads at a normal pace — 200 words of text in a minute. Joshua just finished a novel that took him a total of 10 hours to read. Approximately how long in hours will it take Charise to read the same book?

A. 1.5 hours

B. 2.5 hours

C. 5 hours

D. 6.5 hours

26.

Xander is having a picnic for 78 guests. He plans to serve each guest at least one hot dog. If each package, p, contains eight hotdogs, which inequality could be used to determine how many packages of hotdogs Roger will need to buy?

A. $p \le 78$
B. $8p \le 78$
C. $8p \ge 78$
D. $\frac{p}{8} \ge 78$

27.

Getting into shape requires exercising. According to a fitnes expert, the subject's maximum recommended number of heartbeats per minute (h) can be determined by subtracting the subject's age (a) from 220 and then taking 75% of that value. This relation is expressed by which of the following formulas?

A. $220 = 0.75(h - a)$
B. $0.75h = (220 - a)$
C. $h = 0.75(220 - a)$
D. $0.75h = (a - 220)$

28.

A two-digit number ab is equal to the sum of its tens digit and the square of its units digit. If $a = 8$, find b.

A. 2
B. 6
C. 7
D. 9

29.

Find m.

$$\frac{8}{x-2} + x - 1 = \frac{x^2 - x - m}{x-2}$$

A. −10
B. −9
C. 9
D. 10

30.

The equations $x + y = 15.45$ and $45x + 38y = 623.15$ represents the money collected from concert ticket sales during two class periods. If x represents the cost for each student ticket, what is the cost for each adult ticket y?

A. \$5.15
B. \$8.35
C. \$10.30
D. \$12.35

31.

A video had 80 views when it was posted and later, the number of views increases exponentially. The function $y = 80e^{0.2t}$ models the number of views, where t is the number of days since the video was posted. Which graph represents the given function?

A.

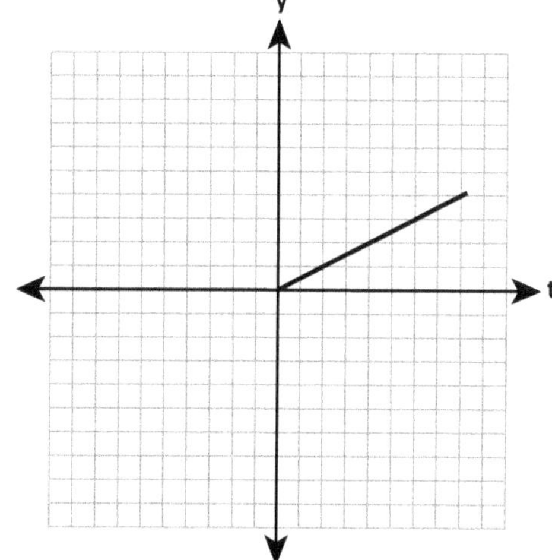

B.

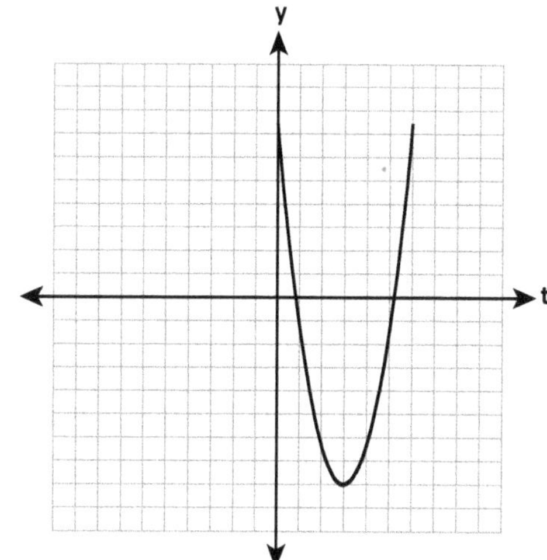

C.

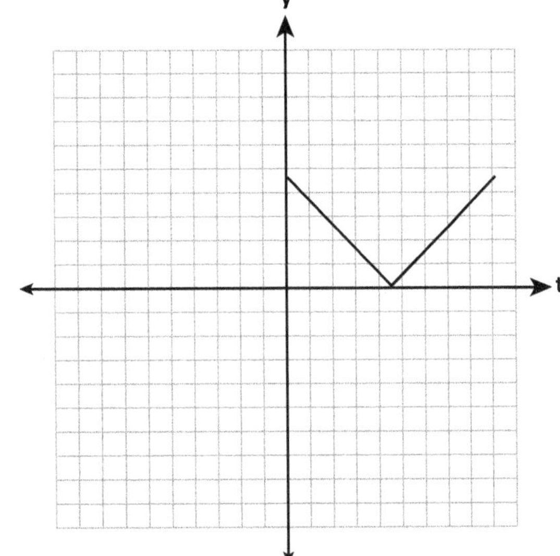

D.

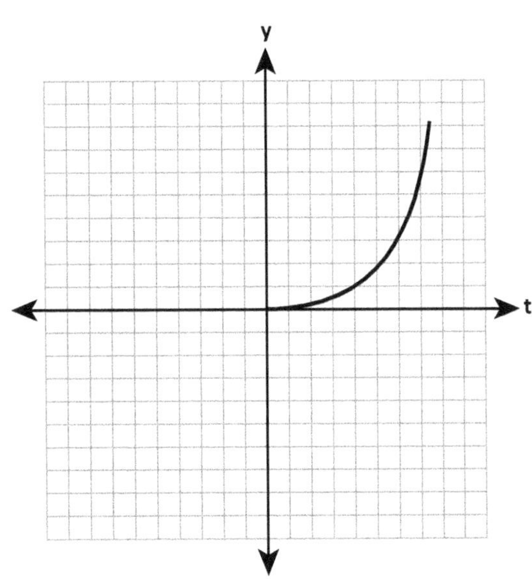

32.

What is the factored form of $3x^2 - 5x - 12$?

A. $(3x-4)(x+3)$
B. $(3x+4)(x-4)$
C. $(3x+4)(x-3)$
D. $(3x+2)(x-3)$

33.

The minimum fine for driving in excess of the speed limit is $25. An additional $6 is added to the minimum fine for each mile per hour in excess of the speed limit. Rachel was issued a $103 fine for speeding in a 55-mph speed limit zone. For driving at what speed, in mph, was Rachel fined?

A. 59 mph
B. 65 mph
C. 68 mph
D. 78 mph

34.

Find y^3 when $y = 3(x - 1)$ and $x = -2$.

A. –6561
B. –847
C. –729
D. –81

35.

Multiply the expressions.

$$(x+4)(x^2-3x+8)$$

A. $x^3 + x^2 + 4x + 24$
B. $x^3 + x^2 - 4x + 32$
C. $2x^3 + 2x^2 + x + 12$
D. $x^3 + 2x^2 + 6x + 12$

36.

Alexa has a cell phone plan that charges $0.7 per minute plus a monthly fee of $15.00. She budgets $29.70 per month for total cell phone expenses without taxes. What is the maximum number of minutes Alexa could use her phone each month in order to stay within her budget?

A. 21
B. 158
C. 188
D. 304

37.

A junior architect made a model of a 5-storey commercial building. The expression $5x^2 + 10x + 5$ represents the building's total height in feet. The expression $2x^2 + 4x + 2$ represents the distance, in feet, between the top of the building and the cafeteria located at the 4th floor.

Which equation represents the distance of the ground floor and the cafeteria?

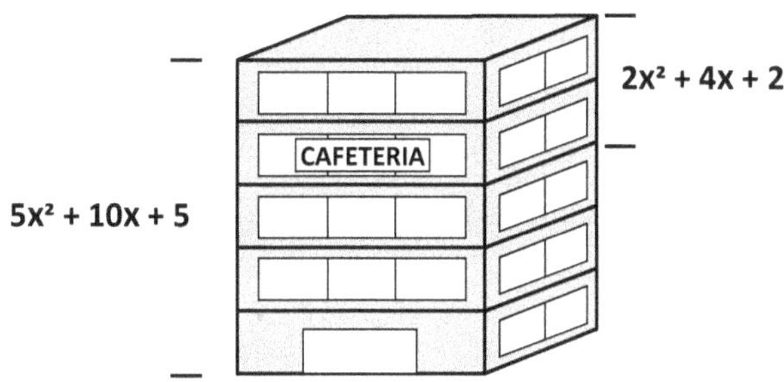

A. $5x^2 + 2x - 3$
B. $10x^2 + 40x + 10$
C. $3x^2 + 6x + 3$
D. $8x^2 + 14x + 7$

38.

What type of solutions are there for the equation $x^3 - 27 = 0$?

A. One real number and two complex numbers
B. Two real numbers and one complex number
C. Three complex numbers
D. Three complex numbers

39.

Anna is a famous maker of souvenir items in her town. She can produce cards (c) with a variable cost of \$3.75. The fixed cost for the use of the machine is \$1300. Which of the following expressions correctly models the cost of producing the cards of paper each day?

A. $1300c + 3.75$
B. $1300 + 3.75c$
C. $1300 - 3.75c$
D. $1300c$

40.

Sample A of 300 marbles was removed from a jar of jellybeans. All of the jellybeans in the jar are one of four colors: red, orange, green, and purple. For the sample, the number of jellybeans of each color is shown in the table below.

Color of the marbles	Number of marbles
Red	45
Orange	60
Green	75
Purple	120

Sample B of marbles was removed from a jar containing 25,000 marbles. If the sample B is indicative of the color distribution in the jar in sample A, which of the following is the best estimate of the number of red marbles in the jar?

A. 2250
B. 3750
C. 6250
D. 10000

41.

75% of the graduating class of Arizona High School had taken at least 6 Chemistry courses. Of the remaining class members, 60% had taken 4 or 5 Chemistry courses. What percent of the graduating class had taken fewer than 4 Chemistry courses?

A. 4%
B. 10%
C. 18%
D. 25%

42.

Which expression is equivalent to $-3x(x-4) - 2x(x+3)$?

A. $-x^2 + 1$
B. $-x^2 + 18x$
C. $-5x^2 + 6x$
D. $-5x^2 + 12x$

43.

An airplane flew for 8 hours at an airspeed of x miles per hour (mph), and for 7 more hours at 325 mph. If the average airspeed for the entire flight was 350 mph, which of the following equations could be used to find x?

A. $8x+7(325)=2(350)$
B. $x+7(325)=35(350)$
C. $x+7(325)=8(350)$
D. $8x+7(325)=15(350)$

44.

What is the sum of the solutions to the equation $9x^2+30x+25=0$?

A. $-\frac{10}{3}$
B. $-\frac{5}{3}$
C. $\frac{5}{3}$
D. $\frac{10}{3}$

45.

Solve for x: $3(x+2)=-3$

A. −3
B. −2
C. 2
D. 3

46.

If $a^x \cdot a^8 = a^{32}$ and $(a^5)^y = a^{20}$, what is the value of $x+y$?

A. 22
B. 26
C. 28
D. 32

47.

A small store sells seasonal berries on sale. During the sale, the store sells packages of blueberries for $4 each and packages of strawberries for $6 each. Joann purchased nine packages of fruit for her sister's dinner party for $40. How many packages of blueberries did she purchase?

A. 4
B. 6
C. 7
D. 9

48.

Which of the following equations represents the given relationship below?

An integer, x, is subtracted from 5. That difference is then multiplied by 2. This product is 18 more than half the original integer.

A. $5(2-x)=\frac{x}{2}-18$
B. $(x-5)=2+18/x$
C. $2(2-5x)=\frac{x}{2}-18$
D. $2(5-x)=\frac{x}{2}+18$

49.

Simplify $\sqrt[3]{16x^5y^4}$.

A. $xy\sqrt[3]{16x^2y}$
B. $2xy\sqrt[3]{2x^2y}$
C. $2x^3y\sqrt[3]{x^2y}$
D. $2yx^2\sqrt[3]{x^2y}$

50.

The production records of factory A and B were compared. Factory A has already produced 18,000 units and can produce 120 units per day. Factory B has produced only 14,500 units but can produce 155 units per day. If *d* represents the number of days (that is, days during which each factory is producing its maximum number of units), which of the following equations could be solved to determine the number of days until A's total production equals B's total production?

A. $18{,}000+120\text{d}=14{,}500+155\text{d}$

B. $18{,}000+155\text{d}=14{,}500+120\text{d}$

C. $(18{,}000+120)\text{d}=(14{,}500+155)\text{d}$

D. $(120+155)\text{d}=18{,}000-14{,}500$

51.

Determine values for m if the vertex of the parabola is V (−6, −4).
$g(x)=x^2+mx+32$.

A. 8
B. 9
C. 15
D. 12

52.

Which fraction represents

$\dfrac{\frac{8}{x-3}+\frac{16x}{x^2-9}}{\frac{4}{x+3}-\frac{10x}{x^2-9}}$ expressed in simplest form?

A. $8\left(\dfrac{x+1}{x+2}\right)$

B. $4\left(\dfrac{x+1}{x+2}\right)$

C. $-4\left(\dfrac{x+1}{x+2}\right)$

D. $-8\left(\dfrac{x-1}{x-3}\right)$

53.

What is the value of x in the solutions of the system of equations below?

$3x+4(x-3)=3(2y-3)-4y$

$3y+2(x-4)=5(y+2)-20$

A. −4
B. 1
C. 2
D. 3

54.

Which statement best describes the lines $-4x+5y=15$ and $-30+10y=8x$?

A. skew
B. perpendicular
C. parallel
D. the same line

55.

What is the inequality that corresponds to the graph below?

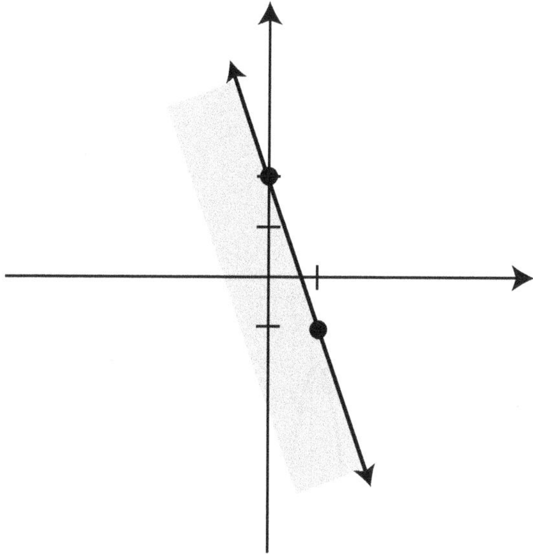

A. $y>3x+2$
B. $y\leq-3x+2$
C. $y\geq-3x+2$
D. $y>3x+2$

56.

Given that the equation $\frac{4x-y}{x+y}=\frac{3}{7}$ is true, what is the value of $\frac{x}{y}$?

A. 0.1
B. 0.4
C. 0.6
D. 1.2

57.

If y = *f*(*x*) is to be reflected across the line *y* = *x*, which of the following graphs represents the result?

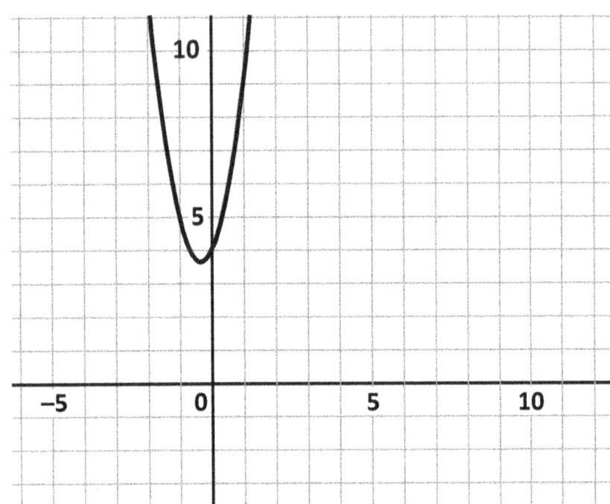

A.

B.

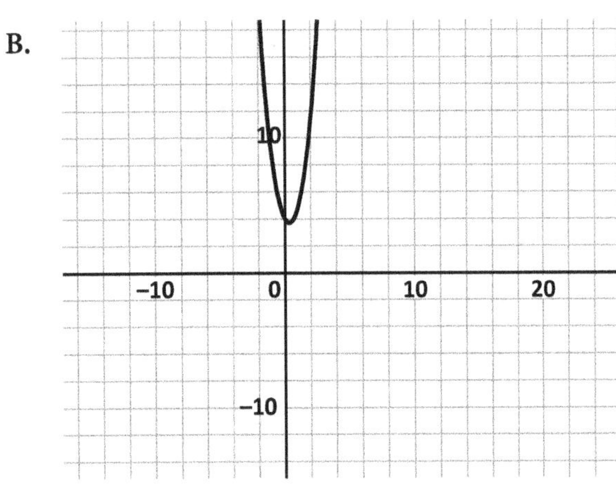

C.

D.

58.

If function f is defined by $f(x)=-3x^3$, then what is the value of f(f(f(1)))?

A. −1594323
B. −2187
C. −81
D. −3

59.

Which fraction is equivalent to $2+\frac{x}{x+1}-\frac{2}{x+1}$?

A. $\frac{3x+1}{3}$

B. $\frac{3x}{x+1}$

C. $\frac{3x-1}{x+1}$

D. $\frac{3}{x+1}$

60.

Which of the following is equivalent to $y = 2x^3 - 4x^2 - 20x - 10$?

A. $(x+2)(x-5)(2x+3)$

B. $2x(x^2 - x - 5)$

C. $2x(x^2 - 2x - 10) - 10$

D. $(x+2)(x-5)\left(x+\frac{1}{2}\right)$

61.

If $\frac{ae}{b} + c = d$, what is e in terms of *a, b, c, and d*?

A. $\frac{e(d-c)}{b}$

B. $b(d-c)-a$

C. $\frac{b(d-c)}{a}$

D. $\frac{d(b-c)}{a}$

62.

Which of the following is true about the graph of $\frac{x-1}{x+3} \geq 0$?

A. The graph is a straight line with a slope of 1.
B. The graph crosses the x-axis at 1 and has an asymptote of 3.
C. The graph is a number with an interval $(-\infty, -3) \cup [1, \infty)$.
D. The graph is a number with an interval $(-\infty, -3) \cup (1, \infty)$.

63.

Which of the following is a root of $12x^2 - 2x = 4$?

A. -4

B. $-\frac{2}{3}$

C. $\frac{1}{2}$

D. $\frac{2}{3}$

64.

If $x:y = 5:2$ and $y:z = 3:2$, what is the ratio of $x:z$?

A. 15:2
B. 2:15
C. 4:2
D. 15:4

65.

Which expression represents $\frac{12x^3 - 6x^2 + 2x}{2x}$ in simplest form?

A. $2x^2 - 6$

B. $2(3x+1)$

C. $6x^2 - 3x + 1$

D. $6x^2 - 2$

66.

Solve for *x*, where $\frac{1}{a} + \frac{1}{b} + \frac{1}{c} \neq 0$.

$$\frac{x-a-b}{c} + \frac{x-b-c}{a} + \frac{x-c-a}{b} = 3$$

A. $a + bc$
B. $ab + c$
C. $a + -b - c$
D. $a + b + c$

67.

Examine the slope of the data in the table. The rate of change is described as

x	y
0.5	9.0
1	8.75
1.5	8.5
2	8.25
2.5	8.0

A. negative
B. positive
C. constant
D. cannot be determined

68.

Solve the value of x in the solution of the given system of equations.

$x-7y=-11$

$5x+2y=-18$

A. -4
B. -1
C. 2
D. 4

69.

A company has weekend business trips and plans to reimburse its staff's personal expenses. It will reimburse $0.80 for every $1.00 a staff member spends, up to $100.00. For the next $200 a staff member spends, the company will reimburse $0.70 for every $1.00 spent. For each additional dollar spent, the company will reimburse $0.60. If a staff member was reimbursed $400.00, approximately how many dollars must she have spent on a weekend business trip?

A. 400
B. 500
C. 600
D. 667

70.

If $5j = 9l - 18$, then $l = ?$

A. $5j-8+18$
B. $\frac{5j+18}{9}$
C. $\frac{5j+8}{18}$
D. $5j+18+8$

71.

What is the y value of the solution of the system of equations below?

$2x+3y=7,\ x+y=3$

A. -1
B. 1
C. 2
D. 3

72.

Jasmine missed her grandmother and took a bicycle to visit her. The trip to her grandma's house was mostly uphill and would take t minutes. On the way home, she rode mostly downhill and was able to travel at an average speed twice that of her trip to her grandma's house. Which of the following expresses the total number of minutes that Jasmine bicycled on her entire trip?

A. $3t$
B. $2t$
C. $t+\frac{1}{2}$
D. $\frac{3t}{2}$

73.

A store charges $25 for a certain type of shoes. This price is 30% more than the amount it costs the shoe store to buy one pair of these shoes. At an end-of–the year sale, sales associates can purchase any remaining shoes at 20% off the shoe store cost. How much would it cost an employee to purchase a pair of shoes of this type during the sale (excluding sales tax)?

A. $12
B. $14
C. $15
D. $16

74.

In a linear equation, the independent variable increases at a constant rate while the dependent variable decreases at a constant rate. The slope of the line is:

A. negative.
B. positive.
C. constant.
D. cannot be determined.

75.

Which inequality best represents the graph below?

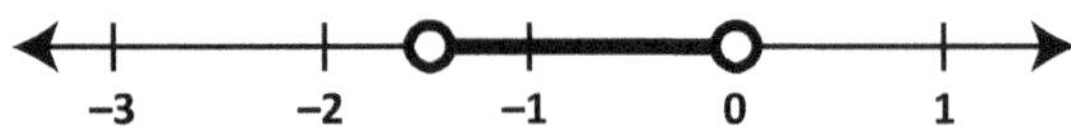

A. $-1.5>x>-1$
B. $x\leq 0$
C. $-0.5>x>0$
D. $-1.5<x<0$

76.

Which of the following describes a true relationship between the functions $f(x) = x^2 - 3x + 4$ and $g(x) = x + 1$ graphed below in the standard (x,y) coordinate plane?

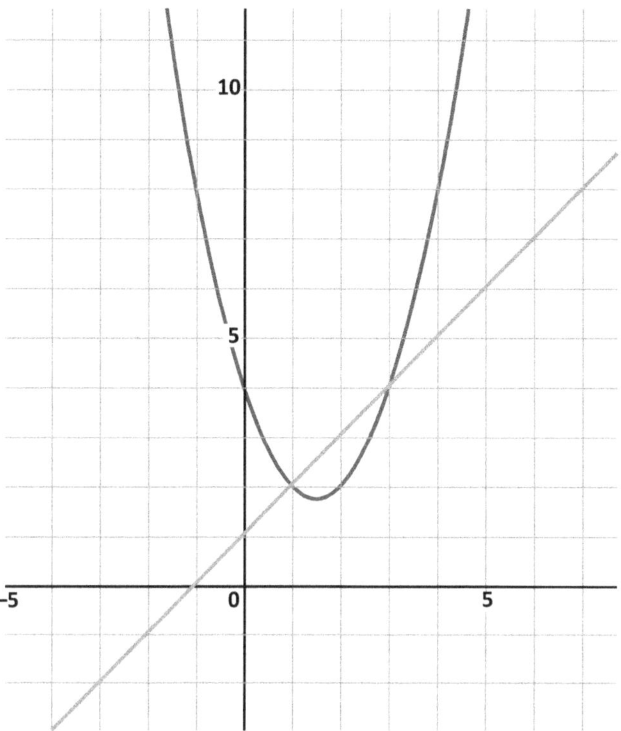

A. $f(x) = g(x)$ for exactly 1 value of x
B. $f(x) = g(x)$ for exactly 2 values of x
C. $f(x) < g(x)$ for all value of x
D. $g(x)$ is the inverse of $f(x)$

77.

Andres is studying her bee farm. She needs to approximate the number of bees in the population, and she realizes that the number of bees, N, is close to 70 more than double the volume of the bee farm, V. Which of the formulas below expresses that approximation?

A. $N = V + 270$
B. $N = 2(V + 70)$
C. $N = 2V + 70$
D. $N = \dfrac{V + 70}{2}$

78.

What is the value of x when $2x + 3 = 3x - 4$?

A. 2
B. 6
C. 7
D. 10

79.

Consider the given system of equations:

$$y = x^2$$
$$ax + by = c$$

For which of the following will there be more than one (x, y) solution, with real-number coordinate, for the system?

A. $a^2 - 4bc \geq c$
B. $a^2 - 4bc = c$
C. $a^2 - 4bc < c$
D. $a^2 - 4bc > c$

80.

Which of the following is the solution statement for the inequality shown below?

$-9 < 1 - 2x < 5$

A. $-2 < x < 5$
B. $-5 < 2x < 5$
C. $-9 < x < 4$
D. $-6 < x < 8$

81.

A yacht moves on a river that has a current of 4 miles per hour. The trip upstream takes 8 hours, while the return trip takes 6 hours. What is the speed of the yacht relative to the water?

A. 20 miles/hour
B. 25 miles/hour
C. 28 miles/hour
D. 30 miles/hour

82.

Thea goes to the Learning Book Club to read a book during her free time. The club charges a \$30 monthly fee, plus \$1.5 per book read in that month. Thea found out that another book club is offering a \$24 monthly fee, plus \$3 per book read in that month. Approximately, how many books must be read in a month for the total charges from each club to be equal?

A. 2
B. 3
C. 4
D. 5

83.

Leonard is drinking a soda as fast as he can. The amount of soda left in the cup (in ml) as a function of time is graphed. How much soda did Sean drink every 5 seconds?

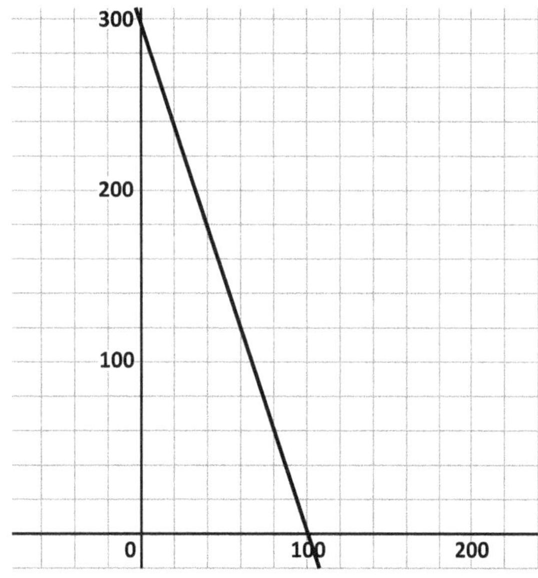

A. −15
B. −3
C. 5
D. 15

84.

Mr. Andrews's burrow lies 3 meters below the ground. He started digging his way deeper into the ground descending 1/5 meters each minute. Which graph represents the relationship between Mr. Andrews elevation to the ground (in meters) and the time (in minutes)?

A.

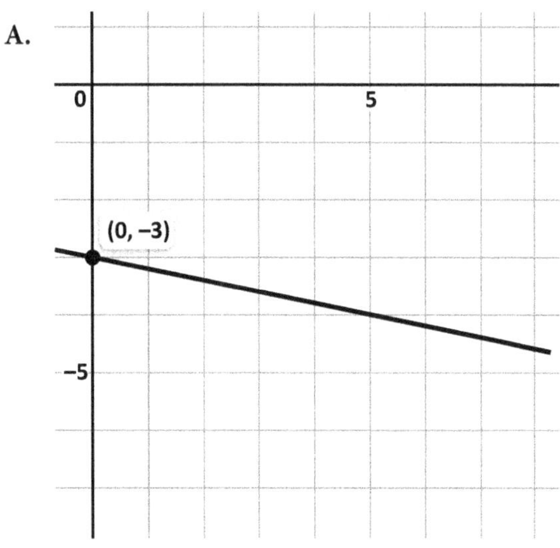

B.

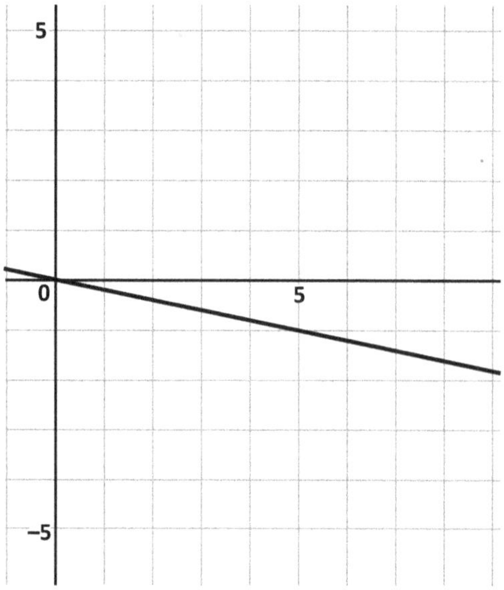

C.

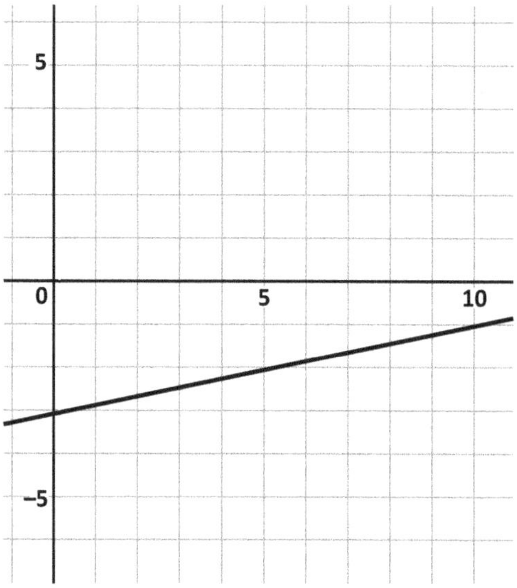

D.

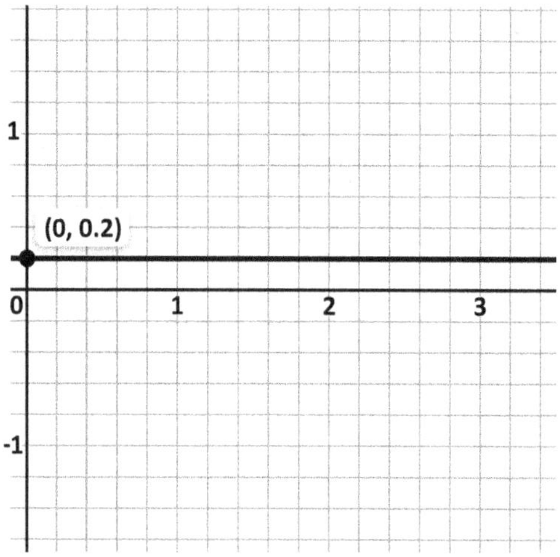

(0, 0.2)

85.

Jane and Lovely bought the same set of notebook and binder. Jane paid \$5.35 for the 3 notebooks and 1 binder. Lovely paid \$6.75 for 4 notebooks and 1 binder. What is the difference between the price of a notebook and a binder?

A. 0.15
B. 0.25
C. 1.15
D. 1.4

86.

Find the unique point that solves the equations simultaneously.

$3x-2y=21$

$3x+4y=3$

A. (−5, −3)
B. (5, −3)
C. (−5, 3)
D. (5, 3)

87.

The graph below shows the forecasted gasoline use for a certain vehicle. Which of the following is the closest estimate of the truck's predicted rate of gasoline use in gallons per mile ?

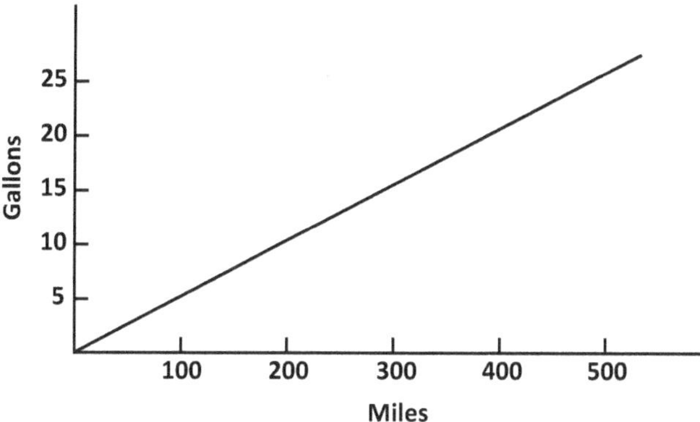

A. 0.05
B. 0.1
C. 0.2
D. 2.0

88.

Joseph can cross a bridge in 6 minutes at a constant rate of 8 kilometers per hour. What is the length of the bridge in meters?

A. $\frac{6}{8}$
B. 48
C. 480
D. 800

89.

A cargo truck is transporting 120 boxes composed of large and small boxes. The large boxes weigh 45 pounds each, the small boxes weigh 35 pounds each. If the truck has a carrying capacity of 4850 pounds, how many large boxes is it carrying?

A. 45
B. 55
C. 65
D. 75

90.

Which of the following is the graph of $2x-3y=-12$ in the standard (x, y) coordinate plane?

A.

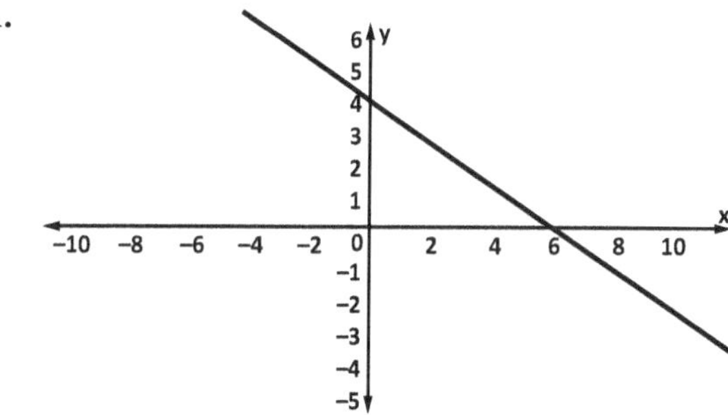

B.

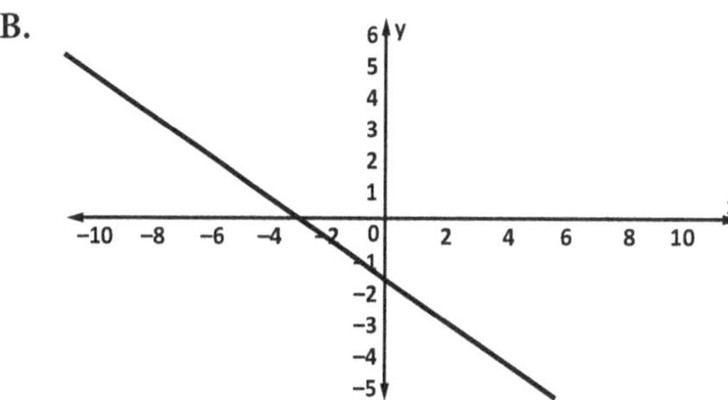

C.

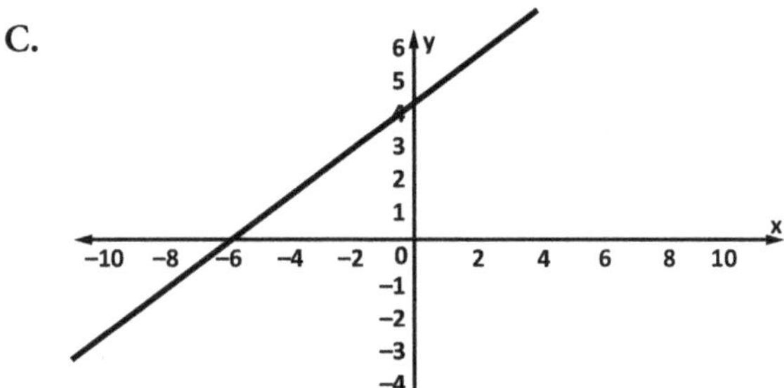

D.

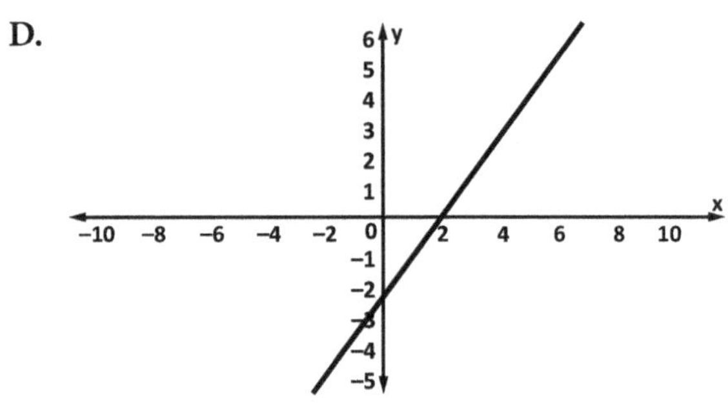

91.

Janet must drive 90 miles to reach the grocery store. If she drives 5 miles every 7 minutes, how long will it take her to reach her destination?

A. 40 minutes
B. 126 minutes
C. 160 minutes
D. 230 minutes

92.

A school offered to pay for the 2 different colors of prom dresses for 120 high school girls. The blue dress was priced at \$75 and the pink dress at \$50. The total budget is \$7000. How many prom dresses of each color can the school purchase for the girls?

A. 80 blue, 40 pink
B. 40 blue, 60 pink
C. 40 blue, 80 pink
D. 60 blue, 80 pink

93.

Using the graph below, find the earnings after 35 hours.

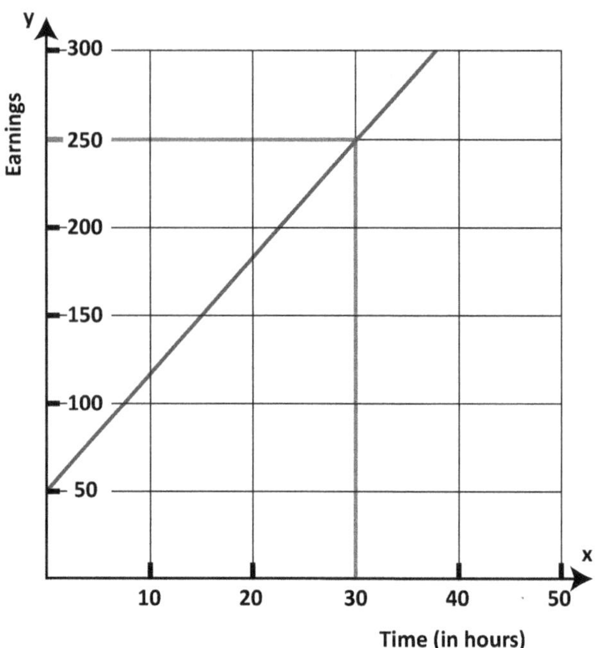

A. 275.00
B. 280.00
C. 283.45
D. 298.45

94.

Andrea drove 20 miles an hour for 15 minutes on the city streets, and then 40 miles an hour for 30 minutes on the highway, 60 miles an hour for 1 hour on the freeway, and finally 20 miles an hour for 15 minutes on city streets. Choose the graph that represents Andreas journey.

A.

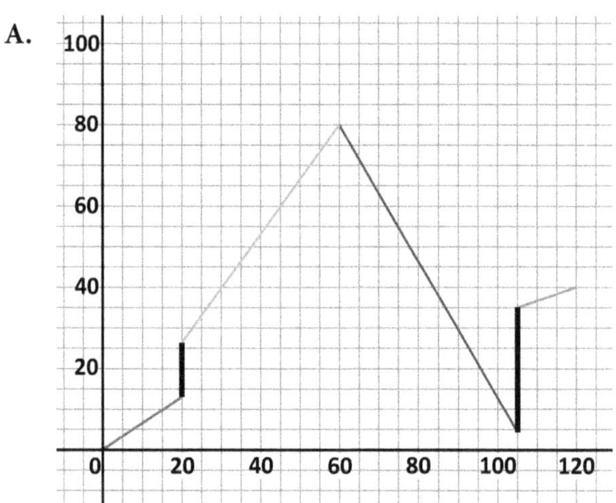

B.

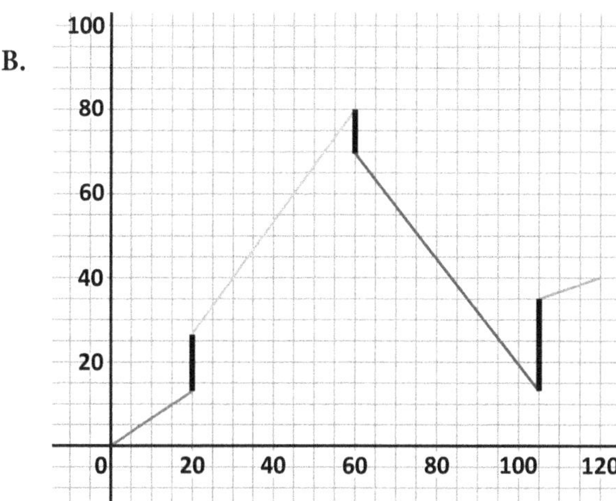

C.

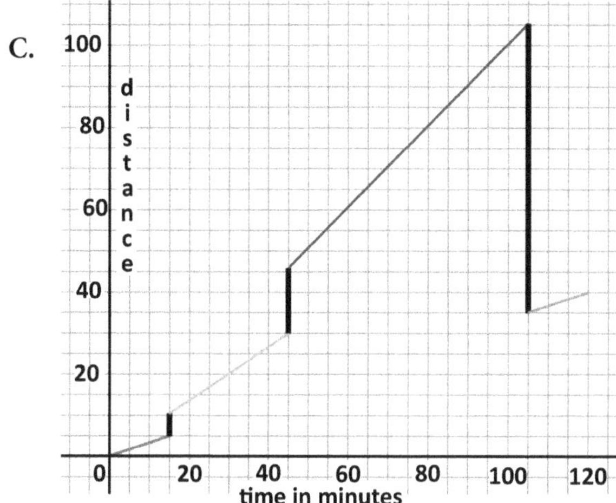

D.

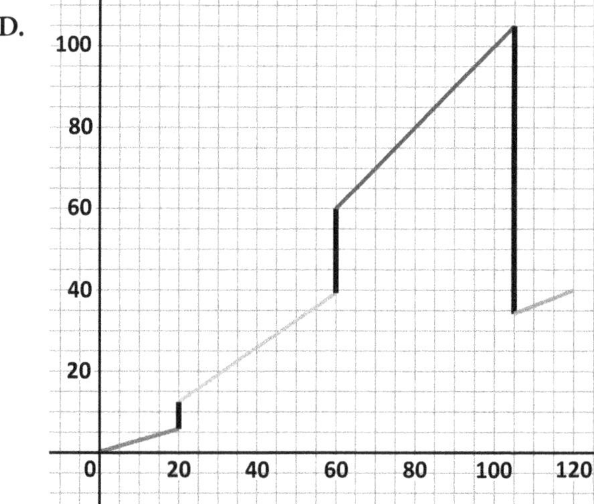

95.

Which of the following equations expresses the relationship between x and y in the table below?

x	y
4	41
7	32
11	20
13	14
16	5

A. $y = -3x + 53$
B. $y = 3x - 45$
C. $y = -3x + 45$
D. $y = 3x - 53$

96.

Which of the following is a polynomial factor of $x^2 - 3x - 54$?

A. $(x - 6)$
B. $(x + 9)$
C. $(x + 3)$
D. $(x + 6)$

97.

On Monday, a local hamburger shop sold a combined total of 450 hamburgers and cheeseburgers. The number of hamburgers sold was two times the number of cheeseburgers sold. How many hamburgers were sold on that day?

A. 150
B. 200
C. 250
D. 300

98.

Abby wants to buy a small rectangular farm. Find the length of the lot whose perimeter is 38 m and whose area is 60 square meters.

A. 4
B. 9
C. 15
D. 18

99.

The equation of a circle with center C is given as $x^2 + y^2 - 4x - 2y + 4 = 0$. Find the radius of the circle.

A. 1
B. 2
C. 3
D. 4

100.

Find the other factor of the polynomial $x^3 - 6x^2 + 11x - 6$, with a factor $x - 1$.

A. $2x^2 - x + 6$
B. $x^2 + 2x + 6$
C. $x^2 - 5x + 6$
D. $x^2 - 2x + 6$

101.

Solve the equation $2x^3 + 13x^2 + 15x$ by factoring.

A. $x(x-5)(2x-3)$
B. $2x(x+5)(2x-3)$
C. $x(2x+5)(x+3)$
D. $x(x+5)(2x+3)$

102.

Determine the maximum of $y = -4x^2 + 24x - 35$.
A. (3, −1)
B. (−3, −1)
C. (3, 1)
D. (−3, 1)

103.

What is the completely simplified form of the expression $\dfrac{12x - 3x - z^3x^2y^2}{2z^3xy - 18}$?

A. $\dfrac{9x}{-18}$

B. $\dfrac{\left(9 - z^3xy^2\right)}{\left(z^3xy - 9\right)}$

C. $\dfrac{x\left(9 - z^3xy^2\right)}{2\left(z^3xy - 9\right)}$

D. $\dfrac{x - z^3xy^2}{2 - z^3xy - 9}$

104.

Determine one of the roots of $12x^2 + 13x + 7 = 12 - 4x$.

A. $-\dfrac{5}{4}$

B. $\dfrac{1}{4}$

C. $\dfrac{3}{4}$

D. $\dfrac{5}{3}$

105.

The attendances y for two movies can be modeled by the following equations, where x is the number of days since the movies opened. When will the attendance for each movie be the same?

$y = -x^2 + 35x + 100$

$y = -5x + 275$

A. $x = 10,\ x = 25$

B. $x = 5,\ x = 35$

C. $x = 15,\ x = 20$

D. $x = 5,\ x = 30$

106.

Find the number of digits in the square root of 4489.

A. 1
B. 2
C. 3
D. 4

107.

The speed of a sports car before the brakes were applied can be estimated by the length of the skid marks left on the road. The formula $s = 2\sqrt{3l}$ can be used to estimate the speed s in miles per hour on wet concrete, where l represents the length of the skid marks in feet. Estimate the speed of the vehicle if the skid marks measure 35 feet.

A. 16.5
B. 18.2
C. 20.5
D. 25.8

108.

Find the cube root of −2197.

A. −15
B. −13
C. 13
D. 15

109.

A square pool is surrounded by a pavement with a uniform width of 1 foot. The combined area of the pool and the pavement is 500 square feet. What is the side length of the pool?

A. 18.00
B. 20.36
C. 21.36
D. 22.36

110.

Find the cube root of −17576.

A. −26
B. −23
C. 23
D. 26

111.

Andrew's backyard is divided into three square areas with Area = 144 square feet. He only wants to fence the outside edge to make one big back yard. How much fencing will he need to buy?

A = 144 ft²

A = 144 ft²   A = 144 ft²

A. 60
B. 84
C. 96
D. 112

112.

Find the number of digits in the square root of 390625.

A. 1
B. 2
C. 3
D. 4

113.

Gina has a bag with cubes. 16 of them are red and 9 are blue. If she makes a square out of all the bricks. How many bricks would be on each side?

A. 3
B. 4
C. 5
D. 6

114.

Ivy is baking a square cake for her friend's birthday. The cake will be served to the guests into 1-inch square pieces. The cake is enough to serve 121 guests and get one piece each. How long should each side of the cake be?

A. 6
B. 8
C. 11
D. 17

115.

Jane has a square flower garden. She plans to renovate it by increasing the width by 1 meter and the length by 3 meters/ The area will be 19 square meters more than the present area. What is the side length of the original garden?

A. 4
B. 5
C. 6
D. 7

116.

If $log_2 x = 3$, then $x = ?$

A. $\frac{1}{log6}$
B. $2log^3$
C. 6
D. 8

117.

Anna and Patrick had a discussion regarding the laws of logarithms. Anna said that the expression $log_3(2y-1)$ can be expanded or simplified using the laws of logarithms. Patrick thinks the opposite. Patrick is indeed correct. Which of the following statements does not help to explain why the laws of logarithms cannot be used to expand or simplify the expression?

A. Each term in the expression does not have the same variable.
B. The expression $2y - 1$ is not raised to a power.
C. $2y$ and 1 are neither multiplied together, nor are they divided into each other.
D. The expression $2y - 1$ cannot be factored.

118.

If $\log_x 16 = 4$ and $\log_2 32 = y$, then $y^x = ?$

A. 2
B. 10
C. 25
D. 32

119.

If $log_a x = b$ and $log_a y = c$, then $log_a (xy)^2 = ?$

A. bc
B. $2bc$
C. $4bc$
D. $2(b + c)$

120.

Which of the following is a value of n that satisfies $log_n 64 = 2$?

A. 6
B. 8
C. 23
D. 32

121.

Let b be an integer greater than 1, then $log_b \frac{b^2}{b^7} = ?$

A. -5
B. -2
C. $-\frac{1}{5}$
D. 5

122.

An audio source can produce a number of decibels modeled by the equation $d = 10log\left(\frac{I}{K}\right)$, where I is the intensity and K is a constant. Determine the number of decibels that an audio can produce whose intensity is 1,000 greater than the value of K.

A. 4
B. 30
C. 100
D. 10000

123.

In the equation $log_4 256 - log_3 9 = log_5 x$, what does x equal to?

A. 15
B. 20
C. 25
D. 30

124.

There are two earthquakes that struck Nepal. One earthquake has $R = 6.9$, $B = 3.2$, and $T = 1.9s$ and the second earthquake has $R = 5.7$, $B = 2.9$, and $T = 1.6s$. The formula for the magnitude of the earthquake is given as $R = \log\left(\frac{a}{T}\right) + B$. How many times larger is the amplitude a in the first earthquake compared to the second earthquake.

A. 1.2 times as large
B. 1.6 times as large
C. 9.4 times as large
D. 15.8 times as large

125.

The value of $log(x)$, is given in the table below. To the nearest 0.1, what is the value of $log(3 \times 10^{500})$?

x	$log(x)$
3	0.5
30	1.5
300	2.5

A. 2.5
B. 5.5
C. 500.5
D. 505.5

Answer Key

Question	Correct	Make your correct answers
1	D	
2	A	
3	C	
4	A	
5	D	
6	B	
7	D	
8	C	
9	A	
10	A	
11	D	
12	B	
13	C	
14	B	
15	D	
16	A	
17	B	
18	D	
19	B	
20	D	
21	B	
22	B	
23	C	
24	D	
25	B	
26	C	
27	C	
28	D	
29	D	
30	C	
31	D	
32	C	

Question	Correct	Make your correct answers
33	C	
34	C	
35	B	
36	A	
37	C	
38	A	
39	B	
40	B	
41	B	
42	C	
43	D	
44	A	
45	A	
46	C	
47	C	
48	D	
49	B	
50	A	
51	D	
52	C	
53	B	
54	D	
55	B	
56	B	
57	C	
58	A	
59	B	
60	C	
61	C	
62	C	
63	D	
64	D	

Question	Correct	Make your correct answers
65	C	
66	D	
67	A	
68	A	
69	C	
70	B	
71	B	
72	D	
73	C	
74	A	
75	D	
76	B	
77	C	
78	C	
79	D	
80	A	
81	C	
82	C	
83	D	
84	A	
85	B	
86	B	
87	A	
88	D	
89	C	
90	C	
91	B	
92	C	
93	C	
94	C	
95	A	
96	D	

Question	Correct	Make your correct answers
97	D	
98	C	
99	A	
100	C	
101	D	
102	C	
103	C	
104	B	
105	B	
106	B	
107	C	
108	B	
109	B	
110	A	
111	C	
112	C	
113	C	
114	C	
115	A	
116	D	
117	D	
118	C	
119	D	
120	B	
121	A	
122	B	
123	C	
124	C	
125	C	

1.

Category: IES
Skill: Scientific notation | **Level:** Easy

Choice D is correct because the obtained principal amount is 786,500 and can be expressed in scientific notation as 78.65×10^4.
Use the formula for continuous compound interest $A = Pe^{rt}$.

$$A = Pe^{rt}$$
$$\$860,568.07 = Pe^{(0.03)(3)}$$
$$\$860,568.07 = P\left(e^{0.09}\right)$$
$$\frac{\$860568.07}{e^{0.09}} = P$$
$$\$786,500 = P$$

Answer can be expressed as 78.65×10^4 in scientific notation.

Choice A is incorrect because 78.65×10^6 is not the correct representation of \$786,500 in scientific notation. **Choice B** is incorrect because 7.865×10^3 is expressed as \$7865 which is less than the obtained value of P. **Choice C** is incorrect because 7.865×10^4 is expressed as \$78650 which is less than the obtained value of P.

2.

Category: IES
Skill: Scientific Notation | **Level:** Medium

Choice A is correct because the current becomes 3.6×10^{-11} after the decrease of 1000 from the original value of the current.

Initial current: 3.6×10^{-8}
Final current after the decrease:

$$\frac{3.6\times10^{-8}}{1000} = \frac{3.6\times10^{-8}}{1\times10^{3}}$$
$$= 3.6\times10^{-8-3} = 3.6\times10^{-11} \text{ amperes}$$

Choice B is incorrect because 3.6×10^{-24} is an underestimate of the obtained final value of the current. **Choice C** is incorrect because 3.6×10^{-5} is greater than the obtained final value of the current. **Choice D** is incorrect because $3.6\times10^{-8/3}$ is not equivalent to the obtained the final value of the current.

3.

Category: PHM
Skill: Scientific Notation | **Level:** Easy

Choice C is correct because 112.1478×10^{-2} is equivalent to 1.121478×10^{0}.

112.1478×10^{-2}, can be expressed as 11.21478×10^{-1} or 1.121478×10^{0}.

Choice A is incorrect because 1.121478×10^{1} is not equivalent to the given decimal. **Choice B** is incorrect because 1.121478×10^{-4} is not equivalent to the given decimal. **Choice D** is incorrect because 11.21478×10^{1} is not equivalent to the given decimal.

4.

Category: PHM
Skill: Scientific Notation | **Level:** Medium

Choice A is correct because 2.5×10^{6} is equivalent to 2.5 million rivets.
To convert the standard form to scientific notation, write 2.5 million in digits (2500000)..
Move the decimal point to the left until there is a non-zero digit to its left. Since you're moving the decimal to the left, the exponent will be positive:
$2500000 = 2.5\times10^{6}$

Choice B is incorrect because 2.5×10^{5} is less than 2.5 million. **Choice C** is incorrect because 2.5×10^{-6} has a negative exponent and does not represent 2.5 million. **Choice D** is incorrect because $2.5\times10^{1/6}$ has a fraction exponent and does not represent 2.5 million.

5.

Category: IES
Skill: Scientific Notation | **Level:** Medium

Choice D is correct because 7.3×10^{-5} is the obtained value after increasing the reaction by 100 times.
Use the property of exponents to obtain the final value.
$7.3\times10^{-7}(100) = 7.3\times10^{-7}(1\times10^{2}) = 7.3\times10^{-7+2} = 7.3\times10^{-5}$

Choice A is incorrect because 7.3×10^{-4} is not equivalent to the obtained value after increasing the reaction by 100 times. **Choice B** is incorrect because 7.3×10^{5} has a positive exponent which is impossible after increasing the reaction by 100 times. **Choice C** is incorrect because 7.3×10^{-9} is not equivalent to the obtained value after increasing the reaction by 100 times.

6.

Category: IES
Skill: Scientific Notation | **Level:** Easy

Choice B is correct because 0.000001 meter is equivalent to 1×10^{-6} meters. To express 0.000001 in scientific notation, move the decimal point to the right up to the first non zero number. Since the movement is to the right, the exponent is -6.

Choice A is incorrect because 10^{-5} meters is greater than the expected value of the measurement. **Choice C** is incorrect because 10^6 meters is not equivalent to 0.000001 meter. **Choice D** is incorrect because 10^{-4} meters is greater than the expected value of the measurement.

7.

Category: PHM
Skill: Scientific Notation | **Level:** Easy

Choice D is correct because the obtained sum is 8.73×10^8.
Add the given numbers.

$$870{,}000{,}000 + 3{,}000{,}000 = 873{,}000{,}000$$

Express the answer in scientific notation.
Move the decimal point so that there is one nonzero digit to the left of the decimal

$$873{,}000{,}000 \text{ becomes } 8.73\times10^8$$

Choice A is incorrect because 8.10×10^8 is less than the obtained sum. **Choice B** is incorrect because 8.73×10^{16} is greater than the obtained sum. **Choice C** is incorrect because 8.73×10^8 is not the sum of the given numbers.

8.

Category: IES
Skill: Scientific Notation | **Level:** Easy

Choice C is correct because the obtained answer is 1393×10^4.

The tuition fee increase is at 15%:

$$1.239\times10^4(1.15) = 1.42485\times10^4$$

Subtract Ann's savings from the new value of the tuition fee:

$$1.42485\times10^4 - 3.15\times10^2 = 1.39335\times10^4$$

Choice A is incorrect because 1.208×10^2 has incorrect coefficient and exponent. **Choice B** is incorrect because 1.208×10^4 has a coefficient 1.208 instead of 1.383. **Choice D** is incorrect because 1.383×10^2 has an exponent of 2 instead of 4.

9.

Category: PHM
Skill: Scientific Notation | **Level:** Medium

Choice A is correct because half-life of uranium-238 is 7.9×10^5 greater than carbon-14.
To find how many times greater is the half-life of uranium-238 than that of carbon-14, divide the half-life of uranium-238 by the half-half life of carbon-14.

$$\frac{4.5\times10^9}{5.7\times10^3} = 0.79\times10^{9-3} = 0.79\times10^6 = 7.9\times10^5$$

Choice B is incorrect because 7.9×10^6 is not equivalent to the obtained value. **Choice C** is incorrect because 7.9×10^{12} is not equivalent to the obtained value. **Choice D** is incorrect because 7.9×10^9 is not equivalent to the obtained value.

10.

Category: IES
Skill: Scientific Notation | **Level:** Medium

Choice A is correct because 7.6×10^2 multiplied by 3 is 2.28×10^3.
The cruising speed is 3 times the speed of sound. Hence,

$$(7.6\times10^2)(3) = 2.28\times10^3.$$

Choice B is incorrect because 22.8×10^3 is not equivalent to the obtained cruising speed. **Choice C** is incorrect because 2.28×10^2 has an incorrect exponent. **Choice D** is incorrect because 2.28×10^4 has an exponent of 4 instead of 3.

11.

Category: PMH
Skill: Equations | **Level:** Easy

Choice D is Correct. Simplifying by distributing the $-x$ and collecting like terms, you have:

$$\left(4x^3+3xy-5\right)-x\left(2x^2-7y+6\right)$$
$$=4x^3+3xy-5-2x^3+7xy-6x$$
$$=\left(4x^3-2x^3\right)+\left(3xy+7xy\right)-6x-5$$
$$=2x^3+10xy-6x-5$$

Choice A is incorrect due to an incorrect sign for the *xy* term and a missing *x* term. **Choice B** is incorrect because the coefficient of *x* should be −6, not −11. **Choice C** is incorrect because both the *xy* term and the *x* term have incorrect signs.

12.

Category: IES & Modeling
Skill: Equations | **Level:** Medium

Choice B is correct because the obtained equation of the distance of the ball with respect to time is $d = 8t + 8$.

Take two points from the table.

$$(t_1, d_1) = (0, 8) \text{ and } (t_2, d_2) = (1, 16)$$

Find the slope.

$$slope = \frac{d_2-d_1}{t_2-t_1} = \frac{16-8}{1-0} = 8$$

Since the table shows that $d = 8$ when $t = 0$, the y-intercept is 8. The equation is $d = 8t + 8$.

Choice A is incorrect because $d = t + 8$ does not represent the given data from the table. **Choice C** is incorrect because $d = 8t + 16$ has incorrect y-intercept. **Choice D** is incorrect because $d = 4t + 8$ has incorrect slope.

13.

Category: PHM
Skill: Equations | **Level:** Hard

Choice C is correct because the obtained value of x is 5.

$$27^{x-5} = 9^{5-x}$$
$$3^{3(x-5)} = 3^{2(5-x)}$$
$$3(x-5) = 2(5-x)$$
$$3x - 15 = 10 - 2x$$
$$3x + 2x = 10 + 15$$
$$5x = 25$$
$$x = 5$$

Choice A is incorrect because 8 is greater than the obtained value of x. **Choice B** is incorrect because 7 is greater than the obtained value of x. **Choice D** is incorrect because 3 is less than the obtained value of x.

14.

Category: PHM
Skill: Equations | **Level:** Easy

Choice B is correct because the obtained answer is 14.
Let x be Gina's age and y be her father's age.
Gina is 25 years younger than his father.

$$x = y - 25.$$

The sum of their ages is 53.

$$x + y = 53$$

To find Gina's age, substitute the value x in the equation, and we get

$$x + y = 53$$
$$y - 25 + y = 53$$
$$2y = 53 + 25$$
$$2y = 78$$
$$y = 39$$
$$x = y - 25$$
$$x = 39 - 25$$
$$x = 14$$

Choice A is incorrect because 7 is too young to be Gina's age. **Choice C** is incorrect because 25. **Choice D** is incorrect because 39

15.

Category: PHM & Modeling
Skill: Equations | **Level:** Hard

Choice D is correct because the second step is

$$\frac{(k+5)}{(k+5)}\cdot\frac{5}{k}+\frac{(k+3)}{(k+5)}\cdot\frac{k}{k}.$$

$$\text{Step 1:}\frac{5}{k}+\frac{k+3}{k+5}$$

For the missing step, find the common denominator of the given expression.

Common denominator is $k(k + 5)$

Hence, Step 2 would be $\frac{(k+5)}{(k+5)}\cdot\frac{5}{k}+\frac{(k+3)}{(k+5)}\cdot\frac{k}{k}$

Choice A is incorrect because $\frac{(k+5)}{(k+5)}\cdot\frac{k}{k}+\frac{(k+3)}{(k+5)}\cdot\frac{5}{k}$ does not represent combining rational expressions by taking the common denominator. **Choice B** is incorrect because $\frac{(k+5)}{(k+5)}+\frac{(k+3)}{(k+5)}+\frac{k}{k}$ does not represent combining rational expressions by taking the common denominator. **Choice C** is incorrect because $\frac{(k+5)}{(k+5)}+\frac{5}{k}+\frac{(k+3)}{(k+5)}+\frac{k}{k}$ does not represent combining rational expressions by taking the common denominator.

16.

Category: IES & Modeling
Skill: Equations | **Level:** Easy

Choice A is correct because the obtained answer is -27.

$$y = x + 3$$
$$(x - y) = -3$$
$$(x - y)^3 = (-3)^3$$
$$(x - y)^3 = -27$$

Choice B is incorrect because -9 is greater than the obtained value. **Choice C** is incorrect because 9 is greater than the obtained value. **Choice D** is incorrect because 27 is greater than the obtained value.

17.

Category: IES
Skill: Equations | **Level:** Easy

Choice B is correct because $yg = (7x+5)(2x+9)$.

Multiply the expressions to find *yg*.

$$yg = (7x+5)(2x+9)$$
$$yg = 14x^2 + 63x + 10x + 45$$
$$yg = 14x^2 + 73x + 45$$

Choice A is incorrect because $(7x+5)(2x-9)$ is not equivalent to the product of the given expressions. **Choice C** is incorrect because $14x^2 + 63x + 45$. the middle term is incorrect. **Choice D** is incorrect because in $14x^2 + 73x + 35$, the last term is incorrect.

18.

Category: IES
Skill: Equations | **Level:** Easy

Choice D is correct because in the obtained answer is

$$\frac{2A}{h} - b_1.$$

$A = \frac{1}{2}h(b_1 + b_2)$ (Multiply both sides by 2)

$2A = h(b_1 + b_2)$ (Divide both sides by h).

$\frac{2A}{h} = (b_1 + b_2)$ (Subtract b_1 from both sides)

$\frac{2A}{h} - b_1 = b_2$

Choice A is incorrect because $\frac{2A}{h} + b_1$ the sign between the terms should have been positive. **Choice B** is incorrect because $\frac{2A}{h+b_1}$ is not equivalent to the equation of b_2. **Choice C** is incorrect because $\frac{2h}{A-b_1}$ is not equivalent to the equation of b_2.

19.

Category: IES & Modeling
Skill: Equations | **Level:** Medium

Choice B is correct because the statement is equivalent to 2*w* – 3, where *w* is the width of the rectangle.

Choice A is incorrect because $l = \frac{1}{2}w + 3$. **Choice C** is incorrect because $l = 3 - 2w$. **Choice D** is incorrect because $l = w - 3$.

20.

Category: IES
Skill: Equations | **Level:** Easy

Choice D is correct because the obtained value of *x* is 7.

$$2x + 4 = 3x - 3$$
$$2x - 3x = -3 - 4$$
$$-x = -7$$
$$x = 7$$

Choice A is incorrect because 1 is less than the obtained value of *x*. **Choice B** is incorrect because 2 is less than the obtained value of *x*. **Choice C** is incorrect because 4 is greater than the obtained value of *x*.

21.

Category: IES
Skill: Equations | **Level:** Easy

Choice B is correct because the absolute value expression's pair of solutions are

$$3x - 4 = 4;\ -(3x-4) = 4$$

$$|3x-4| + 2 = 6$$
$$|3x-4| = 6 - 2$$
$$|3x-4| = 4$$

$$3x - 4 = 4 \qquad -(3x-4) = 4$$

Choice A is incorrect. This may be due to conceptual or calculation error. **Choice C** is incorrect. This may be due to conceptual or calculation error. **Choice D** is incorrect because the first solution is incorrect.

22.

Category: PHM
Skill: Equations | **Level:** Medium

Choice B is correct because it is the obtained value of the distance from the bottom of the tree and the ladder to reach the cat.
Use the Pythagorean theorem to find the value of the distance from the bottom of the tree and the ladder to reach the cat.
Let *c* = 25 be the length of the ladder.
a = 15 be the height of the cat from the ground.

$$c^2 = a^2 + b^2$$
$$25^2 = 15^2 + b^2$$
$$25^2 - 15^2 = b^2$$
$$400 = b^2$$
$$20 = b$$

Choice A is incorrect because 18 is less than the obtained value of the distance from the bottom of the tree and the ladder to reach the cat. **Choice C** is incorrect because 21 is greater than the obtained value of the distance from the bottom of the tree and the ladder to reach the cat. **Choice D** is incorrect because 22 is greater than the obtained value of the distance from the bottom of the tree and the ladder to reach the cat.

23.

Category: IES
Skill: Equations | **Level:** Medium

Choice C is correct because the obtained answer is 90.
Using the Fundamental Counting Principle:
Number of outcomes = product of the choices in each event

$$\begin{aligned}\text{Number of outcomes} &= 6(3)(5)\\ &= 90\end{aligned}$$

Choice A is incorrect because 14 is less than the obtained number of choices. **Choice B** is incorrect because 85 is less than the obtained number of choices. **Choice D** is incorrect because 120 is greater than the obtained number of choices.

24.

Category: PHM
Skill: Equations | **Level:** Easy

Choice D is correct because the obtained answer is

$$y = -4(x-6).$$

$$x = 2t + 5 \qquad \text{express x in terms of t}$$

$$x - 5 = 2t$$

$$\frac{x-5}{2} = t$$

Substitute t into the equation of y.

$$\begin{aligned}y &= 4 - 8t\\ y &= 4 - 8\left(\frac{x-5}{2}\right)\\ y &= 4 - 4(x-5)\\ y &= 4 - 4x + 20\\ y &= -4x + 24\\ y &= -4(x-6)\end{aligned}$$

Choice A is incorrect because $y = -4x + 1$ is not equivalent to the expression of y in terms of x. **Choice B** is incorrect because $y = 8x + 5$ is not equivalent to the expression of y in terms of x. **Choice C** is incorrect because $y = -(8x + 1)$ is not equivalent to the expression of y in terms of x.

25.

Category: PHM
Skill: Equations | **Level:** Medium

Choice B is correct because the obtained answer is 2.5 hours.
Find the number of words Joshua reads in 10 hours.

$$\begin{aligned}\textit{Number of words} &= \textit{speed}\ (\textit{time})\\ \textit{Number of words} &= 200\frac{\textit{words}}{\textit{minute}}(10\ \textit{hours})\\ \textit{Number of words} &= 200\frac{\textit{words}}{\textit{minute}}(10\ \textit{hours})\left(\frac{60\ \textit{minutes}}{1\ \textit{hour}}\right)\\ \textit{Number of words} &= 120000\ \textit{words}\end{aligned}$$

Find the time that Charise can read the 120000 words.

$$\text{Speed} = \frac{800\ \textit{words}}{\textit{minute}}\left(\frac{60\ \textit{minutes}}{1\ \textit{hour}}\right) = 48000\ \textit{words per hour}$$

$$\begin{aligned}\textit{time} &= \frac{\textit{number of words}}{\textit{speed}}\\ \textit{time} &= \frac{120000\ \textit{words}}{48000\ \textit{words / hour}}\\ \textit{time} &= 2.5\ \textit{hours}\end{aligned}$$

Choice A is incorrect because 1.5 hours is less than the obtained value of time. **Choice C** is incorrect because 5 hours is less than the obtained value of time. **Choice D** is incorrect because 6.5 hours is greater than the obtained value of time.

26.

Category: PHM
Skill: Equations | **Level:** Medium

Choice C is correct because the given conditions can be expressed as $8p \geq 78$.

Choice A is incorrect because $p \leq 78$ is not equivalent to the given problem. **Choice B** is incorrect because $8p \leq 78$ is not equivalent to the given problem. **Choice D** is incorrect because $\frac{p}{8} \geq 78$ is not equivalent to the given problem.

27.

Category: IES & Modeling
Skill: Equations | **Level:** Easy

Choice C is correct because $h = 0.75(220 - a)$ is the obtained equation.
Subtracting subject's age (a) from 220

$$(220 - a)$$

Taking 75% of that value

$$h = 0.75(220 - a)$$

Hence, the equation is $h = 0.75(220 - a)$.

Choice A is incorrect because $220 = 0.75(h - a)$ is not a correct representation of the given problem. **Choice B** is incorrect because $0.75h = (220 - a)$ is not a correct representation of the given problem. **Choice D** is incorrect because $0.75h = (a - 220)$ is not a correct representation of the given problem.

28.

Category: IES
Skill: Equations | **Level:** Easy

Choice D is correct because the obtained answer of the ones digit is 9.
Set up the equation.
The two-digit ab can be expressed as $10a + b$.

$$ab = a + b^2$$
$$10a + b = a + b^2$$

Substitute $a = 8$.

$$10a + b = a + b^2$$
$$10(8) + b = 8 + b^2$$
$$80 + b = 8 + b^2$$
$$0 = 8 + b^2 - b - 80$$
$$0 = b^2 - b - 72$$
$$0 = (b - 9)(b + 8)$$

Hence, $b = 9$ or $b = -8$. We will only take the positive number. Hence, the ones digit is 9.

Choice A is incorrect because 2 is not a possible value of the ones digit. **Choice B** is incorrect because 6 does not satisfy the given conditions. **Choice C** is incorrect because 7 is less than the obtained answer.

29.

Category: IES
Skill: Equations | **Level:** Easy

Choice D is correct because the obtained value of m is 10.

$-\frac{8}{x-2} + (x+1) = \frac{x^2 - x - m}{x-2}$ multiply both sides by (x-2).

$$(x-2)\frac{-8}{x-2} + (x+1) = \frac{x^2 - x - m}{x-2}(x-2)$$
$$-8 + (x-2)(x+1) = x^2 - x - m$$
$$-8 + x^2 - x - 2 = x^2 - x - m$$
$$x^2 - x - 10 = x^2 - x - m$$

Comparing LHS and RHS, $m = 10$

Choice A is incorrect because –10 is less than the obtained value of m. **Choice B** is incorrect because –9 is less than the obtained value of m. **Choice C** is incorrect because 9 is less than the obtained value of m.

30.

Category: PHM
Skill: Equations | **Level:** Medium

Choice C is correct because the obtained cost of the adult ticket y is \$10.30.
Let x be the price of the student's ticket and y be the price of an adult's ticket.

$$x + y = 15.45$$
$$45x + 38y = 623.15 \quad (1)$$

Write x in terms of y for equation 1.

$$x = 15.45 - y$$

Substitute the equation of x into equation 2 and solve for y.

$$45x + 38y = 623.15$$
$$45(15.45 - y) + 38y = 623.15$$
$$695.25 - 45y + 38y = 623.15$$
$$-45y + 38y = 623.15 - 695.25$$
$$-7y = -72.1$$
$$y = 10.3 \quad (2)$$

Choice A is incorrect because \$5.15 is the price of the student's ticket. **Choice B** is incorrect because \$8.35 is cheaper than the obtained cost of the adult's ticket. **Choice D** is incorrect because \$12.35 is more expensive than the obtained cost of the adult's ticket.

31.

Category: PHM & Modeling
Skill: Equations | **Level:** Medium

Choice D is correct because it is a graph that represents exponential function.

Choice A is incorrect because the graph shows a linear function. **Choice B** is incorrect because the graph shows a quadratic function. **Choice C** is incorrect because the graph shows an absolute value function.

32.

Category: PHM
Skill: Equations | **Level:** Medium

Choice C is correct

Use the FOIL technique to check the answer:

$$(3x+4)(x-3)$$

Apply FOIL: First: $First: \ 3x \cdot x = 3x^2$

$Outer: \ 3x \cdot (-3) = -9x$

$Inner: \ 4 \cdot x = 4x$

$Last: \ 4 \cdot (-3) = -12$

Now combine the terms: $3x^2 - 9x + 4x - 12 = 3x^2 - 5x - 12$

So, the result is $3x^2 - 5x - 12$, which confirms that the factorization is correct.

Choice A is incorrect as it expands to $3x^2 + 5x - 12$. **Choice B** is incorrect as it expands to $3x^2 - 8x - 16$. **Choice D** is incorrect as it expands to $3x^2 - 7x - 6$.

33.

Category: PHM
Skill: Equations | **Level:** Medium

Choice C is correct because the obtained answer is 68 mph.
Let *x* be the mile per hour excess of speed limit and *y* be the driving speed of Rachel.
Set up the equations.

$$25 + 6x = 103$$
$$x + 55 = y$$

Write equation 2 in terms of x.

$$x + 55 = y$$
$$x = y - 55$$

Substitute the x into equation 1.

$$25 + 6x = 103$$
$$25 + 6(y - 55) = 103$$
$$25 + 6y - 330 = 103$$
$$6y = 103 + 330 - 25$$
$$6y = 408$$
$$y = 68$$

Choice A is incorrect because 59 mph is less than the obtained value of the driving speed. **Choice B** is incorrect because 65 mph is less than the obtained value of the driving speed. **Choice D** is incorrect because 78 mph is greater than the obtained value of the driving speed.

34.

Category: IES & Modeling
Skill: Equations | **Level:** Hard

Choice C is correct because the obtained answer is –729.

y^3 when $y = 3(x-1)$ and $x = -2$.

$$y = 3(x-1)$$
$$y^3 = (3(x-1))^3$$
$$y^3 = (3(-2-1))^3$$
$$y^3 = (3(-3))^3$$
$$y^3 = (-9)^3$$
$$y^3 = -729$$

Choice A is incorrect because –6561 is less than the obtained answer. **Choice B** is incorrect because –847 is less than the obtained answer. **Choice D** is incorrect because –81 is greater than the obtained answer.

35.

Category: PHM
Skill: Equations | **Level:** Easy

Choice B is correct because $x^3 + x^2 - 4x + 32$.

$$(x+4)(x^2 - 3x + 8) = x^3 - 3x^2 + 8x + 4x^2 - 12x + 32$$
$$= x^3 + x^2 - 4x + 32$$

Choice A is incorrect because it gives: $x^3 + x^2 + 4x + 24$
Choice C is incorrect because it gives: $2x^3 + 2x^2 + x + 12$
Choice D is incorrect because it gives: $x^3 + 2x^2 + 6x + 12$

36.

Category: PHM
Skill: Equations | **Level:** Medium

Choice A is correct because the obtained answer is approximately 21 minutes.
Let *x* be the number of minutes.
Set up the equation.

$$0.7x + 15 = 29.5$$

Find x.

$$0.7x = 29.7 - 15$$
$$0.7x = 14.7$$
$$x = 21$$

Choice B is incorrect because 158 is less than the obtained value of the maximum time in minutes.
Choice C is incorrect because 188 is less than the obtained value of the maximum time in minutes.

Choice D is incorrect because 304 is greater than the obtained value of the maximum time in minutes.

37.

Category: IES & Modeling
Skill: Equations | **Level:** Medium

Choice C is correct because the obtained answer is

$$3x^2+6x+3.$$

$5x^2+10x+5$ represents the building's total height in feet
$2x^2+4x+2$ top to 4th floor
Distance of the ground floor and the cafeteria:

$$5x^2+10x+5-(2x^2+4x+2)$$
$$=5x^2+10x+5-2x^2-4x-2$$
$$=5x^2-2x^2+10x-4x+5-2$$
$$=3x^2+6x+3$$

Choice A is incorrect because $5x^2+2x-3$ is not equivalent to the obtained equation. **Choice B** is incorrect because $10x^2+40x+10$ is not equivalent to the obtained equation. **Choice D** is incorrect because $8x^2+14x+7$ is not equivalent to the obtained equation.

38.

Category: PHM
Skill: Equations | **Level:** Easy

Choice A is correct

We are given the cubic equation:

$$x^3-27=0$$

This is a difference of cubes:

$$x^3-27=(x-3)(x^2+3x+9)=0$$
$$x-3=0 \quad \Rightarrow \quad x=3 \quad -a\ real\ root$$

Next, solve the quadratic: $x^2+3x+9=0$
To solve, we get the root of $x^2+3x+9=0$ which produces 2 conjugate complex roots.

Choice B is incorrect because there's only one real solution, not two. **Choice C** is incorrect because one solution is real. **Choice D** is incorrect because the quadratic part has a negative discriminant, so the other two solutions are not real.

39.

Category: IES
Skill: Equations | **Level:** Medium

Choice B is correct because the obtained equation of the cost is 1300 + 3.75*c*.

Let *c* be the number of cards made.
Use the formula for the total cost.

$$Total\ \ cost = Fixed\ Cost + Variable\ Cost$$
$$Total\ \ cost = 1300+3.75c$$

Choice A is incorrect because 1300*c* + 3.75 is not equivalent to the obtained equation. **Choice C** is incorrect because 1300 – 3.75*c* is not equivalent to the obtained equation. **Choice D** is incorrect because 1300*c* is not equivalent to the obtained equation.

40.

Category: PHM & Modeling
Skill: Equations | **Level:** Hard

Choice B is correct because the obtained number of red marbles in Sample B is 3750.
The ratio from Sample A

total marbles: red marbles
300: 45

The ratio of Sample B

total marbles: red marbles
25000: *r*

Distribution of colors from Sample A is proportional to the distribution of colors in Sample B. Hence,

$$300:\ 45=25000:r$$
$$300r=45(25000)$$
$$300r=1125000$$
$$r=3750$$

Choice A is incorrect because 2250 is less than the obtained value of red marbles in Sample B. **Choice C** is incorrect because 6250 is greater than the obtained value of red marbles in Sample B. **Choice D** is incorrect because 10000 is greater than the obtained value of red marbles in Sample B.

41.

Category: IES
Skill: Equations | **Level:** Medium

Choice B is correct because the obtained answer is 10%
Let *x* be the number of students.
Set up the equation.

$0.75x$	at least 6 Chemistry courses
$0.6\ of\ 0.25x$	at least 4 or 5 courses

Find the percentage of those who took less than 4 courses.
$x-0.75x-(0.6)(0.25x)=\ 0.1x$ or 10% of the number of students.

Choice A is incorrect because 4 % is less than the obtained percentage. **Choice C** is incorrect because 18% is greater than the obtained percentage. **Choice D** is incorrect because 25 % is greater than the obtained percentage.

42.

Category: PHM
Skill: Equations | **Level:** Easy

Choice C is correct because the given expression is equivalent to $-5x^2+6x$.

$$=-3x(x-4)-2x(x+3)$$
$$=-3x^2+12x-2x^2-6x$$
$$=-3x^2-2x^2-6x+12x$$
$$=-5x^2+6x$$

Choice A is incorrect because $-x^2+1$ is not equivalent to the given expression. **Choice B** is incorrect because $-x^2+18x$ is not equivalent to the given expression. **Choice D** is incorrect because $-5x^2+12x$ is not equivalent to the given expression.

43.

Category: PHM & Modeling
Skill: Equations | **Level:** Easy

Choice D is correct because the equation is

$$8x+7(325)=15(350).$$

Given:

First 8 hours, speed is x miles per hour (mph).
Next 7 hours, speed is 325 mph
Average air speed is 350 mph

Distance covered first 8 hours $= speed \times time$
$= 8x$

Distance covered next 7 hours $= speed \times time$
$= 7(325)$

The average speed is the total distance over the total time.

Average speed =

$$\frac{distance(first\ 8\ hours)+distance(next\ 7\ hours)}{total\ time}$$

$$350 = \frac{8x+7(325)}{15}$$

$$8x+7(325) = 15(350)$$

The obtained equation is equivalent to Choice D.

Choice A is incorrect because $8x+7(325)=2(350)$

Choice B is incorrect because $x+7(325)=35(350)$

Choice C is incorrect because $x+7(325)=8(350)$

44.

Category: PHM
Skill: Equations | **Level:** Easy

Choice A is correct because $-\frac{10}{3}$ is the obtained sum of the roots of the quadratic equation.

$9x^2+30x+25=0$

Find the roots by factoring the given equation.

$9x^2+30x+25=0$

$(3x+5)(3x+5)=0$

$3x+5=0$	$3x+5=0$
$3x=-5$	$3x=-5$
$x=-\frac{5}{3}$	$x=-\frac{5}{3}$

Choice B is incorrect because $-\frac{5}{3}$ the solution is only $x=-\frac{5}{3}$. **Choice C** is incorrect because $\frac{5}{3}$ is greater than the obtained value of x. **Choice D** is incorrect because $\frac{10}{3}$ is greater than the obtained value of x.

45.

Category: IES
Skill: Equations | **Level:** Easy

Choice A is correct because the obtained value of x is -3.

$$3(x+2)=-3$$
$$3x+6=-3$$
$$3x=-3-6$$
$$3x=-9$$
$$x=-3$$

Choice B is incorrect because -2 is not equivalent to the obtained value of x. **Choice D** is incorrect because 3 is greater than the obtained value of x. **Choice C** is incorrect because 2 is greater than the obtained value of x.

46.

Category: PHM
Skill: Equations | **Level:** Easy

Choice C is correct because the obtained sum of x and y is 28.

Use the product of powers and power of power rules.

$$a^b \cdot a^c = a^{b+c}$$
$$(a^b)^c = a^{bc}$$

$$a^x \cdot a^8 = a^{32}$$
$$a^x \cdot a^8 = a^{x+8} = a^{32}$$
$$x + 8 = 32$$
$$x = 32 - 8$$
$$x = 24$$

$$(a^5)^y = a^{20}$$
$$(a^5)^y = a^{5y} = a^{20}$$
$$5y = 20$$
$$y = 4$$

The sum of x and y is 28.

Choice A is incorrect because 22 is less than the obtained sum of x and y. **Choice B** is incorrect because 26 is less than the obtained sum of x and y. **Choice D** is incorrect because 32 is greater than the obtained sum of x and y.

47.

Category: IES
Skill: Equations | **Level:** Hard

Choice C is correct because the obtained answer is 7.
Set up the equation.

$$4x + 6(9 - x) = 40$$
$$4x + 54 - 6x = 40$$
$$-2x + 54 = 40$$
$$-2x = -14$$
$$x = 7$$

Choice A is incorrect because 4 is less than the obtained number of packages. **Choice B** is incorrect because 6 is less than the obtained number of packages. **Choice D** is incorrect because 9 is greater than the obtained number of packages.

48.

Category: IES
Skill: Equations | **Level:** Hard

Choice D is correct because the obtained equation is $2(5-x) = \frac{x}{2} + 18$.

Let x be the integer.
An integer, x, is subtracted from 5.
$5 - x$

That difference is then multiplied by 2.
$2(5 - x)$

This product is 18 more than half the original integer.

$2(5-x) = \frac{x}{2} + 18$

Choice A is incorrect because $5(2-x) = \frac{x}{2} - 18$ does not represent the given conditions. **Choice B** is incorrect because $(x-5) = 2 + 18/x$ does not represent the given conditions. **Choice C** is incorrect because $2(2-5x) = \frac{x}{2} - 18$ does not represent the given conditions.

49.

Category: PHM
Skill: Equations | **Level:** Easy

Choice B is correct because $2xy\sqrt[3]{2x^2y}$ is equivalent to the given expression.

$$\sqrt[3]{16x^5y^4}$$
$$\sqrt[3]{8(2)x^3x^2y^3y}$$
$$\sqrt[3]{2^3(2)x^3x^2y^3y}$$
$$2xy\sqrt[3]{(2)x^2y}$$
$$2xy\sqrt[3]{2x^2y}$$

Choice A is incorrect because $xy\sqrt[3]{16x^2y}$ is not equivalent to the given expression. **Choice C** is incorrect because $2x^3y\sqrt[3]{x^2y}$ is not equivalent to the given expression. **Choice D** is incorrect because $2yx^2\sqrt[3]{x^2y}$ is not equivalent to the given expression.

50.

Category: IES
Skill: Equations | **Level:** Hard

Choice A is correct because the obtained answer is

18,000 + 120d = 14,500 + 155d.
Writing the expressions.
Factory A: Has already produced 18,000 units and can produce 120 units per day

18,000 + 120(d)

Factory B: Factory B has produced only 14,500 units but can produce 155 units per day

14,500 + 155d

Production of factory A and factory B are equal.

18,000 + 120(d) = 14,500 + 155d

Choice B is incorrect because 18,000 + 155d = 14,500 + 120d does not represent the given conditions. **Choice C** is incorrect because (18,000 + 120)d = (14,500 + 155) does not represent the given conditions. **Choice D** is incorrect because (120 + 155)d = 18,000 – 14,500 does not represent the given conditions.

51.

Category: IES
Skill: Equations | **Level:** Easy

Choice D is correct because the obtained value of m is 12.

Vertex of the parabola is V(–6, –4).

Substitute the values of x and y into the equation and find m.

$$g(x)=x^2+mx+32$$
$$-4=(-6)^2+m(-6)+32$$
$$-4=36-6m+32$$
$$6m=36+4+32$$
$$6m=72$$
$$m=12$$

Choice A is incorrect because 8 is less than the obtained value of m. **Choice B** is incorrect because 9 is less than the obtained value of m. **Choice C** is incorrect because 15 is greater than the obtained value of m.

52.

Category: PHM
Skill: Equations | **Level:** Hard

Choice C is correct because the obtained simplified fraction is $-4\left(\frac{x+1}{x+2}\right)$.

$$\frac{\frac{8}{x-3}+\frac{16x}{x^2-9}}{\frac{4}{x+3}-\frac{10x}{x^2-9}}=\frac{\frac{8(x^2-9)+16x(x-3)}{(x-3)(x^2-9)}}{\frac{4(x^2-9)-10x(x+3)}{(x+3)(x^2-9)}}=$$

$$\frac{8(x^2-9)+16x(x-3)}{(x-3)(x^2-9)}\left(\frac{(x+3)(x^2-9)}{4(x^2-9)-10x(x+3)}\right)$$

$$=\frac{8(x^2-9)+16x(x-3)}{(x-3)}\left(\frac{(x+3)}{4(x^2-9)-10x(x+3)}\right)$$

$$=\frac{8(x-3)(x+3)+16x(x-3)}{(x-3)}\left(\frac{x+3}{4(x-3)(x+3)-10x(x+3)}\right)$$

$$=\frac{(x-3)(8(x+3)+16x)}{(x-3)}\left(\frac{(x+3)}{(x+3)(4(x-3)-10x)}\right)$$

$$=\frac{8(x+3)+16x)}{1}\left(\frac{1}{4(x-3)-10x}\right)$$

$$=\frac{8x+24+16x}{4x-12-10x}$$

$$=\frac{24x+24}{-6x-12}$$

$$=\frac{6(4)(x+1)}{-6(x+2)}$$

$$=-4\left(\frac{x+1}{x+2}\right)$$

Choice A is incorrect because $8\left(\frac{x+1}{x+2}\right)$ is not equivalent to the given rational expression. **Choice B** is incorrect because $4\left(\frac{x+1}{x+2}\right)$ is not equivalent to the given rational expression. **Choice D** is incorrect because $-8\left(\frac{x-1}{x-3}\right)$ is not equivalent to the given rational expression.

53.

Category: PHM
Skill: Equations | **Level:** Hard

Choice B is correct because the obtained value of x is 1.

Simplify each equation.

Equation 1: $3x+4(x-3)=3(2y-3)-4y$

$$3x+4x-12=6y-9-4y$$
$$7x-12=2y-9$$
$$7x-2y=-9+12$$
$$7x-2y=3$$

Equation 2: $3y+2(x-4)=5(y+2)-20$

$$3y+2x-8=5y+10-20$$
$$2x+3y-5y=10-20+8$$
$$2x-2y=-2$$

Solve the system of equations by elimination.

$$7x-2y=3$$
$$-\ (-)2x(+)2y=(+)2$$

$$5x-0=5$$
$$5x=5$$
$$x=1$$

Choice A is incorrect because −4 is greater than the obtained value of *x*. **Choice C** is incorrect because 2 is less than the obtained value of *x*. **Choice D** is incorrect because 3 is greater than the obtained value of *x*.

54.

Category: PHM & Modeling
Skill: Equations | **Level:** Easy

Choice D is correct because both equations are the same when simplified.
Write the line in standard form.
$y = mx + b$

$$-4x + 5y = 15$$
$$5y = 4x + 15$$
$$y = \frac{4}{5}x + 3$$

$$-30 + 10y = 8x$$
$$10y = 8x + 30$$
$$y = 8x + 30$$
$$y = \frac{8}{10}x + \frac{30}{10}$$
$$y = \frac{4}{5}x + 3$$

The two equations are equal and hence, both are the same line.

Choice A is incorrect because the lines are not skew. **Choice B** is incorrect because the lines are not perpendicular. **Choice C** is incorrect because the lines are not parallel.

55.

Category: IES & Modeling
Skill: Equations | **Level:** Easy

Choice B is correct because the $y \le -3x + 2$ represents the given graph.
Find the equation of the line using two points from the graph.
(0, 2) and (1, − 1)

$$\text{Slope} = \frac{y_2 - y_1}{x_2 - x_1} = \frac{-1-2}{1-0} = \frac{-3}{1} = -3$$

The y-intercept is 2.
Hence, equation of the line is $y = -3x + 2$.
Use the test point (0, 0) to identify the inequality symbol.

$$y = -3x + 2$$
$$0 = -3(0) + 2$$
$$0 = 2$$

For the statement to be true, the inequality symbol should be ≤.
Hence, the equation is $y \le -3x + 2$.

Choice A is incorrect because $y > 3x + 2$ has incorrect inequality symbol. **Choice C** is incorrect because $y \ge -3x + 2$ has incorrect inequality symbol. **Choice D** is incorrect because $y > 3x + 2$ has incorrect inequality symbol.

56.

Category: PHM
Skill: Equations | **Level:** Easy

Choice B is correct because the obtained answer is 0.4.

$$\frac{4x - y}{x + y} = \frac{3}{7}$$
$$3(x + y) = 7(4x - y)$$
$$3x + 3y = 28x - 7y$$
$$3x - 28x = -3y - 7y$$
$$-25x = -10y$$
$$-\frac{25x}{y} = -10$$
$$\left(-\frac{1}{25}\right)\left(-\frac{25x}{y}\right) = -10\left(-\frac{1}{25}\right)$$
$$\frac{x}{y} = 0.4$$

Choice A is incorrect because 0.1 is less than the obtained value of x/y. **Choice C** is incorrect because 0.6 is greater than the obtained value of x/y. **Choice D** is incorrect because 1.2 is greater than the obtained value of x/y.

57.

Category: IES & Modeling
Skill: Equations | **Level:** Medium

Choice C is correct because the graph shows the inverse of the given function that is reflected over $y = x$.
Black graph : $y = f(x)$
Dotted line: $y = x$
Grey line: reflection over $y = x$

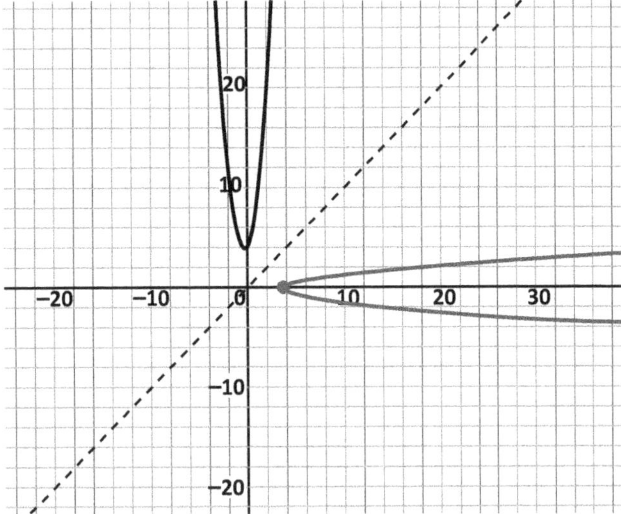

Choice A is incorrect because the graph of A is not reflected across the line $y = x$ but at about x-axis. **Choice B** is incorrect because the graph of B shows does not show a reflection but a translation. **Choice D** is incorrect because the graph of C shows a reflection across the line $y = -x$.

58.

Category: IES & Modeling
Skill: Equations | **Level:** Hard

Choice A is correct because the obtained value of f(f(f(1)) is −1594323.
Find $f(f(f(1))$.

$$f(x) = -3x^3;$$
$$f(1) = -3(1)^3 = -3$$
$$f(f(1)) = f(-3) = -3(-3)^3 = 81$$
$$f(f(f(1))) = f(81) = -3(81)^3 = -1594323$$

Choice B is incorrect because −2187 is not the obtained value. **Choice C** is incorrect because −81 is not the obtained value. **Choice D** is incorrect because −3 is not the obtained value.

59.

Category: PHM
Skill: Equations | **Level:** Easy

Choice B is correct because the simplified form of the expression is $\frac{3x}{x+1}$.

$$2 + \frac{x}{x+1} - \frac{2}{x+1} = \frac{2(x+1)+x-2}{x+1} = \frac{2x+2+x-2}{x+1} = \frac{3x}{x+1}$$

Choice A is incorrect because $\frac{3x+1}{3}$ is the simplified form of the given fractional expression. **Choice C** is incorrect because $\frac{3x-1}{x+1}$ is the simplified form of the given fractional expression. **Choice D** is incorrect because $\frac{3}{x+1}$ is the simplified form of the given fractional expression.

60.

Category: IES
Skill: Equations | **Level:** Easy

Choice C is correct because $2x(x^2 - 2x - 10) - 10$ is equivalent to the given cubic function.

$$y = 2x^3 - 4x^2 - 20x - 10$$
$$y = 2x(x^2 - 2x - 10) - 10$$

Choice A is incorrect because $(x+2)(x-5)(2x+3)$ is not equivalent to the given cubic function. **Choice B** is incorrect because $2x(x^2 - x - 5)$ is not equivalent to the given cubic function. **Choice D** is incorrect because $(x+2)(x-5)\left(x+\frac{1}{2}\right)$ is not equivalent to the given cubic function.

61.

Category: PHM
Skill: Equations | **Level:** Hard

Choice C is correct because $e = \frac{b(d-c)}{a}$.

$$\frac{ae}{b} + c = d$$
$$\frac{ae}{b} = d - c$$
$$ae = b(d-c)$$
$$e = \frac{b(d-c)}{a}$$

Choice A is incorrect because $\frac{e(d-c)}{b}$ is not equivalent to the obtained equation of e. **Choice B** is incorrect because $b(d-c) - a$ is not equivalent to the obtained equation of e. **Choice D** is incorrect because $\frac{d(b-c)}{a}$ is not equivalent to the obtained equation of e.

62.

Category: PHM & Modeling
Skill: Equations | **Level:** Easy

Choice C is correct because the graph of the given inequality is a number line with an interval of

$$(-\infty,-3)\cup[1,\infty).$$

Analyze the given inequality.
Find the critical points (the value of x at which the rational expression becomes zero or undefined).

$$\frac{x-1}{x+3}\geq 0$$

The expression becomes 0 if the numerator is 0. Hence, $x-1=0, x=1$ is a critical point.
The expression becomes undefined if the denominator is 0. Hence, $x+3=0, x=-3$ is a critical point.

We can use the critical points to divide the number line.

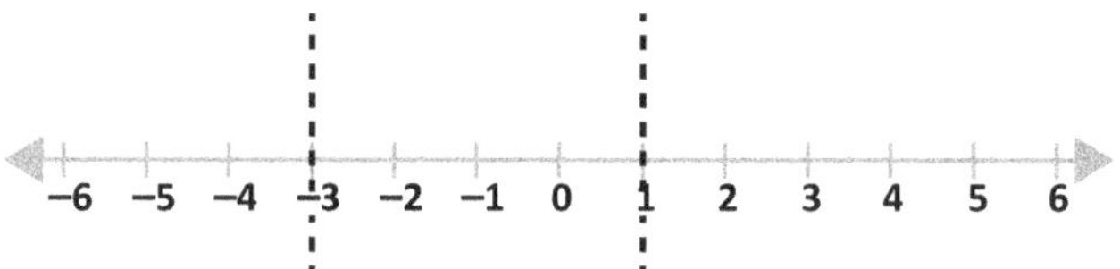

Hence, only ChoiceS C and D are correct that the graph of the given expression is a number line.
Next step is to find the solution of the given rational expression.

From the critical points, the intervals are

$$(-\infty,-3),(-3,1),(1,\infty).$$

Test a value from each interval to identify the solution.

	$(-\infty,-3)$	$(-3,1)$	$(1,\infty)$
$x-1$	-	-	+
$x+3$	-	+	+
$\frac{x-1}{x+3}$	+	-	+

Remember, the critical point is 0 when $x = 1$; hence $x = 1$ is included.
The obtained interval at which the given rational expression is true is at $(-\infty,-3)\cup[1,\infty)$.

Choice A is incorrect because the graph is not a straight line and it has no slope. **Choice B** is incorrect because the graph does not have an asymptote and does not cross the x-axis at 1. **Choice D** is incorrect because the graph is not a horizontal line and does not cross the y-axis at 3.

63.

Category: PHM
Skill: Equations | **Level:** Easy

Choice D is correct because the among the choices, $\frac{2}{3}$ is one of the roots of the given equation.

$$12x^2-2x=4$$
$$12x^2-2x-4=0$$

Use the quadratic equation $x=\frac{-b\pm\sqrt{b^2-4ac}}{2a}$.

$$x=\frac{-b\pm\sqrt{b^2-4ac}}{2a}$$

$$x=\frac{-(-2)\pm\sqrt{(-2)^2-4(12)(-4)}}{2(12)}$$

$$x=\frac{2\pm 14}{24}$$

$$x=\frac{2}{3}\qquad x=-\frac{1}{2}$$

Choice A is incorrect because −4 is not one of the roots of the given equation. **Choice B** is incorrect because $-\frac{2}{3}$ is not one of the roots of the given equation. **Choice C** is incorrect because $\frac{1}{2}$ is not one of the roots of the given equation.

64.

Category: PHM
Skill: Equations | **Level:** Medium

Choice D is correct because the obtained answer is $15:4$.

Given:

$$x:y=5:2 \text{ and } y:z=3:2,$$
$$x:y=15:6 \text{ and } y:z=6:4$$

Therefore,

$$x:y=15:4$$

Choice A is incorrect because $15:2$ is not equal to the obtained ratio of $x:z$. **Choice B** is incorrect because $2:15$ is not equal to the obtained ratio of $x:z$. **Choice C** is incorrect because $4:2$ is not equal to the obtained ratio of $x:z$.

65.

Category: PHM
Skill: Equations | **Level:** Easy

Choice C is correct because the simplified form of the given expression is $6x^2-3x+1$.

$$\frac{12x^3-6x^2+2x}{2x}=\frac{2x\left(6x^2-3x+1\right)}{2x}=6x^2-3x+1$$

Choice A is incorrect because $2x^2-6$ is not equivalent to the obtained simplified form of the expression. **Choice B** is incorrect because $2(3x+1)$ is not equivalent to the obtained simplified form of the expression. **Choice D** is incorrect because $6x^2-2$ is not equivalent to the obtained simplified form of the expression.

66.

Category: PHM
Skill: Equations | **Level:** Hard

Choice D is correct because the obtained answer is $a+b+c$.

$$\frac{x-a-b}{c}+\frac{x-b-c}{a}+\frac{x-c-a}{b}=3$$

$$\frac{x-(a+b)}{c}+\frac{x-(b+c)}{a}+\frac{x-(c+a)}{b}=3$$

$$\frac{x}{c}-\frac{(a+b)}{c}+\frac{x}{a}-\frac{(b+c)}{a}+\frac{x}{b}-\frac{(c+a)}{b}=3$$

$$\frac{x}{c}+\frac{x}{a}+\frac{x}{b}=3+\frac{(a+b)}{c}+\frac{(b+c)}{a}+\frac{(c+a)}{b}$$

$$\frac{x}{c}+\frac{x}{a}+\frac{x}{b}=1+\frac{(a+b)}{c}+1+\frac{(b+c)}{a}+1+\frac{(c+a)}{b}$$

$$\frac{x}{c}+\frac{x}{a}+\frac{x}{b}=\left(\frac{c}{c}+\frac{(a+b)}{c}\right)+\left(\frac{a}{a}+\frac{(b+c)}{a}\right)+\left(\frac{b}{b}+\frac{(c+a)}{b}\right)$$

$$\frac{x}{c}+\frac{x}{a}+\frac{x}{b}=\frac{a+b+c}{c}+\frac{a+b+c}{a}+\frac{a+b+c}{b}$$

$$x\left(\frac{1}{c}+\frac{1}{a}+\frac{1}{b}\right)=\frac{a+b+c}{c}+\frac{a+b+c}{a}+\frac{a+b+c}{b}$$

$$x\left(\frac{1}{c}+\frac{1}{a}+\frac{1}{b}\right)=\frac{1}{c}(a+b+c)+\frac{1}{a}(a+b+c)+\frac{1}{b}(a+b+c)$$

$$x\left(\frac{1}{c}+\frac{1}{a}+\frac{1}{b}\right)=\left(\frac{1}{c}+\frac{1}{a}+\frac{1}{b}\right)(a+b+c)$$

$$x=(a+b+c)$$

Choice A is incorrect because $a+bc$ is not equivalent to the obtained equation of x. **Choice B** is incorrect because $ab+c$ is not equivalent to the obtained equation of x. **Choice C** is incorrect because $a+-b-c$ is not equivalent to the obtained equation of x.

67.

Category: PHM & Modeling
Skill: Equations | **Level:** Easy

Choice A is correct because from the table, as x increases, the value of y decreases. Hence, the slope is negative.

Choice B is incorrect because the data from the table is not increasing. Therefore, slope is not positive. **Choice C** is incorrect because the data from the table is not constant. **Choice D** is incorrect because the slope can be determined from the data from the table.

68.

Category: PHM
Skill: Equations | **Level:** Easy

Choice A is correct because the obtained value of x is -4.

$$x-7y=-11$$
$$5x+2y=-18$$

Write the equation 1 in terms of y.

$$y=\frac{11+x}{7}$$

$$5x+2\left(\frac{11+x}{7}\right)=-18$$

$$5x+\frac{22+2x}{7}=-18$$

$$\frac{5x(7)+22+2x}{7}=-18$$

$$\frac{37x+22}{7}=-18$$

$$37x+22=-18(7)$$

$$37x+22=-126$$

$$37x=-126-22$$

$$37x=-148$$

$$x=-4$$

Choice B is incorrect because -1 is less than the obtained value of x. **Choice C** is incorrect because 2 is greater than the obtained value of x. **Choice D** is incorrect because 4 is greater than the obtained value of x.

69.

Category: PHM
Skill: Equations | **Level:** Medium

Choice C is correct because to reimburse \$400, the staff should have spent \$600 from their personal pocket.

Given :
First \$100 → reimbursed at **\$0.80 per \$1**
→ Reimbursed: 0.80 × 100 = 80

Next \$200 → reimbursed at **\$0.70 per \$1**
→ Reimbursed: 0.70 × 200 = 140

Remaining reimbursement:
400 – 220 = 180
This part is reimbursed at **\$0.60 per \$1**, so:

Amount spent beyond \$300: $\frac{180}{0.60} = 300$

Total spent:

100(first tier) + 200(second tier) + 300(final tier) = 600

Choice A is incorrect because 400 is less than the obtained amount. **Choice B** is incorrect because 500 is less than the obtained amount. **Choice D** is incorrect because 667 is greater than the obtained amount.

70.

Category: PHM
Skill: Equations | **Level:** Easy

Choice B is correct because the obtained equation of l is $\frac{5j+18}{8}$.

$$5j = 9l - 18$$
$$5j + 18 = 9l$$
$$\frac{5j+18}{9} = l$$

Choice A is incorrect because $5j - 8 + 18$ is not equivalent to the obtained equation of l. **Choice C** is incorrect because $\frac{5j+8}{18}$ is not equivalent to the obtained equation of l. **Choice D** is incorrect because $5j + 18 + 8$ is not equivalent to the obtained equation of l.

71.

Category: PHM
Skill: Equations | **Level:** Easy

Choice B is correct because the obtained value of y is 1.
Solve by substitution.

$$2x + 3y = 7,$$
$$x + y = 3 \quad \text{---->} \quad x = 3 - y$$
$$2x + 3y = 7$$
$$2(3 - y) + 3y = 7$$
$$6 - 2y + 3y = 7$$
$$-2y + 3y = 7 - 6$$
$$y = 1$$

Choice A is incorrect because –1 is less than the obtained value of y. **Choice C** is incorrect because 2 is greater than the obtained value of y. **Choice D** is incorrect because 3 is greater than the obtained value of y.

72.

Category: IES
Skill: Equations | **Level:** Medium

Choice D is correct because the total time is expressed as $\frac{3t}{2}$.

$$Speed = \frac{distance}{time}$$

Speed uphill is slower than speed downhill. So she traveled d distance in t minutes and $(1/2)t$ on her way back because she went twice as fast, so it took her half as long.
Distance covered is equal.

Total time would be: $t + \frac{1}{2}t = \frac{3t}{2}$.

Choice A is incorrect because $3t$ does not represent the total time traveled. **Choice B** is incorrect because $2t$ does not represent the total time traveled. **Choice C** is incorrect because $t + \frac{1}{2}$ does not represent the total time traveled.

73.

Category: IES
Skill: Equations | **Level:** Medium

Choice C is correct because the obtained value of the sneakers purchased by an employee is \$15.

Store selling price = \$25.
This is 30% more than cost.
So, 130% of cost is \$25.
Cost = 25/1.30 = 250/13 = 19.23

Price after 20% discount:
Employee price = 0.80 × 19.23 = 15.38 ≈ 15

Choice A is incorrect because \$12 is less than the obtained value of the shoes. **Choice B** is incorrect because \$14 is less than the obtained value of the shoes. **Choice D** is incorrect because \$16 is greater than the obtained value of the shoes.

74.

Category: PHM
Skill: Equations | **Level:** Easy

Choice A is correct because the slope will be negative. Slope of the equation is the ratio between the dependent variable and the independent variable.

$$Slope = \frac{y}{x} = \frac{decreasing}{increasing}$$

Hence, slope is negative.

Choice B is incorrect because the slope is not positive. **Choice C** is incorrect because the slope is not constant. **Choice D** is incorrect because a relationship can be determined from the given information.

75.

Category: IES & Modeling
Skill: Equations | **Level:** Easy

Choice D is correct because the number line represents $-1.5 < x < 0$.
Identify the end points of the graph. The left side is −1.5 and the right side is 0.
Since it shows an open point, −1.5 and 0 are excluded in the graph. Hence, the answer is $-1.5 < x < 0$.

Choice A is incorrect because $-1.5 > x > -1$ does not represent the given number line. **Choice B** is incorrect because $x \leq 0$ does not represent the given number line. **Choice C** is incorrect because $-1.5 > x > 0$ does not represent the given number line.

76.

Category: IES & Modeling
Skill: Equations | **Level:** Easy

Choice B is correct because the given graph shows that $f(x) = g(x)$ for exactly 2 values of x.

Given: $f(x) = x^2 - 3x + 4$
$g(x) = x + 1$

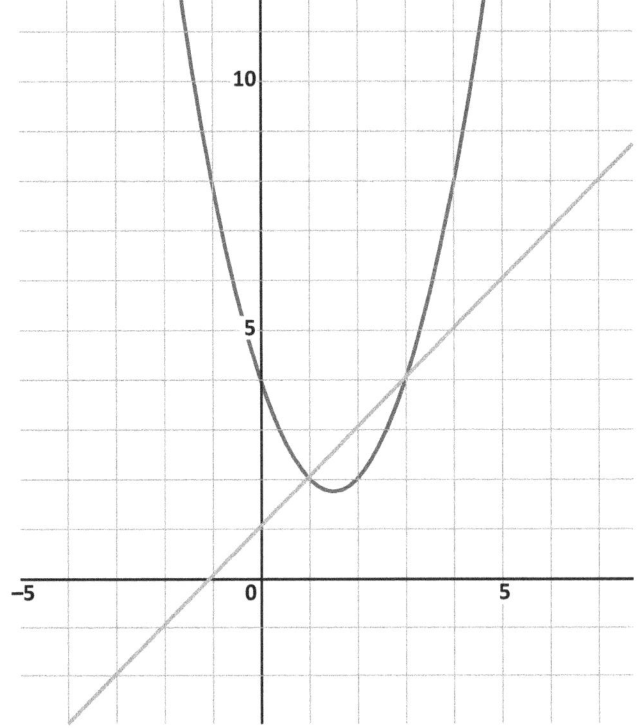

Analyze each choices.
For Choice A and Choice B:
Find $f(x) = g(x)$.

$$\begin{aligned} f(x) &= g(x) \\ x^2 - 3x + 4 &= x + 1 \\ x^2 - 3x - x &= 1 - 4 \\ x^2 - 4x &= -3 \\ x^2 - 4x + 3 &= 0 \\ (x-1)(x-3) &= 0 \end{aligned}$$

$$(x-1) = 0 \qquad (x-3) = 0$$
$$x = 1 \qquad x = 3$$

This shows that $f(x) = g(x)$ for exactly 2 values of x. Hence, **Choice A** is incorrect and **Choice B** is correct. The graph also shows that the two given graphs intersect at two points.

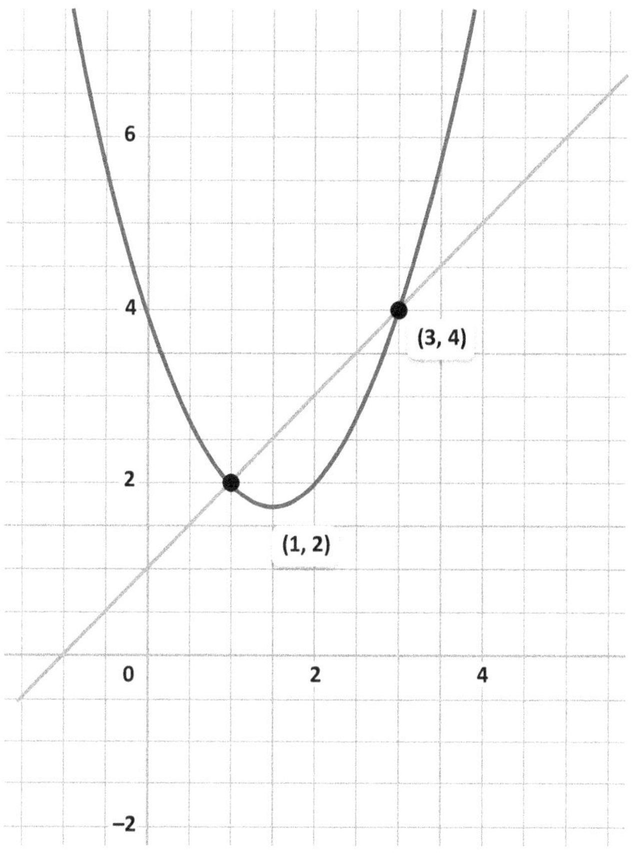

For Choice C:

Looking at the graph, $f(x) < g(x)$ when $(-\infty, 1] \cup [3, 4]$ and $f(x) > g(x)$ when $[1, 3]$.

Choice C is incorrect. $f(x) < g(x)$ is not true for all value of x.

For Choice D:

Find the inverse of $f(x)$.

The graph of $f(x)$ is parabolic while the graph of $g(x)$ is a line. The inverse of a quadratic function $f(x)$ is just the reflection of its graph across the line $y = x$. Hence, $g(x)$ is not the inverse of $f(x)$.

Choice A is incorrect because there are two values of x at which $f(x) = g(x)$ as shown in the graph. **Choice C** is incorrect because the statement is not true. **Choice D** is incorrect because $g(x)$ is not the inverse of $f(x)$

77.

Category: PHM & Modeling
Skill: Equations | **Level:** Medium

Choice C is correct because $N = 2V + 70$ is the obtained equation.

Let N be the number of bees.
70 more than double the volume of the bee farm, V

$$N = 2V + 70$$

Choice A is incorrect because $N = V + 270$ is not equivalent to the given conditions. **Choice B** is incorrect because $N = 2(V + 70)$ is not equivalent to the given conditions. **Choice D** is incorrect because $N = \frac{V + 70}{2}$ is not equivalent to the given conditions.

78.

Category: PHM
Skill: Equations | **Level:** Easy

Choice C is correct because the obtained value $x = 7$.

$$2x + 3 = 3x - 4$$
$$2x - 3x = -3 - 4$$
$$-1x = -7$$
$$x = 7$$

Choice A is incorrect because 2 is less than the obtained value of x. **Choice B** is incorrect because 6 is less than the obtained value of x. **Choice D** is incorrect because 10 is greater than the obtained value of x.

79.

Category: PHM
Skill: Equations | **Level:** Easy

Choice D is correct because $a^2 - 4bc > c$ will give the system of equations more than 1 solution.
Given:

$$y = x^2$$
$$ax + by = c$$

Substitute equation 1 to equation 2.

$$ax + bx^2 = c$$

Arrange terms in standard form.

$$bx^2 + ax = c \quad ; \quad Ax^2 + Bx = C$$

Hence, A=b, B=a, C=c

Using determinants where there are two distinct roots.

$b^2 - 4ac > 0$, substitute the variables.

Substituting the variables, $a^2 - 4bc > 0$.

Choice A is incorrect because $a^2 - 4bc \geq c$ will not give more than 1 solution. **Choice B** is incorrect because $a^2 - 4bc = c$ will not give more than 1 solution. **Choice C** is incorrect because $a^2 - 4bc < c$ will not give more than 1 solution.

80.

Category: PHM
Skill: Equations | **Level:** Hard

Choice A is correct because the obtained solution of the inequality is $-2 < x < 5$.

If $a < u < b$, then $a < u$ and $u < b$.

$$-9 < 1 - 2x < 5$$

$$\begin{array}{ll} -9 < 1 - 2x & 1 - 2x < 5 \\ -9 - 1 < -2x & -2x < 5 - 1 \\ -10 < -2x & -2x < 4 \\ 5 > x & x > -2 \end{array}$$

Hence, the answer is $-2 < x < 5$.

Choice B is incorrect because $-5 < 2x < 5$ is not a true statement for the solution of the given inequality. **Choice C** is incorrect because $-9 < x < 4$ is not a true statement for the solution of the given inequality. **Choice D** is incorrect because $-6 < x < 8$ is not a true statement for the solution of the given inequality.

81.

Category: IES
Skill: Linear equations | **Level:** Hard

Choice C is correct because the speed of the yacht relative to the water is 28 miles per hour.

Let the speed of the yacht relative to the water be x miles/hour.

Upstream trip:

Speed of the yacht relative to the water: $x - 4$ miles/hour

Time to travel upstream: 8 hours

Distance of the yacht is $d = speed(time) = (x - 4)8$

Downstream trip:

Speed of the yacht relative to the water: $x + 4$ miles/hour

Time to travel upstream: 6 hours

Distance of the yacht is $d = speed(time) = (x + 4)6$

Distance between upstream trip and downstream trip is the same. Hence,

$$(x - 4)8 = (x + 4)6$$
$$8x - 32 = 6x + 24$$
$$8x - 6x = 24 + 32$$
$$2x = 56$$
$$x = 28 \text{ miles/hour}$$

Choice A is incorrect because 20 miles/hour is less than the obtained value of the speed of the yacht relative to the water. **Choice B** is incorrect because 25 miles/hour is close to the obtained value of the speed but not accurate. **Choice D** is incorrect because 30 miles/hour is greater than the obtained value of the speed of the yacht relative to the water.

82.

Category: PHM
Skill: Linear equations | **Level:** Medium

Choice C is correct because 4 books is the number that makes the monthly charges equal.

Learning Book Club :
$y = 30 + 1.5x$

Another Club : $y = 24 + 3x$

$$y = y$$
$$30 + 1.5x = 24 + 3x$$
$$30 - 24 = 3x - 1.5x$$
$$6 = 1.5x$$
$$4 = x$$

Choice A is incorrect because 2 is less than the obtained value. **Choice B** is incorrect because 3 is less than the obtained value. **Choice D** is incorrect because 5 is greater than the obtained value.

83.

Category: PHM & Modeling
Skill: Linear equations | **Level:** Hard

Choice D is correct because the obtained decrease in the amount of soda every 5 seconds is 15 ml.

Find the slope of the graph by taking two distinct points. In the graph we have $(x_1, y_1) = (0,300)$ and $(x_2, y_2) = (100,0)$

$$slope = \frac{(y_2 - y_1)}{(x_2 - x_1)} = \frac{(0 - 300)}{(100 - 0)} = -3$$

The meaning of the slope is that every second, the decrease in the amount of soda is 3 ml which is also equal to the amount drunk by Leonard. Hence, every 5 seconds, the decrease is $3(5) = 15$.

Choice A is incorrect because -15 indicates a negative value which should have been a positive since it asks **Choice B** is incorrect because -3 is the slope and not the amount of soda drunk. **Choice C** is incorrect because 5 is less than the obtained amount.

84.

Category: IES & Modeling
Skill: Linear equations | **Level:** Medium

Choice A is correct because the graph shows that at the initial point, the value of y is at -3 and the slope of the

line is ⅕.
Given:

Initial point : 3 meters below the ground.

Rate of digging: descending 1/5 meters each minute.

Based on the given, the y-intercept is at (0,–3). Since the rate is descending 1/5 meters each minute, the slope of the graph is –1/5.
Let's sketch the graph.
Plot the y-intercept.

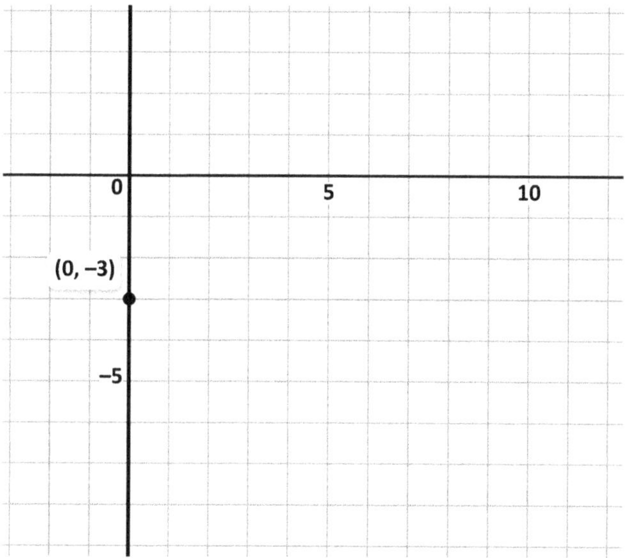

From point (0,–3), move 1 unit down and 5 units to the right.

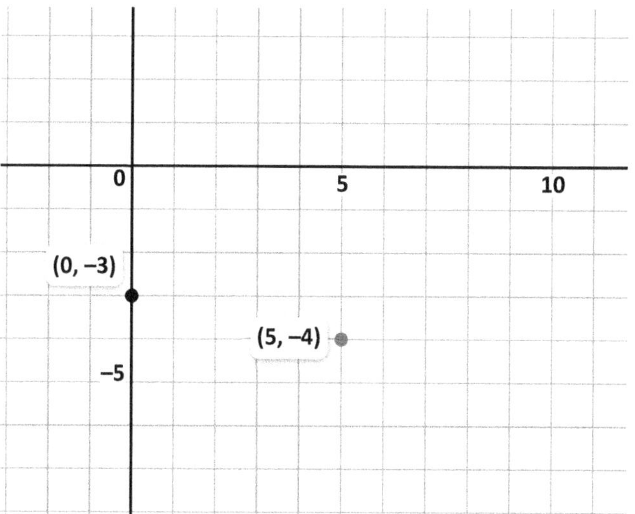

Connect the points to make the line.

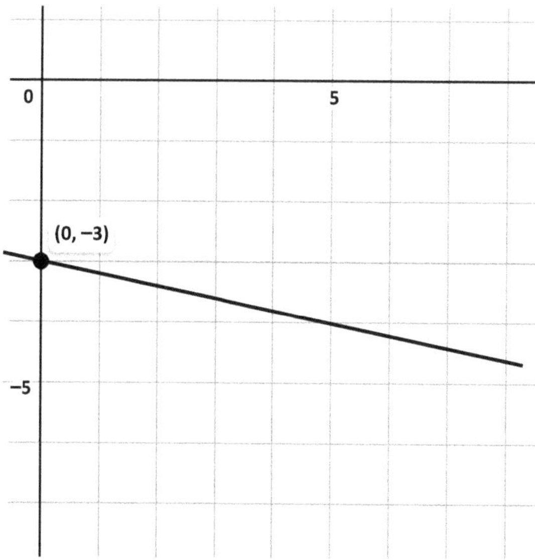

The final graph matches the Choice A.

Choice B is incorrect because the graph shows that the initial distance of Mr. Andrews from the ground is 0. **Choice C** is incorrect because the graph shows a positive slope which means that Mr. Andrews is going up. **Choice D** is incorrect because the graph is a horizontal line which interprets that there is no movement in Mr. Andrews's distance from the ground as time is running.

85.

Category: PHM
Skill: Linear equations | **Level:** Medium

Choice B is correct because the obtained value of the difference in the price between a notebook and a binder is 0.25.

Let x be the price of the notebook.
Let y be the price of the binder.

Set up the equation.

$$3x + y = 5.35$$

$$4x + y = 6.75$$

Solve by elimination.

$$3x + y = 5.35$$

$$-(4x + y = 6.75)$$

$$-x = -1.4$$

$$x = 1.4$$

Substitute the value of x into equation 1 to find y.

$$3(1.4)+y=5.35$$
$$y=5.35-4.2$$
$$y=1.15$$

The difference in the price is $1.4-1.15=0.25$.

Choice A is incorrect because 0.15 is less than the obtained value of the difference in the price between a notebook and a binder. **Choice C** is incorrect because 1.15 is the price of the binder. **Choice D** is incorrect because 1.4 is the price of the notebook.

86.

Category: PHM
Skill: Linear equations | **Level:** Easy
Choice B is correct because the obtained point is $(5,-3)$.
Use elimination method.

$$3x-2y=21$$
$$-3x-4y=-3$$
$$-6y=18$$
$$y=-3$$

Substitute the obtained value of y into any of the equations.

$$3x-2y=21$$
$$3x-2(-3)=21$$
$$3x+6=21$$
$$3x=21-6$$
$$3x=15$$
$$x=5$$

Hence, the point is $(5,-3)$.

Choice A is incorrect because $(-5,-3)$ is not a solution to the given system. **Choice C** is incorrect because $(-5,3)$ is not a solution to the given system. **Choice D** is incorrect because $(5,3)$ is not a solution to the given system.

87.

Category: PHM & Modeling
Skill: Linear equations | **Level:** Easy

Choice A is correct because it is the closest approximation of the rate of gasoline use in gallons per mile.
We take two points from the graph.
Close estimated points are (0,0) and (100,5). Find the slope between two points.

$$slope=\frac{y_2-y_1}{x_2-x_1}=\frac{5-0}{100-0}=0.05$$

This means that the predicted rate of gasoline use is 0.05 gallons per mile.

Choice B is incorrect because 0.1 is greater than the obtained value of the rate of gasoline use. **Choice C** is incorrect because 0.2 is not equivalent to the obtained value of the rate of gasoline use. **Choice D** is incorrect because 2.0 is an overestimation of the rate of gasoline use.

88.

Category: IES
Skill: Linear equations | **Level:** Easy

Choice D is correct because the obtained answer is 800.

$$Speed = Distance\,/\,Time$$
$$Distance=Speed(Time)$$
$$Distance=8\frac{km}{h}(6minutes)$$

Convert the speed to $\frac{m}{minute}$.

$$Distance=8\frac{km}{h}\left(\frac{1h}{60minutes}\right)\left(\frac{1000m}{1km}\right)(6minutes)$$
$$Distance=133\frac{m}{minute}(6minutes)$$
$$Distance=800m$$

Choice A is incorrect because $\frac{6}{8}$ meters is too short **Choice C** is incorrect because 480 is less than the obtained answer. **Choice B** is incorrect because 48 meters is too short.

89.

Category: PHM
Skill: Linear equations | **Level:** Hard

Choice C is correct because 65 is the obtained number of large boxes.
Given:
Total boxes: 120
Weight of large box: 45 pounds
Weight of small box: 35 pounds

Write the equation.
Let x be the number of small boxes and y be the number of large boxes.

$$x+y=120$$
$$35x+45y=4850$$

Find y.
Rewrite the first equation in terms of x.

$$x=120-y$$

Substitute this equation to equation 2.

$$35x + 45y = 4850$$
$$35(120 - y) + 45y = 4850$$
$$4200 - 35y + 45y = 4850$$
$$-35y + 45y = 4850 - 4200$$
$$10y = 650$$
$$y = 65$$

Choice A is incorrect because 45 is less than the obtained number of the large box. **Choice B** is incorrect because 55 is not equivalent to the obtained number of the large box. **Choice D** is incorrect because 75 is greater than the obtained number of the large box.

90.

Category: PHM
Skill: Linear equations | **Level:** Medium

Choice C is correct. Since the equation is a linear function, you can find the x and y-intercepts to determine the correct graph.

Setting $x = 0$, the y-intercept is,

$$2(0) - 3y = -12$$
$$-3y = -12$$
$$y = 4$$

Setting $y = 0$, the x-intercept is,

$$2x - 3(0) = -12$$
$$2x = -12$$
$$x = -6$$

So, the correct graph is Choice C.

Choice A is incorrect. This has an x-intercept 6 of and y-intercept of 4. **Choice B** is incorrect. This has an x-intercept –3 of and y-intercept of –1.5. **Choice D** is incorrect. This has an x-intercept 2 of and y-intercept of –3.

91.

Category: IES
Skill: Linear equations | **Level:** Medium

Choice B is correct because the obtained answer is 126 minutes.
Given:

Distance: 90 miles

Speed: $\dfrac{5\,miles}{7\,minutes}$

Find t.

$$t = \frac{distance}{speed}$$
$$t = \frac{90\,miles}{\frac{5\,miles}{7\,minutes}}$$
$$t = 90\,miles\left(\frac{7\,minutes}{5\,miles}\right)$$
$$t = 126\,minutes$$

Choice A is incorrect because 40 minutes is less than the obtained answer. **Choice C** is incorrect because 160 minutes is greater than the obtained answer. **Choice D** is incorrect because 230 minutes is greater than the obtained answer.

92.

Category: IES
Skill: Linear equations | **Level:** Medium

Choice C is correct because the obtained answer is 40 blue, 80 pink.
Let b be the number of blue dressed and p be the number of pink dresses.
Set up the equation.

$$b + p = 120$$
$$75b + 50p = 7000$$

Solve for p

$$b + p = 120$$
$$b = 120 - p$$
$$75b + 50p = 7000$$
$$75(120 - p) + 50p = 7000$$
$$9000 - 75p + 50p = 7000$$
$$-75p + 50p = 7000 - 9000$$
$$-25p = -2000$$
$$p = 80$$

Solve for b.

$$b + p = 120$$
$$b + 80 = 120$$
$$b = 120 - 80$$
$$b = 40$$

Choice A is incorrect because 80 blue, 40 pink is not a solution to the obtained system of equations. **Choice B** is incorrect because 40 blue, 60 pink has an incorrect value of pink dresses. **Choice D** is incorrect because 60 blue, 80 pink has an incorrect value of blue dresses.

93.

Category: IES & Modeling
Skill: Linear equations | **Level:** Easy

Choice C is correct because the value of y when $x = 35$ is 283.45.
Take two points from the graph.
Find the equation of the line.

$$slope = \frac{250-50}{30-0} = \frac{200}{30} = 6.67$$

The y intercept is 50 because as per the graph when $x = 0$, $y = 50$.
Hence, equation of the line is:

$$y = 6.67x + 50$$

Find y when $x = 35$.

$$y = 6.67(35) + 50$$
$$y = 283.45$$

Choice A is incorrect because 275.00 is less than the obtained value of y. **Choice B** is incorrect because 280.00 is less than the obtained value of y. **Choice D** is incorrect because 298.45 is greater than the obtained value of y.

94.

Category: IES & Modeling
Skill: Linear equations | **Level:** Hard

Choice C is correct because it represents the graph of the Andrea's journey in distance over time.
Given:

- drove 20 miles an hour for 15 minutes on the city streets,
- 40 miles an hour for 30 minutes on the highway
- 60 miles an hour for 1 hour on the freeway, and finally
- 20 miles an hour for 15 minutes on city street.

We let t be the time it takes for Andrea to travel.
Let d be the distance traveled and s be the speed.

When $t = 0$, $d = 0$. So the starting point is at the origin.
When $0 < t < 15$,

$$speed = 20\, miles\ per\ hour = 20/60\, miles\ per\ minute.$$

From the graph, we eliminate Choices A, B and D because the first journey is from $t = 0$ *to* $t = 15$.

Choice A is incorrect because the graph shows the time for the first journey incorrectly. It should have been at $t = 0$ *to* $t = 15$. **Choice B** is incorrect because the graph shows the time for the first journey incorrectly. It should have been at $t = 0$ *to* $t = 15$. **Choice D** is incorrect because the graph shows the time for the first journey incorrectly. It should have been at $t = 0$ *to* $t = 15$.

95.

Category: PHM
Skill: Linear equations | **Level:** Easy

Choice A is correct because the values in the given table follows the equation

$$y = -3x + 53.$$

Take 2 points and find the slope.

$$(4,41)\ \&(16,5)$$

$$\text{Slope} = \frac{y_2 - y_1}{x_2 - x_1} = \frac{5-41}{16-4} = \frac{-36}{12} = -3$$

The slope should be negative; hence, eliminate Choices B and D.
Find the y-intercept.

$$y = mx + b$$
$$41 = -3(4) + b$$
$$41 = 42 + b$$
$$53 = b$$

Hence, the equation is $y = -3x + 53$

Choice B is incorrect because $y = 3x - 45$ is not equivalent to the given values of x and y shown in the table. **Choice C** is incorrect because $y = -3x + 45$ has an incorrect y intercept. **Choice D** is incorrect because $y = 3x - 53$ has an incorrect slope.

96.

Category: PHM
Skill: System of equations | **Level:** Easy

Choice D is correct because the factors of $x^2 - 3x - 54$ are $(x-9)(x+6)$.

$x^2 - 3x - 54$ ---- the last term has a factor of $(9\, and\, 6)$
the middle term is the sum of the factors of the last term.

$$-54 = (-9)(6)$$
$$-3 = (-9) + (6)$$

Hence, the factors of $x^2 - 3x - 54$ are $(x-9)(x+6)$.

Choice A is incorrect because $(x-6)$ is not a factor of the given expression. **Choice B** is incorrect because $(x+9)$ is not a factor of the given expression. **Choice C** is incorrect because $(x+3)$ is not a factor of the given expression.

97.

Category: PHM
Skill: System of equations | **Level:** Medium

Choice D is correct because the obtained number of hamburgers is 300.

Set up the system of equations.
Let x be the number of hamburgers and y be the number of cheeseburgers.

$$x+y=450$$
$$x=2y$$
$$2y+y=450$$
$$3y=450$$
$$y=150$$

Find x.

$$x+y=450$$
$$x+150=450$$
$$x=450-150$$
$$x=300$$

Choice A is incorrect because 150 is the obtained number of cheeseburgers. **Choice B** is incorrect because 200 is less than the obtained number of hamburgers. **Choice C** is incorrect because 250 less than the obtained number of hamburgers.

98.

Category: PHM
Skill: System of equations | **Level:** Medium

Choice C is correct because the obtained length of the rectangular farm is 15 m.
Formula for the perimeter: $P=2L+2W$
Formula for the Area: $A=LW$
where L is the length and W is the width.
Substitute the given values into the equation.
$38=2L+2W$ (equation 1)
$60=LW$ (equation 2)
Simplify equation 1.

$$38=2L+2W \text{ divide both sides by 2}$$
$$19=L+W$$

Substitute $W=\dfrac{60}{L}$ into equation 1.

$$19=L+W$$
$$19=L+\frac{60}{L}$$
$$19=\frac{60+L^2}{L}$$
$$L^2-19L+60=0$$

Factor the obtained equation.

$$L^2-19L+60=0$$
$$(L-4)(L-15)=0$$

Possible values of L : $L=4, L=15$. Since the length is greater than the width, we take $L=15$ *and* $W=4$.

Choice A is incorrect because 4 is less than the obtained length of the rectangular farm. **Choice B** is incorrect because 9 is less than the obtained length of the rectangular farm. **Choice D** is incorrect because 18 is greater than the obtained length of the rectangular farm.

99.

Category: IES
Skill: System of equations | **Level:** Medium

Choice A is correct because the obtained radius is 1.

$$x^2+y^2-4x-2y+4=0$$

Combine like terms.

$$x^2-4x+y^2-2y+4=0$$

Complete the square.

$$(x^2-4x)+(y^2-2y)=-4$$
$$(x^2-4x+4)+(y^2-2y+1)=-4+4+1$$
$$(x-2)^2+(y-1)^2=1$$

Choice B is incorrect because 2 is greater than the obtained value of r. **Choice C** is incorrect because 3 is greater than the obtained value of r. **Choice D** is incorrect because 4 is not the obtained value of r.

100.

Category: PHM
Skill: System of equations | **Level:** Easy

Choice C is correct because x^2-5x+6 is the obtained factor of the given polynomial.
$x^3-6x^2+11x-6$, with a factor $x-1$
Use synthetic division to find the other factor of

$$x^3-6x^2+11x-6.$$

1	1	-6	11	-6
		1	-5	6
	1	-5	6	0

The obtained coefficients are: 1, -5, 6, 0
All the coefficients except the last one are the coefficients of the quotient; the last coefficient is the remainder. Thus, the quotient is x^2-5x+6 and the remainder is 0.

Choice A is incorrect because $2x^2-x+6$ has incorrect first and second terms. **Choice B** is incorrect because x^2+2x+6 has an incorrect second term. **Choice D** is incorrect because x^2-2x+6 has an incorrect second term.

101.

Category: IES & Modeling
Skill: System of equations | **Level:** Easy

Choice D is correct because $x(x+5)(2x+3)$ is the obtained factor of the given polynomial.

Given: $2x^3+13x^2+15x$
Take out the common term x.

$$x(2x^2+13x+15)$$

Factor out completely $2x^2+13x+15$.

$$2x^2+13x+15 \quad \text{---->} \quad ax^2+bx+c$$

Take note that from the polynomial, $ac=30$, $b=13$.
Hence, the second term can be expanded to 10 and 3.

$$x(2x^2+13x+15)$$
$$x(2x^2+10x+3x+15)$$
$$x[(2x^2+10x)+(3x+15)]$$
$$x[(2x(x+5)+3(x+5)]$$
$$x[(x+5)(2x+3)]$$
$$x(x+5)(2x+3)$$

Choice A is incorrect because $x(x-5)(2x-3)$ has incorrect signs for the second and third factor. **Choice B** is incorrect because $2x(x+5)(2x-3)$ has an incorrect first term. **Choice C** is incorrect because $x(2x+5)(x+3)$ is not equivalent to the given polynomial.

102.

Category: PHM & Modeling
Skill: System of equations | **Level:** Hard

Choice C is correct because $y=-4x^2+24x-35$ has a maximum at $(3,1)$.
Transform the equation to the vertex formula of quadratic equation.

$$y=-4x^2+24x-35$$
$$y=-4(x^2-6x)-35$$
$$y=-4(x^2-6x+9)-35+36$$
$$y=-4(x-3)^2+1$$
$$y=-4(x-3)^2+1,$$

Comparing this to the vertex equation $y=a(x-h)^2+k$ where the maximum of the vertex is at (h, k).
Hence, the maximum is at (3,1)

Choice A is incorrect because $(3,-1)$ has an incorrect sign for the y-intercept. **Choice B** is incorrect because $(-3,-1)$ has incorrect signs for the x and y-intercept. **Choice D** is incorrect because $(-3,1)$ has an incorrect sign for the x-intercept.

103.

Category: PHM
Skill: System of equations | **Level:** Easy

Choice C is correct because the expression can be simplified as $\frac{x(9-z^3xy^2)}{2(z^3xy-9)}$.

Find the common term for both the numerator and the denominator.

$$\frac{12x-3x-z^3x^2y^2}{2z^3xy-18}=\frac{9x-z^3x^2y^2}{2(z^3xy-9)}=\frac{x(9-z^3xy^2)}{2(z^3xy-9)}$$

Choice A is incorrect because $\frac{9x}{-18}$ is not the correct simplified form of the given expression. **Choice B** is incorrect because $\frac{(9-z^3xy^2)}{(z^3xy-9)}$ is not the correct simplified form of the given expression. **Choice D** is incorrect because $\frac{x-z^3xy^2}{2-z^3xy-9}$ is not the correct simplified form of the given expression.

104.

Category: IES
Skill: System of equations | **Level:** Hard

Choice B is correct because $\frac{1}{4}$ is one of the roots of.

$$12x^2+13x+7=12-4x$$
$$12x^2+13x+4x+7-12=0$$
$$12x^2+17x-5=0$$

Use the quadratic equation to find the roots.

$$x=\frac{-b\pm\sqrt{b^2-4ac}}{2a}$$
$$x=\frac{-17\pm\sqrt{17^2-4(12)(-5)}}{2(12)}$$
$$x=\frac{-17\pm23}{24}$$
$$x=\frac{1}{4},\ x=-\frac{5}{3}$$

Choice A is incorrect because $-\frac{5}{4}$ the denominator is incorrect. **Choice C** is incorrect because $\frac{3}{4}$ is not one of the roots of the quadratic equation. **Choice D** is incorrect because $\frac{5}{3}$ is positive. One of the factors is $-\frac{5}{3}$.

105.

Category: PHM & Modeling
Skill: System of equations | **Level:** Medium

Choice B is correct because when x=5 and x=35, the number of attendees are equal.

Given: $y=-x^2+35x+100$
$y=-5x+275$

Find x.

$$y=y$$
$$-x^2+35x+100=-5x+275$$
$$-x^2+35x+5x+100-275=0$$
$$-x^2+40x-175=0$$
$$-\left(x^2-40x+175\right)=0$$
$$-(x-35)(x-5)=0$$
$$x-35=0 \qquad x-5=0$$
$$x=35 \qquad x=5$$

Choice A is incorrect because when $x=10$, $x=25$ attendees don't have the same number for both movies. **Choice C** is incorrect because when $x=15$, $x=20$ attendees don't have the same number for both movies. **Choice D** is incorrect because when $x=5$, $x=30$ attendees don't have the same number for both movies.

106.

Category: IES
Skill: Roots | **Level:** Easy

Choice B is correct because the number of digits is 2.

Number of digits in 4489 is 4.
Since 4 is even, then the number of digits in the square root is $\frac{n}{2}=\frac{4}{2}=2$.

Choice A is incorrect because 1 is less than the obtained number of digits in the square root of 4489. **Choice C** is incorrect because 3 is greater than the obtained number of digits in the square root of 4489. **Choice D** is incorrect because 4 is greater than the obtained number of digits in the square root of 4489.

107.

Category: PHM
Skill: Roots | **Level:** Medium

Choice C is correct because the obtained answer is 20.5
Find the speed s if $l=35$.

$$s=2\sqrt{3l}$$
$$s=2\sqrt{3(35)}$$
$$s=2\sqrt{105}$$
$$s=20.5$$

Choice A is incorrect because 16.5 is less than the obtained speed 20.5. **Choice B** is incorrect because 18.2 is less than the obtained speed 20.5. **Choice D** is incorrect because 25.8 is greater than the obtained speed 20.5.

108.

Category: PHM
Skill: Roots | **Level:** Easy

Choice B is correct because the square root of −2197 is −13.

Find out the prime factorization of 2197.
The prime that can divide 2197 and have a whole number quotient is 13.

$$2197=13\times13\times13$$
$$-2197=(-13)\times(-13)\times(-13)$$

Hence, the cube root of −2197 is −13.

Choice A is incorrect because −15 is not a prime factor of −2197. **Choice C** is incorrect because 13 is positive. The cube root of a negative number is negative. **Choice D** is incorrect because 15 is not a prime of −2197.

109.

Category: IES
Skill: Roots | **Level:** Medium

Choice B is correct because the width of the swimming pool is 20.36.

Area of the pool and the pavement = 500 square feet.
Let s be the width of the swimming pool.
The pavement is 1 foot long and each side is added by 2 feet.

Write the equation.
Area of the square pool:

$$A=s^2$$

Since the area A=500 is the combination of the pavement and the pool:

$$A=(s+2)^2$$
$$500=(s+2)^2$$

$$\sqrt{500} = (s+2)$$

$$22.36 = (s+2)$$
$$22.36 - 2 = s$$
$$20.36 = s$$

Choice A is incorrect because 18.00 is less than the obtained width of the swimming pool. **Choice C** is incorrect because 21.36 is less than the obtained width of the swimming pool. **Choice D** is incorrect because 22.36 is greater than the obtained width of the swimming pool.

110.

Category: PHM
Skill: Roots | **Level:** Easy

Choice A is correct because the square root of −17576 is −26.

Find out the prime factorization of 17576.

$$17576 = 2(8788)$$
$$17576 = 2(2)(4394)$$
$$17576 = 2(2)(2)(2197)$$
$$17576 = 2(2)(2)(13)(169)$$
$$17576 = 2(2)(2)(13)(13)(13)$$
$$17576 = 2^3(13)^3$$
$$17576 = 26^3$$
$$-17576 = (-26)\times(-26)\times(-26)$$

Hence, the cube root of −17576 is −26.

Choice B is incorrect because −23 is not the cube root of −17576. **Choice C** is incorrect because 23 is positive.The cube root of a negative number is negative. **Choice D** is incorrect because 26 is positive.The cube root of a negative number is negative.

111.

Category: IES
Skill: Roots | **Level:** Hard

Choice C is correct because the total fencing is 96 feet.

Find one side of the square.

$$A = s^2$$
$$144 = s^2$$
$$144 = s^2$$
$$\sqrt{144} = s$$
$$12 = s$$

Based on the figure, there are 8 sides that need to be fenced. Hence,

$$\text{Total fencing } = 12(8) = 96$$

Choice A is incorrect because 60 is less than the obtained total fence. **Choice B** is incorrect because 84 is less than the obtained total fence. **Choice D** is incorrect because 122 is greater than the obtained total fence.

112.

Category: IES
Skill: Roots | **Level:** Easy

Choice C is correct because the number of digits in the square root of 390625 is 3.
Number of digits in 390625 is 6.
Since 6 is even, then the number of digits in the square root is

$$\frac{n}{2} = \frac{6}{2} = 3.$$

Choice A is incorrect because 1 is less than the obtained number of digit. **Choice B** is incorrect because 2 is less than the obtained number of digit. **Choice D** is incorrect because 4 is greater than the obtained number of digit.

113.

Category: PHM
Skill: Roots | **Level:** Hard

Choice C is correct because the bigger square should have 5 bricks.

There are 16 red bricks and 9 blue bricks and a total of 25 bricks.

Let x be the side of the bigger square.

$$A = x^2$$
$$25 = x^2$$
$$\sqrt{25} = x$$
$$5 = x$$

Choice A is incorrect because 3 is less than the obtained value of x. **Choice B** is incorrect because 4 is less than the obtained value of x. **Choice D** is incorrect because 6 is greater than the obtained value of x.

114.

Category: PHM
Skill: Roots | **Level:** Medium

Choice C is correct because the side length of the cake is 11.

There are 121 guests. The side length of one slice of cake is 1-inch.
Let x be the side length of the cake.

$$A = s^2$$
$$121 = s^2$$
$$\sqrt{121} = s$$
$$11 = s$$

Choice A is incorrect because 6 is less than the obtained value of the side length of the cake. **Choice B** is incorrect because 8 is less than the obtained value of the side length of the cake. **Choice D** is incorrect because 17 is greater than the obtained value of the side length of the cake.

115.

Category: IES
Skill: Roots | **Level:** Medium

Choice A is correct because the side length of the original garden is 4 meters.

Area of the original garden : $A = s^2$

Area of the new garden: $A + 19 = (s+1)(s+3)$
Find s.

$$A + 19 = (s+1)(s+3)$$
$$A = (s+1)(s+3) - 19$$
$$s^2 = s^2 + 4s + 3 - 19$$
$$s^2 = s^2 + 4s - 16$$
$$s^2 - s^2 = 4s - 16$$
$$16 = 4s$$
$$4 = s$$

Choice B is incorrect because 5 is greater than the obtained value of the side of the garden. **Choice C** is incorrect because 6 is greater than the obtained value of the side of the garden. **Choice D** is incorrect because 7 is greater than the obtained value of the side of the garden.

116.

Category: PHM
Skill: Logarithmic equations | **Level:** Medium

Choice D is correct because the value of x in the given logarithmic function is 8.

$log_2 x = 3$ is equivalent to $x = 2^3 = 8$

Choice A is incorrect because $\frac{1}{log\,6}$ is not equivalent to the value of x. **Choice B** is incorrect because $2log^3$ is not equivalent to the value of x. **Choice C** is incorrect because 6 is less than the obtained value of x.

117.

Category: PHM & Modeling
Skill: Logarithmic equations | **Level:** Medium

Choice D is correct because the statement is not an issue for the given expression to be non-expandable using the laws of logarithms.
The given logarithm is
$log_3(2y-1)$.
The statement for Choice D is "The expression $2y-1$ cannot be factored.
To be able to expand the given logarithm, the argument inside the logarithm which is
$(2y-1)$ should either be a product, a quotient or an exponent.
Let's analyze each choice.
Choice A: Each term in the expression does not have the same variable.
This is a true statement but does not directly explain why the logarithmic laws are not applicable.
Choice B: The expression $2y-1$ is not raised to a power.
This is a true statement. It also makes sense because it is not raised to a power so the quotient rule is not applicable.
Choice C: $2y$ and 1 are neither multiplied together, nor are they divided into each other.
This is a true statement. It also makes sense because it is not a product or a quotient so the product and quotient rule are not applicable.
Choice D: The expression $2y-1$ cannot be factored.
This is a false statement. This does not make sense because being non-factorable is not relevant in expanding the given logarithm.

Choice A is incorrect because the statement is a valid reason to prove that the laws of logarithms can't be used to expand or simplify the given expression. **Choice B** is incorrect because the statement is true and can be a valid reason to prove that the laws of logarithms can't be used to expand or simplify the given expression. **Choice C** is incorrect because it is a valid reason to prove that the laws of logarithms can't be used to expand or simplify the given expression.

118.

Category: PHM
Skill: Logarithmic equations | **Level:** Medium

Choice C is correct. Using the properties of logarithms, $\log_x 16 = 4$ then $x^4 = 16$ so, $x = 2$, and $\log_2 32 = y$ then $2^y = 32$ so, $y = 5$. Then, $5^2 = 25$.

Choice A is incorrect. This is the value of x. **Choice B** is incorrect. This is the product of 2 and 5. **Choice D** is incorrect. This calculates the expression as 25.

119.

Category: PHM & Modeling
Skill: Logarithmic equations | **Level:** Easy

Choice D is correct because $log_a(xy)^2$ is equivalent to $2(b+c)$.

Given: $log_a x = b$ and $log_a y = c$
Use the addition and product laws of logarithms.
$log_a x + log_a y = log_a xy$
$log_a x^2 = 2log_a x$
then $log_a(xy)^2 = 2(log_a x + log_a y) = 2(b+c)$.

Choice A is incorrect because *bc* is not equivalent to $log_a(xy)^2$. **Choice B** is incorrect because *2bc* is not equivalent to $log_a(xy)^2$. **Choice C** is incorrect because *4bc* is not equivalent to $log_a(xy)^2$.

120.

Category: IES
Skill: Logarithmic equations | **Level:** Easy

Choice B is correct because the obtained value of *n* is 8.
The $log_n 64 = 2$ can be expressed as $n^2 = 64$.

$$n^2 = 64$$
$$n = \sqrt{64}$$
$$n = 8$$

Choice A is incorrect because 6 is less than the obtained value. **Choice C** is incorrect because 23 is greater than the obtained value. **Choice D** is incorrect because 32 overestimated the given value.

121.

Category: PHM
Skill: Logarithmic equations | **Level:** Medium

Choice A is correct because for every integer *b*,

$$log_b \frac{b^2}{b^7} = -5.$$

Use the properties of logarithm:
Quotient property of logarithm:

$$log_b \frac{x}{y} = log_b x - log_b y$$

Power property of logarithm: $log_b x^2 = 2log_b x$

Inverse property of logarithm: $log_b b = 1$

For any integer *b*, $log_b \frac{b^2}{b^7} = log_b b^2 - log_b b^7$

$$log_b \frac{b^2}{b^7} = 2log_b b - 7log_b b$$
$$log_b \frac{b^2}{b^7} = 2(1) - 7(1)$$
$$log_b \frac{b^2}{b^7} = -5$$

Choice B is incorrect because -2 is greater than the obtained value of $log_b \frac{b^2}{b^7}$.
Choice C is incorrect because $-\frac{1}{5}$ is not the obtained value of $log_b \frac{b^2}{b^7}$.
Choice D is incorrect because 5 is greater than the obtained value of $log_b \frac{b^2}{b^7}$.

122.

Category: PHM & Modeling
Skill: Logarithmic equations | **Level:** Medium

Choice B is correct because the obtained value of *d* is 30 if intensity is 1,000 greater than the value of *K*.

Let $K = 1$, $I = 1000$. Substitute these values into the equation.

$$d = 10log\left(\frac{I}{K}\right)$$
$$d = 10log\left(\frac{1000}{1}\right)$$
$$d = 10log(1000)$$
$$log(1000) \text{ is equivalent to } 3$$
$$d = 10(3)$$
$$d = 30$$

Choice A is incorrect because 4 is less than the obtained value of *d*. **Choice C** is incorrect because 100 is greater than the obtained value of d. **Choice D** is incorrect because 1000 is greater than the obtained value of *d*.

123.

Category: IES
Skill: Logarithmic equations | **Level:** Medium

Choice C is correct because the obtained value of *x* is 25.

Let's evaluate each logarithmic expression.

$$log_4 256 - log_3 9 = log_5 x$$

$log_4 256 = a$ can be expressed as $4^a = 256$

$$4^a = 4^4$$
$$a = 4$$

$log_3 9 = b$ can be expressed as $3^a = 9$

$$3^b = 3^2$$
$$b = 2$$

$$log_4 256 - log_3 9 = log_5 x$$
$$4 - 2 = log_5 x$$
$$2 = log_5 x$$
$$x = 5^2$$
$$x = 25$$

Choice A is incorrect because 15 is less than the obtained value of *x*. **Choice B** is incorrect because 20 is less than the obtained value of *x*. **Choice D** is incorrect because 30 is greater than the obtained value of *x*.

124.

Category: PHM
Skill: Logarithmic equations | **Level:** Hard

Choice C is correct because the obtained answer is 9.4.
Earthquake A:

$$R = log\left(\frac{a}{T}\right) + B$$
$$6.9 = log\left(\frac{a}{1.9}\right) + 3.2$$
$$6.9 - 3.2 = log\left(\frac{a}{1.9}\right)$$
$$3.7 = log\left(\frac{a}{1.9}\right)$$
$$9522.55 = a$$

Earthquake B:

$$R = log\left(\frac{a}{T}\right) + B$$
$$5.7 = log\left(\frac{a}{1.6}\right) + 2.9$$
$$5.7 - 2.9 = log\left(\frac{a}{1.6}\right)$$
$$2.8 = log\left(\frac{a}{1.6}\right)$$
$$1009.53 = a$$

$$\frac{amplitude\ A}{ampitude\ B} = \frac{9522.55}{1009.53} = 9.4$$

Choice A is incorrect because 1.2 is an underestimation of the obtained value. **Choice B** is incorrect because 1.6 is less than the obtained value. **Choice D** is incorrect because 15.8 is an overestimation of the obtained value.

125.

Category: IES
Skill: Logarithmic equations | **Level:** Medium

Choice C is correct because the obtained answer is 500.5.
Expand the given logarithm applying the logarithmic rules.

Use the product rule: $log(3 \times 10^{500})$

$$log(3) + log(10^{500})$$

Apply the exponent rule: $log(3) + log(10^{500})$

$$log(3) + 500\ log(10)$$

Apply identity rule: $log(3) + 500\ log(10)$

$$log(3) + 500\ (1)$$
$$log(3) + 500$$

From the table, $log(3) = 0.5$, hence, $log(3) + 500 = 0.5 + 500 = 500.5$.

Choice A is incorrect because 2.5 is less than the obtained answer. **Choice B** is incorrect because 5.5 is not equivalent to the given logarithm. **Choice D** is incorrect because 505.5 is greater than the obtained value.

This page is intentionally left blank

Chapter 5
Functions Practice Questions

1.

Find a formula for the general term a_n of the sequence, assuming that the pattern of the first few terms continues.

$\left\{4, -1, \frac{1}{4}, -\frac{1}{16}, \frac{1}{64}, ..\right\}$

A. $a_n = 4(\frac{1}{4})^{n-1}$

B. $a_n = 4(-\frac{1}{4})^{n-1}$

C. $a_n = 4 + (-\frac{1}{4})^{n-1}$

D. $a_n = 4 - (-\frac{1}{4})^{n-1}$

2.

Bill is completing a data entry job where he makes a bonus on the number of rows of data completed. If he was able to make $25 his first hour and then was able to increase the amount he makes by an additional $3 per hour each hour, how much did he make in total after eight hours of work?

A. $49
B. $284
C. $309
D. $568

3.

In the given arrangement below, how many such letters are followed by a symbol and then a number?
D?1K#$3G@!4W6P%5I8T>J&8L?

A. one
B. two
C. three
D. four

4.

What is the next term in the geometric sequence 80, 20, 5, ...?

A. $\frac{-4}{5}$

B. $\frac{1}{2}$

C. 1

D. $\frac{5}{4}$

5.

In an arithmetic sequence the value of a_3 is 18 and the value of a_{15} is −18. What is the value of the first term in the sequence?

A. 24
B. 30
C. 35
D. 36

6.

Two bells in the city ring at different times. One bell rings every 12 hours and the other bell rings every 5 hours. At the beginning of each week, both bells are reset and will ring together at midnight on Sunday and then will continue to ring according to their set schedules until the following week when they are reset again. After their reset, when is the next day and time that they will ring together again?

A. Monday at Noon
B. Tuesday at Noon
C. Wednesday at Midnight
D. Thursday at Midnight

7.

The first term in an arithmetic sequence is −11. The common difference of the sequence is 3. What is the sum of the first 10 terms of this sequence?

A. 25
B. 50
C. 55
D. 80

8.

A finite arithmetic sequence has 8 terms with the first term being 17 and the fourth term being 26. What is the sum of the sequence?

A. 55
B. 220
C. 350
D. 440

9.

A theater show can sell as many tickets as there are theater seats. The theater has a total of 15 rows of seats. The first row has 10 seats and 2 seats are added per row after the first row. How many seats are in the 15th row?

A. 12
B. 28
C. 38
D. 40

10.

Find the 10th term of the given sequence 7,19,31,43,...

A. 98
B. 115
C. 112
D. 128

11.

The first term of an arithmetic sequence is 8. The common ratio is –3. What is the value of the seventh term in the sequence?

A. –52488
B. –17496
C. 5832
D. 17488

12.

The first element of a pattern consists of four dots. The next element in the pattern includes the first row of four dots and then another row of five. Then the next element includes one row of four dots, another row of five dots, and a third row of six dots. How many total dots will there be in the fourth element?

A. 9
B. 15
C. 22
D. 30

13.

What is the fifth term in a geometric sequence whose third term is 44 and eighth term is –1408?

A. –352
B. –44
C. 176
D. 704

14.

A bacteria population doubles in size every day. The original population size was 100 bacteria. Which equation best represents this scenario?

A. $y = 100(2)^x$
B. $y = 100(2)^{x-1}$
C. $y = 2x + 100$
D. $y = x^2 + 100$

15.

A framing company offers 8 different sizes of picture frames, each one 10% greater in area of the previous size. If the smallest size that they offer has an area of 100 square centimeters, what is the approximate size of their largest picture frame?

A. 125 cm^2
B. 150 cm^2
C. 195 cm^2
D. 200 cm^2

16.

Two trains depart from a station at different times on different tracks. Both trains make the same loop and return to the station multiple times throughout the day. Train A returns to the station every 45 minutes and train B returns to the station every 18 minutes. If the trains leave the station at the same time, how many minutes will pass before they are both at the station at the same time?

A. 45 minutes
B. 90 minutes
C. 100 minutes
D. 120 minutes

17.

The first number in a geometric series is −3 and the common ratio is −4. What is the value of the eighth term?

A. −12288
B. −3072
C. 49152
D. 196608

18.

If 5 is the first term and 45 is the third term of a geometric progression, what is the fifth term?

A. 90
B. 125
C. 405
D. 1215

19.

Over a two-week period, the temperature rose four degrees from the previous day on a consistent basis. Based on this trend, if the temperature starts at 45 degrees Fahrenheit, on day one, what would the temperature have risen to by day five?

A. 49
B. 53
C. 57
D. 61

20.

How many terms are in the geometric sequence 2, 4, 8, …, 128?

A. 5
B. 6
C. 7
D. 8

21.

For any real number x such that $x > -8$ in the equation below, which of the following statements must be true of the number represented by y?

$y = -\sqrt{x+8}$

A. y is irrational
B. $y < 0$
C. $y > 0$
D. y is imaginary

22.

The graph of $y = 2 - 4\cos(x - \Pi)$ is shown in the standard (x, y) coordinate plane below. What is the range of y?

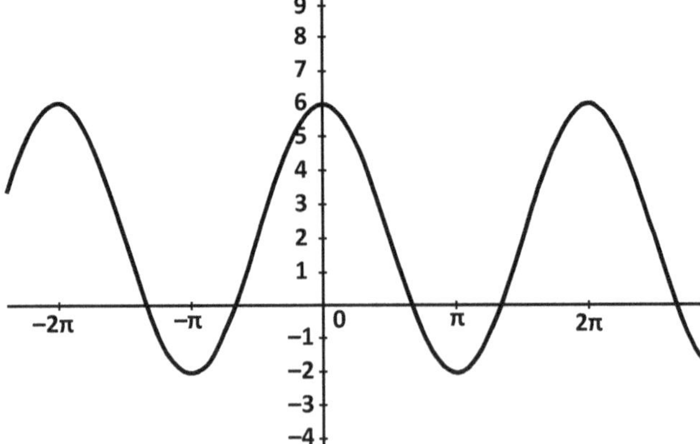

A. $-6 \leq y \leq 6$
B. $-2 \leq y \leq 6$
C. $-4 \leq y \leq 2$
D. $-2 \leq y \leq 4$

23.

A graph of a function has points at (−2, 6), (0, 2), and (2, 6). Which of the following functions best represents this graph?

A. $y = x^2 + 2$
B. $y = x^2 - 4$
C. $y = 2x + 10$
D. $y = 2^x + 3$

24.

Experimental data is represented in the standard (x, y) coordinate plane by a scatterplot consisting of five points as shown on the graph below: $(-1, 3)$, $(0, 9)$, $(-3, -1)$, $(1, 15)$, and $(-4, -2)$. When all possible real values for a, b, and c are considered, which of the following functions best fits the experimental data?

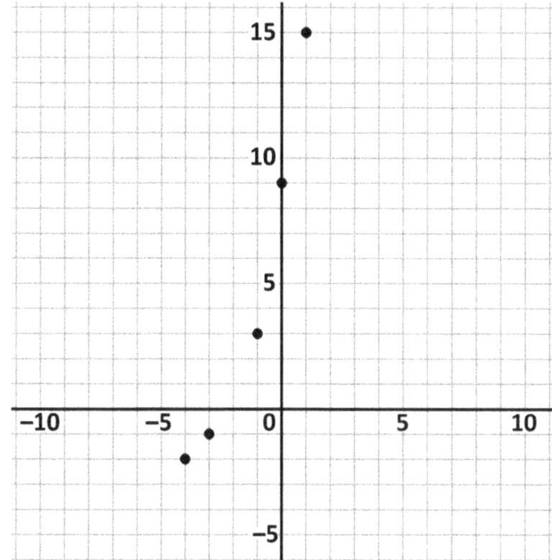

A. $y = ax$
B. $y = a + b(c)^x$
C. $y = a + b(\log_c x)$
D. $y = ax^2 + bx + c$

25.

Which of the following expressions is equivalent to $(3x - 4)(-x + 5)$?

A. $(3x + 4)(x + 5)$
B. $(-3x - 4)(-x - 5)$
C. $(-3x + 4)(x - 5)$
D. $(3x + 4)(-x - 5)$

26.

A polynomial, $f(x)$, has the following values:
$f(-1) = -8$
$f(-2) = -5$
$f(0) = -3$
$f(1) = 8$
$f(2) = 10$
Between which 2 consecutive integers, if any, must $f(x)$ have a zero?

A. -2 and -1
B. 0 and 1
C. 1 and 2
D. $f(x)$ need not have a zero.

27.

Which of the following expressions is equivalent to $y = 2(x - 5) + 6$?

A. $y = 2x + 11$
B. $y = 2x - 4$
C. $y - 6 = 2x - 5$
D. $y + 5 = x - 6$

28.

A function $f(x)$ is defined as $f(x) = -5x^2 + 3$. What is the value of $f(f(-2))$?

A. -1442
B. -87
C. 25
D. 103

29.

The function $a\Theta b$ is defined as $ab + 2a - 2b$. What is the value of $3\Theta 2$

A. 2
B. 4
C. 6
D. 8

30.

Over which of the following intervals is the graph of f constant?

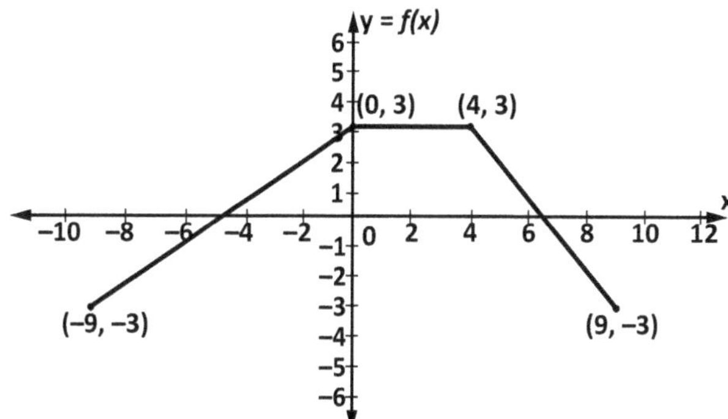

A. $[-9, 0]$
B. $[0, 9]$
C. $[0, 4]$
D. $[4, 9]$

31.

Given the domain for x is {−4, −3, −2, −1, 0, 1, 2, 3, 4, 5}, what is the complete solution set for the function $y = x + 3$?

A. {−1, 0, 1}
B. {−2, −1, 0, 1, 2, 3}
C. {−1, 0 , 1, 2, 3, 4, 5, 6, 7, 8}
D. {−1, 0 , 1, 2, 3, 4, 5, 6, 7, 8, 9, 10}

32.

Which of the following expressions is equivalent to $(4x + 1)(x - 2)$?

A. $4x^2 - 7x - 2$
B. $4x^2 - 3x - 3$
C. $3x^2 + 3x - 2$
D. $4x^2 - x - 2$

33.

For what value of x does the equation $y = 4x - x^2$ have its maximum value for x?

A. 0
B. 2
C. 4
D. 8

34.

Which of the following expressions is equivalent to $b(3 - \text{b}) - 6(b + 4)$?

A. $\text{b}^2 - 3\text{b} + 4$
B. $-\text{b}^2 - 3\text{b} + 20$
C. $-\text{b}^2 - 3\text{b} - 24$
D. $-\text{b}^2 - 9\text{b} - 24$

35.

A function is defined by $f(x) = -3x + 8$ and its domain is the set of integers from 1 to 20 inclusive. For how many values of x is $f(x)$ negative?

A. 17
B. 18
C. 19
D. 20

36.

The function $f(x)$ is defined as $f(x) = -2x^3 + 4x^2$. What is $f(-3)$?

A. 18
B. 54
C. 90
D. 360

37.

A city had 5 inches of snow on the ground when another snowstorm hit. The snow fell at a rate of 1.25 inches per hour. The relationship between depth of the snow and time that passed can be expressed as a linear relationship between d, depth in inches, and t, time in hours.
Which expression best matches this relationship?

A. $d = 1.25t - 5$
B. $d = 5t + 1.25$
C. $d = 1.25t + 5$
D. $d = 6.25t$

38.

What is the set of real solutions for $|x^2| - |6x| - 7 = 0$?

A. {−7}
B. {−7, 7}
C. {0, 7}
D. {0, −7, 7}

39.

For all $x > 0$, which of the following is equivalent to $\frac{1}{x+2} + \frac{1}{x}$?

A. $\frac{1}{x(x+2)}$

B. $\frac{2x+2}{x(x+2)}$

C. $\frac{x+1}{x(x+2)}$

D. $\frac{x+1}{x+2}$

40.

The amount of products an assembly line finishes is based on the function $f(x)$ which is determined by the hour of the day. Since there are more workers at different periods of the day, the function $f(x)$ can vary as follows:

$$f(x)=\begin{cases} 2x+4 & 0<x\le 5 \\ 3x+15 & 5<x<8 \\ x^2-45 & 8\le x\le 12 \end{cases}$$

What is the maximum number of products produced at any given hour of the day?

A. 14
B. 39
C. 50
D. 99

41.

The equation $f(x) = \dfrac{2x^2-32}{x^2-7x}$ has 2 vertical asymptotes and 1 horizontal asymptote. What is the horizontal asymptote?

A. $x = 0$
B. $x = 7$
C. $y = 0$
D. $y = 2$

42.

If $f(x) = x^2 + 3x + 8$, evaluate $f(-1)$.

A. 4
B. 6
C. 7
D. 8

43.

A baseball was thrown into the air at a time of $t = 0$ seconds. The location of the ball over a period of t seconds was recorded to determine it reached its maximum height of 15 meters at a time of 4 seconds. The baseball hit the ground at a time of 8 seconds. What is the average speed of the baseball from $t = 4$ and $t = 8$?

A. 1.5 meters per second
B. 2.5 meters per second
C. 3.75 meters per second
D. 4.5 meters per second

44.

Which of the following intervals is the domain of the function $f(x) = \dfrac{x+4}{x^2-2x-24}$?

A. $(-\infty, 6) \cup (6, \infty)$
B. $(-\infty, -4]$ and $[6, \infty)$
C. $(-\infty, -4]$
D. $(-\infty, -4) \cup (-4, \infty)$

45.

The domain of $f(x) = \dfrac{x-4}{x^2-16}$ is the set of all real numbers EXCEPT:

A. −4
B. 0
C. 2
D. 4

46.

If $f(x) = 2^x$ and $g(x) = -4$, then $-f(g(x)) = $?

A. −16
B. $-\sqrt{8}$
C. $-\dfrac{1}{16}$
D. 4

47.

Define the functions $f(x)$ and $g(x)$ such that $f(x) = -5x$ and $g(x) = \sqrt{x+6}$. For all such x that $x \geq -6$, which of the following expressions is equal to $g(f(x))$?

A. $-5\sqrt{x+6}$
B. $-5x\sqrt{x+6}$
C. $\sqrt{-5x^2-30x}$.
D. $\sqrt{-5x+6}$

48.

Find $(f \circ g)(5)$, given

$f(x) = x^2+3x+12$ *and* $g(x) = -(3x+15)$.

A. −12
B. −8
C. 12
D. 15

49.

Given the functions $f(x) = x^2 + 5$ and $g(x) = x - 6$, which of the following expressions is $f(g(x))$?

A. $x^2 - 12x + 41$
B. $x^2 - 6x + 36$
C. $x^2 - 12x - 25$
D. $x^2 - 11$

50.

If $f(x) = x + 8$ and $g(x) = 4$, what is the value of $f(g(x))$?

A. 8
B. 12
C. 16
D. 32

51.

Given that $f(x) = x^2 - 9$ and $g(x) = x - 2$, what are all of the values of x for which $f(g(x)) = 0$?

A. −1 and 5
B. −1 and −2
C. 0 and 3
D. 4 and 6

52.

For functions f and g defined by $f(x) = 8x - 9$ and $g(x) = 6$, what is the value of $f(g(x))$?

A. 6
B. 18
C. 36
D. 39

53.

Consider the 2 functions $f(x) = 3x + 4$ and $g(x) = -2x + b$ where b is a real number. If $f(g(x)) = -6x + 13$, then b = ?

A. 0
B. 2
C. 3
D. 7

54.

Let the polynomial functions $f(x)$ and $g(x)$ be defined as $f(x) = x^2 + 8x - 13$ and $g(x) = x^2 - 6x + 7$. Let $h(x) = f(x) - g(x)$. What is $h(5)$?

A. −10
B. 30
C. 50
D. 90

55.

The function $f(x)$ is defined as $f(x) = x + 5$.
What is the value of $f(f(f(x)))$?

A. $x + 10$
B. $x + 15$
C. $x + 25$
D. $3x + 15$

56.

What is the slope of a line, in the standard (x, y) coordinate plane, that is parallel to the line $3x - 2y = 8$?

A. −4
B. $-\frac{2}{3}$
C. $\frac{3}{2}$
D. 3

57.

A company charges \$50 for the first 10 orders of a part and then \$40 for each additional part ordered. Which of the following expressions represents the cost of x parts, where $x > 10$?

A. $y = 40x + 50$
B. $y = 40x + 100$
C. $y = 50x + 400$
D. $y = 50x + 10$

58.

The graph below displays the linear function $ay + bx = c$. If $0 < \frac{a}{b} < 1$, then which of the following linear equations would have the greatest slope?

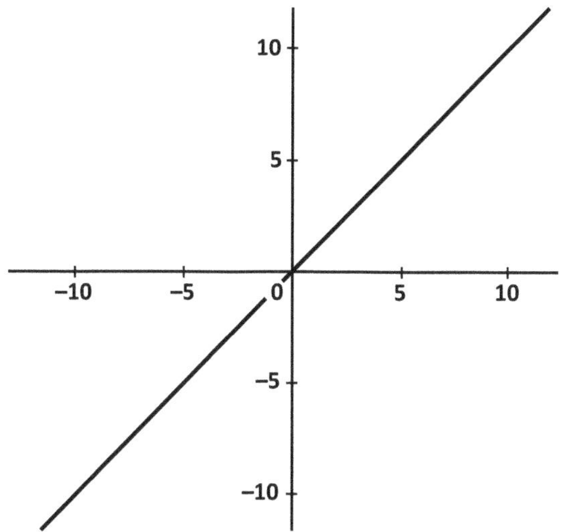

A. $ax + by = c$
B. $ax - by = c$
C. $-bx + ay = c$
D. $-bx - ay = c$

59.

In the standard (x, y) coordinate plane, the line with the equation $y + \frac{1}{4} = \frac{5}{8}(x - \frac{3}{4})$ has a slope of:

A. $\frac{1}{4}$
B. $\frac{5}{16}$
C. $\frac{5}{8}$
D. $\frac{3}{4}$

60.

Pedro ran at a constant speed and recorded his distance, d, in feet from a reference point a certain amount of feet from his home based on time, t, in minutes from $t = 2$ minutes to $t = 10$ minutes.

t	2	4	6	8	10
d	385	745	1105	1465	1825

Which of the following equations represents this relationship between d and t?

A. $d = 180t + 25$
B. $d = 200t + 50$
C. $d = 250t + 40$
D. $d = 300t + 55$

61.

In the standard (x, y) coordinate plane below, the line through the points $(0, -3)$ and $(6, 0)$ is graphed. Which of the following values is the slope of any line that is in this plane and perpendicular to the graphed line?

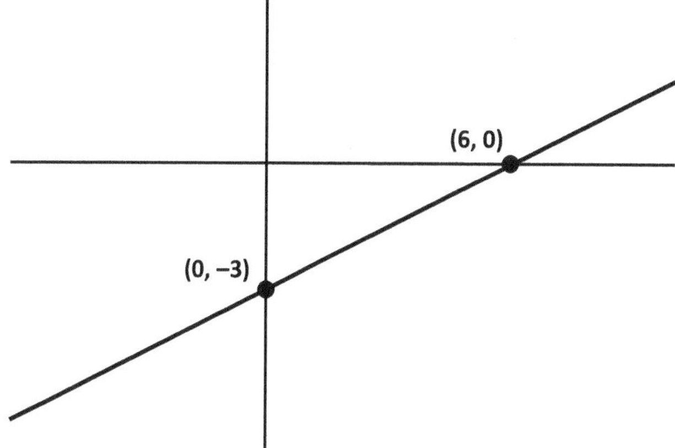

A. −2
B. −0.5
C. 0.5
D. 1

62.

Find the equation of the line in slope-intercept form and its graph if a line passes through points (0, 5) and (−5, −10).

A. $y = 5x + 3$,

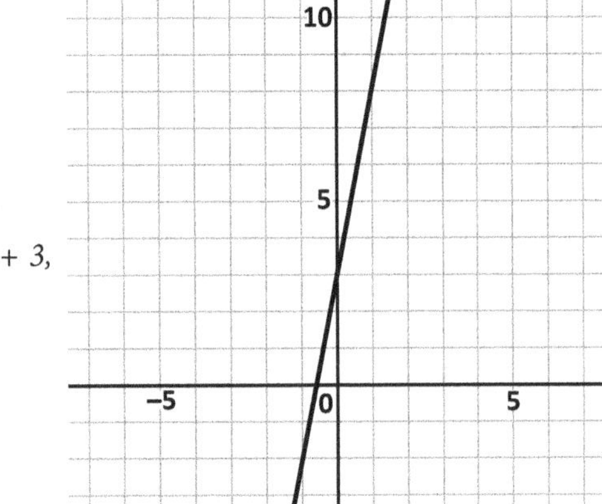

B. $y = 3x + 3$,

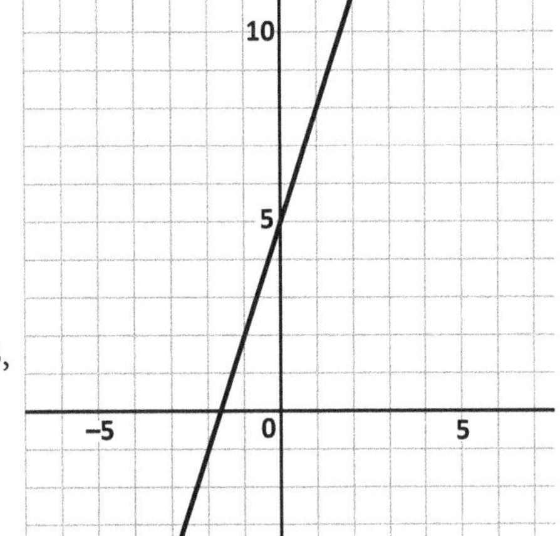

C. $y = 3x + 5$,

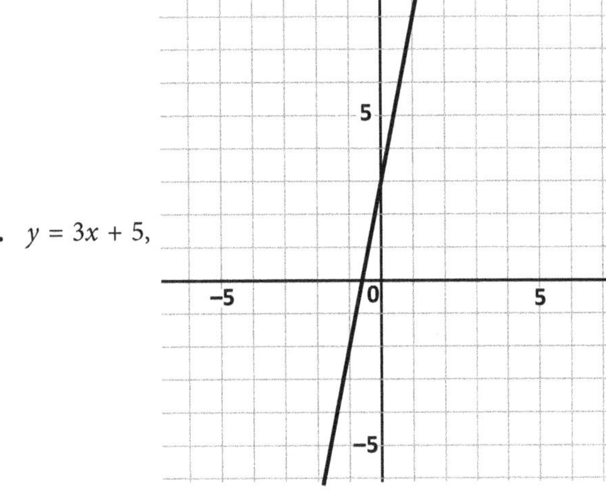

D. $y = 3x + 5$,

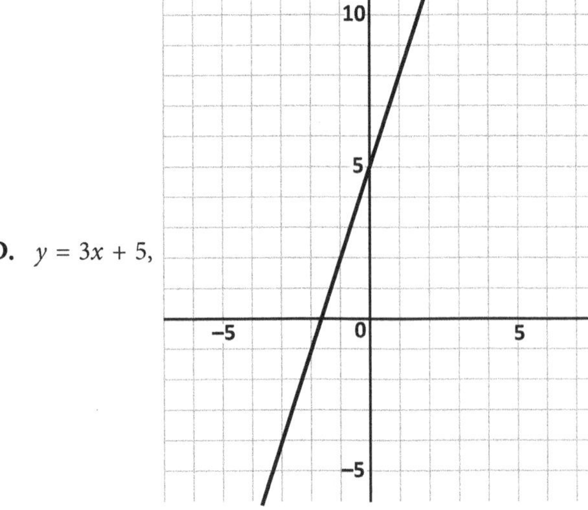

63.

What is the slope of a line that is perpendicular to the graph of a line whose equation is $3x - 5y = 4$?

A. $-\frac{5}{3}$

B. $-\frac{4}{5}$

C. $\frac{3}{5}$

D. $\frac{5}{3}$

64.

Erwin wants to order a photo album to print his vacation pictures in. The photo album itself costs $25 and each included picture costs $0.05. Which of the following equations gives the total cost of the photo album and pictures, *c*, if p pictures are ordered by Erwin?

A. $c = 25p + 0.05$
B. $c = 0.05p + 25$
C. $c = 25.05p$
D. $c = 25p$

65.

Line shown below is parallel to the line through the points (3, 8) and (x, 10). Find the value of x.

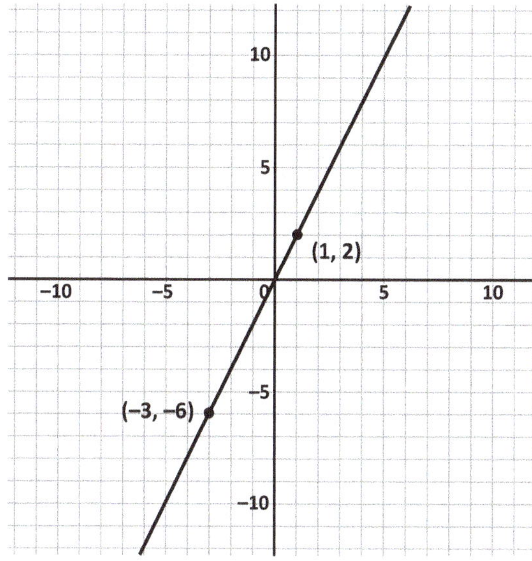

A. 3
B. 4
C. 8
D. 9

66.

For the equation $-4x + 24y = 6$, which of the following expressions gives y in terms of x?

A. $\frac{1}{6}x + \frac{1}{4}$
B. $x + 4$
C. $6x + 16$
D. $\frac{1}{6}x + 16$

67.

Pierre uses the water from his rain barrel to water his plants. The barrel started with 50 gallons of water and Pierre used it at a rate of 9 gallons per minute. Which of the following is a relationship between the volume, v, in gallons of the water in the rain barrel and the time, t, in minutes that the water is being used?

A. $v = 9t - 50$
B. $v = 50t - 9$
C. $v = -9t + 50$
D. $v = -9t$

68.

What is the slope of the line given by the equation $4x - 10y = -15$?

A. $\frac{2}{5}$
B. $\frac{3}{2}$
C. 4
D. 10

69.

Students performed an experiment to record the distance a ball rolled while moving at a constant rate. The distance of the ball, d, in meters based on the amount of time that had passed in seconds, is recorded in the table below from $t = 1$ to $t = 5$ seconds. Which of the following equations represents this relationship between d and t?

t	1	2	3	4	5
d	19	22	25	28	31

A. $d = 5t + 13$
B. $d = t + 12$
C. $d = 3t + 16$
D. $d = 6t + 10$

70.

What is the slope of a line that has a y-intercept of −3 and is perpendicular to a line whose equation is $3x + 4y = -5$?

A. −5
B. −3
C. $-\frac{3}{4}$
D. $\frac{4}{3}$

71.

What is the slope of any line parallel to the line $6x + 8y = 1$?

A. −6
B. $\frac{-3}{4}$
C. 1
D. $\frac{4}{3}$

72.

A line in the standard (x, y) coordinate plane passes through the points (4, 7) and (7, 1). The slope of line:

A. is positive.
B. is negative.
C. is zero.
D. is undefined.

73.

What is the slope of a line in the standard (x, y) coordinate plane that contains the points (5, −3) and (8, 6)?

A. −3
B. $\frac{1}{3}$
C. 1
D. 3

74.

In the standard (x,y) coordinate plane, what is the slope of the line that is perpendicular to the line $5x - 7y = 14$?

A. $-\frac{7}{5}$
B. $-\frac{1}{5}$
C. $\frac{5}{7}$
D. 5

75.

What is the slope of the line $4x + 5y = -10$ that is graphed in the standard (x, y) coordinate plane?

A. −4
B. $-\frac{5}{2}$
C. $-\frac{4}{5}$
D. $\frac{2}{5}$

76.

The graph of the function $f(x) = \sqrt{-log\left(\frac{1}{4}x\right)}$ is shown in the standard (x, y) coordinate plane below. The function is defined for values of x strictly between which of the following pairs of numbers?

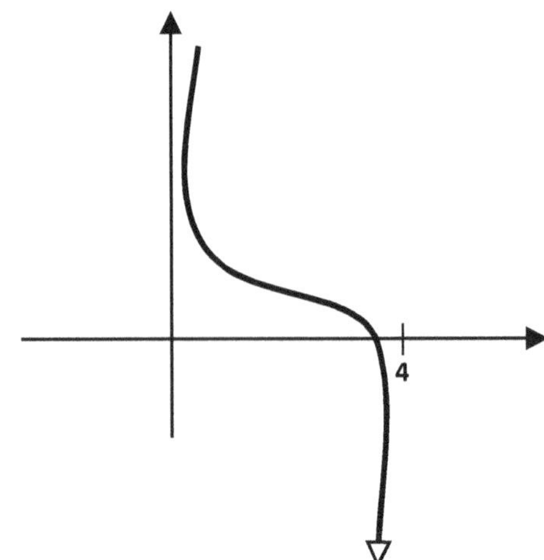

A. 0 and $\frac{1}{4}$
B. $-\frac{1}{4}$ and $\frac{1}{4}$
C. 0 and 4
D. −4 and 4

77.

What is the minimum degree possible for the polynomial function whose graph is shown in the standard (x,y) coordinate plane below?

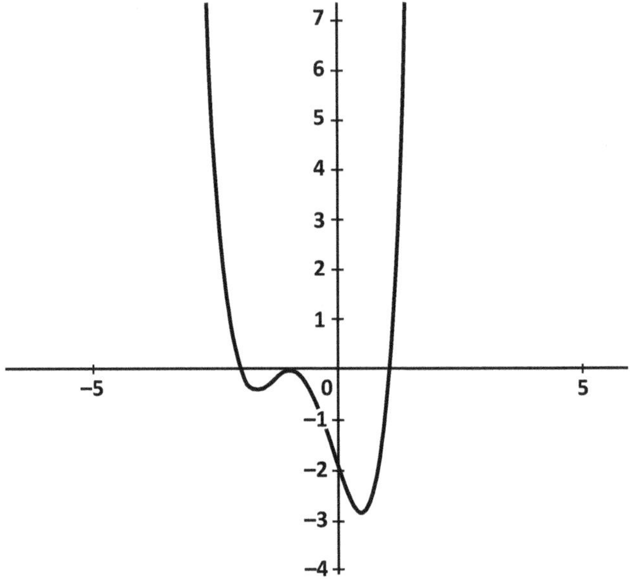

A. 1
B. 2
C. 3
D. 4

78.

Which of the following statements is true about the graph of the function $y = f(x)$ shown below?

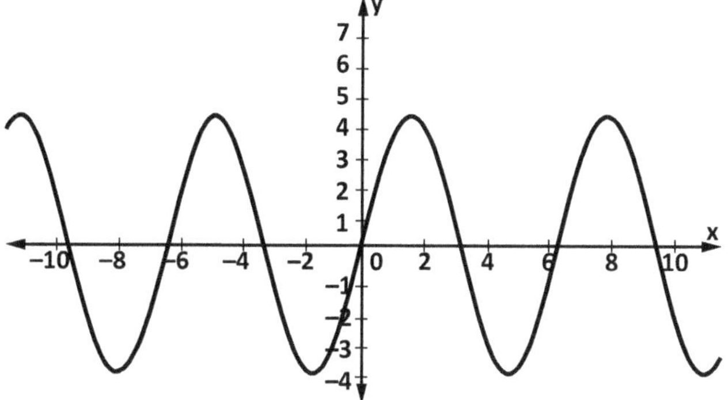

A. Its graph has symmetry about the x-axis.
B. The domain is for the function is $-4 \le y \le 4$
C. The graph has y-axis symmetry.
D. The graph has symmetry about the origin.

79.

Point A(2, 4) is shown in the standard (x, y) coordinate plane below. Point A is reflected across the line $x = 5$ and after the reflection is labeled B. What are the coordinates of B?

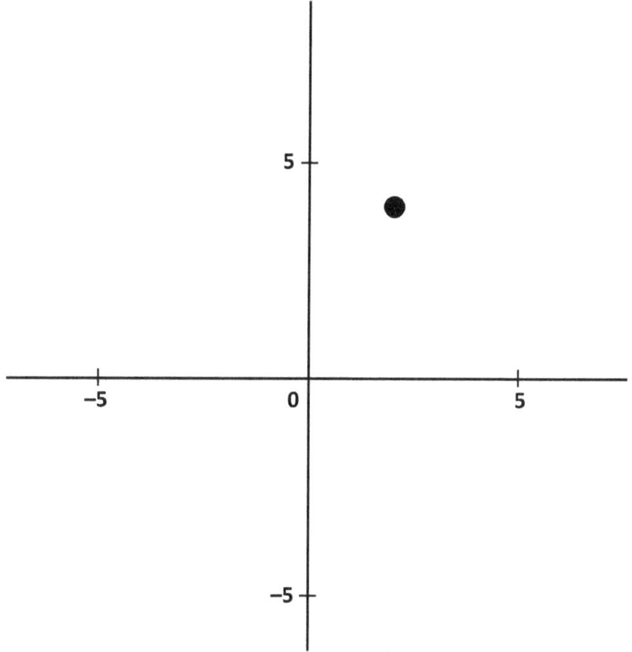

A. (2, 9)
B. (7, 4)
C. (8, 4)
D. (2, 5)

80.

One of the following equations determines the graph in the standard (x, y) coordinate plane below. Which one?

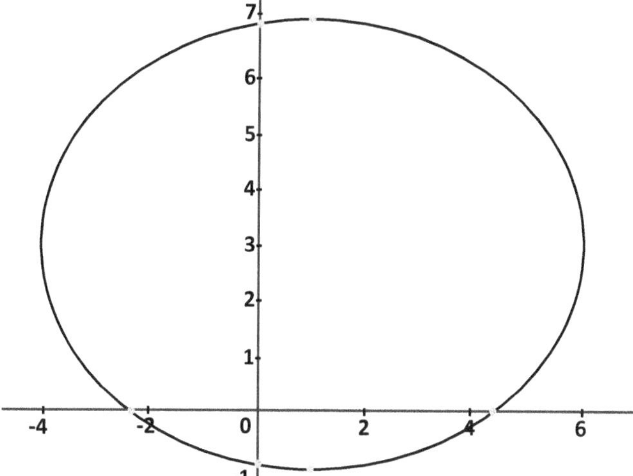

A. $\frac{(x-1)^2}{25} + \frac{(y-3)^2}{16} = 1$

B. $\frac{(x+1)^2}{25} + \frac{(y+3)^2}{16} = 1$

C. $\frac{(x-1)^2}{16} + \frac{(y-3)^2}{25} = 1$

D. $\frac{(x+1)^2}{5} + \frac{(y+3)^2}{4} = 1$

81.

The graph of which of the following functions has the largest maximum value?

A. $y = -3x^2 + 5$
B. $y = -x^2 + 7$
C. $y = -|x+2| + 3$
D. $y = 4sinx$

82.

Margo is selling brownies at her school's bake sale. She paid $7.50 for her supplies and is charging $1.50 per brownie. Her profit is found by subtracting her expenses from her income. Which of the following graphs represents her profit as a function of the number of brownies she sells?

A.

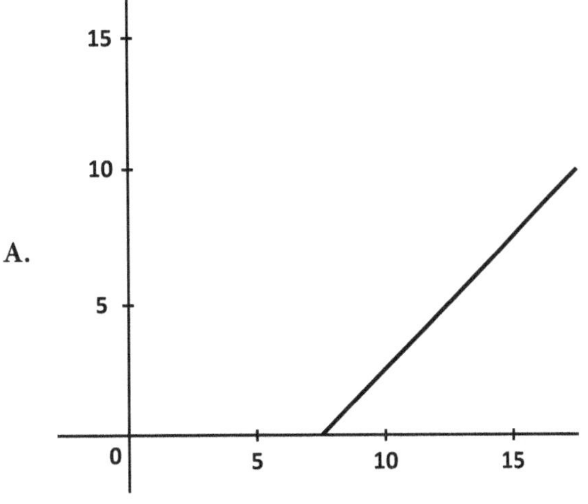

B.

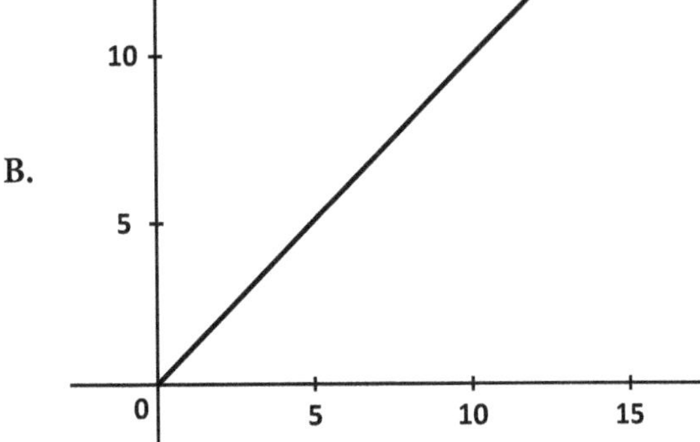

C.

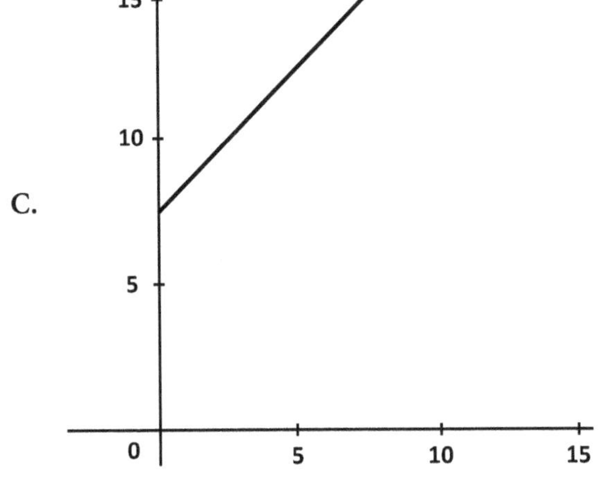

D.

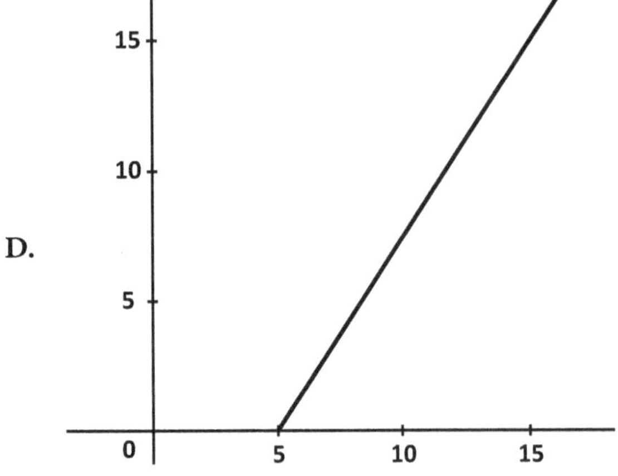

83.

The equation $f(x)$ is graphed on the (x, y) coordinate plane below. What is the value of $f(3)$?

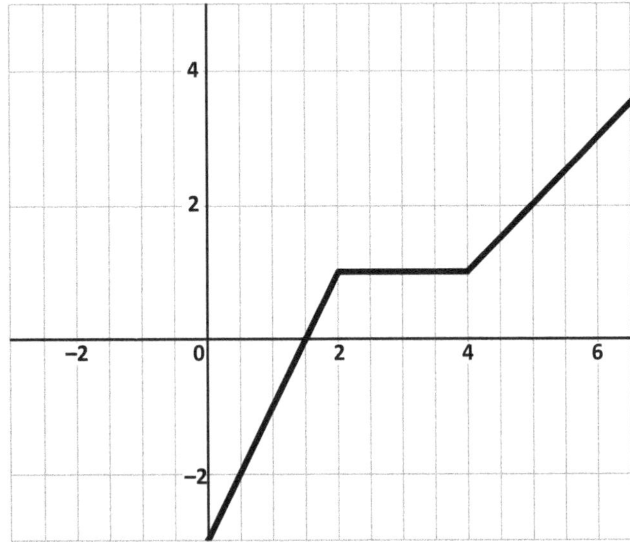

A. 0
B. 1
C. 3
D. 5

84.

A circle with the equation $(x + 4)^2 + (y - 2)^2 = 25$ is graphed in the (x, y) coordinate plane below. If the circle was to be shifted right 3 and down 4, what would be the new coordinates of the center of the circle?

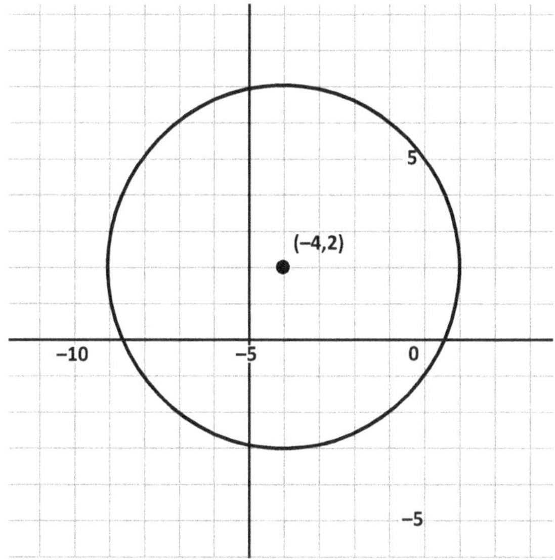

A. $(-1, -2)$
B. $(0, 1)$
C. $(-4, -6)$
D. $(2, 5)$

85.

Which of the following equations determines the circle shown in the standard (x, y) coordinate plane below?

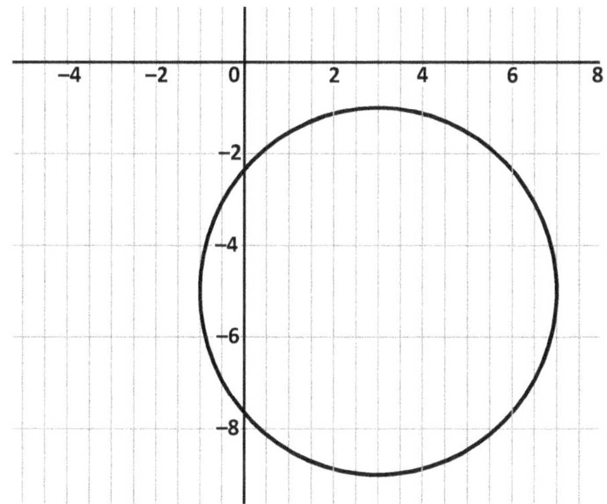

A. $(x + 5)^2 + (y - 3)^2 = 16$
B. $(x - 3)^2 + (y + 5)^2 = 16$
C. $(x + 5)^2 + (y - 3)^2 = 25$
D. $(x - 3)^2 + (y + 5)^2 = 25$

86.

A city had 5 inches of snow on the ground when another snowstorm hit. The snow fell at a rate of 1.25 inches per hour. The relationship between depth of the snow and time that passed can be expressed as a linear relationship between d, depth, and t, time in hours. One of the following graphs in the standard (x, y) coordinate plane models the equation for positive values of x and y. Which one?

A. 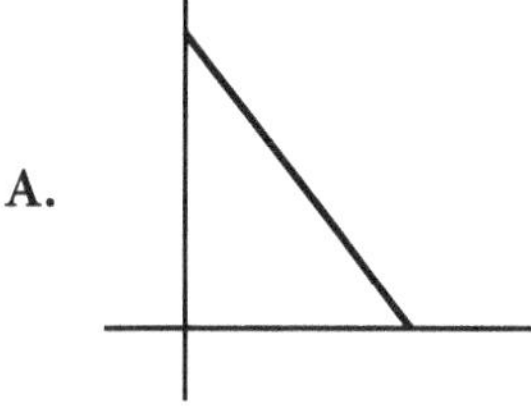

B. 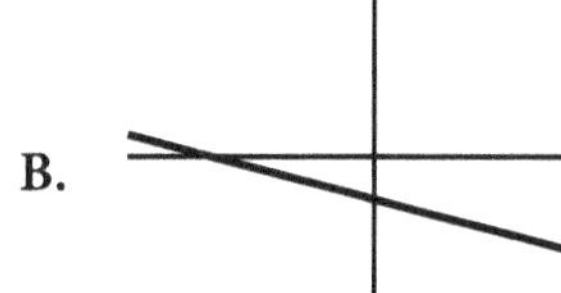

C. 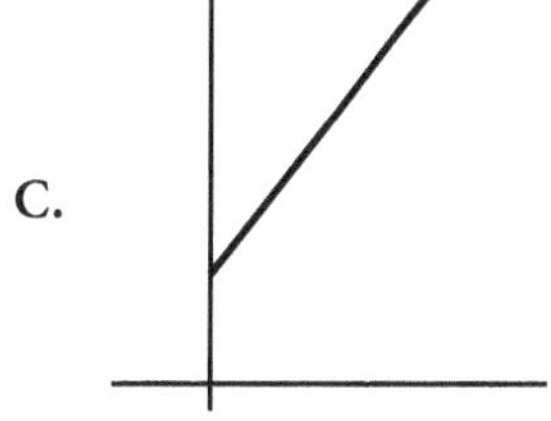

D. 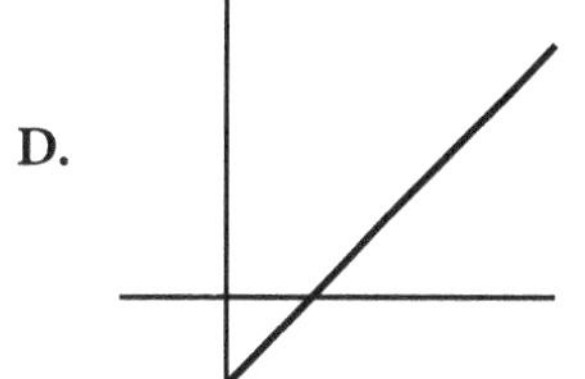

87.

For the graphs of $y = f(x)$ and $y = g(x)$ shown in the standard (x, y) coordinate plane below, which of the following values of x is $g(x) - f(x) = 9$?

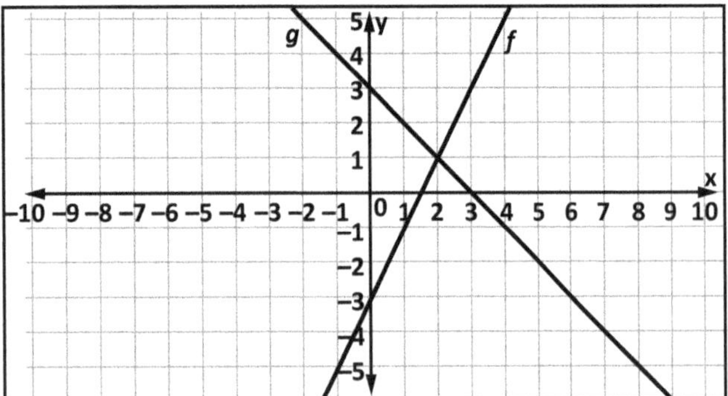

A. -1
B. 0
C. 2
D. 3

88.

The graph of the quadratic function in the form $y = ax^2 + bx + c$ where a, b, and c are constants is shown in the standard (x, y) coordinate plane below. Which statement is true about the constants?

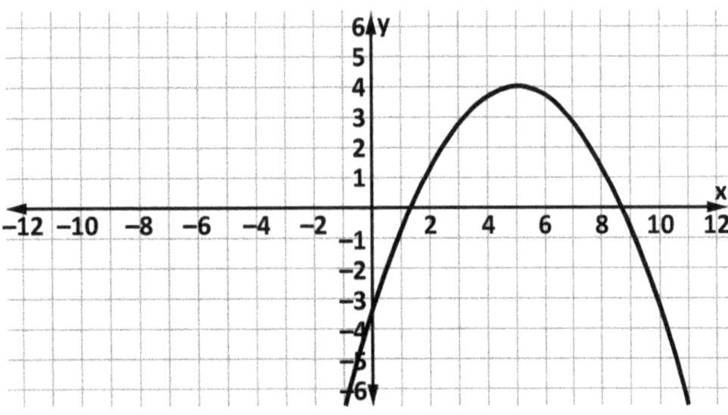

A. $a > 0$ and $c > 0$
B. $a < 0$ and $c < 0$
C. $a > 0$ and $c < 0$
D. $a > 0$ and $b = 0$

89.

A series of transformations are applied to the graph in the standard (x, y) coordinate plane below. The graph is reflected across the y-axis and then translated 5 units up. The resulting graph is one of the following graphs. Which one?

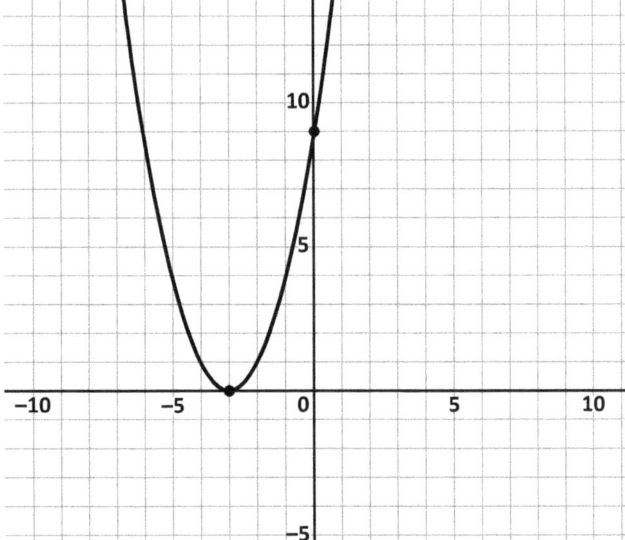

A.

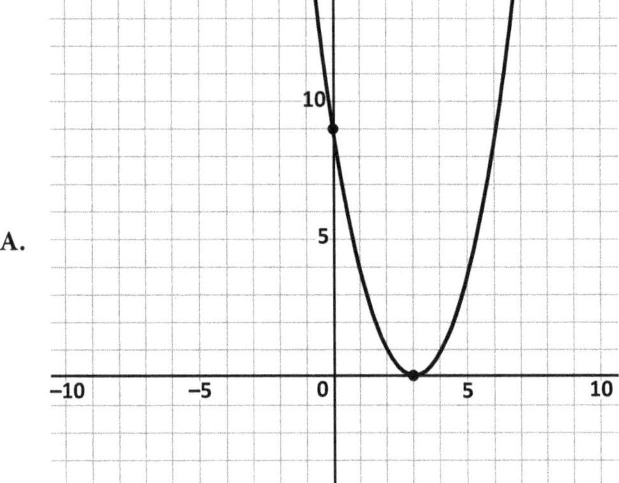

B.

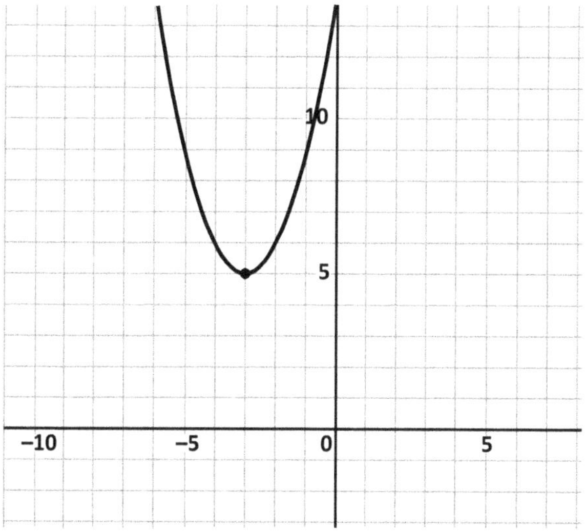

C.

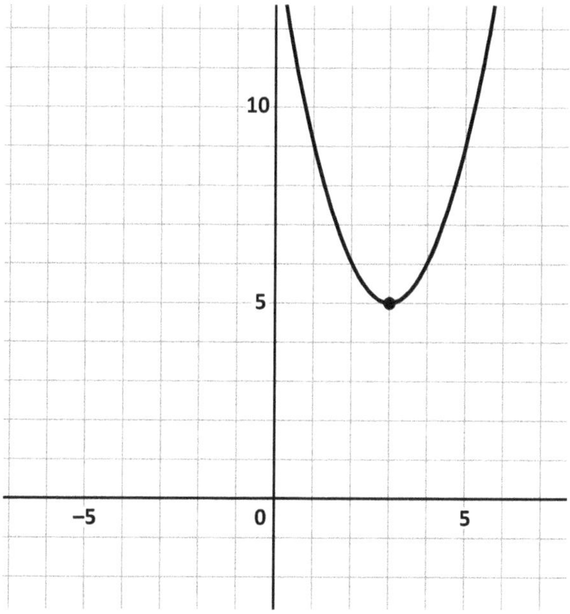

D.

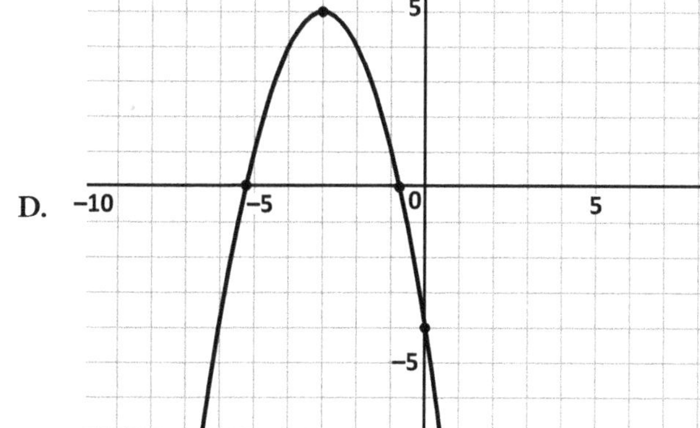

90.

The following graph is defined for all values of x EXCEPT:

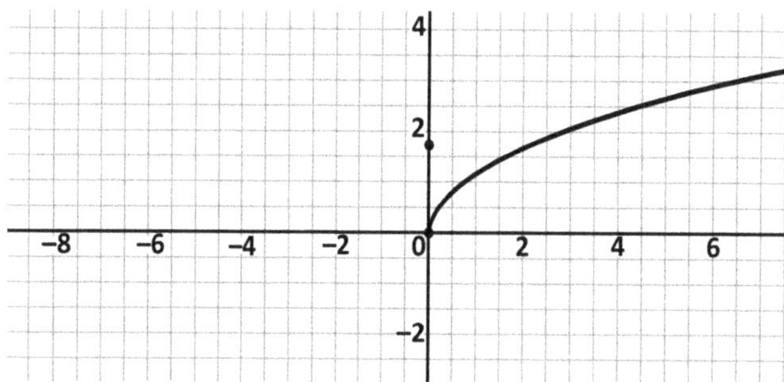

A. -1
B. 0
C. 1
D. 2

91.

The amount of products an assembly line finishes is based on the function $f(x)$ which is determined by the hour of the day. Since there are more workers at different periods of the day, the function $f(x)$ can vary as follows:

$$f(x) = \begin{cases} 2x + 4 & 0 < x \leq 5 \\ 3x + 15 & 5 < x < 8 \\ x^2 - 45 & 8 \leq x \leq 12 \end{cases}$$

Which graph best matches this piecewise function?

A.

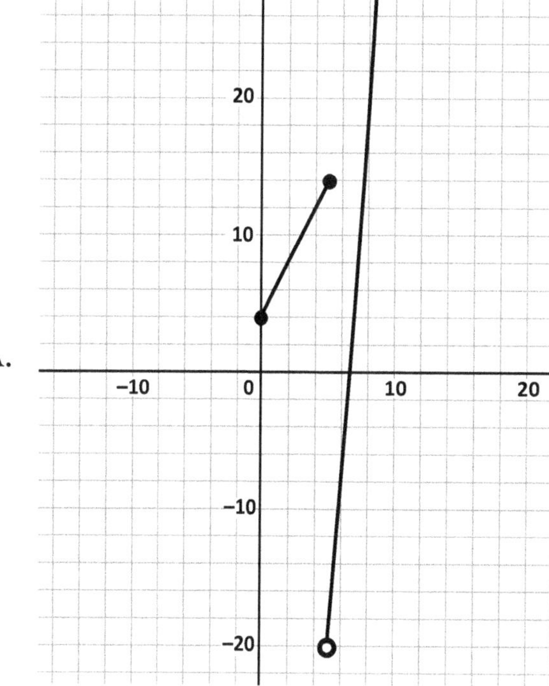

B.

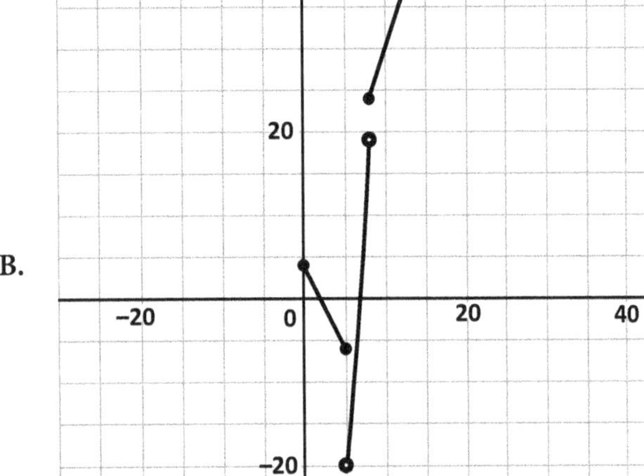

C.

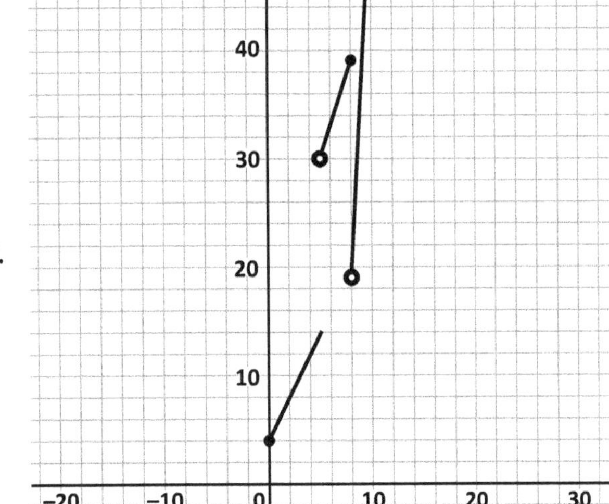

D.

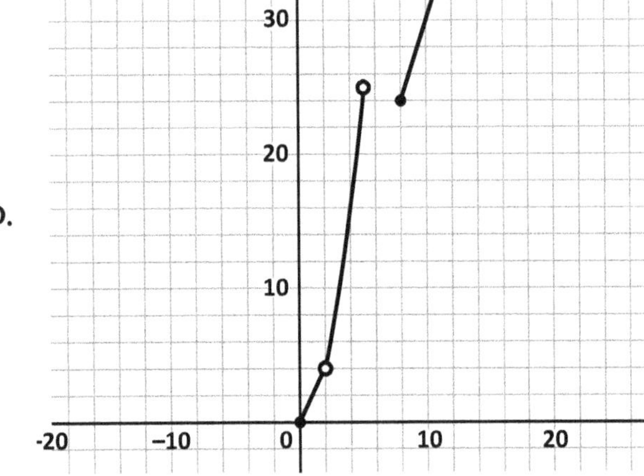

92.

The function $f(x) = 3x + 6$ in the (x, y) coordinate plane is shifted down 8 units. What is the new equation of the function?

A. $f(x) = 8x + 6$
B. $f(x) = -5x + 6$
C. $f(x) = 3x - 2$
D. $f(x) = 3x + 14$

93.

A baseball was thrown into the air at a time of $t = 0$ seconds. The location of the ball over a period of t seconds was recorded to determine it reached its maximum height of 15 meters at a time of 4 seconds. The baseball hit the ground at a time of 8 seconds. Which of the following equations best matches this scenario?

A. $f(x) = (x - 15)^2 + 4$
B. $f(x) = (x - 4)^2 + 15$
C. $f(x) = \frac{15}{16}(x + 4)^2 + 15$
D. $f(x) = -\frac{15}{16}(x - 4)^2 + 15$

94.

What is the maximum value of the function $f(x) = 3\sin(x) + 3$ as graphed in the (x, y) coordinate plane below?

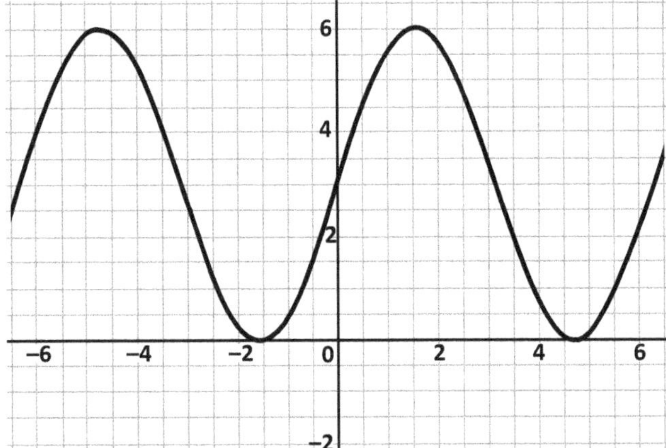

A. 0
B. 3
C. 6
D. 10

95.

The function $f(x)$ is graphed in the coordinate plane below. Which of the following is the equation for $f(x)$?

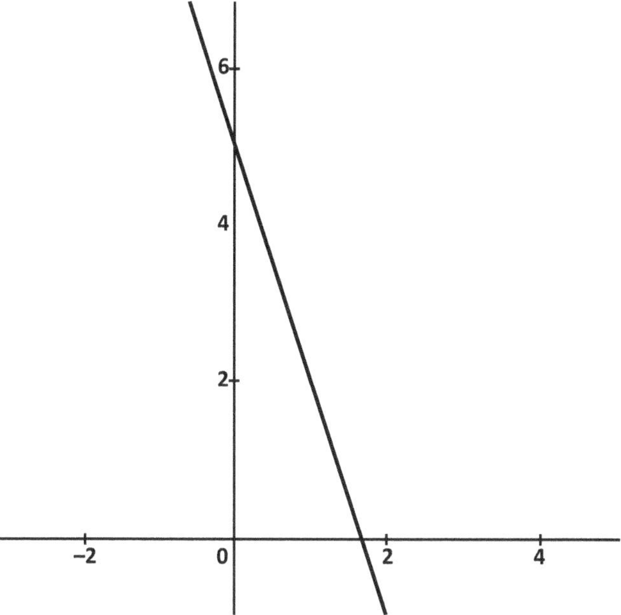

A. $y = -3x + 5$
B. $y = -x + 3$
C. $y = 2x - 3$
D. $y = 3x - 1$

96.

The sine function $f(x)$ is graphed on the coordinate plane below. Which of the following is the amplitude of the function?

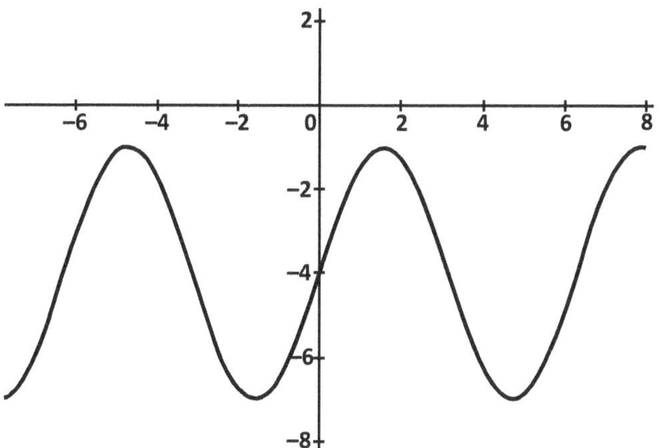

A. 2
B. 3
C. 4
D. 5

97.

Which of the following is equal to (sin 30°)(cos 60°) + (sin 60°)(cos 30°)?

A. sin (30° – 60°)
B. sin (30°+ 60°)
C. cos (30° – 60°)
D. cos (30° + 60°)

98.

A cosine function is shown in the standard (x, y) coordinate plane below.

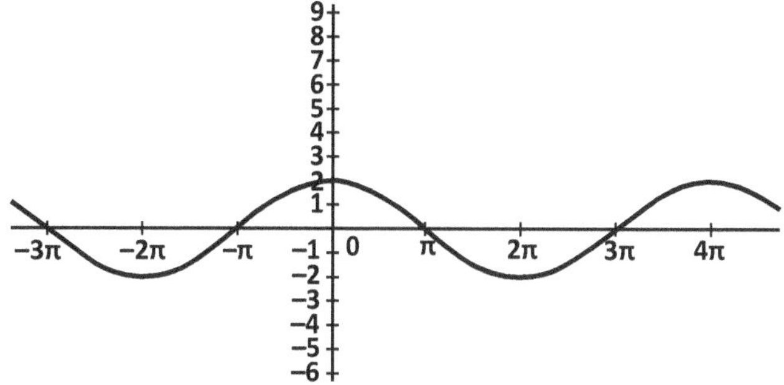

One of the following equations represents this function. Which one?

A. $y = 2 \cos x$
B. $y = 2 \cos\left(\frac{x}{2}\right)$
C. $y = \cos(2x)$
D. $y = \frac{1}{2} \cos x$

99.

What is the amplitude of the function $y = 4 \sin x$?
A. 1
B. 2
C. 3
D. 4

100.

What is the amplitude of the function $y = \cos x$?
A. 1
B. 2
C. 3
D. 4

101.

What is the amplitude of $g(x) = cos\left(\frac{2\pi}{3}x\right) + 1$?

A. $\frac{2}{3}$
B. 1
C. 2
D. 3

102.

What is the amplitude of the function $y = \frac{1}{4}\sin(x + \Pi)$?

A. $\frac{1}{4}$
B. $\frac{1}{2}$
C. 1
D. 4

103.

What is the amplitude of the function $f(x) = 5\cos(2x + 3) - 4$?

A. 2
B. 3
C. 4
D. 5

104.

For $0^\circ < a^\circ < 90^\circ$ and $0 < b < 1$, when $\sin a^\circ = b$, which of the following expressions is equivalent to $\sin(2a^\circ)$?

A. 0
B. 1
C. $a^2 - b^2$
D. $2b\sqrt{1-b^2}$

105.

Which of the following expressions is equivalent to $\tan\theta$ if θ is in the 1st quadrant?

A. $1 - \sec\theta$
B. $\sec\theta - 1$
C. $\sec^2\theta - 1$
D. $\sqrt{\sec^2\theta - 1}$

Answer Key

Question	Correct	Make your correct answers
1	B	
2	B	
3	C	
4	D	
5	A	
6	B	
7	A	
8	B	
9	C	
10	B	
11	C	
12	C	
13	C	
14	B	
15	C	
16	B	
17	C	
18	C	
19	D	
20	C	
21	B	
22	B	
23	A	
24	B	
25	C	
26	B	
27	B	
28	A	
29	D	
30	C	
31	C	
32	A	

Question	Correct	Make your correct answers
33	B	
34	C	
35	B	
36	C	
37	C	
38	B	
39	B	
40	D	
41	D	
42	B	
43	C	
44	A	
45	A	
46	C	
47	D	
48	C	
49	A	
50	B	
51	A	
52	D	
53	C	
54	C	
55	B	
56	C	
57	B	
58	C	
59	C	
60	A	
61	A	
62	D	
63	A	
64	B	

Question	Correct	Make your correct answers
65	B	
66	A	
67	C	
68	A	
69	C	
70	D	
71	B	
72	B	
73	D	
74	A	
75	C	
76	C	
77	D	
78	D	
79	C	
80	A	
81	B	
82	D	
83	B	
84	A	
85	B	
86	C	
87	A	
88	B	
89	C	
90	A	
91	C	
92	C	
93	D	
94	C	
95	A	
96	B	

Question	Correct	Make your correct answers
97	B	
98	B	
99	D	
100	A	
101	B	
102	A	
103	D	
104	D	
105	D	

1.

Category: PHM
Skill: Series, Sequences and Consecutive numbers |
Level: Easy

Choice B is correct because the obtained answer is

$$a_n = 4(-\frac{1}{4})^{n-1}.$$

Given: $\left\{4, -1, \frac{1}{4}, -\frac{1}{16}, \frac{1}{64}, \ldots\right\}$

The general equation is $a_n = a_1 r^{n-1}$.
Find the value of r.

$$r = \frac{a_2}{a_1} = \frac{-1}{4} = -\frac{1}{4}$$

Use the general equation for geometric series.

$$a_n = a_1 r^{n-1}$$

$$a_n = 4(-\frac{1}{4})^{n-1}$$

Choice A is incorrect because $a_n = 4(\frac{1}{4})^{n-1}$ does not represent the general equation of the given series.
Choice C is incorrect because $a_n = 4 + (-\frac{1}{4})^{n-1}$ does not represent the general equation of the given series.
Choice D is incorrect because $a_n = 4 - (-\frac{1}{4})^{n-1}$ does not represent the general equation of the given series.

2.

Category: PHM
Skill: Series, Sequences and Consecutive numbers |
Level: Hard

Choice B is correct because you can use the arithmetic sums formula to determine how much Bill made in total. To find the sum of an arithmetic series, use the equation $S = \frac{1}{2}(a_n + a_1)$. You already know the first term is \$25, but you need to determine the last term which would be how much Bill made for the eighth hour of his shift. You can determine this by finding the equation for the series and then evaluating for a_8.
The equation for an arithmetic series that can be used for this scenario is $a_n = a_1 + d(n - 1)$. Plugging into this equation will yield the new formula $a_n = 25 + 3(n - 1)$ which will simplify to be $a_n = 25 + 3n - 3 = 3n + 22$. To find a_8, plug in $n = 8$ to get $a_8 = 3(8) + 22 = 46$.
Now you can solve for the sum by plugging in.
$S = \frac{1}{2}(a_n + a_1) = \frac{1}{2}(25 + 46) = \$284$.

Choice A is incorrect because this would assume he made \$25 the first hour and \$3 for each hour after which is a misinterpretation of the problem. **Choice C** is incorrect because this would result from an error in addition. **Choice D** is incorrect because this would result from multiplying by 8 and not dividing by 2 to find the sum.

3.

Category: PHM
Skill: Series, Sequences and Consecutive numbers |
Level: Easy

Choice C is correct because there are three arrangements where a letter is followed by a symbol then a number.
Given: D ?1*K*#\$3*G*@! 4*W*6*P*%5*I*8*T* > *J*&8*L*?
Find the arrangements where a letter is followed by a symbol then a number.

D?1 , *P*%5 , *J*&8

Hence, there are 3 arrangements.

Choice A is incorrect because there are more than one arrangement in the given pattern. **Choice B** is incorrect because there are more than two arrangements in the given pattern. **Choice D** is incorrect because there are less than four arrangements in the given pattern.

4.

Category: PHM
Skill: Series, Sequences and Consecutive numbers |
Level: Easy

Choice D is correct because the given series has a common ratio of $\frac{1}{4}$ meaning each term is multiplied by $\frac{1}{4}$ or divided by 4 each time. The next term after 5 would be $5 \times \frac{1}{4}$ which equals $\frac{5}{4}$.

Choice A is incorrect because this does not use the correct common ratio. **Choice B** is incorrect because this does not use the correct common ratio. **Choice C** is incorrect because this does not use the correct common ratio.

5.

Category: IES & Modeling
Skill: Series, Sequences and Consecutive numbers |
Level: Medium

Choice A is correct because the first term of the sequence can be calculated through the formula $a_n = a_1 + d(n - 1)$. The common difference can be determined by subtracting the values of a_3 and a_{15} to get 36 and then dividing by the number of steps between term 3 and 15. It takes 12 steps to get from term 3 to 15, so 36 divided by 12 will yield a common difference of 3. Since the numbers are getting smaller, this common difference should also be negative.

Using $a_3 = 18$, the formula can then be written as $18 = a_1 - 3(3 - 1)$ which will simplify to be $18 = a_1 - 6$. Adding the 6 over will result in the first term being found to be 24.

Choice B is incorrect because this results from a math error when calculating the formula. **Choice C** is incorrect because this results from a math error when calculating the formula. **Choice D** is incorrect because this results from a math error when calculating the formula.

6.

Category: IES
Skill: Series, Sequences and Consecutive numbers |
Level: Medium

Choice B is correct because the least common multiple of 12 and 5 is 60. This means 60 hours must pass between synchronous bell rings. Counting 60 hours after midnight on Sunday would be 2 days and 12 hours later which would be noon on Tuesday.

Choice A is incorrect because this time is not a common multiple of both bell schedules. **Choice C** is incorrect because this time is not a common multiple of both bell schedules. **Choice D** is incorrect because this time is not a common multiple of both bell schedules.

7.

Category: PHM
Skill: Series, Sequences and consecutive numbers modeling | **Level:** Medium

Choice A is correct because to find the sum of the series, first find the value of the 10th term using the formula $a_n = a_1 + d(n - 1)$. Plug-in the given information to get the expression for the tenth term to be $a_{10} = -11 + 3(10 - 1) = -11 + 3(9) = -11 + 27 = 16$. Now plug this value into the expression to find the sum:

$$S = \frac{n}{2}(a_n + a_1) = \frac{10}{2}(-11 + 27) = 25.$$

Choice B is incorrect because this results from a calculation error. **Choice C** is incorrect because this results from a calculation error. **Choice D** is incorrect because this results from a calculation error.

8.

Category: IES & Modeling
Skill: Series, Sequences and Consecutive numbers |
Level: Medium

Choice B is correct because to find the sum of an arithmetic series, use the summation formula $S = \frac{n}{2}(a_n + a_1)$. To fill this in, first identify the value of the last term using the known information. The common difference can be found by subtracting the value of the first term and the fourth term then dividing by 3 since there are 3 steps from the first term to the fourth term. This will result in $\frac{26-17}{3} = 3$. Use this in the formula $a_n = a_1 + d(n - 1)$ to get the expression to find the 8th term as $a_8 = 17 + 3(8 - 1) = 17 + 3(7) = 17 + 21 = 38$. Now, plug into the sum formula to get $S = \frac{8}{2}(17 + 38) = 220$.

Choice A is incorrect because this is just the sum of the first and last term. **Choice C** is incorrect because this results from a calculation error. **Choice D** is incorrect because this is the sum before being divided in half.

9.

Category: IES
Skill: Series, Sequences and Consecutive numbers |
Level: Easy

Choice C is correct because to find the number of seats in the 15th row, use the arithmetic sequence formula $a_n = a_1 + d(n - 1)$. Based on the given information, this can be filled in to be equal to $a_{15} = 10 + 2(15 - 1) = 10 + 2(14) = 10 + 28 = 38$.

Choice A is incorrect because this is the number of seats in the second row. **Choice B** is incorrect because this results from a calculation error that does not account for the first row having 10 seats. **Choice D** is incorrect because this is more than the number of seats.

10.

Category: PHM
Skill: Series, Sequence, and consecutive numbers|
Level: Easy

Choice B is correct because the obtained answer is 115.

Given: $a_1 = 7$, $n = 10$, $d = 12$

$$a_n = a_1 + (n - 1)d$$
$$a_{10} = 7 + (10 - 1)12$$
$$a_{10} = 7 + (9)12$$
$$a_{10} = 115$$

Choice A is incorrect because 98 is less than the obtained answer. **Choice C** is incorrect because 112 is less than the obtained answer. **Choice D** is incorrect because 128 is greater than the obtained answer.

11.

Category: PHM
Skill: Series, Sequences and Consecutive numbers |
Level: Easy

Choice C is correct because geometric sequences can be evaluated using the formula of $a_n = a_1(r^{n-1})$. Plug-in the given information to find $a_7 = 8(-3)^{7-1} = 5832$.

Choice A is incorrect because this results from a calculation error. **Choice B** is incorrect because this results from a calculation error. **Choice D** is incorrect because this results from a calculation error.

12.

Category: PHM
Skill: Series, Sequences and Consecutive numbers |
Level: Medium

Choice C is correct because the fourth element has one row of four, one row of five, one row of six, and one row of seven dots. Adding these all together will get you $4 + 5 + 6 + 7 = 22$.

Choice A is incorrect because this is the total for the second element. **Choice B** is incorrect because this is the total for the third element. **Choice D** is incorrect because this is the total for the fifth element.

13.

Category: PHM
Skill: Series, Sequences and Consecutive numbers |
Level: Hard

Choice C is correct because you can use the equation of a geometric sequence to identify the fifth term of the sequence. A geometric sequence follows the equation $a_n = a_1(r^{n-1})$. The common ratio can be determined by dividing the eighth term by the third term and then taking the fifth root since there are five steps between them. Dividing −1408 by 44 yields −32, which has the fifth root of −2.

Plug this back into the equation and use a_3 to evaluate for a_1: $a_3 = a_1(-2^{3-1})$. Simplify to get $44 = a_1(-2^2)$ which then simplifies to be $44 = 4a_1$. Divide both sides by 4 to find the first term equals 11.

Now, to solve for the fifth term, use the full equation $a_5 = 11(-2^{5-1}) = 176$.

Choice A is incorrect because this is the sixth term of the sequence. **Choice B** is incorrect because this term does not exist in the sequence. **Choice D** is incorrect because this is the seventh term of the sequence.

14.

Category: PHM
Skill: Series, Sequences and Consecutive numbers |
Level: Easy

Choice B is correct because this scenario will follow the pattern of a geometric sequence following the formula $y = a(r)^{x-1}$. Plugging in the known information where a is the initial population size and r is the rate you will get the formula $y = 100(2)^{x-1}$.

Choice A is incorrect because this does not represent the starting value of the population correctly.
Choice C is incorrect because this is an arithmetic sequence. **Choice D** is incorrect because this represents a quadratic relationship, not a geometric.

15.

Category: IES
Skill: Series, Sequences and Consecutive numbers |
Level: Hard

Choice C is correct because to find the largest possible size use a geometric sequence formula of $a_n = a_1(r^{n-1})$. Plugging in the known information can help with finding a_1 by using the information for the 8th term: $a_8 = 100\,(1.1^{8-1})$. Simplifying will yield $a_8 = 100*1.948$ and then dividing will result in approximately 195 as the largest area of a frame offered.

Choice A is incorrect because this is smaller than the largest possible size. **Choice B** is incorrect because this is smaller than the largest possible size. **Choice D** is incorrect because this is larger than the largest possible size.

16.

Category: PHM & Modeling
Skill: Series, Sequences and Consecutive numbers |
Level: Medium

Choice B is correct because to determine when the two trains will next be at the station together, you need to find the LCM of 18 and 45. This would be 90.

Choice A is incorrect because 45 is not a multiple of 18. **Choice C** is incorrect because neither train will be at the station after 100 minutes. **Choice D** is incorrect because neither train will be at the station after 120 minutes.

17.

Category: PHM & Modeling
Skill: Series, Sequences and Consecutive numbers |
Level: Easy

Choice C is correct because to determine the value of a term in a geometric series use the expression $a_n = a_1(r^{n-1})$. Based on the given information this expression would be equal to $a_8 = -3(-4^{8-1}) = 49152$.

Choice A is incorrect because this results from a calculation error. **Choice B** is incorrect because this results from a calculation error. **Choice D** is incorrect because this results from a calculation error.

18.

Category: IES
Skill: Series, Sequences and Consecutive numbers |
Level: Medium

Choice C is correct because to determine the value of a term in a geometric series use the expression $a_n = a_1(r^{n-1})$. To find *r*, divide 45 by 5 and then take the square root to get 3 as the common ratio. Based on the given information the equation would be $a_5 = 5(3^{5-1}) = 405$.

Choice A is incorrect because this results from a calculation error. **Choice B** is incorrect because this results from a calculation error. **Choice D** is incorrect because this results from a calculation error.

19.

Category: PHM
Skill: Series, Sequences and Consecutive numbers |
Level: Medium

Choice D is correct because the fifth term can be found by using the expression to evaluate arithmetic equations of $a_n = a_1 + d(n - 1)$. In this scenario, $a_5 = 45 + 4(5 - 1) = 61$ degrees.

Choice A is incorrect because this is not the temperature on day five. **Choice B** is incorrect because this is not the temperature on day five. **Choice C** is incorrect because this is not the temperature on day five.

20.

Category: IES
Skill: Series, Sequences and Consecutive numbers |
Level: Easy

Choice C is correct because you can use the formula $a_n = a_1\, r^{n-1}$ to solve for the number of terms in the series. Plug-in the given values of $128 = 2(2)^{n-1}$ and then solve for n by simplifying the expression to be $128 = 2^n$. The seventh power of 2 will get you 128 which means there are 7 terms.

Choice A is incorrect because there are more than 5 terms in the series. **Choice B** is incorrect because there are more than 6 terms in the series. **Choice D** is incorrect because there are less than 8 terms in the series.

21.

Category: PHM & Modeling
Skill: Evaluation of functions, domain and range |
Level: Medium

Choice B is correct because if $x > -8$ that would result in a positive value under the square root. However, there is a negative outside of the square root expression which means all values of y under this condition are negative.

Choice A is incorrect because y is only irrational for some values and not all. **Choice C** is incorrect because y cannot be greater than 0. **Choice D** is incorrect because y is not imaginary as the square root would yield a real number.

22.

Category: PHM & Modeling
Skill: Evaluation of functions, domain and range |
Level: Medium

Choice B is correct because the range can be determined by evaluating the maximum and minimum from the graph. The maximum y-value is at 6 and the minimum y-value is at −2. This matches the range of $-2 \le y \le 6$.

Choice A is incorrect because this includes values outside the range. **Choice C** is incorrect because this includes values outside the range. **Choice D** is incorrect because this includes values outside of the range.

23.

Category: IES
Skill: Evaluation of functions, domain and range |
Level: Easy

Choice A is correct because from the provided information, the graph can be visualized to be a quadratic since there are two of the same outputs for two different inputs: (−2, 6) and (2, 6). Plugging into the two quadratic equations would yield $y = x^2 + 2$ as the best answer because that works best for all the given values.

Choice B is incorrect because this does not match the given points. **Choice C** is incorrect because this does not match the given points. **Choice D** is incorrect because this does not match the given points.

24.

Category: IES & Modeling
Skill: Evaluation of functions, domain and range |
Level: Hard

Choice B is correct because when the points are plotted in the (x, y) plane, they resemble a exponential rate of change as seen in the graph below:

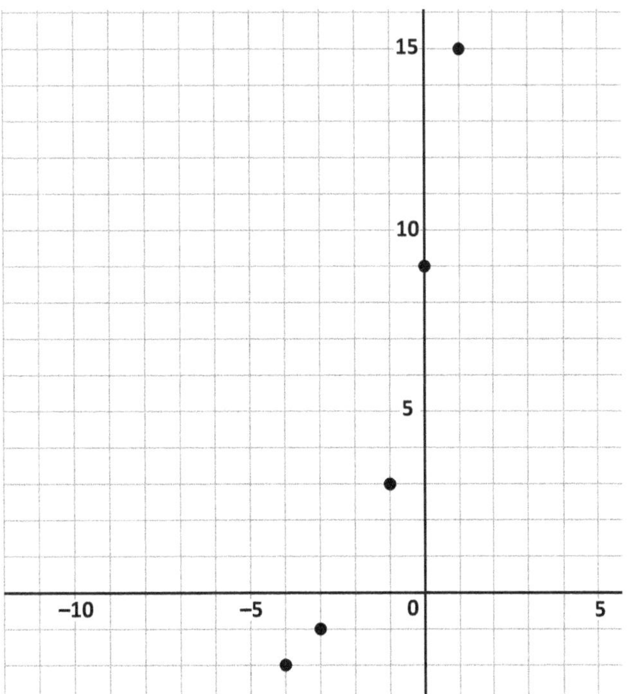

The equation $y = a + b(c)^x$ can be used to express exponential growth.

Choice A is incorrect because a linear function would not be the line of best fit. **Choice C** is incorrect because a logarithmic function would not be the line of best fit. **Choice D** is incorrect because a quadratic function would not be the line of best fit.

25.

Category: IES
Skill: Evaluation of functions, domain and range |
Level: Medium

Choice C is correct because expanding the original function and the given function will result in the same equation. Distributing $(3x - 4)(-x + 5)$ will result in $-3x^2 + 15x + 4x - 20$ which simplifies to be $-3x^2 + 19x - 20$. Distributing $(-3x + 4)(x - 5)$ results in $-3x^2 + 15x + 4x - 20$ which also simplifies to be $-3x^2 + 19x - 20$.

Choice A is incorrect because it expands to be $3x^2 + 19x + 20$. **Choice B** is incorrect because it expands to be $3x^2 + 19x + 20$. **Choice D** is incorrect because it expands to be $-3x^2 - 19x - 20$

26.

Category: PHM
Skill: Evaluation of functions, domain and range |
Level: Hard

Choice B is correct because for a given polynomial, a zero will occur when there is a change in sign of the value of $f(x)$. From $f(0)$ to $f(1)$, the number changes from Negative to Positive indicating a cross over the x-axis which is where a zero would occur.

Choice A is incorrect because no change in sign occurs. **Choice C** is incorrect because no change in sign occurs. **Choice D** is incorrect because no change in sign occurs.

27.

Category: PHM & Modeling
Skill: Evaluation of functions, domain and range |
Level: Easy

Choice B is correct because to simplify $y = 2(x - 5) + 6$, distribute and then combine like terms. Distributing will result in $y = 2x - 10 + 6$, which then simplifies to be $y = 2x - 4$.

Choice A is incorrect because this results from an addition error when simplifying. **Choice C** is incorrect because this is an incorrect rearrangement of the given equation. **Choice D** is incorrect because this is an incorrect rearrangement of the given equation.

28.

Category: PHM
Skill: Evaluation of functions, domain and range |
Level: Easy

Choice A is correct because to solve, plug in -2 for x in the function $f(x)$. This will yield the value $f(-2) = -5(-2)^2 + 3 = -17$. Then plug this solution into $f(x)$ again to get $f(f(2)) = f(-17) = -5(-17)^2 + 3 = -1442$.

Choice B is incorrect because this results from a miscalculation. **Choice C** is incorrect because this results from a miscalculation. **Choice D** is incorrect because this results from a miscalculation.

29.

Category: PHM
Skill: Evaluation of functions, domain and range |
Level: Medium

Choice D is correct because $3\Theta2$ means that $a = 3$ and $b = 2$ into the given expression. To solve, plug-in the numbers accordingly into the equation given. The new equation will be equal to 3(2) + 2(3) – 2(2) which simplifies to be 8.

Choice A is incorrect because this results from a calculation error. **Choice B** is incorrect because this results from a calculation error. **Choice C** is incorrect because this results from a calculation error.

30.

Category: PHM & Modeling
Skill: Evaluation of functions, domain and range |
Level: Easy

Choice C is correct. The graph of f is constant over an interval (the x-values) where the y-values for any point on the graph are the same over the interval. The points on the graph from $0 \leq x \leq 4$ have y-coordinate of 3 so the graph is constant from [0, 4].

Choice A is incorrect. The graph is increasing for the interval [–9, 0] **Choice B** is incorrect. The graph is constant and decreasing for the interval [0, 9]. **Choice D** is incorrect. The graph is decreasing for the interval [4, 9].

31.

Category: IES & Modeling
Skill: Evaluation of functions, domain and range |
Level: Medium

Choice C is correct because the solution set is found by evaluating all possible y values based on the given domain. Plug each value of the domain in to get the complete list of y-values. For example, the lowest x-value is –4, which would yield y = –4 + 3 = –1 as the lowest number in the range. Continue plugging in numbers until you get the complete range set in Choice C.

Choice A is incorrect because this does not include all possible range values. **Choice B** is incorrect because this does not include all possible range values. **Choice D** is incorrect because this includes extra values outside the range.

32.

Category: IES
Skill: Evaluation of functions, domain and range |
Level: Easy

Choice A is correct because this is the result after distributing and simplifying the given expression. First, distribute to get $4x^2 + x - 8x - 2$ and then combine like terms to get the final result of $4x^2 - 7x - 2$.

Choice B is incorrect because this results from a math error when simplifying. **Choice C** is incorrect because this results from a math error when simplifying.
Choice D is incorrect because this results from a math error when simplifying.

33.

Category: IES
Skill: Evaluation of functions, domain and range |
Level: Medium

Choice B is correct because to evaluate the maximum of a quadratic function, you can use the expression $x = \frac{-b}{2a}$ to determine the x-coordinate. Plugging in the numbers from the expression will give you $x = \frac{-(4)}{2(-1)} = 2$.

Choice A is incorrect because this is the y-intercept and not the maximum value. **Choice C** is incorrect because this is the y-coordinate of the vertex. **Choice D** is incorrect because this is not the maximum y-value.

34.

Category: IES
Skill: Evaluation of functions, domain and range |
Level: Easy

Choice C is correct because this is the result when you distribute and combine like terms. After distributing, you will get the expression $3b - b^2 - 6b - 24$. Rearranging and collecting like terms will result in the expression $-b^2 - 3b - 24$.

Choice A is incorrect because this results from a math error when distributing. **Choice B** is incorrect because this results from a math error when distributing. **Choice D** is incorrect because this results from a math error when distributing.

35.

Category: PHM
Skill: Evaluation of functions, domain and range |
Level: Medium

Choice B is correct because to determine which values of x will result in a negative, plug-in numbers starting with 1 to evaluate if they are positive or negative. For $f(1)$ and $f(2)$, the result is still positive. Once you reach $f(3)$, the result becomes negative which would indicate x-values of 3-20 will result in negative $f(x)$ values.

Choice A is incorrect because there are more values in the domain that result in negative values for $f(x)$. **Choice C** is incorrect because there are 2 values in the domain that result in positive values for $f(x)$. **Choice D** is incorrect because there are values in the domain that result in positive values for $f(x)$.

36.

Category: IES & Modeling
Skill: Evaluation of functions, domain and range |
Level: Easy

Choice C is correct because you can plug in −3 for x to solve. This will result in the function equating $-2(-3)^3 + 4(-3)^2$ which simplifies to equal 90.

Choice A is incorrect because this results from a math error when simplifying. **Choice B** is incorrect because this results from a math error when simplifying. **Choice D** is incorrect because this results from a math error when simplifying.

37.

Category: PHM
Skill: Evaluation of functions, domain and range |
Level: Medium

Choice C is correct because the relationship should follow the form $y = mx + b$, where m is the slope or rate of change and b is the y-intercept or starting point. Based on the given word problem, the starting value of the depth of snow will be 5 inches and the rate of change will be 1.25 which makes the full expression $y = 1.25x + 5$.

Choice A is incorrect because it does not match the given relationship between variables. **Choice B** is incorrect because it does not match the given relationship between variables. **Choice D** is incorrect because it does not match the given relationship between variables.

38.

Category: IES & Modeling
Skill: Evaluation of functions, domain and range |
Level: Medium

Choice B is correct because you can solve the expression by removing the absolute value sign and solving for the two possible cases. If $x \geq 0$, the equation would be $x^2 - 6x - 7 = 0$ which factors to be $(x - 7)(x + 1) = 0$. In this instance, the solution would be $x = 7$, since x cannot be −1 due to the constraint that $x \geq 0$.
If $x < 0$, the equation would be $x^2 + 6x - 7 = 0$, which would factor to be $(x - 1)(x + 7) = 0$. The solution to this set-up is $x = -7$.

Choice A is incorrect because this does not account for all solutions. **Choice C** is incorrect because this includes solutions outside the answer. **Choice D** is incorrect because this includes solutions outside the answer.

39.

Category: IES
Skill: Evaluation of functions, domain and range |
Level: Hard

Choice B is correct because you need to find a common denominator to combine the two fractions. The common denominator will be $x(x + 2)$. This would mean that the first expression should be multiplied by $\frac{x}{x}$ to get $\frac{x}{x(x+2)}$ and the second expression should be multiplied by $\frac{x+2}{x+2}$ to get $\frac{x+2}{x(x+2)}$. Now add together $\frac{x}{x(x+2)} + \frac{x+2}{x(x+2)}$ to get $\frac{2x+2}{x(x+2)}$.

Choice A is incorrect because this does not account for finding a common denominator and instead is just the two expressions multiplied. **Choice C** is incorrect because this results from an incorrect simplification of terms. **Choice D** is incorrect because this results from an incorrect simplification of terms.

40.

Category: PHM
Skill: Evaluation of functions, domain and range |
Level: Medium

Choice D is correct because the maximum number of products will occur when the expression equals $f(x) = x^2 - 45$ and $x = 12$. Plugging this into the expression will yield $f(12) = 12^2 - 45 = 99$.

Choice A is incorrect because this is not the largest y-value possible. **Choice B** is incorrect because this is not the largest y-value possible. **Choice C** is incorrect because this is not the largest y-value possible.

41.

Category: IES
Skill: Evaluation of functions, domain and range |
Level: Hard

Choice D is correct because the horizontal asymptote of a function is found by comparing the powers of the numerator and denominator and should also take the form of a $y = a$ expression where a is a constant. Since the highest power of the numerator and the denominator is 2, then the ratio of the coefficients of the highest power will give you the value of the asymptote. In this case that would be 2.

Choice A is incorrect because this would be a vertical asymptote. **Choice B** is incorrect because this would be a vertical asymptote. **Choice C** is incorrect because this would be the horizontal asymptote if the power of the denominator was greater than the numerator.

42.

Category: PHM & Modeling
Skill: Evaluation of functions, domain and range
Level: Easy

Choice B is correct because the obtained answer is 6.

Substitute $x = -1$ into the function.

$$f(x) = x^2 + 3x + 8$$
$$f(-1) = (-1)2 + 3(-1) + 8$$
$$f(-1) = 1-3 + 8$$
$$f(-1) = 9-3$$
$$f(-1) = 6$$

Hence, the answer is Choice B.

Choice A is incorrect because 4 is less than the obtained answer. **Choice C** is incorrect because 7 is greater than the obtained answer. **Choice D** is incorrect because 8 is greater than the obtained answer.

43.

Category: PHM
Skill: Evaluation of functions, domain and range |
Level: Easy

Choice C is correct because to find the average speed between those two times, use the formula $\frac{\Delta d}{\Delta t}$. For $t = 4$ to $t = 8$, this will be $\frac{15-0}{8-4}$. This will simplify to be $\frac{15}{4}$ or 3.75 meters per second.

Choice A is incorrect because this results from a calculation error. **Choice B** is incorrect because this results from a calculation error. **Choice D** is incorrect because this results from a calculation error.

44.

Category: PHM
Skill: Evaluation of functions, domain and range |
Level: Hard

Choice A is correct because the range of a rational function is found by simplifying the expression and setting the denominator equal to 0. Factoring the denominator will result in the expression $(x + 4)(x - 6)$. The factor $(x + 4)$ cancels out with the numerator so the remaining factor $x - 6$ can be set equal to 0 to determine that the domain cannot be equal to 6. To express this in interval notation use the union statement $(-\infty, 6) \cup (6, \infty)$.

Choice B is incorrect because this includes the canceled out value of 4. **Choice C** is incorrect because this uses the numerator to evaluate the domain. **Choice D** is incorrect because this uses the numerator to evaluate the domain.

45.

Category: PHM
Skill: Evaluation of functions, domain and range |
Level: Medium

Choice A is correct because the restriction on the domain will result from evaluating when the denominator will equal 0. To determine this, first factor the denominator using the difference of squares to get $(x + 4)(x - 4)$. The factor $(x - 4)$ will cancel with the numerator so the only factor that restricts the domain is $x + 4$. Setting this equal to zero will find the value of x that is not possible: $x + 4 = 0$ will solve to be $x = -4$.

Choice B is incorrect because this value is within the domain. **Choice C** is incorrect because this value is within the domain. **Choice D** is incorrect because this value is within the domain because it is canceled out by the numerator.

46.

Category: PHM
Skill: System of functions | **Level:** Medium

Choice C is correct because the composite function $-f(g(x))$ can be simplified to equal $-\frac{1}{16}$. To solve, plug-in $g(x)$ into x in the function $f(x)$ to get $f(-4) = 2^{-4}$. A value to a negative exponent represents the reciprocal which would be $\frac{1}{2^4}$ which is equal to $\frac{1}{16}$. Since there is a negative sign out in front of the composite function, the result will also be negative which equals $-\frac{1}{16}$.

Choice A is incorrect because this does not account for the negative exponent. **Choice B** is incorrect because this is a misinterpretation of the exponent. **Choice D** is incorrect because this would be the result if the exponent was a fraction and not negative.

47.

Category: PHM & Modeling
Skill: System of functions | **Level:** Medium

Choice D is correct because the notation $g(f(x))$ indicates replacement of the variable x within the function $g(x)$ by the function $f(x)$. Plugging $f(x)$ into $g(x)$ will result in $\sqrt{-5x+6}$.

Choice A is incorrect because this is equivalent to $f(g(x))$. **Choice B** is incorrect because this is an incorrect understanding of how to find $f(g(x))$. **Choice C** is incorrect because this would incorrectly result from the entire function under the square being multiplied by $f(x)$.

48.

Category: PHM
Skill: System of functions | **Level:** Easy

Choice C is correct because the obtained answer is 12.
Given:

$$f(x)=x^2+3x+12 \text{ and } g(x)=-(3x-15)$$

Find $(f \circ g)(5)$.

$$(f \circ g)(x)=(-3x+15)^2+3(-3x+15)+12$$

$$(f \circ g)(x)=9x^2-90x+225-9x+45+12$$

$$(f \circ g)(x)=9x^2-99x+282$$

$$(f \circ g)(5)=9(5)^2-99(5)+282$$

$$(f \circ g)(5)=12$$

Choice A is incorrect because −12 is less than the obtained answer. **Choice B** is incorrect because −8 is less than the obtained answer. **Choice D** is incorrect because 15 is greater than the obtained answer.

49.

Category: PHM
Skill: System of functions | **Level:** Medium

Choice A is correct because to find $f(g(x))$, plug $g(x)$ into $f(x)$ and simplify. When $g(x)$ is plugged into $f(x)$ the result is $f(g(x)) = (x - 6)^2 + 5$. This can be expanded by distributing the expression $(x - 6)^2$ which yields $f(x) = x^2 - 12x + 36 + 5$ which simplifies to $x^2 - 12x + 41$.

Choice B is incorrect because this would not account for the 5 added to the expression in $f(x)$. **Choice C** is incorrect because this results from a math error when simplifying. **Choice D** is incorrect because this is the result of $g(f(x))$.

50.

Category: PHM
Skill: System of functions | **Level:** Easy

Choice B is correct because to find $f(g(x))$, plug $g(x)$ into $f(x)$ as x. This will result in the equation $f(g(x)) = 4 + 8$, which simplifies to be 12.

Choice A is incorrect because this results from a calculation error. **Choice C** is incorrect because this results from a calculation error. **Choice D** is incorrect because this results from a calculation error.

51.

Category: IES & Modeling
Skill: System of functions | **Level:** Medium

Choice A is correct because to find where the composite function is equal to 0, first substitute in $g(x)$ for x in the function $f(x)$. This will yield $f(g(x)) = (x - 2)^2 - 9$ which can then be expanded through distribution to be $f(g(x)) = x^2 - 4x - 5$. Setting the expression equal to 0 and factoring will yield $0 = (x - 5)(x + 1)$. To determine the solution, set each factor equal to 0 to get $x - 5 = 0$ and $x + 1 = 0$. Solving both will get you $x = 5$ and $x = -1$.

Choice B is incorrect because this would be the x-intercepts for $f(x)$ and $g(x)$ separately. **Choice C** is incorrect because these are not the x-intercepts of the composite function. **Choice D** is incorrect because these are not the x-intercepts of the composite function.

52.

Category: IES & Modeling
Skill: System of functions | **Level:** Easy

Choice D is correct because to find $f(g(x))$, plug $g(x)$ for x in the expression $f(x)$. This would result in $f(g(x)) = 8(6) - 9$ which simplifies to be 39.

Choice A is incorrect because this results from a calculation error. **Choice B** is incorrect because this results from a calculation error. **Choice C** is incorrect because this results from a calculation error.

53.

Category: IES
Skill: System of functions | **Level:** Medium

Choice C is correct because to evaluate b, plug $g(x)$ into x in the function $f(x)$ and set equal to the provided answer of $-6x + 13$. This would result in $-6x + 13 = 3(-2x + b) + 4$. Simplify the right-hand side to get $-6x + 13 = -6x + 3b + 4$. Then combine like terms to solve for b by first removing $-6x$ from both sides and subtractive over 4. This will yield $9 = 3b$. Divide both sides by 3 to get $b = 3$.

Choice A is incorrect because this would not result in the given composite function. **Choice B** is incorrect because this would not result in the given composite function. **Choice D** is incorrect because this would not result in the given composite function.

54.

Category: IES
Skill: System of functions | **Level:** Hard

Choice C is correct because $h(5)$ can be found by subtracting the two expressions and then plugging in 2. To subtract $f(x) - g(x)$, write out the equations as $x^2 + 8x - 13 - (x^2 - 6x + 7)$ and distribute the negative to get $x^2 + 8x - 13 - x^2 + 6x - 7$. Combine like terms to determine the function $h(x) = 14x - 20$. Plug in 5 to get $h(5) = 14(5) - 20 = 50$.

Choice A is incorrect because this results from a math error when subtracting the functions. **Choice B** is incorrect because this results from a math error when simplifying. **Choice D** is incorrect because this results from a math error when simplifying.

55.

Category: IES
Skill: System of functions | **Level:** Easy

Choice B is correct because you can input $f(x)$ into itself twice to solve. The first input would be equal to $f(f(x))$ which equals $(x + 5) + 5$ and simplifies to be $x + 10$. The second input would be $f(f(f(x)))$ and that would equal $(x + 10) + 5$ which simplifies to be $x + 15$.

Choice A is incorrect because this would just be the value of $f(f(x))$. **Choice C** is incorrect because this results from an addition error. **Choice D** is incorrect because this results from a miscalculation of the composite function.

56.

Category: IES
Skill: Slope-intercept form of a linear equation |
Level: Medium

Choice C is correct because the slope of the given equation is $\frac{3}{2}$ and a parallel line would have the same slope. To find the slope of the given equation, it needs to be rearranged into slope-intercept form. To do this, first subtract $3x$ and then divide by -2 to get $y = \frac{3}{2}x - 4$.

Choice A is incorrect because this is the y-intercept of the given function. **Choice B** is incorrect because this is the slope of the line perpendicular to the equation. **Choice D** is incorrect because this would be based on a misinterpretation of the slope.

57.

Category: IES
Skill: Slope-intercept form of a linear equation |
Level: Hard

Choice B is correct because the expression can be initially written as $y = \$50(10) + \$40(x - 10)$. Simplifying and distributing would result in the expression $y = 500 + 40x - 400$, which then becomes $y = 40x + 100$.

Choice A is incorrect because it does not account for the first 10 parts costing \$50 each. **Choice C** is incorrect because it incorrectly places 50 as the rate per additional part and identifies the incorrect starting point. **Choice D** is incorrect because it incorrectly places 50 as the rate per additional part and identifies the incorrect starting point.

58.

Category: IES & Modeling
Skill: Slope-intercept form of a linear equation |
Level: Hard

Choice C is correct because if $0 < \frac{a}{b} < 1$ that means $a < b$ since a divided by b would create a fraction. If a is less than b, each of the equations can be evaluated and their slopes compared. For $-bx + ay = c$, the slope-intercept form would be $y = \frac{b}{a}x + \frac{c}{a}$. The slope would be $\frac{b}{a}$ which would be greater than 1 and larger than all other slopes.

Choice A is incorrect because the slope would be $\frac{-a}{b}$ which is less than 1. **Choice B** is incorrect because the slope would be $\frac{a}{b}$ which is less than 1. **Choice D** is incorrect because the slope would be $-\frac{b}{a}$ which is less than 1.

59.

Category: IES & Modeling
Skill: Slope-intercept form of a linear equation |
Level: Easy

Choice C is correct because the given expression is in point-slope form which matches the formula $y - y_1 = m(x - x_1)$. The value m represents the slope which would make the slope of the given expression $\frac{5}{8}$.

Choice A is incorrect because this is the y-value in the point-slope formula. **Choice B** is incorrect because this results from a misunderstanding of the slope. **Choice D** is incorrect because this is the x-value in the point-slope formula.

60.

Category: PHM
Skill: Slope-intercept form of a linear equation |
Level: Medium

Choice A is correct because the slope can be found by finding the difference between two points. Using $t = 2$ and $t = 4$, Pedro walked a total of 360 feet in 2 minutes which would equal 180 feet in 1 minute. Then plug in another point to determine the reference starting point. This can be found with $t = 6$ to get $1105 = 180(6) + b$ which results in $b = 25$. This matches with the equation $d = 180t + 25$.

Choice B is incorrect because it does not match with the given information. **Choice C** is incorrect because it does not match with the given information. **Choice D** is incorrect because it does not match with the given information.

61.

Category: PHM & Modeling
Skill: Slope-intercept form of a linear equation |
Level: Hard

Choice A is correct because the slope of the graph can be determined by using the given points and plugging into the slope formula for rise over run of $\frac{y_2 - y_1}{x_2 - x_1}$.

Plugging in the given points of (0, –3) and (6, 0) will yield $\frac{0-(-3)}{6-0} = \frac{3}{6} = \frac{1}{2}$. The slope of a line that is perpendicular to this would be the negative reciprocal. The negative reciprocal of $\frac{1}{2}$ is –2.

Choice B is incorrect because this is not the negative reciprocal of the slope. **Choice C** is incorrect because this is the slope of the given graph. **Choice D** is incorrect because this is not the negative reciprocal of the slope.

62.

Category: IES & Modeling
Skill: Slope-intercept form of a linear equation |
Level: Easy

Choice D is correct because the obtained answer is $y = 3x + 5$ and its graph is:

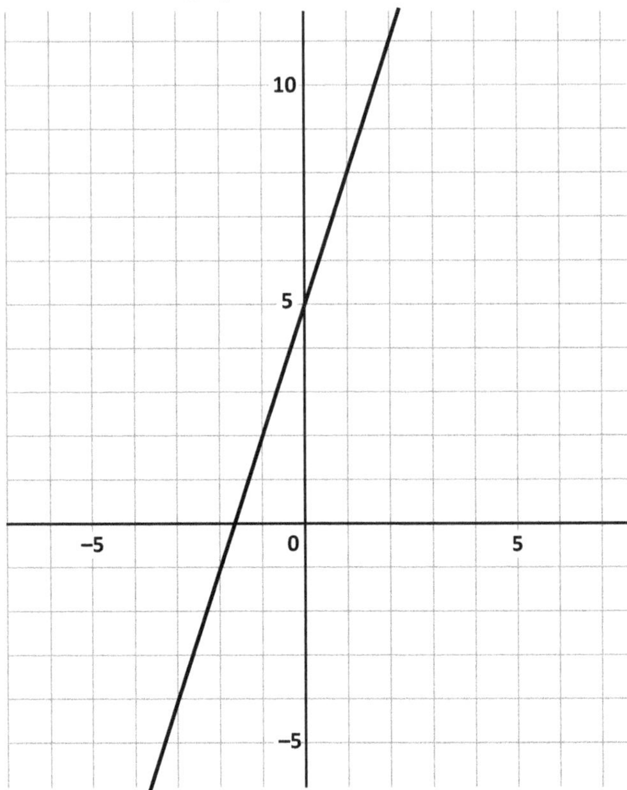

Find the slope and the y-intercept of the given points.

$$m = \frac{y_2 - y_1}{x_2 - x_1} = \frac{-15}{-5} = 3$$

Use the point (0, 5) to find the y-intercept.

$$y = mx + b$$
$$5 = 3(0) + b$$
$$5 = b$$

Hence, the equation of the line is $y = 3x + 5$.
For the graph, plot points $(0,5)$ *and* $(-5,-10)$ and connect.

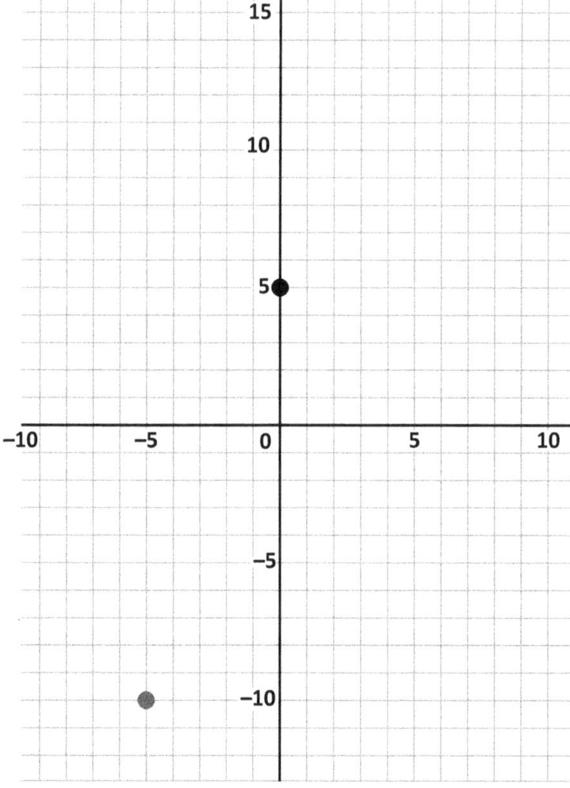

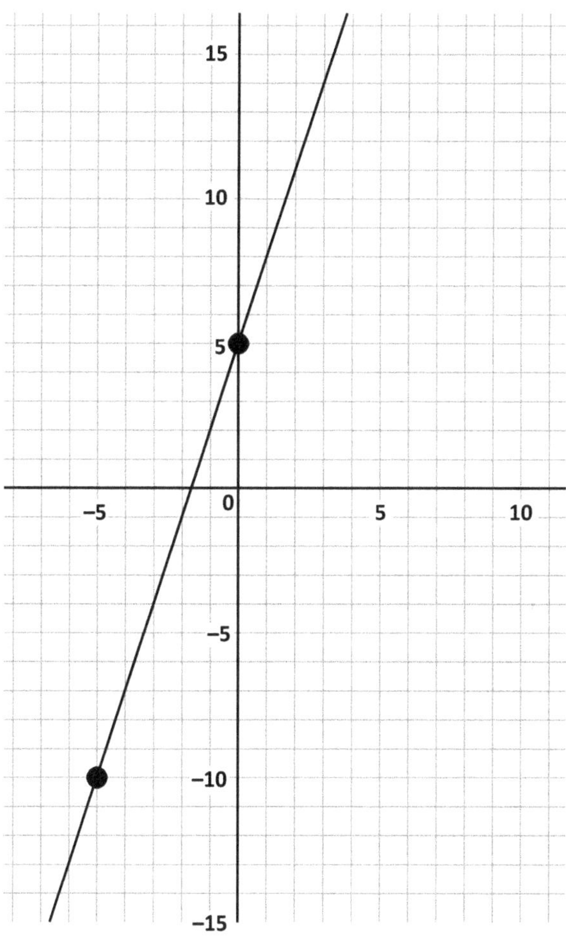

Choice A is incorrect because both the equation and the graph are incorrect. **Choice B** is incorrect because both the equation and the graph are incorrect. **Choice C** is incorrect because given graph does not represent the given

63.

Category: PHM
Skill: Slope-intercept form of a linear equation |
Level: Medium

Choice A is correct. In slope-intercept form $3x - 5y = 4$ is $y = \frac{3}{5}x - \frac{4}{5}$ so, the slope is $m = \frac{3}{5}$.
A perpendicular line's slope is the negative reciprocal so, $m = -\frac{5}{3}$

Choice B is incorrect. This is the y-intercept of the given line **Choice C** is incorrect. This is the slope of the given line. **Choice D** is incorrect. This only takes the reciprocal of the slope of the given line.

64.

Category: PHM
Skill: Slope-intercept form of a linear equation |
Level: Easy

Choice B is correct because the standard form of a linear relationship will be in slope intercept form which is $y = mx + b$. The slope, or rate of change, is represented by m and the y-intercept, or starting value, is represented by b. Using the information from the word problem, the resulting equation will be $c = 0.05p + 25$.

Choice A is incorrect because this is the incorrect relationship between variables. **Choice C** is incorrect because this is the incorrect relationship between variables. **Choice D** is incorrect because this is the incorrect relationship between variables.

65.

Category: PHM and Modeling
Skill: Slope-intercept form of a linear equation |
Level: Hard

Choice B is correct because the obtained answer is 4.

Take two points from the line shown in the graph.

Find the slope of the line through the points (1, 2) and (–3, –6).

$$m = \frac{y_2 - y_1}{x_2 - x_1} = \frac{-6-2}{-3-1} = \frac{-8}{-4} = 2$$

The line through the points (3,8) and (x, 10) has a slope parallel to the slope of the line through the points (1, 2) and (–3, –6).

Parallel slope : 2

$$y = mx + b$$
$$8 = 2(3) + b$$
$$8 = 6 + b$$
$$2 = b$$
$$y = mx + b$$
$$10 = 2x + 2$$
$$10 - 2 = 2x$$
$$8 = 2x$$
$$4 = x$$

Hence, the answer is Choice B.

Choice A is incorrect because 3 is less than the obtained value of x. **Choice C** is incorrect because 8 is greater than the obtained value of x. **Choice D** is incorrect because 9 is greater than the obtained value of x.

66.

Category: IES
Skill: Slope-intercept form of a linear equation |
Level: Easy

Choice A is correct because the question is asking you to rearrange the equation in terms of y. To do this, first add $4x$ and then divide by 24. This will yield $y = \frac{1}{6}x + \frac{1}{4}$ when simplified.

Choice B is incorrect because this is not the correct slope or y-intercept. **Choice C** is incorrect because this is not the correct slope or y-intercept. **Choice D** is incorrect because this forgets to divide 16 by 24 as well.

67.

Category: PHM & Modeling
Skill: Slope-intercept form of a linear equation |
Level: Easy

Choice C is correct because the answers are given in slope-intercept form which follows the formula $v = mt + b$, where v = volume of water remaining (in gallons), t is time in minutes, m is the rate of change and b is the starting value. According to the given problem, the rate of change is –9 gallons per minute and the starting value is 50 gallons. These key points match with the equation $v = -9t + 50$.

Choice A is incorrect because it has a positive slope and a negative y-intercept. **Choice B** is incorrect because it mixes up the slope and y-intercept. **Choice D** is incorrect because it does not include a y-intercept.

68.

Category: IES
Skill: Slope-intercept form of a linear equation |
Level: Medium

Choice A is correct because to identify the slope of the line, the equation must be rewritten in slope-intercept form. To do this, first subtract $-4x$ from both sides to get $-10y = -4x - 15$. Then divide both sides by -10 to get $y = \frac{2}{5}x + \frac{3}{2}$. The slope of this function is $\frac{2}{5}$.

Choice B is incorrect because this is the y-intercept, not the slope. **Choice C** is incorrect because this is the coefficient in front of x before the equation is put into the correct form. **Choice D** is incorrect because this is the coefficient in front of y which does not represent the slope.

69.

Category: PHM
Skill: Slope-intercept form of a linear equation |
Level: Medium

Choice C is correct because plugging in the first two points of (1, 19) and (2, 22) will match with this equation. If 1 is plugged in for t, then the result would be $d = 3(1) + 16$ which simplifies to be $d = 19$. If 2 is plugged in for t, then the result would be $d = 3(2) + 16$ which simplifies to be $d = 22$.

Choice A is incorrect because this function does not work with all given data points. **Choice B** is incorrect because this function does not work with all given data points. **Choice D** is incorrect because this function does not work with all given data points.

70.

Category: PHM
Skill: Slope-intercept form of a linear equation |
Level: Medium

Choice D is correct.
In slope intercept form $3x + 4y = -5$ is

$$3x + 4y = -5$$
$$4y = -5 - 3x$$
$$y = -\frac{3}{4}x - \frac{5}{4}$$

So, the slope of the line is $m = -\frac{3}{4}$. The slope of the perpendicular line has a slope that is the negative or opposite reciprocal so, $m = \frac{4}{3}$ for the perpendicular line.

Choice A is incorrect. This may result from conceptual error. **Choice B** is incorrect. This is the *y*-intercept of the line. **Choice C** is incorrect. This is the slope of the line.

71.

Category: IES
Skill: Slope-intercept form of a linear equation |
Level: Medium

Choice B is correct because the given formula can be rearranged into slope-intercept form to identify its slope. Subtract 6*x* and divide by 8 to get $y = \frac{-3}{4}x + \frac{1}{8}$.

The slope of this expression is $\frac{-3}{4}$ and a parallel line would have the same slope.

Choice A is incorrect because this does not match the slope of the given expression. **Choice C** is incorrect because this does not match the slope of the given expression. **Choice D** is incorrect because this is the slope of a perpendicular line.

72.

Category: PHM
Skill: Slope-intercept form of a linear equation |
Level: Medium

Choice B is correct because to find the slope with the given coordinates, use the expression for slope of $\frac{y_2 - y_1}{x_2 - x_1}$. Plugging in the given information will yield

$\frac{1-7}{7-4} = \frac{-6}{3} = -2$. This is a negative slope.

Choice A is incorrect because the slope of the line is negative. **Choice C** is incorrect because the slope of the line is negative. **Choice D** is incorrect because the slope of the line is negative.

73.

Category: PHM
Skill: Slope-intercept form of a linear equation |
Level: Easy

Choice D is correct because to find the slope of a line based on two points, use the expression $\frac{y_2 - y_1}{x_2 - x_1}$.

Plugging into this expression will yield $\frac{6-(-3)}{8-5}$ which simplifies to be $\frac{9}{3}$ which is 3.

Choice A is incorrect because the slope is not negative. **Choice B** is incorrect because this would be based on dividing change in *x* by change in *y*. **Choice C** is incorrect because this is less than the actual slope.

74.

Category: PHM
Skill: Slope-intercept form of a linear equation |
Level: Medium

Choice A is correct because the given equations slope can be found by changing it into slope-intercept form. To do this, subtract 5x and divide by −7 to get $y = \frac{5}{7}x - 2$. The slope of this line is $\frac{5}{7}$. Perpendicular lines have slopes that are negative reciprocals of each other. The negative reciprocal of $\frac{5}{7}$ is $-\frac{7}{5}$.

Choice B is incorrect because this results from a misunderstanding of how to find slope. **Choice C** is incorrect because this is the slope of the given equation, not the perpendicular slope. **Choice D** is incorrect because this would be the coefficient in front of *x* before rearranging into slope-intercept form.

75.

Category: PHM
Skill: Slope-intercept form of a linear equation |
Level: Easy

Choice C is correct. Convert the equation from standard form to slope intercept form, $y = mx + b$ to determine the slope *m*.

$$4x + 5y = -10$$
$$5y = -4x - 10$$
$$y = -\frac{4}{5}x - 2$$
$$\text{So, } m = -\frac{4}{5}.$$

Choice A is incorrect. This is the negative coefficient of *x*. **Choice B** is incorrect. This may result from conceptual or calculation error. **Choice D** is incorrect. This may result from conceptual or calculation error.

76.

Category: PHM
Skill: Graphed functions | **Level:** Medium

Choice C is correct because the question is asking for the domain of the function. The domain can be found based on analyzing the graph and determining which x values are possible. The least x-value possible is 0 and the greatest x-value possible is 4.

Choice A is incorrect because the x-values of the graph go up to 4. **Choice B** is incorrect because the x-values of the graph do not go into the negatives. **Choice D** is incorrect because the x-values of the graph do not go into the negatives.

77.

Category: IES & Modeling
Skill: Graphed functions | **Level:** Hard

Choice D is correct because to determine the degree of a polynomial function based on the graph, you can look at how many times the function crosses or touches the x-axis. The graph passes through the x-axis once in the negative x-value and once in the positive x-values. It then touches, then bounces off the x-axis at another point in the negatives. A bounce off the x-axis indicates a double zero at that value. Therefore, there are a total of 4 zeros which would make this a fourth degree polynomial.

Choice A is incorrect because the given graph has a total of four zeros. **Choice B** is incorrect because the given graph has a total of four zeros. **Choice C** is incorrect because the given graph has a total of four zeros.

78.

Category: PHM
Skill: Graphed functions | **Level:** Easy

Choice D is correct. Rotating the graph around the origin produces the original graph of the function. The graph of a function that has origin symmetry is a combination of both types of reflections. (B looks correct, but that is not the domain, it is the range.)

Choice A is incorrect. The graph has symmetry about the origin not the x-axis. **Choice B** is incorrect. This is not the domain, it is the range. **Choice C** is incorrect. The graph has symmetry about the origin not the y-axis.

79.

Category: PHM
Skill: Graphed functions | **Level:** Medium

Choice C is correct because a reflection over a line will place the point symmetrically over the line. This means the new location of the point will have the same y-coordinate, but a new x-coordinate that is proportionally located. The graph below shows the point is currently located 3 away from the line $x = 5$. This means when reflected, it will also be 3 away on the other side of the line. To find this, add 3 to the x-value of 5 to get a new x-value placement at 8. The final location of coordinate B will be at (8, 4)

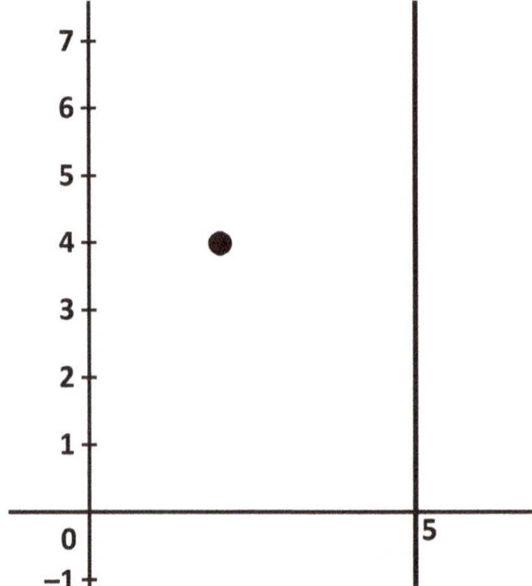

Choice A is incorrect because this would be a reflection over a horizontal line. **Choice B** is incorrect because this would be a translation of 5 right which is not the same as a reflection. **Choice D** is incorrect because this would be a reflection over a horizontal line.

80.

Category: PHM & Modeling
Skill: Graphed functions | **Level:** Hard

Choice A is correct because the equation of an ellipse is typically written in the standard form of $\frac{(x-h)^2}{a^2} + \frac{(y-k)^2}{b^2} = 1$. From the given graph, it can be determined that the center of the ellipse would be in the first quadrant which would make (h, k) positive. Then it would appear that the x-axis is the major axis because the radius in the horizontal direction is larger than the vertical radius. Choice A matches all of these points with a center at (1, 3) and a major axis radius of 5 and a minor axis radius of 4.

Choice B is incorrect because the center would be located at (-1, -3) which is incorrect based on the graph. **Choice C** is incorrect because the major and minor axis are switched. **Choice D** is incorrect because the major and minor axis radii should be squared.

81.

Category: PHM
Skill: Graphed functions | **Level:** Easy

Choice B is correct. The maximum for A is 5. The maximum for B is 7. The maximum for C is 3. The maximum for D is 4.

Choice A is incorrect. 7 is greater than 5. **Choice C** is incorrect. 7 is greater than 3. **Choice D** is incorrect. 7 is greater than 4.

82.

Category: IES & Modeling
Skill: Graphed functions | **Level:** Easy

Choice D is correct because the equation for profit can be found to be $y = 1.5x - 7.50$ since Margo makes $1.50 per brownie and she must take away her cost of $7.50 before she makes a profit. This matches with choice D, since this equation would have a x-intercept at $x = 5$ which shows her breakeven point.

Choice A is incorrect because it does not correctly match the values in the scenario. **Choice B** is incorrect because it does not correctly match the values in the scenario. **Choice C** is incorrect because it does not correctly match the values in the scenario.

83.

Category: PHM
Skill: Graphed functions | **Level:** Easy

Choice B is correct because $f(3)$ would be the value of the y-coordinate from the graph that matches the x-coordinate of 3. This would be 1 based on the graph.

Choice A is incorrect because this does not match the graph. **Choice C** is incorrect because this does not match the graph. **Choice D** is incorrect because this does not match the graph.

84.

Category: IES & Modeling
Skill: Graphed functions | **Level:** Medium

Choice A is correct because the current center of the circle sits at (−4, 2). If the circle was to be shifted right 3 and down 4, the center would move the same. This would mean the new location of the center of the circle would be located at (−4 + 3, 2 − 4) which would be (−1. −2).

Choice B is incorrect because this moves the center right 4 and down 3. **Choice C** is incorrect because this is the wrong transformation of the center. **Choice D** is incorrect because this is the wrong transformation of the center.

85.

Category: PHM
Skill: Graphed functions | **Level:** Medium

Choice B is correct because the center of the circle can be determined to be (3, −5) and the radius is 4. Utilizing the standard form of the equation of a circle, $(x - h)^2 + (y - k)^2 = r^2$, then the equation can be determined to be $(x - 3)^2 + (y + 5)^2 = 16$.

Choice A is incorrect because it has the wrong coordinates for the center of the circle. **Choice C** is incorrect because it has the wrong radius of the circle. **Choice D** is incorrect because it has the wrong center and radius.

86.

Category: IES & Modeling
Skill: Graphed functions | **Level:** Easy

Choice C is correct because the y-intercept should be positive and the slope should be positive as well. The only graph with both of these characteristics is **Choice C.**

Choice A is incorrect because the slope is negative. **Choice B** is incorrect because the slope and y-intercept is negative. **Choice D** is incorrect because the y-intercept is negative.

87.

Category: PHM & Modeling
Skill: Graphed functions | **Level:** Easy

Choice A is correct. The y-coordinate for g minus the y-coordinate for f must be 9 for the corresponding points on f and g that have the same x-coordinate. Now,

$$g(-1) - f(-1) = 4 - (-5) = 4 + 5 = 9.$$

Choice B is incorrect because you get, $g(0) - f(0) = 6$.
Choice C is incorrect because you get, $g(2) - f(2) = 0$
Choice D is incorrect because you get, $g(3) - f(3) = -3$.

88.

Category: PHM & Modeling
Skill: Graphed functions | **Level:** Easy

Choice B is correct. The graph of a parabola opens down when a is a negative value. The y-intercept for the graph of a parabola is the value of c. So, $a < 0$ and $c = -4 < 0$. The value for b could be positive, negative, or zero depending on the values for a and c so more information is needed to determine the sign of b.

Choice A is incorrect. This may result from conceptual error. **Choice C** is incorrect. This may result from conceptual error. **Choice D** is incorrect. This may result from conceptual error.

89.

Category: PHM
Skill: Graphed functions | **Level:** Medium

Choice C is correct because a reflection over the y-axis would place the majority of the graph in the first quadrant. The translation upward should also be reflected in the graph and the one that matches best is choice G.

Choice A is incorrect because this is just reflected across the y-axis. **Choice B** is incorrect because this is just a translation upward. **Choice D** is incorrect because this applies the wrong translation.

90.

Category: IES & Modeling
Skill: Graphed functions | **Level:** Easy

Choice A is correct because the graph is defined at all values greater than −1 which means the domain is restricted by $x = -1$.

Choice B is incorrect because 0 is included in the domain of the function. **Choice C** is incorrect because 1 is included in the domain of the function. **Choice D** is incorrect because 2 is included in the domain of the function.

91.

Category: IES & Modeling
Skill: Graphed functions | **Level:** Hard

Choice C is correct because the graph has all of the correct functions and the locations that indicate the correct domain and range of each in the graph.

Choice A is incorrect because it does not match the functions given. **Choice B** is incorrect because it does not match the functions given. **Choice D** is incorrect because it does not match the functions given.

92.

Category: IES
Skill: Graphed functions | **Level:** Easy

Choice C is correct because when a function is shifted up or down, the y-value is manipulated. If the equation is moved down 8, then 8 is subtracted from the original function. This would create the new expression $f(x) = 3x + 6 - 8$ which would simplify to be $f(x) = 3x - 2$.

Choice A is incorrect because this is a manipulation of the x-variable, not the y-variable. **Choice B** is incorrect because this is a manipulation of the x-variable, not the y-variable. **Choice D** is incorrect because this incorrectly moves the function up 8.

93.

Category: IES & Modeling
Skill: Graphed functions | **Level:** Medium

Choice D is correct because all answers are given in vertex form, so it is important to find the vertex form of the equation. To do this, use the vertex form of a quadratic equation which equals $y = a(x - h)^2 + k$. The values h and k represent the vertex or maximum so the equation can be adjusted to be $y = a(x - 4)^2 + 15$. To find the value of a, plug-in the x-intercept of (8, 0). This will result in $0 = a(8 - 4)^2 + 15$. Simplify to get $0 = 16a + 15$. Subtract 15 and divide by 16 on both sides to find that a $= -\frac{15}{16}$. The full equation will therefore be $f(x) = -\frac{15}{16}(x - 4)^2 + 15$.

Choice A is incorrect because this switches the vertex coordinates. **Choice B** is incorrect because this does not account for the given x-intercept. **Choice C** is incorrect because the coefficient should be negative.

94.

Category: PHM
Skill: Graphed functions | **Level:** Medium

Choice C is correct because the maximum value of the graph is when the y-value reaches its greatest value. This occurs at $y = 6$.

Choice A is incorrect because this is the minimum of the graph. **Choice B** is incorrect because this is the midline of the graph. **Choice D** is incorrect because this is greater than the maximum.

95.

Category: PHM
Skill: Graphed functions | **Level:** Easy

Choice A is correct because the given graph has a negative slope and a positive y-intercept at 5. Only Choice A and Choice B have negative slopes, but **Choice A** has a y-intercept at 5.

Choice B is incorrect because it does not have the correct slope or y-intercept. **Choice C** is incorrect because it has a positive slope. **Choice D** is incorrect because it has a positive slope.

96.

Category: PHM & Modeling
Skill: Trigonometric functions | **Level:** Medium

Choice B is correct because the amplitude of a sine function is the average difference between the maximum and minimum points. The maximum of the sine function can be identified to be –1 based on the graph and the minimum is –7. Subtracting these together and dividing by 2 would yield an absolute value of 3 as the average distance.

Choice A is incorrect because the average difference between the maximum and minimum is not 2. **Choice C** is incorrect because the average difference between the maximum and minimum is not 4. **Choice D** is incorrect because the average difference between the maximum and minimum is not 5.

97.

Category: PHM
Skill: Trigonometric functions | **Level:** Hard

Choice B is correct because the given expression is the trigonometric identity that follows the rule $\sin(a + b) = (\sin a)(\cos b) + (\cos a)(\sin b)$. In this scenario a = 30 and $b = 60$, making the complete identity $\sin(30 + 60) = (\sin 30)(\cos 60) + (\cos 30)(\sin 60)$.

Choice A is incorrect because it applies the incorrect relationship. **Choice C** is incorrect because it applies the incorrect relationship. **Choice D** is incorrect because it applies the incorrect relationship.

98.

Category: IES & Modeling
Skill: Trigonometric functions | **Level:** Medium

Choice B is correct because it has the correct amplitude and period to match the graph. The amplitude of the function in the graph is 2 since the maximum is also 2. The period is found by identifying how long the function takes to complete one cycle. In this case, the period is 4Π which means the value of x will be divided by 2 since the period is doubled. These changes best match with the formula

$$y = 2\cos\left(\frac{x}{2}\right).$$

Choice A is incorrect because it does not account for the change in the period of the function. **Choice C** is incorrect because it does not have the correct amplitude or period. **Choice D** is incorrect because it does not have the correct amplitude or period.

99.

Category: PHM
Skill: Trigonometric functions | **Level:** Easy

Choice D is correct because to determine the value of the amplitude of a trigonometric function, you will look at the value in front of the function itself. In this case, there is a 4 in front of the sine function so the amplitude is 4. Alternatively, you can graph the function and determine the maximum of the function to evaluate the amplitude.

Choice A is incorrect because the value in front of the sin expression is not 1. **Choice B** is incorrect because the value in front of the sin expression is not 2. **Choice C** is incorrect because the value in front of the sin expression is not 3.

100.

Category: IES & Modeling
Skill: Trigonometric functions | **Level:** Easy

Choice A is correct because the amplitude of a standard cosine function is always 1 unless there is a coefficient in front of the expression.

Choice B is incorrect because this is larger than the amplitude. **Choice C** is incorrect because this is larger than the amplitude. **Choice D** is incorrect because this is larger than the amplitude.

101.

Category: IES
Skill: Trigonometric functions | **Level:** Easy

Choice B is correct because the amplitude of the given equation is 1.
Given:

$$g(x) = cos\left(\frac{2\pi}{3}x\right) + 1$$

Compare the given equation to the $g(x) = Acos\left(B(x - C)\right) + D$, where A is the amplitude.

$$g(x) = Acos\left(B(x - C)\right) + D$$
$$g(x) = cos\left(\frac{2\pi}{3}x\right) + 1$$

Amplitude: $|A| = 1$

Choice A is incorrect because $\frac{2}{3}$ is not the amplitude of the trigonometric equation. **Choice C** is incorrect because 2 is not the amplitude of the trigonometric equation. **Choice D** is incorrect because 3 is not the amplitude of the trigonometric equation.

102.

Category: IES
Skill: Trigonometric functions | **Level:** Easy

Choice A is correct because the value of the coefficient in front of the trigonometric equation determines the amplitude of the function. In this function, the value is $\frac{1}{4}$ so the amplitude is the same.

Choice B is incorrect because this does not match the given expression's amplitude. **Choice C** is incorrect because this does not match the given expression's amplitude. **Choice D** is incorrect because this does not match the given expression's amplitude.

103.

Category: PHM & Modeling
Skill: Trigonometric functions | **Level:** Easy

Choice D is correct because this is the value of the coefficient in front of the cosine function. The amplitude is always the *a* value in the standard form of $f(x) = a\cos(bx + c) + d$.

Choice A is incorrect because this number represents a horizontal transformation, not the amplitude. **Choice B** is incorrect because this number represents a translation, not the amplitude. **Choice C** is incorrect because this number represents a translation, not the amplitude.

104.

Category: IES
Skill: Trigonometric functions | **Level:** Hard

Choice D is correct because $\sin(2a) = 2\sin(a)\cos(a)$. If $\sin(a) = b$, use substitution to determine that $\sin(2a) = 2b\cos(a)$. You can relate sin and cos through the formula $\sin^2 a + \cos^2 a = 1$ and rearrange to get $\cos(a) = \sqrt{1-sin^2(a)}$. Substitute in b to find $\cos(a) = \sqrt{1-b^2}$. The final solution will therefore be $2b\sqrt{1-b^2}$.

Choice A is incorrect because this would only hold true for certain values of *a* and *b*. **Choice B** is incorrect because this would only hold true for certain values of *a* and *b*. **Choice C** is incorrect because this results from *a* misinterpretation of relationships between a and *b*.

105.

Category: PHM
Skill: Trigonometric functions | **Level:** Easy

Choice D is correct. Using the trigonometric identity $1+\tan^2\theta = \sec^2\theta$, you get,

$$1+\tan^2\theta = \sec^2\theta$$
$$\tan^2\theta = \sec^2\theta - 1$$
$$\sqrt{\tan^2\theta} = \sqrt{\sec^2\theta - 1}$$
$$\tan\theta = \sqrt{\sec^2\theta - 1}$$

Choice A is incorrect. This may result from incorrect operation. **Choice B** is incorrect. This takes the square root of $\sec^2\theta$ and 1 separately in the 3rd line of the solution above. **Choice C** is incorrect. This neglects to take the square root of the 2nd line in the solution above

Chapter 6

Geometry Practice Questions

1.

The equations $y = 4 - \frac{1}{2}(x-2)^2$ and $y = x - 2$ are graphed in the standard (x, y) coordinate plane below. Which of the following is the solution set for the system of the given equations?

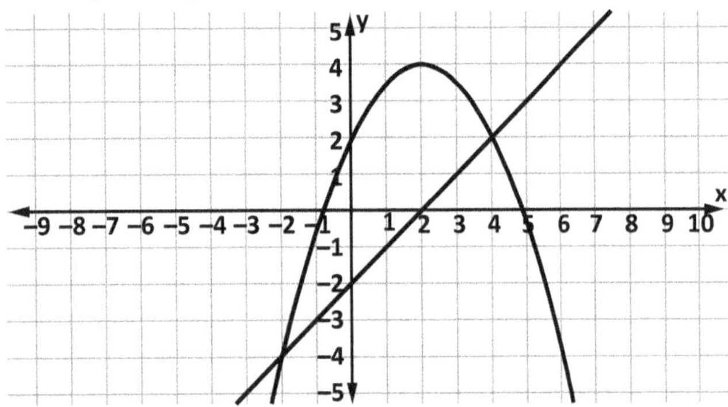

A. (0, −2) and (0, 2)
B. (−2, −4) and (4, 2)
C. (−4, −2) and (2, 4)
D. (−1, 0), (2, 0) and (5, 0)

2.

The midpoint of the line segment joining points (−2, 7) and (4, −3) is:

A. (1, 2)
B. (8, 5)
C. (8, −5)
D. (−1, 2)

3.

The point (2, 5) is shown in the standard (x, y) plane below and its distance from points A, B, C, D *and* E. Which of the following point has a distance the same as that of points A, B, C, D *and* E from point (2, 5)?

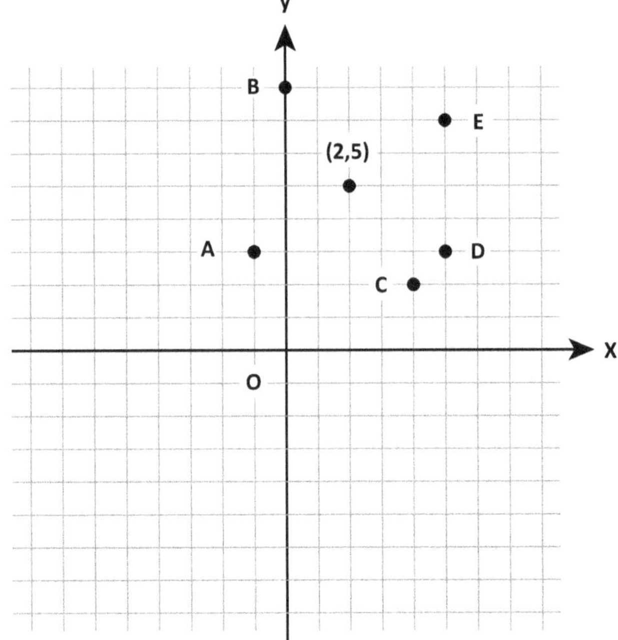

A. (0, 2)
B. (2, 1)
C. (3, 1)
D. (−1, 1)

4.

In the (x, y) plane below, points of the triangle are given. Find the area of the triangle.

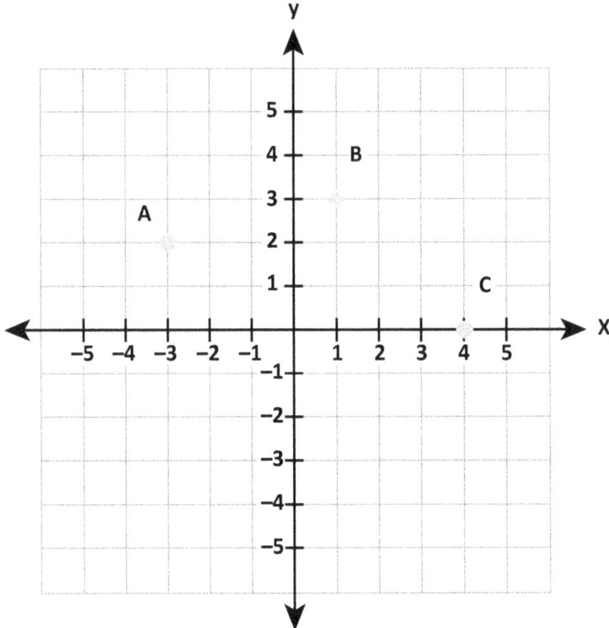

A. 5.5
B. 7.5
C. 7
D. 8

5.

In the figure shown below, $ABCD$ is a rectangle, $EFGH$ is a square, and $\underline{CD}$ is the diameter of a semicircle. Point K is at the origin, $\underline{AB}$ and $\underline{EF}$. Points E and F lie on $\underline{AB}$. The 3 given lengths are in meters.

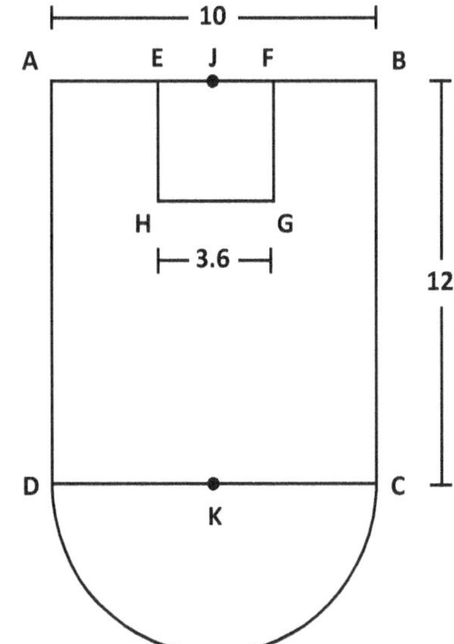

What is the total area of the figure?
A. 152
B. 159
C. 162
D. 182

6.

The graph of a circle in the standard (x, y) coordinate plane that is tangent to the x-axis at 4 and the y-axis at −4 is shown below. Which of the following is the equation of the circle?

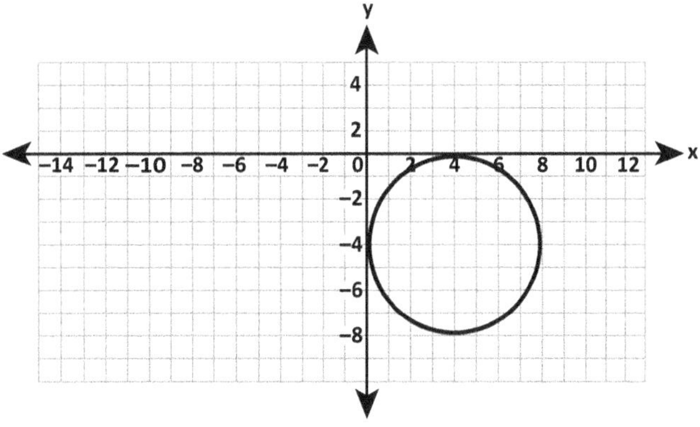

A. $(x - 4)^2 + (y - 4)^2 = 4$
B. $(x - 4)^2 + (y + 4)^2 = 16$
C. $(x + 4)^2 + (y - 4)^2 = 16$
D. $x^2 + y^2 = 4$

7.

As shown in the figure below, Triangle *ABC* has vertices *A*(8, 2), *B*(0, 6), and *C*(−3, 2). Point *C* can be moved along a certain line, with points *A* and *B* remaining stationary, and the area of ΔABC will not change. What is the slope of that line?

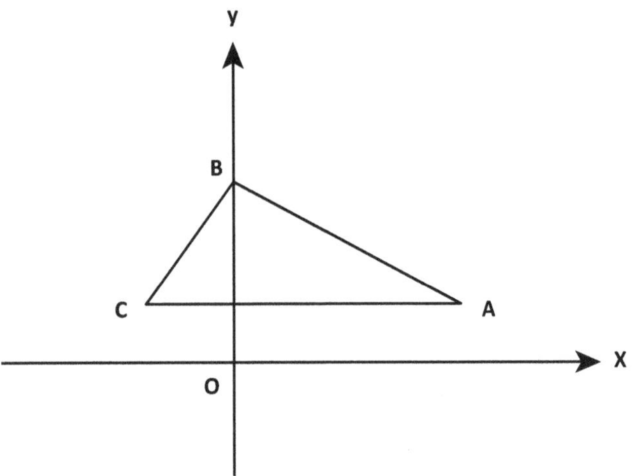

A. $-\frac{1}{2}$
B. 0
C. $\frac{1}{2}$
D. $\frac{4}{3}$

8.

Find the coordinates of the midpoint of the line segment joining *A*(3, −1) and *B*(−2, −5).

A. $\left(\frac{1}{2},3\right)$
B. $\left(-\frac{1}{2},3\right)$
C. $\left(-\frac{1}{2},-3\right)$
D. $\left(\frac{1}{2},-3\right)$

9.

The vertices of a triangle are (−1, −2),(−1, −5),(−4, −5). Find the coordinates of a congruent triangle that lies in Quadrant I.

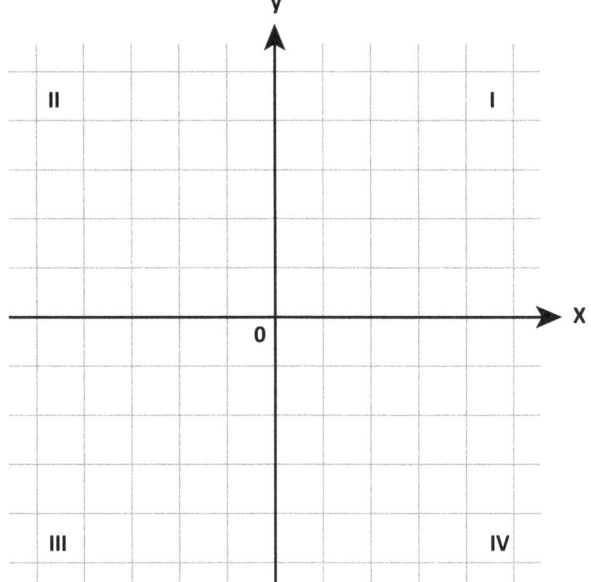

A. (1, 2), (1, 5), (4, 5)
B. (−1, 2), (−1, 5), (−4, 5)
C. (1, −2), (1, 5), (4, −5)
D. (1,−2), (−1, 5), (4, −5)

10.

The vertices of a triangle are (1, 2), (4, 2), (4, 5). When the triangle is graphed in the standard (x, y) coordinate plane below, what percent of the total area of the Triangle lies in Quadrant I?

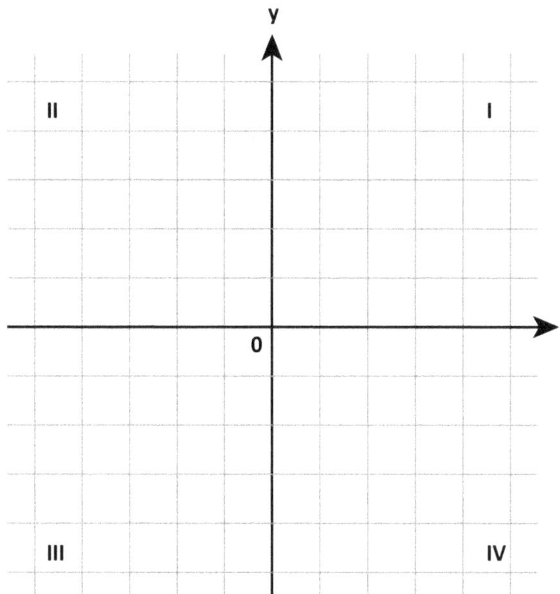

A. 25%
B. 50%
C. 75%
D. 100%

11.

In the figure below, line *a* is parallel to line *b*, and line *c* is a transversal crossing both *a* and *b*. Which of the following lists has 3 angles equal?

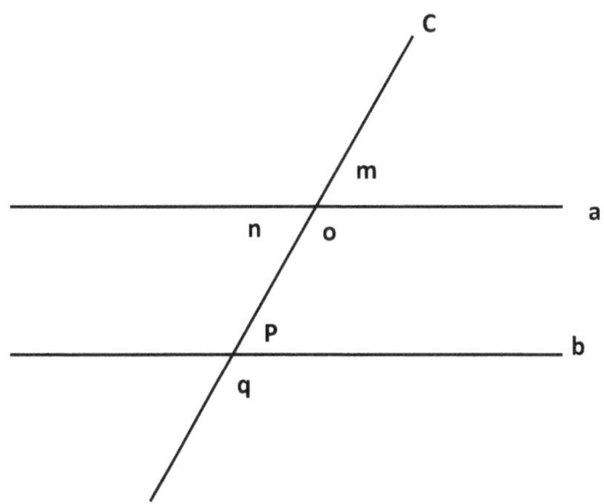

A. $\angle n, \angle p, \angle q$
B. $\angle n, \angle o, \angle q$
C. $\angle m, \angle p, \angle q$
D. $\angle m, \angle n, \angle p$

12.

In the figure below, $m\angle BOC = 125^\circ$, and $m\angle DOC = d + 13^\circ$. Which of the following represents the expression for the measure of angle *BOD*?

A. $112^\circ + d$
B. $112^\circ - d$
C. $138^\circ + d$
D. $d - 112^\circ$

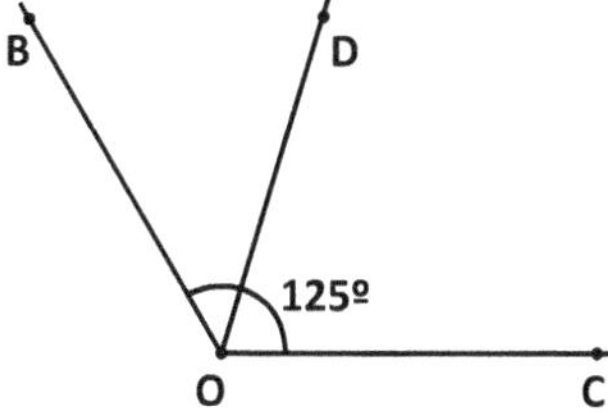

13.

Find the measure of $\angle B$ if $\angle BCD$ is an obtuse angle.

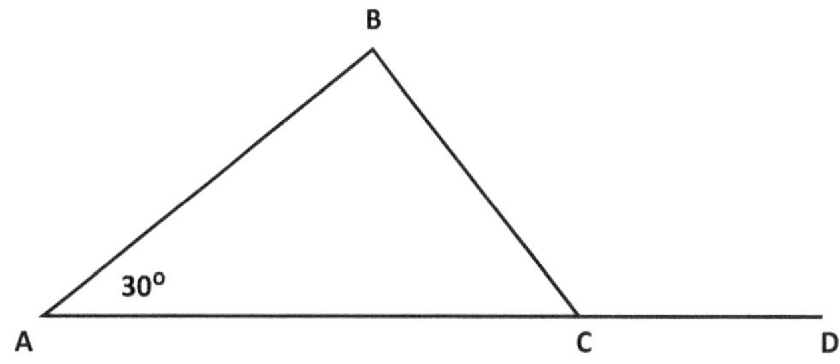

A. $0 < B < 90°$
B. $30 < B < 120°$
C. $60 < B < 150°$
D. $60 < B < 180°$

14.

Which of the following statements MUST be true?

I. $\angle A \simeq \angle D$
II. $\angle A \simeq \angle E$
III. $\angle C \simeq \angle F$

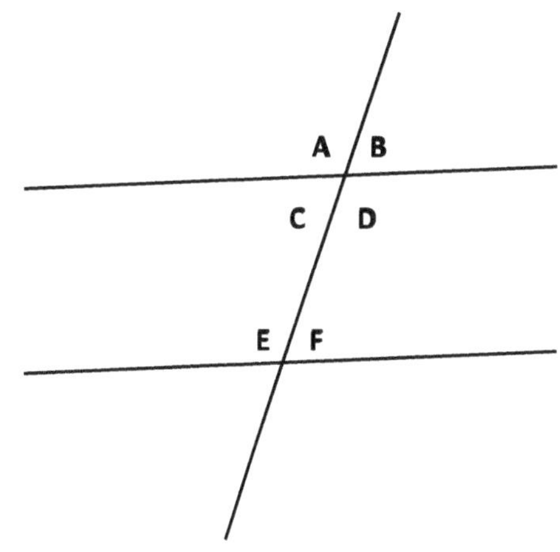

A. I only
B. II only
C. I and II only
D. I, II and III

15.

The points with coordinates $(-5,0)$, $(5q^2, 10q)$ *and* $(5p^2, 10q)$ are collinear. What is the value of pq where $p \neq q$?

A. $-p^2$
B. p^2
C. q^2
D. $-q^2$

16.

What is the measure of the following angle?

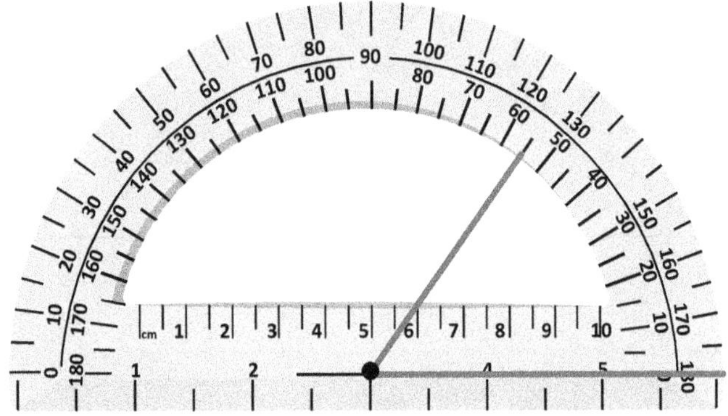

A. 55°
B. 65°
C. 125°
D. 130°

17.

The measure of angle T is

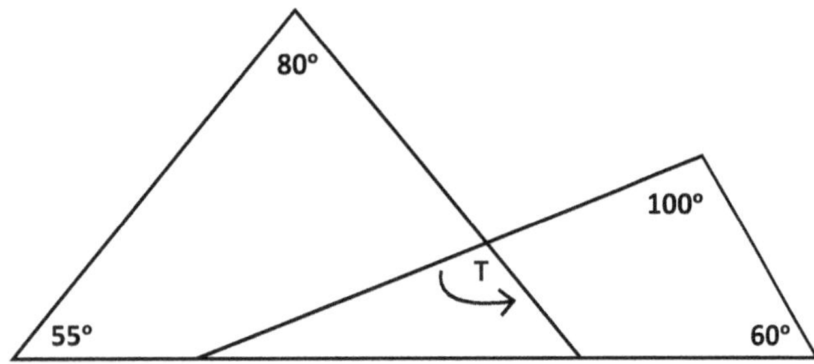

A. 95°
B. 105°
C. 115°
D. 125°

18.

Which line could be parallel to $4x - 4y = 4$?

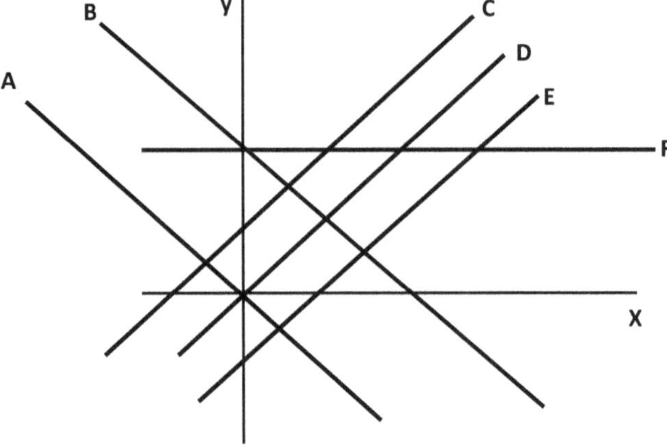

A. C, D
B. C, D, E
C. F
D. A, B

19.

Point P divides the line segment joining $R(-1,3)$ and $S(9,8)$ in ratio $k:1$. If P lies on the line $x - y + 2 = 0$, then value of k is:

A. $\frac{1}{3}$
B. $\frac{1}{2}$
C. $\frac{2}{3}$
D. $\frac{3}{2}$

20.

Convert 810° to radians.

A. $\frac{9}{2}\pi$
B. $\frac{8}{2}\pi$
C. 6π
D. 9π

21.

In triangle LMN, find the length of altitude of $\overline{LO}$ if the given vertices are $L(1, 3)$, $M(4, 5)$, $N(6, 2)$.

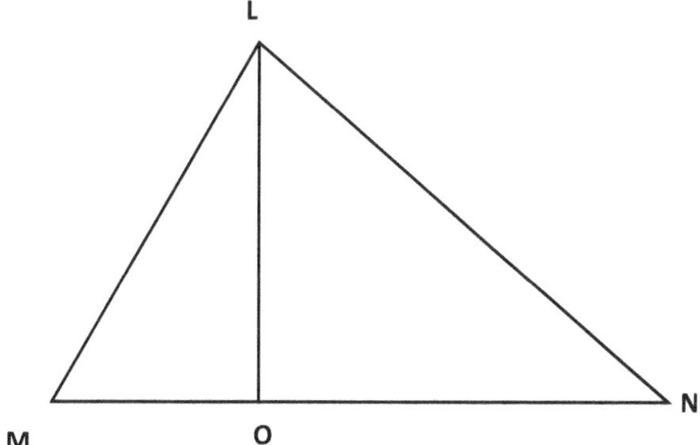

A. $\sqrt{13}$

B. $2\sqrt{13}$

C. 13

D. $13\sqrt{13}$

22.

If the graph of $y = \sqrt[3]{x}$ is reflected about the x-axis then translated horizontally to the right 3 units, which of the following represents the transformed graph?

A. $y = \sqrt[3]{-x+3}$

B. $y = -\sqrt[3]{x} - 3$

C. $y = -\sqrt[3]{x-3}$

D. $y = \sqrt[3]{-x} + 3$

23.

Which statement is false about parallelogram ABCD shown below?

A. AC = BD

B. AD = BC

C. $\angle A = \angle C$

D. $\angle C + \angle D = 180°$

24.

Allison has a rectangular garden whose perimeter is 26 units. Which of the following cannot be dimensions of the rectangle?

A. 1 and 12

B. 4 and 9

C. 8 and 5

D. 10 and 6

25.

Refer to the figure shown below. In an isosceles triangle ΔABC, length of $\overline{AB}$ is equal to the length of $\overline{AC}$ and the measure of $\angle A$ is 40°. Points B,C and D are collinear. Find the measure of the exterior angle ACD.

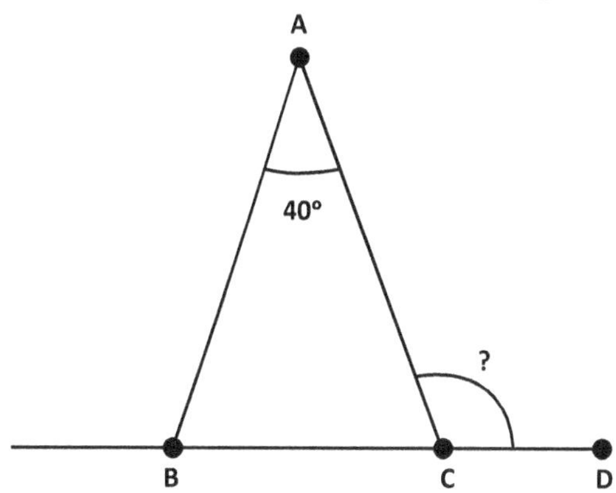

A. 60°

B. 80°

C. 110°

D. 160°

26.

Alice wants to fence a grazing pasture. Each north/south and east/west post is set 10 feet apart. The diagonal posts are northwest and southeast. What is the perimeter of the fence?

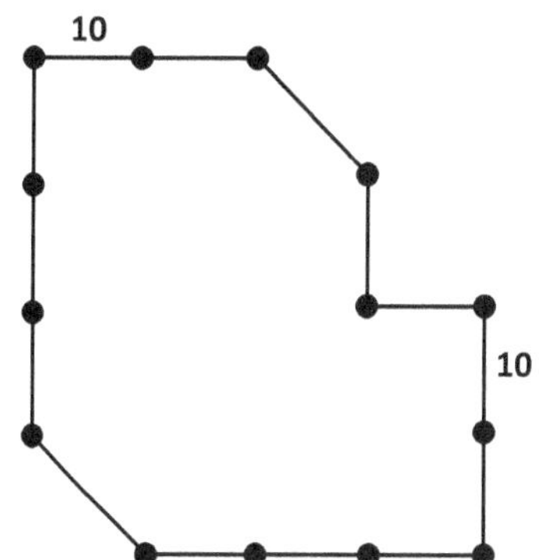

A. 120

B. $120 + 10\sqrt{2}$

C. $120 + 20\sqrt{2}$

D. 140

27.

A mango tree is planted on level ground as shown in the figure below. It is supported by wires of equal length. The mango tree is perpendicular to the ground. The wires are tied 3 feet above the ground with endpoints at C and Z, which are equidistant from the mango tree. Which statement explains how you can prove $\angle C \cong \angle Z$?

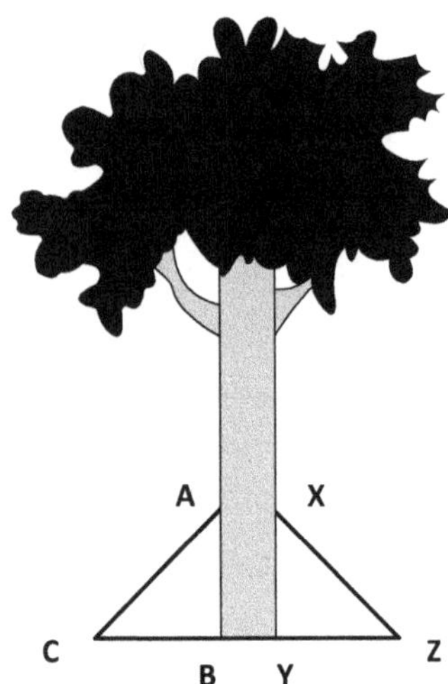

A. $\Delta ABC \cong \Delta XYZ$ by AAS theorem, and $\angle C \cong \angle Z$ because corresponding parts of congruent triangles are congruent.
B. $\angle C \cong \angle Z$ by AA theorem
C. $\angle C \cong \angle Z$ by ASA theorem
D. $\Delta ABC \cong \Delta XYZ$ by SSS theorem, and $\angle C \cong \angle Z$ because corresponding parts of congruent triangles are congruent.

28.

You push a wheelbarrow that has a single wheel straight across a driveway. The radius of the wheel is 6 inches. If the wheel rotated 20 times, approximately how many feet did you push the wheelbarrow?

A. 31
B. 63
C. 125
D. 189

29.

The triangle ABO shown below is reflected over the y-axis, then the triangle in quadrant 2 is reflected over the x-axis. Find the perimeter of the 3 triangle area.

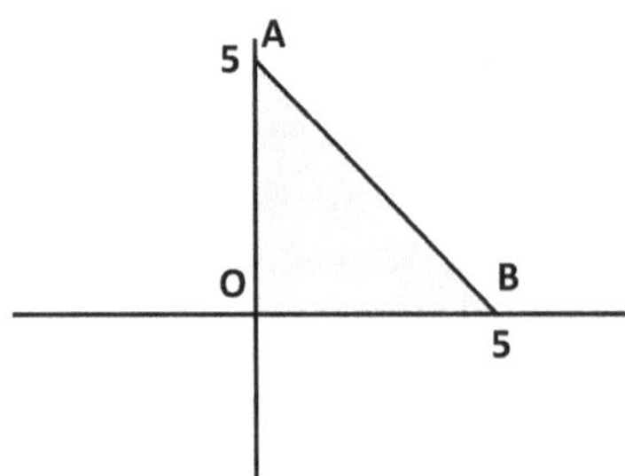

A. $10+15\sqrt{2}$
B. 15
C. 25
D. $30+15\sqrt{2}$

30.

The graph of which of the following lines passes through the center of the graph of a circle whose equation is $(x-5)^2+(y-3)^2=36$?

A. $y=2x-7$
B. $y=x+2$
C. $y=\frac{3}{5}x+1$
D. $y=\frac{3}{5}x-1$

31.

The area of a square is 169 cm^2. What is the area of the square formed with the diagonal of the original square as its side? Identify the figure

A. 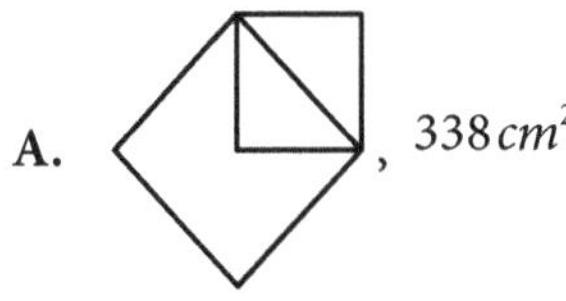, $338\,cm^2$

B. 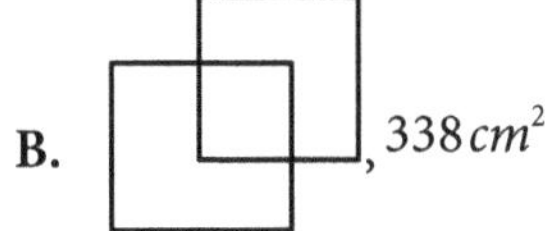, $338\,cm^2$

C. 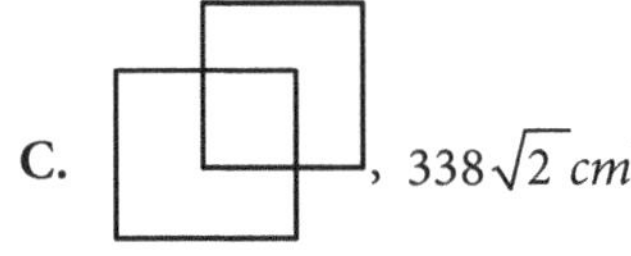, $338\sqrt{2}\ cm^2$

D. , $338\sqrt{2}\ cm^2$

32.

Anne bought a 10" × 13" wooden picture frame that can hold an 8" × 10" glossy photo. What is the area of the wood portion of the frame?

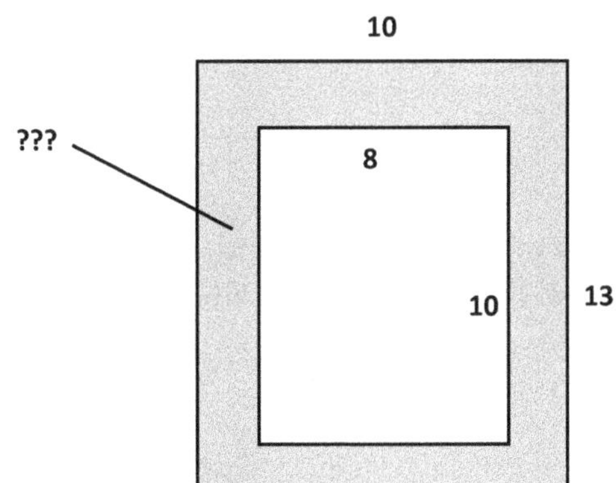

A. 45 in^2
B. 50 in^2
C. 55 in^2
D. 80 in^2

33.

Sophia wanted to fence a rectangular field into four equal parts. She wants the division to be parallel to the width of the rectangular field. What is the total cost to fence a 12 × 6 meters rectangular field if the fence is $3 per meter?

A. $144
B. $162
C. $172
D. $184

34.

A triangle has one side that is 16 inches long and a perimeter of 66 inches. The length of the other two sides have a ratio of 2:3. What is the length, in inches, of the longest side of the triangle?

A. 24
B. 30
C. 48
D. 52

35.

What is the area of ΔABD?

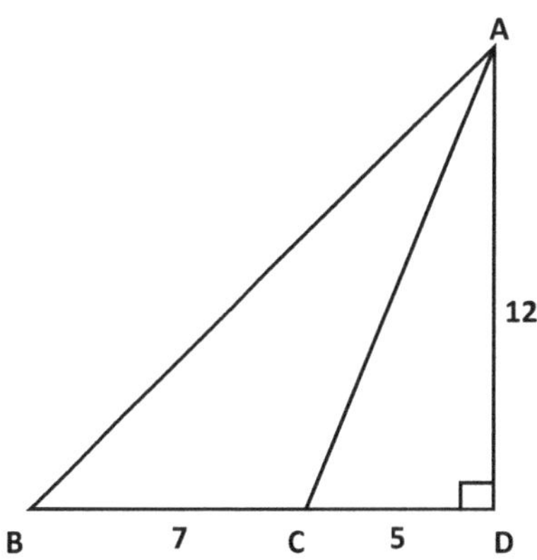

A. 48
B. 56
C. 72
D. 81

36.

While training for a marathon, Shane decided to run from home at E, through the park C, along road to D, and then straight back home. How far did Shane run?

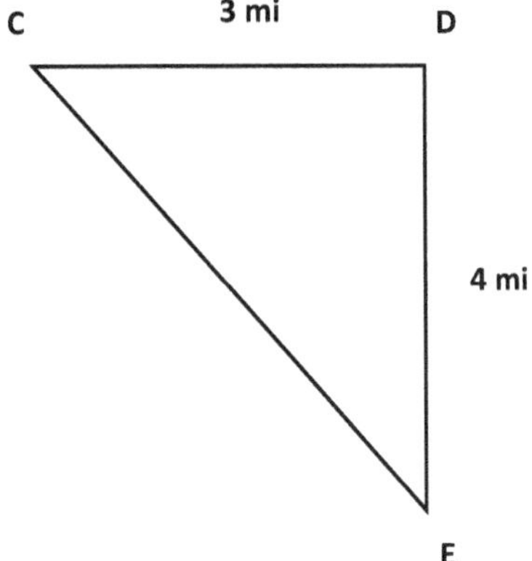

A. 7 mi
B. 10 mi
C. 12 mi
D. 16 mi

37.

In the figure below, $\Delta ABC \sim \Delta EFG$, $a = 12$ units, $c = 5$ units, and $e = 8$ units. What is the length of g in units?

A. $\frac{3}{10}$

B. $\frac{10}{3}$

C. $\frac{96}{5}$

D. $\frac{15}{2}$

A, B, C, 5, 12; E, F, G, 8

38.

Find the equation and the graph of an ellipse whose vertices are at (±4, 0) and the foci are (±2, 0) centered at the origin.

A. 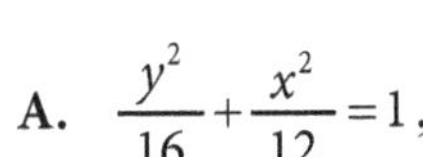 $\frac{y^2}{16}+\frac{x^2}{12}=1,$

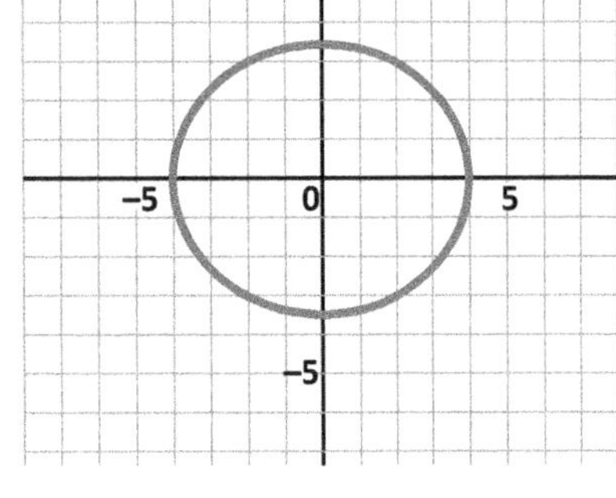

B. 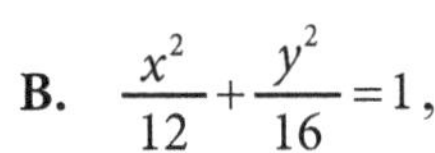 $\frac{x^2}{12}+\frac{y^2}{16}=1,$

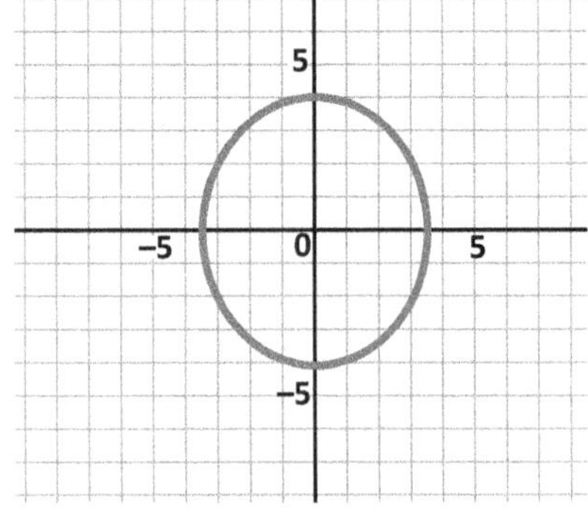

C. $\frac{x^2}{16}+\frac{y^2}{12}=1,$

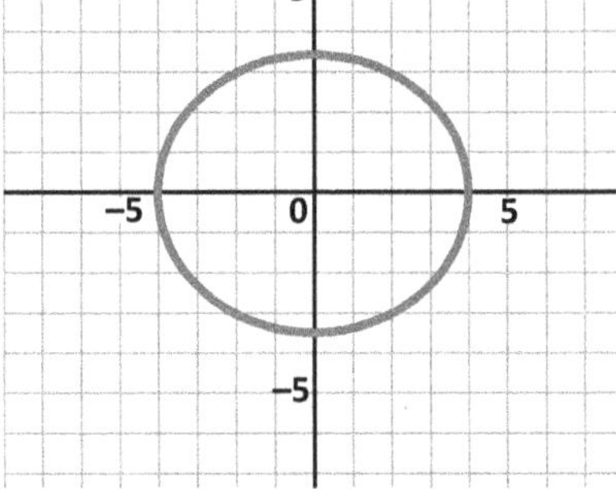

D. $\frac{x^2}{16}+\frac{y^2}{12}=1,$

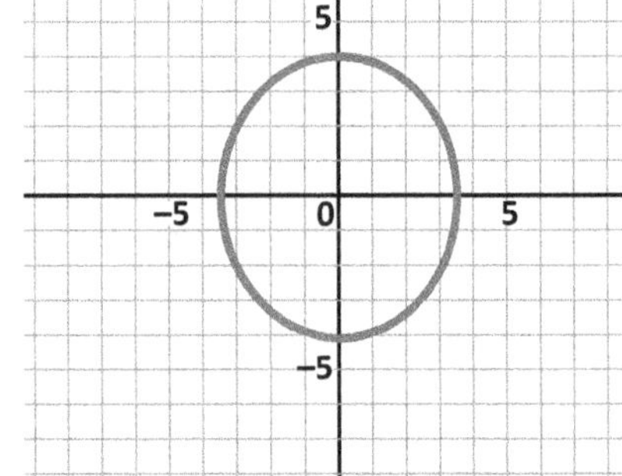

39.

The lengths of $\overline{DE}$, $\overline{EF}$, $\overline{FG}$, in units, are given in the figure below. Find the area of ΔDEG.

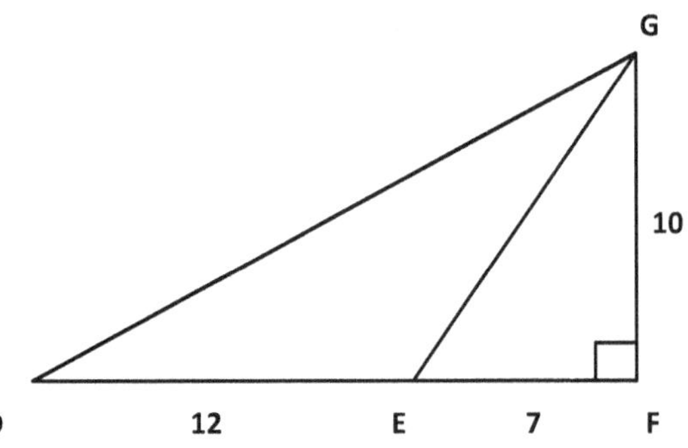

A. 50
B. 60
C. 70
D. 80

40.

Lovely draws a star as shown below. Determine if it has rotational symmetry. If it does, give the smallest angle of rotation needed for the figure to appear unmoved.

A. 45°
B. 65°
C. 72°
D. 90°

41.

James bought a lampshade which is the shape of a part of a cone and its top and bottom ends are circles with circumferences 30 cm and 40 cm respectively. The perpendicular distance between the ends is 6 cm. Determine the ratio of the area of the upper circle to the lower circle in a lampshade.

A. 2:3
B. 11:6
C. 3:5
D. 9:16

42.

In a figure below, a circle is circumscribed within a square with sides 12 ft. What is the area of the circle to the nearest square foot?

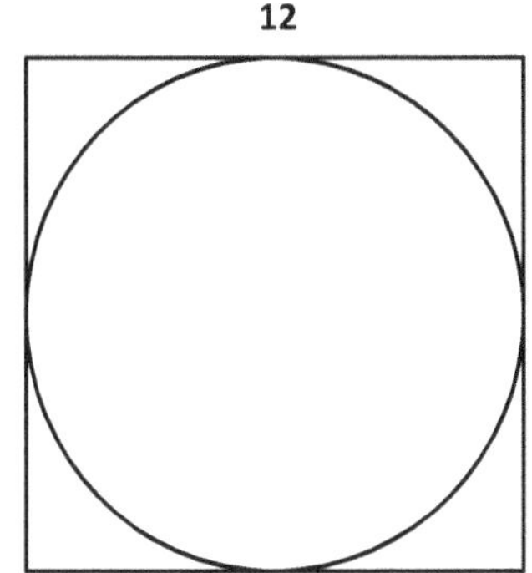

A. 108
B. 113
C. 386
D. 456

43.

Triangles *ABC* is similar to triangle *KLM* (whose lengths are given in centimeters as shown below). What is the perimeter of ΔABC?

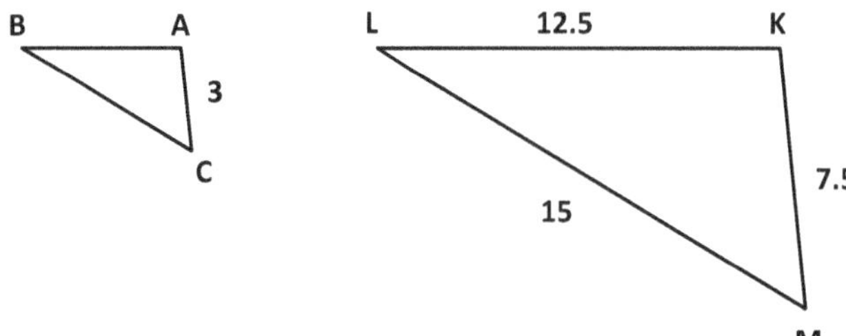

A. 11
B. 12
C. 14
D. 16

44.

Steve planned to create a roof for his dog's house with a shape of a triangle on one side. He planned to use an equilateral triangle with a side length of 8 cm. Find the length of the altitude of the triangle.

A. $2\sqrt{3}$
B. $3\sqrt{2}$
C. $3\sqrt{4}$
D. $4\sqrt{3}$

45.

The figure shows a quadrilateral *ABCD*. What is the measure of $\angle C$?

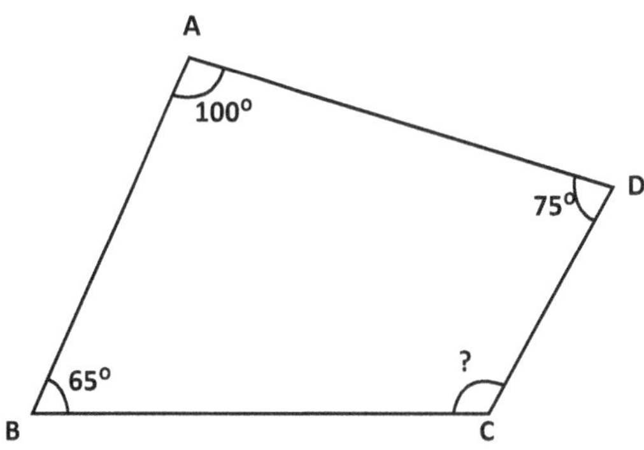

A. 80°
B. 110°
C. 120°
D. 140°

46.

Find the equation of the circle whose endpoints of its diameter are $(-1, 2)$ and $(4, 7)$.

A. $(x-\frac{9}{2})^2+(y-\frac{3}{2})^2=\frac{25}{2}$

B. $(x-\frac{3}{2})^2+(y-\frac{9}{2})^2=\frac{25}{2}$

C. $(x-\frac{1}{2})^2+(y-\frac{3}{2})^2=\frac{25}{5}$

D. $(x-\frac{1}{3})^2+(y-\frac{3}{2})^2=\frac{25}{2}$

47.

Find the x intercepts of the circle with the given equation $(x-6)^2+(y+3)^2=16$.

A. $7\pm\sqrt{6}$

B. $2\pm\sqrt{5}$

C. $-6\pm\sqrt{7}$

D. $6\pm\sqrt{7}$

48.

Two triangles are similar as shown in the figure below. The lengths of their sides are also shown. What is the value of y in terms of x?

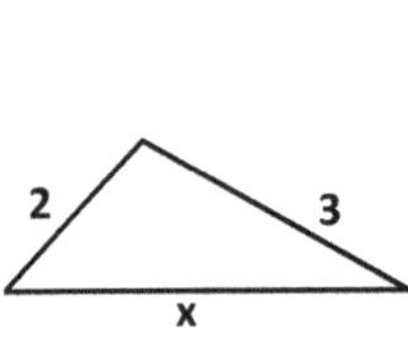

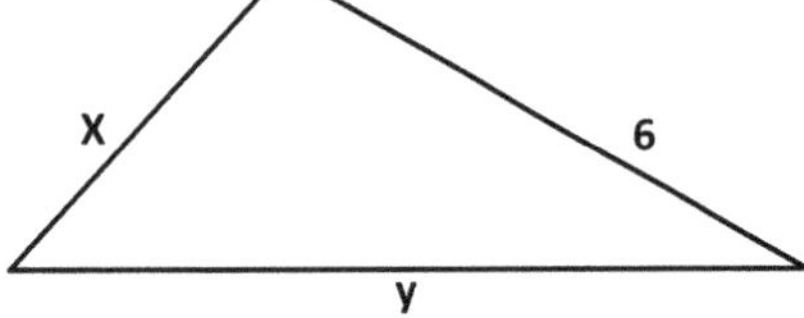

A. $y=2x^2$

B. $y=\frac{x^2}{2}$

C. $y=\frac{2}{x^2}$

D. $y=2x$

49.

Two identical circles which are inscribed in a square of side 10 cm touch each other as shown. Find the circumference of one of the circles.

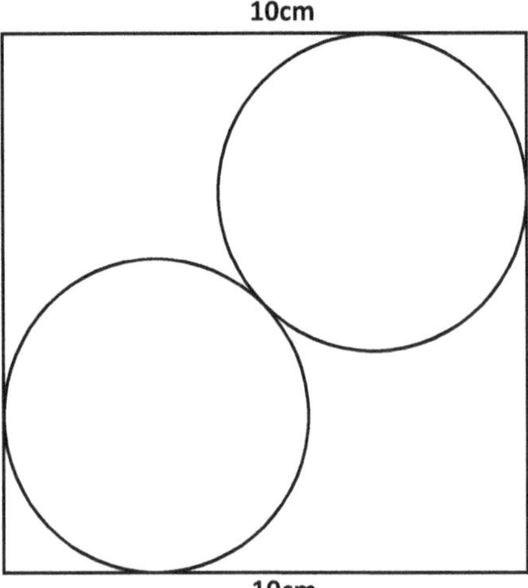

A. 12.2
B. 16.5
C. 18.4
D. 20.5

50.

The side lengths of a triangle is exactly 12:14:15. Another triangle is similar to the first, the shortest side being 8 inches long. To the nearest tenth of an inch, what is the length of the longest side of the second triangle?

A. 6.4
B. 9.3
C. 10.0
D. 11.0

51.

If 2 sides of an isosceles triangle have lengths 6 and 14, then the third side must be:

A. 6
B. 8
C. 10
D. 14

52.

If the angle between two radii of a circle is 110°, then the angle between the tangents at the ends of the radii is:

A. 40°
B. 50°
C. 70°
D. 90°

53.

A room is 20 m long and 18 m broad. Find the cost of carpeting the room with a carpet of width 1.5 m at the rate of 60 per meter.

A. $11,400
B. $14,000
C. $14,400
D. $14,800

54.

Find the angles ($\angle P$, $\angle Q$, $\angle R$) of the triangle if $a + b = 120°$ and $a - c = 30°$.

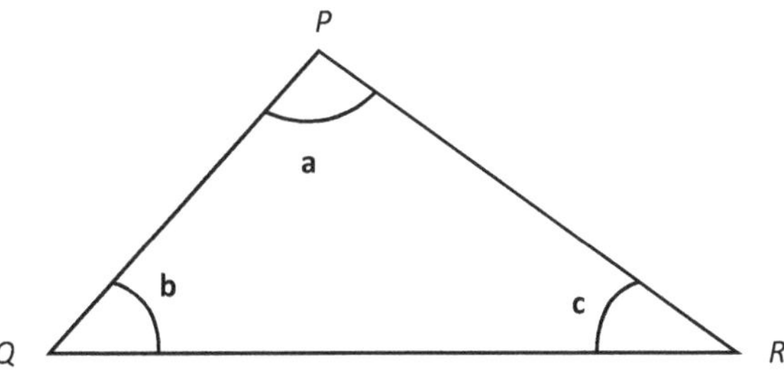

A. $\angle P = 90^0$, $\angle Q = 60^0$, $\angle R = 30^0$
B. $\angle P = 90^0$, $\angle Q = 30^0$, $\angle R = 60^0$
C. $\angle P = 60^0$, $\angle Q = 30^0$, $\angle R = 90^0$
D. $\angle P = 30^0$, $\angle Q = 60^0$, $\angle R = 90^0$

55.

The perimeter of an isosceles triangle is 3.6 m and its base is 30 cm shorter than each of the equal sides. What is the area (in m^2) of the triangle?

A. 0.2 m^2
B. 0.4 m^2
C. 0.6 m^2
D. 0.8 m^2

56.

The equation of circle with center (1, –2) and radius 4 cm is:

A. $x^2 + y^2 + 2x - 4y = 16$
B. $x^2 + y^2 + 2x - 4y = 11$
C. $x^2 + y^2 + 2x + 4y = 16$
D. $x^2 + y^2 - 2x + 4y = 11$

57.

If a triangle has an area of 24 square cm, what is its base if the height is 3 cm?

A. 12
B. 16
C. 18
D. 20

58.

A piece of wire 120 cm long is bent successively in the shape of an equilateral triangle, a square and a circle. Then, the area will be the largest in the shape of?

A. equilateral triangle
B. circle
C. square
D. All shapes are equal.

59.

The area of a square is given as 225 square units. Using the perimeter of a square formula, calculate its perimeter.

A. 40 square units
B. 60 square units
C. 70 square units
D. 80 square units

60.

The area of a parallelogram is 56 square meters. What will be the area of the two triangles that can be formed from this parallelogram?

A. Each triangle will have an area of 112 square meters.
B. The area of each triangle will be 56 square meters divided by 2.
C. The area of each triangle will be 56 square meters divided by 3.
D. There is no way to determine the area of the triangles formed from the parallelogram.

61.

Use the trapezoid midsegment theorem to find the measure of *ST*.

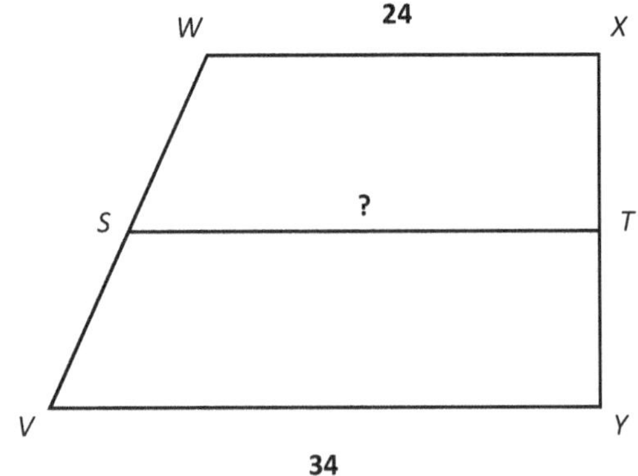

A. 25
B. 29
C. 30
D. 32

62.

The radio signal from the transmitter site of the radio station can be received only within a radius of 52 miles in all directions from the transmitter site. A map of the region of coverage of the radio signal is shown below in the standard (x, y) coordinate plane, with the transmitter site at the origin and 1 coordinate unit representing 1 mile.

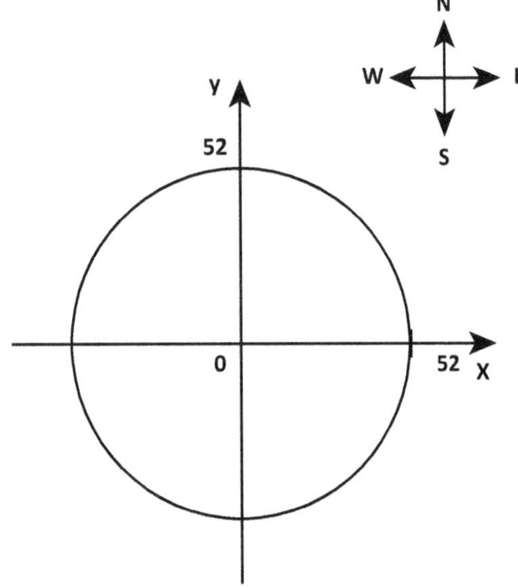

Which of the following is an equation of the circle shown on the map?

A. $x^2 - y^2 = 52^2$
B. $x^2 + y^2 = 52^2$
C. $x^2 - y^2 = 52$
D. $x^2 + y^2 = 52$

63.

If the length of a diagonal of a square is $(a + b)$, then the area of the square is:

A. $A = \frac{a^2 + 2ab + b^2}{2}$

B. $A = \frac{a^2 + b^2}{2}$

C. $A = \frac{a^2 + b}{2}$

D. $A = \frac{a + b}{2}$

64.

Jericho wants to know how tall a building in his neighborhood is. Since he can't directly measure the height of the building he decided to use the properties of right triangles. He walks 100 feet from the base of the building and looks up to the top. He estimates the angle from his vantage point to the top of the building to be 75 degrees. How tall is the building?

A. 237.2 ft
B. 327.3 ft
C. 337.2 ft
D. 373.2 ft

65.

Let $\Delta ABC \sim \Delta DEF$. If sides $a = 18$, $d = 3$, and $c = 42$, what is the length of side f?

A. $\frac{7}{9}$
B. 6
C. 7
D. 252

66.

A 10×24 rectangle is inscribed in a circle. What is the circumference of the circle?

A. 16π
B. 20π
C. 26π
D. 36π

67.

If one of the sides of a rectangle is increased by 20% & the other is increased by 5%, find the percent value by which the area changes.

A. 16 %
B. 22 %
C. 26 %
D. 33 %

68.

A rectangle has an area of 33 cm^2. Its length is two more than thrice its width. Find the perimeter of the rectangle.

A. 15
B. 22
C. 28
D. 33

69.

There is a rectangular garden of 220 meters by 70 meters. A path of 4 meters is built around the garden. What is the area of the path?

A. 1122
B. 1144
C. 1234
D. 1342

70.

Mae purchased a CD that was 5 inches in diameter. What is the circumference of the CD?

A. 2.5π
B. 3π
C. 5π
D. 6π

71.

A tablecloth has a length of 150 inches and breadth of 120 inches. How much lace will be required to complete the border?

A. 360
B. 450
C. 540
D. 600

72.

A circle is inside a regular hexagon. The perimeter of the regular hexagon is 84 cm. Find the difference between the area of the circle and the regular hexagon.

A. 35.8
B. 45.3
C. 47.4
D. 50.1

73.

In the given figure, area of the triangle ABC is $80 cm^2$ and BC = 10 cm, then what is the side (in cm) of the square PQRS?

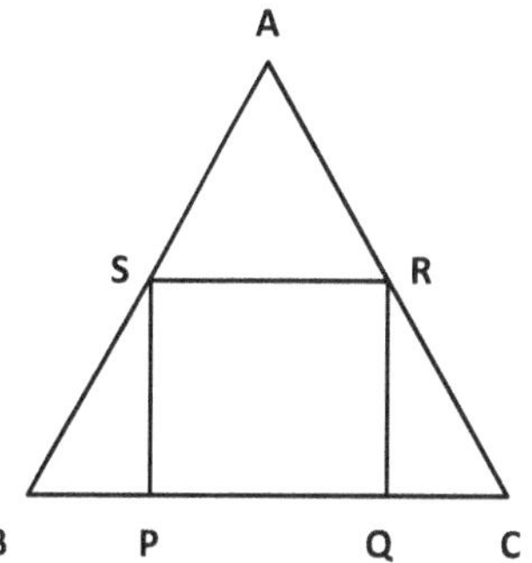

A. 13/80
B. 80/13
C. 8/13
D. 13/10

74.

Jhanica is converting a 12-foot-by-15-foot room in her house to a craft room. She will install the tiles herself but will have JC installation build and install the cabinets. Refer to the drawing scale below (0.25 inch represents 2 ft).

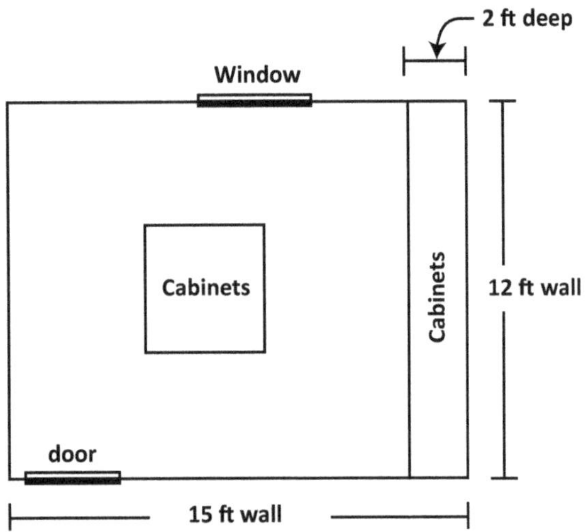

Cabinets will be installed along one of the 12-foot walls from floor to ceiling, and 4 cabinets that are each 3 feet tall will be installed in the middle of the room. These are the only cabinets that will be installed, and each of them will be 2 feet wide and 2 feet deep. JC Installations has given Jhanica an estimate of $2,150.00 for building and installing the cabinets.

A 15-foot wall is how many inches in the square drawing?

A. 1.05
B. 1.75
C. 1.875
D. 2.5

75.

For the right triangle shown in the figure below, which statement is true about angles θ and α ?

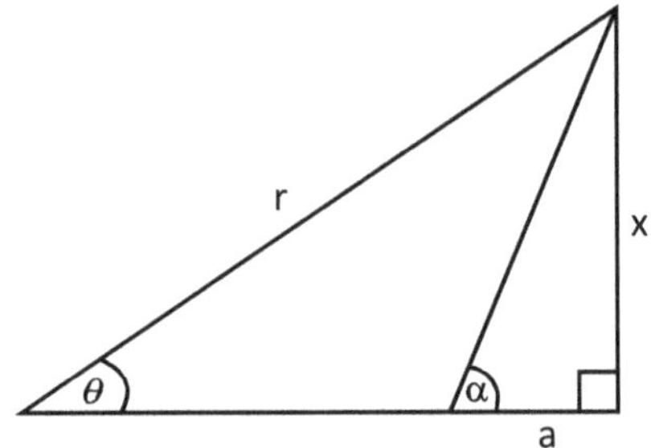

A. $\frac{tan\alpha}{tan\theta}=\frac{y}{a}$

B. $\frac{tan\theta}{tan\alpha}=\frac{y}{a}$

C. $tan\alpha \times tan\theta = ay$

D. $y\ tan\alpha = a\ tan\theta$

76.

Refer to the given figures below. The base of the pyramid has the same area as the base of the cylinder. The height of the cylinder is twice the height of the pyramid. What is the ratio of the volume of the pyramid to the volume of the cylinder?

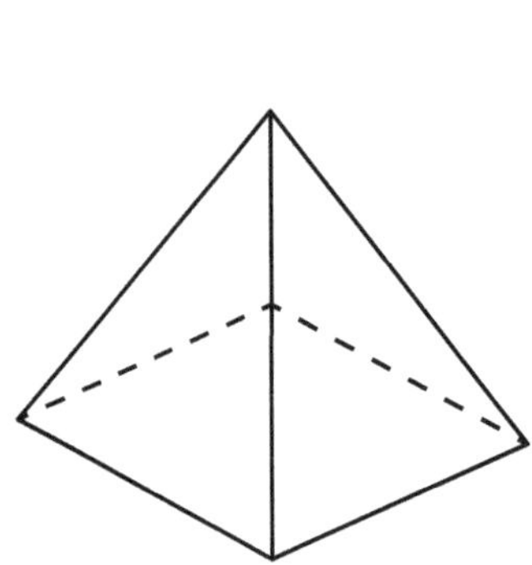

A. 1:3
B. 1:6
C. 3:2
D. 6:1

77.

Anna wants to paint the outside part of a wooden box. The box is 12 inches long, 3 inches wide and x inches high. Which of the following equations represent the amount of paint Anna needs to use to cover the box?

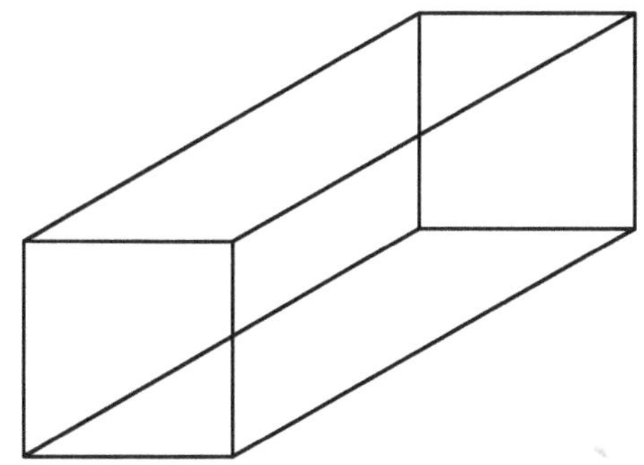

A. $30x + 72$
B. $72x + 30$
C. $30x - 72$
D. $-30x - 72$

78.

A sphere is inscribed in a cube with a diagonal of $3\sqrt{3}$ *ft*. Which expression represents the relationship between the side length s and the diameter of the sphere d, and the value of the diameter of the sphere?

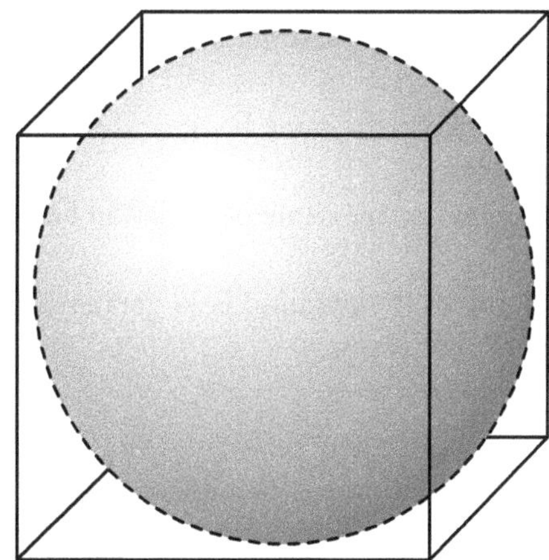

A. $s=d,\ d=3$
B. $s-d,\ d=\sqrt{3}$
C. $\frac{s}{d},\ d=2$
D. $s+d,\ d=3+\sqrt{3}$

79.

A cubical block weighs 6 pounds. If the sides are all doubled, then the new block will weigh

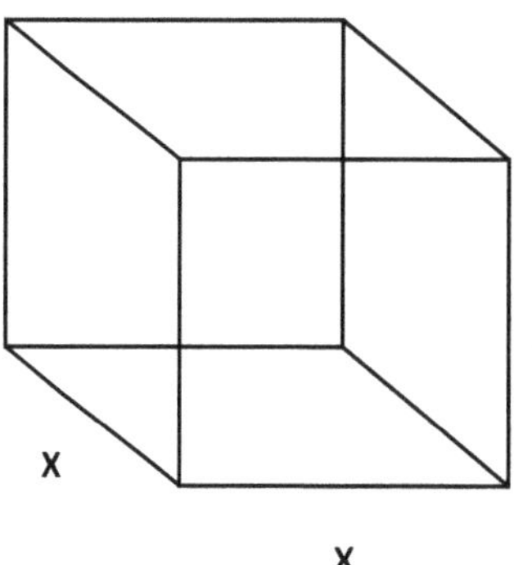

A. 24
B. 36
C. 48
D. 56

80.

Find the surface area of the given pyramid

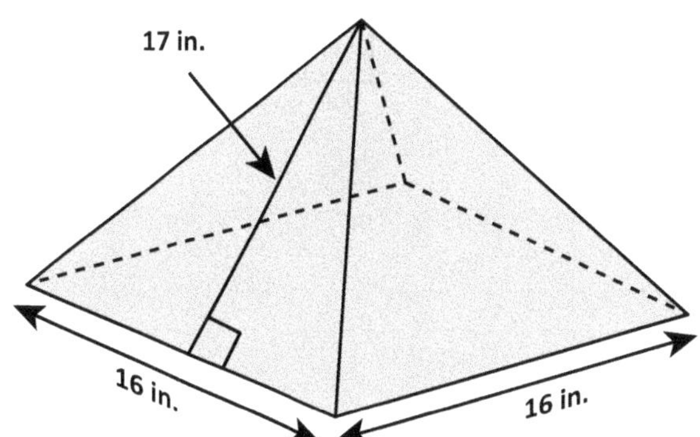

A. 450 in^2
B. 600 in^2
C. 800 in^2
D. 900 in^2

81.

The first cuboid is filled with orange juice. How much orange juice will be left if it is filled in the second cuboid?

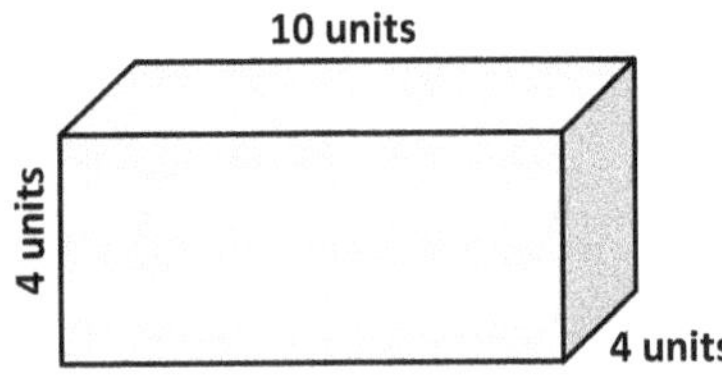

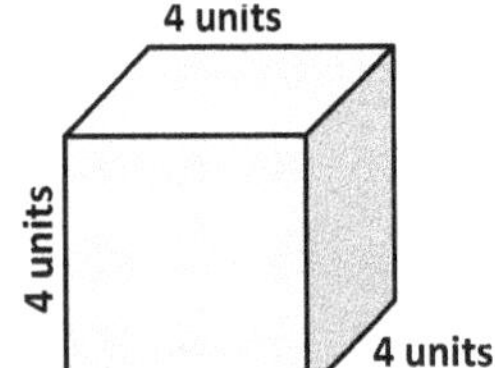

A. 86 units
B. 96 units
C. 106 units
D. 116 units

82.

Which arrangement shows increasing volume of the given prisms?

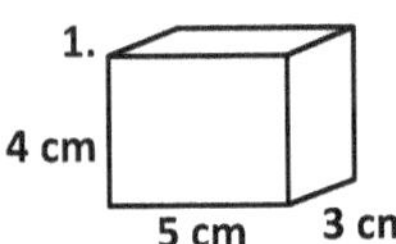

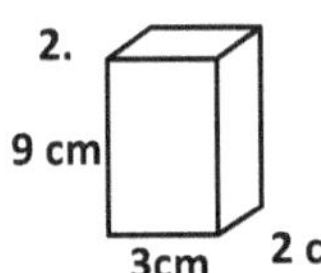

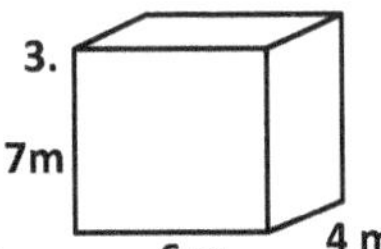

A. 1, 2, 3
B. 2, 1, 3
C. 3, 2, 1
D. 3, 1, 2

83.

Approximately 7.5 gallons of water can fill 1 cubic foot. How many gallons of water would be in a cylindrical water tank with diameter 20 feet and height 12 feet, if it was full?

A. 18,174.30 gallons
B. 20,274.33 gallons
C. 24,100.33 gallons
D. 28,274.33 gallons

84.

The ratio of the heights of a right circular cone and a right circular cylinder is 4:3 and the ratio of the radii of their bases is 7:3. If the volume of the cylinder is 810 cm^3, then the volume (in cm^3) of the cone is:

A. 1360 cm^3
B. 1560 cm^3
C. 1960 cm^3
D. 2160 cm^3

85.

Find the volume of a cylinder if the circumference of its base is 66 cm and height cylinder 40 cm. (Use $\pi = \frac{22}{7}$).

A. 11,235
B. 12,435
C. 13,860
D. 15,352

86.

A square pyramid with side 10 cm has a volume of 400 cm^3. Find the total surface area of the pyramid.

A. 280
B. 330
C. 360
D. 450

87.

Which statement correctly describes the volume of the two figures?

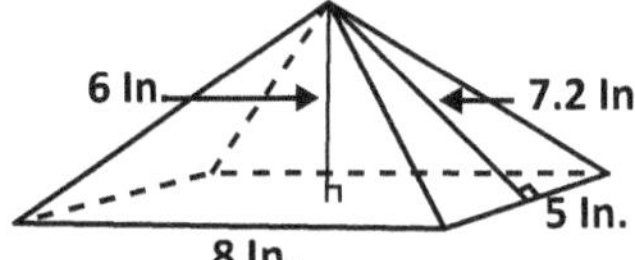

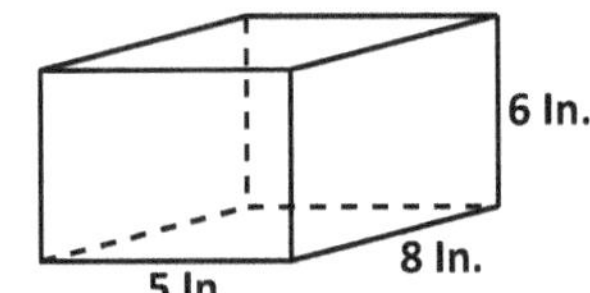

A. The volume of the pyramid is ⅓ the volume of the prism.
B. The volumes are the same because the dimensions are the same.
C. The volumes are the same because the bases are the same.
D. The volume of the pyramid is ⅓ greater than the volume of the prism.

88.

Determine the surface area of a square pyramid with slant height 12 and base side of 8.

A. 124
B. 256
C. 305
D. 350

89.

The base of a right pyramid is a square and the length of the side of the square is 32 cm and height of the pyramid is 12 cm. What is the total surface area of the square pyramid?

A. 1947
B. 2003
C. 2304
D. 2560

90.

A trailer truck travelled 1.2 km up a ramp that is horizontally inclined at an angle of $49°18'$. Find the height at which the truck stopped, giving the answer in meters to one decimal place.

A. 750
B. 850
C. 910
D. 1050

91.

Which expression if equivalent to $\cos(-\theta)$?

A. $-\sin(\theta)$
B. $-\cos(\theta)$
C. $\cos(\theta)$
D. $-\sin(-\theta)$

92.

Which of the following statements is true about the graph of the function $y = f(x)$ shown below?

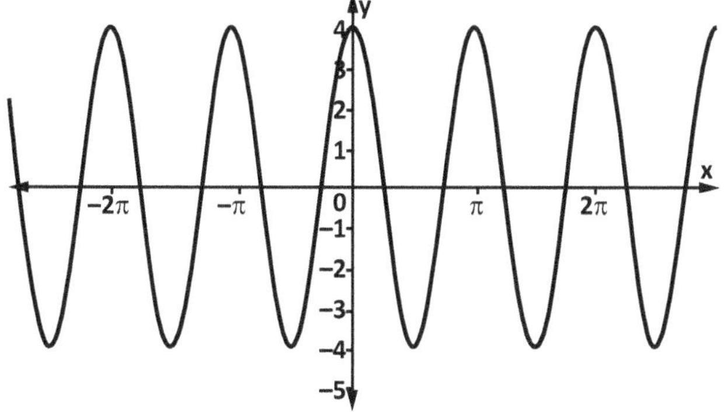

A. It has a period of 2π.
B. It has a period of π.
C. It is an odd function.
D. It has x-axis symmetry.

93.

A plane travels 800 meters along the runway before taking off at an angle 15°. It travels further 1,000 meters at this angle as shown in the figure below. Work out the distance of the plane from its starting point. Give your answer to 2 decimal places.

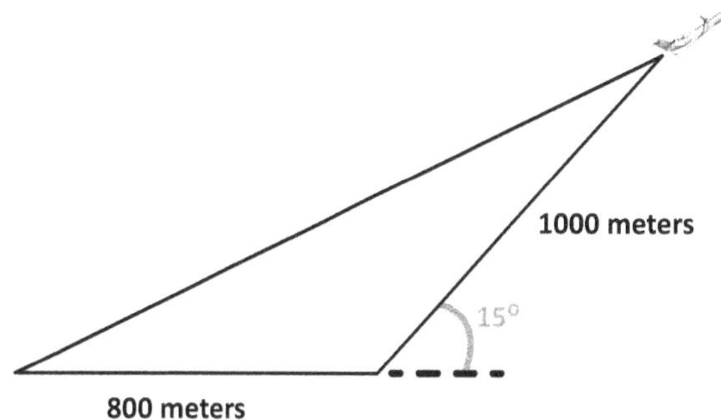

A. 1542.79
B. 1784.79
C. 1875.81
D. 1945.47

94.

Standing in a lighthouse, 150 feet above the shore, Ben spotted a boat at an angle of depression of 11 degrees. How far away is the boat from the shore?

A. 550
B. 772
C. 850
D. 972

95.

If $\sin B = \frac{3}{5}$ and $\tan B < 0$, then $\cos B = ?$

A. $-\frac{4}{5}$
B. $-\frac{2}{5}$
C. $\frac{2}{5}$
D. $\frac{4}{5}$

96.

An object 4 feet tall casts a 3-foot shadow when the angle of elevation of the sun is θ. What is $\tan\theta$?

A. $\frac{3}{5}$

B. $\frac{3}{4}$

C. $\frac{4}{3}$

D. $\frac{5}{3}$

97.

What is the cosine of angle A in right angle ABC below?

A. $\frac{\sqrt{3}}{5}$

B. $\frac{\sqrt{5}}{2}$

C. $\frac{\sqrt{2}}{3}$

D. $\frac{\sqrt{5}}{3}$

98.

What is the length of the line segment joining the midpoints of $\overline{AC}$ and $\overline{BC}$ in right triangle ΔABC shown below?

A. 4.5
B. 15
C. 21
D. 30

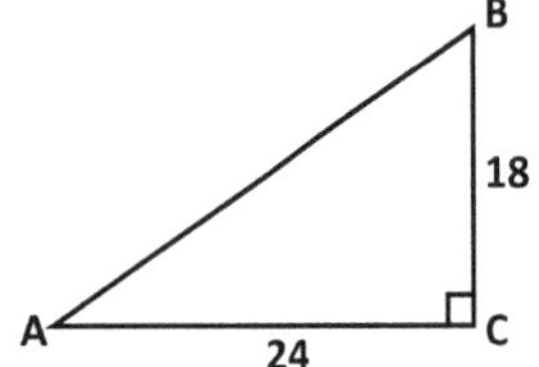

99.

An angle B is in standard position on the xy-coordinate plane. The initial side is on the x-axis, and the terminal side passes through (–3, 7). Find $\cot B$.

A. $-\frac{7}{3}$

B. $-\frac{3}{7}$

C. $\frac{3}{7}$

D. $\frac{7}{3}$

100.

The sides of a triangle are 5, 12 and 13 inches long. What is the angle between the 2 shortest sides?

A. 75°

B. 80°

C. 90°

D. 110°

101.

A geodetic engineer took and recorded the measurements shown in the figure below. If the engineer wants to use these 3 measurements to calculate the length of the pond, which of the following would be the most directly applicable?

A. The Pythagorean theorem
B. A formula for the area of a triangle
C. The law of cosines.
D. The ratios for the side lengths of 45° – 45° – 90°

102.

What is the period for the sinusoidal graph shown in the standard (x, y) coordinate system below?

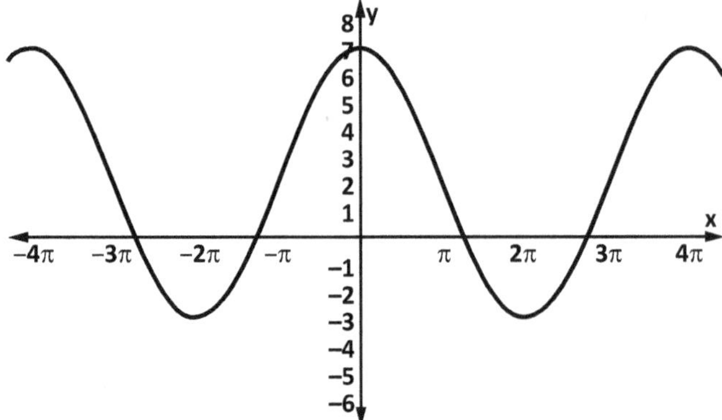

A. 2π
B. 7
C. 10
D. 4π

103.

Solve the equation: $2cos\theta - 3 = -5$, $0 \leq \theta < 2\pi$.

A. $\pi/2$

B. $\pi/4$

C. π

D. 2π

104.

The town surveyor has to stake the lot markers for a new public park beside an existing building lot. The engineering department gave this sketch. How much chain-link fence will be needed to enclose the entire park?

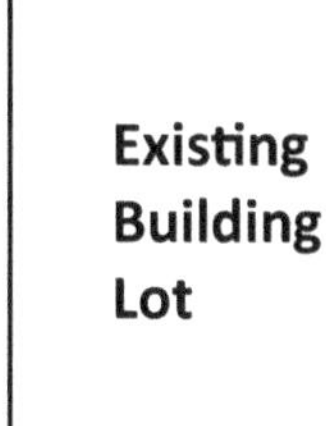

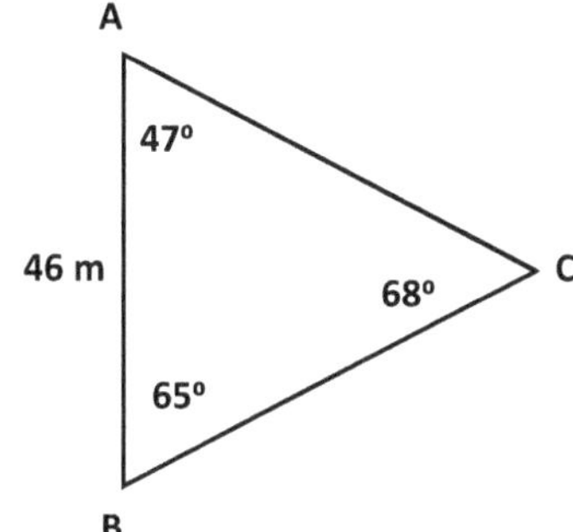

A. 126

B. 135

C. 145

D. 150

105.

If $sin A = \frac{12}{13}$, *and* $tan A = -\frac{12}{5}$, *then cos* $A = ?$

A. $-\frac{12}{13}$

B. $\frac{4}{13}$

C. $-\frac{13}{12}$

D. $-\frac{5}{13}$

Answer Key

Question	Correct	Make your correct answers
1	B	
2	A	
3	A	
4	B	
5	B	
6	B	
7	A	
8	D	
9	A	
10	D	
11	D	
12	B	
13	C	
14	D	
15	A	
16	A	
17	C	
18	B	
19	C	
20	A	
21	A	
22	C	
23	A	
24	D	
25	C	
26	C	
27	D	
28	B	
29	A	
30	A	
31	A	
32	B	

Question	Correct	Make your correct answers
33	B	
34	B	
35	C	
36	C	
37	B	
38	D	
39	B	
40	C	
41	D	
42	B	
43	C	
44	D	
45	C	
46	B	
47	D	
48	B	
49	C	
50	C	
51	D	
52	C	
53	C	
54	B	
55	C	
56	D	
57	B	
58	B	
59	B	
60	B	
61	B	
62	B	
63	A	
64	D	

Question	Correct	Make your correct answers
65	C	
66	C	
67	C	
68	C	
69	B	
70	C	
71	C	
72	C	
73	B	
74	C	
75	A	
76	B	
77	A	
78	A	
79	C	
80	C	
81	B	
82	D	
83	D	
84	C	
85	C	
86	C	
87	A	
88	B	
89	C	
90	C	
91	C	
92	B	
93	B	
94	B	
95	A	
96	C	

Question	Correct	Make your correct answers
97	D	
98	B	
99	B	
100	C	
101	C	
102	D	
103	C	
104	B	
105	D	

1.

Category: PHM & Modeling
Skill: Coordinate geometry | **Level:** Easy

Choice B is correct. The solution set are the points of intersection for the graphs of the 2 functions.

Choice A is incorrect because this is the y-intercepts for the 2 graphs. **Choice C** is incorrect because this reverses the coordinates for the points of intersection. **Choice D** is incorrect because this states the x-intercepts of the 2 graphs.

2.

Category: PHM & Modeling
Skill: Coordinate geometry | **Level:** Easy

Choice A is correct because the obtained midpoint is $(1,2)$.

Use the midpoint formula.

$$(x_m, y_m) = \left(\frac{x_1+x_2}{2}, \frac{y_1+y_2}{2}\right)$$

$$(x_m, y_m) = \left(\frac{-2+4}{2}, \frac{7+(-3)}{2}\right)$$

$$(x_m, y_m) = \left(\frac{2}{2}, \frac{4}{2}\right)$$

$$(x_m, y_m) = (1,2)$$

Choice B is incorrect because (8, 5) is not the midpoint of the given points. **Choice C** is incorrect because (8, –5) is not the midpoint of the given points. **Choice D** is incorrect because (–1, 2) is not the midpoint of the given points.

3.

Category: PHM & Modeling
Skill: Coordinate geometry | **Level:** Hard

Choice A is correct because $(0,2)$ has the same distance as the other points from $(2,5)$.
Find the distance of points A, B, C, D, E from point $(2,5)$ using the distance formula.

Point A$(-1,3)$ to point $(2,5)$.

$$d = \sqrt{(-1-2)^2+(3-5)^2} = \sqrt{(-3)^2+(-2)^2} = \sqrt{9+4} = \sqrt{13}$$

Point B$(0,8)$ to point $(2,5)$.

$$d = \sqrt{(0-2)^2+(8-5)^2} = \sqrt{(-2)^2+(3)^2} = \sqrt{4+9} = \sqrt{13}$$

Point C$(4,2)$ to point $(2,5)$.

$$d = \sqrt{(4-2)^2+(2-5)^2} = \sqrt{(2)^2+(-3)^2} = \sqrt{4+9} = \sqrt{13}$$

Point D$(5,3)$ to point $(2,5)$.

$$d = \sqrt{(5-2)^2+(3-5)^2} = \sqrt{(3)^2+(-2)^2} = \sqrt{9+4} = \sqrt{13}$$

Point E$(5,7)$ to point $(2,5)$.

$$d = \sqrt{(5-2)^2+(7-5)^2} = \sqrt{(3)^2+(2)^2} = \sqrt{9+4} = \sqrt{13}$$

Analyze each choices if the given point is $\sqrt{13}$ from point $(2,5)$.
Choice A: $(0,2)$ to point $(2,5)$.

$$d = \sqrt{(0-2)^2+(2-5)^2} = \sqrt{(-2)^2+(-3)^2} = \sqrt{4+9} = \sqrt{13}$$

Choice B: $(2,1)$ to point $(2,5)$.

$$d = \sqrt{(2-2)^2+(1-5)^2} = \sqrt{(0)^2+(-4)^2} = \sqrt{16} = 4$$

Choice C: $(3,1)$ to point $(2,5)$.

$$d = \sqrt{(3-2)^2+(2-5)^2} = \sqrt{(1)^2+(-3)^2} = \sqrt{1+9} = \sqrt{10}$$

Choice D: $(-1,1)$ to point $(2,5)$.

$$d = \sqrt{(-1-2)^2+(1-5)^2} = \sqrt{(-3)^2+(-4)^2} = \sqrt{9+16} = 5$$

Choice B is incorrect because length of (2,1) from (2,5) is not the same. **Choice C** is incorrect because length of (3,1) from (2,5) is not the same. **Choice D** is incorrect because length of (–1,1) from (2,5) is not same.

4.

Category: IES
Skill: Coordinate geometry | **Level:** Easy

Choice B is correct because the obtained answer is 7.5.

$$\text{Let } (x_1, y_1) = A(-3,2)$$
$$(x_2, y_2) = B(1,3)$$
$$(x_3, y_3) = C(4,0)$$

Use the equation

$$A = \frac{1}{2}|x_1(y_2-y_3)+x_2(y_3-y_1)+x_3(y_1-y_2)|$$

$$A = \frac{1}{2}|-3(3-0)+1(0-2)+4(2-3)|$$

$$A = \frac{1}{2}|-9+(-2)+(-4)|$$

$$A = \frac{1}{2}|-15|$$

$$A = 7.5$$

Choice A is incorrect because 5.5 is less than the obtained area of the triangle. **Choice C** is incorrect because 7 is less than the obtained area of the triangle. **Choice D** is incorrect because 8 is greater than the obtained area of the triangle.

5.

Category: IES & Modeling
Skill: Coordinate geometry | **Level:** Easy

Choice B is correct because the obtained area of the figure is 159.
The total area of the figure is the sum of the areas of the rectangle and a semi circle.
Area of the rectangle = $lw = 12 \times 10 = 120m^2$.
Area of the semi circle = $\frac{1}{2}\pi r^2 = \frac{1}{2}\pi(5)^2 = 39.27m^2$
Total area is 120 + 39.27 = 159.27 or approximately 159.

Choice A is incorrect because 152 is less than the obtained total area of the figure. **Choice C** is incorrect because 162 is greater than the obtained total area of the figure. **Choice D** is incorrect because 182 is greater than the obtained total area of the figure.

6.

Category: IES & Modeling
Skill: Coordinate geometry | **Level:** Hard

Choice B is correct. The center of the circle is the intersection of the horizontal line through the point of tangency (0, – 4) and the vertical line through the point of tangency at (4, 0).
So, the center (h, k) is (4, – 4). The radius can be found by counting vertically or horizontally the distance from the center of the circle to either point of tangency. So, $r = 4$.
Substituting the center and radius into the standard form for a circle

$$(x - h)^2 + (y - k)^2 = r^2$$
$$(x - 4)^2 + (y + 4)^2 = 16$$

Choice A is incorrect because it places the center at (4, 4), which is above the x-axis, not below. Also, the radius is $\sqrt{4} = 2$, not 4. **Choice C** is incorrect because it places the center at (–4, 4), which does not match the tangency points on the x-axis at (4, 0) or y-axis at (0, –4).
Choice D is incorrect because it places the center at (0, 0) and the radius is $\sqrt{4} = 2$, which does not match the given tangency points.

7.

Category: IES & Modeling
Skill: Coordinate geometry | **Level:** Medium

Choice A is correct because the obtained answer is $-\frac{1}{2}$.
Find the area of the new position of C using the formula $A(8,2), B(0,6)$, and $C(-3,2)$.

Let $A(8,2) = (x_1, y_1), B(0,6) = (x_2, y_2)$, and $C(x_3, y_3)$

$$A = \frac{1}{2}\left|x_1(y_2 - y_3) + x_2(y_3 - y_1) + x_3(y_1 - y_2)\right|$$
$$A = \frac{1}{2}\left|8(6 - y_3) + 0(y_3 - 2) + x_3(2 - 6)\right|$$
$$A = \frac{1}{2}\left|48 - 8y_3 - 4x_3\right|$$

Area is constant if $48 - 8y_3 - 4x_3$ remains constant.

$$48 - 8y_3 - 4x_3 = k$$
$$8y_3 + 4x_3 = 48 - k$$

Let $48 - k$ be the constant

$$2y_3 + x_3 = C$$

Find the slope of the obtained equation.

$$2y_3 + x_3 = C$$
$$2y_3 = -x_3 + C$$
$$y_3 = -\frac{1}{2}x_3 + C$$

Hence, the slope of the line is $-\frac{1}{2}$.

Choice B is incorrect because 0 is greater than the obtained answer. **Choice C** is incorrect because $\frac{1}{2}$ is greater than the obtained answer. **Choice D** is incorrect because $\frac{4}{3}$ is greater than the obtained answer.

8.

Category: PHM & Modeling
Skill: Coordinate geometry | **Level:** Easy

Choice D is correct because the obtained answer is $\left(\frac{1}{2}, -3\right)$.

Use the midpoint formula.

$$midpoint = \left(\frac{x_1 + x_2}{2}, \frac{y_1 + y_2}{2}\right) = \left(\frac{3 + (-2)}{2}, \frac{-1 + (-5)}{2}\right)$$
$$= \left(\frac{1}{2}, \frac{-6}{2}\right) = \left(\frac{1}{2}, -3\right).$$

Choice A is incorrect because $\left(\frac{1}{2}, 3\right)$ has an incorrect sign for the y-coordinate.

Choice B is incorrect because $\left(-\frac{1}{2}, 3\right)$ has an incorrect sign for both the x and y-coordinate.

Choice C is incorrect because $\left(-\frac{1}{2}, -3\right)$ has an incorrect sign for the x-coordinate.

9.

Category: PHM & Modeling
Skill: Coordinate geometry | **Level:** Medium

Choice A is correct because the obtained answer is (1, 2), (1, 5), (4, 5).

Plot the given points.

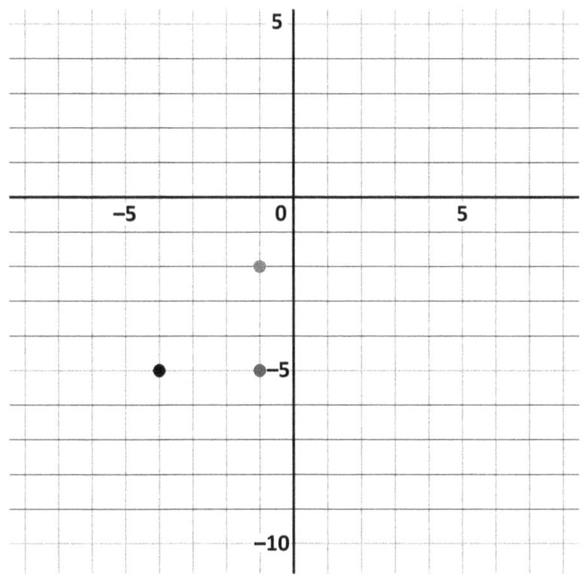

The points lie in Quadrant III.
To find a congruent triangle in Quadrant I, transform the points into positive.
Hence, (1, 2), (1, 5), (4, 5) lie in Quadrant I and is congruent to the given triangle.

Choice B is incorrect because (−1, 2), (−1, 5), (−4, 5) do not lie in Quadrant I. **Choice C** is incorrect because (1, −2), (1, 5), (4, −5) do not lie in Quadrant I. **Choice D** is incorrect because (1, −2), (−1, 5), (4, −5) do not lie in Quadrant I.

10.

Category: IES & Modeling
Skill: Coordinate geometry | **Level:** Medium

Choice D is correct because the obtained answer is 100%.

Plot the given points.

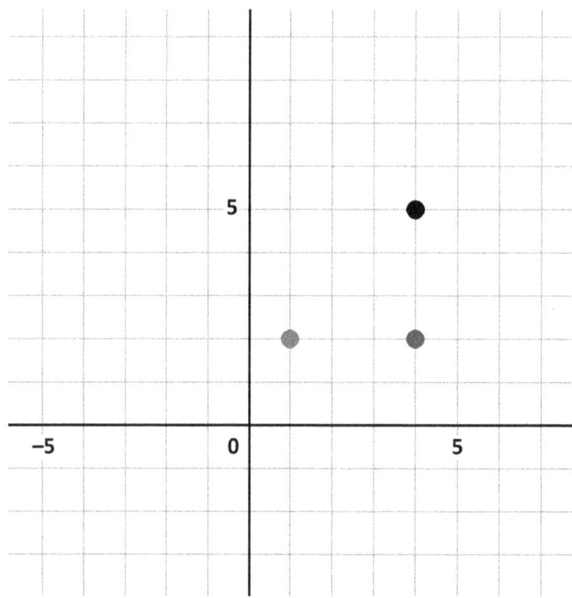

The 3 points lie in Quadrant 1. Hence, percentage of the area of the triangle formed that falls in Quadrant I is 100%.

Choice A is incorrect because 25% does not represent the total area of the rectangle lies in Quadrant I. **Choice B** is incorrect because 50% does not represent the total area of the rectangle lies in Quadrant I. **Choice C** is incorrect because 75% does not represent the total area of the rectangle lies in Quadrant I.

11.

Category: PHM & Modeling
Skill: Lines and angles | **Level:** Easy

Choice D is correct because angles $\angle m$, $\angle n$, $\angle p$ are angles with the same measure.

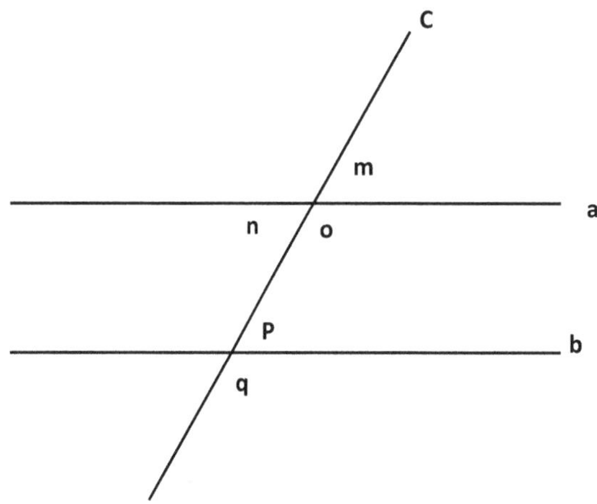

Use the parallel lines properties.
Alternate angles are equal. $\angle n = \angle p$.
Corresponding angles are equal. $\angle m = \angle p$
Hence, $\angle m, \angle n, \angle p$ are angles with the same measure.

Choice A is incorrect because in $\angle n, \angle p, \angle q$, $\angle n$ is not equal to the measure of $\angle p$ *and* $\angle q$. **Choice B** is incorrect because in $\angle n, \angle o, \angle q$ $\angle n$ is not equal to the measure of $\angle o$ *and* $\angle q$. **Choice C** is incorrect because in $\angle m, \angle p, \angle q$, is not equal to the measure of $\angle m$ *and* $\angle q$

12.

Category: PHM
Skill: Lines and angles | **Level:** Easy

Choice B is correct. Since segment OD divides $\angle BOC$ into two parts you have,

$$\angle BOD + \angle DOC = \angle BOC$$

Substituting in the given values you get,

$$\angle BOD + (d + 13^\circ) = 125^\circ$$

$$\angle BOD = 125^\circ - (d + 13^\circ)$$

$$\angle BOD = 112^\circ - d$$

Choice A is incorrect. This may result from incorrect sign for d. **Choice C** is incorrect. This may result if $m\angle DOC = -d - 13°$. **Choice D** is incorrect. This may result from incorrect signs.

13.

Category: PHM & Modeling
Skill: Lines and Angles | **Level:** Medium

Choice C is correct because the obtained answer is $60 < B < 150°$.

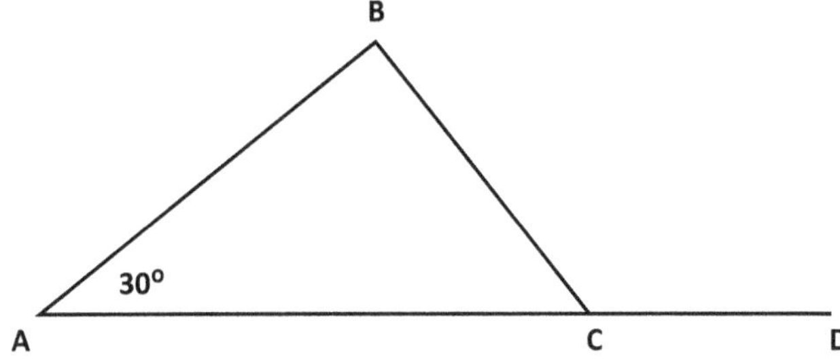

Given: $\angle BCD$ is an obtuse angle.
By exterior angle theorem, the exterior angle is the sum of the two opposite interior angles.

Hence, $m\angle A + m\angle B = m\angle BCD$

$$30^o + m\angle B = m\angle BCD$$

From Triangle ABC, $m\angle A + m\angle B + m\angle C = 180^o$

$$30^o + m\angle B + m\angle C = 180^o$$

$$m\angle B + m\angle C = 180^o - 30^o$$

$$m\angle B + m\angle C = 150^o$$

$$m\angle B = 150^o - m\angle C$$

$m\angle C$ and $m\angle BCD$ are supplementary angles. Hence, $m\angle BCD + m\angle C = 180^o$.

Analyze the given choices.
Choice A: $0 < B < 90^o$. Given that $m\angle BCD$ is obtuse, it should be greater than 90°.

Using this $30^o + m\angle B = m\angle BCD$, if $B = 0^o$ *to* $B = 60^o$, it will give a value of $m\angle BCD$ as an acute angle or a right triangle. Hence, this range is not possible.
Choice B: $30 < B < 120^o$
Using this $30^o + m\angle B = m\angle BCD$, if $B = 31^o$ *to* $B = 60^o$, it will give a value of $m\angle BCD$ as an acute angle or a right triangle. Hence, this range is not possible.
Choice C: $60 < B < 150^o$
Using this $30^o + m\angle B = m\angle BCD$, if $B = 61^o$ *to* $B = 149^o$, it will give a value of $m\angle BCD$ as an obtuse angle. Hence, this range is possible.
Choice D: $60 < B < 180^o$
Using this $30^o + m\angle B = m\angle BCD$, if $B = 61^o$ *to* $B = 179^o$, it will give a value of $m\angle BCD$ as an obtuse angle. But for $B = 150^o$ *to* $B = 179^o$, it will affect the given measure of angle $\angle A$, hence this range is not possible.

Choice A is incorrect because $0 < B < 90^o$, has possible values that will make $\angle BCD$ an acute angle. **Choice B** is incorrect because $30 < B < 120^o$, has possible values that will make $\angle BCD$ an acute angle. **Choice D** is incorrect because $60 < B < 180^o$, 150° *to* 180° values for B is not possible for $\angle BCD$

14.

Category: IES
Skill: Lines and angles | **Level:** Easy

Choice D is correct because statements I, II and III are true statements.

Given:

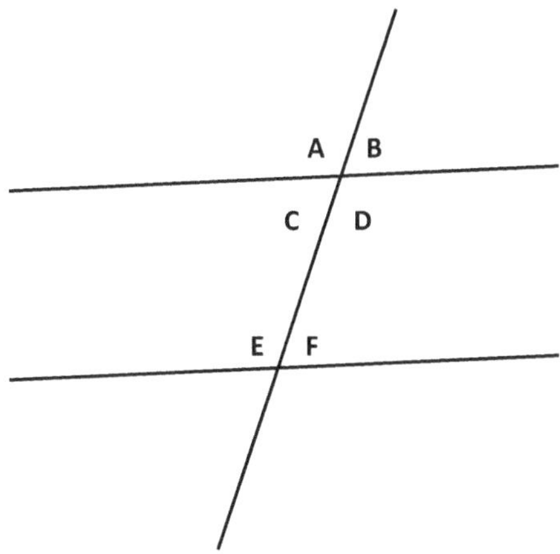

Use the properties of angles in parallel lines.

Corresponding angles are congruent:

Opposite angles are congruent.

Alternate angles are congruent.

I . $\angle A \simeq \angle D$
II. $\angle A \simeq \angle E$
III. $\angle C \simeq \angle F$

$\angle A \simeq \angle D$ because they are opposite angles.
$\angle A \simeq \angle E$ because they are corresponding angles.
$\angle C \simeq \angle F$ because they are alternate angles.
Hence, statements I, II and III are true.

Choice A is incorrect because it's not only statement I that is true. **Choice B** is incorrect because it's not only statement II that is true. **Choice C** is incorrect because it's not only statements I and II that are true.

15.

Category: PHM
Skill: Lines and angles | **Level:** Easy

Choice A is correct because the obtained answer is $-p^2$.

Write the slope between points using the formula $m = \frac{y_2 - y_1}{x_2 - x_1}$.

Between points $(-5,0) and (5q^2,10q)$.

$$m = \frac{10q - 0}{5q^2 + 5} = \frac{10q}{5q^2 + 5}$$

Between points $(-5,0) and (5p^2,10q)$.

$$m = \frac{10q - 0}{5p^2 + 5} = \frac{10q}{5p^2 + 5}$$

Equate the slope for collinearity.

$\frac{10q}{5q^2 + 5} = \frac{10q}{5p^2 + 5}$ Cancel 10q on both sides.

$$\frac{1}{5q^2 + 5} = \frac{1}{5p^2 + 5}$$

$$5q^2 + 5 = 5p^2 + 5$$

$$5q^2 = 5p^2$$

$$q^2 = p^2$$

Given the condition that $p \neq q$,

$q^2 = p^2$ then $q = \pm p$, then $q = -p$

Find pq.

$$pq = p(-p) = -p^2$$

Choice B is incorrect because p^2 is not the obtained answer. **Choice C** is incorrect because q^2 is not the obtained answer. **Choice D** is incorrect because $-q^2$ is not the obtained answer.

16.

Category: IES
Skill: Lines and angles | **Level:** Medium

Choice A is correct because the obtained angle is 55°.

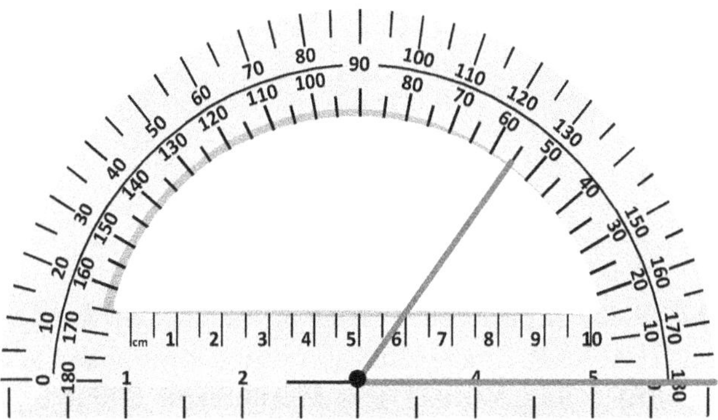

Start reading from where one ray of the angle is lined up and look for the spot where the other ray crosses the protractor. Hence, angle is 55°.

Choice B is incorrect because 65° is greater than the obtained angle. **Choice C** is incorrect because 125° is greater than the obtained angle. **Choice D** is incorrect because 130° is greater than the obtained angle.

17.

Category: IES
Skill: Lines and angles | **Level:** Hard

Choice C is correct because the obtained answer is 115°.

Assign labels to the vertices of the triangles.

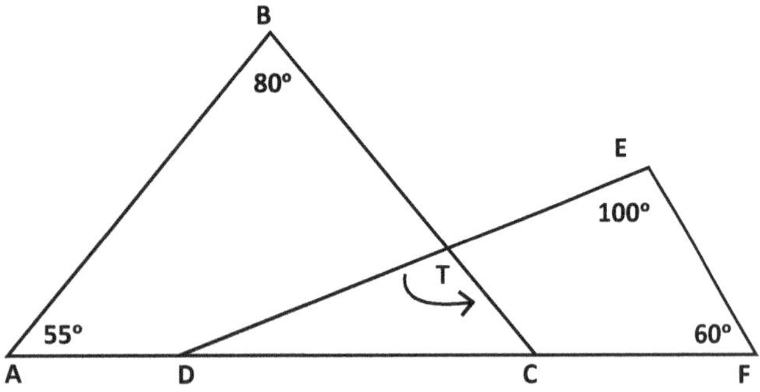

Find angle C in triangle ABC using the angle property of a triangle.

$$180^o = A + B + C$$
$$180^o = 55^o + 80^o + C$$
$$180^o = 135^o + C$$
$$180^o - 135^o = C$$
$$45^o = C$$

Find angle D in triangle EDF using the angle property of a triangle.

$$180^o = E + D + F$$
$$180^o = 100^o + D + 60^o$$
$$180^o = 160^o + D$$
$$180^o - 160^o = D$$
$$20^o = D$$

Find angle T in triangle DTC using the angle property of a triangle.

$$180^o = D + T + C$$
$$180^o = 20^o + T + 45^o$$
$$180^o = 65^o + T$$
$$180^o - 65^o = D$$
$$115^o = T$$

Choice A is incorrect because 95º is less than the obtained angle. **Choice B** is incorrect because 105º is less than the obtained angle. **Choice D** is incorrect because 125º is greater than the obtained angle.

18.

Category: IES & Modeling
Skill: Lines and angles | **Level:** Medium

Choice B is correct because the lines parallel to $4x - 4y = 4$ are C, D, and E.

Find the slope of $4x - 4y = 4$ by rewriting this to slope-intercept form.

$$4x - 4y = 4$$
$$-4y = 4 - 4x$$
$$y = x - 1$$

The slope of the given equation is positive. Hence, the parallel lines are lines that have positive slopes. Hence, lines C, D, and E is the answer.

Choice A is incorrect because lines C, D are not the only lines parallel to $4x - 4y = 4$. **Choice C** is incorrect because line F is not parallel to $4x - 4y = 4$. **Choice D** is incorrect because lines A, B are not parallel to $4x - 4y = 4$.

19.

Category: PHM
Skill: Lines and angles | **Level:** Hard

Choice C is correct because the obtained answer is $\frac{2}{3}$.

Use the Section Formula

The coordinates of point P, dividing the segment RS in the ratio k :1, are:

$$P = \left(\frac{k \times 9 + 1 \times (-1)}{k+1}, \frac{k \times 8 + 1 \times 3}{k+1}\right) = \left(\frac{9k-1}{k+1}, \frac{8k+3}{k+1}\right)$$

Since P lies on the line $x - y + 2 = 0$, substitute the coordinates of P into the equation:

$$\left(\frac{9k-1}{k+1}\right) - \left(\frac{8k+3}{k+1}\right) + 2 = 0$$

Simplify:

$$\frac{9k - 1 - (8k+3)}{k+1} + 2 = 0$$
$$\frac{9k - 1 - 8k - 3}{k+1} + 2 = 0$$
$$\frac{k-4}{k+1} + 2 = 0$$

Multiply both side by $k + 1$:

$$k - 4 + 2(k+1) = 0$$
$$k - 4 + 2k + 2 = 0$$
$$3k - 2 = 0 \Rightarrow k = \frac{2}{3}$$

Choice A is incorrect because $\frac{1}{3}$ is less than the obtained answer. **Choice B** is incorrect because $\frac{1}{2}$ is less than the obtained answer. **Choice D** is incorrect because $\frac{3}{2}$ is greater than the obtained answer.

20.

Category: IES & Modeling
Skill: Lines and angles | **Level:** Easy

Choice A is correct because the obtained value is $\frac{9}{2}\pi$.

$$810^o \times \frac{\pi}{180^o} = \frac{9}{2}\pi$$

Choice B is incorrect because $\frac{8}{2}\pi$ is not equivalent to 810°. **Choice C** is incorrect because 6π is not equivalent to 810°. **Choice D** is incorrect because 9π is not equivalent to 810°.

21.

Category: PHM
Skill: Two-dimensional shapes | **Level:** Easy

Choice A is correct because the obtained answer is $\sqrt{13}$.
Given : Vertice of the triangle: $L(1,3), M(4,5), N(6,2)$
Find the length of the base using the distance formula.

$$d = \sqrt{(x_2 - x_1)^2 + (y_2 - y_1)^2}$$
$$d = \sqrt{(4-6)^2 + (5-2)^2}$$
$$d = \sqrt{(-2)^2 + (3)^2}$$
$$d = \sqrt{4+9}$$
$$d = \sqrt{13}$$

Find the area of the triangle using the Shoelace Theorem.

$$A = \frac{1}{2}\left|1(5-2) + 4(2-3) + 6(3-5)\right|$$
$$A = \frac{1}{2}\left|1(3) + 4(-1) + 6(-2)\right|$$
$$A = \frac{1}{2}\left|3 - 4 - 12\right|$$
$$A = \frac{1}{2}\left|-13\right|$$
$$A = \frac{13}{2}$$

Find the altitude.

$$h = \frac{2A}{d}$$
$$h = \frac{2\left(\frac{13}{2}\right)}{\sqrt{13}}$$
$$h = \frac{13}{\sqrt{13}}$$
$$h = \frac{13}{\sqrt{13}} \cdot \frac{\sqrt{13}}{\sqrt{13}}$$
$$h = \frac{13\sqrt{13}}{13}$$
$$h = \sqrt{13}$$

Choice B is incorrect because $13\sqrt{13}$ is greater than $\sqrt{13}$. **Choice C** is incorrect because 13 is greater than $\sqrt{13}$. **Choice D** is incorrect because $2\sqrt{13}$ is greater than $\sqrt{13}$.

22.

Category: PHM
Skill: Two-dimensional shapes | **Level:** Easy

Choice C is correct. Reflecting the graph about the x-axis transforms the equation to $y = -\sqrt[3]{x}$. A horizontal translation to the right 3 units transforms $y = -\sqrt[3]{x}$ to $y = -\sqrt[3]{x-3}$.

Choice A is incorrect. It shifts left 3 instead of right 3. **Choice B** is incorrect. It shifts down 3. **Choice D** is incorrect. It shifts up 3.

23.

Category: PHM
Skill: Two-dimensional shapes | **Level:** Easy

Choice A is correct. AC = BD only if the parallelogram is a rectangle. For a parallelogram opposite sides are congruent so Choice B is true, opposite angles are congruent so Choice C is true, and consecutive angles are supplementary so Choice D is also correct.

Choice B is incorrect. Based on the explanation above, this is true. **Choice C** is incorrect. Based on the explanation above, this is true. **Choice D** is incorrect. Based on the explanation above, this is true.

24.

Category: IES
Skill: Two-dimensional shapes | **Level:** Medium

Choice D is correct because 10 and 6 can't be the dimension of the rectangle.
Analyze the given choices.
Choice A: 1 and 12

$$P = 2l + 2w$$
$$26 = 2(1) + 2(12)$$
$$26 = 2 + 24$$
$$26 = 26$$

Choice B: 4 and 9

$$P = 2l + 2w$$
$$26 = 2(4) + 2(9)$$
$$26 = 8 + 18$$
$$26 = 26$$

Choice C: 8 and 5

$$P = 2l + 2w$$

$$26 = 2(8) + 2(5)$$
$$26 = 16 + 10$$
$$26 = 26$$

Choice D: 10 and 6

$$P = 2l + 2w$$
$$26 = 2(10) + 2(6)$$
$$26 = 20 + 12$$
$$26 \neq 32$$

Choice A is incorrect because 1 and 12 are possible dimensions of the rectangle. **Choice B** is incorrect because 4 and 9 are possible dimensions of the rectangle. **Choice C** is incorrect because 8 and 5 are possible dimensions of the rectangle.

25.

Category: IES & Modeling
Skill: Two-dimensional shapes | **Level:** Easy

Choice C is correct because the obtained answer is 110°.

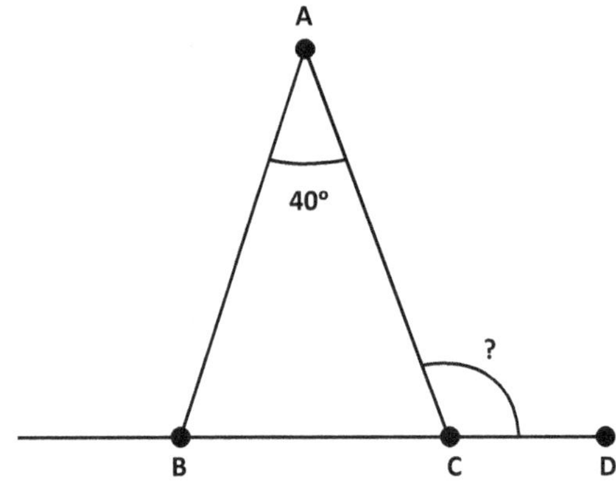

Since length of $\overline{AB}$ is equal to the length of $\overline{AC}$ then angle B and C are equal.
Let x be the measure of angle B and C.
Find x using the angle property of the triangle.

$$\angle B + \angle C + \angle A = 180°$$
$$x + x + 40° = 180°$$
$$2x = 180° - 40°$$
$$2x = 140°$$
$$x = 70°$$

Use the exterior angle theorem to find the measure of angle ACD.

$$\angle ACD = \angle A + \angle B$$
$$\angle ACD = 40° + 70°$$
$$\angle ACD = 110°$$

Choice A is incorrect because 60° is less than the obtained value of the exterior angle. **Choice B** is incorrect because 80° is less than the obtained value of the exterior angle. **Choice D** is incorrect because 160° is greater than the obtained value of the exterior angle.

26.

Category: PHM
Skill: Two-dimensional shapes | **Level:** Medium

Choice C is correct because the obtained answer is

$$120 + 20\sqrt{2}$$

Given:

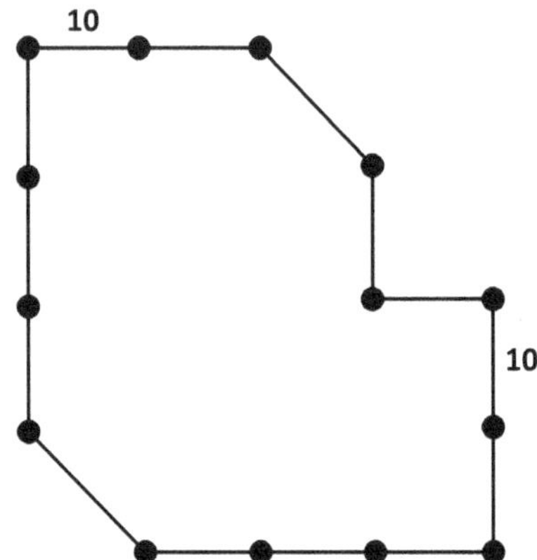

Identify the number of sides in the given figure.
Number of 10 units : 12
Number of diagonals: 2
Find the measure of the diagonal.

$$c^2 = a^2 + b^2$$
$$c^2 = 10^2 + 10^2$$
$$c^2 = 2(100)$$
$$c = 10\sqrt{2}$$

Find the perimeter:

$$P = 12(10\,units) + 2(10\sqrt{2})units$$
$$P = 120\,units + 20\sqrt{2}\ units$$
$$P = 120 + 20\sqrt{2}\ units$$

Choice A is incorrect because 120 is less than the obtained perimeter. **Choice B** is incorrect because $120 + 10\sqrt{2}$ is less than the obtained perimeter. **Choice D** is incorrect because 140 is less than the obtained perimeter.

27.

Category: PHM & Modeling
Skill: Two-dimensional shapes | **Level:** Medium

Choice D is correct because the required proof is $\Delta ABC \cong \Delta XYZ$ by SSS theorem, and $\angle C \cong \angle Z$ because corresponding parts of congruent triangles are congruent.
Figure:

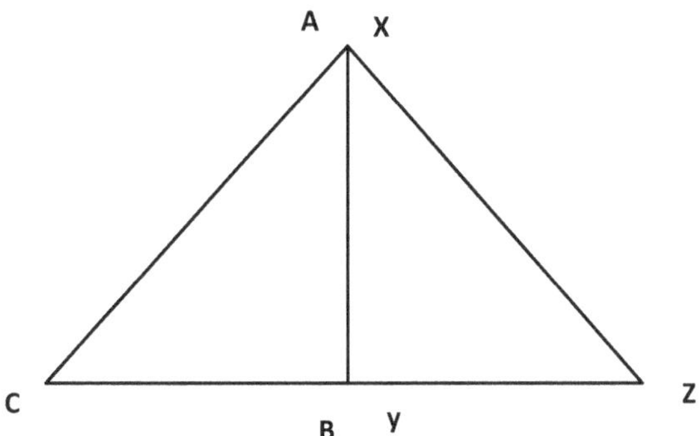

Analyze the given:

- wires of equal length. $\overline{AC} = \overline{XZ}$
- wires are tied 3 feet above the ground $\overline{AB} = \overline{XY}$
- C and Z, which are equidistant from the mango tree $\overline{CB} = \overline{ZY}$

Hence, $\Delta ABC \simeq \Delta XYZ$ by SSS theorem.
By CPCTC (corresponding parts of congruent triangles are congruent), $\angle C \cong \angle Z$.

Choice A is incorrect because $\Delta ABC \simeq \Delta XYZ$ is not congruent by AAS theorem. **Choice B** is incorrect because AA theorem does not exist. **Choice C** is incorrect because $\angle C \cong \angle Z$ is not congruent by ASA theorem.

28.

Category: IES & Modeling
Skill: Two-dimensional shapes | **Level:** Medium

Choice B is correct. One rotation of the wheel encompasses the circumference of the wheel so, C = 2π(6) = 12π. Rotating 20 then 12π × 20 = 753.98 inches or 62.83 feet which is approximately 63 feet.

Choice A is incorrect because it uses 6π as the circumference of the wheel. **Choice C** is incorrect because it uses 24π as the circumference of the wheel. **Choice D** is incorrect because it uses the area of the circle to determine its circumference.

29.

Category: IES
Skill: Two-dimensional shapes | **Level:** Easy

Choice A is correct because the obtained perimeter of the final figure is $10+15\sqrt{2}$.
Given:
Triangle ABO shown below is reflected over the y-axis, then the triangle in quadrant 2 is reflected over the x-axis.

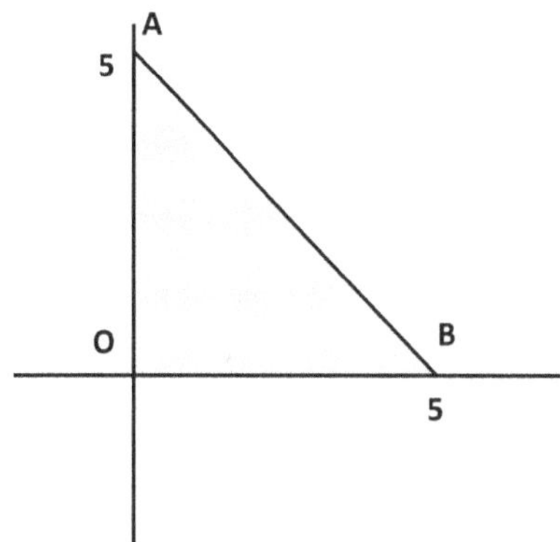

Original figure:

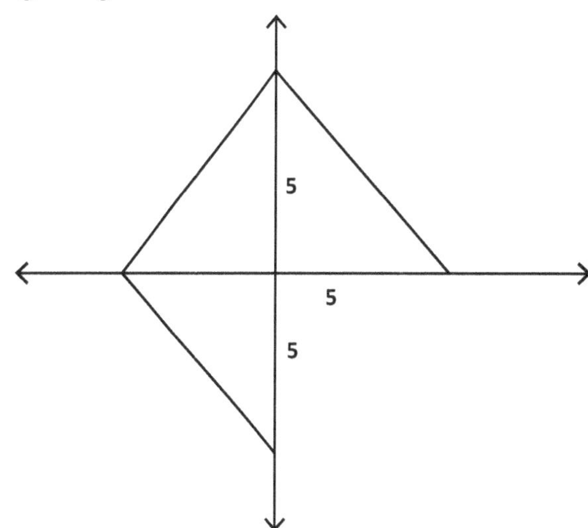

New figure:
Use Pythagorean theorem to find the measure of the diagonal.

$$c^2 = a^2 + b^2$$
$$c^2 = 5^2 + 5^2$$
$$c = 5\sqrt{2}$$

The perimeter of the new figure is

$$P = 5 + 5\sqrt{2} + 5\sqrt{2} + 5\sqrt{2} + 5$$
$$P = 10 + 15\sqrt{2}$$

Choice B is incorrect because 15 is less than the obtained perimeter. **Choice C** is incorrect because 25 is less than the obtained perimeter. **Choice D** is incorrect because $30+15\sqrt{2}$ is greater than the obtained perimeter.

30.

Category: PHM
Skill: Two-dimensional shapes | **Level:** Easy

Choice A is correct. Substitute the center of the circle (5, 3) into the answer choices to see which equation is a solution. Substituting the center into $y = 2x - 7$ you get,

$$3 = 2(5) - 7$$
$$3 = 10 - 7$$
$$3 = 3$$

choice A is the correct choice. The other answer choices do not yield an equality when substituting the center.

Choice B is incorrect. This does not yield an equality when substituting the center. **Choice C** is incorrect. This does not yield an equality when substituting the center. **Choice D** is incorrect. This does not yield an equality when substituting the center.

31.

Category: IES & Modeling
Skill: Two-dimensional shapes | **Level:** Easy

Choice A is correct because the obtained figure is also a square as shown in Choice A and the area is 338 cm^2.
Given: Area of the original square: 169 cm^2.
The side of the new figure is the diagonal of the original square .
Use the formula for the diagonal of the square formula.

$$d = s\sqrt{2}$$
$$d = 13\sqrt{2}$$

The side of the new figure is $13\sqrt{2}$.
Area of the new figure.

$$A = s^2 = (13\sqrt{2})^2 = 169(2) = 338\,cm^2$$

Choice B is incorrect because the figure is incorrect. **Choice C** is incorrect because the figure and the value of the area are incorrect. **Choice D** is incorrect because the value of the area is incorrect.

32.

Category: PHM
Skill: Two-dimensional shapes | **Level:** Medium

Choice B is correct because the obtained area of the wood part of the frame is 50 in^2.

The area of the frame is $A = 10'' \times 13'' = 130\,in^2$
The area of the photo paper is $A = 8'' \times 10'' = 80\,in^2$

The area of the wooden part is the difference between the area of the frame and the area of the photo paper.

$$A = 130\,in^2 - 80\,in^2 = 50\,in^2$$

Choice A is incorrect because 45 in^2 is less than the obtained area. **Choice C** is incorrect because 55 in^2 is greater than the obtained area. **Choice D** is incorrect because 80 in^2 is greater than the obtained area.

33.

Category: PHM
Skill: Two-dimensional shapes | **Level:** Medium

Choice B is correct because the obtained answer is \$162.

Given: Fence : width = 6 meters, length =12 meters

Fenced parallel to the width of the rectangular field, hence additional 3 fences inside the rectangle.

Find the perimeter of the rectangular field including the inner fence.

$$P = 2l + 2w + 3w$$
$$P = 2(12)+2(6)+3(6)$$
$$P = 24+12+18$$
$$P = 54 \text{ meters}$$

Find the total cost of fencing the rectangular field.

Total cost = Perimeter (Price of the fence per meter)
Total cost = 54(\$3)
Total cost = \$162

Choice A is incorrect because \$144 is less than the obtained answer. **Choice C** is incorrect because \$172 is greater than the obtained answer. **Choice D** is incorrect because \$184 is greater than the obtained answer.

34.

Category: PHM
Skill: Two-dimensional shapes | **Level:** Easy

Choice B is correct because the longest side of the triangle is 30 inches.

Given: Perimeter of the triangle = 66 inches, One side = 16, ratio of two sides : 2: 3

Let x be the proportionality constant of the unknown sides of the triangle.

Find the value of x using the formula of the perimeter.

$$P = 16 + 2x + 3x$$
$$66 = 16 + 2x + 3x$$
$$50 = 5x$$
$$10 = x$$

Sides of the triangle: given side : 16
Unknown side: $2x = 2(10) = 20$
Unknown side: $3x = 3(10) = 30$
Hence, the longest side is 30 inches.

Choice A is incorrect because 24 is less than the obtained value. **Choice C** is incorrect because 48 is greater than the obtained value. **Choice D** is incorrect because 52 is greater than the obtained value.

35.

Category: PHM
Skill: Two-dimensional shapes | **Level:** Easy

Choice C is correct because the obtained answer is 72.
Given: base of $\Delta ABD = \underline{BD} = \underline{BC} + \underline{CD} = 7 + 5 = 12$
height of $\Delta ABD = \underline{AD} = 12$
Find the area of ΔABD.

$$A = \frac{1}{2}bh$$
$$A = \frac{1}{2}(12)(12)$$
$$A = \frac{1}{2}(144)$$
$$A = 72$$

Choice A is incorrect because 48 is less than the obtained value. **Choice B** is incorrect because 56 is less than the obtained value. **Choice D** is incorrect because 81 is greater than the obtained value.

36.

Category: PHM & Modeling
Skill: Two-dimensional shapes | **Level:** Medium

Choice C is correct because the obtained answer is 12 mi.
Given: $\overline{CD} = 3mi, \overline{DE} = 4mi$
Unknown: Perimeter of the triangle
Find $\overline{EC}$ using Pythagorean theorem

$$\overline{EC}^2 = \overline{CD}^2 + \overline{DE}^2$$
$$\overline{EC}^2 = 3^2 + 4^2$$
$$\overline{EC}^2 = 9 + 16$$
$$\overline{EC}^2 = 25$$
$$\overline{EC} = \sqrt{25}$$
$$\overline{EC} = 5$$

To find the total distance that Shane ran, we use the perimeter of the triangle.

$$Perimeter = \underline{CD} + \underline{DE} + \underline{EC}$$
$$Perimeter = 3 + 4 + 5$$
$$Perimeter = 12\,mi$$

Choice A is incorrect because 7 mi is less than the obtained value. **Choice B** is incorrect because 10 mi is less than the obtained value. **Choice D** is incorrect because 16 mi is greater than the obtained value.

37.

Category: IES & Modeling
Skill: Two-dimensional shapes | **Level:** Medium

Choice B is correct. We are looking for the side across from angle G, or side EF. Since $\Delta ABC \sim \Delta EFG$, the ratio of the corresponding sides of the 2 triangles are equal. Then,

$$\frac{5}{g} = \frac{12}{8}$$
$$12g = 40$$
$$g = \frac{40}{12} = \frac{10}{3}$$

Choice A is incorrect. This is the reciprocal of the correct answer. **Choice C** is incorrect. This may result from incorrect use of formula. **Choice D** is incorrect. This may result from incorrect use of formula and the given.

38.

Category: PHM & Modeling
Skill: Two-dimensional shapes | **Level:** Hard

Choice D is correct because the answer is $\frac{x^2}{16} + \frac{y^2}{12} = 1$.

Given: Vertices: $(\pm 4, 0)$, Foci: $(\pm 2, 0)$, Center: $(0,0)$
From the given, the distance from the center to each vertex is the semi-major axis, $a = 4$.
The foci are $(2,0)$ and $(-2,0)$, meaning the distance from the center to each focus is $c = 2$.
Graph the points.

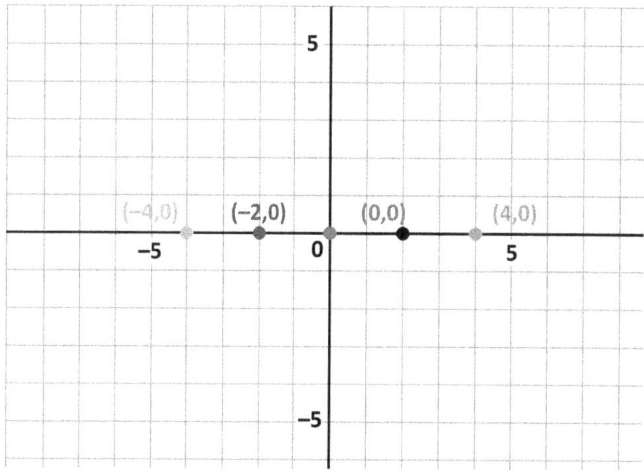

Find the value of b using the relationship $c^2 = a^2 - b^2$.

$$c^2 = a^2 - b^2$$
$$2^2 = 4^2 - b^2$$
$$b^2 = 4^2 - 2^2$$
$$b^2 = 16 - 4$$
$$b^2 = 12$$
$$b = \sqrt{12}$$

The ellipse has horizontal major axis, hence, use the formula $\frac{x^2}{a^2} + \frac{y^2}{b^2} = 1$.

$$\frac{x^2}{4^2} + \frac{y^2}{\left(\sqrt{12}\right)^2} = 1.$$

$$\frac{x^2}{16} + \frac{y^2}{12} = 1$$

The graph is .

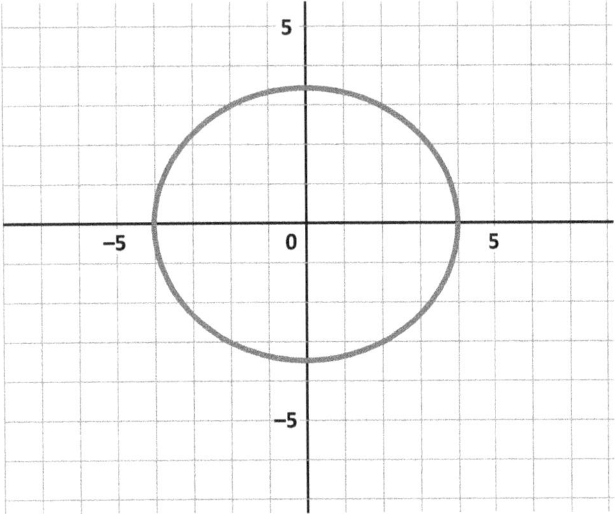

Hence, **Choice D is correct.**

Choice A is incorrect because the equation does not represent the ellipse. **Choice B** is incorrect because both the equation and the graph do not represent the ellipse. **Choice C** is incorrect because the graph does not represent the ellipse.

39.

Category: IES & Modeling
Skill: Two-dimensional shapes | **Level:** Hard

Choice B is correct because the obtained area of triangle DEG is 60 square units.
Area of triangle DEG = Area of triangle DGF - Area of triangle EGF
Area of triangle DGF = $\frac{1}{2}(12+7)(10) = \frac{1}{2}(190) = 95$

Area of triangle EGF = $\frac{1}{2}(7)(10) = \frac{1}{2}(70) = 35$

Area of triangle DEG = Area of triangle DGF – Area of triangle EGF
= 95 – 35
=60

Choice A is incorrect because 50 is less than the obtained area of triangle DEG is 60 square units. **Choice C** is incorrect because 70 is greater than the obtained area of triangle DEG is 60 square units. **Choice D** is incorrect because 80 is greater than the obtained area of triangle DEG is 60 square units.

40.

Category: IES & Modeling
Skill: Two-dimensional shapes | **Level:** Medium

Choice C is correct because the obtained answer is 72°.
The geometric figure is a star with 5 vertices.
The smallest angle of rotation is

$$\frac{360^o}{no.of\ vertices} = \frac{360^o}{5} = 72^o.$$

Choice A is incorrect because 45° is not the minimum angle of rotation of the given figure. **Choice B** is incorrect because 65° is not the minimum angle of rotation of the given figure. **Choice D** is incorrect because 90° is not the minimum angle of rotation of the given figure.

41.

Category: PHM
Skill: Two-dimensional shapes | **Level:** Hard

Choice D is correct because the obtained answer is 9:16.
Use the circumference formula to find the radius of the two circles.

$$C_1 = 30cm \qquad r = \frac{c_1}{2\pi} = \frac{30}{2\pi} = \frac{15}{\pi}cm$$

$$C_1 = 40cm \qquad r = \frac{c_1}{2\pi} = \frac{40}{2\pi} = \frac{20}{\pi}cm$$

Find the areas of the circles.

$$A_1 = \pi r_1^2 = \pi(\frac{15}{\pi})^2 = \frac{225}{\pi}$$
$$A_2 = \pi r_2^2 = \pi(\frac{20}{\pi})^2 = \frac{400}{\pi}$$

The ratio of the areas is

$$\frac{A_1}{A_2} = \frac{\frac{225}{\pi}}{\frac{400}{\pi}} = \frac{225}{400} = \frac{9}{16}.$$ Answer is 9:16.

Choice A is incorrect because 2:3 is not the obtained answer. **Choice B** is incorrect because 11:6 is not the obtained answer. **Choice C** is incorrect because 3:5 is not the obtained answer.

42.

Category: PHM & Modeling
Skill: Two-dimensional shapes | **Level:** Medium

Choice B is correct because the obtained answer is 113.

The side of the square is 12. The diameter of the circle is also equal to 12.

The radius of the circle is $r = \frac{d}{2} = \frac{12}{2} = 6$.

The area of the circle is $A = \pi r^2 = \pi(6)^2 = 113$.

Choice A is incorrect because 108 is less than the obtained answer. **Choice C** is incorrect because 386 is less than the obtained answer. **Choice D** is incorrect because 452 is greater than the obtained answer.

43.

Category: IES & Modeling
Skill: Two-dimensional shapes | **Level:** Easy

Choice C is correct because the obtained perimeter of triangle ABC is 14 centimeters.
Find the side lengths BA and BC using properties of similar triangles.

$$\frac{BA}{LK} = \frac{AC}{KM}$$

$$\frac{BA}{12.5} = \frac{3}{7.5}$$

$$7.5BA = 37.5$$

$$BA = 5$$

$$\frac{BC}{LM} = \frac{AC}{KM}$$

$$\frac{BC}{15} = \frac{3}{7.5}$$

$$7.5BC = 45$$

$$BC = 6$$

Find the perimeter of triangle ABC.

$$P = BA + BC + AC$$

$$P = 5 + 6 + 3$$

$$P = 14$$

Choice A is incorrect because 11 is less than the obtained perimeter of triangle ABC. **Choice B** is incorrect because 12 is less than the obtained perimeter of triangle ABC. **Choice D** is incorrect because 16 is greater than the obtained perimeter of triangle ABC.

44.

Category: PHM
Skill: Two-dimensional shapes | **Level:** Medium

Choice D is correct because the obtained answer is $4\sqrt{3}$.
In an equilateral triangle, the formula of the altitude is

$$h = \frac{a\sqrt{3}}{2}.$$

In the problem, $a = 8$.

Hence, $h = \frac{a\sqrt{3}}{2} = \frac{8\sqrt{3}}{2} = 4\sqrt{3}$.

Choice A is incorrect because $2\sqrt{3}$ is less than the obtained value. **Choice B** is incorrect because $3\sqrt{2}$ is less than the obtained value. **Choice C** is incorrect because $3\sqrt{4}$ is less than the obtained value.

45.

Category: PHM
Skill: Two-dimensional shapes | **Level:** Easy

Choice C is correct because the obtained answer is 120°.

The total measure of the angle in a quadrilateral is 360°.

$$360° = A + B + C + D$$

$$360° = 100° + 65° + C + 75°$$

$$360° = 240° + C$$

$$360° - 240° = C$$

$$120° = C$$

Choice A is incorrect because 80° is less than the obtained angle. **Choice B** is incorrect because 110° is less than the obtained angle. **Choice D** is incorrect because 140° is greater than the obtained angle.

46.

Category: PHM & Modeling
Skill: Two-dimensional shapes | **Level:** Easy

Choice B is correct because the obtained answer is

$$(x - \frac{3}{2})^2 + (y - \frac{9}{2})^2 = \frac{25}{2}.$$

Given: endpoints of its diameter are $(-1,2)$ and $(4,7)$.
Use the formula for the circle, $(x-h)^2 + (y-k)^2 = r^2$.
Find the center of the circle (h,k) and the radius.
For the center (h,k), use the midpoint formula.

$$m=\left(\frac{x_1+x_2}{2},\frac{y_1+y_2}{2}\right)=\left(\frac{-1+4}{2},\frac{2+7}{2}\right)=\left(\frac{3}{2},\frac{9}{2}\right)$$

Hence, center (h,k) is $\left(\frac{3}{2},\frac{9}{2}\right)$.

Find the radius using the distance formula.

$$d=\sqrt{(x_2-x_1)^2+(y_2-y_1)^2}$$
$$d=\sqrt{(4-(-1))^2+(7-2)^2}$$
$$d=\sqrt{(5)^2+(5)^2}$$
$$d=\sqrt{25+25}$$
$$d=\sqrt{50}$$
$$d=5\sqrt{2} \quad \text{diameter of the circle.}$$

Radius $=\frac{diameter}{2}=\frac{5\sqrt{2}}{2}$.

Use the formula for the circle,

$$(x-h)^2+(y-k)^2=r^2$$
$$(x-\frac{3}{2})^2+(y-\frac{9}{2})^2=(\frac{5\sqrt{2}}{2})^2$$
$$(x-\frac{3}{2})^2+(y-\frac{9}{2})^2=\frac{25(2)}{4}$$
$$(x-\frac{3}{2})^2+(y-\frac{9}{2})^2=\frac{25}{2}$$

Choice A is incorrect because the equation does not represent the given circle. **Choice C** is incorrect because the equation does not represent the given circle. **Choice D** is incorrect because the equation does not represent the given circle.

47.

Category: IES & Modeling
Skill: Two-dimensional shapes | **Level:** Easy

Choice D is correct because the obtained answer is $6\pm\sqrt{7}$.

To find the x-intercept, let $y=0$.

$$(x-6)^2+(y+3)^2=16$$
$$(x-6)^2+(0+3)^2=16$$
$$(x-6)^2+9=16$$
$$(x-6)^2=16-9$$
$$(x-6)^2=7$$
$$(x-6)=\pm\sqrt{7}$$
$$x=6\pm\sqrt{7}$$

Choice A is incorrect because $7\pm\sqrt{6}$ is greater than obtained value. **Choice B** is incorrect because $2\pm\sqrt{5}$ is less than obtained value. **Choice C** is incorrect because $-6\pm\sqrt{7}$ is less than obtained value.

48.

Category: IES & Modeling
Skill: Two-dimensional shapes | **Level:** Easy

Choice B is correct because the obtained answer is $y=\frac{x^2}{2}$.

Use the SSS Similar triangle rule.

$$\frac{x}{y}=\frac{2}{x}$$
$$2y=x(x)$$
$$2y=x^2$$
$$y=\frac{x^2}{2}$$

Choice A is incorrect because $y=2x^2$ does not represent y in terms of x. **Choice C** is incorrect because $y=\frac{2}{x^2}$ does not represent y in terms of x. **Choice D** is incorrect because $y=2x$ does not represent y in terms of x.

49.

Category: IES
Skill: Two-dimensional shapes | **Level:** Medium

Choice C is correct because the obtained answer is 18.4.

Find the radius of one circle using the formula $r=\frac{a+b-c}{2}$. The diagonal of the square is $10\sqrt{2}$.

$$r=\frac{10+10-10\sqrt{2}}{2}=10-5\sqrt{2}$$

Find the circumference of one circle.

$$C=2\pi r=2\pi\left(10-5\sqrt{2}\right)=18.4$$

Choice A is incorrect because 12.2 is less than the obtained value. **Choice B** is incorrect because 16.5 is less than the obtained value. **Choice D** is incorrect because 20.5 is greater than the obtained value.

50.

Category: PHM
Skill: Two-dimensional shapes | **Level:** Medium

Choice C is correct because the obtained answer is 10.0.

Find the scaling factor.

$$Scaling\ factor = \frac{shortest\ side}{shortest\ side\ in\ the\ ratio} = \frac{8}{12} = \frac{2}{3}$$

Find the longest side.

$$longest\ side = scaling\ factor \times longest\ side\ in\ the\ ratio$$

$$longest\ side = \frac{2}{3} \times 15$$

$$longest\ side = \frac{30}{3}$$

$$longest\ side = 10$$

Choice A is incorrect because 6.4 is less than the obtained answer. **Choice B** is incorrect because 9.3 is less than the obtained answer. **Choice D** is incorrect because 11.0 is greater than the obtained answer.

51.

Category: IES
Skill: Two-dimensional shapes | **Level:** Easy

Choice D is correct because the obtained answer is 14.
Use the triangle inequality theorem.
It states that if given a triangle with sides of length a, b, and c, it must be true that $a + b > c$, $a + c > b$, and $b + c > a$.
Since the triangle is an isosceles, the possible value of the third side is either 6 or 14.
If the third side is 6, use the triangle inequality theorem.
$6 + 6 > 14$
$12 > 14$
This is false, hence, 6 is not a possible value of the third side.
If the third side is 14, use the triangle inequality theorem.
$14 + 6 > 14$ true
$14 + 14 > 6$ true
Hence, the third side should be 14.

Choice A is incorrect because 6 is less than the obtained answer. **Choice B** is incorrect because 8 is less than the obtained answer. **Choice C** is incorrect because 10 is less than the obtained answer.

52.

Category: PHM & Modeling
Skill: Two-dimensional shapes | **Level:** Easy

Choice C is correct because the obtained answer is 70°.
The angle between the tangent ends of two radii is given by the formula = 180° – central angle.
The angle between the tangent ends of two radii is given by the formula =
180° – 110° = 70°

Choice A is incorrect because 40° is less than the obtained angle. **Choice B** is incorrect because 50° is less than the obtained angle. **Choice D** is incorrect because 90° is greater than the obtained angle.

53.

Category: PHM
Skill: Two-dimensional shapes | **Level:** Medium

Choice C is correct because the obtained answer is 14,400.
Find the area of the room.

$$A = 20 \times 18 = 360\,m^2$$

Find the length of the carpet needed.

$$length\ of\ the\ carpet = \frac{Area\ of\ the\ room}{width\ of\ the\ carpet} = \frac{360\,m^2}{1.5\,m} = 240\,m$$

Cost of carpeting = $240\,m(\$60)$ = \$14,400

Choice A is incorrect because \$11,400 is less than the obtained cost. **Choice B** is incorrect because \$14,000 is less than the obtained cost. **Choice D** is incorrect because \$14,800 is greater than the obtained cost.

54.

Category: PHM
Skill: Two-dimensional shapes | **Level:** Hard

Choice B is correct because the obtained answer is $\angle P = 90°$, $\angle Q = 30°$, $\angle R = 60°$.
Given: $a + b = 120^o, a - c = 30^o$.
Use the angle property of triangles.

$$a + b + c = 180^o$$
$$120^o + c = 180^o$$
$$c = 180^o - 120^o$$
$$c = 60^o$$
$$\angle R = c = 60^o$$

Substitute the obtained value of c into $a - c = 30^o$ to find a.

$$a - c = 30^o$$
$$a - 60^0 = 30^o$$
$$a = 30^o + 60^o$$
$$\angle P = a = 90^o$$

Substitute the value of a into $a + b = 120^o$ to find b.

$$a + b = 120^o$$
$$90^o + b = 120^o$$
$$b = 120^o - 90^o$$

$$b = 30^o$$

Choice A is incorrect because $\angle Q$ and $\angle R$ are incorrect. **Choice C** is incorrect because all angles are incorrect. **Choice D** is incorrect because $\angle P$ and $\angle R$ are incorrect.

55.

Category: PHM & Modeling
Skill: Two-dimensional shapes | **Level:** Medium

Choice C is correct because the obtained answer is $0.6m^2$.
Let x be the side of the isosceles triangle.
We know that $30cm = 0.3m$.

$$Perimeter = x + x + (x - 0.3)$$
$$3.6 = x + x + (x - 0.3)$$
$$3.6 + 0.3 = x + x + x$$
$$3.9 = 3x$$
$$1.3 = x$$

Base of the triangle: 1.3 - 0.3 = 1
Find the area of the triangle.

$$Area = \frac{1}{2} base(height)$$
$$Area = \frac{1}{2}(1)\left(\sqrt{a^2 - \frac{b^2}{4}}\right)$$
$$Area = \frac{1}{2}(1)\left(\sqrt{1.3^2 - \frac{1^2}{4}}\right)$$
$$Area = \frac{1}{2}(1)(1.2)$$
$$Area = 0.6m^2$$

Choice A is incorrect because $0.2m^2$ is less than the obtained area. **Choice B** is incorrect because $0.4m^2$ is less than the obtained area. **Choice D** is incorrect because $0.8m^2$ is greater than the obtained area.

56.

Category: PHM & Modeling
Skill: Two-dimensional shapes | **Level:** Easy

Choice D is correct because the obtained answer is $x^2 + y^2 - 2x + 4y = 11$.
Use the equation for the circle, $(x-h)^2 + (y-k)^2 = r^2$, where (h,k) is the center of the circle.

$$(x-h)^2 + (y-k)^2 = r^2$$
$$(x-1)^2 + (y+2)^2 = 4^2$$

We can expand the equation:

$$x^2 - 2x + 1 + y^2 + 4y + 4 = 16$$
$$x^2 - 2x + y^2 + 4y = 16 - 1 - 4$$
$$x^2 + y^2 - 2x + 4y = 11$$

Choice A is incorrect because $x^2 + y^2 + 2x - 4y = 16$ does not represent the given circle. **Choice B** is incorrect because $x^2 + y^2 + 2x - 4y = 11$ does not represent the given circle. **Choice C** is incorrect because $x^2 + y^2 + 2x + 4y = 16$ does not represent the given circle.

57.

Category: PHM
Skill: Two-dimensional shapes | **Level:** Easy

Choice B is correct because the obtained answer is 16.

$$A = \frac{1}{2}bh$$
$$24 = \frac{1}{2}b(3)$$
$$16 = b$$

Choice A is incorrect because 12 is less than the obtained answer. **Choice C** is incorrect because 18 is greater than the obtained answer. **Choice D** is incorrect because 20 is greater than the obtained answer.

58.

Category: PHM
Skill: Two-dimensional shapes | **Level:** Medium

Choice B is correct because the obtained answer is circle.
Find the area of each shape given that P = 120 cm.

Equilateral Triangle: $P = s + s + s$

$$120 = 3s$$
$$40 = s$$

Each side is 40 cm.

$$A = \frac{\sqrt{3}}{4}s^2 = \frac{\sqrt{3}}{4}(40)^2 = 692.8$$

Square: $P = s + s + s + s$

$$120 = 4s$$
$$30 = s$$

Each side is 30 cm.

$$A = s^2 = (30)^2 = 900$$

Circle: $C = 2\pi r$

$$120 = 2\pi r$$
$$\frac{60}{\pi} = r$$

$$A = \pi r^2 = \pi(\frac{60}{\pi})^2 = 1146.5$$

Hence, the circle has the largest area among the shapes

Choice A is incorrect because the triangle does not have the largest area. **Choice C** is incorrect because the triangle does not have the largest area. **Choice D** is incorrect because the shapes do not have equal area.

59.

Category: PHM & Modeling
Skill: Two-dimensional shapes | **Level:** Easy

Choice B is correct because the obtained answer is 60 square units.
Find the side length.

$$A = s^2$$
$$225 = s^2$$
$$\sqrt{225} = s$$
$$15 = s$$

Find the perimeter.

$$P = 4s = 4(15) = 60$$

Choice A is incorrect because 40 is less than the obtained perimeter. **Choice C** is incorrect because 70 is greater than the obtained perimeter. **Choice D** is incorrect because 80 is greater than the obtained perimeter.

60.

Category: IES & Modeling
Skill: Two-dimensional shapes | **Level:** Medium

Choice B is correct because the obtained answer is the area of each triangle will be 56 square meters divided by 2.

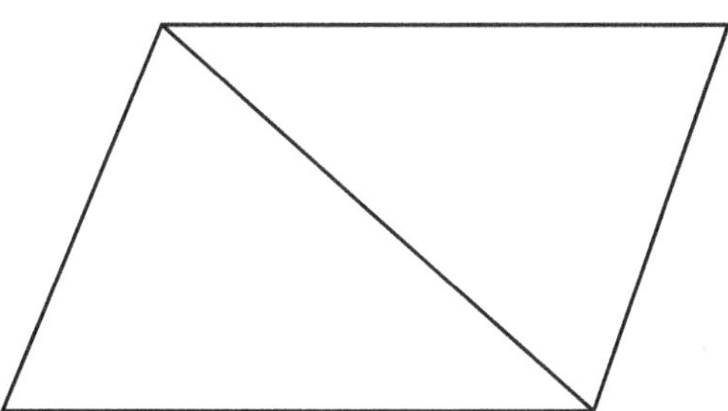

Two triangles can be formed from a parallelogram. Since Area of the parallelogram is 56, then each triangle will have an area of 56/2 = 28.

Choice A is incorrect because area will not double. **Choice C** is incorrect because it is stated that there will be two triangles formed and not 3. **Choice D** is incorrect because triangles can be formed from the parallelogram.

61.

Category: PHM
Skill: Two-dimensional shapes | **Level:** Medium

Choice B is correct because the obtained answer is 29.

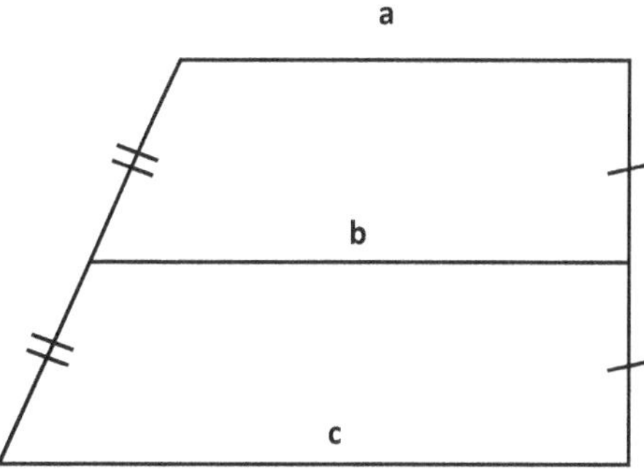

Use the midsegment theorem.

$$b = \frac{a+c}{2} = \frac{24+34}{2} = \frac{58}{2} = 29$$

Choice A is incorrect because 25 is less than the obtained value. **Choice C** is incorrect because 30 is greater than the obtained value. **Choice D** is incorrect because 32 is greater than the obtained value.

62.

Category: IES
Skill: Two-dimensional shapes | **Level:** Hard

Choice B is correct because the obtained answer is $x^2 + y^2 = 52^2$.
Since, the center of the circle lies in the origin, use the equation $x^2 + y^2 = r^2$.

The radius of the circle is 52. Hence, the equation of the circle is $x^2 + y^2 = 52^2$.

Choice A is incorrect because $x^2 - y^2 = 52^2$ does not represent the equation of the given circle. **Choice C** is incorrect because $x^2 + y^2 = 52$ does not represent the equation of the given circle. **Choice D** is incorrect because $x^2 + y^2 = 52$ does not represent the equation of the given circle.

63.

Category: IES & Modeling
Skill: Two-dimensional shapes | **Level:** Hard

Choice A is correct because the obtained answer is

$$A = \frac{a^2 + 2ab + b^2}{2}.$$

The diagonal of the square has an equation $d = s\sqrt{2}$.

If $d = a + b$, then $a + b = s\sqrt{2}$. Solve for s.

$$a+b=s\sqrt{2}$$
$$\frac{a+b}{\sqrt{2}}=s$$

Find the area of the square.

$$A=s^2=(\frac{a+b}{\sqrt{2}})^2=\frac{(a+b)^2}{2}=\frac{a^2+2ab+b^2}{2}$$

Choice B is incorrect because $A=\frac{a^2+b^2}{2}$ is not the obtained expression for the area of the square. **Choice C** is incorrect because $A=\frac{a^2+b}{2}$ is not the obtained expression for the area of the square.

Choice D is incorrect because $A=\frac{a+b}{2}$ is not the obtained expression for the area of the square.

64.

Category: PHM & Modeling
Skill: Two-dimensional shapes | **Level:** Medium

Choice D is correct because the obtained answer is 373.2 ft.

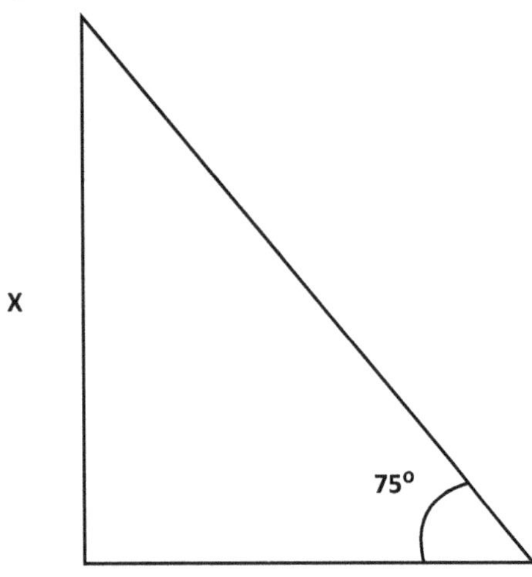

$$tan75^o=\frac{x}{100}$$
$$x=tan75^o\left(100\right)$$
$$x=373.2$$

Choice A is incorrect because 237.2 ft is less than the obtained value. **Choice B** is incorrect because 327.3 ft is less than the obtained value. **Choice C** is incorrect because 337.2 ft is less than the obtained value.

65.

Category: IES
Skill: Two-dimensional shapes | **Level:** Easy

Choice C is correct. Since $\Delta ABC\sim\Delta DEF,\frac{a}{d}=\frac{c}{f}.$

Substituting you have,

$$\frac{18}{3}=\frac{42}{f}$$
$$6=\frac{42}{f}$$
$$6f=42$$
$$f=7$$

Choice A is incorrect. This uses the ratio $\frac{3}{42}=\frac{f}{18}$ to find f.

Choice B is incorrect. This may result from $\frac{a}{d}$. **Choice D** is incorrect. This uses the ratio $\frac{3}{18}=\frac{42}{f}$ to find f.

66.

Category: PHM
Skill: Two-dimensional shapes | **Level:** Easy

Choice C is correct because the obtained value is 26π

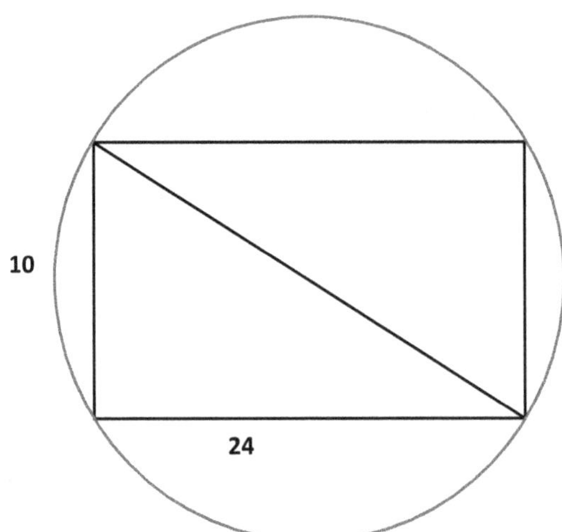

Find the diagonal of the rectangle using Pythagorean theorem

$$c^2=a^2+b^2$$
$$c^2=10^2+24^2$$
$$c^2=676$$
$$c=26$$

As shown in the figure, c is the diameter of the circle. Find the circumference.

$$C=\pi d=26\pi$$

Choice A is incorrect because 16π is less than the obtained circumference. **Choice B** is incorrect because 20π is less than the obtained circumference. **Choice D** is incorrect because 36π is greater than the obtained circumference.

67.

Category: IES
Skill: Two-dimensional shapes | **Level:** Medium

Choice C is correct because the obtained answer is 26 %.

Original Area of the rectangle : $A = LW$

New area of the rectangle: $A = (1.20L)(1.05W)$

$A = 1.26LW$

This means that the new area of the rectangle is 26% of the original area.

Choice A is incorrect because 16 % is less than the obtained answer. **Choice B** is incorrect because 22 % is less than the obtained answer. **Choice D** is incorrect because 33 % is less than the obtained answer.

68.

Category: IES & Modeling
Skill: Two-dimensional shapes | **Level:** Medium

Choice C is correct because the obtained answer is 28.

Given:

$$A = 33, L = 3W + 2$$

Find the value of L and W.

$$A = LW$$

$$33 = (3W + 2)W$$

$$33 = 3W^2 + 2W$$

$$0 = 3W^2 + 2W - 33$$

Find the value of W using a quadratic equation.

$$W = 3 \; or \; W = -11/3$$

Neglect the negative value of W. Hence, W=3.

$$L = 3W + 2 = 3(3) + 2 = 11$$

Find the perimeter using the obtained dimensions.

$$P = 2L + 2W$$

$$P = 2(11) + 2(3)$$

$$P = 28$$

Choice A is incorrect because 15 is less than the obtained perimeter. **Choice B** is incorrect because 22 is less than the obtained perimeter. **Choice D** is incorrect because 33 is greater than the obtained perimeter.

69.

Category: PHM & Modeling
Skill: Two-dimensional shapes | **Level:** Hard

Choice B is correct because the obtained answer is 1144.

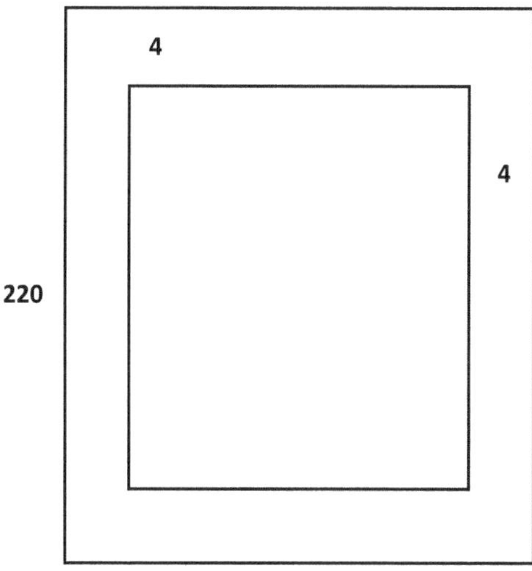

Find the area of the rectangular garden.

$$A = 220 \times 70 = 15400$$

Find the area of the inner garden by subtracting 4 meters from the length and the width of the rectangular garden.

$$A = 216 \times 66 = 14256$$

The area of the path is the difference between the areas.

$$A = 15400 - 14256 = 1144$$

Choice A is incorrect because 1122 is less than the obtained area. **Choice C** is incorrect because 1234 is greater than the obtained area. **Choice D** is incorrect because 1342 is greater than the obtained area.

70.

Category: IES
Skill: Two-dimensional shapes | **Level:** Easy

Choice C is correct because the obtained answer is 5π.

Use the formula for the circumference of a circle.

$$C = \pi d = 5\pi$$

Choice A is incorrect because 2.5π is less than the obtained circumference. **Choice B** is incorrect because 3π is less than the obtained circumference. **Choice D** is incorrect because 6π is greater than the obtained circumference.

71.

Category: IES
Skill: Two-dimensional shapes | **Level:** Medium

Choice C is correct because the obtained answer is 540.

Given: L = 150, W = 120

Find the perimeter.

$$P = 2L + 2W = 2(150) + 2(120) = 300 + 240 = 540$$

Choice A is incorrect because 360 is less than the obtained perimeter. **Choice B** is incorrect because 450 is less than the obtained perimeter. **Choice D** is incorrect because 600 is greater than the obtained perimeter.

72.

Category: PHM
Skill: Two-dimensional shapes | **Level:** Easy

Choice C is correct because the obtained answer is 47.4.
Given: Perimeter = 84.
Sides of the hexagon = $Perimeter / 6 = 84 / 6 = 14$.
Find the area of the hexagon using the formula

$$A = \frac{3\sqrt{3}}{2} s^2.$$

$$A = \frac{3\sqrt{3}}{2} s^2$$

$$A = \frac{3\sqrt{3}}{2} (14)^2$$

$$A = \frac{3\sqrt{3}}{2} (196)$$

$$A = 294\sqrt{3}$$

Find the radius of the inscribed circle.

The radius is equal to the apothem of the hexagon given by $r = \frac{\sqrt{3}}{2} s$.

$$r = \frac{\sqrt{3}}{2} s = \frac{\sqrt{3}}{2}(14) = 7\sqrt{3}$$

Find the area of the circle.

$$A = \pi r^2 = \pi(7\sqrt{3})^2 = \pi(49 \times 3) = 147\pi$$

Difference of the area is $A = A_{hexagon} - A_{circle}$

$$A = 294\sqrt{3} - 147\pi$$

$$A \approx 47.4 cm^2$$

Choice A is incorrect because 35.8 is less than the obtained answer. **Choice B** is incorrect because 45.3 is less than the obtained answer. **Choice D** is incorrect because 50.1 is greater than the obtained answer.

73.

Category: IES & Modeling
Skill: Two-dimensional shapes | **Level:** Medium

Choice B is correct because the obtained answer is 80/13.

Find the height given the Area of the triangle.

$$A = \frac{1}{2} bh$$

$$80 = \frac{1}{2}(10)h$$

$$80 = 5h$$

$$16 = h$$

Sides of the square are equal. Similar triangles can be established from the figure. $ASR \sim ABC$.
Let x be the side of the square.

$$\frac{BC}{SR} = \frac{AD}{AM}$$

$$\frac{10}{x} = \frac{16}{16 - x}$$

$$16x = 10(16 - x)$$

$$16x = 160 - 10x)$$

$$16x + 10x = 160$$

$$26x = 160$$

$$x = 80/13$$

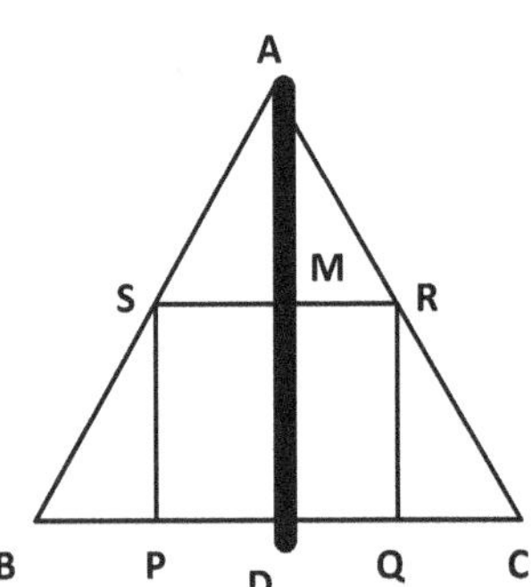

Choice A is incorrect because 13/80 is less than the obtained value. **Choice C** is incorrect because 8/13 is less than the obtained value. **Choice D** is incorrect because 13/10 is less than the obtained value.

74.

Category: PHM & Modeling
Skill: Two-dimensional shapes | **Level:** Medium
Choice C is correct because the obtained answer is 1.875

$$15\,ft \times \frac{0.25 inch}{2\,ft} = 1.875 inches$$

Choice A is incorrect because 1.05 is less than the obtained answer. **Choice B** is incorrect because 1.75 is less than the obtained answer. **Choice D** is incorrect because 2.5 is greater than the obtained answer.

75.

Category: IES
Skill: Two-dimensional shapes | **Level:** Medium

Choice A is correct because the obtained answer is

$$\frac{tan\alpha}{tan\theta}=\frac{y}{a}.$$

For the right triangle with vertex angle θ, $tan\theta=\frac{x}{y}$, and for the right triangle with the vertex angle α, $tan\alpha=\frac{x}{a}$.

The ratio and $tan\theta$ to $tan\alpha$, is, $\frac{tan\alpha}{tan\theta}=\frac{\frac{x}{a}}{\frac{x}{y}}=\frac{x}{a}\times\frac{y}{a}=\frac{y}{a}$

Hence, the answer is Choice A

Choice B is incorrect because this is the reciprocal of the correct value. **Choice C** is incorrect because multiplying the expressions for $tan\alpha$ and $tan\theta$ we get $\frac{x^2}{ay}$

Choice D is incorrect because this expression is not derived from the identity involving the product of tangents.

76.

Category: PHM & Modeling
Skill: Three-dimensional shapes | **Level:** Hard

Choice B is correct because the obtained answer is $1:6$.
Given: pyramid and cylinder with the same base
Height of the cylinder is twice the height of the pyramid.

$$\text{Volume of pyramid}=\frac{lwh}{3}$$

$$\text{Volume of cylinder}=\pi r^2h$$

Express the volumes in terms of Area of the base.
Let B be the area of the base. Take note that the height of the cylinder is twice that of the pyramid.

$$\text{Base area of pyramid}=lw=B$$

$$\text{Base area of cylinder}=\pi r^2=B$$

$$\text{Volume of pyramid}=\frac{1}{3}Bh$$

$$\text{Volume of cylinder}=Bh$$

Find the ratio of the volume of the pyramid to the volume of the cylinder.

$$\frac{Volume\,of\,pyramid}{Volume\,of\,cylinder}=\frac{\frac{1}{3}Bh}{2Bh}=\frac{\frac{1}{3}}{2}=\frac{1}{3}\left(\frac{1}{2}\right)=\frac{1}{6}$$

Hence the ratio of the volume of the pyramid to the volume of the cylinder is $\frac{1}{6}$.

Choice A is incorrect because $1:3$ is not equal to the obtained ratio. **Choice C** is incorrect because $3:2$ is not equal to the obtained ratio. **Choice D** is incorrect because $6:1$ is not equal to the obtained ratio.

77.

Category: PHM & Modeling
Skill: Three-dimensional shapes | **Level:** Medium

Choice A is correct because the obtained surface area is $30x + 72$.
Given: A cuboid with dimension 12 inches long, 3 inches wide and x inches high.
Find the equation that represents the surface area of the cuboid.
Use the formula for the surface area S of a cuboid.

$$S = 2(lw + lh + wh)$$
$$S = 2(12(3) + 12(x) + 3(x))$$
$$S = 2(36 + 15x)$$
$$S = 72 + 30x$$
$$S = 30x + 72$$

Choice B is incorrect because $72x + 30$ does not represent the surface area of the cuboid. **Choice C** is incorrect because $30x–72$ does not represent the surface area of the cuboid. **Choice D** is incorrect because $-30x–72$ does not represent the surface area of the cuboid.

78.

Category: IES & Modeling
Skill: Three-dimensional shapes | **Level:** Hard

Choice A is correct because the obtained answer is $s=d,\ d=3$.
The diameter of the sphere inscribed in the cube equals the side length of the cube.
Hence, $s=d$ is the correct expression.
To find the side length of the cube, we are given the cube's space diagonal, $diagonal=3\sqrt{3}$ ft., and we can use the relationship between the side length and the diagonal of a cube: $diagonal=s\sqrt{3}$.

$$diagonal=s\sqrt{3},\ s=d(diameter)$$

$$3\sqrt{3}=d\sqrt{3}$$

$$3=d$$

Choice B is incorrect because $s-d$, $d=\sqrt{3}$ does not represent the relationship between the side length s and the diameter of the sphere d. The value of d is also incorrect. **Choice C** is incorrect because $\frac{s}{d}$, $d=2$ does not represent the relationship between the side length s and the diameter of the sphere d. The value of d is also incorrect. **Choice D** is incorrect because $s+d$, $d=3+\sqrt{3}$ does not represent the relationship between the side length s and the diameter of the sphere d. The value of d is also incorrect.

79.

Category: PHM
Skill: Three-dimensional shapes | **Level:** Hard

Choice C is correct because the obtained answer is 48.

Given: Original weight of the block is 6 pounds.

Find the new weight of the block by comparing the original volume to the new volume.

Original volume = $V = x^3 = 6$
For the new volume, all sides are doubled.
New volume = $V = (2x)^3 = 8x^3 = 8(6) = 48$

Choice A is incorrect because 24 is less than the obtained value. **Choice B** is incorrect because 36 is less than the obtained value. **Choice D** is incorrect because 56 is greater than the obtained value.

80.

Category: IES
Skill: Three-dimensional shapes | **Level:** Hard

Choice C is correct because the obtained answer is 800 in^2.
Find the surface area of the square pyramid.

$$S = Area\ of\ the\ base + 4(Area\ of\ the\ triangles)$$
$$S = s^2 + 4\left(\frac{1}{2}bh\right)$$
$$S = 16^2 + 4\left(\frac{1}{2}(16)(17)\right)$$
$$S = 256 + 544$$
$$S = 800 \text{ in}^2$$

Choice A is incorrect because 450 in is less than the obtained surface area of the pyramid. **Choice B** is incorrect because 600 in is less than the obtained surface area of the pyramid. **Choice D** is incorrect because 900 in is greater than the obtained surface area of the pyramid.

81.

Category: PHM
Skill: Three-dimensional shapes | **Level:** Easy

Choice B is correct because the obtained volume is 96 units.
First cuboid: $V = l \times w \times h$
$$V = 10 \times 4 \times 4$$
$$V = 160\, units^3$$
Seond cuboid:
$$V = l \times w \times h$$
$$V = 4 \times 4 \times 4$$
$$V = 64\, units^3$$
Orange juice left if it fills the second cuboid
$$V = V_1 - V_2$$
$$V = 160 - 64$$
$$V = 96\, units^3$$

Choice A is incorrect because 86 is less than the remaining volume. **Choice C** is incorrect because 106 is greater than the remaining volume. **Choice D** is incorrect because 116 is greater than the remaining volume.

82.

Category: PHM & Modeling
Skill: Three-dimensional shapes | **Level:** Easy

Choice D is correct because the arrangement of increasing volumes of the given prisms is 3, 1, 2.
Find the volumes of each given prisms.

Prism 1: $4 \times 5 \times 3 = 60\ cm^2$
Prism 2: $9 \times 3 \times 2 = 54\ cm^2$
Prism 3: $7 \times 6 \times 4 = 168\ m^2$

Hence, increasing volume is Prism 3, Prism 1, Prism 2.

Choice A is incorrect because the arrangement 1, 2, 3 is not in increasing volume. **Choice B** is incorrect because the arrangement 2, 1, 3 is not in increasing volume. **Choice C** is incorrect because the arrangement 3, 2, 1 is not in increasing volume.

83.

Category: PHM
Skill: Three-dimensional shapes | **Level:** Medium

Choice D is correct because the obtained answer is 28,274.33 gallons.
Given: 7.5 gallons of water can fill 1 cubic foot.
Diameter of cylindrical tank – 20 ft, height 12 feet.
Find the volume of the cylindrical tank.

$$V = \pi r^2 h$$
$$V = \pi(10)^2(12)$$
$$V = 1200\pi$$
$$V \approx 3769.91\,ft^3$$

Volume in gallons:

$$V \approx 3769.91\,ft^3 \times \frac{7.5\,gallons}{1\,ft^3} = 28{,}274.33\,gallons$$

Choice A is incorrect because 18,174.30 gallons is less than the obtained value. **Choice B** is incorrect because 20,274.33 gallons is less than the obtained value. **Choice C** is incorrect because 24,100.33 gallons is less than the obtained value.

84.

Category: IES & Modeling
Skill: Three-dimensional shapes | **Level:** Medium

Choice C is correct because the obtained answer is 1960 cm^3.
Given: $h_{right\ circular\ cone} : h_{right\ circular\ cylinder} = 4:3$

$r_{right\ circular\ cone} : r_{right\ circular\ cylinder} = 7:3$

$V_{right\ circular\ cylinder} = 810$

Let the ratio be $h_{cone} = 4x$, $h_{cylinder} = 3x$

$r_{right\ circular\ cone} = 7y \quad r_{right\ circular\ cylinder} = 3y$

Find the volume of the cylinder.

$$V_{cylinder} = \pi r^2 h \qquad \text{substitute the ratios}$$
$$V_{cylinder} = \pi(3y)^2(3x)$$
$$810 = \pi 9y^2 3x$$
$$810 = 27\pi xy^2$$
$$\frac{810}{27\pi} = xy^2$$
$$xy^2 = \frac{30}{\pi}$$

Find the volume of the cone.

$$V_{cone} = \frac{1}{3}\pi r^2 h \qquad \text{substitute the ratios}$$
$$V_{cone} = \frac{1}{3}\pi(7y)^2(4x)$$
$$V_{cone} = \frac{1}{3}\pi 49y^2 4x$$
$$V_{cone} = \frac{1}{3}196\pi y^2 x$$
$$V_{cone} = \frac{196}{3}\pi xy^2$$

Substitute $xy^2 = \frac{30}{\pi}$ into the equation.

$$V_{cone} = \frac{196}{3}\pi xy^2$$
$$V_{cone} = \frac{196}{3}\pi\frac{30}{\pi}$$
$$V_{cone} = \frac{196}{3}\pi\frac{30}{\pi}$$
$$V_{cone} = \frac{5880}{3}$$
$$V_{cone} = 1960\ cm^3$$

Choice A is incorrect because 1360 cm^3 is less than the obtained answer. **Choice B** is incorrect because 1560 cm^3 is less than the obtained answer. **Choice D** is incorrect because 2160 cm^3 is Greater than the obtained answer.

85.

Category: PHM
Skill: Three-dimensional shapes | **Level:** Easy

Choice C is correct because the obtained answer is 13,860.
Given: $C = 66\ cm$, $h = 40$
Find the radius.

$$C = 2\pi r$$
$$66 = 2\left(\frac{22}{7}\right)r$$
$$10.5 = r$$

Find the volume of the cylinder.

$$V = \pi r^2 h = \left(\frac{22}{7}\right)(10.5)^2(40) = 13860$$

Choice A is incorrect because 11,235 is less than the obtained volume. **Choice B** is incorrect because 12,435 is less than the obtained volume. **Choice D** is incorrect because 15,352 is greater than the obtained volume.

86.

Category: PHM
Skill: Three-dimensional shapes | **Level:** Easy

Choice C is correct because the obtained answer is 360.
Given : s =10, V = 400
Find the height using the volume of the square pyramid.

$$V = a^2\frac{h}{3}$$
$$400 = 10^2\frac{h}{3}$$
$$12 = h$$

Find the surface area of the square pyramid.

$$SA = a^2 + 2a\sqrt{\frac{a^2}{4} + h^2} = 10^2 + 2(10)\sqrt{\frac{10^2}{4} + 12^2} = 360$$

Choice A is incorrect because 280 is less than the obtained value. **Choice B** is incorrect because 330 is less than the obtained value. **Choice D** is incorrect because 450 is greater than the obtained value.

87.

Category: IES & Modeling
Skill: Three-dimensional shapes | **Level:** Easy

Choice A is correct because the obtained answer is the volume of the pyramid is ⅓ the volume of the prism.
Volume of the rectangular prism: $V = lwh = 8(5)(6) = 240$.
Volume of the rectangular pyramid: $V = 1/3\ lwh = 1/3\ (8)(5)(6) = 80$.
Hence, the volume of the pyramid is ⅓ the volume of the prism.

Choice B is incorrect because the pyramid and the prism don't have the same volume. **Choice C** is incorrect because the pyramid and the prism don't have the same volume **Choice D** is incorrect because the prism has greater volume than a pyramid.

88.

Category: IES
Skill: Three-dimensional shapes | **Level:** Easy

Choice B is correct because the obtained surface area is 256 units.
Given: slant height = 12
Base = 8
Use the formula $SA = 2bs + b^2$.

$$SA = 2(8)(12) + (8)^2$$
$$SA = 192 + 64$$
$$SA = 256$$

Choice A is incorrect because 124 is less than the obtained surface area. **Choice C** is incorrect because 305 is greater than the obtained surface area. **Choice D** is incorrect because 350 is greater than the obtained surface area.

89.

Category: IES
Skill: Three-dimensional shapes | **Level:** Easy

Choice C is correct because the obtained answer is 2304.
Use the formula for the surface area of the pyramid.

$$SA = a^2 + 2a\sqrt{\frac{a^2}{4} + h^2}$$
$$SA = 32^2 + 2(32)\sqrt{\frac{32^2}{4} + 12^2}$$
$$SA = 2304$$

Choice A is incorrect because 1947 is less than the obtained answer. **Choice B** is incorrect because 2003 is less than the obtained answer. **Choice D** is incorrect because 2560 is greater than the obtained answer.

90.

Category: IES
Skill: Three-dimensional shapes | **Level:** Medium

Choice C is correct because the obtained answer is 910.
We know that $\sin A = \frac{opp}{hyp}$, $1^\circ = 60'$, $1000m = 1km$.

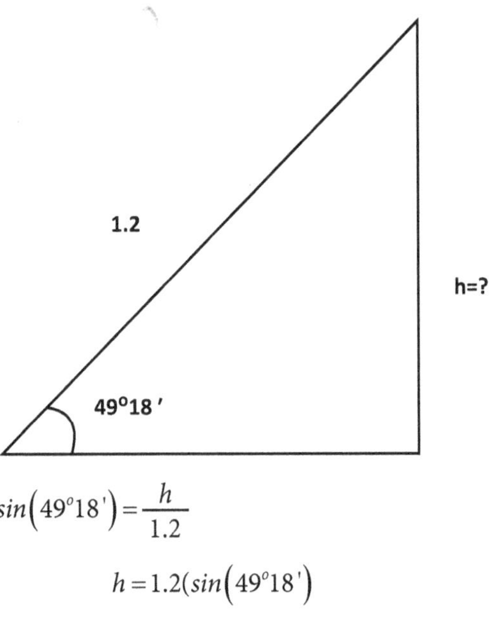

$$\sin(49^\circ 18') = \frac{h}{1.2}$$
$$h = 1.2(\sin(49^\circ 18'))$$
$$h = 0.910\,km$$
$$h = 0.910\,km \times \frac{1000\,m}{1\,km} = 910\,m$$

Choice A is incorrect because 750 is less than the obtained height. **Choice B** is incorrect because 850 is less than the obtained height. **Choice D** is incorrect because 1050 is greater than the obtained height.

91.

Category: PHM
Skill: Trigonometry | **Level:** Easy

Choice C is correct. For $y = f(x)$ is even if $f(-x) = f(x)$, and odd if $f(-x) = -f(x)$. Cosine is an even function so, $\cos(-\theta) = \cos(\theta)$.

Choice A is incorrect. This is the answer for $\sin(-\theta)$. **Choice B** is incorrect. This assumes cosine is an odd function. **Choice D** is incorrect. This may result from conceptual error.

92.

Category: PHM
Skill: Trigonometry | **Level:** Easy

Choice B is correct. To find the period, count the horizontal distance from one point on the graph to the next point where the domain repeats itself. This can easily be done by counting from the maximum point of (0, 4) to the next maximum point to the right of (0, π).

Choice A is incorrect. This is the fundamental period for the graph of cosine or sine. **Choice C** is incorrect. The function is even (has symmetry about the y-axis). **Choice D** is incorrect. The function is even (has symmetry about the y-axis).

93.

Category: PHM
Skill: Trigonometry | **Level:** Hard

Choice B is correct because the obtained answer is 1784.79.
Find the angle between the path of the plane. Let this be angle C.

$$\angle C = 180^o - 15^o = 165^o$$

Find the distance of the plane from the starting point using Cosine Law. Let's denote this as c and

$$a = 800, b = 1000.$$

$$c^2 = a^2 + b^2 - 2ab\cos C$$

$$c^2 = 800^2 + 1000^2 - 2(800)(1000)\cos 165^o$$

$$c^2 = 3185481.32$$

$$c = 1784.79$$

Choice A is incorrect because 1542.79 is less than the obtained value. **Choice C** is incorrect because 1875.81 is greater than the obtained value. **Choice D** is incorrect because 1945.47 is greater than the obtained value.

94.

Category: IES & Modeling
Skill: Trigonometry | **Level:** Medium

Choice B is correct because the obtained answer is 772.

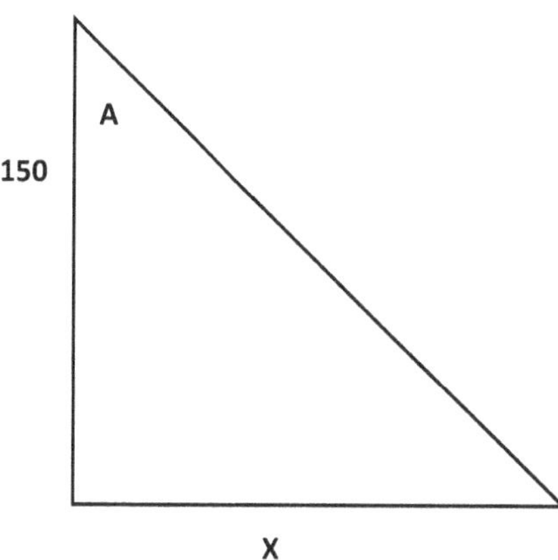

Find the angle A.

$$A = 90^o - 11^o = 79^o$$

Find x using tangent function.

$$\tan A = \frac{opposite}{adjacent} = \frac{x}{150}$$

$$\tan 79^o = \frac{x}{150}$$

$$x = 150(\tan 79^o)$$

$$x \approx 772$$

Choice A is incorrect because 550 is less than the obtained value. **Choice C** is incorrect because 850 is less than the obtained value. **Choice D** is incorrect because 972 is less than the obtained value.

95.

Category: IES
Skill: Trigonometry | **Level:** Easy

Choice A is correct because the obtained answer is $-\frac{4}{5}$.

Given: $\sin B = \frac{3}{5}$ and $\tan B < 0$,

We know that $\sin\theta = \frac{opposite}{hypothenus}, \cos\theta = \frac{adjacent}{hypothenus}$.

Find the adjacent side using Pythagorean Theorem.

$$c^2 = a^2 + b^2$$

$$5^2 = 3^2 + b^2$$

$$25 - 9 = b^2$$

$$16 = b^2$$

$$4 = b$$

Hence, adjacent side is 4.

Given that $tan\,B < 0$, the adjacent side must be negative.

$$\cos B = \frac{adjacent}{hypothenus}$$

$$\cos B = \frac{-4}{5}$$

$$\cos B = -\frac{4}{5}$$

Choice B is incorrect because $-\frac{2}{5}$ is greater than obtained value. **Choice C** is incorrect because $\frac{2}{5}$ is greater than obtained value. **Choice D** is incorrect because $\frac{4}{5}$ is greater than obtained value.

96.

Category: IES & Modeling
Skill: Trigonometry | **Level:** Medium

Choice C is correct because the obtained answer is $\frac{4}{3}$.

Illustrate the problem.

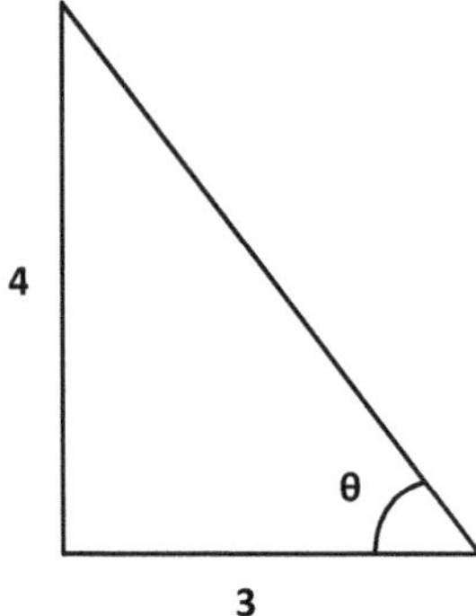

$$tan\theta = \frac{opposite}{adjacent} = \frac{4}{3}$$

Choice A is incorrect because $\frac{3}{5}$ is not the ratio for the tangent θ. **Choice B** is incorrect because $\frac{3}{4}$ is not the ratio for the tangent θ. **Choice D** is incorrect because $\frac{5}{3}$ is not the ratio for the tangent θ.

97.

Category: IES & Modeling
Skill: Trigonometry | **Level:** Easy

Choice D is correct because the obtained answer is $\frac{\sqrt{5}}{3}$.

We know that $\cos A = \frac{adjacent}{hypotenuse}$.

Find the adjacent side of angle A using the pythagorean theorem.

$$c^2 = a^2 + b^2$$
$$3^2 = 2^2 + b^2$$
$$9 = 4 + b^2$$
$$9 - 4 = b^2$$
$$5 = b^2$$
$$\sqrt{5} = b$$

Find $\cos A$.

$$\cos A = \frac{adjacent}{hypotenuse} = \frac{\sqrt{5}}{3}.$$

Choice A is incorrect because $\frac{\sqrt{3}}{5}$ is not the obtained ratio for cos A. **Choice B** is incorrect because $\frac{\sqrt{5}}{2}$ is not the obtained ratio for cos A. **Choice C** is incorrect because $\frac{\sqrt{2}}{3}$ is not the obtained ratio for cos A.

98.

Category: IES
Skill: Trigonometry | **Level:** Hard

Choice B is correct. Let D be the midpoint of $\overline{AC}$ and E be the midpoint of $\overline{BC}$, then $\overline{CD} = 12$ and $\overline{CE} = 9$ for right triangle ΔDEC shown below.

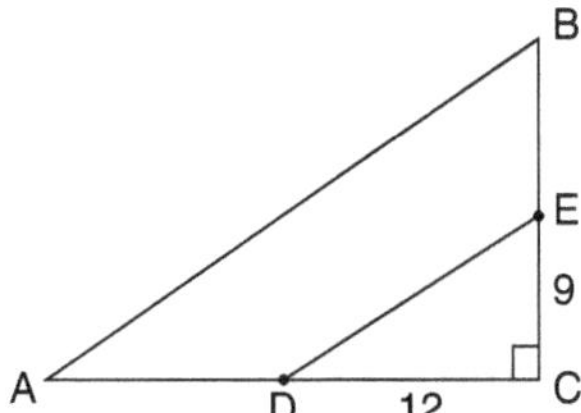

Hypotenuse $\overline{DE}$ is the line segment joining midpoints D and E. Then,

$$\overline{DE}^2 = 9^2 + 12^2$$
$$\overline{DE}^2 = 225$$
$$\overline{DE} = 15$$

Choice A is incorrect. This is ¼ *BC*. **Choice C** is incorrect. This is the average of sides *AC* and *BC*. **Choice D** is incorrect. This is the length of *AB*.

99.

Category: PHM & Modeling
Skill: Trigonometry | **Level:** Easy

Choice B is correct because the obtained answer

is $-\frac{3}{7}$.

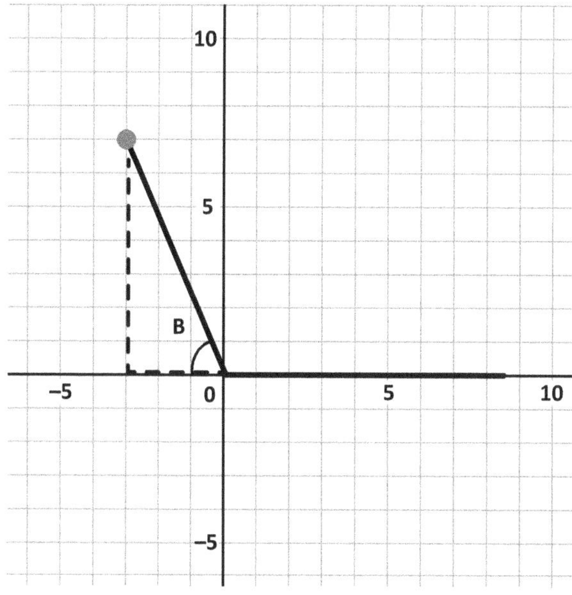

$$cot\ B = \frac{adjacent}{opposite} = \frac{-3}{7} = -\frac{3}{7}$$

Choice A is incorrect because $-\frac{7}{3}$ is not the ratio of $cot\ B$. **Choice C** is incorrect because $\frac{3}{7}$ is not the ratio of $cot\ B$. **Choice D** is incorrect because $\frac{7}{3}$ is not the ratio of $cot\ B$

100.

Category: PHM
Skill: Trigonometry | **Level:** Easy
Choice C is correct because the obtained answer is 90°.
Find the angle between 5 and 12 using the cosine rule.

$$\cos C = \frac{a^2 + b^2 - c^2}{2ab}$$

$$\cos C = \frac{5^2 + 12^2 - 13^2}{2(5)(12)}$$

$$\cos C = \frac{0}{120}$$

$$\cos C = 0$$

$$C = 90^o$$

Choice A is incorrect because 75° is less than the obtained angle. **Choice B** is incorrect because 80° is less than the obtained angle. **Choice D** is incorrect because 110° is greater than the obtained angle.

101.

Category: PHM
Skill: Trigonometry | **Level:** Medium

Choice C is correct because the answer is to use the law of cosines.
It is used to calculate the sides or angles of a triangle when lengths of the two sides and the angle between them are known.

Choice A is incorrect because the Pythagorean theorem can't be used. **Choice B** is incorrect because area is not unknown. **Choice D** is incorrect because the triangle is not isosceles.

102.

Category: PHM & Modeling
Skill: Trigonometry | **Level:** Easy

Choice D is correct. The period is the interval along the x-axis where the graph reproduces itself. It is easiest to find the period by counting horizontally from maximum point to maximum point, or minimum point to the minimum point on the graph. The interval from the maximum point of (0, 7) to or minimum point to the minimum point on the graph. The interval from the maximum point of (0, 7) to (4π, 7) is 4π.

Choice A is incorrect. This is the fundamental period for a sinusoidal graph **Choice B** is incorrect. This is the maximum value of the graph. **Choice C** is incorrect. This is the difference in the maximum and minimum y-values of the graph.

103.

Category: IES
Skill: Trigonometry | **Level:** Medium

Choice C is correct because the obtained answer is π.

$$2cos\theta - 3 = -5$$

$$2cos\theta = -5 + 3$$

$$2cos\theta = -2$$

$$cos\theta = -1$$

$$\theta = \pi$$

The general solution of cosine is $x = 2\pi n + \alpha$ .Hence, general solution is $x = 2\pi n + \pi$.
Since the given condition is $0 \le \theta < 2\pi$, then the solution to the equation is just π.

Choice A is incorrect because $\pi / 2$ is not a solution to the given trigonometric equation. **Choice B** is incorrect because $\pi / 4$ is not a solution to the given trigonometric equation. **Choice D** is incorrect because 2π is not a solution to the given trigonometric equation.

104.

Category: PHM & Modeling
Skill: Trigonometry | **Level:** Medium

Choice B is correct because the obtained answer is 135.
Use the sine Law to find the side lengths AC, BC.

$$\frac{sin68^o}{46} = \frac{sin65^o}{AC}$$

$$AC = \frac{sin65^o(46)}{sin68^o}$$

$$AC = 44.96$$

$$\frac{sin68^o}{46} = \frac{sin70^o}{BC}$$

$$AC = \frac{sin65^o(46)}{sin70^o}$$

$$AC = 44.365$$

Perimeter = AB + AC + BC
= 46 + 44.96 +44.365
≈ 135

Choice A is incorrect because 126 is less than the obtained answer. **Choice C** is incorrect because 145 is greater than the obtained answer. **Choice D** is incorrect because 150 is greater than the obtained answer.

105.

Category: PHM
Skill: Trigonometry | **Level:** Hard

Choice D is correct because the obtained answer is $-\frac{5}{13}$.

We know that

$sin\ A = \frac{opposite}{hypotenuse}$, $tan\ A = \frac{opposite}{adjacent}$, $cos\ A = \frac{adjacent}{hypotenuse}$.

Hence, hypotenuse = 13, opposite side = 12, adjacent side = –5.

Hence, $cos\ A = \frac{adjacent}{hypotenuse} = \frac{-5}{13} = -\frac{5}{13}$.

Choice A is incorrect because $-\frac{12}{13}$ does not represent the ratio of cos A. **Choice B** is incorrect because $\frac{4}{13}$ does not represent the ratio of cos A. **Choice C** is incorrect because $-\frac{13}{12}$ does not represent the ratio of cos A.

Chapter 7

Statistics and Probability Practice Questions

1.

The probability of a flight being delayed for any length of time due to a mechanical issue is 12%. What is the probability that there will **not** be a delay on a round trip (a flight to your destination and a flight back)?

A. 1%
B. 12%
C. 24%
D. 77%

2.

You randomly choose a coin from a container having 15 pennies, 10 nickels, and 22 dimes. What is the probability that you do not choose a penny?

A. 0.21
B. 0.32
C. 0.53
D. 0.68

3.

A hotel logs the number of days a hotel patron spends the night in one of their rooms. The distribution table is given below.

No. of nights spent	Frequency
2	59
3	45
4	32
5	18
6	9

What is the probability that a person spends the night in one of their rooms for more than 4 days?

A. 0.17
B. 0.20
C. 0.36
D. 0.64

4.

If the probability of an event *A* is 0.4 and the probability of event *B* is 0.6, how do you find *P*(not *A* and not *B*)?

A. $P\left(\overline{A} \cap \overline{B}\right)=0.2$

B. $P\left(\overline{A} \cap \overline{B}\right)=0.8$

C. $P\left(\overline{A} \cup \overline{B}\right)=0.8$

D. $P\left(\overline{A} \cup \overline{B}\right)=0.2$

5.

Identify the favorable outcome in the given situation. The probability of drawing a red card or a card with a face (king, queens, or jack) from a standard deck of 52 cards.

A. Favorable outcomes = (Red cards)+(Face cards)–(Red face cards)
B. Favorable outcomes = (Red cards)+(Face cards)+(Red face cards)
C. Favorable outcomes = (Red cards)+(Face cards)
D. Favorable outcomes = (Red cards)–(Face cards)

6.

What is the probability of making a perfect score on a 5-question multiple choice quiz that has 4 answer choices?

A. $\frac{1}{1024}$

B. $\frac{1}{625}$

C. $\frac{1}{120}$

D. $\frac{1}{20}$

7.

You and a friend are among 6 people that are chosen at random for an experiment that requires 2 people. What is the probability that both you and your friend are chosen?

A. $\frac{1}{30}$

B. $\frac{1}{15}$

C. $\frac{1}{6}$

D. $\frac{1}{5}$

8.

In a survey at an elementary school, it was found that 4 out of every 5 students do not like spinach. If two students at the school are chosen at random where the first student chosen can be chosen again, what is the probability that they both like spinach?

A. $\frac{1}{25}$

B. $\frac{2}{5}$

C. $\frac{3}{5}$

D. $\frac{16}{25}$

9.

A bag contains 5 green and 3 blue balls. Two balls are picked at random. What is the probability that both are of the same colour?

A. $\frac{C_1^5 * C_1^3}{C_2^8}$

B. 0.5

C. $\frac{C_2^5}{C_2^8} + \frac{C_2^3}{C_2^8}$

D. $\frac{C_2^5 * C_2^3}{C_2^8}$

10.

What is the probability of making a perfect score on a 4-question multiple choice quiz that has 5 answer choices, if you answer each question randomly?

A. $\frac{4}{625}$

B. $\frac{1}{625}$

C. $\frac{5}{625}$

D. $\frac{20}{625}$

11.

The blood types of 150 people were determined for a study as shown in the figure below.

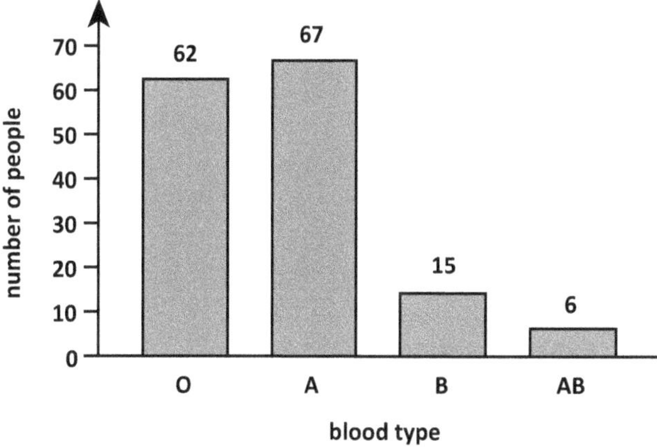

If 1 person from this study is randomly selected, what is the probability that this person has either Type A or Type AB blood?

A. $\frac{62}{150}$

B. $\frac{66}{150}$

C. $\frac{68}{150}$

D. $\frac{73}{150}$

12.

In a room there are 8 couples. Out of them, 4 people are selected at random. The probability that they may be couple is:

A. $\frac{{}^{8}C_4}{{}^{16}C_4}$

B. $\frac{{}^{8}C_2}{{}^{16}C_8}$

C. $\frac{{}^{8}C_2}{{}^{8}C_4}$

D. $\frac{{}^{8}C_2}{{}^{16}C_4}$

13.

A test group of men and women are given a drug or a placebo. Forty-two percent of the group are men and it is known that thirty-five percent of the men are given a placebo. If a person from the group is chosen at random, what is the probability that it will be a man that was given a placebo?

A. 0.15
B. 0.23
C. 0.58
D. 0.65

14.

If A and B are two events such that $P(A) \neq 0$ and $P(B|A) = 1$, then

A. $A \subset B$

B. $B = \phi$

C. $B \subset A$

D. None of these

15.

Find the probability of getting one or two heads if a coin is tossed thrice.

A. $\frac{4}{5}$

B. $\frac{5}{8}$

C. $\frac{3}{4}$

D. $\frac{6}{4}$

16.

There are three mangoes and three apples in a box. If two fruits are chosen at random, the probability that one is a mango and the other is an apple is

A. $\frac{2}{3}$

B. $\frac{3}{5}$

C. $\frac{1}{3}$

D. $\frac{4}{5}$

17.

James has a pouch with three marbles in it: one is red, one blue, one orange. If he randomly selects two marbles without replacing them, what is the probability that he selects first the orange then the blue?

A. $\frac{1}{9}$

B. $\frac{1}{8}$

C. $\frac{1}{6}$

D. $\frac{2}{3}$

18.

A jar contains y black colored balls and x yellow colored balls. Two balls are pulled from the jar without replacement. What is the probability that the first ball is black and the second one is yellow?

A. $\frac{y^2 - y}{x^2 + y^2 + 2xy - (x + y)}$

B. $\frac{xy - y}{x^2 + y^2 + 2xy - (x - y)}$

C. $\frac{xy - y}{x^2 + y^2 + 2xy - (x + y)}$

D. $\frac{xy}{x^2 + y^2 + 2xy - (x + y)}$

19.

A piggy bank contains 12 nickels, 27 dimes, and 16 quarters. How many dimes will need to be added to the piggy bank if the probability of randomly selecting a dime will be $\frac{3}{4}$?

A. 1
B. 10
C. 25
D. 57

20.

A person spins the wheel and is rewarded the amount indicated by the pointer. What is the expected value of a spin?

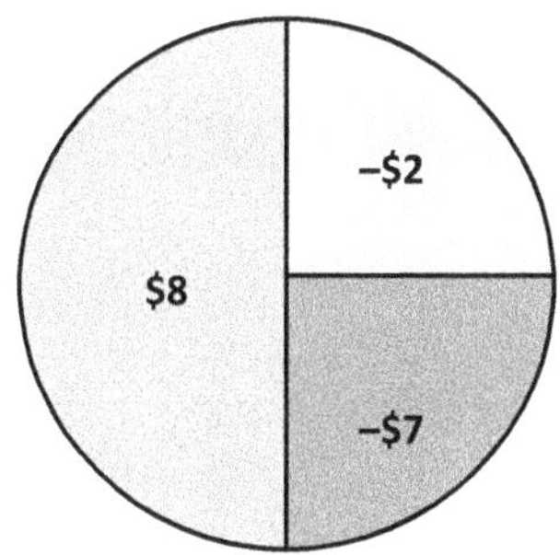

A. –$1.25
B. –$0.75
C. $1.00
D. $1.75

21.

Determine whether this table represents a probability distribution.

x	*P(x)*
0	0.05
1	0.1
2	0.3
3	0.6

A. No
B. Yes
C. Maybe
D. No enough information

22.

Out of 50 people that like candy bars or spinach or both, 42 like candy bars and 18 like spinach. If a person is selected at random from the 50 people surveyed, what is the probability that the person likes both candy bars and spinach?

A. 0.16
B. 0.2
C. 0.36
D. 0.5

23.

If you roll a 6-sided die where each side is numbered 1 through 6, and flip a two-headed coin labeled heads and tail respectively, at the same time, what is the probability the you roll a 4 with the die and get a tails with the coin flip?

A. $\frac{1}{12}$
B. $\frac{1}{6}$
C. $\frac{1}{2}$
D. $\frac{2}{3}$

24.

The probability of randomly choosing a green marble from a bag containing green, red, and blue marbles is $\frac{1}{5}$. If there are 11 red marbles and 5 blue marbles, how many green marbles must be in the bag?

A. 4
B. 5
C. 16
D. 20

25.

An 18 member committee has 4 officers. The committee needs a non-officer to take notes during the meetings and decides to select someone randomly. If Jhanica is a member of the committee, but NOT an officer, what is the probability that she will be selected to take notes?

A. 0
B. $\frac{1}{14}$
C. $\frac{1}{6}$
D. $\frac{1}{18}$

26.

A high school's graduating class has 250 people. Sixty percent of the graduating class are male, and eighty-two percent of the graduating class will go to a four-year college. What is the probability that a person chosen in the graduating class will be male that attends a four-year college?

A. 0.13
B. 0.22
C. 0.49
D. 0.78

27.

One hundred thirty people were surveyed about their preference for certain kinds of fruit. One hundred of them preferred apples, 50 of them preferred oranges, and 20 of them preferred both apples and oranges. What is the probability that a person chosen at random only prefers apples?

A. 0.15
B. 0.23
C. 0.62
D. 0.77

28.

The circle graph below shows the distribution of registered voters, by age, for a community. Registered voters are randomly selected from this distribution to be called for a duty. What are the odds (in the age range: not in the age range) that the first person called for duty is in the age range of 25–35 years?

Distribution of Registered Voters by Age

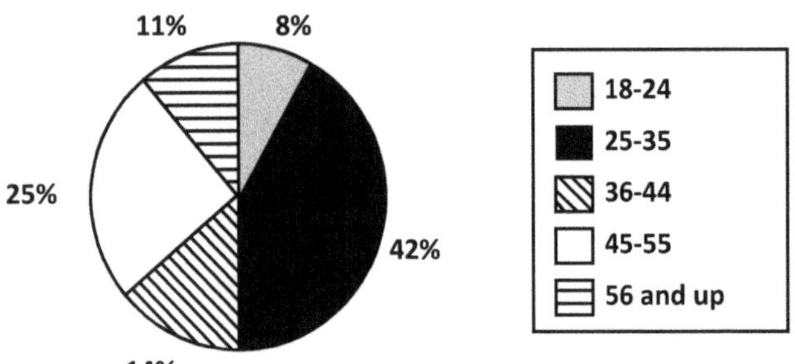

A. 1:3
B. 7:8
C. 7:43
D. 21:29

29.

In a box, there are 8 red, 7 blue and 6 green balls. One ball is picked up randomly. Which of the following solutions show the probability that it is neither red nor green?

A. $P(\text{not green and not red}) = \frac{\text{No of blue balls}}{\text{Total number of balls}} = \frac{7}{21} = \frac{1}{3}$

B. $P(\text{not green and not red}) = \frac{\text{No of blue balls}}{\text{Total number of red and green}} = \frac{7}{14} = \frac{1}{2}$

C. $P(\text{not green and not red}) = \frac{\text{No of red balls}}{\text{Total number of green}} = \frac{8}{6}$

D. $P(\text{not green and not red}) = \frac{\text{No of green balls}}{\text{Total number of red}} = \frac{6}{8}$

30.

Eloise rolled two dices. She then did something with the two numbers shown. Here is a sample space diagram showing all the possible outcomes:

		Dice 2					
		1	2	3	4	5	6
Dice 1	1	0	1	2	3	4	5
	2	1	0	1	2	3	4
	3	2	1	0	1	2	3
	4	3	2	1	0	1	2
	5	4	3	2	1	0	1
	6	5	4	3	2	1	0

What did Eloise do with the two numbers shown on the dice?

A. Add the numbers in the two dice together
B. Subtract the bigger number in any dice to the other smaller number
C. Multiply the numbers on the dice
D. Subtract the number on dice 2 from dice 1

31.

John asked 50 people whether they like Hawaiian pizza or pepperoni pizza.

35 people like Hawaiian pizza.
20 people like both.
5 people like neither.

John picked one of the 50 people at random. Given that the person he chose likes pepperoni pizza, find the probability that they don't like Hawaiian pizza.

A. $\frac{1}{2}$

B. $\frac{1}{3}$

C. $\frac{1}{5}$

D. $\frac{2}{5}$

32.

There are 18 girls and 12 boys in a class. $\frac{2}{9}$ of the girls and $\frac{1}{4}$ of the boys walk to school. One of the students who walks to school is chosen at random. Find the probability that the student is a boy.

A. $\frac{12}{30}$

B. $\frac{3}{7}$

C. $\frac{1}{4}$

D. $\frac{3}{12}$

33.

Data were collected on 100 students regarding their class and major. The data is summarized in the following contingency table.

			Class		
		Sophomore	Junior	Senior	
	Undeclared	19	5	6	30
Major	Business	5	17	16	38
	Science	5	6	21	32
		29	28	43	100

What is the probability of randomly selecting a sophomore or an undeclared student?

A. 0.19
B. 0.29
C. 0.40
D. 0.59

34.

Janice, Sandra, and 13 other people are members of the community planning committee. The committee decides to select a president and vice president randomly from its 15 members. What is the probability that Janice will be president and Sandra will be vice president?

A. $\frac{1}{132}$

B. $\frac{1}{220}$

C. $\frac{1}{210}$

D. $\frac{1}{6}$

35.

Of 155 students that were surveyed, 125 took an English course, 75 took an advanced math course, and 45 took both an English course and an advanced math course. If a student that was surveyed was chosen at random, what is the probability the student only took an advanced math class?

A. 0.19
B. 0.29
C. 0.48
D. 0.81

36.

The below Venn diagram shows the cardinality of each set. Use this to find the cardinality of given $(A \cap B \cap C^c)$.

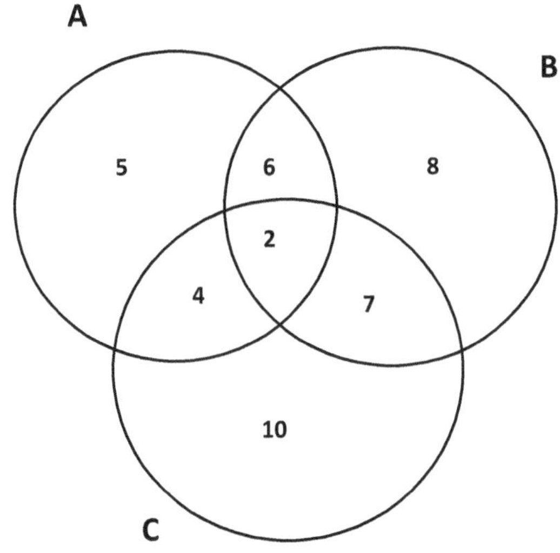

A. 4
B. 5
C. 6
D. 7

37.

Consider the given data sets $7, 8, X, 3$. What is the formula of the variance in terms of the missing number X?

A. $\sigma^2 = \frac{1}{4}\sum_{i=1}^{4}(x_i - X)^2$

B. $\sigma^2 = \frac{1}{4}[(7-\mu)^2 + (8-\mu)^2 + (X-\mu)^2 + (3-\mu)^2]$

C. $\sigma^2 = \frac{1}{4}[(7-(\frac{18+x}{4}))^2 + (8-(\frac{18+x}{4}))^2 + (X-(\frac{18+x}{4}))^2 + (3-(\frac{18+x}{4}))^2]$

D. $\sigma^2 = \frac{1}{4}[(7-X)^2 + (8-X)^2 + (X-X)^2 + (3-X)^2]$

38.

Identify the data set with the highest standard deviation without calculation.

A. 3, 32, 53, 64, 64, 63
B. 10, 10, 10, 10, 10, 11
C. 100, 200, 300, 400, 500, 500
D. 1000, 2000, 3000, 4000, 5000, 6000

39.

The cost of 3 items, including tax, on a menu at a restaurant are fish \$9.50, roast beef \$11.25, and chicken \$8.75. You buy one of the items and hand the cashier a \$50 bill. You are still hungry, so you purchase a second item with the change the cashier gave you after your first purchase. If you received \$31.75 in change after your 2nd purchase, which menu items did you buy?

A. Fish and chicken
B. Fish and roast beef
C. Chicken and roast beef
D. Fish both times

40.

Andrew wants an 84 average for the grading period in his math class. There are 5 assignments for the class each having equal weight. If Andrew scored an 85, 85, 75, and 92 on his first 4 assignments, what must he make on his fifth assignment to have an 84 average for the grading period?

A. 75
B. 83
C. 84
D. 85

41.

Julian wants to have an average grade of 85 in his Chemistry course. There are 5 assignments that are graded for the course, each having an equal weight. If Julian scores grades of 79, 84, 92, and a 79 on his first four assignments, what must his median score be if he is to end up with an average grade of 85?

A. 79
B. 84
C. 85
D. 88

42.

Which Venn diagram below has $(X \cap Y^c) U Z$ shaded?

A.

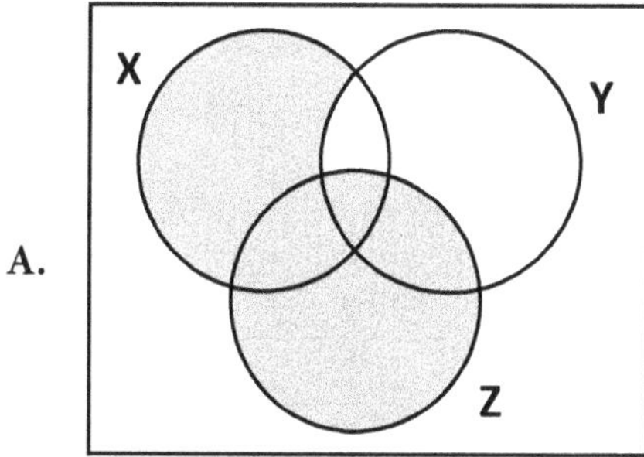

B.

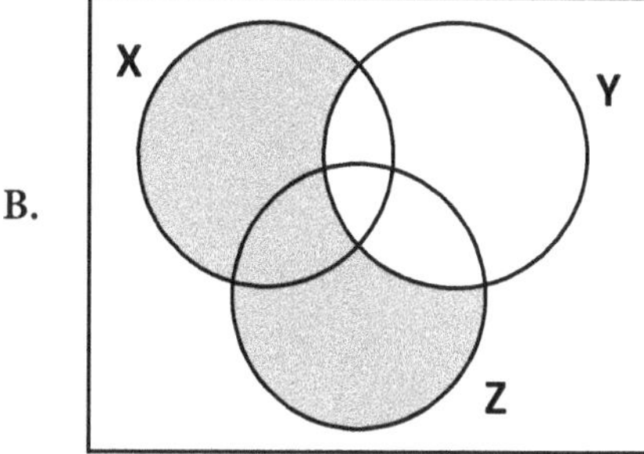

C.

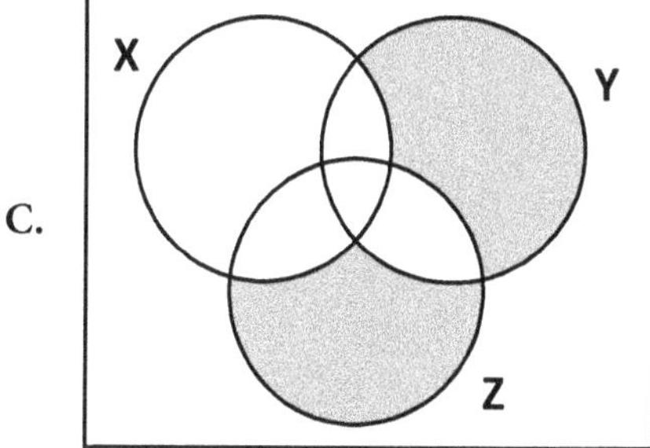

D.

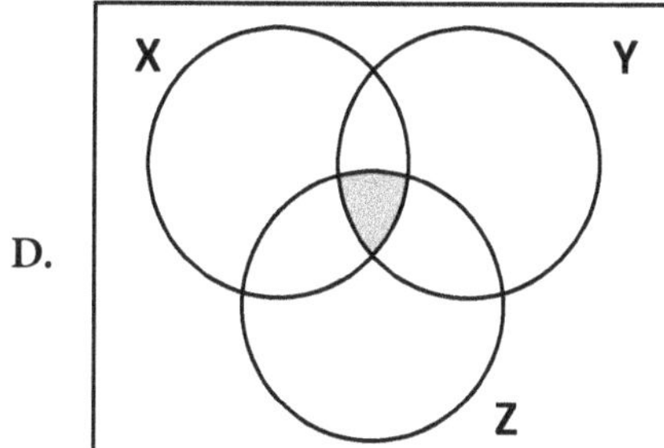

43.

The stem-leaf plot given below shows the grades for a test in Andrew's science class. Andrew's score is the median score for the class. What grade did Andrew make on the test?

Stem	Leaf
5	0
6	1, 8, 9
7	0, 4, 4, 5, 5
8	2, 6, 6, 6, 6, 8
9	0, 1, 5, 5

A. 75
B. 79
C. 82
D. 86

44.

Find the median of the following data: 26, 20, 30, 30, 20, 24, 30, 31.

A. 20
B. 26
C. 28
D. 30

45.

Compute the weighted mean for the following data.

x_i	Weight (W_i)
19	12
17	30
14	28
13	10
18	10

A. 16
B. 18
C. 20
D. 24

46.

What is the sum of the mean and mode for the set {7, 9, 1, 14, 2, 16, 7}?

A. 1
B. 7
C. 8
D. 15

47.

Derrick has scores of 73, 93, 87, and 91 on 4 of his quizzes in science. What is the difference in his median score and mean score?

A. 1
B. 2
C. 3
D. 4

48.

A random sample of 20 GRE scores from 2010 is listed below. Calculate the sample mean and standard deviation.
29, 26, 13, 23, 23, 25, 17, 22, 17, 19, 12, 26, 30, 30, 18, 14, 12, 26, 17, 18

A. 20.50, 5.79
B. 20.50, 5.94
C. 20.85, 5.79
D. 20.85, 5.94

49.

The average (arithmetic mean) test score for all the students in a class is 83. The average score of b boys in the class was 79, while that of g girls was 87. What is the ratio of b to g?

A. 2:1
B. 3:1
C. 1:1
D. 1:3

50.

The random variable x represents the number of credit cards that adults have along with the corresponding probabilities. Find the mean and standard deviation.

x	$P(x)$
0	0.07
1	0.68
2	0.21
3	0.03
4	0.01

A. mean: 1.23; sd: 0.44
B. mean: 1.30; sd: 0.32
C. mean: 1.30; sd: 0.44
D. mean: 1.23; sd: 0.66

51.

If $A = \{1, 2, 3\}, B = \{3, 4\}$ *and* $C = \{4, 5, 6\}$ then $A \cup (B \cap C)$ is equal to

A. $\{1, 2, 3, 4\}$

B. $\{3\}$

C. $\{1, 2, 3, 4, 5, 6\}$

D. $\{1,2\}$

52.

Set A = {7, 21, 11, 9, 1, 3, 11}. If the mean, median, and mode are the same for set B and set B contains 13 numbers, then the sum of the numbers in set B is?

A. 63
B. 81
C. 117
D. 143

53.

For a set of 7 numbers, the mean is 45. The median of the set is 42 and the mode is 51. What is the sum of the other four numbers in the set?

A. 14
B. 150
C. 171
D. 228

54.

Jerry needs an average test score of 75 to pass his math class. The class gives five equally-weighted tests, and his first four scores were 57, 63, 90 and 72. What score does he need to receive on his final test to pass his class?

A. 60
B. 75
C. 93
D. 100

55.

The table below shows the distribution of Science scores for a sample of students enrolled in 1999.

Science	Frequency
15	1
16	1
17	10
18	7
19	13
20	9
21	7
22	7
23	13
24	4
25	3
26	4
27	0
28	3
29	1
30	1

Select the statement that is true.

A. 17 students had scores of 10
B. 42 students had scores of 13
C. A and B both true
D. A, B and C are all false.

56.

The mean marks of 58 boys is 32 and the mean of 42 girls in the same class is 38. Then formula of the mean and the value of the mean of all 100 students is:

A. $\frac{32+42}{2}$, 37.0
B. $\frac{58(32)+42(38)}{(58+42)}$, 34.5
C. $\frac{58(21)+42(38)}{100}$, 37.0
D. $\frac{58-42}{58}$, 37.5

57.

If A = {2, 3, 4, 6, 8}, B = {3, 4, 5, 10}, C = {4, 5, 6, 8, 11}. Find the Venn diagram that represents the given set.

A.

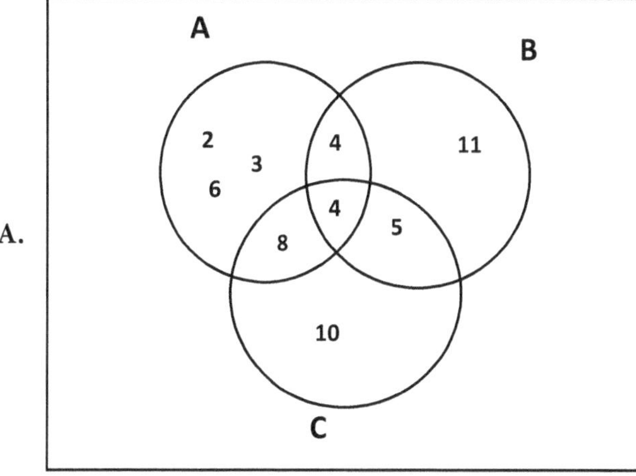

B.

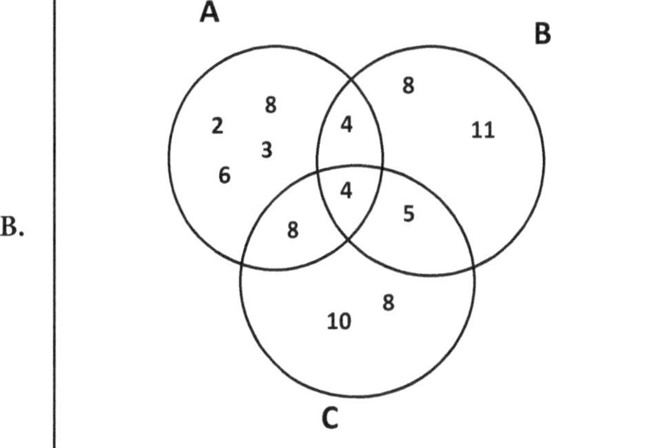

C.

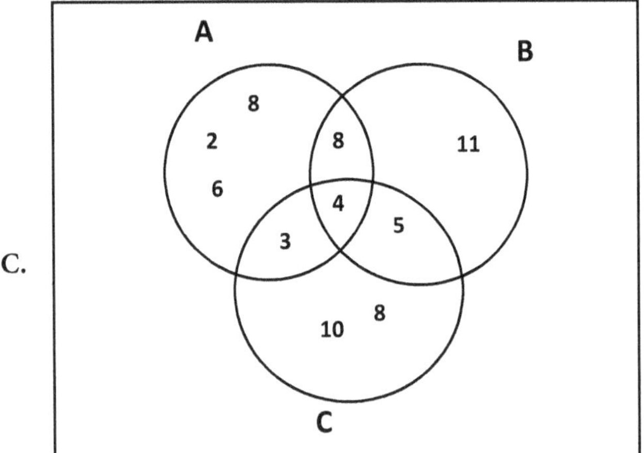

D.

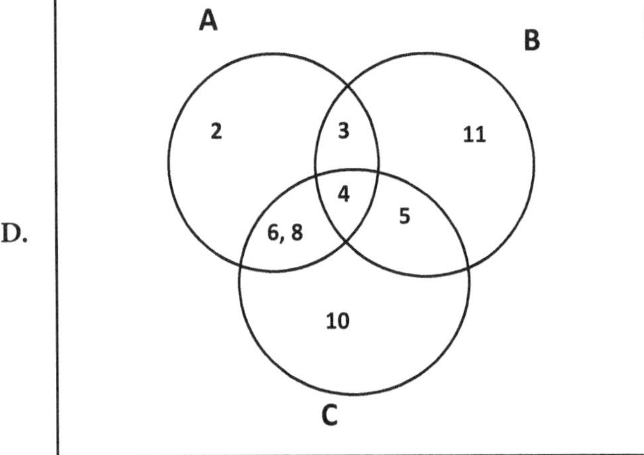

58.

The stem–leaf plot below shows your favorite basketball's team scores for the first 9 games of the season.

Stem	Leaf
5	5, 7
6	1, 3, 4, 9
7	1, 1
8	3

For example, a score of 63 is represented by stem value of 6 and a leaf value of 3.

What is the sum of the mean and mode score for the first 9 games?

A. 125
B. 129
C. 135
D. 137

59.

Given that

$$U = \{0, 2, 9, 11, 12, 13, 15, 16, 17, 18, 19\}$$
$$A = \{9, 11, 12, 15, 17\}$$
$$B = \{0, 2, 9, 12, 17,\}$$

Represent the information on a Venn diagram.

A.

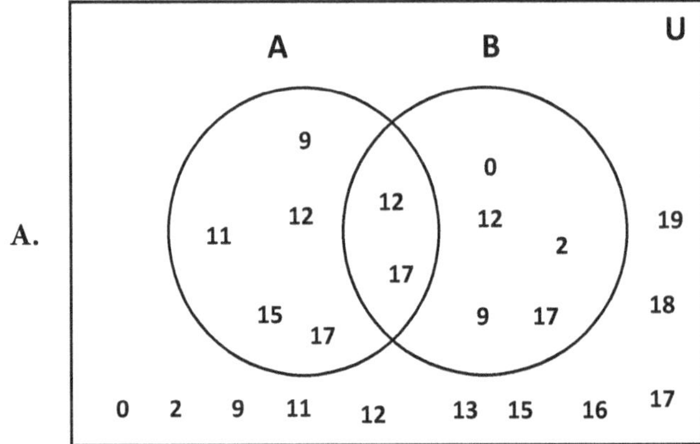

B.

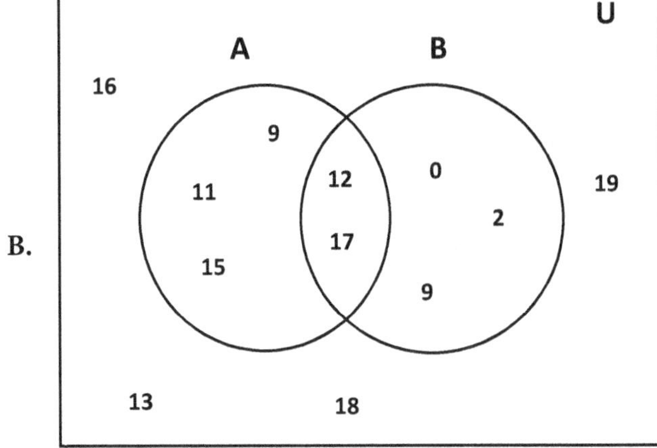

C.

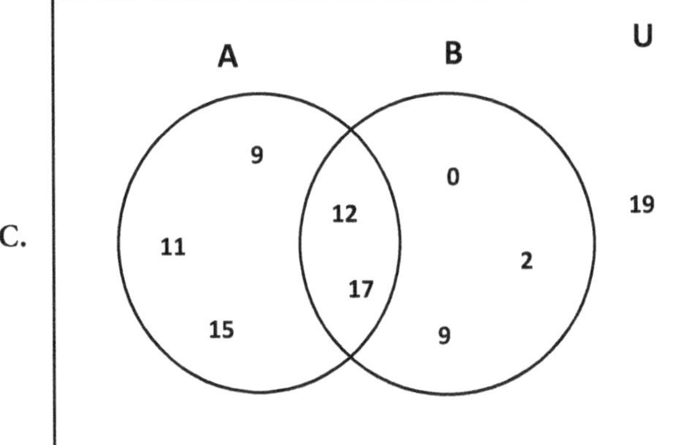

D. 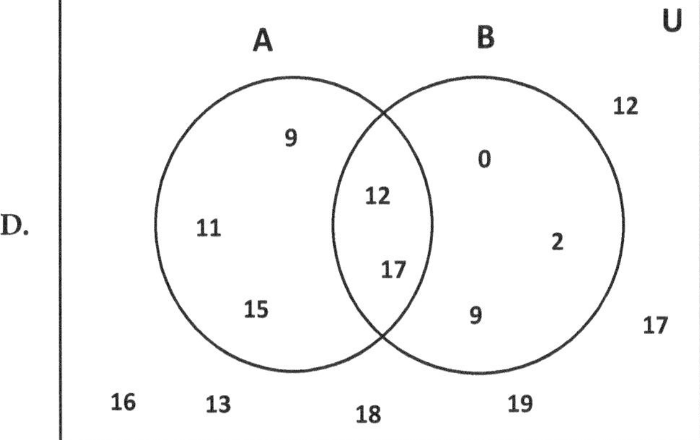

60.

Jason asked 7 of his classmates if they passed or failed the most recent test in science class. Three of the seven students said they failed the test. How many students can Jason predict passed the test if the class has 42 students?

A. 10
B. 18
C. 21
D. 24

61.

The stem–leaf plot below shows the grades of each assignment in a math class for a grading period. For example, grade of 94 is represented by stem value of 9 and a leaf value of 4. If each assignment carries an equal weight, what must the value for *n* be for your average to be an 80?

Stem	Leaf
5	2
6	*n*, 8
7	3, 9, 9
8	1, 5, 5, 5, 8
9	2, 4, 8

A. 0
B. 1
C. 3
D. 5

62.

If $A = \{5, 6\}$ *and* $B = \{7, 8\}$, then what is the number of relations from A to B?

A. 2^3
B. 2^2
C. 2^4
D. None of the above.

63.

Find the median of an even data set:

9, 10, 3, 5, 9, 8, 10, 3

A. 5.0
B. 6.5
C. 8.5
D. 9.5

64.

Which of the following is set B?

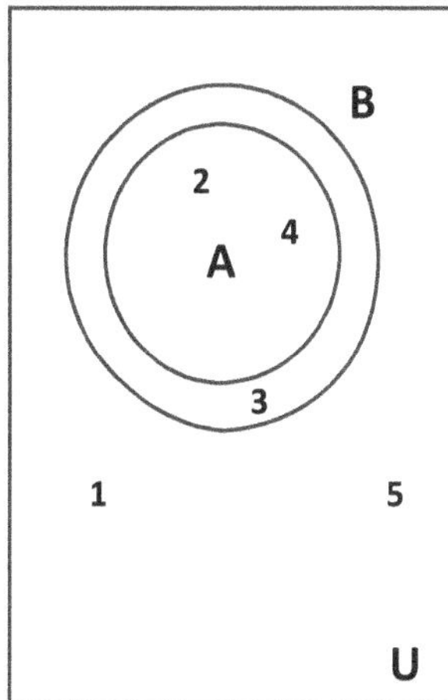

A. {1, 2, 3, 4, 5}
B. {2,4}
C. {2,3,4}
D. {3}

65.

Suppose the mean of 5 numbers increases by $\frac{1}{3}$. Which of the following statements must be true?

A. The sum of the 5 numbers must increase by $\frac{5}{3}$ of the original mean.
B. The sum of the 5 numbers must increase by $\frac{1}{3}$ of the original mean.
C. The sum of the 5 numbers must increase by $\frac{4}{3}$ of the original mean.
D. The sum of the 5 numbers must increase by $\frac{1}{3}$ of the new mean.

66.

Jeanette wants to get an accurate reading on how many miles per gallon her car gets on a tank of fuel. She does 5 trials and finds that her car gets 23.1, 23.8, 23.7, 23.8, and 23.1 miles per gallon for each tank of fuel used. What is the sum of the median and mean of the 5 trials?

A. 23.5
B. 46.6
C. 47.2
D. 47.3

67.

A set of data consists of the following 5 numbers: 0, 2, 4, 6, and 8. Which two numbers, if added to create a set of 7 numbers, will result in a new standard deviation that is close to the standard deviation for the original 5 numbers?

A. –1 and 9
B. 4 and 4
C. 3 and 5
D. 2 and 6

68.

Consider two data sets for item 68 –70.

Set A : $n=15;\ \bar{x}=30$ Set B : $n=50;\ \bar{x}=30$

Supposing the number 20 is included as an additional data value in Set A, compute $\bar{x}$ for the new data set.

A. 20.00
B. 29.00
C. 29.38
D. 30.20

69.

A survey was done to 43 students, 30 of them like mathematics and 29 students like English. Which Venn diagram shows the correct representation of the problem?

A.

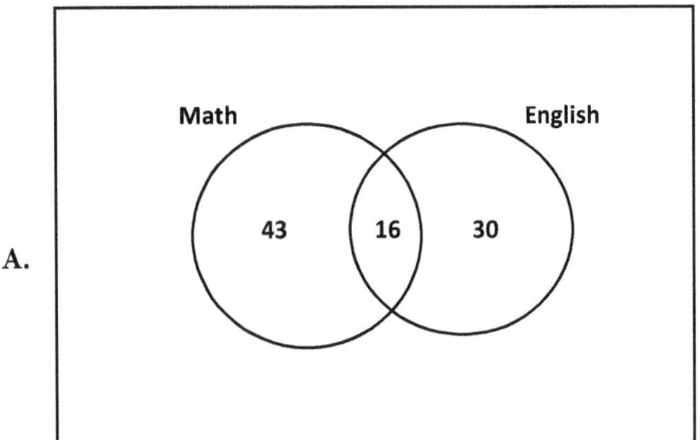

B.

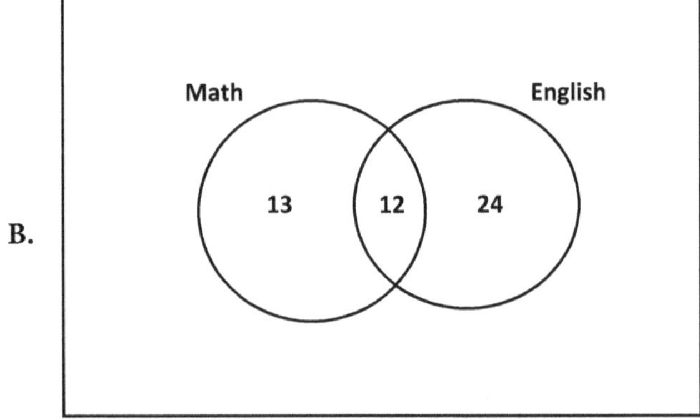

C.

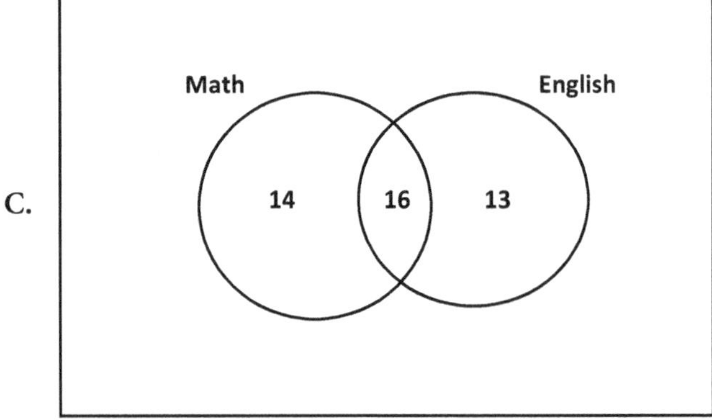

D.

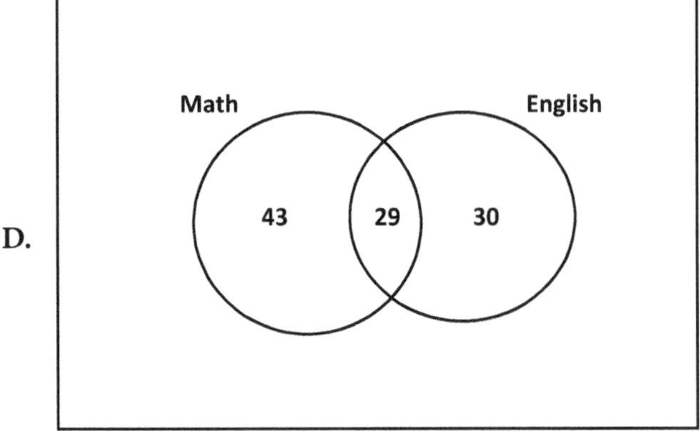

70.

If X={3, 6, 8} and Y={1, 6, 9, 10}, then find the number of proper subsets of $X \cup Y$.

A. 61
B. 64
C. 65
D. 63

71.

If $A=\{1, 2, 3, 4\}$, $B=\{2, 4, 6, 8\}$ *and* $C=\{3, 4, 5, 6\}$, the value of $A-\{B\cap C\}$ is:

A. $\{1\}$

B. $\{2,3,4,5\}$

C. $\{1,2,3\}$

D. $\{0\}$

72.

Of the 200 candidates who were interviewed for a position at a call center, 100 had a two-wheeler, 70 had a credit card and 140 had a mobile phone. 40 of them had both, a two-wheeler and a credit card, 30 had both, a credit card and a mobile phone and 60 had both, a two wheeler and mobile phone and 10 had all three. Which of the following correctly represents the formula for the people who had none of the three? Let *T for two–wheeler, C for creditcard* αvδ *M for mobilephone.*

A. $200-|T\cup C\cup M|$

B. $200-|T\cap C\cap M|$

C. $|T\cap C\cap M|-200$

D. $190-|T\cap C\cap M|$

73.

There are 80 students in Year 8.
15 students study French (F) and German (G).
39 students study German
53 students study French
3 students do not study French or German.

Complete the Venn diagram below by finding the values of x and y.

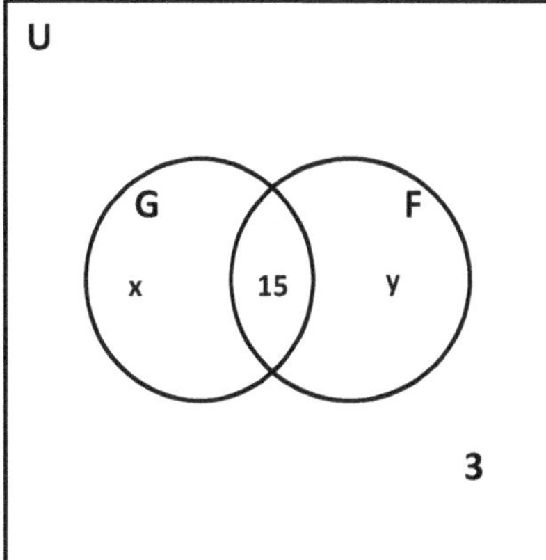

A. $x = 38, y = 24$
B. $x = 28, y = 34$
C. $x = 14, y = 28$
D. $x = 24, y = 38$

74.

Which of the following Venn Diagram shows $A-(B\cap C)$?

A.

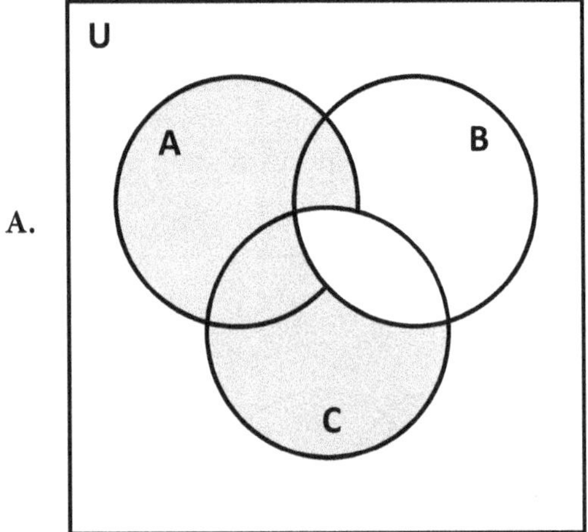

B.

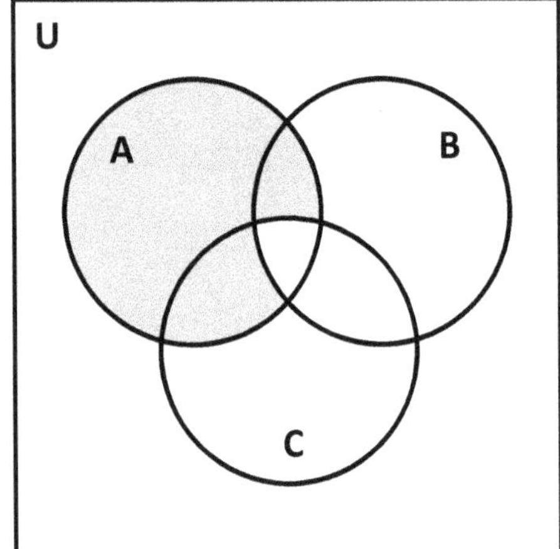

C.

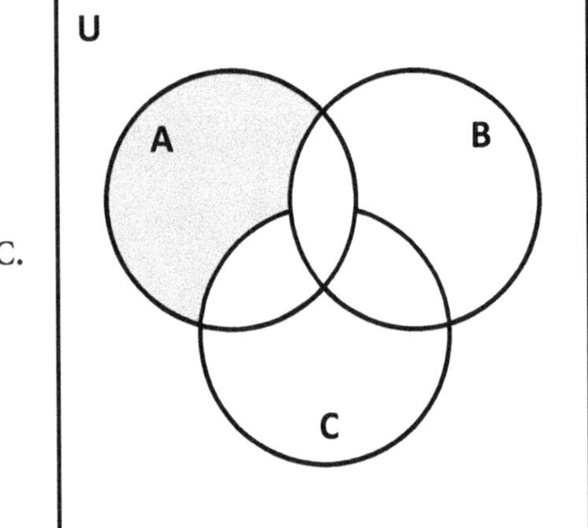

D.

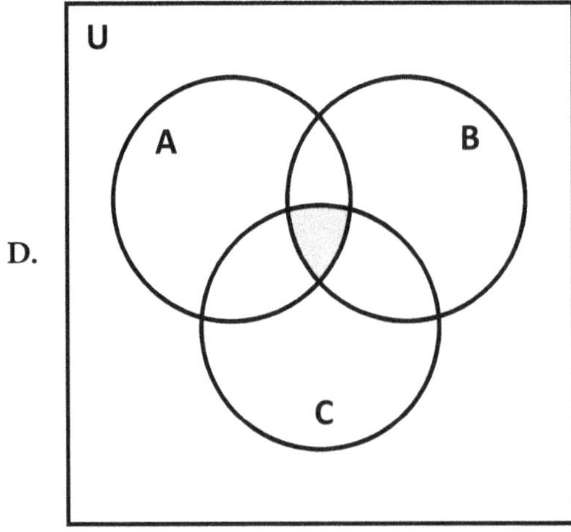

75.

Which of the following data sets has the largest standard deviation?

A. 2, 3, 4, 5, 6
B. 301, 34, 306, 308, 311
C. 350, 350, 350, 350, 350
D. 888.5, 888.6, 888.7, 888.8, 888.9

76.

In the following distribution, if the mean of the distribution is 86, then the correct mean formula in terms of p is _____.

Wages (in $)	50–60	60–70	70–80	80–90	90–100	100–110
Number of workers	5	3	4	P	2	13

A. $86=\dfrac{2325p+85p}{27}$

B. $86=\dfrac{2325p+85}{27+p}$

C. $86=\dfrac{2325+85p}{27+p}$

D. $86=\dfrac{2325+85p}{27p+p}$

77.

If the mode of the following data is 7, the the value of k in the data set 3, 8, 6, 7, 1, 6, 10, 6, 7, $2k + 5$, 9, 7, and 13 is:

A. 1
B. 3
C. 4
D. 7

78.

Most states in the United States have license plate numbers that contain 7 values. If there are 3 letters from the alphabet followed by 4 digits from 0 through 9, how many combinations of license plate numbers can a state have if the letters and digits can be repeated?

A. 2,600
B. 11,232,000
C. 78,624,000
D. 175,760,000

79.

Miss Smith drives 4 hours at an average speed of 30 miles per hour. Then she drives 2 hours at a speed of 45 miles per hour. What is her average speed for the whole trip?

A. 20 miles per hour
B. 25 miles per hour
C. 35 miles per hour
D. 45 miles per hour

80.

Which of the following two sets are disjoint?

A. {1, 3, 5} and {1, 3, 6}
B. {1, 2, 3} and {1, 2, 3}
C. {1, 3, 5} and {2, 3, 4}
D. {1, 3, 5} and {2, 4, 6}

81.

Angela scores 17, 19, 13, 24 and 14 points in the first five games of a seven-game basketball season. If the scoring leader in Angela's league averages 18 points per game, how many points must Angela score in the final two games combined to end the season with the highest scoring average in the league AND have a higher scoring average than any other player?

A. 32
B. 37
C. 40
D. 43

82.

What is the sum of the mean and the median for the set {9, 5, 2, 6, 13}?

A. 6
B. 7
C. 13
D. 42

83.

Cayden has 3 shirts, 2 pair of pants, and one pair of shoes. An outfit consists of 1 of the shirts worn with one pair of paints, and one pair of shoes. How many distinct outfits can Cayden wear?

A. 3
B. 5
C. 6
D. 12

84.

Below is a stem-leaf plot for the temperature, in degrees Fahrenheit, taken at various times during a day. For example, a temperature of 43 is represented by stem value of 4 and a leaf value of 3. What is the difference, in degrees Fahrenheit, between the mean temperature and the mode for that day?

Stem	Leaf
4	2, 4, 7
5	1, 1, 4
6	0, 2, 4, 5
7	1, 3

A. 0
B. 4
C. 6
D. 7

85.

The intersection of the sets {1, 2, 3, 4, 5} and {1, 2, 6, 7, 8} is the set ______.

A. {1, 2}
B. {5, 6}
C. {2, 5}
D. {2, 8}

86.

In a group of 60 people, 29 prefer cold beverages and 40 prefer hot beverages, and each prefers at least one of the two. Which of the following Venn diagram shows how many people like coffee and tea?

A.

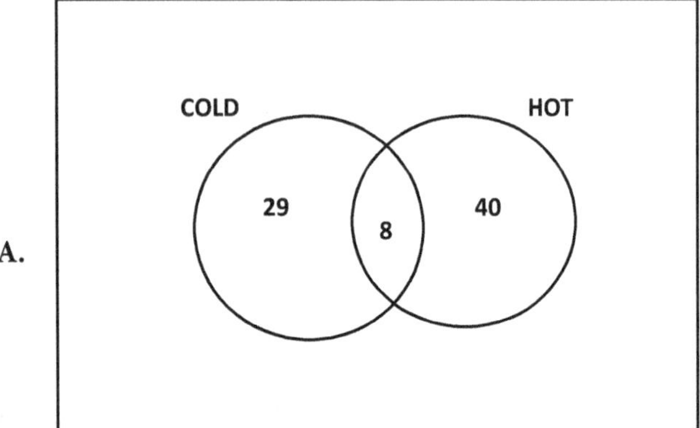

B.

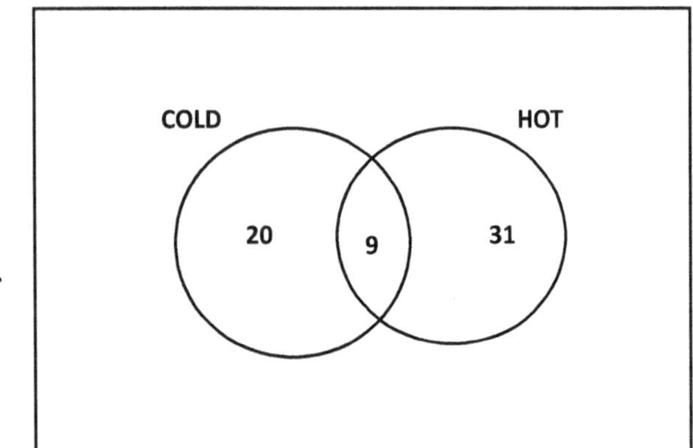

C.

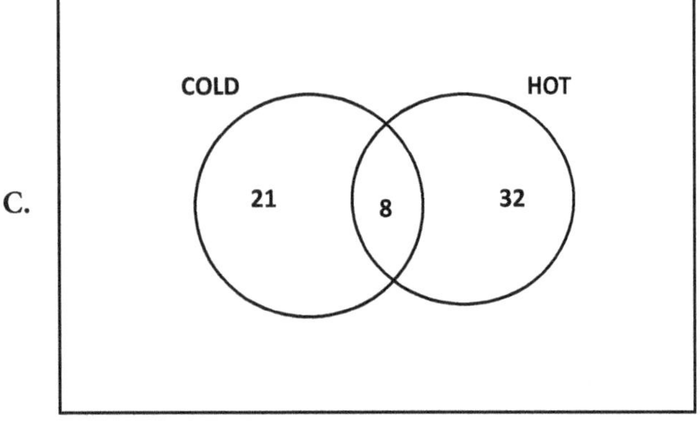

D.

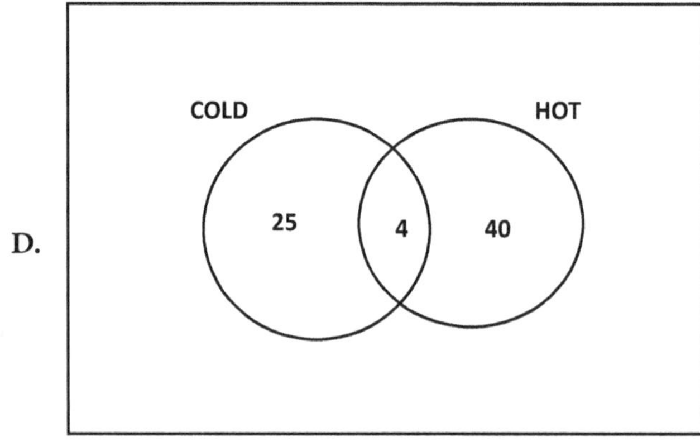

87.

Find the mean number of children per family for the sample from the following table and its formula.

Number of children	Number of families
0	8
1	16
2	22
3	14
4	6
5	4
6	2

A. $Mean = \frac{\Sigma(\neq of\ children \times \neq of\ families)}{\Sigma(\neq of\ families)}$, 3.14

B. $Mean = \frac{\Sigma(\neq of\ children \times \neq of\ families)}{\Sigma(\neq of\ children)}$, 2.19

C. $Mean = \frac{\Sigma(\neq of\ children \times \neq of\ families)}{\Sigma(\neq of\ children)}$, 3.14

D. $Mean = \frac{\Sigma(\neq of\ children \times \neq of\ families)}{\Sigma(\neq of\ families)}$, 2.19

88.

Given the following sets:

A = {2, 4, 6, 8, 10, 12}
B = {1, 3, 5, 8, 10, 12}
C = {7, 8, 9, 10, 11, 12, 13}

Which of the following represent the set {8,10,12}?

A. $(A \cup B) \cup (B \cap C)$
B. $(A \cup B) \cap (B \cup C)$
C. $(A \cap B) \cup (B \cap C)$
D. $(A \cup B) \cup (B \cap C)$

89.

In a survey, it was found that 21 people read English newspapers, 26 people read Hindi newspapers, and 29 people read regional language newspapers. If 14 people read both English and Hindi newspapers; 15 people read both Hindi and regional language newspapers; 12 people read both English and regional language newspapers and 8 read all types of newspapers; how many people were surveyed?

A. 35
B. 43
C. 59
D. 65

90.

If balls X, Y and Z are added to the group of five balls at the left, the standard deviation of the volume of the 5 balls will be _________ the standard deviation of the volume of the new 8 balls.

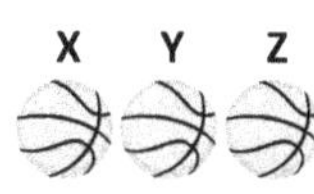

A. will be about the same
B. will be greater than
C. will be less than
D. cannot be computed since the balls are of different sizes

91.

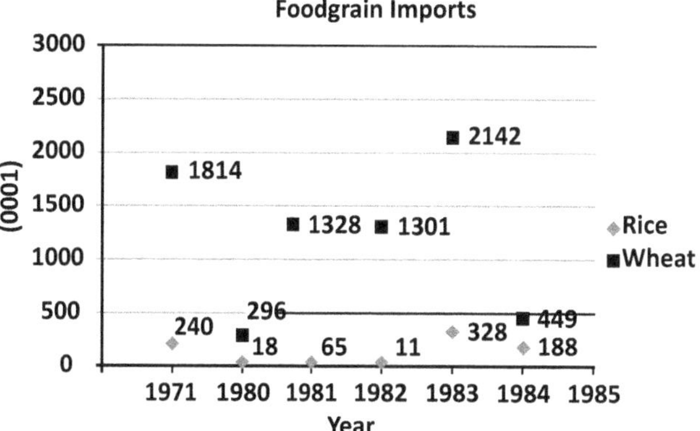

The total value of food grains (rice and wheat) imported during these years are given below:

1971: $1.56 B
1980: $0.78 B
1981: $5.23 B
1982: $2.93 B
1983: $6.12 B
1984: $1.69 B

What percent of the volume of the total imports of food grains are wheat from 1980–84?

A. 66%
B. 75%
C. 90%
D. 95%

92.

150 students were asked if they prefer a bird (B), a cat (C), or a dog (D) as a pet. The result is shown in the Venn diagram below. Which of the following statements is true?

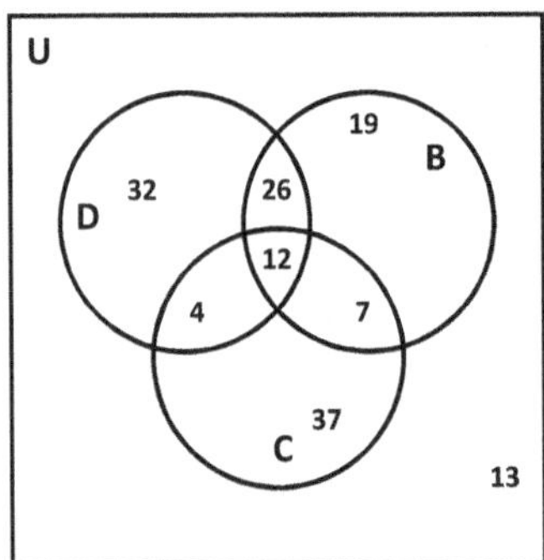

A. likes dog: 74
Likes cat: 60
Likes bird: 64
Don't like pets: 13
Likes dog or bird: 100
Likes Bird or Cat: 105
Likes dog or cat: 118

B. likes dog: 60
Likes cat: 74
Likes bird: 74
Don't like pets: 10
Likes dog or bird: 110
Likes Bird or Cat: 150
Likes dog or cat: 180

C. likes dog: 70
Likes cat: 60
Likes bird: 70
Don't like pets: 10
Likes dog or bird: 105
Likes Bird or Cat: 125
Likes dog or cat: 120

D. likes dog: 74
Likes cat: 60
Likes bird: 74
Don't like pets: 13
Likes dog or bird: 110
Likes Bird or Cat: 105
Likes dog or cat: 118

93.

The histogram below represents the lifespan of a random sample of a particular type of insect. Identify the relationship between the mean and median.

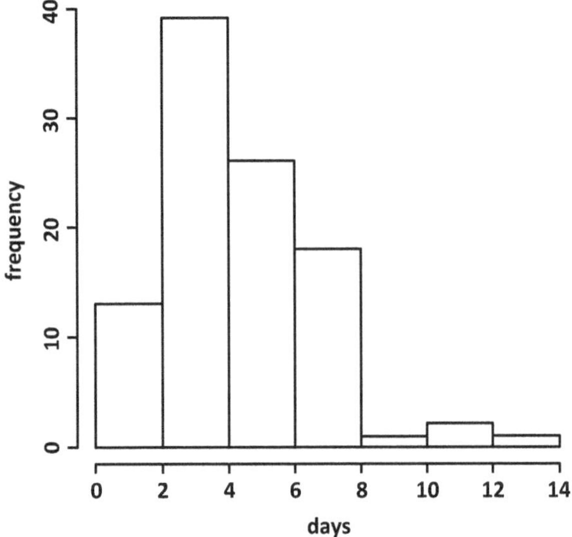

A. mean = median
B. mean ≈ median
C. mean < median
D. mean > median

94.

Refer to the following graph.

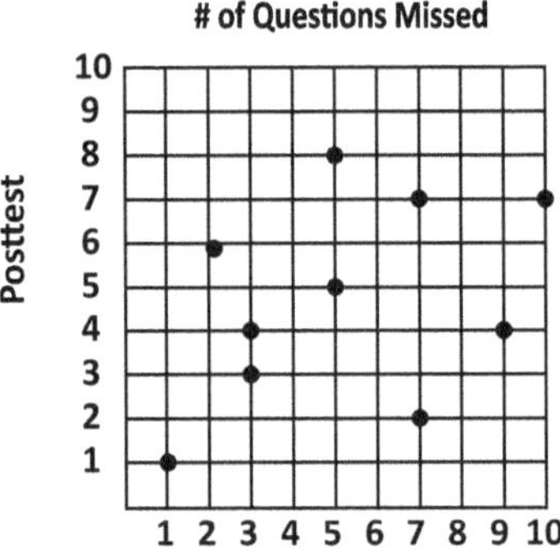

Key: Each orderd pair represents the score (pretest, posttest) for one student

Mr. Andy made a scatterplot to compare the number of questions each student missed on their pretest and post test.

How many of Mr. Andy's 10 students missed the same number of questions on both tests?

A. 2
B. 4
C. 8
D. 10

95.

A survey was conducted among 200 people about how they like to travel. The results are displayed in the Venn diagram below. How many people don't like to fly in an airplane?

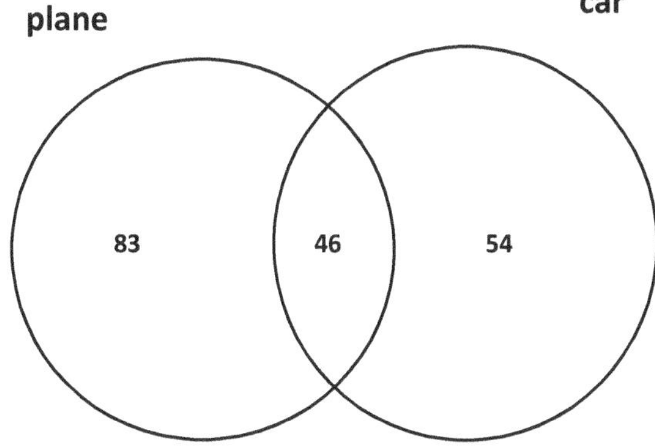

A. 51
B. 61
C. 71
D. 83

96.

The shipping rate for customers at International Parcel Shipping contains a fee per package and a price per ounce for that package. The table and its corresponding line graph below gives the fee and the price per ounce.

Weight (ounces)	Fee	Price per ounce
Fewer than 8	$2.00	$0.75
8–15	$5.00	$0.50
16 or more	$7.00	$0.25

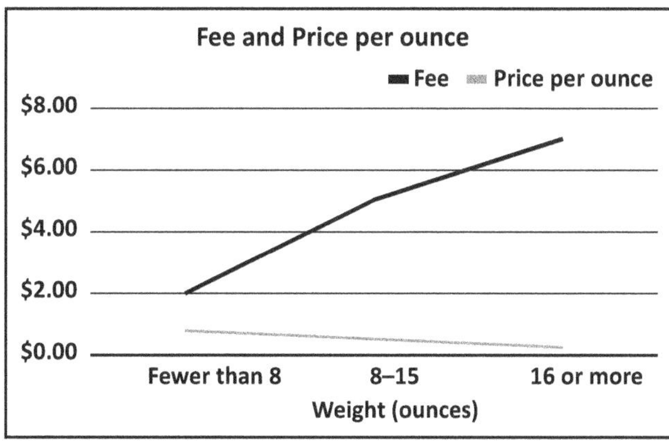

What is the equation used and its value to calculate for how much is Evan going to pay to ship one package that weighs 14 ounces?

A. $y = 7x + 0.25$, $12.00
B. $y = 2x + 0.75$, $8.50
C. $y = 5x + 0.50$, $12.00
D. $y = 0.50x + 5$, $12.00

97.

The pie chart, given below, shows the results from a survey of percentage of people that preferred a genre for watching a movie. What are the odds of a person preferring an action movie to a preferring comedy?

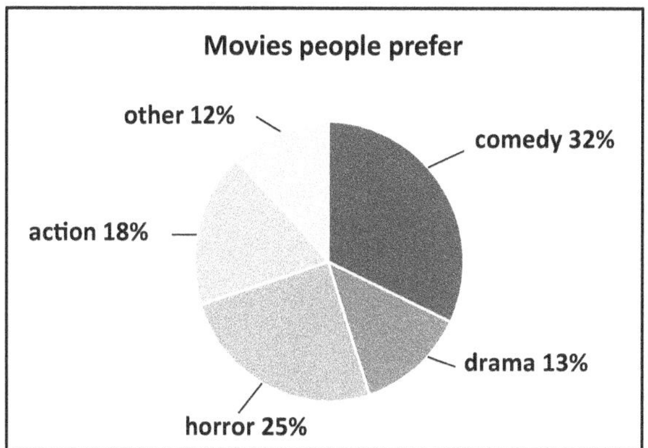

A. 9:16
B. 9:25
C. 9:41
D. 9:50

98.

Study the graph below carefully and answer the question.

(Production in million units)

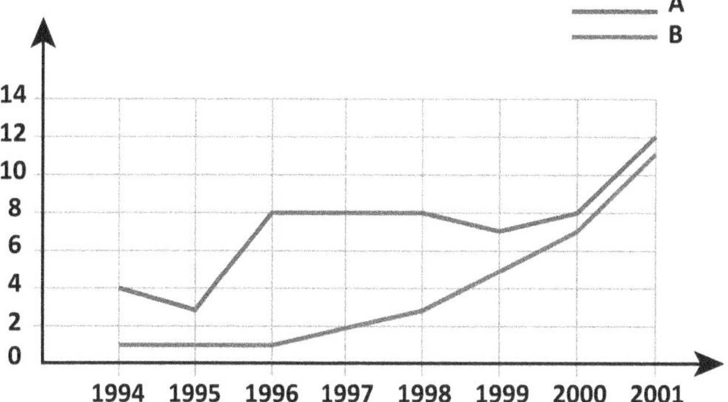

Production of two companies A & B over the years is as shown in the figure. For company A, what is the percent decrease in production from 1998 to 1999?

A. 11%
B. 12.5%
C. 25%
D. 40%

99.

The pie chart given below shows the results from a survey of the percentage of different ways people get to work each day. If 45 people that were surveyed walked to work, how many people from the survey drove a car to work?

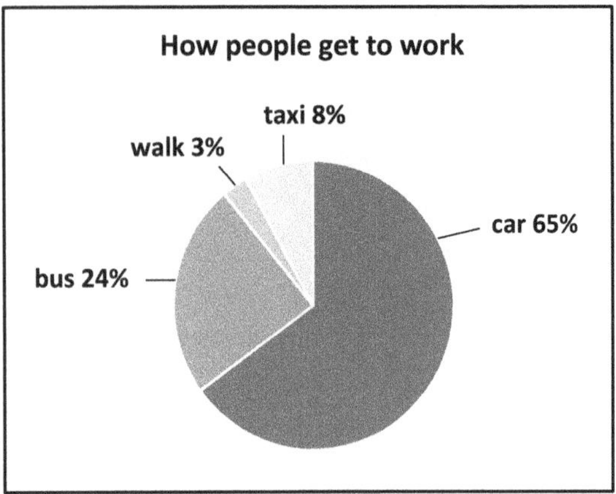

A. 69
B. 175
C. 975
D. 1000

100.

Thirty people are surveyed to determine their preference for one of 4 fruits. The results are in the bar graph displayed below. What is the probability that a person chosen at random prefers bananas or apples as their preferred fruit?

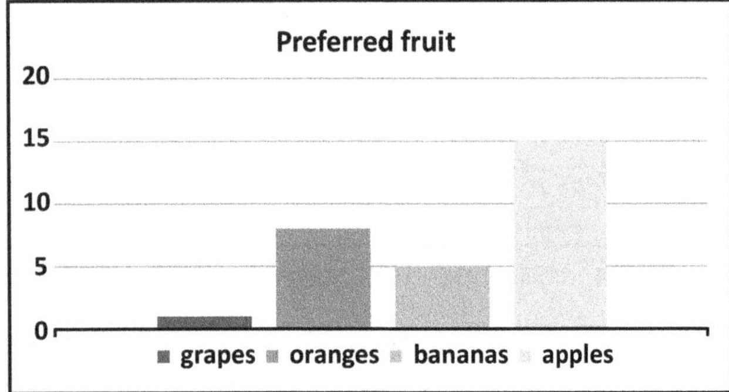

A. 0.45
B. 0.55
C. 0.67
D. 0.98

101.

Given that A and B are independent events, which of the following statements is correct?

A. $P(A|B) = P(A)$ and $P(B|A) = P(B)$
B. $P(AB) = 0$
C. $P(AB) = P(A) + P(B)$
D. Choice A and B both

102.

In how many different ways can the letters of the word JUDGE be arranged in a way that the vowels are already together?

A. 16
B. 20
C. 48
D. 124

103.

How many 4-digit positive integers divisible by 3 can be formed using only the digits {1, 3, 4, 6, 7} such that no digit appears more than once in a number?

A. 12
B. 24
C. 48
D. 72

104.

Let m be men and n for women. They are to be seated in a row where no two women sit together. If $m > n$, then the number of ways in which they can be seated, is

A. $\dfrac{(m-1)(m+1)!}{(m-n+1)!}$

B. $\dfrac{m!(m-1)!}{(m-n+1)!}$

C. $\dfrac{m!(m+1)!}{(m-n+1)!}$

D. None of these

105.

From a group of 7 men and 6 women, five persons are to be selected to form a committee so that at least 3 men are there on the committee. In how many ways can it be done?

A. 564
B. 645
C. 735
D. 756

106.

If $P_r^{10} : P_{r+1}^{12} = 1:22$, then the expansion of the given

A. $\frac{10!}{(10-r)!} : \frac{12!}{(12-(r-1)!)} = 1:22$

B. $\frac{10!}{(10-r)!} : \frac{12!}{(12-(r+1)!)} = 1:22$

C. $\frac{10!}{(10-r)!} : \frac{12!}{(12+(r-1)!)} = 1:22$

D. $\frac{10!}{(10-r)!} : \frac{12!}{(12-(r+1))!} = 1:22$

107.

Which situation illustrates combination?

A. Assembling a jigsaw puzzle
B. Four people posing for pictures
C. Picking 6 balls from a basket of 13 balls
D. Determining the top three winners in a Science Quiz Bee

108.

Suppose you secure your bike using a combination lock. Later, you realized that you forgot the 4-digit code. You only remembered that the code contains the digits 1, 2, 5, and 9. How many possible codes are there?

A. 12
B. 24
C. 36
D. 48

109.

If Jericho has 12 shirts, 6 pairs of jeans and 3 pairs of sneakers, how many possibilities can she dress himself up for the day?

A. 54
B. 108
C. 216
D. 312

110.

Find out the number of distinctive words that can be formed using the word GOOD.

A. 12
B. 16
C. 24
D. 48

Answer Key

Question	Correct	Make your correct answers
1	D	
2	D	
3	A	
4	A	
5	A	
6	A	
7	B	
8	A	
9	C	
10	B	
11	D	
12	D	
13	A	
14	A	
15	C	
16	B	
17	C	
18	D	
19	D	
20	D	
21	A	
22	B	
23	A	
24	A	
25	B	
26	C	
27	C	
28	D	
29	A	
30	B	
31	B	
32	B	

Question	Correct	Make your correct answers
33	C	
34	C	
35	A	
36	C	
37	C	
38	D	
39	A	
40	B	
41	B	
42	A	
43	C	
44	C	
45	A	
46	D	
47	C	
48	D	
49	C	
50	D	
51	A	
52	C	
53	C	
54	C	
55	D	
56	B	
57	D	
58	D	
59	B	
60	B	
61	B	
62	C	
63	C	
64	C	

Question	Correct	Make your correct answers
65	A	
66	C	
67	D	
68	C	
69	C	
70	D	
71	A	
72	A	
73	D	
74	B	
75	B	
76	C	
77	A	
78	D	
79	C	
80	D	
81	C	
82	C	
83	C	
84	C	
85	A	
86	B	
87	D	
88	C	
89	B	
90	C	
91	C	
92	A	
93	D	
94	B	
95	C	
96	D	

Question	Correct	Make your correct answers
97	A	
98	B	
99	C	
100	C	
101	A	
102	C	
103	C	
104	C	
105	D	
106	D	
107	C	
108	B	
109	C	
110	A	

1.

Category: IES
Skill: Probability | **Level:** Medium

Choice D is correct. The probability that there will not be a delay for your flight is 100% – 12% = 88% or 0.88. One flight being delayed due to a mechanical issue is independent of any other flight so, the probabilities that the flights will not be delayed will be multiplied to determine the probability that there will not be a delay for the round trip. Then,

$$0.88 \times 0.88 = 0.7744 \approx 0.77 \text{ or } 77\%.$$

Choice A is incorrect. This may result from calculation or conceptual error. **Choice B** is incorrect. This is the probability of delay for one flight. **Choice C** is incorrect. This is twice the delay probability for one flight.

2.

Category: PHM
Skill: Probability | **Level:** Easy

Choice D is correct. There are 15 + 10 + 22 = 47 coins in the container. If a coin is not a penny, it must be a nickel or a dime. There are 10 + 22 = 32 coins that are not pennies in the container. The probability is,

$$P(\text{not a penny}) = \frac{32}{47} = 0.68.$$

Choice A is incorrect. This is the probability of choosing a nickel. **Choice B** is incorrect. This is the probability of choosing a penny instead of not choosing one. **Choice C** is incorrect. This may result from $\frac{25}{47}$.

3.

Category: PHM
Skill: Probability | **Level:** Easy

Choice A is correct. The frequency table tells you there are 163 people that spend from 2 to 6 days at the hotel. 27 people spend more than 4 days (5 or 6 days) at the hotel so, the probability is $\frac{27}{163} = 0.17$.

Choice B is incorrect. This is the probability of spending 4 nights. **Choice C** is incorrect. This includes 4 nights spent when determining the probability. **Choice D** is incorrect. This is the probability of less than 4 days.

4.

Category: PHM & Modeling
Skill: Probability | **Level:** Easy

Choice A is correct because $P(\overline{A} \cap \overline{B}) = 0.2$.

Events A and B are two independent events. Find

$$P(\text{not } A \text{ and not } B).$$

$$\text{If } P(B)=0.6, \text{ then } P(\text{not } B)=1-P(B)=1-0.6=0.4$$

$$\text{If } P(A)=0.4, \text{ then } P(\text{not } A)=1-P(A)=1-0.4=0.6$$

$$P(\overline{A} \cap \overline{B})=0.4(0.6)=0.24$$

The symbol $\cap$ and "and" indicates intersection.

Choice B is incorrect because the value is 0.8 which is greater than the obtained value of 0.2. **Choice C** is incorrect because the symbol used in for "or". **Choice D** is incorrect because the symbol used in for "or".

5.

Category: PHM & Modeling
Skill: Probability | **Level:** Medium

Choice A is correct because the obtained answer is Favorable outcomes = (Red cards)+(Face cards)-(Red face cards).

Identify the total number of favorable outcomes.

Red cards : There are 26 red cards (13 hearts + 13 diamonds).

Face cards: There are 12 face cards (3 face cards per suit × 4 suits)

However, let's consider that there are both red and face cards.

Red face cards: There are 6 red face cards (3 face heart cards and 3 face diamond cards)

Hence, the favorable outcomes is

Favorable outcomes = (Red cards) + (Face cards) - (Red face cards)

Choice B is incorrect because red face cards should have been subtracted and not added. **Choice C** is incorrect because it failed to consider the red face cards. **Choice D** is incorrect because it failed to consider the red face cards.

6.

Category: PHM
Skill: Probability | **Level:** Medium

Choice A is correct. The probability of answering any one question correctly is $\frac{1}{4}$. Each question is answered independently so each probability is multiplied to get

$$\frac{1}{4}\times\frac{1}{4}\times\frac{1}{4}\times\frac{1}{4}\times\frac{1}{4}=\frac{1}{1024}.$$

Choice B is incorrect. This may result if the probability of answering each question is $\frac{1}{5}\times\frac{1}{5}\times\frac{1}{5}\times\frac{1}{5}$. **Choice C** is incorrect. This may result if the probability of answering each question is $\frac{1}{5!}$. **Choice D** is incorrect. This adds the denominator of each probability for each question.

7.

Category: PHM
Skill: Probability | **Level:** Medium

Choice B is correct. The probability of one of you being chosen 1st is $\frac{2}{6}$. The probability that the other person is chosen 2nd is $\frac{1}{5}$ since one of the 6 people has been chosen. The events of choosing a person at random are independent so the probability is $\frac{2}{6}\times\frac{1}{5}=\frac{2}{30}=\frac{1}{15}$.

Choice A is incorrect. Assumes the probability of one of you chosen first is $\frac{1}{6}$. **Choice C** is incorrect. The probabilities of one person being chosen 1st. **Choice D** is incorrect. The probabilities of one person being chosen 2nd.

8.

Category: PHM
Skill: Probability | **Level:** Medium

Choice A is correct. Since $\frac{4}{5}$ of the students in the survey do not like spinach, $\frac{1}{5}$ do. Also, since a student chosen at random can be chosen again, the probability that the 2nd student chosen at random is also $\frac{1}{5}$.
The events of choosing a student at random that likes spinach are independent of each other so, the multiplication property can be used to get a probability of $\frac{1}{5}\times\frac{1}{5}=\frac{1}{25}$ that both students chosen will like spinach.

Choice B is incorrect. This may result from a wrong understanding of probability. **Choice C** is incorrect. This may result from conceptual error. **Choice D** is incorrect. This is the probability that both students chosen do not like spinach.

9.

Category: IES & Modeling
Skill: Probability | **Level:** Easy

Choice C is correct because the obtained answer is

$$\frac{C_2^5}{C_2^8}+\frac{C_2^3}{C_2^8}.$$

Total number of balls = $5G+3B=8$
No. of ways in which 2 balls can be picked = ${}^8C_2$

Probability of picking both balls as green = $\frac{{}^5C_2}{{}^8C_2}$

Probability of picking both balls as blue = $\frac{{}^3C_2}{{}^8C_2}$

Required probability $\frac{C_2^5}{C_2^8}+\frac{C_2^3}{C_2^8}$

Choice A is incorrect because $\frac{C_1^5 * C_1^3}{C_2^8}$ is not equivalent to the obtained probability. **Choice B** is incorrect because 0.5 is not equivalent to the obtained probability. **Choice D** is incorrect because $\frac{C_2^5 * C_2^3}{C_2^8}$ is not equivalent to the obtained probability.

10.

Category: PHM
Skill: Probability | **Level:** Easy
Choice B is correct. Since each question has 5 answer choices, the probability of getting any one question correct is $\frac{1}{5}$. Each question is answered independently so, the probability of getting all 4 questions correct (which would be a perfect score) is the product of each question's probability or $\frac{1}{5}\times\frac{1}{5}\times\frac{1}{5}\times\frac{1}{5}=\frac{1}{625}$.
Choice A is incorrect. This may result from wrong probability calculations. **Choice C** is incorrect. This may result from wrong probability calculations. **Choice D** is incorrect.This may result from wrong probability calculations.

11.

Category: IES & Modeling
Skill: Probability | **Level:** Medium

Choice D is correct because the obtained answer is $\frac{73}{150}$.
Number of people: 150

Number of people with Type A or Type AB = 67 + 6 = 73
The formula for the probability is

$$P(Type\ A\ or\ Type\ AB) = \frac{Number\ of\ people\ with\ Type\ A\ or\ Type\ AB}{Total\ number\ of\ people}$$

$$P(Type\ A\ or\ Type\ AB) = \frac{73}{150}$$

Choice A is incorrect because it is not equivalent to the obtained probability. **Choice B** is incorrect because it is not equivalent to the obtained probability. **Choice C** is incorrect because it is not equivalent to the obtained probability.

12.

Category: PHM & Modeling
Skill: Probability | **Level:** Easy

Choice D is correct because the obtained probability is

$$\frac{{}^{8}C_2}{{}^{16}C_4}.$$

Given:
In a room, there are 8 couples

8 couples = 16 people

If we select 4 people out of 16 people then, ${}^{16}C_4$

Now, we have to select four people - they may be a couple.

So, we have to select two couples from 8 couples.

Favorable cases = ${}^{8}C_2$

Hence, required probability = $\frac{{}^{8}C_2}{{}^{16}C_4}$

Choice A is incorrect because it is not equivalent to the required probability. **Choice B** is incorrect because it is not equivalent to the required probability. **Choice C** is incorrect because it is not equivalent to the required probability.

13.

Category: PHM
Skill: Probability | **Level:** Medium

Choice A is correct. Of the 42% of the men in the group 35% are given a placebo, so there is 35% of 42% or $0.35 \times 0.42 = 0.147$ or a probability of 0.15 of choosing a man that was given a placebo.

Choice B is incorrect. This may result from wrong assumption and calculation of probability. **Choice C** is incorrect. This may result from wrong calculation of probability. **Choice D** is incorrect. This may result from wrong calculation of probability.

14.

Category: PHM & Modeling
Skill: Probability | **Level:** Medium

Choice A is correct because the obtained answer is $A \subset B$.

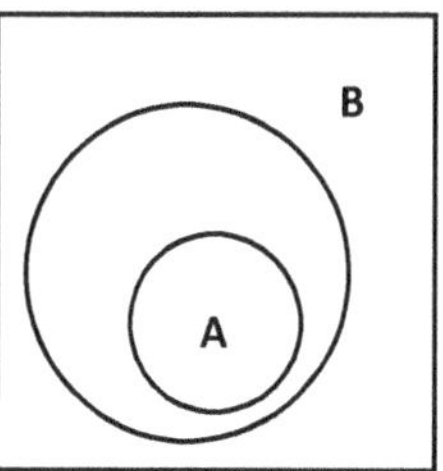

Given $P(B|A) = 1$

$$P(B|A) = \frac{P(A \cap B)}{P(A)} = 1$$

$$P(A \cap B) = P(A)$$

$$(A \cap B) = A$$

So, every element of A is in B, but B has more elements. $A \subset B$

Choice B is incorrect because $B = \phi$ is not true.
Choice C is incorrect because $B \subset A$ is not true.
Choice D is incorrect because Choice A is true.

15.

Category: PHM & Modeling
Skill: Probability | **Level:** Medium

Choice C is correct because the probability of getting one or two heads is $\frac{3}{4}$.

If a coin is tossed thrice, possible outcomes are:

$$S = \{HHT, HTH, THH, THT, TTH, HTT, TTT, HHH\}$$

Let A be an event where a coin is tossed thrice and gets one or two heads.

$$A = \{HHT, HTH, THH, THT, TTH, HTT\}$$

There are 6 out of 8 possible outcomes in getting one or two heads. Hence,

$$P(A) = \frac{6}{8}$$

$$P(A) = \frac{3}{4}$$

Choice A is incorrect because $\frac{4}{5}$ is not equivalent to the obtained value. **Choice B** is incorrect because $\frac{5}{8}$ is less than the obtained probability. **Choice D** is incorrect because $\frac{6}{4}$ is greater than 1.

16.

Category: IES & Modeling
Skill: Probability | **Level:** Easy

Choice B is correct because the obtained probability is $\frac{3}{5}$.

Given: Total fruits = 3 + 3 = 6

Total possible ways = ${}^{6}C_2 = 15$

Favourable ways = ${}^{3}C_1 \times {}^{3}C_1 = 9$

Required Probability = $\frac{9}{15} = \frac{3}{5}$

Choice A is incorrect because $\frac{2}{3}$ is greater than the obtained value. **Choice C** is incorrect because $\frac{1}{3}$ is less than the obtained value. **Choice D** is incorrect because $\frac{4}{5}$ is greater than the obtained value.

17.

Category: IES
Skill: Probability | **Level:** Easy

Choice C is correct because the obtained value is $1/6$.
Given: One is red, one blue, one orange
Selecting two marbles without replacement.

Selecting orange first: $\frac{1}{3}$

Selecting blue after the orange: $\frac{1}{2}$

Combining the probabilities : $\frac{1}{3} \times \frac{1}{2} = \frac{1}{6}$

Choice A is incorrect because $\frac{1}{9}$ is less than the obtained value. **Choice B** is incorrect because $\frac{1}{8}$ is less than the obtained value. **Choice D** is incorrect because $\frac{2}{3}$ is greater than the obtained value.

18.

Category: PHM & Modeling
Skill: Probability | **Level:** Easy

Choice D is correct because the obtained probability is

$$\frac{xy}{x^2 + y^2 + 2xy - (x + y)}.$$

Number of black balls = y
Number of yellow balls = x
Total number of balls = $x + y$

Probability of Black ball first = $\frac{y}{x+y}$
No. of balls remaining after removing one = $x + y - 1$

Probability of pulling second ball as Yellow = $\frac{x}{x+y-1}$
Required probability =

$$\frac{y}{(x+y)}\frac{x}{(x+y-1)} = \frac{xy}{x^2 + y^2 + 2xy - (x + y)}$$

Choice A is incorrect because it does not represent the required probability. **Choice B** is incorrect because it does not represent the required probability. **Choice C** is incorrect because it does not represent the required probability.

19.

Category: PHM & Modeling
Skill: Probability | **Level:** Medium

Choice D is correct. Let n be the number of dimes that need to be added, then the number of dimes that will be in the piggy bank is 27 + n, and the number of coins will be 55 + n. The probability of randomly selecting a dime is,

$$\frac{27+n}{55+n} = \frac{3}{4}$$

Cross multiplying and solving for n,

$$\frac{27+n}{55+n} = \frac{3}{4}$$

$$4(27+n) = 3(55+n)$$

$$108 + 4n = 165 + 3n$$

$$n = 57$$

So, 57 dimes need to be added.

Choice A is incorrect because 1 is lower than 57.
Choice B is incorrect because 10 is lower than 57.
Choice C is incorrect because 25 is lower than 57.

20.

Category: IES & Modeling
Skill: Probability | **Level:** Easy

Choice D is correct because the obtained answer is the obtained answer is $1.75.
Make a probability table from the given spinner.

Probability	Net Gain
1/2	$8
1/4	–$2
1/4	–$7

Find the expected value.

$$E(X)=\sum_{i=1}^{n}(X_i)(P(X_i)$$

$$E(X)=(1/2)(8)+(1/4)(-\$2)+(1/4)(-\$7)$$

$$E(X)=4-1/2-7/4$$

$$E(X)=1.75$$

Choice A is incorrect because –$1.25 is less than the obtained expected value. **Choice B** is incorrect because –$0.75 is less than the obtained expected value.
Choice C is incorrect because $1.00 is less than the obtained expected value.

21.

Category: IES & Modeling
Skill: Probability | **Level:** Easy

Choice A is correct because the table does not represent probability distribution.
Check the range of the probabilities. It should be less than 1.
All probabilities are less than 1.

Check if the sum of the probabilities is equal to 1.
0.05+0.1+0.3+0.6 =1.05
The sum does not equal to 1, hence, the given table does not represent probability distribution.

Choice B is incorrect because the table does not represent probability distribution **Choice C** is incorrect because the table does not represent probability distribution **Choice D** is incorrect because there is enough information to tell if the table does represent probability distribution or not.

22.

Category: IES & Modeling
Skill: Probability | **Level:** Hard

Choice B is correct. The Venn diagram below shows the relationships of a person that likes candy bars, spinach, or both.

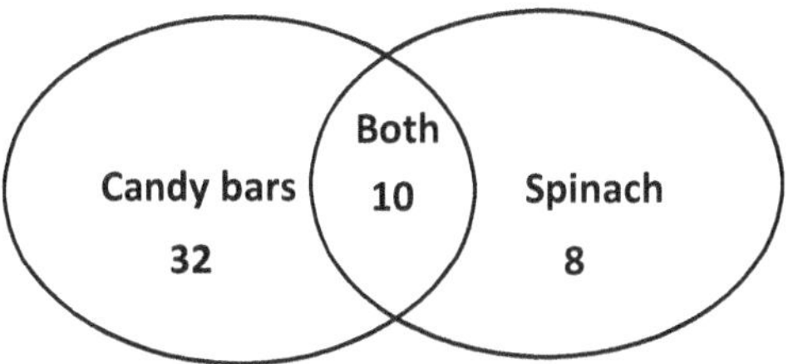

Since 42 out of 50 people surveyed like candy bars, the remaining 8 must only like spinach. Similarly, 18 out of 50 people like spinach, so the remaining 32 people must only like candy bars. Thus, out of the 50 people surveyed, 10 must like both candy bars and spinach. The probability that a person chosen likes both candy bars and spinach out of the 50 people surveys is $\frac{10}{50}=0.2$.

Choice A is incorrect. This may result from conceptual error. **Choice C** is incorrect. This is the probability of liking spinach, not both. **Choice D** is incorrect. This is the assumed half of the people liking both, $\frac{25}{50}$.

23.

Category: PHM
Skill: Probability | **Level:** Medium

Choice A is correct. The probability of rolling a 4 with the die is $\frac{1}{6}$ and the probability of getting a tails with the coin flip is $\frac{1}{2}$. Since one event has no bearing on the other, the events are independent so the product of each is taken to find the combined probability. Now, $\frac{1}{6}\times\frac{1}{2}=\frac{1}{12}$.

Choice B is incorrect. This is the probability of rolling a 4. **Choice C** is incorrect. This is the probability of getting tails. **Choice D** is incorrect. This combines the individual probabilities.

24.

Category: PHM
Skill: Probability | **Level:** Medium

Choice A is correct Let g be the number of green marbles. The probability of choosing a green marble is,

$$\frac{g}{g+11+5}=\frac{1}{5}.$$

Solving for g,

$$\frac{g}{g+16}=\frac{1}{5}$$
$$5g=g+16$$
$$4g=16$$
$$g=4$$

So, there must be 4 green marbles in the bag.

Choice B is incorrect. This is the number of blue marbles. **Choice C** is incorrect. This adds the red and blue marbles. **Choice D** is incorrect. This is the total number of marbles needed.

25.

Category: IES & Modeling
Skill: Probability | **Level:** Medium

Choice B is correct because the obtained answer is $\frac{1}{14}$.

Given:

Total members : 18
Number of Officers: 4
Non- officers –18-4 = 14

Jhanica is a non-officer. Probability that she will be chosen is:

$$\text{Probability} = \frac{\text{favorable outcome}}{\text{total number of outcome}}$$

$$\text{Probability} = \frac{1}{14}$$

Choice A is incorrect because 0 is less than the obtained value. **Choice C** is incorrect because $\frac{1}{6}$ is greater than the obtained value. **Choice D** is incorrect because $\frac{1}{18}$ is less than the obtained value.

26.

Category: PHM
Skill: Probability | **Level:** Medium

Choice C is correct. Of the graduating class, $0.60 \times 250 = 150$ are male. Of the males in the graduating class, $0.82 \times 150 = 123$ will attend a four-year college. So, the probability that a person chosen in the graduating class will be male that attends a four-year college is $\frac{123}{250} = 0.49$. Note that 82% of 60% is $0.82 \times 0.60 = 0.49$.

Choice A is incorrect. This is too low and may result from wrong multiplication. **Choice B** is incorrect. This may result from 0.82 – 0.60. **Choice D** is incorrect. This may result from adding 0.60 and 0.18.

27.

Category: PHM
Skill: Probability | **Level:** Medium

Choice C is correct. Since 100 people prefer apples and 20 of them prefer both apples and oranges then, 100 – 20 = 80 people in the survey prefer only apples. The probability that a person chosen at random prefers only apples out of the130 people in the survey is $\frac{80}{130} = 0.62$.

Choice B is incorrect. This is the probability of a person preferring both apples and oranges. **Choice A** is incorrect. This is the probability of a person only preferring oranges. **Choice D** is incorrect. This is the probability of a person preferring apples.

28.

Category: IES & Modeling
Skill: Probability | **Level:** Hard

Choice D is correct because the obtained answer is 21:29.

What are the odds (in the age range: not in the age range) that the first person called for duty is in the age range of 25–35 years?

In the age range : 25-35 – 42%

not in the age range: 18-24 – 8%

36-44 – 14%

45-55 – 25%

56 and up – 11%

Total percentage: 58%

odds (in the age range: not in the age range) is 42:58 or 21:29.

Choice A is incorrect because 1:3 does not represent the given odds. **Choice B** is incorrect because 7:8 does not represent the given odds. **Choice C** is incorrect because 7:43 does not represent the given odds.

29.

Category: IES & Modeling
Skill: Probability | **Level:** Medium

Choice A is correct because the obtained answer is $\frac{1}{3}$

The probability of neither green or red ball means the probability of the blue balls.

Total number of balls = 8 red + 7 blue + 6 green =21 balls.

$$P = \frac{No\,of\ favorable\,outcomes}{Total\,number\ of\ outcomes}$$

$$P(not\ green\,and\,not\ red) = \frac{No\,of\ blue\,balls}{Total\,number\ of\ balls} = \frac{7}{21} = \frac{1}{3}$$

Choice B is incorrect because the formula used is incorrect. **Choice C** is incorrect because the denominator is incorrect. **Choice D** is incorrect because the formula used is incorrect.

30.

Category: PHM & Modeling
Skill: Probability | **Level:** Easy

Choice B is correct because Eloise subtracted the bigger number in any dice to the other smaller number.
Analyze the given table.

		Dice 2					
		1	2	3	4	5	6
Dice 1	1	0	1	2	3	4	5
	2	1	0	1	2	3	4
	3	2	1	0	1	2	3
	4	3	2	1	0	1	2
	5	4	3	2	1	0	1
	6	5	4	3	2	1	0

Looking at the first column and the first row, Eloise subtracted the bigger number in any dice to the other smaller number.

Choice A is incorrect because the given method is incorrect. **Choice C** is incorrect because the given method is incorrect. **Choice D** is incorrect because the given method is incorrect.

31.

Category: IES
Skill: Probability | **Level:** Hard

Choice B is correct because the obtained answer is $\frac{1}{3}$.

Given:

N = 50 people

Let $H = 35$, number of people who like Hawaiian pizza.

$P = ?$ number of people who like Hawaiian pizza.

$H \cap P = 20$ number of people who like both.
U

$N \setminus H \cup P$ =5 number of people who like neither.

Let's first find the number of people who only like pepperoni pizza.

Use the principle of inclusion-exclusion.

$$|H \cup P| = |H| + |P| - |H \cap P| \text{ and}$$

$$|H \cap P| = N - |N \setminus H \cap P|$$

$$|H \cup P| = |H| + |P| - |H \cap P|$$

$$N - |N \setminus H \cup P| = |H| + |P| - |H \cap P|$$

$$50 - 5 = 35 + |P| - 20$$

$$|P| = 50 - 5 - 35 + 20$$

$$|P| = 30$$

$$|P| - |H \cap P| = 30 - 20 = 10$$

Hence, the number of people who only like pepperoni pizza is 10.

Find the probability that a person who likes pepperoni pizza does not like Hawaiian pizza. This is $P(H^c \mid P)$, where H^c represents the complement of H (not liking Hawaiian pizza).

Use the conditional probability .

$$P(H^c \mid P) = \frac{P(H^c \cap P)}{P(P)}$$

$$P(H^c|P) = \frac{\frac{10}{50}}{\frac{30}{50}} = \frac{10}{30} = \frac{1}{3}$$

Choice A is incorrect because $\frac{1}{2}$ is greater than the obtained value. **Choice C** is incorrect because $\frac{1}{5}$ is less than the obtained value. **Choice D** is incorrect because $\frac{2}{5}$ is greater than the obtained value.

32.

Category: IES & Modeling
Skill: Probability | **Level:** Easy

Choice B is correct because the obtained answer is $\frac{3}{7}$.

Given: No. of Girls : 18
No. of Boys: 12

Portion of girls who walk to school: $\frac{2}{9}(18)=4$

Portion of boys who walk to school: $\frac{1}{4}(12)=3$

Probability of a boy who walks to school

$$=\frac{\text{Number of boys who walks}}{\text{total number of walkers}}$$

$$=\frac{3}{7}.$$

Choice A is incorrect because $\frac{12}{30}$ is less than the obtained answer. **Choice C** is incorrect because $\frac{1}{4}$ is less than the obtained answer. **Choice D** is incorrect because $\frac{3}{12}$ is less than the obtained answer.

33.

Category: IES
Skill: Probability | **Level:** Easy

Choice C is correct because the obtained answer is 0.40.
Let S be sophomore and U be an undeclared student.
To find the probability of randomly selecting a sophomore or an undeclared student, use the formula,

$$P(S or U)=P(S)+P(U)-P(S and U)$$

$$P(S or U)=29+30-19$$

$$P(S or U)=40$$

Probability $=\frac{Favored\ outcome}{total\ outcome}=\frac{40}{100}=0.40.$

Choice A is incorrect because 0.19 is less than the obtained probability. **Choice B** is incorrect because 0.29 is less than the obtained probability. **Choice D** is incorrect because 0.59 is greater than the obtained probability.

34.

Category: IES
Skill: Probability | **Level:** Medium

Choice C is correct because the obtained probability that Janice will be the president and Sandra will be the vice president is $\frac{1}{210}$.

There are 15 members in the committee.
The president can be chosen in 15 ways, after which, 14 ways to choose a vice president.

$$15\times14=210$$

The probability of choosing Janice as the president and Sandra as the vice president has only 1 specific arrangement.

Hence, probability is $=\frac{favorable\ outcome}{total\ outcome}=\frac{1}{210}$.

Choice A is incorrect because $\frac{1}{132}$ is greater than the obtained value. **Choice B** is incorrect because $\frac{1}{220}$ is less than the obtained value. **Choice D** is incorrect because $\frac{1}{6}$ is greater than the obtained value.

35.

Category: PHM & Modeling
Skill: Probability | **Level:** Medium

Choice A is correct. Thirty students took only an advanced math course, since 45 of the 75 students that took an advanced math course also took an English course. So, the probability that a student only took an advanced course is

$$\frac{30}{155}=0.19.$$

Choice B is incorrect. This is the probability that a student took both an English course and an advanced math course. **Choice C** is incorrect. This is the probability that a student took an advanced math course. **Choice D** is incorrect. This is the probability that a student took an English course.

36.

Category: IES & Modeling
Skill: Sets of numbers | **Level:** Easy

Choice C is correct because the cardinality of $(A\cap B\cap C^c)$ is 6.

First let's find $A\cap B$:

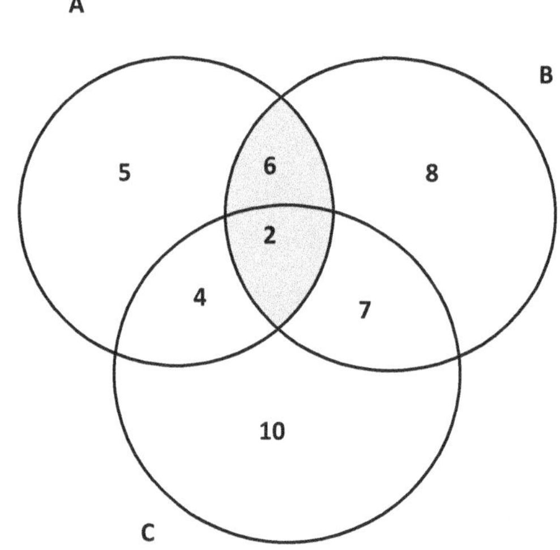

The figure below shows C^c:

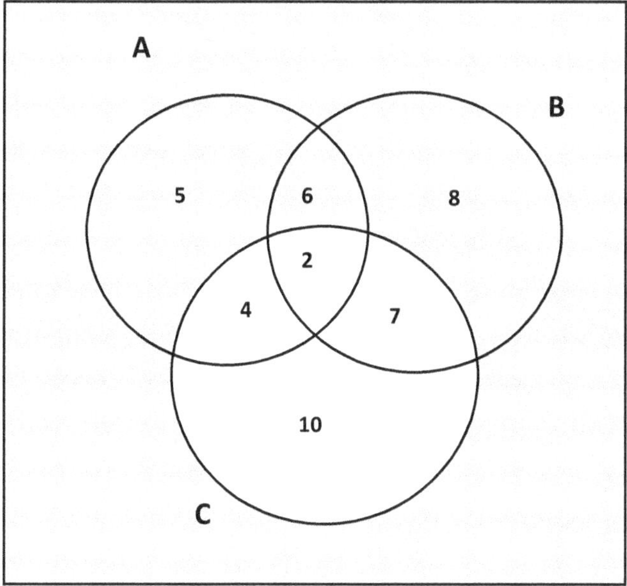

Then, $(A \cap B) \cap C^c)$ is

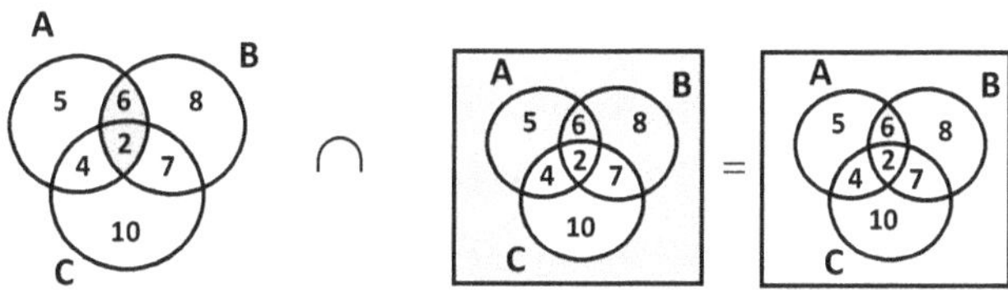

Then the cardinality of $\left(A \cap B \cap C^c\right)$ is 6.

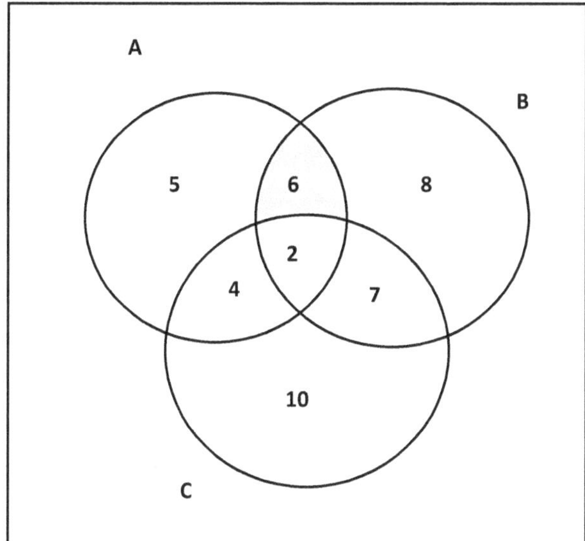

Choice A is incorrect because 4 is not the cardinality of $\left(A \cap B \cap C^c\right)$. **Choice B** is incorrect because 5 is not the cardinality of $\left(A \cap B \cap C^c\right)$. **Choice D** is incorrect because 7 is not the cardinality of $\left(A \cap B \cap C^c\right)$.

37.

Category: PHM & Modeling
Skill: Sets of numbers | **Level:** Hard

Choice C is correct because the obtained formula of the variance in terms of X is

$$\sigma^2 = \frac{1}{4}[(7-\left(\frac{18+x}{4}\right))^2 + (8-\left(\frac{18+x}{4}\right))^2.$$
$$+(X-\left(\frac{18+x}{4}\right))^2 + \left(3-\left(\frac{18+x}{4}\right)\right)^2\Big]$$

Find the mean of the given data set.

$$\mu = \frac{7+8+X+3}{4} = \frac{18+X}{4}$$

Formula of variance is $\sigma^2 = \frac{1}{4}\sum_{i=1}^{4}(x_i - \mu)^2$

The expanded form is $\sigma^2 = \frac{1}{4}\sum_{i=1}^{4}(x_i - \mu)^2$

$$\sigma^2 = \frac{1}{4}[(7-\mu)^2 + (8-\mu)^2 + (X-\mu)^2 + \left(3-\mu\right)^2\Big]$$
$$\sigma^2 = \frac{1}{4}[(7-\left(\frac{18+x}{4}\right))^2 + (8-\left(\frac{18+x}{4}\right))^2$$
$$+(X-\left(\frac{18+x}{4}\right))^2 + \left(3-\left(\frac{18+x}{4}\right)\right)^2\Big]$$

Choice A is incorrect because the formula is used X instead of the mean μ.
Choice B is incorrect because the formula is not in terms of X.
Choice D is incorrect because the mean μ is not X.

38.

Category: PHM
Skill: Sets of numbers | **Level:** Hard

Choice D is correct because it has the greatest standard deviation.

Without calculating the standard deviation, analyze the choices.

Choice A: 3, 32, 53, 64, 64, 63
The data set suggests a fairly spread out (3 to 64) which suggests a moderate standard deviation.

Choice B: 10, 10, 10, 10, 10, 11
The set is the same except for one outlier (11). Because of this, the standard deviation will be small and is almost close to 0.

Choice C: 100, 200, 300, 400, 500, 500
The set has a regular pattern with the repeated value (500). Hence, the spread is quite large, suggesting a moderate standard deviation.

Choice D: 1000, 2000, 3000, 4000, 5000, 6000
The set increases significantly, thus implying a large spread. Large spreads result in a higher standard deviation.

Choice A is incorrect because it does not have the largest standard deviation. **Choice B** is incorrect because it has small or close to zero standard deviation. **Choice C** is incorrect because it has a moderate standard deviation.

39.

Category: IES & Modeling
Skill: Sets of numbers | **Level:** Medium

Choice A is correct You spend \$50 – \$31.75 = \$18.25 for both menu items. Only the combination of the fish and chicken cost \$18.25 since \$9.50 + \$8.75 = \$18.25.

Choice B is incorrect. Fish and roast beef cost \$20.75 which would have \$29.25 left. **Choice C** is incorrect. Chicken and roast beef cost \$20 which would have \$30 left. **Choice D** is incorrect. Fish both times cost \$19 which would have \$31 left.

40.

Category: IES & Modeling
Skill: Sets of numbers | **Level:** Medium

Choice B is correct Let n be the 5th score. The formula for the average is $\frac{85+85+75+92+n}{5}=84$. Solving for n you have,

$$\frac{85+85+75+92+n}{5}=84$$
$$\frac{337+n}{5}=84$$
$$337+n=420$$
$$n=83$$

Choice A is incorrect. This is the first term of the set in ascending order. **Choice C** is incorrect. This is the mean. **Choice D** is incorrect. This is the median of the given scores.

41.

Category: IES
Skill: Sets of numbers | **Level:** Medium

Choice B is correct Let n be the grade for the 5th assignment. The average is,

$$\frac{79+84+92+79+n}{5}=85$$
$$\frac{334+n}{5}=85$$
$$334+n=425$$
$$n=91$$

Arranging the five scores from least to greatest you have 79, 79, 84, 91, 92.
So, the median score is an 84

Choice A is incorrect. This is Julian's score on two assignments. **Choice C** is incorrect. This is the average score Julian wants to have. **Choice D** is incorrect. This is the average score if Julian receives a score of 106 on the last assignment.

42.

Category: IES & Modeling
Skill: Sets of numbers | **Level:** Hard

Choice A is correct because the obtained answer is

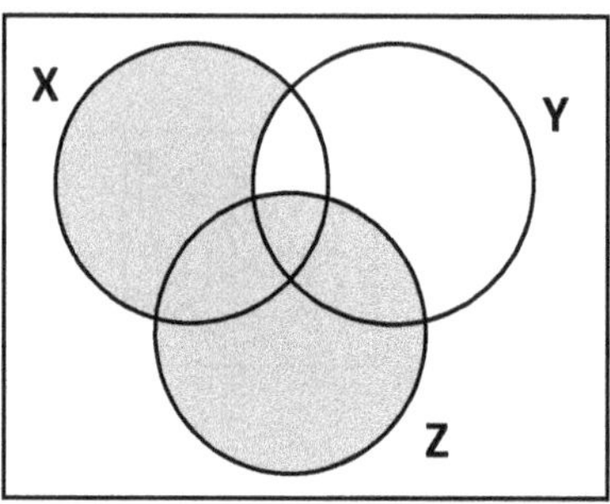

Find the $X \cap Y^c$.

$X \cap Y^c$ which is the set of things in X which are not in Y. Hence, you need to shade at least the regions numbered 1 and 2 in the picture below.

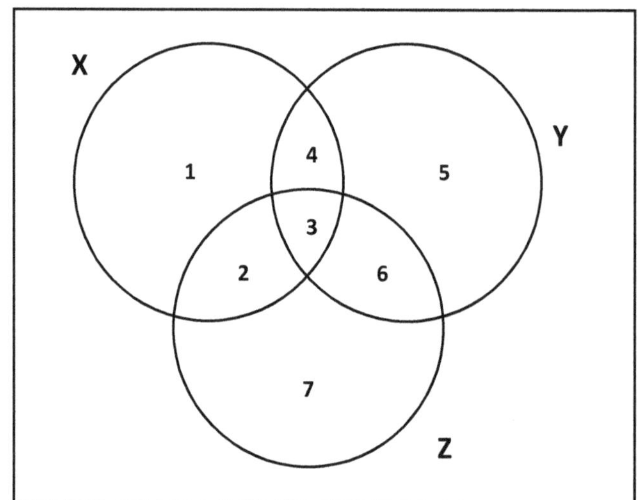

Then you need to add all the regions in Z which consist of the regions numbered 2, 3, 6 and 7.

Hence the answer is 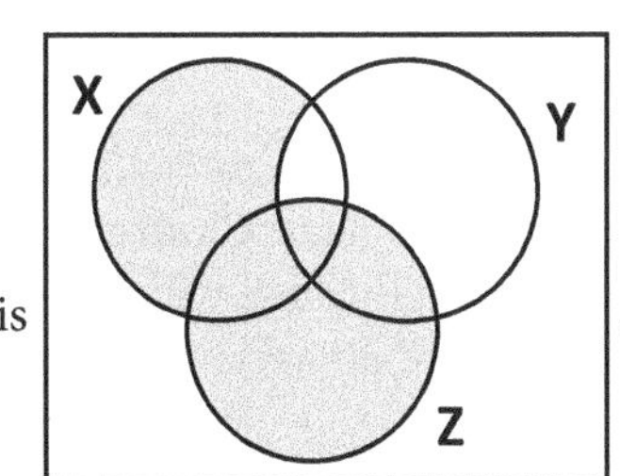

.

Choice B is incorrect because the Venn diagram shown does not represent. **Choice C** is incorrect because the Venn diagram shown does not represent **Choice D** is incorrect because the Venn diagram shown does not represent.

43.

Category: IES & Modeling
Skill: Sets of numbers | **Level:** Medium

Choice C is correct Andrew scores in order from least to greatest are, {50, 61, 68, 69, 70, 74, 74, 75, 75, 82, 86, 86, 86, 86, 88, 90, 91, 95, 95}. The median is the middle score. Since there a total of 19 scores, the 10th score of an 82 is the median score.

Choice A is incorrect. This is one of the scores. **Choice B** is incorrect. This is the mean score. **Choice D** is incorrect. This is the mode.

44.

Category: PHM
Skill: Sets of numbers | **Level:** Easy

Choice C is correct because the obtained median is 28.

Arranged the given data in ascending order.

$$20, 20, 24, 26, 30, 30, 30, 31$$

Total number of data points is 8.
The median is the average of the middle values, 4th and 5th digit.

$$\text{Median } \frac{26+30}{2} = \frac{56}{2} = 28$$

Choice A is incorrect because 20 is less than the obtained median. **Choice B** is incorrect because 26 is less than the obtained median. **Choice D** is incorrect because 30 is greater than the obtained median.

45.

Category: PHM
Skill: Sets of numbers | **Level:** Hard

Choice A is correct because the obtained weighted mean is 16.

Use the formula for the weighted mean to find the weighted mean of the given data set.

$$WeightedMean = \frac{\Sigma(x_i \cdot W_i)}{\Sigma W_i}$$

Given:

$$x_i = \{19, 17, 14, 13, 18\}$$

$$W_i = \{12, 30, 28, 10, 10\}$$

Compute for the sum of $x_i \cdot W_i$.

$$\Sigma(x_i \cdot W_i) = (19(12)) + (17(30)) + (14(28)) + (13(10)) + (18(10))$$

$$\Sigma(x_i \cdot W_i) = 228 + 510 + 392 + 130 + 180$$

$$\Sigma(x_i \cdot W_i) = 1440$$

Compute for the sum of weights $\Sigma W_{i.}$

$$\Sigma W_i = 12 + 30 + 28 + 10 + 10 = 90$$

$$WeightedMean = \frac{\Sigma(x_i \cdot W_i)}{\Sigma W_i} = \frac{1440}{90} = 16$$

Choice B is incorrect because 18 is greater than the obtained value. **Choice C** is incorrect because 20 is greater than the obtained value. **Choice D** is incorrect because 24 is greater than the obtained value.

46.

Category: IES
Skill: Sets of numbers | **Level:** Easy

Choice D is correct. The mean or average for the set is $\frac{7+9+1+14+2+16+7}{7} = \frac{56}{7} = 8$. The mode is the number that occurs most often in the set so, the mode is 7. The sum of the mean and mode is 8 + 7 = 15.

Choice A is incorrect. This is the minimum of the set. **Choice B** is incorrect. This is the mode. **Choice C** is incorrect. This is the mean.

47.

Category: IES
Skill: Sets of numbers | **Level:** Easy

Choice C is correct. Putting the scores in order, 73, 87, 91, 93, the median is the average of 87 and 91. So, the median is 89. The mean is $\frac{73+93+87+91}{4}$ = 86. The difference in the median and mean is 3.

Choice A is incorrect. This may result if the mean is 88.
Choice B is incorrect. This may result if the mean is 87.
Choice D is incorrect. This may result if the mean is 85.

48.

Category: PHM & Modeling
Skill: Sets of numbers | **Level:** Hard
Choice D is correct because the obtained value of mean and sd is 20.85, 5.94.

The number of scores: 20

Mean $\mu =$

$$\frac{29+26+13+23+23+25+17+22+17+19+12+26+30+30+18+14+12+26+17+18}{20}$$

Mean = $\mu = 20.85$

Standard Deviation $s = \sqrt{\frac{\Sigma(x_i - \mu)^2}{n-1}}$

Arrange the data in the table.

x_i	frequency	$(x_i - \mu)^2$	$(x_i - \mu)^2$ (*frequency*)
12	2	$(12-20.85)^2$	$78.3225(2) = 156.645$
13	1	$(13-20.85)^2$	$61.6225(1) = 61.6225$
14	1	$(14-20.85)^2$	$46.9225(1) = 46.9225$
17	3	$(17-20.85)^2$	$14.8225(3) = 44.4675$
18	2	$(18-20.85)^2$	$8.1225(2) = 16.245$
19	1	$(19-20.85)^2$	$3.4225(1) = 3.4225$
22	1	$(22-20.85)^2$	$1.3225(1) = 1.3225$
23	2	$(23-20.85)^2$	$4.6225(2) = 9.245$
25	1	$(25-20.85)^2$	$17.2225(1) = 17.2225$
26	3	$(26-20.85)^2$	$26.5225(3) = 79.5675$
29	1	$(29-20.85)^2$	$66.4225(1) = 66.4225$
30	2	$(30-20.85)^2$	$83.7225(2) = 167.445$

$\Sigma(x_i - \mu)^2$ (*frequency*) = 156.645 + 61.6225 + 46.9225 + 44.4675 + 16.245 + 3.4225 + 1.3225 + 9.245 + 17.2225 + 79.5675 + 66.4225 + 167.445
= 670.55

$$s = \sqrt{\frac{\Sigma(x_i - \mu)^2}{n-1}} = \sqrt{\frac{670.55}{20-1}} = \sqrt{\frac{670.55}{19}} = \sqrt{35.29} = 5.94$$

SD = 5.94

Choice A is incorrect because both mean and sd do not match the obtained values. **Choice B** is incorrect because mean do not match the obtained values. **Choice C** is incorrect because sd do not match the obtained values.

49.

Category: IES
Skill: Sets of numbers | **Level:** Easy

Choice C is correct because the obtained answer is $1:1$.

Total score of class = $79b + 87g$
Total score of class = $83(b + g)$

Find the ratio.

$$79b + 87g = 83(b+g)$$
$$79b + 87g = 83b + 83g$$
$$79b - 83b = -87g + 83g$$
$$79b - 83b = -87g + 83g$$
$$-4b = -4g$$
$$b = g$$

Hence, ratio is 1:1

Choice A is incorrect because $2:1$ does not correspond to the obtained ratio. **Choice B** is incorrect because $3:1$ does not correspond to the obtained ratio. **Choice D** is incorrect because $1:3$ does not correspond to the obtained ratio.

50.

Category: IES
Skill: Sets of numbers | **Level:** Easy

Choice D is correct because the obtained answer is mean: 1.23; sd: 0.66.

Find the mean. Use the mean formula.

$$\mu = \Sigma|xP(x)|$$

$$\mu = 0(0.07) + 1(0.68) + 2(0.21) + 3(0.03) + 4(0.01)$$

$$\mu = 1.23$$

Find the standard deviation. Using the standard deviation formula for grouped data.

$$\sigma = \sqrt{\Sigma(x-\mu)^2 \cdot P(x)}$$

$\Sigma(x - \mu)^2 \cdot P(x) = (0-1.23)^2(0.07) + (1-1.23)^2(0.68) + (2-1.23)^2(0.21) + (3-1.23)^2(0.03) + (4-1.23)^2(0.01)$
$= 0.105903 + 0.035972 + 0.124509 + 0.093987 + 0.076729$
$= 0.4371$

$$\sigma = \sqrt{\Sigma(x-\mu)^2 \cdot P(x)}$$

$$\sigma = \sqrt{0.4371}$$

$$\sigma \approx 0.66$$

Choice A is incorrect because the value of sd is incorrect. **Choice B** is incorrect because both the mean and sd are incorrect. **Choice C** is incorrect because both the mean and sd are incorrect.

51.

Category: PMH & Modeling
Skill: Sets of numbers | **Level:** Medium

Choice A is correct because $A \cup (B \cap C)$ is equal to $\{1,2,3,4\}$.

$$A = \{1,2,3\}, B = \{3,4\}, C = \{4,5,6\}$$
$$(B \cap C) = \{4\}$$
$$A \cup (B \cap C) = \{1,2,3,4\}$$

Choice B is incorrect because it is not equivalent to the obtained set. **Choice C** is incorrect because it is not equivalent to the obtained set. **Choice D** is incorrect because it is not equivalent to the obtained set.

52.

Category: PHM
Skill: Sets of numbers | **Level:** Easy

Choice C is correct. You only need the mean, $\bar{x}$, and the number of elements, n in set B to find its sum, S. The formula to find the mean is $\bar{x} = \frac{S}{n}$. Now, the mean for set A is,

$\bar{x} = \frac{7+21+11+9+1+3+11}{7} = \frac{63}{7} = 9$. So, the mean for set B is also 9. Then,

$$9 = \frac{S}{13}$$
$$S = 9 \times 13$$
$$S = 117$$

The sum for set B is 117.

Choice A is incorrect because the mean is not a whole number, which is unlikely to match median and mode. **Choice B** is incorrect because the mean is not a whole number, which is unlikely to match median and mode. **Choice D** is incorrect because it uses the mean of 11 when calculating the sum.

53.

Category: IES
Skill: Sets of numbers | **Level:** Medium

Choice C is correct. You know 3 of the numbers must be 42, 51, and 51 since they are the median and the mode for the set. Let x_4, x_5, x_6, x_7 be the other 4 numbers in the set.

Using the mean of the set you get,

$$\frac{42+51+51+x_4+x_5+x_6+x_7}{7} = 45$$
$$\frac{144+x_4+x_5+x_6+x_7}{7} = 45$$
$$144+x_4+x_5+x_6+x_7 = 315$$
$$x_4+x_5+x_6+x_7 = 171$$

So, the sum of the other 4 numbers is 171.

Choice A is incorrect. This may result from conceptual or calculation error. **Choice B** is incorrect. This may result from conceptual or calculation error. **Choice D** is incorrect. This may result from conceptual or calculation error.

54.

Category: PHM
Skill: Sets of numbers | **Level:** Easy

Choice C is correct because the obtained answer is 93.

Given:

Jerry's first 4 scores: 57, 63,90 and 72
Average score to pass = 75

Find the 5th score using the formula for the average.

$$Average = \frac{Total\ score}{no.\ of\ test}.$$

Find the total score.

$$57 + 63 + 90 + 72 + x = 282 + x$$

Number of test = 5

$$Average = \frac{Total\ score}{no.\ of\ test}$$
$$75 = \frac{282+x}{5}$$
$$282 + x = 75(5)$$

$$282 + x = 375$$
$$x = 375 - 282$$
$$x = 93$$

Choice A is incorrect because 60 is less than the obtained value of the 5th score. **Choice B** is incorrect because 75 is less than the obtained value of the 5th score. **Choice D** is incorrect because 100 is greater than the obtained value of the 5th score.

55.

Category: IES & Modeling
Skill: Sets of numbers | **Level:** Hard

Choice D is correct because Choice A, B and C are false statements.

Analyze each choice.

Choice A

Looking at the table. There are 10 students who got a score of 17 in Science. Hence, choice A is an incorrect statement.

Choice B

Looking at the table. No one got a score of 13 in Science. Hence, choice B is an incorrect statement.

Choice A is incorrect because it is a false statement. **Choice B** is incorrect because it is a false statement. **Choice C** is incorrect because both A and B are false.

56.

Category: PHM & Modeling
Skill: Sets of numbers | **Level:** Medium

Choice B is correct because the obtained answer is

$$\frac{58(32)+42(38)}{(58+42)}, 34.5.$$

Mean marks for 58 boys = 32,
$58 \times 32 = 1856$

Mean marks for 42 girls = 38,
$42 \times 38 = 1596$

Total mean mark

$$\frac{\textit{total mean score for boys} + \textit{total mean score for girls}}{\textit{total number of student}}$$

$$\text{Total mean mark } \frac{58(32)+42(38)}{(58+42)}$$

$$\text{Total mean mark } \frac{3452}{100}$$

$$\text{Total mean mark } 34.5$$

Choice A is incorrect because both the mean formula and value are incorrect. **Choice C** is incorrect because the mean value is incorrect **Choice D** is incorrect because both the mean formula and value are incorrect.

57.

Category: IES & Modeling
Skill: Sets of numbers | **Level:** Easy

Choice D is correct because it represents the given set.

If A = {2,3,4,6,8}, B = {3,4,5,10}, C = {4,5,6,8,11}. Find the Venn diagram that represents the given set.

$A = \{2,3,4,6,8\}$, $B = \{3,4,5,10\}$, $C = \{4,5,6,8,11\}$

Analyze the given set.

$A \cap B = \{3,4\}$

$A \cap C = \{4,6,8\}$

$B \cap C = \{4,5\}$

$A \cap B \cap C = \{4\}$

Draw the Venn Diagram.

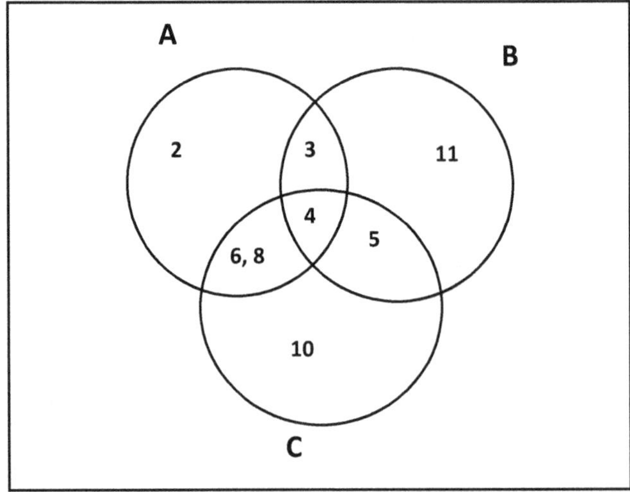

Choice A is incorrect because it does not present the given set. **Choice B** is incorrect because it does not present the given set. **Choice C** is incorrect because it does not present the given set.

58.

Category: IES & Modeling
Skill: Sets of numbers | **Level:** Medium

Choice D is correct. Converting the stem–leaf scores to standard numbers, the set of scores is {55, 57, 61, 63, 64, 69, 71, 71, 83}.

The mode is 71 and the mean or average is,

$$\bar{x} = \frac{55+57+61+63+64+69+71+71+83}{9}$$
$$= \frac{594}{9}$$
$$= 66$$

The sum of the mean and mode is 71 + 66 = 137.

Choice A is incorrect. This may result if the mean is 54.
Choice B is incorrect. This may result if the mean is 58.
Choice C is incorrect. This may result if the mean is 64.

59.

Category: IES & Modeling
Skill: Sets of numbers | **Level:** Easy

Choice B is correct because the Venn diagram that represents the given is

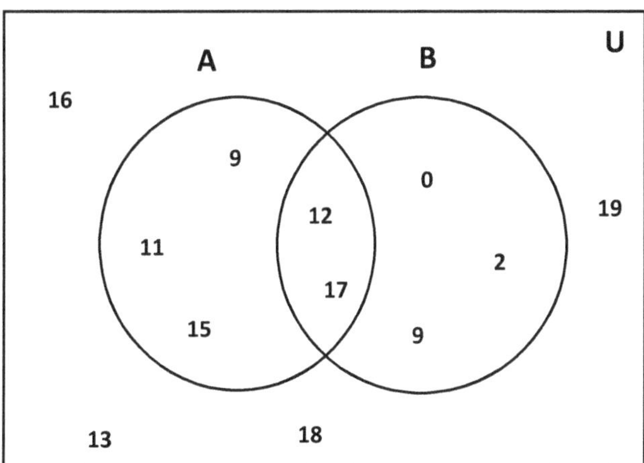

Make a Venn Diagram.

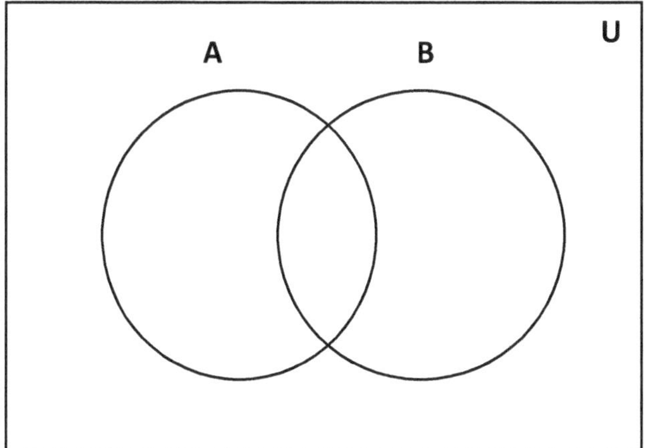

Identify $A \cap B$ and write the numbers in the Venn Diagram.

$$A = \{9, 11, 12, 15, 17\}$$
$$B = \{0, 2, 9, 12, 17,\}$$
$$A \cap B = \{12, 17\}$$

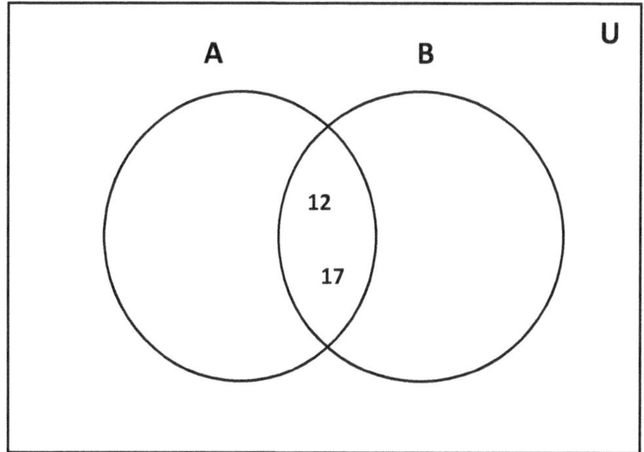

Identify the numbers that are only A and only B. Write down in the Venn Diagram.

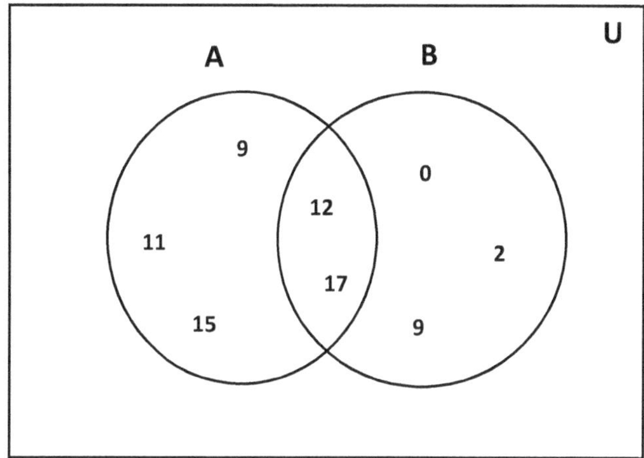

Identify $A^c \cap B^c$.

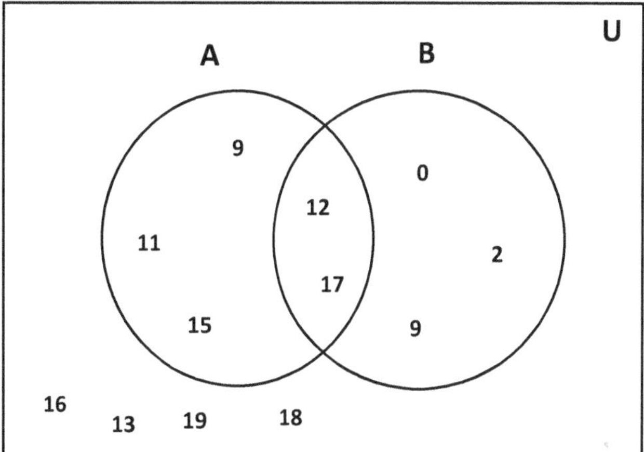

Choice A is incorrect because the Venn diagram does not show the given data set. **Choice C** is incorrect because the Venn diagram does not show the given data set. **Choice D** is incorrect because the Venn diagram does not show the given data set.

60.

Category: PHM
Skill: Sets of numbers | **Level:** Medium

Choice B is correct. $\frac{3}{7}$ of the students surveyed failed the test. Of 42 students in the class, $\frac{3}{7}\times 42 = 18$ failed the test, according to the survey.

Choice A is incorrect. This is the sum of 3 and 7. **Choice C** is incorrect. This is the number of students that passed the test. **Choice D** is incorrect. This is the difference between 42 and 3.

61.

Category: IES & Modeling
Skill: Sets of numbers | **Level:** Medium

Choice B is correct. Converting the stem–leaf assignment scores to standard numbers, the set of scores is {52, *x*, 68, 73, 79, 79, 81, 85, 85, 85, 88, 92, 94, 98} where *x* is the unknown assignment score in the 60's.

The average, $\overline{x}$, is,

$$\overline{x} = \frac{52+x+68+73+79+79+81+85+85+85+88+92+94+98}{14}$$

$$80 = \frac{x+1059}{14}$$

$$1120 = x+1059$$

$$x = 61$$

So, there must be an assignment score of 61 for your average to be an 80, then $n = 1$.

Choice A is incorrect. This may result from calculation error. **Choice C** is incorrect. This may result from calculation error. **Choice D** is incorrect. This may result from calculation error.

62.

Category: IES & Modeling
Skill: Sets of numbers | **Level:** Medium

Choice C is correct because the obtained answer is 2^4

A relation of two sets is the cartesian product $A\times B$ of the two sets.

$$A\times B = \{(5,7),(5,8),(6,7),(6,8)\}$$

The number of subset is $2^n = 2^4$

Choice A is incorrect because 2^3 is less than the obtained value. **Choice B** is incorrect because 2^2 is less than the obtained value. **Choice D** is incorrect because an answer can be determined from the choices.

63.

Category: IES
Skill: Sets of numbers | **Level:** Easy

Choice C is correct because the obtained answer is 8.

Number of data: 8
The median is the 4th number and the 5th number.

Arrange the given data.

3, 3, 5, 8, 9, 9, 10, 10

The fourth number is 8 and the fifth number is 9.

Hence, median is $\frac{8+9}{2} = 8.5$

Choice A is incorrect because 5 is less than the obtained value. **Choice B** is incorrect because 6 is less than the obtained value. **Choice D** is incorrect because 9 is greater than the obtained value.

64.

Category: PHM & Modeling
Skill: Sets of numbers | **Level:** Easy

Choice C is correct because the elements in set B are {2,3,4}.

Choice A is incorrect because there are elements not part of set B. **Choice B** is incorrect because there's a missing element 3. **Choice D** is incorrect because 3 is not the only element of set B.

65.

Category: PHM
Skill: Sets of numbers | **Level:** Hard

Choice A is correct Let S_1 be the sum of the 5 numbers, and $\overline{x}$ be the original mean. Then, $S_1 = 5\cdot\overline{x}$.

Increase the mean by $\frac{1}{3}$ then the new mean is $\frac{4}{3}\cdot\overline{x}$ so, the new sum, $S_2 = \frac{20}{3}\cdot\overline{x}$.

The differnce in the new sum and original is the how much the sum of the orignal 5 numbers must increase. Now,

$$S_2 - S_1 = \frac{20}{3}\cdot\overline{x} - 5\cdot\overline{x} = \frac{5}{3}\overline{x}\cdot$$

So the original sum must increase by $\frac{5}{3}$ of the original mean whenever the original mean increases by $\frac{1}{3}$.

Choice B is incorrect. The sum of the 5 numbers must increase by $\frac{5}{3}$ of the original mean and not $\frac{1}{3}$. **Choice C** is incorrect. The sum of the 5 numbers must increase by $\frac{5}{3}$ of the original mean and not $\frac{4}{3}$. **Choice D** is incorrect. The sum of the 5 numbers must increase by $\frac{5}{3}$ of the original mean and not $\frac{1}{3}$ of the new mean.

66.

Category: IES & Modeling
Skill: Sets of numbers | **Level:** Medium

Choice C is correct. Order the data to get the median. 23.1, 23.1, 23.7, 23.8, 23.8 so, the median is 23.7. The mean is, $\frac{23.1 + 23.8 + 23.7 + 23.8 + 23.1}{5} = 23.5$. So, the sum of the median and mode is 23.7 + 23.5 = 47.2.

Choice A is incorrect. This is the mean. **Choice B** is incorrect. This uses a median of 23.1 when finding the sum. **Choice D** is incorrect. This uses a mode of 23.8 when finding the sum.

67.

Category: PHM
Skill: Sets of numbers | **Level:** Hard

Choice D is correct because the obtained answer is 2 and 6.

Original data set: $n = 5$, 0,2,4,6,8

Find the mean and standard deviation.

$$Mean = \mu = \frac{sum\ of\ all\ data\ points}{number\ of\ data\ points} = \frac{0+2+4+6+8}{5} = 4$$

Standard Deviation

$$= \sqrt{\frac{\Sigma(x_i - \mu)^2}{N}}$$
$$= \sqrt{\frac{(0-4)^2 + (2-4)^2 + (4-4)^2 + (6-4)^2 + (8-4)^2}{5}}$$
$$= \sqrt{\frac{(-4)^2 + (-2)^2 + (0)^2 + (2)^2 + (4)^2}{5}}$$
$$= \sqrt{\frac{16 + 4 + 4 + 16}{5}}$$
$$= \sqrt{\frac{40}{5}}$$
$$= \sqrt{8}$$
$$= 2.83$$

Analyze the choices.

Choice A: –1 and 9

$$Mean = \mu = \frac{sum\ of\ all\ data\ points}{number\ of\ data\ points}$$
$$= \frac{0+2+4+6+8+(-1)+9}{7} = 4$$

Standard Deviation

$$= \sqrt{\frac{\Sigma(x_i - \mu)^2}{N}}$$
$$= \sqrt{\frac{(0-4)^2 + (2-4)^2 + (4-4)^2 + (6-4)^2 + (8-4)^2 + (-1-4)^2 + (9-4)^2}{5}}$$
$$= \sqrt{\frac{(-4)^2 + (-2)^2 + (0)^2 + (2)^2 + (4)^2 + (-5)^2 + (+5)^2}{7}}$$
$$= \sqrt{\frac{16 + 4 + 0 + 4 + 16 + 25 + 25}{7}}$$
$$= \sqrt{\frac{90}{7}}$$
$$= \sqrt{12.86}$$
$$= 3.59$$

Choice B: 4 and 4

$$Mean = \mu = \frac{Sum\ of\ all\ data\ points}{number\ of\ data\ points}$$
$$= \frac{0+2+4+6+8+4+4}{7} = 4$$

Standard Deviation

$$= \sqrt{\frac{\Sigma(x_i - \mu)^2}{N}}$$
$$= \sqrt{\frac{(0-4)^2 + (2-4)^2 + (4-4)^2 + (6-4)^2 + (8-4)^2 + (4-4)^2 + (4-4)^2}{5}}$$
$$= \sqrt{\frac{(-4)^2 + (-2)^2 + (0)^2 + (2)^2 + (4)^2 + (0)^2 + (0)^2}{7}}$$
$$= \sqrt{\frac{16 + 4 + 0 + 4 + 16 + 0 + 0}{7}}$$
$$= \sqrt{\frac{40}{7}}$$
$$= \sqrt{5.71}$$
$$= 2.39$$

Choice C: 3 and 5

$$Mean = \mu = \frac{Sum\ of\ all\,data\ points}{number\,of\ datapoints}$$
$$= \frac{0+2+4+6+8+3+5}{7} = 4$$

Standard Deviation

$$=\sqrt{\frac{\Sigma(x_i-\mu)^2}{N}}$$

$$=\sqrt{\frac{(0-4)^2+(2-4)^2+(4-4)^2+(6-4)^2+(8-4)^2+(3-4)^2+(5-4)^2}{5}}$$

$$=\sqrt{\frac{(-4)^2+(-2)^2+(0)^2+(2)^2+(4)^2+(-1)^2+(1)^2}{7}}$$

$$=\sqrt{\frac{16+4+0+4+16+1+1}{7}}$$

$$=\sqrt{\frac{42}{7}}$$

$$=\sqrt{6}$$

$$=2.42$$

Choice D: 2 and 6

Standard Deviation

$$=\sqrt{\frac{\Sigma(x_i-\mu)^2}{N}}$$

$$=\sqrt{\frac{(0-4)^2+(2-4)^2+(4-4)^2+(6-4)^2+(8-4)^2+(2-4)^2+(6-4)^2}{5}}$$

$$=\sqrt{\frac{(-4)^2+(-2)^2+(0)^2+(2)^2+(4)^2+(-2)^2+(2)^2}{7}}$$

$$=\sqrt{\frac{16+4+0+4+16+4+4}{7}}$$

$$=\sqrt{\frac{48}{7}}$$

$$=\sqrt{6.86}$$

$$=2.62$$

The two numbers added to create a set of 7 numbers that resulted in a new standard deviation that is close to the standard deviation for the original 5 numbers is 2 and 6.

Choice A is incorrect because adding -1 and 9 will not give a standard deviation close to the standard deviation for the original 5 numbers. **Choice B** is incorrect because adding 4 and 4 will not give a standard deviation close to the standard deviation for the original 5 numbers. **Choice C** is incorrect because adding 3 and 5 will not give a standard deviation close to the standard deviation for the original 5 numbers.

68.

Category: IES & Modeling
Skill: Sets of numbers | **Level:** Easy

Choice C is correct because the obtained answer is 29.38.

Set A : $n=15$; $\bar{x}=30$

An addition of 20 to the data value set in A. The new $\bar{x}$ is
Sum of original values $= 15\times 30=450$

Addition of 20 $= 450+20=470$

New mean $=\dfrac{470}{n+1}=\dfrac{470}{15+1}=\dfrac{470}{16}=29.38$

Choice A is incorrect because 20.00 is less than the obtained answer. **Choice B** is incorrect because 29.00 is less than the obtained answer. **Choice D** is incorrect because 30.20 is greater than the obtained answer.

69.

Category: IES and Modeling
Skill: Sets of numbers | **Level:** Hard
Choice C is correct because the Venn diagram represents the given situation.
Total number of student : 43
Likes Math $|M|=30$
Likes English: $|E|=29$
Find the number of students who like both $|M\cap E|$.
$|M\cap E|=|M|+|E|-|M\cup E|$
$|M\cap E|=30+29-43|$
$|M\cap E|=16|$

Math Only: 30 – 16 =14
English Only: 29 – 16 =13

Hence, the Venn diagram is

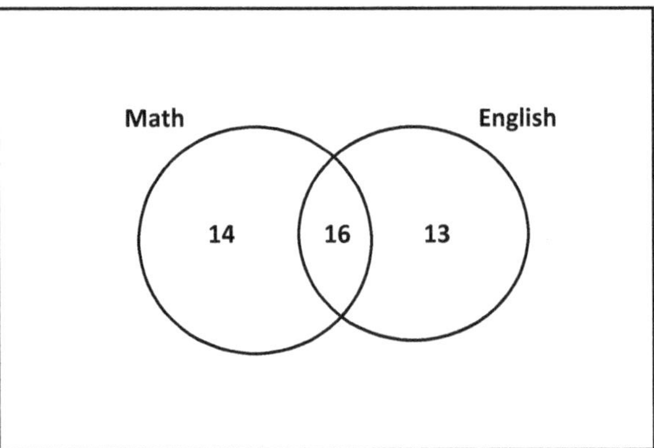

Choice A is incorrect because it does not represent the given situation. **Choice B** is incorrect because it does not represent the given situation. **Choice D** is incorrect because it does not represent the given situation.

70.

Category: IES
Skill: Sets of numbers | **Level:** Easy

Choice D is correct because the obtained answer is 63.
Given: X={3, 6, 8} and Y={1, 6, 9, 10}
then, $X\cup Y$ ={1, 3, 6, 8, 9, 10} has 6 elements.
The total number of subsets of a set with 6 elements is
$2^n=2^6=64$

The number of proper subsets is
$2^n - 1 = 2^6 - 1 = 64 - 1 = 63$
Hence, the answer is Choice D.
Choice A is incorrect because 61 is less than the obtained value. **Choice B** is incorrect because 64 is greater than the obtained value. **Choice C** is incorrect because 65 is greater than the obtained value.

71.

Category: PHM & Modeling
Skill: Sets of numbers | **Level:** Easy

Choice A is correct because $A - \{B \cup C\} = \{1\}$.

$$A = \{1, 2, 3, 4,\} \; B = \{2, 4, 6, 8\} \; C = \{3, 4, 5, 6\}$$

$$B \cup C = \{2, 3, 4, 5, 6, 8\}$$

$$A - \{B \cup C\} = \{1, 2, 3, 4\} - \{2, 3, 4, 5, 6, 8\} = \{1\}$$

Choice B is incorrect because the given set does not satisfy the given equation. **Choice C** is incorrect because the given set does not satisfy the given equation.
Choice D is incorrect because the given set does not satisfy the given equation.

72.

Category: IES & Modeling
Skill: Sets of numbers | **Level:** Easy

Choice A is correct because the obtained answer is
$200 - |T \cup C \cup M|$.
Let
$n|T|$ - number of people with two-wheeler
$n|C|$ - number of people with credit card
$n|M|$ - number of people with mobile phone
$n|T \cap C|$ - number of people with both two-wheeler and credit card
$n|C \cap M|$ -number of people with credit card and mobile phone
$n|T \cap M|$ - number of people with two-wheeler and mobile phone
$n|T \cap C \cap M|$ - number of people with two-wheeler, credit card, and mobile phone

Find the number of candidates with none of these items.

200 – the number of candidates with at least one.

Find the number of candidates with at least one.
$|T \cup C \cup M| = |T| + |C| + |M| - |T \cap C| - |C \cap M| - |T \cap M| + |T \cap C|M|$

Hence, the formula that represents for the number of the people who had none of the three is 200 – the number of candidates with at least one.

$$200 - |T \cup C \cup M|$$

Choice B is incorrect because it does not correctly represent the formula for the people who had none of the three. **Choice C** is incorrect because it does not correctly represent the formula for the people who had none of the three. **Choice D** is incorrect because it does not correctly represent the formula for the people who had none of the three.

73.

Category: IES & Modeling
Skill: Sets of numbers | **Level:** Easy

Choice D is correct because the obtained answer is

$$x = 24, \; y = 38.$$

The Venn diagram shows the unknown as students who study German only and French only.

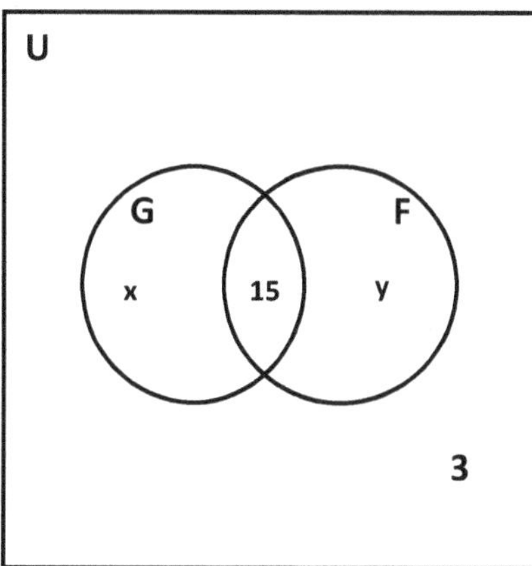

39 students study German

$$x + 15 = 39$$
$$x = 39 - 15$$
$$x = 24$$

53 students study French

$$y + 15 = 53$$
$$y = 53 - 15$$
$$y = 38$$

Hence, the answer is Choice D.

Choice A is incorrect because $x = 38, y = 24$ does not represent the given unknowns in the Venn diagram.
Choice B is incorrect because $x = 28, y = 34$ does not represent the given unknowns in the Venn diagram.
Choice C is incorrect because $x = 14, y = 28$ does not represent the given unknowns in the Venn diagram.

74.

Category: PHM & Modeling
Skill: Sets of numbers | **Level:** Hard

Choice B is correct because the obtained answer is

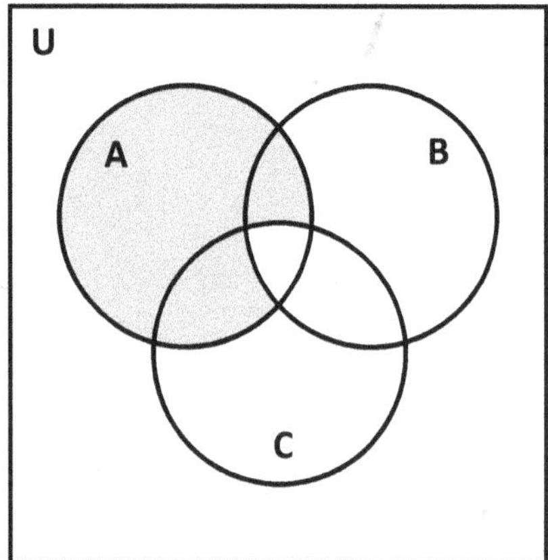

Draw the Venn Diagram.

Let's start to draw A then $(B \cap C)$

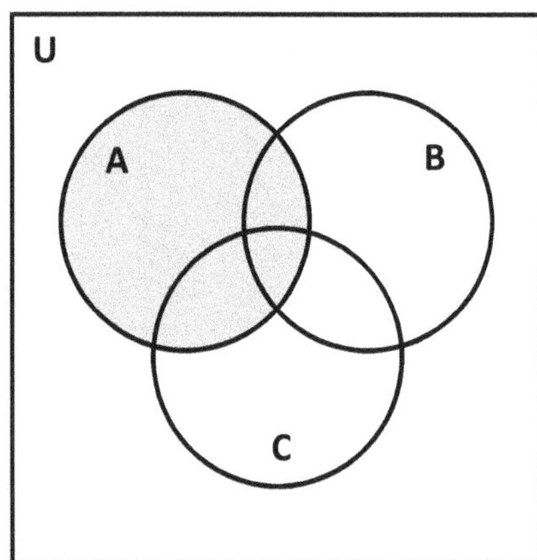

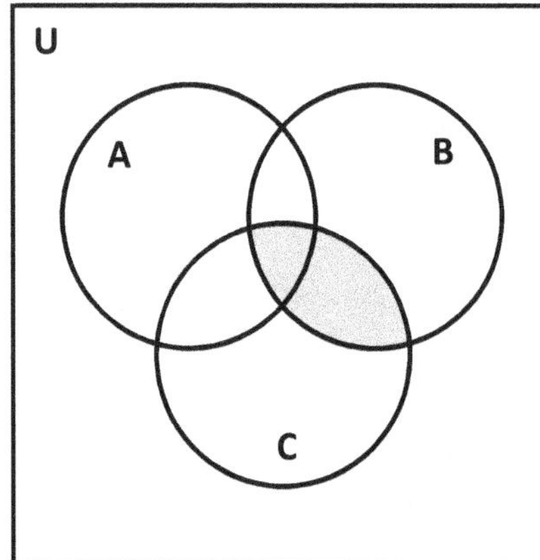

$A-(B \cap C)$ means that the difference between $(B \cap C)$ and A.

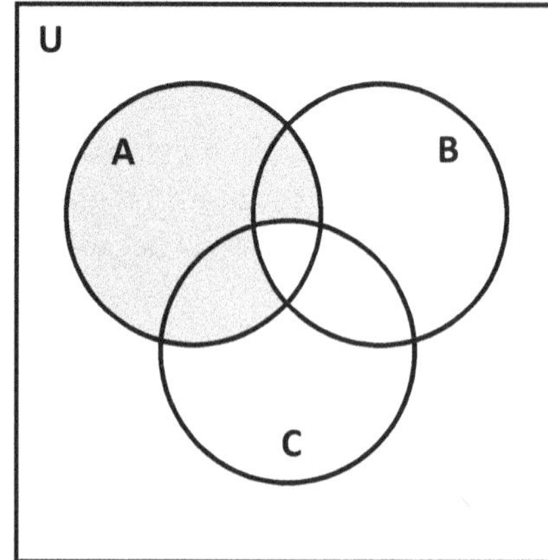

Hence, the answer is Choice B.

Choice A is incorrect because does not represent the given information. **Choice C** is incorrect because does not represent the given information. **Choice D** is incorrect because does not represent the given information.

75.

Category: PHM
Skill: Sets of numbers | **Level:** Easy

Choice B is correct because 301,34,306,308,311 has the largest standard deviation.

Find the mean of the given set from each choice and analyze the standard deviation.

Standard deviation is the measure of how dispersed the data from the mean.

Choice A: 2,3,4,5,6

$$Mean = \frac{2+3+4+5+6}{5} = 4$$

The data is symmetrically distributed around the mean with small differences, so the standard deviation will be small.

Choice B: 301,34,306,308,311

$$Mean = \frac{301+34+306+308+311}{5} = 252$$

The numbers 34 and 311 are far from the mean, indicating a large spread. This data set is likely to have the largest standard deviation.

Choice C: 350,350,350,350,350

$$Mean = \frac{350+350+350+350+350}{5} = 350$$

All deviations are 000 because all values are equal, so the standard deviation is 0.

Choice D: 888.5, 888.6, 888.7, 888.9

$$Mean = \frac{888.5 + 888.6 + 888.7 + 888.8 + 888.9}{5} = 888.7$$

The values are very close to each other, indicating a small spread and thus a small standard deviation.

Choice A is incorrect because the set has lesser standard deviation. **Choice C** is incorrect because the set has lesser standard deviation. **Choice D** is incorrect because the set has lesser standard deviation.

76.

Category: PHM & Modeling
Skill: Sets of numbers | **Level:** Easy

Choice C is correct because the obtained mean formula is $86 = \frac{2325 + 85p}{27 + p}$.

Find the midpoints (x of the wages).

$$x = \frac{Lower\ limit + upper\ limit}{2}$$

Midpoints: 55, 65, 75, 85, 95 and 105
The frequencies are: $f = 5, 3, 4, p, 2, 13$

Mean is $\frac{\Sigma fx}{\Sigma f}$

Find Σf

$$\Sigma f = 5 + 3 + 4 + p + 2 + 13 = 27 + p$$

Find Σfx

$$\Sigma fx = (5 \times 55) + (3 \times 65) + (4 \times 75) + (p \times 85) + (2 \times 95) + (13 \times 105)$$

$$\Sigma fx = 275 + 195 + 300 + 85p + 190 + 1365$$

$$\Sigma fx = 2325 + 85p$$

Substitute to the mean formula.

$$\bar{x} = \frac{\Sigma fx}{\Sigma f}$$

$$86 = \frac{2325 + 85p}{27 + p}$$

Hence, the correct answer is C.

Choice A is incorrect because the denominator is incorrect. **Choice B** is incorrect because the numerator is incorrect. **Choice D** is incorrect because the denominator is incorrect.

77.

Category: PHM
Skill: Sets of numbers | **Level:** Hard

Choice A is correct because the obtained value of k is 1.

Given: 3, 8, 6, 7, 1, 6, 10, 6, 7, $2k + 5$, 9, 7, and 13

Mode is the number that appears most frequent in the data set.

Looking at the data set, 6 appears 3 times and 7 appears 3 times.

Since, 7 is the mode, it means it appears the most frequent, hence, $2k + 5 = 7$.

Solve for k.

$$2k + 5 = 7$$

$$2k = 7 - 5$$

$$2k = 2$$

$$k = 1$$

Choice B is incorrect because 3 is greater than the obtained value of k. **Choice C** is incorrect because 4 is greater than the obtained value of k. **Choice D** is incorrect because 7 is an overestimation of the obtained value of k.

78.

Category: PHM
Skill: Sets of numbers | **Level:** Medium

Choice D is correct There are 26 letters to choose from for the first 3 values and 10 number to choose from for the last four values. Since each letter and number can be used repeatedly the total number of combinations is $26 \times 26 \times 26 \times 10 \times 10 \times 10 \times 10 = 175,760,000$.

Choice A is incorrect. This may results from $26 \times 10 \times 10$. **Choice B** is incorrect. This may result from calculation error.**Choice C** is incorrect. This assumes the letters and numbers cannot be repeated.

79.

Category: PHM
Skill: Sets of numbers | **Level:** Medium
Choice C is correct because the average speed is 35 miles per hour.
First distance: $t = 4$

$s = 30$ mi/h
$d = st = 30(4) = 120$ miles

Second distance: t = 2

s = 45 mi/h
d = st = 45(2) = 90 miles

Average speed =

$$\frac{total\ distance}{total\ time} = \frac{120 + 90}{4 + 2} = \frac{210}{6} = 35\frac{mi}{h}$$

Choice A is incorrect because 20 miles per hour is less than the obtained average speed. **Choice B** is incorrect because 25 miles per hour is less than the obtained average speed. **Choice D** is incorrect because 45 miles per hour is less than the obtained average speed.

80.

Category: IES
Skill: Sets of numbers | **Level:** Easy

Choice D is correct because {1,3,5} and {2,4,6} are disjoint.

Two sets are disjoint if they don't have a common element. Analyze the choices.

Choice A: {1,3,5} and {1,3,6} have common elements {1,3}
Choice B: {1,2,3} and {1,2,3} have common elements {1,2,3}
Choice C: {1,3,5} and {2,3,4}have common elements {3}
Choice D: {1,3,5} and {2,4,6}have no common elements.

Choice A is incorrect because {1,3,5} and {1,3,6} have common elements. **Choice B** is incorrect because {1,2,3} and {1,2,3}have common elements. **Choice C** is incorrect because {1,3,5} and {2,3,4}have common elements.

81.

Category: IES
Skill: Sets of numbers | **Level:** Medium

Choice C is correct because the obtained answer is 40.
Points from the first five games = 17 + 19 + 13 + 24 + 14 = 87 points
Let x be the sum of the scores for the last 2 games.
Set up the inequality where the mean of the scores is greater than 18.

$$\frac{87+x}{7}>18$$
$$87+x>126$$
$$x>126-87$$
$$x>39$$

To get a mean higher than the scoring average of other players, Angela should score 40 in the final two games.

Choice A is incorrect because 32 is less than the obtained answer. **Choice B** is incorrect because 37 is less than the obtained answer. **Choice D** is incorrect because 43 is less than the obtained answer.

82.

Category: PHM
Skill: Sets of numbers | **Level:** Medium

Choice C is correct Order the set to find the median, {2, 5, 6, 9, 13}. So, the median is 6. The mean is $\frac{2+5+6+9+13}{5}=7$. The sum of the mean and median is
6 + 7 =13.

Choice A is incorrect. This is the median. **Choice B** is incorrect. This is the mean. **Choice D** is incorrect. This is the product of the mean and median.

83.

Category: PHM
Skill: Sets of numbers | **Level:** Medium

Choice C is correct. For each of the 3 shirts you have a combination of choosing 2 pairs of pants and 1 pair of shoes, so you can make 2 outfits by choosing 1 of the shirts. This can be done 3 times with the shirts for a total of $3\times2=6$.

Choice A is incorrect. This is the number of shirts **Choice B** is incorrect. This may result from miscalculations. **Choice D** is incorrect. This is twice the distinct outfit he can wear.

84.

Category: IES & Modeling
Skill: Sets of numbers | **Level:** Medium
Choice C is correct. The mode is 51 and the means is,

$$\frac{42+44+47+51+51+54+60+62+64+65+71+73}{12}=57.$$

So, the difference is 57 – 51 = 6.

Choice A is incorrect because it uses the median of 57 as the mode when finding the difference. **Choice B** is incorrect because it calculates the mean as 55 when finding the difference. **Choice D** is incorrect because it calculates the mean as 58 when finding the difference.

85.

Category: BHM
Skill: Sets of numbers | **Level:** Easy

Choice A is correct because the intersection of the given sets is {1,2}

The intersection of two sets consists of the elements that are present in both sets.

Hence, the intersection of the set is {1,2}

Choice B is incorrect because both {5,6} are not elements of both sets. **Choice C** is incorrect because in {2,5}, 5 is not an element of both sets. **Choice D** is incorrect because in {2,8}, 8 is not an element of both sets.

86.

Category: IES & Modeling
Skill: Sets of numbers | **Level:** Hard

Choice B is correct because the obtained answer is

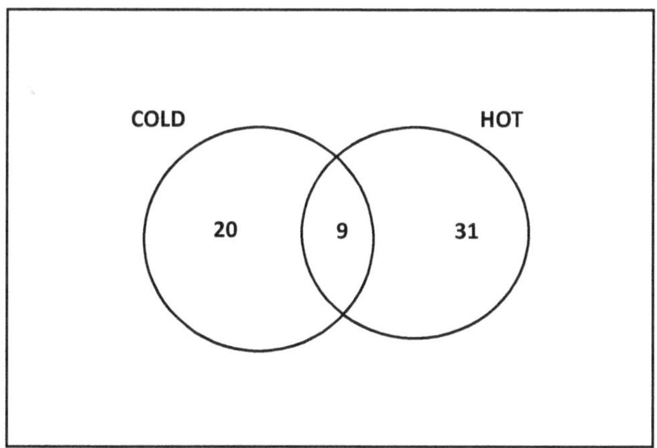

Given: 60 people, 29 prefer cold beverages and 40 prefer hot beverages

Let's make a Venn diagram with 2 overlapping circles.

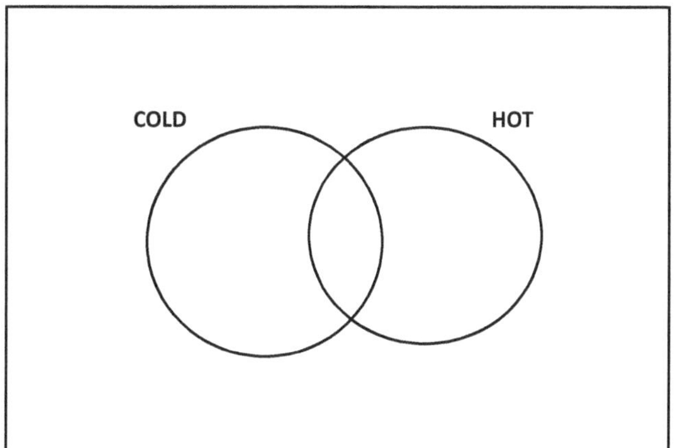

We use the equation $A \cap B = A + B - A \cup B$

$A \cap B = 29 + 40 - 60$
$A \cap B = 9$

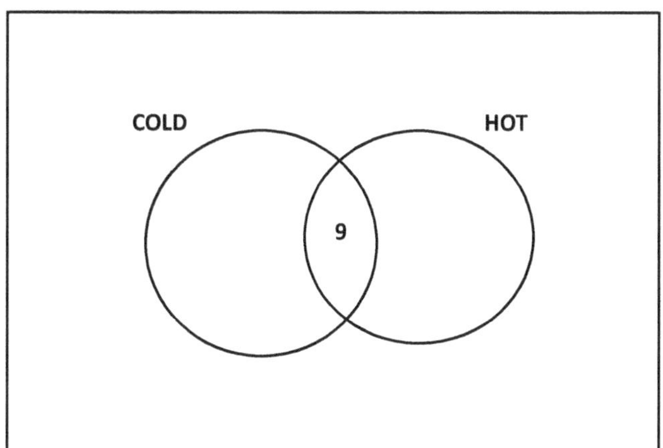

Since, 29 likes cold drinks and 9 likes both hot and cold, 29-9=20 likes only cold drinks.

40 likes hot drinks and 9 likes both hot and cold, 40-9=31 likes only hot drinks.

Hence, the Venn diagram is

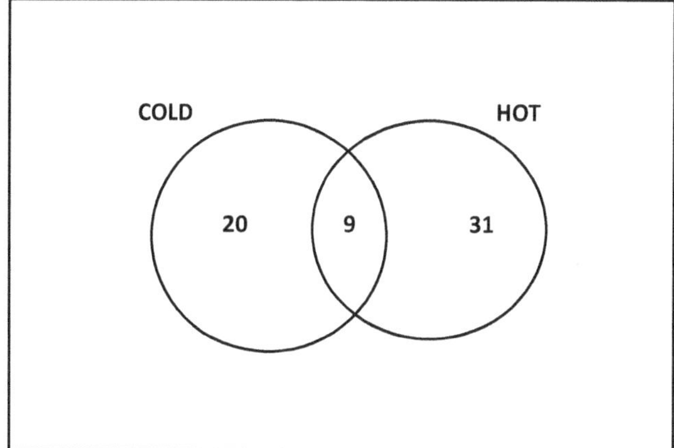

Choice A is incorrect because the Venn diagram does not represent the given problem. **Choice C** is incorrect because the Venn diagram does not represent the given problem. **Choice D** is incorrect because the Venn diagram does not represent the given problem.

87.

Category: PHM & Modeling
Skill: Sets of numbers | **Level:** Easy

Choice D is correct because the obtained answer is

$$Mean = \frac{\Sigma(\neq of\ children \times \neq of\ families)}{\Sigma(\neq of\ families)} = 2.19.$$

$$Mean = \frac{\Sigma(\neq of\ children \times \neq of\ families)}{\Sigma(\neq of\ families)}$$

$$Mean = \frac{0(8)+1(16)+2(22)+3(14)+4(6)+5(4)+6(2)}{8+16+22+14+6+4+2}$$

$$Mean = \frac{158}{72}$$

$$Mean = 2.19$$

Choice A is incorrect because the obtained value is incorrect. **Choice B** is incorrect because the formula is incorrect. **Choice C** is incorrect because both the formula and the o obtained value are incorrect.

88.

Category: IES & Modeling
Skill: Sets of numbers | **Level:** Easy

Choice C is correct because the obtained set represents

$$(A \cap B) \cup (B \cap C).$$

Looking at set $A = \{2,4,6,8,10,12\}$, $B = \{1,3,5,8,10,12\}$,

$C = \{7,8,9,10,11,12,13\}$

Find $(A \cup B)$, $(A \cap B)$, $(B \cup C)$, $(B \cap C)$.

$$(A \cup B) = \{1,2,3,4,5,6,8,10,12\}$$
$$(A \cap B) = \{8,10,12\}$$
$$(B \cup C) = \{1,3,5,7,8,9,10,11,12,13\}$$
$$(B \cap C) = \{8,10,12\}$$

Analyze the choices.

Choice A: $(A \cup B) \cup (B \cap C)$

$$(A \cup B) = \{1,2,3,4,5,6,8,10,12\}$$
$$(B \cap C) = \{8,10,12\}$$
$$(A \cup B) \cup (B \cap C) = \{1,2,3,4,5,6,8,10,12\}$$

Choice B: $(A \cup B) \cap (B \cup C)$

$$(A \cup B) = \{1,2,3,4,5,6,8,10,12\}$$
$$(B \cup C) = \{1,3,5,7,8,9,10,11,12,13\}$$
$$(A \cup B) \cap (B \cup C) = \{1,3,5,8,10,12\}$$

Choice C: $(A \cap B) \cup (B \cap C)$

$$(A \cap B) = \{8,10,12\}$$
$$(B \cap C) = \{8,10,12\}$$
$$(A \cap B) \cup (B \cap C) = \{8,10,12\}$$

Choice D: $(A \cup B) \cup (B \cap C)$

$$(A \cup B) = \{1,2,3,4,5,6,8,10,12\}$$
$$(B \cap C) = \{8,10,12\}$$
$$(A \cup B) \cup (B \cap C) = \{1,2,3,4,5,6,8,10,12\}$$

Hence, answer is $(A \cap B) \cup (B \cap C) = \{8,10,12\}$.

Choice A is incorrect because the symbols between the sets A, B and B, C are incorrect. **Choice B** is incorrect because the symbols between the sets A,B and B,C are incorrect. **Choice D** is incorrect because the symbols between the sets A,B and B,C are incorrect.

89.

Category: PHM
Skill: Sets of numbers | **Level:** Hard

Choice B is correct because the obtained value is 43.
Given:
Let |E| be the no of people reading English newspaper – 21
|H| be the no of people reading Hindi – 26
|R| be the no of people reading Regional – 29
$|E \cap H|$ be the no of people reading English and Hindi – 14
$|H \cap R|$ be the no of people reading Hindi and Regional –15
$|E \cap R|$ be the no of people reading English and Regional –12
$|H \cap R \cap E|$ be the no of people readingAll types –8
Find the total number of people surveyed $|H \cup R \cup E|$.

$$|H \cup R \cup E| = |E| + |H| + |R| - |E \cap H| - |H \cap R| - |E \cap R| + |H \cap R \cap E|$$
$$|H \cup R \cup E| = 21 + 26 + 29 - 14 - 15 - 12 + 8$$
$$|H \cup R \cup E| = 43$$

There are a total of 43 people surveyed.

Choice A is incorrect because 35 is less than the obtained value. **Choice C** is incorrect because 59 is greater than the obtained value. **Choice D** is incorrect because 65 is greater than the obtained value.

90.

Category: PHM & Modeling
Skill: Sets of numbers | **Level:** Hard

Choice C is correct because the obtained answer will be less than.

Let's analyze the given figure.

Volume of the original 5 balls

Volume of the new set of 8 balls

When the balls X, Y and Z are added to the original 5 balls, there will be more variability in volume compared to the original set of 5 balls. This resulted to a large variety of sizes as well as the variety in volume.

When the individual data points are spread out quite a bit the data has a high SD. On the other had, if the data set has a smaller SD, you can infer that the data points are closer to the mean.

Hence, the standard deviation of the volume of the 5 balls will be less than the standard deviation of the volume of the new 8 balls.

Choice A is incorrect because the given statement is not true. **Choice B** is incorrect because the new standard deviation is greater than the original sd. **Choice D** is incorrect because the standard deviation can still be computed even though the balls are in different sizes.

91.

Category: IES & Modeling
Skill: Charts | **Level:** Easy

Choice C is correct because the obtained answer is 90%

Adding up the approximate quantity of wheat and dividing it by the total quantity of food grains (i.e. wheat + rice) will give us

$$\approx 5516/6126 \approx 90\%$$

Choice A is incorrect because 66% is less than the obtained answer. **Choice B** is incorrect because 75% is less than the obtained answer. **Choice D** is incorrect because 95% is greater than the obtained answer.

92.

Category: IES & Modeling
Skill: Charts | **Level:** Hard

Choice A is correct because the obtained answer is

Likes dog: 74
Likes cat: 60
Likes bird: 74
Don't like pets: 13
Likes dog or bird: 100
Likes Bird or Cat: 105
Likes dog or cat: 118

Look at the Venn diagram.

Likes dog: 32 + 4 + 12 + 26 = 74

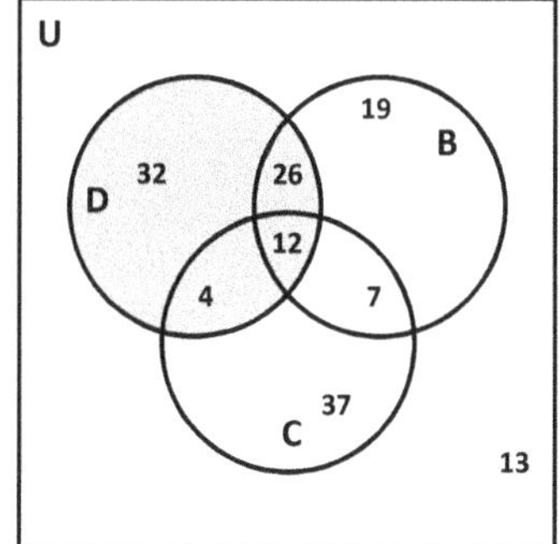

Likes cat: 4 + 12 + 7 + 37 = 60

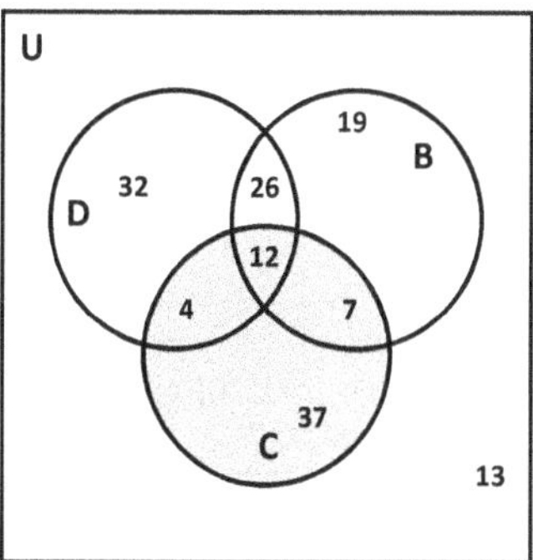

Likes bird: 12 + 26 + 19 + 7 = 64

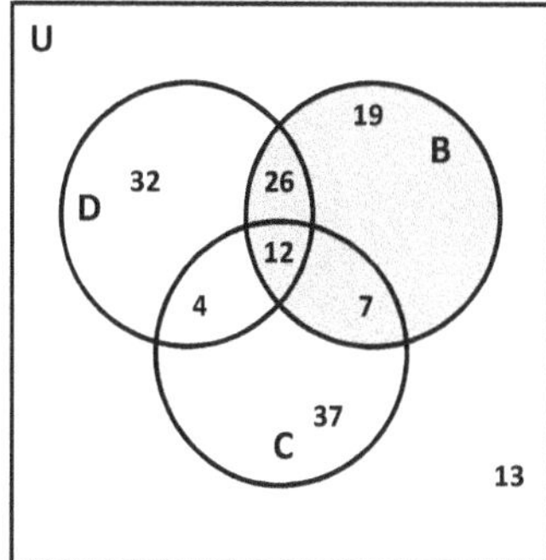

Don't like pets: 13

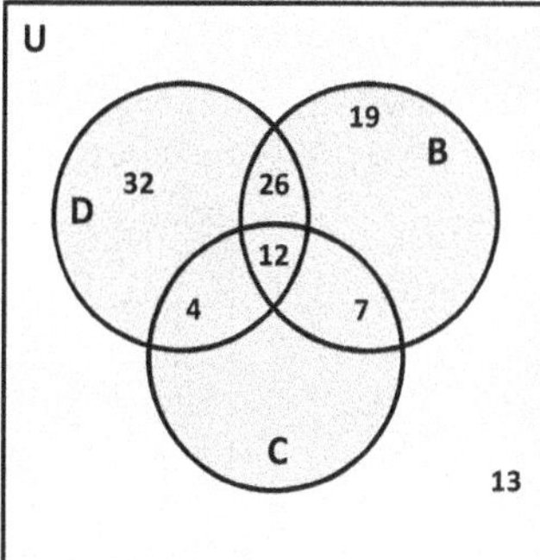

Likes dog or bird: 32 + 26 + 12 + 4 + 19 + 7 = 100

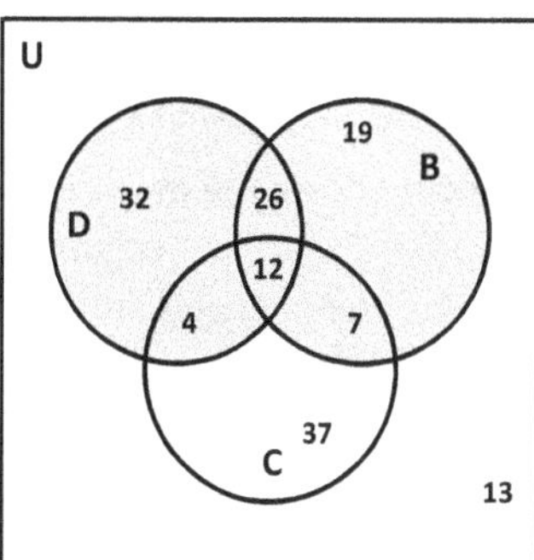

Likes Bird or Cat: 4 + 12 + 26 + 19 + 7 + 37 = 105

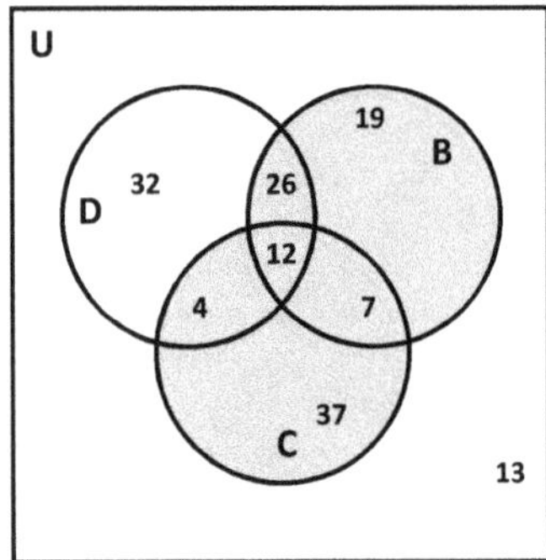

Likes dog or cat: 32 + 4 + 12 + 26 + 7 + 37 = 118

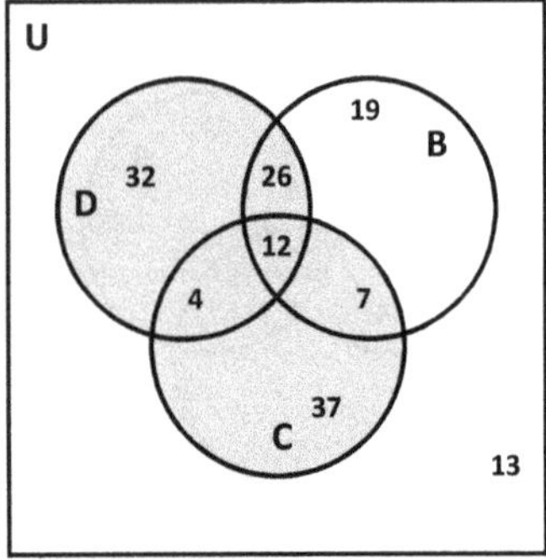

Hence, the answer is Choice A.
Choice B is incorrect because does not represent the given Venn diagram. **Choice C** is incorrect because does not represent the given Venn diagram. **Choice D** is incorrect because does not represent the given Venn diagram.

93.

Category: IES & Modeling
Skill: Charts | **Level:** Hard

Choice D is correct because the obtained answer is mean > median.
The skewness of the graph determines the mean of the data. The given histogram is skewed to the right. The mode is often less than the median, which is less than the mean. Hence, the answer is **Choice D**.

Choice A is incorrect because the mean is not equal to the median. **Choice B** is incorrect because the mean is not approximately equal to the median **Choice C** is incorrect because the mean is not less than the median.

94.

Category: PHM & Modeling
Skill: Charts | **Level:** Easy

Choice B is correct because the obtained number of students who missed the same number on both tests is 4.

Choice A is incorrect because 2 is less than the obtained value. **Choice C** is incorrect because 8 is greater than the obtained value. **Choice D** is incorrect because 10 is greater than the obtained value.

95.

Category: PHM & Modeling
Skill: Charts | **Level:** Easy

Choice C is correct because the obtained answer is 71.

Total people who like to fly in an airplane:

People who like only planes: 83

People who like both planes and cars: 46

So, the total number of people who like to fly is:

$$83 + 46 = 129$$

Total people who don't like to fly in an airplane: Since there are 200 people in total and 129 like to fly, the number of people who don't like to fly is:

$$200 - 129 = 71$$

So, 71 people don't like to fly in an airplane.

Choice A is incorrect because 51 is less than the obtained value. **Choice B** is incorrect because 61 is less than the obtained value. **Choice D** is incorrect because 83 is greater than the obtained value.

96.

Category: IES & Modeling
Skill: Charts | **Level:** Easy

Choice D is correct because the obtained answer is $y = 0.50x + 5$, \$12.00.

Evan's package is 14 ounces. Hence, the fee is \$5.00 and the price per ounce is \$0.50.

Set up the equation.

Let x be the number of ounces and y be the total payment for the shipment.

$$y = 0.50x + 5$$

$$y = 0.50(14) + 5$$

$$y = 12$$

Choice A is incorrect because the equation is incorrect. **Choice B** is incorrect because both the equation and the value are incorrect. **Choice C** is incorrect because the value is incorrect.

97.

Category: IES & Modeling
Skill: Charts | **Level:** Medium

Choice A is correct. Since 18% prefer action and 32% prefer comedy, the ratio 18:32 can be simplified to 9:16.

Choice B is incorrect. This may result if the ratio is 18:50. **Choice C** is incorrect. This may result if the ratio is 18:81. **Choice D** is incorrect. This may result if the ratio is 18:100.

98.

Category: IES & Modeling
Skill: Charts | **Level:** Easy

Choice B is correct because the obtained answer is 12.5%

Company A's production in 1998 = 8 million units;
Company A's production in 1999 = 7 million units;
Difference in production 1998 to 1999 for company A = 8 –7 = 1; Original production = 8
Using the formula : % Decrease = (Decrease in production/Original production) × 100

Required percentage decrease = $\frac{8-7}{8} = \frac{1}{8} \times 100$

Therefore, there was a decrease of 12.5 %.

Choice A is incorrect because 11% is less than the obtained answer. **Choice C** is incorrect because 25% is greater than the obtained answer. **Choice D** is incorrect because 40% is greater than the obtained answer.

99.

Category: IES & Modeling
Skill: Charts | **Level:** Medium

Choice C is correct. 3% of the people walked to work. Since 45 people walked to work, the number of people in the survey can be determined by dividing 45 by 3% then, $\frac{45}{0.03} = 1500$. So, there are 1500 people in the survey.

65 of 1500 people drove a car to work then, $0.65 \times 1500 = 975$ people drove a car to work.

Choice A is incorrect. This might be a random guess due to conceptual error. **Choice B** is incorrect. This might be a random guess due to conceptual error. **Choice D** is incorrect. This might be a random guess due to conceptual error.

100.

Category: PHM & Modeling
Skill: Charts | **Level:** Easy

Choice C is correct. Twenty of the thirty people prefer bananas or apples so, $\frac{20}{30} = 0.67$.

Choice A is incorrect. This may result from wrong use of formula and calculation. **Choice B** is incorrect. This may result from wrong use of formula and calculation. **Choice D** is incorrect. This may result from wrong use of formula and calculation.

101.

Category: PHM & Modeling
Skill: Permutation and combination | **Level:** Medium

Choice A is correct because the statement is true considering that A and B are independent events.

Analyze the given choices:

Definition of Independent events. It implies that the occurrence of one event does not affect the probability of the other event.

Choice A:

$P(A|B) = P(A)$ means that the probability of A given B is just the probability of A.
$P(B|A) = P(B)$ means that the probability of B given A is just the probability of B.
Hence, this statement is correct.

Choice B:

$P(AB) = 0$ is incorrect. If events A and B are independent, the probability of both events occurring is not necessarily zero. For independent events, $P(AB) = P(A) \cdot P(B)$, and this is nonzero unless either P(A)orP(B) is zero.

Choice C:

$P(AB) = P(A) + P(B)$ is incorrect. RHS should have been the product and not the sum.

Choice B is incorrect because the statement is not always true. **Choice C** is incorrect because the RHS of the statement is sum and not product of the probabilities of A and B. **Choice D** is incorrect because Choice B is a false statement.

102.

Category: IES
Skill: Permutation and combination | **Level:** Medium

Choice C is correct because the obtained answer is 48.

Count the number of letters in the given word:

JUDGE = 5 letters   vowels are U, E = 2 letters

Vowels should always stay alongside, hence we treat U and E as 1 block.

There will now be 4 letters, J, D, G and the block U, E. Arrangement would be 4! = 24.

Within the block U, E, it can be arranged as 2! = 2.

Calculating the total arrangement would be 4!(2!) = 24(2) = 48.

Choice A is incorrect because 16 has less arrangement than the obtained value. **Choice B** is incorrect because 20 has less arrangement than the obtained value. **Choice D** is incorrect because 124 is an overestimate of the obtained value.

103.

Category: PHM
Skill: Permutation and combination | **Level:** Medium

Choice C is correct because the obtained answer is 48.
Understand the conditions.

- The number is a 4 -digit integer
- Divisible by 3
- The digits used are {1,3,4,6,7) and not repeated

The sum of the available digits is 1+3+4+6+7 = 21 which is divisible by 3.

Find the numbers to exclude so that the sum of the digits of a 4-digit number is divisible by 3.

Exclude 1 digit from the available digits and determine if it is divisible by 3.

Excluding 1 : 3+4+6+7 = 20 (not divisible by 3)
Excluding 3 : 1+4+6+7 = 18 (divisible by 3)
Excluding 4 : 1+3+6+7 = 17 (not divisible by 3)
Excluding 6 : 1+3+4+7 = 15 (divisible by 3)
Excluding 7 : 1+3+4+6 = 14 (not divisible by 3)

Hence, the possible combinations of digits are {1,4,6,7} and {1,3,4,7}

Find the permutation of the possible combinations of digits.

{1,4,6,7} = 4!   And   {1,3,4,7} = 4!

Hence, 4!+4! = 24 + 24 = 48

Choice D is incorrect because 72 is greater than the obtained answer. **Choice B** is incorrect because 24 is less than the obtained answer. **Choice A** is incorrect because 12 is less than the obtained answer.

104.

Category: PHM & Modeling
Skill: Permutation and combination | **Level:** Medium

Choice C is correct because the obtained answer is

$$\frac{m!(m+1)!}{(m-n+1)!}.$$

Find the seating arrangement:

Given: m be men and n for women. They are to be seated in a row where no two women sit together.

- m men can be arranged to sit in $m!$ ways
- Since no two women can sit together then, there are only $m + 1$ places available for women to sit.
- So, n women can be arranged to sit in $m + 1$ places in ${}^{m+1}P_n$ ways

Hence, the total number of ways in which m men and n women are to be seated in a row so that no two women sit together are

$$= m!\left({}^{m+1}P_n\right)$$

$$= m!\left(\frac{(m+1)!}{(m-n+1)!}\right)$$

$$= \frac{m!(m+1)!}{(m-n+1)!}$$

Choice A is incorrect because the numerator is incorrect. **Choice B** is incorrect because the numerator is incorrect. **Choice D** is incorrect because an answer is obtained from the given choices.

105.

Category: PHM
Skill: Permutation and Combination | **Level:** Medium

Choice D is correct because the obtained answer is 756.

Given: 7 - men , 6- women

Selecting 5 to form a committee with at least 3 men in the committee.

Identify the cases:

3 men and 2 women
4 men and 1 women
5 men and 0 women

Find the number of ways for each case.

Case 1: 3 men and 2 women.

$$= C_3^7 \times C_2^6$$
$$= 35 \times 15$$
$$= 525$$

Case 2: 4 men and 1 woman .

$$= C_4^7 \times C_1^6$$
$$= 35 \times 6$$
$$= 210$$

Case 3: 5 men and 0 woman.

$$= C_5^7 \times C_0^6$$
$$= 21 \times 1$$
$$= 21$$

Total ways: 525 + 210 + 21 = 756.
Choice A is incorrect because 564 is less than the obtained value. **Choice B** is incorrect because 645 is less than the obtained value. **Choice C** is incorrect because 735 is less than the obtained value.

106.

Category: IES & Modeling
Skill: Permutation and combination | **Level:** Easy

Choice D is correct because the obtained expansion is $\frac{10!}{(10-r)^2} : \frac{12!}{(12-(r+1)!} = 1.22.$.
The expansion of $P_r^n = \frac{n!}{(n-r)!}$. Use this to expand the given equation.

Expand P_r^{10}.
$$P_r^n = \frac{n!}{(n-r)!}$$
$$P_r^{10} = \frac{10!}{(10-r)!}$$

Expand P_{r+1}^{12}
$$P_r^n = \frac{n!}{(n-r)!}$$
$$P_{r+1}^{12} = \frac{12!}{((12-(r+1)))!}$$

Hence,
$$P_r^{10} : P_{r+1}^{12} = 1:22$$
$$\frac{10!}{(10-r)!} : \frac{12!}{((12-(r+1)))!} = 1:22$$

Choice A is incorrect because it does not represent the expansion of the given equation. **Choice B** is incorrect because it does not represent the expansion of the given equation. **Choice C** is incorrect because it does not represent the expansion of the given equation.

107.

Category: PHM & Modeling
Skill: Permutation and combination | **Level:** Easy

Choice C is correct because it represents Combination.
Combination - order of selection does not matter
Permutation - order of selection matters

Analyze the choices.

Choice A: Assembling a jigsaw puzzle

Involves arranging pieces in order. Hence, not a combination.

Choice B: Four people posing for pictures

Involves arranging in specific order. Hence, not a combination.

Choice C: Picking 6 balls from a basket of 13 balls

Selecting 6 balls from a basket does not involve taking specific order. Hence, a Combination.

Choice D: Determining the top three winners in a Science Quiz Bee

Involves arranging in specific order (first, second, third place). Hence, not a combination.

Choice A is incorrect because it does not represent Combination. **Choice B** is incorrect because it does not represent Combination. **Choice D** is incorrect because it does not represent Combination.

108.

Category: PHM
Skill: Permutation and combination | **Level:** Easy

Choice B is correct because the obtained answer is 24.

Given: The code is a 4-digit code.
Use digits 1, 2, 5, and 9
must appear exactly once in the code.

The order of the digits matters. Hence, this is a permutation problem because the order of the digits is important.

Formula for permutations:

$$P(n, r) = n!$$

Here, $n = 4$ (the total number of digits), and all 4 digits are used:

$$P(4, 4) = 4! = 4 \times 3 \times 2 \times 1 = 24$$

Hence, there are 24 possible codes.

Choice A is incorrect because 12 is less than the obtained value. **Choice C** is incorrect because 36 is greater than the obtained value. **Choice D** is incorrect because 48 is greater than the obtained value.

109.

Category: PHM
Skill: Permutation and combination | **Level:** Easy

Choice C is correct because the obtained answer is 216.

$$Total\ Possibilities = (Number\ of\ shirts) \times (Number\ of\ pair\ of\ jeans) \times (Number\ of\ pair\ of\ sneakers)$$

Substitute the given values:

$$Total\ Possibilities = 12 \times 6 \times 3 = 216$$

Hence, Jericho can dress herself in 216 different ways.

Choice A is incorrect because 54 is less than the obtained value. **Choice B** is incorrect because 108 is less than the obtained value. **Choice D** is incorrect because 312 is greater than the obtained value.

110.

Category: PHM
Skill: Permutation and combination | **Level:** Easy

Choice A is correct because the obtained answer is 12.
Number of letters: n=4

The frequency of letters: G - 1, O-2 , D-1

$$\text{Number of distinct arrangements} = \frac{n!}{p_1!p_2!....p_k!}$$

Applying the formula

$$\text{Number of distinct arrangements} = \frac{4!}{1!2!1!} = \frac{24}{2} = 12$$

Choice B is incorrect because 16 is greater than the obtained value. **Choice C** is incorrect because 24 is greater than the obtained value. **Choice D** is incorrect because 48 is greater than the obtained value.

Chapter 8
ACT Math Practice Test #1

Mark Your Answers For Test 1 Here

Date: ________

Marking Directions: Mark only one oval for each question. Fill in responese completely. Erase errors cleanly without smudging.

Correct mark: ○◎○○

1 Ⓐ Ⓑ Ⓒ Ⓓ	9 Ⓐ Ⓑ Ⓒ Ⓓ	17 Ⓐ Ⓑ Ⓒ Ⓓ	25 Ⓐ Ⓑ Ⓒ Ⓓ	33 Ⓐ Ⓑ Ⓒ Ⓓ	41 Ⓐ Ⓑ Ⓒ Ⓓ
2 Ⓕ Ⓖ Ⓗ Ⓙ	10 Ⓕ Ⓖ Ⓗ Ⓙ	18 Ⓕ Ⓖ Ⓗ Ⓙ	26 Ⓕ Ⓖ Ⓗ Ⓙ	34 Ⓕ Ⓖ Ⓗ Ⓙ	42 Ⓕ Ⓖ Ⓗ Ⓙ
3 Ⓐ Ⓑ Ⓒ Ⓓ	11 Ⓐ Ⓑ Ⓒ Ⓓ	19 Ⓐ Ⓑ Ⓒ Ⓓ	27 Ⓐ Ⓑ Ⓒ Ⓓ	35 Ⓐ Ⓑ Ⓒ Ⓓ	43 Ⓐ Ⓑ Ⓒ Ⓓ
4 Ⓕ Ⓖ Ⓗ Ⓙ	12 Ⓕ Ⓖ Ⓗ Ⓙ	20 Ⓕ Ⓖ Ⓗ Ⓙ	28 Ⓕ Ⓖ Ⓗ Ⓙ	36 Ⓕ Ⓖ Ⓗ Ⓙ	44 Ⓕ Ⓖ Ⓗ Ⓙ
5 Ⓐ Ⓑ Ⓒ Ⓓ	13 Ⓐ Ⓑ Ⓒ Ⓓ	21 Ⓐ Ⓑ Ⓒ Ⓓ	29 Ⓐ Ⓑ Ⓒ Ⓓ	37 Ⓐ Ⓑ Ⓒ Ⓓ	45 Ⓐ Ⓑ Ⓒ Ⓓ
6 Ⓕ Ⓖ Ⓗ Ⓙ	14 Ⓕ Ⓖ Ⓗ Ⓙ	22 Ⓕ Ⓖ Ⓗ Ⓙ	30 Ⓕ Ⓖ Ⓗ Ⓙ	38 Ⓕ Ⓖ Ⓗ Ⓙ	
7 Ⓐ Ⓑ Ⓒ Ⓓ	15 Ⓐ Ⓑ Ⓒ Ⓓ	23 Ⓐ Ⓑ Ⓒ Ⓓ	31 Ⓐ Ⓑ Ⓒ Ⓓ	39 Ⓐ Ⓑ Ⓒ Ⓓ	
8 Ⓕ Ⓖ Ⓗ Ⓙ	16 Ⓕ Ⓖ Ⓗ Ⓙ	24 Ⓕ Ⓖ Ⓗ Ⓙ	32 Ⓕ Ⓖ Ⓗ Ⓙ	40 Ⓕ Ⓖ Ⓗ Ⓙ	

MATHEMATICS TEST

50 Minutes—45 Questions

DIRECTIONS: Solve each problem, choose the correct answer, and then fill in the corresponding oval on your answer document.

Do not linger over problems that take too much time. Solve as many as you can; then return to the others in the time you have left for this test.

You are permitted to use a calculator on this test. You may use your calculator for any problems you choose, but some of the problems may best be done without using a calculator.

Note: Unless otherwise stated, all of the following should be assumed.

1. Illustrative figures are NOT necessarily drawn to scale.
2. Geometric figures lie in a plane.
3. The word line indicates a straight line.
4. The word average indicates arithmetic mean.

DO YOUR FIGURING HERE.

1. Ms Santiago throws out the lowest test score and takes the average of the remaining test scores to determine a student's overall test score for the semester. Lovely earned the following test scores in Ms Santiago's class this semester: 78, 83, 95, 64, and 79. What is the overall test score did Lovely earn in Ms Santiago's class this semester?

A. 80.75
B. 83.75
C. 85.50
D. 90.25

2. In an institution 75 pupils have pencils, 87 have sharpeners, 93 have rulers. 25 have both pencils and sharpeners, 30 have both pencils and rulers while 47 have both sharpeners and rulers. Each pupil has at least one of the three items. There are a total of 160 pupils.

Which Venn diagram illustrates this information?

F.

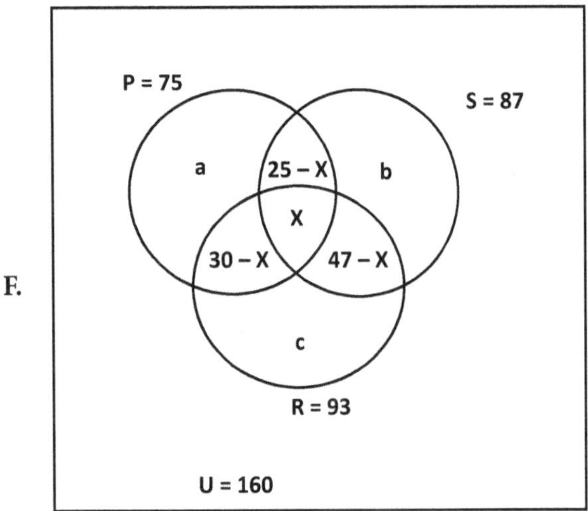

DO YOUR FIGURING HERE.

G.

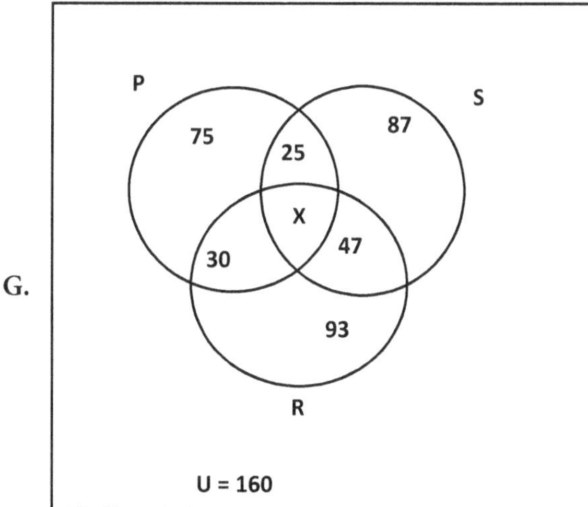

H.

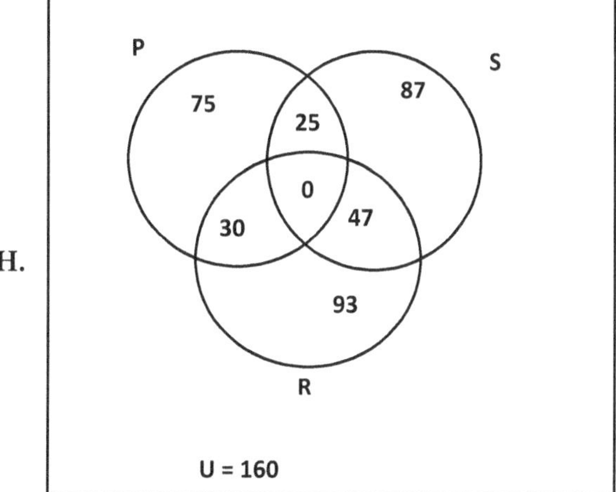

J.

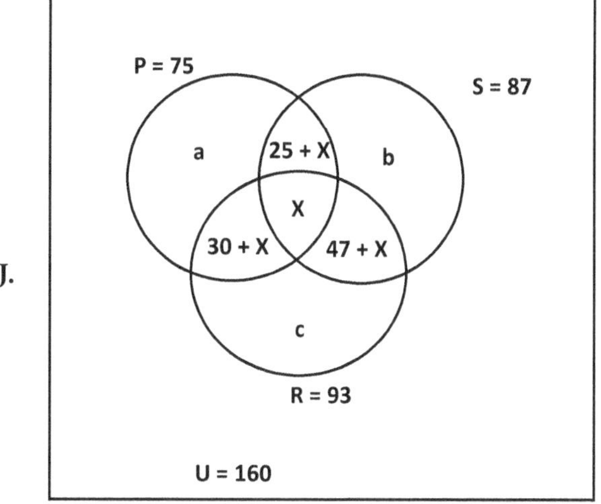

GO ON TO THE NEXT PAGE.

DO YOUR FIGURING HERE.

3. Patricia's grade for her statistics class is determined by her test average, quiz average, and homework average. The test average carries a weight of 50% of her grade, quiz average has a weight of 30%, and homework accounts for 20% of her grade. If her test and quiz averages are 86 and 88 respectively, what needs to be her homework average if she is to have a grade of 85 for the class?

A. 78
B. 81
C. 87
D. 90

4. In diagram shown below, points A, C, and E are colinear. ΔABC has an exterior angle measuring 142°. What is the measure of angle C in degrees?

F. 38
G. 42
H. 57
J. 85

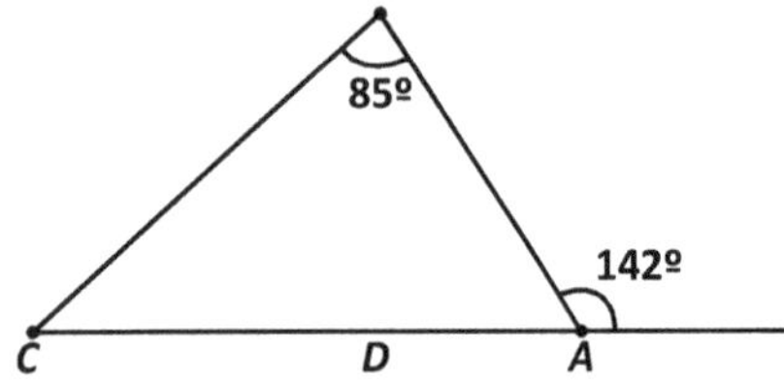

5. Which of the following expressions is a factor of $16x^2 - 49$?

A. $8x + 7$
B. $8x - 7$
C. $4x^2 + 7$
D. $4x - 7$

6. Which of the following matrices represents the sum of $\begin{bmatrix} 2 & 4 \\ 6 & 8 \end{bmatrix} + \begin{bmatrix} 1 & 3 \\ 5 & 7 \end{bmatrix}$?

F. $\begin{bmatrix} 3 & 7 \\ 11 & 15 \end{bmatrix}$

G. $\begin{bmatrix} 3 & 7 \\ 10 & 15 \end{bmatrix}$

H. $\begin{bmatrix} 3 & 7 \\ 11 & 16 \end{bmatrix}$

J. $\begin{bmatrix} 1 & 4 \\ 5 & 8 \end{bmatrix}$

DO YOUR FIGURING HERE.

7. What amount of ounces of frozen peas costing \$0.03 for each ounce should be added to 14 ounces of diced frozen carrots costing \$0.06 for each ounce to make a bag of frozen peas and carrots which costs \$0.05 for each ounce?

A. 7
B. 14
C. 20
D. 28

8. Which of the following represents the combined graph of $y = 2x + 4$ and $y = 2x^2 + 4$

F.

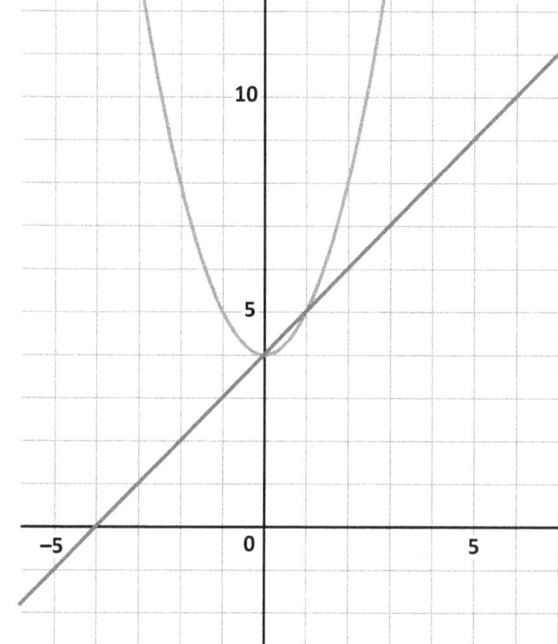

GO ON TO THE NEXT PAGE.

DO YOUR FIGURING HERE.

G. 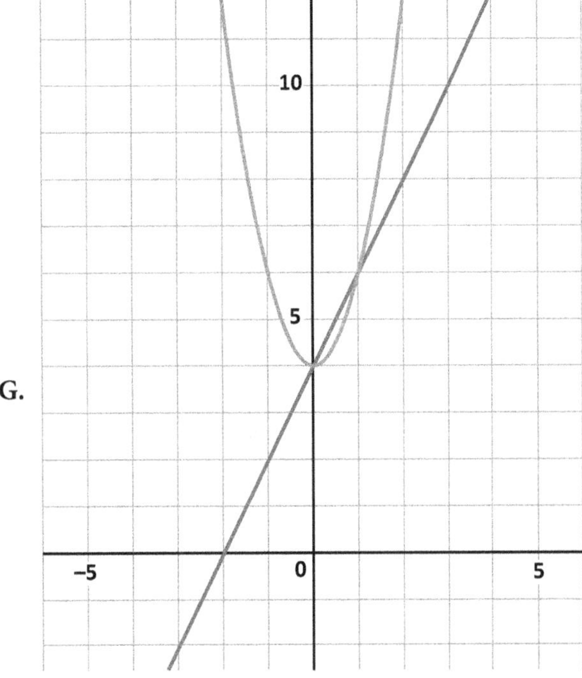

H. 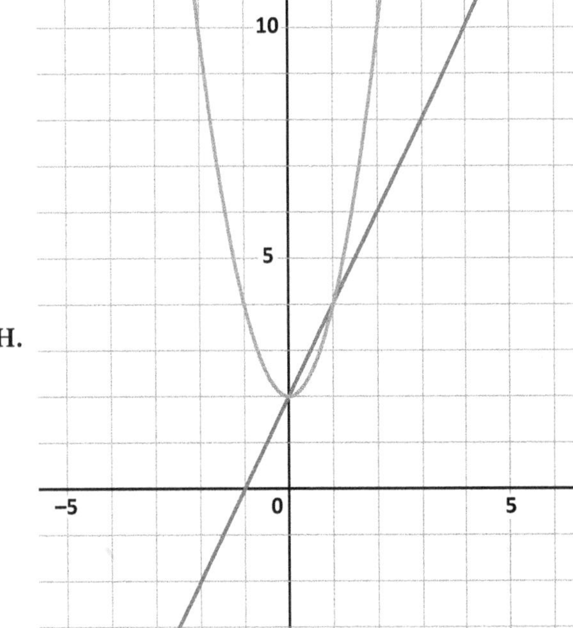

DO YOUR FIGURING HERE.

J. 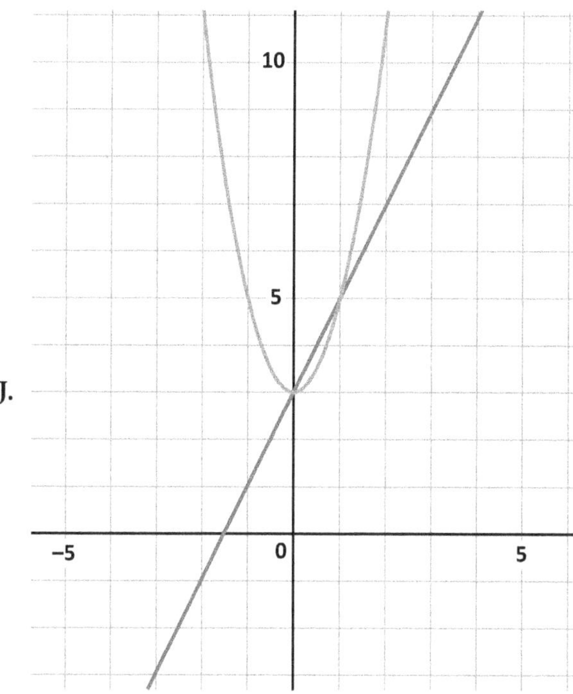

9. Which of the following statements is true for x if $2^{x^2-2x} = 2^3$?

A. $x = 3$ only
B. $x = -1$ only
C. $x = -1$ or 3
D. $x = -3$ only

10. Every 3 minutes you can answer 4 questions on a multiple-choice test. How long will it take to answer an 84 multiple-choice test?

F. 49 minutes
G. 63 minutes
H. 84 minutes
J. 112 minutes

GO ON TO THE NEXT PAGE.

DO YOUR FIGURING HERE.

11. Lance and Andrew left their campsite by raft and paddled downstream at an average speed of 12 km/h. They turned around and paddled back upstream at an average rate of 4 km/h. The total trip took 1 hour. After how much time did the campers turn around downstream?

A. $\frac{1}{5}$ hours

B. $\frac{1}{4}$ hours

C. $\frac{1}{3}$ hours

D. $\frac{1}{2}$ hours

12. Three identical dice are rolled. The probability that the same number will appear on each of them is _______.

F. $\frac{1}{36}$

G. $\frac{3}{36}$

H. $\frac{1}{6}$

J. $\frac{1}{5}$

13. What is the period for the graph of $y = 4\cos\left(\frac{x}{2}\right)$?

A. $\frac{\pi}{2}$

B. π

C. 2π

D. 4π

14. If (4, 3) is a solution to the system, $ax + by = 5$ and $ax - by = 11$ where a and b are constants, then which of the following must be the values for a and b?

F. $a = 4, b = 3$

G. $a = 5, b = 11$

H. $a = 2, b = -1$

J. $a = -1, b = 2$

DO YOUR FIGURING HERE.

15. Which expression is equivalent to $\frac{6xy^2 - 12x^5y}{2xy^3}$?

A. $\frac{3-4x^4}{y}$

B. $\frac{3y-6x^4}{y^2}$

C. $\frac{3x-6x^4}{y}$

D. $3 - 6x^4$

16. C, F, and E lie on the same ray as shown in the diagram below. The ratio of CF to FE is 3:1. Which of the following statements must be true?

C F E

F. FE = 4CE

G. FE = $\frac{1}{3}$CE

H. FE = $\frac{3}{4}$CE

J. CF = $\frac{3}{4}$CE

17. Bacteria is grown in a petri dish. Initially, the petri dish is $\frac{1}{10}$ full of the bacteria. Every hour the bacteria is fed a solution and the amount in the petri dish doubles in value. Which equation represents how full, F, the petri dish is of bacteria where h is time, in hours?

A. $F = \frac{1}{10} + (2)^h$

B. $F = 2 + \frac{1}{10}^h$

C. $\left(2 + \frac{1}{10}\right)^h$

D. $F = \frac{1}{10}(2)^h$

18. Simplify $(3 + 2i)(1 - 4i) + 2i(5i)$ where $i^2 = -1$.

F. $-15 - 10i$

G. $21 + 10i$

H. $21 - 10i$

J. $1 - 10i$

GO ON TO THE NEXT PAGE.

DO YOUR FIGURING HERE.

19. What is a formula for the nth term, a_n, in the sequence of terms {11, 7, 3, −1, …}?

A. $a_n = 15 - 4n$
B. $a_n = 11 - 4n$
C. $a_n = 11(4^n)$
D. $a_n = 11\ (-\ 4^n)$

20. What is the perimeter of ΔABC shown in the figure below?

F. 39.9
G. 45.6
H. 48.1
J. 82.5

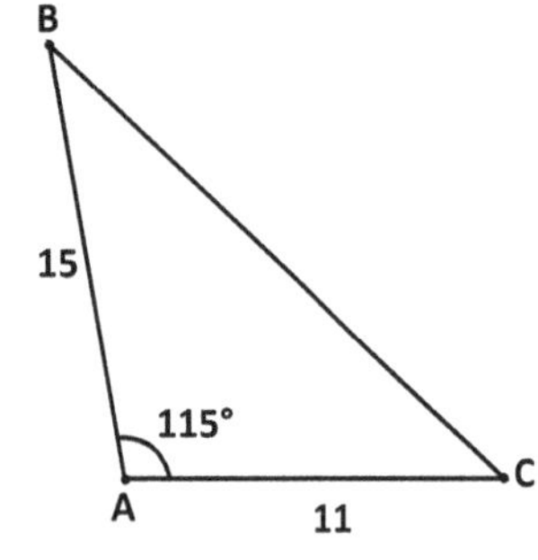

21. The engineer proposed trapezoidal landscape design is shown in the figure below, with dimensions given feet. The trapezoid consists of a right triangle and a square divided into isosceles right triangles. The unshaded regions are covered with white stones, the shaded [art will be black stones.What is the area, in square feet, of the black stones?

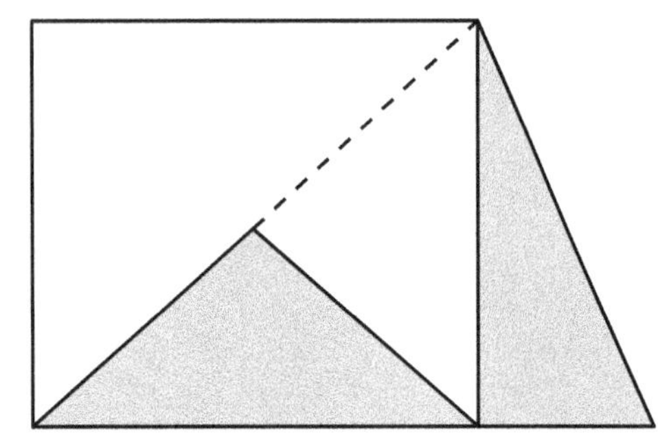

A. 25
B. 30
C. 32
D. 50

DO YOUR FIGURING HERE.

22. A mixture containing 5% of an insecticide is mixed with 3 quarts of another mixture that contains 9% of the same insecticide. How many quarts of the 5% mixture should be used to produce a mixture that is 8% of the insecticide?

F. 1
G. 2
H. 3
J. 4

23. An initial investment of \$10,000 has an amount, A, that is modeled by the function $A = 10{,}000e^{0.08t}$ where t is time in years. Approximately how many years will it take for the initial investment to double in value?

A. 9
B. 15
C. 18
D. 29

24. A circle with center O contains points A, C, D, and E shown below. If $\angle ACE = 82^\circ$, what is the measure, in

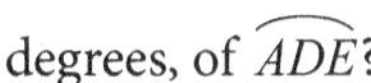

degrees, of $\widehat{ADE}$?

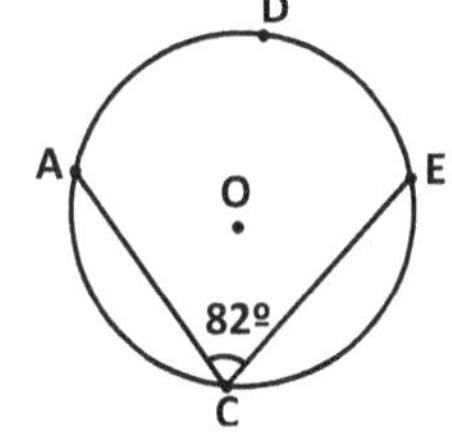

F. 41°
G. 82°
H. 90°
J. 164°

25. Below is the graph of a function in the form $y = ax^2 + c$ where a and c are constants. Which of the following must be true for a and c?

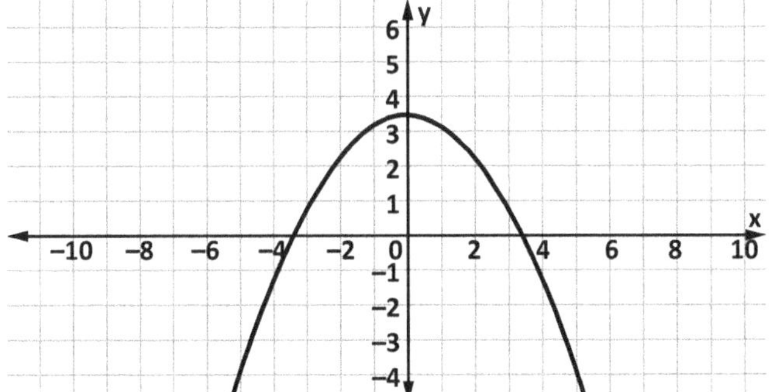

A. $a > 0$ and $c < 0$
B. $a < 0$ and $c > 0$
C. $a > 0$ and $c > 0$
D. $a < 0$ and $c < 0$

GO ON TO THE NEXT PAGE.

DO YOUR FIGURING HERE.

26. Simplify $3x - (y^2 + 2xy) + 4(x - y)$ if $x = 5$ and $y = -2$.

F. -39
G. 43
H. 59
J. 67

27. Ding's Diner advertised this daily lung special: "Choose 1 item from each column - only \$4.95!" Thus, each daily lunch special consists of a salad, a soup, a sandwich, and a drink.

Salad	Soup	Sandwiches	Drinks
Cole slaw Lettuce Potato	Onion Tomato	Meat loaf Chicken Hamburger Ham Tenderloin	Milk Cola Coffee Tea

How many different daily lunch specials are possible?

A. 30
B. 40
C. 120
D. 340

28. The graph of f is transformed to produce the graph of g shown below. Which of the following statements best describes the transformation?

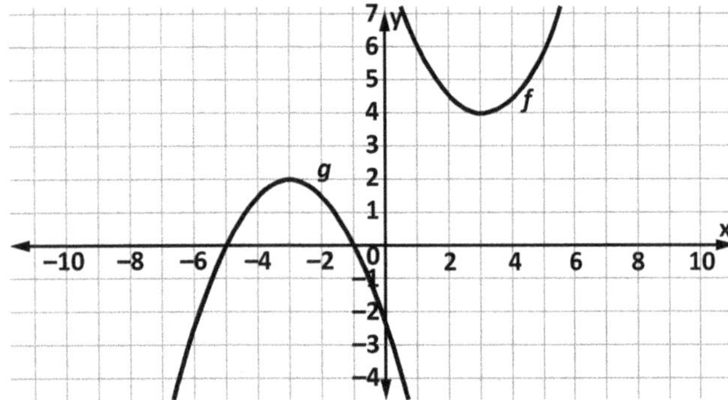

F. The graph of f is reflected across the x-axis, then shifted horizontally to the left 3 units.
G. The graph of f is reflected across the y-axis, then shifted vertically down 2 units.
H. The graph of f is reflected across the y-axis, shifted horizontally to the left 3 units, then shifted vertically up 6 units.
J. The graph of f is reflected across the x-axis, shifted horizontally to the left 6 units, then shifted vertically up 6 units.

DO YOUR FIGURING HERE.

29. Given a and b are positive integers, what is $\frac{40 \times 10^a}{2 \times 10^b}$ expressed in scientific notation?

A. $2 \times 10^{a-b-1}$
B. $2 \times 10^{a+b+1}$
C. $2 \times 10^{a+b-1}$
D. $2 \times 10^{a-b+1}$

30. Which statement is true for the shaded region between $y = -x^2 + 4x + 3$ and $y = x - 4$?

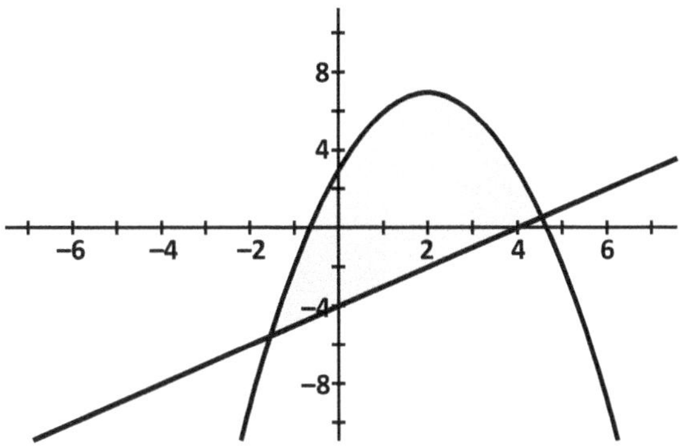

F. $-x^2 - 3x + 7 \leq 0$
G. $-x^2 - 3x + 7 \geq 0$
H. $-x^2 + 3x + 7 \geq 0$
J. $x^2 + 3x - 7 \leq 0$

31. Find the length of $\overline{BC}$ for ΔABC shown below.

A. 12.8
B. 19
C. 21.5
D. 35.9

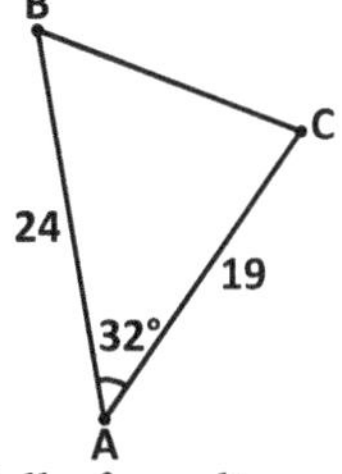

32. Your car's gasoline tank is one-half full of gasoline when you decide to take a trip. You drive and use two-thirds of the remaining gasoline before filling the tank at a gas station. If the tank holds 18 gallons of gasoline full, how much gasoline did you put into the tank?

F. 3
G. 9
H. 15
J. 18

GO ON TO THE NEXT PAGE.

DO YOUR FIGURING HERE.

33. From an airport, a helicopter flies to the roof of a skyscraper. The skyscraper is 125 miles due west and 35 miles due south of the airport. To the nearest mile, how far is the skyscraper from the airport?

A. 100
B. 120
C. 125
D. 130

34. Find two consecutive integers if the sum of four times the smaller integer and three less than the larger integer is 523.

F. 261 and 262
G. 53 and 54
H. 100 and 101
J. 105 and 106

35. If $0 < x < 1$, which expression has the smallest value?

A. x^2
B. $\sqrt{x}$
C. $\frac{x}{2}$
D. $x - x$

36. An applicant must pass a written test and a driving test. Past records show that 80% of the applicants pass the written test and 60% of those who have passed the written test pass the driving test. If there are a total of 1000 , how many applicants would you expect to get a driver's license?

F. 360
G. 420
H. 480
J. 520

37. If $\frac{2p-q}{p+2q} = \frac{8}{9}$, what is the product of p and q?

A. 2
B. 5
C. 7
D. 10

DO YOUR FIGURING HERE.

38. Albert's car averages 25 miles per gallon of gasoline. Gas cost $2.45 per gallon. From an empty gas tank, Albert spends $36.75 to fill the tank. How far can Albert drive in his car before it runs out of gas?

F. 345 miles
G. 375 miles
H. 500 miles
J. 735 miles

39. The Venn diagram below shows the number of students who want to participate in the different extracurricular activities. If a student is randomly chosen, what is the probability that the student participates in athletics or drama?

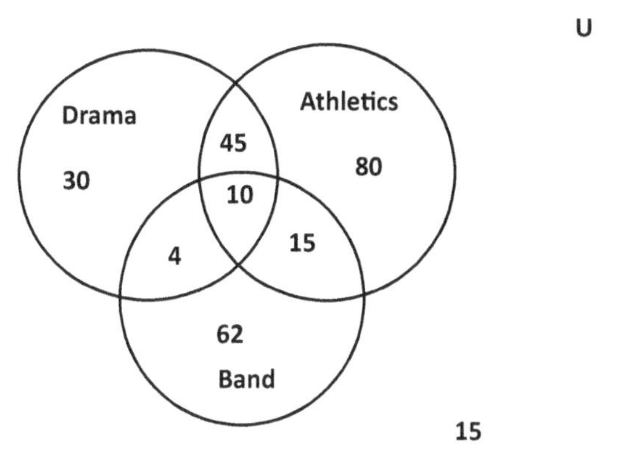

A. 0.50
B. 0.56
C. 0.70
D. 0.75

40. 152 is 8 less than 4 times some number. What must be the number?

F. 19.5
G. 36
H. 40
J. 160

41. Let $p = qr^2 - q$. If $p = 120$ and $q = 8$, $r > 0$, then $r =$?

A. 4
B. 8
C. 16
D. 20

GO ON TO THE NEXT PAGE.

DO YOUR FIGURING HERE.

42. What is the sum of the mode and the median for the set containing $\{5x, 2x, x, 6x, x, 7x, 3x, 10x\}$?

F. $4x$
G. $5x$
H. $6x$
J. $7x$

43. A circular solid metal pipe 6 feet long has a radius of 2 feet. From the center of one end of the circular pipe, a circle is bored out with a drill press all the way through the pipe. The circular bore has a radius of 6 inches. A cross section of the circular pipe and the circular bore is shown below.

After the circle is bored through, what will be the approximate volume, in cubic feet, of metal in the pipe?

A. 24
B. 66
C. 71
D. 75

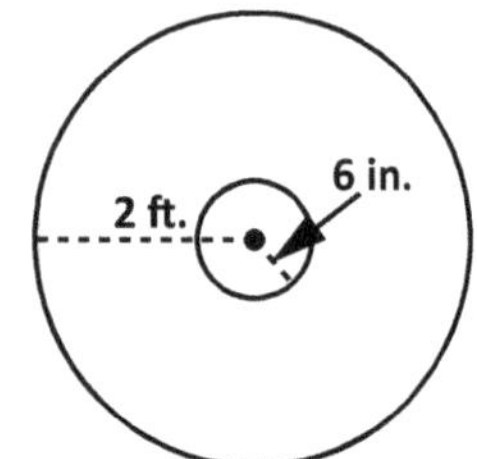

44. If Jonathan increases his caloric intake, he hopes to gain the weight he needs to be able to play football. Below is a table of values for the increase in daily calories each week for a five-week period in Johnathan's diet and the weight he has gained each week. What appears to be the relationship for the weight gained each week in terms of the calories added to his diet?

Increase in Calories	Weight gained (lbs.)
200	0.4
400	0.8
800	1.6
1500	3.0
2000	4.0

F. The relationship is exponential.
G. The relationship is quadratic.
H. The relationship is linear.
J. There is no relationship.

DO YOUR FIGURING HERE.

45. Andrew's drawer has 20 socks in it: 10 white socks, 4 black socks, 4 blue socks, and 2 red socks. If Andrew randomly takes two socks out of the drawer, what is the probability they will be the same color? Round your answer to the nearest thousandth.

A. 0.003
B. 0.100
C. 0.237
D. 0.305

GO ON TO THE NEXT PAGE.

Answer Key

Question	Correct	Make your correct answers
1	B	
2	F	
3	A	
4	H	
5	D	
6	F	
7	A	
8	G	
9	C	
10	G	
11	B	
12	F	
13	D	
14	H	
15	B	
16	J	
17	D	
18	J	
19	A	
20	H	
21	C	
22	F	
23	A	

Question	Correct	Make your correct answers
24	J	
25	B	
26	H	
27	C	
28	J	
29	D	
30	H	
31	A	
32	H	
33	D	
34	J	
35	D	
36	H	
37	D	
38	G	
39	C	
40	H	
41	A	
42	G	
43	C	
44	H	
45	D	

1.

Category: IES
Skill: Sets of numbers | **Level:** Easy

Choice B is correct because Lovely's overall test score for the semester is 83.75.
Identify the lowest test score:
The test scores are: 78, 83, 95, 64, and 79.
The lowest score is 64.

Remove the lowest test score:
After removing 64, the remaining scores are: 78, 83, 95, and 79.

Calculate the average of the remaining test scores:
Add up the remaining scores:

$$78 + 83 + 95 + 79 = 335$$

Divide the sum by the number of remaining test scores (4 scores):

$$\frac{335}{4} = 83.75$$

So, Lovely's overall test score for the semester is 83.75.

Choice A is incorrect because 80.75 is less than the obtained test score. **Choice C** is incorrect because 85.50 is greater than the obtained test score. **Choice D** is incorrect because 90.25 is greater than the obtained test score.

2.

Category: IES & Modeling
Skill: Sets of numbers | **Level:** Easy

Choice F is correct because the Venn diagram that illustrates the given information is

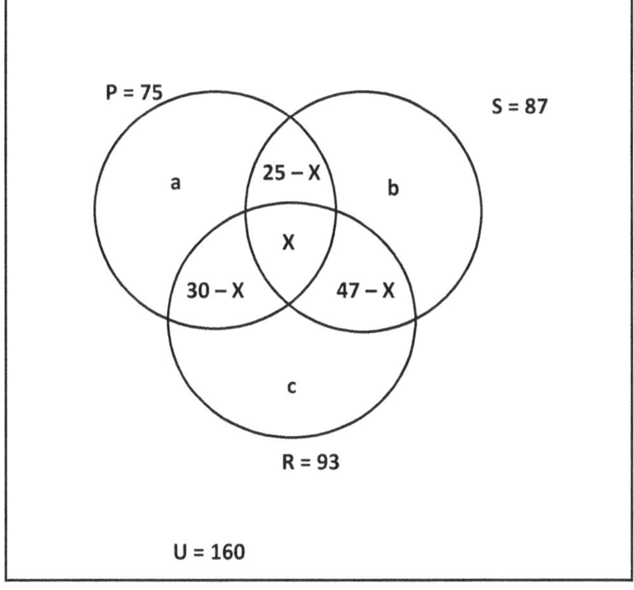

Analyze the given data.
75 pupils have pencils,
87 have sharpeners,
93 have rulers
25 have both pencils and sharpeners,
30 have both pencils and rulers while
47 have both sharpeners and rulers.
Each pupil has at least one of the three items.
There are a total of 160 pupils.

Make a Venn diagram.

Let P stands for pencils, S for sharpeners, R for rulers, U be the total number of pupils.

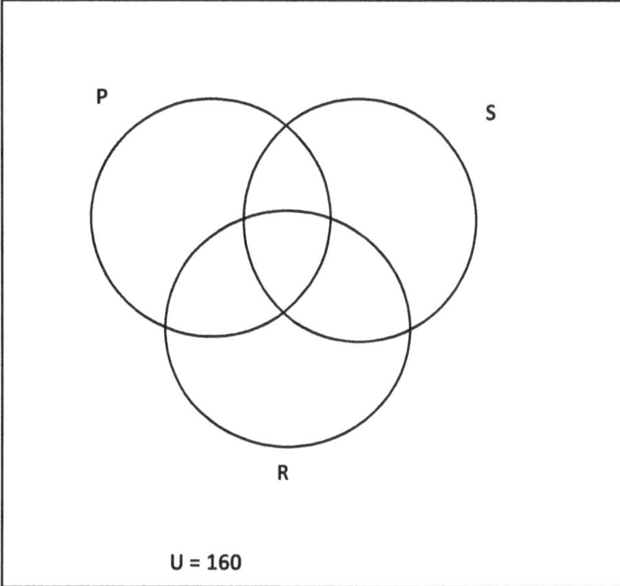

Label the given information.

P	75 pupils have pencils,
S	87 have sharpeners,
R	93 have rulers
(*P and S only*)	25 have both pencils and sharpeners,
(*P and R only*)	30 have both pencils and rulers while
(*S and R only*)	47 have both sharpeners and rulers.
	Each pupil has at least one of the three items.
U	There are a total of 160 pupils.

Let x be $(P \cap R \cap S)$, let a be P only, b be S only and c be R only.

Follow the Venn diagram below and draw the Venn diagram that represents the problem.

GO ON TO THE NEXT PAGE.

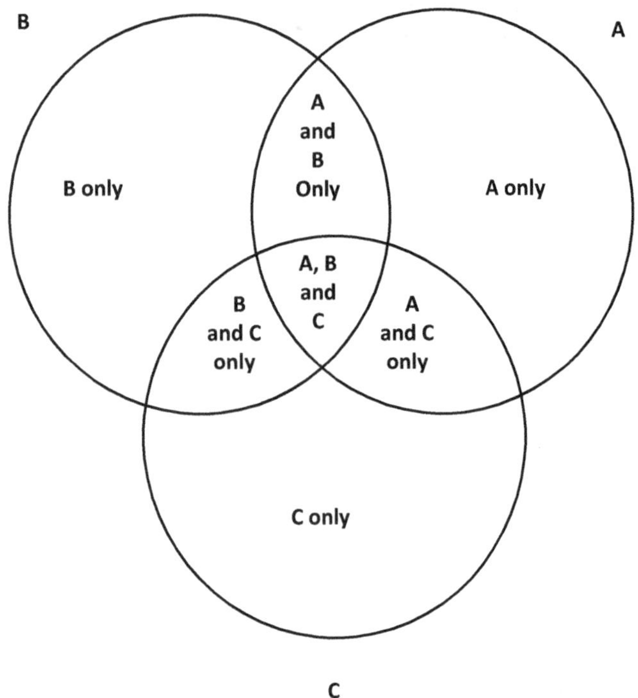

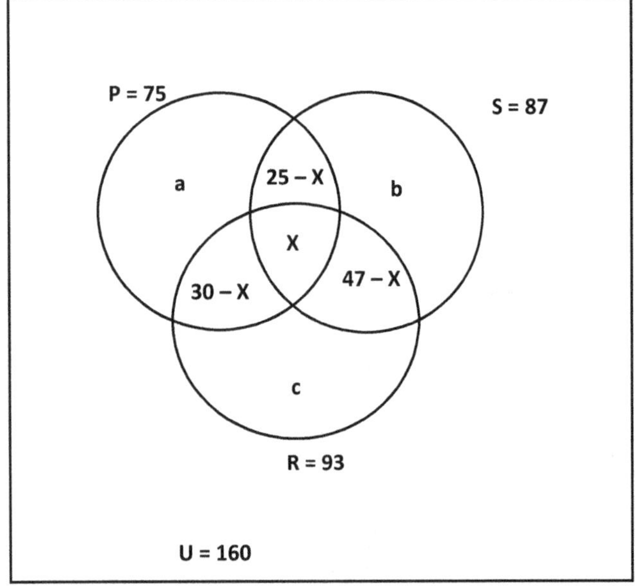

Choice G is incorrect because does not represent the given information. **Choice H** is incorrect because does not represent the given information. **Choice J** is incorrect because does not represent the given information.

3.

Category: PHM & Modeling
Skill: Sets of numbers | **Level:** Medium

Choice A is correct. Let x be her homework average, then $0.5 \times 86 + 0.3 \times 88 + 0.2x = 85$. Solving for x,

$$\begin{aligned} 0.5 \times 86 + 0.3 \times 88 + 0.2x &= 85 \\ 43 + 26.4 + 0.2x &= 85 \\ 69.4 + 0.2x &= 85 \\ 0.2x &= 15.6 \\ x &= 78 \end{aligned}$$

Choice B is incorrect. This equally weighs the test, quiz, and homework average. **Choice C** is incorrect. This is her assumed grade for her statistics class. **Choice D** is incorrect. This equally weighs the test, quiz, and homework average.

4.

Category: PHM
Skill: Lines and angles | **Level:** Medium

Choice H is correct. The exterior angle for a triangle is the sum of its two remote interior angles. Angle *BAE* is an exterior angle for the triangle and angles B and C are its remote interior angles.

So,

$$\begin{aligned} \angle BAE &= \angle B + \angle C \\ 142 &= 85 + \angle C \\ \angle C &= 57 \end{aligned}$$

Choice F is incorrect. This is the measure of $\angle BAC$. **Choice G** is incorrect. This may be due to calculation error. **Choice J** is incorrect. This may be due to calculation error.

5.

Category: PHM
Skill: Equations | **Level:** Medium

Choice D is correct. $16x^2 - 49$ is a difference of two perfect squares that can be factored using $a^2 - b^2 = (a-b)(a+b)$ where $a = 4x$ and $b = 7$ so,

$$16x^2 - 49 = (4x-7)(4x+7).$$

Choice A is incorrect. This is not a factor of the given expression. **Choice B** is incorrect. This is not a factor of the given expression. **Choice C** is incorrect. This is not a factor of the given expression.

6.

Category: PHM
Skill: Matrices | **Level:** Easy

Choice F is correct. To add matrices, add the corresponding elements to get

GO ON TO THE NEXT PAGE.

$$\begin{bmatrix} 2 & 4 \\ 6 & 8 \end{bmatrix} + \begin{bmatrix} 1 & 3 \\ 5 & 7 \end{bmatrix} = \begin{bmatrix} 2+1 & 4+3 \\ 6+5 & 8+7 \end{bmatrix} = \begin{bmatrix} 3 & 7 \\ 11 & 15 \end{bmatrix}$$

Choice G is incorrect. The 3rd position is a miscalculation. **Choice H** is incorrect. The 4th position is a miscalculation. **Choice J** is incorrect. This may be due to calculation error.

7.

Category: IES
Skill: Equations | **Level:** Hard

Choice A is correct. Let x be the number of ounces of frozen peas, then the total cost of peas is $0.03x$. The total cost of frozen carrots is $0.06 \times 14 = 0.84$. The total cost for the mixture of peas and carrots is $0.05(x + 14)$.

Adding the frozen peas and carrots to get the mixture you have,

$$0.03x + 0.84 = 0.05(x + 14)$$
$$3x + 84 = 5(x + 14)$$
$$3x + 84 = 5x + 70$$
$$-2x = -14$$
$$x = 7$$

7 ounces of frozen peas need to be added.

Choice B is incorrect. This is twice the ounce of frozen peas that need to be added. **Choice C** is incorrect. This may result from calculation error. **Choice D** is incorrect. This is 4 times the ounce of frozen peas that need to be added.

8.

Category: IES & Modeling
Skill: Equations | **Level:** Hard

Choice G is correct because the graph represents the given linear and quadratic equations.
Given: $y = 2x + 4$ and $y = 2x^2 + 4$

Find the point of intersection of the given equations.

$$y = y$$
$$2x + 4 = 2x^2 + 4$$
$$0 = 2x^2 - 2x + 4 - 4$$
$$0 = 2x^2 - 2x$$
$$0 = 2x(x - 1)$$
$$2x = 0 \qquad (x - 1) = 0$$
$$x = 0 \qquad x = 1$$

Substitute the obtained values of x to obtain y.

When $x = 0$, $\quad y = 2x + 4$
$y = 2(0) + 4$
$y = 4$

When $x = 1$, $\quad y = 2x + 4$
$y = 2(1) + 4$
$y = 6$

Looking at the graphs in the choices, Choice B has intersection at $(0, 4)$ *and* $(1, 6)$.

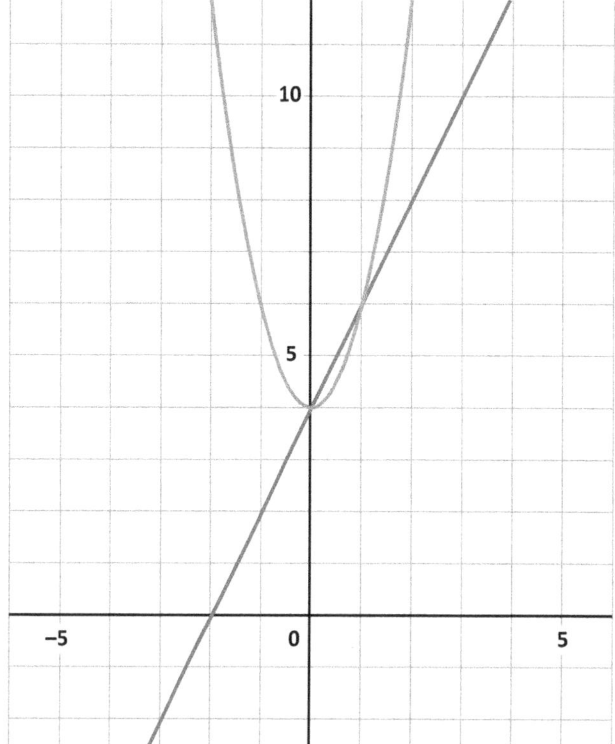

Choice F is incorrect because the graph did not represent the given linear and quadratic equations. **Choice H** is incorrect because the graph did not represent the given linear and quadratic equations. **Choice J** is incorrect because the graph did not represent the given linear and quadratic equations.

9.

Category: PHM
Skill: Equations | **Level:** Easy

Choice C is correct. Using the one-to-one property for exponential equations you have,

$$x^2 - 2x = 3$$
$$x^2 - 2x - 3 = 0$$
$$(x + 1)(x - 3) = 0$$
$$x + 1 = 0 \text{ or } x - 3 = 0$$
$$x = -1 \text{ or } x = 3$$

GO ON TO THE NEXT PAGE.

Choice A is incorrect. 3 is not the only solution. $x = -1$ also satisfies the equation. **Choice B** is incorrect. -1 is not the only solution. $x = 3$ also satisfies the equation. **Choice D** is incorrect. Substituting $x = -3$ into the exponent 2^{x^2-2x} yields 2^{15} which is not equal to 2^3.

10.

Category: IES
Skill: Scientific notation | **Level:** Medium

Choice G is correct. Simplifying the ratio $\frac{3 \text{ minutes}}{4 \text{ questions}}$ you can answer $\frac{\frac{3}{4}\text{minutes}}{1 \text{ questions}}$ which is $\frac{3}{4}$ minutes per questions. In 84 questions, you will take $84 \times \frac{3}{4} = 63$ minutes.

Choice F is incorrect. This can answer 65 questions
Choice H is incorrect. This can answer 112 questions
Choice J is incorrect. This can answer 149 questions

11.

Category: IES
Skill: Equations | **Level:** Medium

Choice B is correct because the obtained answer is $\frac{1}{4}$ hours.

Downstream : Rate : 12 km/h
Time = t
Distance = 12 t

Upstream: Rate : 4 km/h
Time = (1-t)
Distance = 4 (1-t)

Find t.
Distance Downstream = Distance Upstream

$$12t = 4(1-t)$$
$$12t = 4 - 4t$$
$$12t + 4t = 4$$
$$16t = 4$$
$$t = \frac{1}{4} \text{ hours}$$

Choice A is incorrect because $\frac{1}{5}$ hours is greater than the obtained time. **Choice C** is incorrect because $\frac{1}{3}$ hours is greater than the obtained time. **Choice D** is incorrect because $\frac{1}{2}$ hour is less than the obtained time.

12.

Category: IES
Skill: Probability | **Level:** Medium

Choice F is correct because the obtained answer is $\frac{1}{36}$.

Total outcome when a dice is rolled 3 times
$= 6 \times 6 \times 6 = 216$

Probability that outcomes have the same number = 6

Probability $= \frac{6}{216} = \frac{1}{36}$

Choice G is incorrect because $\frac{3}{36}$ is not the obtained probability. **Choice H** is incorrect because $\frac{1}{6}$ is not the obtained probability. **Choice J** is incorrect because $\frac{1}{5}$ is not the obtained probability.

13.

Category: PHM
Skill: Trigonometry | **Level:** Medium

Choice D is correct. For the graph of the function in the form $y = a\cos(bx)$, the period is $\frac{2\pi}{|b|}$.

For $y = 4\cos\left(\frac{x}{2}\right)$, $b = \frac{1}{2}$. So, the period is

$$\frac{2\pi}{\left|\frac{1}{2}\right|} = 2\pi \cdot \frac{2}{1} = 4\pi.$$

Choice A is incorrect. This may be due to conceptual error. **Choice B** is incorrect. This may be due to conceptual error. **Choice C** is incorrect. This is half the period.

14.

Category: PHM
Skill: System of equations | **Level:** Medium

Choice H is correct. Substitute $x = 4$ and $y = 3$ into the system to find a and b.

$$4a + 3b = 5$$
$$+(4a - 3b = 11)$$
$$8a = 16$$
$$a = 2$$

Substituting a=2 into the 1st equation you get, $4(2) + 3b = 5$ then, $b = -1$.

Choice F is incorrect. Uses the given solution for the values of a and b. **Choice G** is incorrect. Uses the solutions for the 2 equations written in terms of a and b. **Choice J** is incorrect. Reverses the correct values for a and b.

GO ON TO THE NEXT PAGE.

15.
Category: PHM
Skill: Equations | **Level:** Medium

Choice B is correct. The GCF in the numerator and denominator is $2xy$. Simplifying you get,

$$\frac{6xy^2 - 12x^5y}{2xy^3} = \frac{\cancel{2xy}(3y - 6x^4)}{\cancel{2xy}(y^2)} = \frac{3y - 6x^4}{y^2}$$

Choice A is incorrect. $6xy^2$ and $2xy^3$ are reduced by 2 but $12x^5 y$ is reduced by 3. **Choice C** is incorrect. $6xy^2$ and $2xy^3$ have a common factor of y^2 but $12x^5 y$ does not when the expression is simplified. **Choice D** is incorrect. This may result from calculation error.

16.
Category: IES
Skill: Number line and absolute value | **Level:** Medium

Choice J is correct. Since CF is 3 parts of CE and FE is 1 part of CE so, CF is three-fourths of CE and FE is one-fourth of CE. This correlates to option D, CF = ¾CE

Choice F is incorrect. FE is one-fourth of CE. **Choice G** is incorrect. FE is one-fourth of CE. **Choice H** is incorrect. FE is one-fourth of CE.

17.
Category: PHM
Skill: Equations | **Level:** Medium

Choice D is correct. Since the bacteria is doubling in value, F can be represented by an exponential function, $F = P(a)^h$ where P is the initial amount, h is the time, in hours, it takes for P to grow by a. Substituting $P = \frac{1}{10}$, $a = 2$, you get $F = \frac{1}{10}(2)^h$.

Choice A is incorrect. This may result from wrong use of formula in calculation. **Choice B** is incorrect. This may result from wrong use of formula in calculation. **Choice C** is incorrect. This may result from wrong use of formula in calculation.

18.
Category: PHM
Skill: Real and complex number systems | **Level:** Easy

Choice J is correct. $(3 + 2i)(1 - 4i) + 2i(5i) = 3 - 10i - 8i^2 + 10i^2 = 3 - 10i + 8 - 10 = 1 - 10i$.

Choice F is incorrect. This converts $-8i^2$ to -8 when simplifying. **Choice G** is incorrect. This converts $10i^2$ to 10 when simplifying. **Choice H** is incorrect. This converts $10i^2$ to 10 when simplifying.

19.
Category: PHM
Skill: Series, sequences and consecutive numbers | **Level:** Medium

Choice A is correct. The common difference, d, of the sequence is $7 - 11 = 3 - 7 = -1 - 3 = -4$. Using $a_n = a_1 + d(n - 1)$ you get $a_n = 11 - 4(n - 1) = 11 - 4n + 4 = 15 - 4n$.

Choice B is incorrect. This uses $a_n = a_1 + d(n)$ as the nth term. **Choice C** is incorrect. This appears to be geometric sequences. **Choice D** is incorrect. This appears to be geometric sequences.

20.
Category: IES & Modeling
Skill: Two-dimensional shapes | **Level:** Hard

Choice H is correct. Since SAS (side included angle and side) are given, the law of cosines can be used to find the remaining side. Let a be the side opposite angle A, $b = 11$ and $c = 15$ for $a^2 = b^2 + c^2 - 2bc\cos A$,

$$a^2 = 11^2 + 15^2 - 2(11)(15)\cos(115)$$
$$a^2 = 121 + 225 - 330\cos(115)$$
$$a^2 = 485.46$$
$$a = 22.1$$

So, the perimeter is 11 + 15 + 22.1 = 48.1.

Choice F is incorrect. This uses the law of cosines by using *sin*115° formula instead of *cos*115° **Choice G** is incorrect. This assumes a is the hypotenuse for a right triangle. **Choice J** is incorrect. This assumes ABC is a right triangle and finds the area using sides 11 and 15.

21.
Category: IES & Modeling
Skill: Two-dimensional shapes | **Level:** Hard

Choice C is correct because the obtained answer is 32.

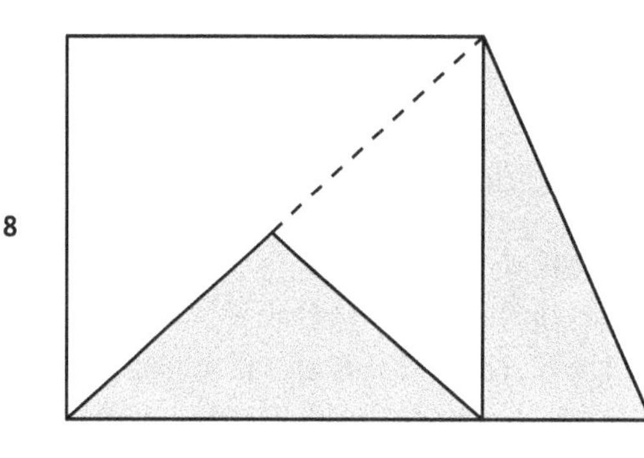

The black stones are composed of two triangles. To find its area, use the formula for the area of triangles.

$$A_{total} = A_{triangle\,1} + A_{triangle\,2}$$
$$A_{total} = \frac{1}{2}bh + \frac{1}{2}bh$$
$$A_{total} = \frac{1}{2}(8\times 4) + \frac{1}{2}(12-8)(8)$$
$$A_{total} = \frac{1}{2}(32) + \frac{1}{2}(32)$$
$$A_{total} = \frac{1}{2}(32) + \frac{1}{2}(32)$$
$$A_{total} = 32$$

Choice A is incorrect because 25 is less than the obtained area of the black stone. **Choice B** is incorrect because 30 is less than the obtained area of the black stone. **Choice D** is incorrect because 50 is greater than the obtained area of the black stone.

22.
Category: IES
Skill: Number line and absolute value | **Level:** Hard

Choice F is correct Let x be the number of quarts that contain the 5% insecticide mixture, then the % mixture contains $0.05x$ quarts of insecticide. The 9% mixture contains $0.09 \times 3 = 0.27$ quarts of insecticide. The 8% mixture contains $0.08(x + 3)$ quarts of insecticide. Combining the 5% and (5 mixtures to produce the 8% mixture you get,

$$0.05x + 0.27 = 0.08(x+3)$$
$$5x + 27 = 8(x+3)$$
$$5x + 27 = 8x + 24$$
$$-3x = -3$$
$$x = 1$$

So, 1 quart is needed to produce a mixture that is 8% insecticide.

Choice G is incorrect. This may result from calculation error. **Choice H** is incorrect. This may result from calculation error. **Choice J** is incorrect.This may result from calculation error.

23.
Category: PHM
Skill: Function evaluation | **Level:** Medium

Choice A is correct You can use the rule of 72, $\frac{72}{r}$ where r is the interest rate, to approximate the time an investment will double in value. The given equation is the continuous compounded amount. $A = Pe^{rt}$ where r the interest rate. Be careful to state the interest rate as a standard number, not in its decimal form when using the rule of 72. So, $r = 0.08 = 8\%$ and the investment will double in approximately $\frac{72}{8} = 9$ years.

Choice B is incorrect. This may result if the rate is 4.8.
Choice C is incorrect. This may result if the rate is 4.
Choice D is incorrect. This may result if the rate is 3.6.

24.
Category: PHM
Skill: Lines and angles | **Level:** Easy

Choice J is correct. The measure of an inscribed angle is one-half the measure of the arc it inscribes in a circle. In the diagram, $\angle ACE$ inscribes $\overset{\frown}{ADE}$ then,

$$\angle ACE = \frac{1}{2}\overset{\frown}{ADE}$$
$$82 = \frac{1}{2}\overset{\frown}{ADE}$$
$$\overset{\frown}{ADE} = 164^\circ$$

Choice F is incorrect. This is half of the inscribed angle.
Choice G is incorrect. This is the measure of $\angle$ACE.
Choice H is incorrect. A common distractor. 90° is often mistakenly chosen when dealing with semicircles or perpendicular diameters.

25.
Category: PHM
Skill: Graphed functions | **Level:** Medium

Choice B is correct. The graph of the function in the form $f(x) = ax^2 + c$ is a parabola that opens up if $a > 0$ and opens down if $a < 0$. Additionally, c is the y-intercept. Since the graph opens down, $a < 0$, and since the y-intercept is 3.5, $c > 0$.

Choice A is incorrect. This shows a parabola that opens up and the y-intercept is less than 0. **Choice C** is incorrect. This shows a parabola that opens up. **Choice D** is incorrect. This shows the y-intercept is less than 0

26.
Category: PHM
Skill: Equations | **Level:** Easy

Choice H is correct. Substituting the values for x and y and simplifying you get, $3(5) - ((-2)^2 + 2 \times 5 \times (-2)) + 4(5 - (-2)) = 15 - (4 - 20) + 4(7) = 15 + 16 + 28 = 59$.

Choice F is incorrect. This switches x and y when evaluating the expression. **Choice G** is incorrect. This evaluates $(x - y)$ as $(5 - 2)$. **Choice J** is incorrect. This evaluates $y^2 + 2xy$ as $(-4 - 20)$.

GO ON TO THE NEXT PAGE.

27.
Category: IES & Modeling
Skill: Number line and absolute value | **Level:** Hard

Choice C is correct because the obtained answer is 120.

Give:

Salads: 3 choices (Cole slaw, Lettuce, Potato)

Soups: 2 choices (Onion, Tomato)

Sandwiches: 5 choices (Meat loaf, Chicken, Hamburger, Ham, Tenderloin)

Drinks: 4 choices (Milk, Cola, Coffee, Tea)

Total Combinations:

Total Specials = (Number of Salads) × (Number of Soups) × (Number of Sandwiches) × (Number of Drinks)

Substitute the values:

Total Specials = 3 × 2 × 5 × 4 = 120

There are 120 different daily lunch specials possible.

Choice A is incorrect because 30 is less than the obtained answer. **Choice B** is incorrect because 40 is less than the obtained answer. **Choice D** is incorrect because 340 is greater than the obtained answer.

28.
Category: PHM & Modeling
Skill: Two-dimensional shapes | **Level:** Medium

Choice J is correct. Let's focus on transforming the vertex for the graph of *f* to the graph of *g*. Reflecting the graph of *f* across the *x*-axis first moves the vertex of the graph to (3, –4). Next shifting the graph transformed graph of *f* to the left 6 units moves the vertex to (–3, –4). Finally, shifting the transformed graph of *f* up 6 units takes the vertex to (–3, 2) which is the vertex for the graph of *g*.

Choice F is incorrect because after reflecting across the *x*-axis, the horizontal shift of only 3 units does not bring the vertex to its new location. **Choice G** is incorrect because the graph is reflected across the *x*-axis, not the *y*-axis. **Choice H** is incorrect because the reflection is across the wrong axis.

29.
Category: IES
Skill: Scientific notation | **Level:** Hard

Choice D is correct because the obtained answer is $2\times10^{a-b+1}$.

$$\frac{40\times10^{a}}{2\times10^{b}}=20\times10^{a-b}$$
$$=(2\times10)\times10^{a-b}$$
$$=(2\times10^{1})\times10^{a-b}$$
$$=2\times10^{a-b+1}$$

Choice A is incorrect because $2\times10^{a-b-1}$ does not represent the scientific notation of the given expression. **Choice B** is incorrect because $2\times10^{a+b+1}$ does not represent the scientific notation of the given expression. **Choice C** is incorrect because $2\times10^{a+b-1}$ does not represent the scientific notation of the given expression.

30.
Category: PHM
Skill: Coordinate geometry | **Level:** Medium

Choice H is correct. For the shaded region, the graph of the parabola lies above the line, so the *y* values for the parabola will be greater than the *y* values for the line. Since $y=-x^2+4x+3$ and $y = x - 4$ you get,

$$-x^2+4x+3\geq x-4$$
$$-x^2+3x+7\geq 0$$

Choice F is incorrect. The sign of the linear term is 3 not −3 and inequality is flipped. **Choice G** is incorrect. The sign of the linear term is 3 not −3. **Choice J** is incorrect. The sign of the quadratic and constant term is wrong and inequality is flipped.

31.
Category: IES
Skill: Two-dimensional shapes | **Level:** Hard

Choice A is correct. Since you are given two sides and an included angle for the triangle, you can use the law of cosines to find the side opposite the included angle, $\overline{BC}$. Now,

$$\overline{BC}^2=19^2+24^2-2(19)(24)\cos 32^\circ$$
$$\overline{BC}^2=361+576-773.42$$
$$\overline{BC}^2=163.58$$
$$\overline{BC}=12.8$$

Choice B is incorrect. This assumes ΔABC is an isosceles triangle where $\overline{BC}=\overline{AC}$. **Choice C** is incorrect. This incorrectly uses the law of sines to find $\overline{BC}$. **Choice D** is incorrect. This assumes angle C is a right angle, so the Pythagorean Theorem was used to find $\overline{BC}$.

GO ON TO THE NEXT PAGE.

32.
Category: PHM
Skill: Scientific notation | **Level:** Medium

Choice H is correct. You have $\frac{1}{2}\times 18 = 9$ gallons of gasoline when you decide to take a trip. You have $\frac{1}{3}\times 9 = 3$ gallons of gasoline left in the tank when you are at the gas station, so you will need to put 18 – 3 = 15 gallons of gasoline to fill the car.

Choice F is incorrect. This appears to only calculate the amount of gasoline you have left in the tank when you are at the gas station. **Choice G** is incorrect. This is the amount of gasoline left when you decide to take a trip. **Choice J** is incorrect. This is the amount of gasoline for a full tank.

33.
Category: IES
Skill: Two-dimensional shapes | **Level:** Medium

Choice D is correct. The distances form a right angle with the legs being 125 miles and 35 miles. The hypotenuse, *c*, is the distance of the skyscraper from the airport in miles. Then,

$$c^2 = 125^2 + 35^2$$
$$c^2 = 15,625 + 1225$$
$$c^2 = 16,850$$
$$c = 129.808$$
$$c \approx 130$$

Choice A is incorrect. This may result from calculation error **Choice B** is incorrect. This may result from calculation error **Choice C** is incorrect. This is the length of one of the legs of the triangle.

34.
Category: PHM
Skill: Series, sequences and consecutive numbers |
Level: Medium

Choice J is correct. Let *n* be the smaller integer. Then, *n* + 1 is the larger, consecutive (next) integer. Then, $4n+[(n+1)-3]=523$. Solving for *n*,

$$4n+[(n+1)-3]=523$$
$$5n-2=523$$
$$5n=525$$
$$n=105$$

So, the consecutive integers are 105 and 106.

Choice F is incorrect. Substituting 261 for *n* yields 1303 ≠ 523, which is too large. **Choice G** is incorrect. Substituting 53 for *n* yields 263 ≠ 523, which is too low. **Choice H** is incorrect. Substituting 100 for *n* yields 498 ≠ 523, which is too low.

35.
Category: PHM
Skill: Real and complex number systems |
Level: Medium

Choice D is correct. Choose a number between 0 and 1 and substitute it into the choices to see which has the smallest value. Let $x = \frac{1}{2}$ then, $x^2 = \left(\frac{1}{2}\right)^2 = \frac{1}{4} > 0$, $\sqrt{x} = \sqrt{\frac{1}{2}} > 0$, $\frac{x}{2} = \frac{\frac{1}{2}}{2} = \frac{1}{4} > 0$, $x - x = \frac{1}{2} - \frac{1}{2} = 0$, and $x = \frac{1}{2} > 0$. So, **choice D** is the smallest value.

Choice A is incorrect. Based on the explanation above, its value is greater than 0. **Choice B** is incorrect. Based on the explanation above, its value is greater than 0. **Choice C** is incorrect. Based on the explanation above, its value is greater than 0.

36.
Category: IES
Skill: Probability | **Level:** Easy

Choice H is correct because the obtained value is 480.

Total participants = 1000

Number of participants who pass the written test;

80% of the participants = 0.8*1000 = 800

60 % of those who pass = 0.6*800 = 480

Choice F is incorrect because 360 is less than the obtained value. **Choice G** is incorrect because 420 is less than the obtained value. **Choice J** is incorrect because 520 is greater than the obtained value.

37.
Category: PHM
Skill: Equations | **Level:** Medium

Choice D is correct. Setting the numerators and denominators equal gives you the system of equations,

$$2p - q = 8$$
$$p + 2q = 9$$

Multiply the first equation by 2 and use the elimination method to find *p*,

GO ON TO THE NEXT PAGE.

$$2(2p-q=8)$$
$$p+2q=9$$
$$4p-2q=16$$
$$p+2q=9$$
$$5p=25$$
$$p=5$$

Substituting p = 5 into the first equation you get,

$$2(5)-q=8$$
$$10-q=8$$
$$q=2$$

The product of p and q is $5\times2=10$.

Choice A is incorrect. This is the value of q. **Choice B** is incorrect. This is the value of p. **Choice C** is incorrect. This is the value of $q + p$.

38.
Category: IES & Modeling
Skill: Sets of numbers | **Level:** Hard

Choice G is correct. To find how many gallons of gas the gas tank can hold, divide the cost to fill the tank by the cost per gallon of gas. So, there are $\frac{36.75}{2.45}=15$ gallons of gas in the gas tank when it is filled. Next, to determine how far Albert can travel in the car before running out of gas, multiply the number of gallons in the gas tank by the miles per gallon the car averages to get, $15\times25=375$ miles.

Choice F is incorrect. This may result if the gas tank can hold 13.8 gallons of gas. **Choice H** is incorrect. This may result if the gas tank can hold 20 gallons of gas. **Choice J** is incorrect. This may result if the gas tank can hold 29.4 gallons of gas.

39.
Category: IES & Modeling
Skill: Sets of numbers | **Level:** Hard

Choice C is correct because te obtained answer is 0.70.

Find the total number of students.

30 + 45 + 10 + 4 + 80 + 15 + 62 + 15 = 261

Find the number of student who participates in athletics or drama.

30 + 45 + 10 + 4 + 80 + 15 = 184

Find the probability of student who participates in athletics or drama.

$$Probability=\frac{No.of\ favourable\,outcome}{Total\,number\ of\ outcome}$$
$$Probability=\frac{184}{261}$$
$$Probability=0.70$$

Choice A is incorrect because 0.50 is less than the obtained probability. **Choice B** is incorrect because 0.56 is less than the obtained probability. **Choice D** is incorrect because 0.75 is greater than the obtained probability.

40.
Category: PHM
Skill: Real and Complex number systems |
Level: Medium

Choice H is correct. Let x be the number then,
$152 = 4x - 8$
$160 = 4x$
$x = 40$

Choice F is incorrect. Uses $8x - 4$ when solving for x.
Choice G is incorrect. Uses $8 - 4x$ when solving for x.
Choice J is incorrect. This is the value of $4x$.

41.
Category: PHM
Skill: Real and Complex number systems |
Level: Easy

Choice A is correct Substituting p and q and solving for r,

$$120=8r^2-8$$
$$128=8r^2$$
$$16=r^2$$
$$\pm4=r$$

So, $r = 4$ only since r must be greater than 0.

Choice B is incorrect. This is the value of q. **Choice C** is incorrect. This is the value of $2q$. **Choice D** is incorrect. This is the value of $2q + r$.

42.
Category: PHM
Skill: Sets of numbers | **Level:** Medium

Choice G is correct. Ordering the values in the set you have, $\{x, x, 2x, 3x, 5x, 6x, 7x, 10x\}$. The mode is the value that occurs most often, x. Since there are an even number of values in the set, the median is the average of the 2 most "middle" values, $3x$ and $5x$. So, the median is $4x$. The sum of the median and mode is $x + 4x = 5x$.

GO ON TO THE NEXT PAGE.

Choice F is incorrect. This is the median. **Choice H** is incorrect. This uses $5x$ as the median when finding the sum of the mode and median. **Choice J** is incorrect. This uses $6x$ as the median when finding the sum of the mode and median.

43.
Category: IES & Modeling
Skill: Three-dimensional shapes | **Level:** Hard

Choice C is correct You need to subtract the volume of the right circular cylinder created from boring a hole in the center of the metal pipe from the volume of the right circular cylinder that is the metal pipe. The volume, V_m of the metal pipe is $V_m = \pi(2)^2 \cdot 6 = 24\pi$ cubic feet, and the volume, V_b, of the hole in the metal pipe is $V_b = \pi(0.5)^2 \cdot 6 = 1.5\pi$ cubic feet. So, $V_m - V_b = 24\pi - 1.5\pi = 70.69$ or 71 cubic feet.

Choice A is incorrect. This may result from $(2)^2 \cdot 6$. **Choice B** is incorrect. This may result from using incorrect formulas. **Choice D** is incorrect. This is the volume of the metal pipe.

44.
Category: PHM & Modeling
Skill: Function Evaluation | **Level:** Medium

Choice H is correct. The relationship between the weight Johnathan gained and the increase in calories is linear. The difference between any 2 values of weight gained divided by the difference between any 2-corresponding increase in calories is 0.002. For example, $\frac{0.8-0.4}{400-200} = 0.002$.

Choice F is incorrect. The relationship is linear and not exponential. **Choice G** is incorrect. The relationship is linear and not quadratic. **Choice J** is incorrect. There is a relationship between the weight gained and the increase in calories.

45.
Category: IES
Skill: Probability | **Level:** Hard

Choice D is correct because the obtained answer is 0.305

Given:

20 socks where 10 are white, 4 black, 4 blue,2 red socks

To find the probability, find the favorable outcomes as well as the total outcomes.

$$Probability = \frac{Favorable\ outcome}{Total\ outcome}$$

Total outcomes is the number of ways to choose 2 socks from 20 socks.

$$\binom{n}{r} = \frac{n!}{r!(n-r)!} = \frac{20!}{2!(20-2)!} = \frac{20!}{2!(18)!} = 190$$

Find the favorable outcome. The probability that the socks will be the same color.

White socks: $= \frac{10!}{2!(10-2)!} = \frac{10!}{2!(8)!} = 45$

Black socks: $= \frac{4!}{2!(4-2)!} = \frac{4!}{2!(2)!} = 6$

Blue socks: $= \frac{4!}{2!(4-2)!} = \frac{4!}{2!(2)!} = 6$

Red socks: $= \frac{2!}{2!(2-2)!} = \frac{2!}{2!(0)!} = 1$

Add the favorable outcomes: 45+6+6+1=58

Hence, the probability is

$$Probability = \frac{Favorable\ outcome}{Total\ outcome} = \frac{58}{190} = 0.305$$

Choice A is incorrect because 0.003 is less than the obtained value. **Choice B** is incorrect because 0.100 is less than the obtained value. **Choice C** is incorrect because 0.237 is less than the obtained value.

GO ON TO THE NEXT PAGE.

Chapter 9
ACT Math Practice Test #2

Mark Your Answers For Test 2 Here

Date: ________

Marking Directions: Mark only one oval for each question. Fill in responese completely. Erase errors cleanly without smudging.

Correct mark: ○◉○○

1 Ⓐ Ⓑ Ⓒ Ⓓ	9 Ⓐ Ⓑ Ⓒ Ⓓ	17 Ⓐ Ⓑ Ⓒ Ⓓ	25 Ⓐ Ⓑ Ⓒ Ⓓ	33 Ⓐ Ⓑ Ⓒ Ⓓ	41 Ⓐ Ⓑ Ⓒ Ⓓ
2 Ⓕ Ⓖ Ⓗ Ⓙ	10 Ⓕ Ⓖ Ⓗ Ⓙ	18 Ⓕ Ⓖ Ⓗ Ⓙ	26 Ⓕ Ⓖ Ⓗ Ⓙ	34 Ⓕ Ⓖ Ⓗ Ⓙ	42 Ⓕ Ⓖ Ⓗ Ⓙ
3 Ⓐ Ⓑ Ⓒ Ⓓ	11 Ⓐ Ⓑ Ⓒ Ⓓ	19 Ⓐ Ⓑ Ⓒ Ⓓ	27 Ⓐ Ⓑ Ⓒ Ⓓ	35 Ⓐ Ⓑ Ⓒ Ⓓ	43 Ⓐ Ⓑ Ⓒ Ⓓ
4 Ⓕ Ⓖ Ⓗ Ⓙ	12 Ⓕ Ⓖ Ⓗ Ⓙ	20 Ⓕ Ⓖ Ⓗ Ⓙ	28 Ⓕ Ⓖ Ⓗ Ⓙ	36 Ⓕ Ⓖ Ⓗ Ⓙ	44 Ⓕ Ⓖ Ⓗ Ⓙ
5 Ⓐ Ⓑ Ⓒ Ⓓ	13 Ⓐ Ⓑ Ⓒ Ⓓ	21 Ⓐ Ⓑ Ⓒ Ⓓ	29 Ⓐ Ⓑ Ⓒ Ⓓ	37 Ⓐ Ⓑ Ⓒ Ⓓ	45 Ⓐ Ⓑ Ⓒ Ⓓ
6 Ⓕ Ⓖ Ⓗ Ⓙ	14 Ⓕ Ⓖ Ⓗ Ⓙ	22 Ⓕ Ⓖ Ⓗ Ⓙ	30 Ⓕ Ⓖ Ⓗ Ⓙ	38 Ⓕ Ⓖ Ⓗ Ⓙ	
7 Ⓐ Ⓑ Ⓒ Ⓓ	15 Ⓐ Ⓑ Ⓒ Ⓓ	23 Ⓐ Ⓑ Ⓒ Ⓓ	31 Ⓐ Ⓑ Ⓒ Ⓓ	39 Ⓐ Ⓑ Ⓒ Ⓓ	
8 Ⓕ Ⓖ Ⓗ Ⓙ	16 Ⓕ Ⓖ Ⓗ Ⓙ	24 Ⓕ Ⓖ Ⓗ Ⓙ	32 Ⓕ Ⓖ Ⓗ Ⓙ	40 Ⓕ Ⓖ Ⓗ Ⓙ	

MATHEMATICS TEST

50 Minutes—45 Questions

DIRECTIONS: Solve each problem, choose the correct answer, and then fill in the corresponding oval on your answer document.

Do not linger over problems that take too much time. Solve as many as you can; then return to the others in the time you have left for this test.

You are permitted to use a calculator on this test. You may use your calculator for any problems you choose, but some of the problems may best be done without using a calculator.

Note: Unless otherwise stated, all of the following should be assumed.

1. Illustrative figures are NOT necessarily drawn to scale.
2. Geometric figures lie in a plane.
3. The word line indicates a straight line.
4. The word average indicates arithmetic mean.

DO YOUR FIGURING HERE.

1. Determine the two numbers whose arithmetic mean is 126, given the ratio between them is 3.

A. 84 and 168
B. 63 and 189
C. 72 and 216
D. 85 and 255

2. 2 and 20 are the least and greatest numbers in a list of 7 real numbers. The median of the list is 6, and the number 3 occurs most often in the list. Which of the following could be the average (arithmetic mean) of the numbers in the list?

I. 7
II. 8.5
III. 10

F. I only
G. II and III only
H. I and III only
J. I, II , only

GO ON TO THE NEXT PAGE.

DO YOUR FIGURING HERE.

3. Refer to the given table below. Suppose another solution has been measured in Experiment 2 and the mass of the solution in the graduated cylinder was 67.54 grams with a density of 1.35 g/ml. What is the average of the 6 solutions?

Experiment 2		
Solution	**Mass of solution**	**Density**
6	52.51	1.05
7	55.70	1.11
8	57.53	1.15
9	60.63	1.21
19	64.64	1.29

A. 1.16
B. 1.18
C. 1.19
D. 1.21

4. In the diagram below, $\angle ABC = 137^\circ$ and BD divides $\angle ABC$ so that $\angle CBD$ is 11 degrees less than 3 times $\angle ABD$. What is the measure of $\angle CBD$ in degrees?

F. 37
G. 80
H. 85
J. 100

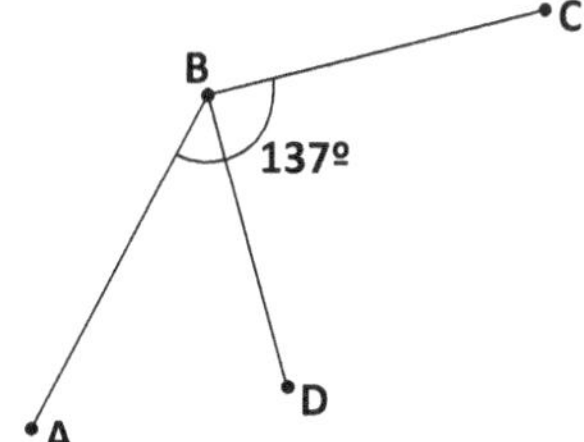

5. Which of the following expressions is equivalent to $x^2 + 16x$?

A. $(x-4)^2 - 64$
B. $(x+4)^2 + 64$
C. $(x-8)^2 - 64$
D. $(x+8)^2 - 64$

6. If $A = \begin{pmatrix} 0 & 3 \\ 4 & -2 \end{pmatrix}$ and $kA = \begin{pmatrix} 0 & 6b \\ 12a & 24 \end{pmatrix}$ then the values of k, a, and b respectively are

F. −12,−4, 6
G. −12,−4,−6
H. 12,−4,−6
J. 12, 4, 6

GO ON TO THE NEXT PAGE.

DO YOUR FIGURING HERE.

7. From home, Karen walks to the grocery store at a rate of 3 miles per hour. Ten minutes later, her brother Nick rides his bicycle to the grocery store at a rate of 15 miles per hour. Nick catches up with Karen before reaching the grocery store. How many minutes did it take Nick to catch up with his sister?

A. 5
B. 12.5
C. 22.5
D. 33.3

8. Find the equation and the graph that corresponds to the given table below.

x	1	2	3	4
y	7	13	19	25

F. $y = 6x + 1$,

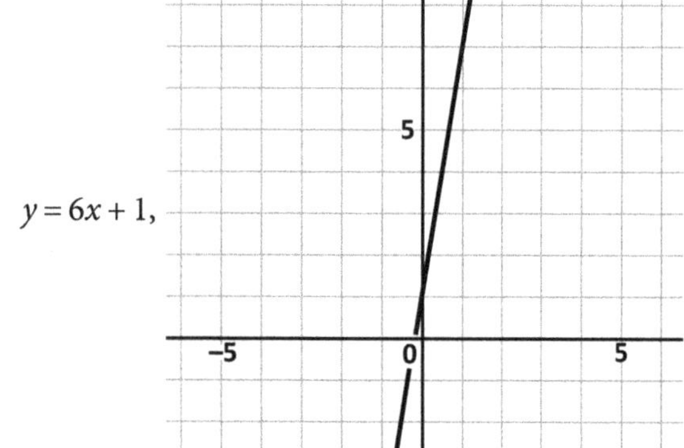

G. $y = 2x + 6$,

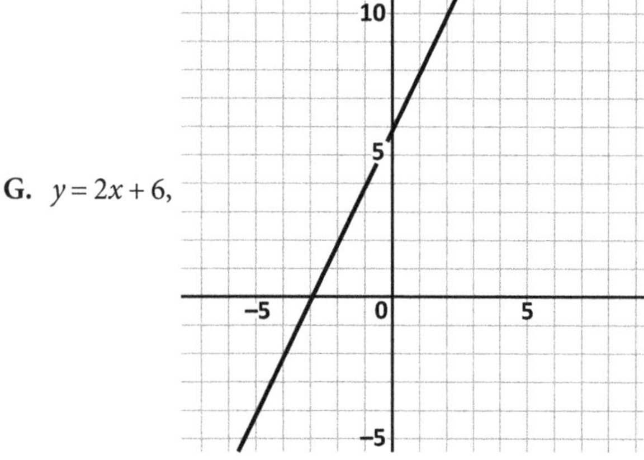

GO ON TO THE NEXT PAGE.

DO YOUR FIGURING HERE.

H. $y = 2x + 3$,

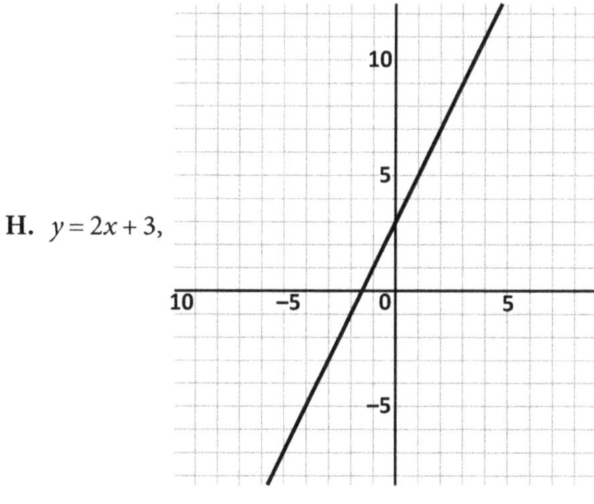

J. $y = x + 6$,

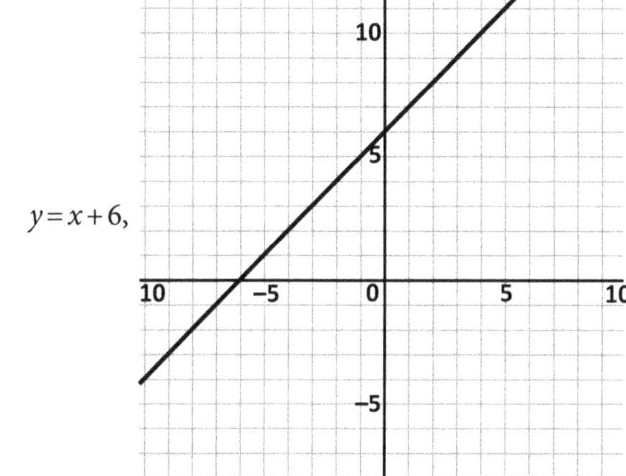

9. Which of the following is equivalent to $y = x^2 + 8x - 5$?

   A. $y = (x-4)^2 - 21$
   B. $y = (x+4)^2 - 21$
   C. $y = (x+4)^2 + 11$
   D. $y = (x+8)^2 - 21$

10. Todd can rake the leaves in his yard in 4 hours. Patty can rake the leaves in Todd's yard in 7 hours. Working together, how many hours will it take them to rake the leaves in Todd's yard?

   F. 2.5
   G. 3.5
   H. 4
   J. 5.5

GO ON TO THE NEXT PAGE.

DO YOUR FIGURING HERE.

11. An animal doctor recommends that each day a certain hamster should eat 25 calories per pound of the hamster's weight, plus an additional 11 calories. Which equation and answer represents this situation, where c is the total calories the veterinarian recommends the hamster should eat each day if the hamster's weight is $w = 5$ pounds?

A. $c = 11w + 25, 80$ *calories*
B. $c = 25w - 11, 114$ *calories*
C. $c = 25w + 11, 136$ *calories*
D. $c = 2w + 25, 35$ *calories*

12. The 54 members of the Math club will choose a student government representative. The members decided to choose at random. The representative cannot be any of the 5 officers of the club. What is the probability that Jane, who is a member of the club but not an officer will be chosen?

F. $\frac{1}{49}$
G. $\frac{1}{54}$
H. $\frac{5}{49}$
J. $\frac{5}{54}$

13. For what values of θ is $|\sin\theta| \leq 1$ if θ is an angle in the first or second quadrant?

A. $0^\circ < \theta < 90^\circ$
B. $180^\circ < \theta < 270^\circ$
C. $0^\circ < \theta < 180^\circ$
D. $270^\circ < \theta < 360^\circ$

GO ON TO THE NEXT PAGE.

DO YOUR FIGURING HERE.

14. Which of the following is the equation for a parabola that has its vertex at (4, 3) and passes through (6, –1)?

F. $y=-(x-6)^2-1$
G. $y=-(x+6)^2-1$
H. $y=(x-6)^2+1$
J. $y=-(x-4)^2+3$

15. Which expression is equivalent to $x^2 - 18x$?

A. $(x + 9)^2 - 81$
B. $(x - 9)^2 - 81$
C. $(x - 9)^2 + 81$
D. $(x + 9)^2 + 81$

16. The temperature of oil in a car is recorded in the table below for the first 5 minutes after the car is turned off.

Time (minutes)	Temperature (°F)
0	275
1	262
2	242
3	202
4	152
5	91

Which of the following statements is true about the temperature?

F. The temperature of the oil is decreasing at an increasing rate.
G. The temperature of the oil is decreasing at a decreasing rate.
H. The temperature of the oil is decreasing at a constant rate.
J. The temperature of the oil is inversely proportional to time.

17. Which expression is a factor of $8x^3-125$?

A. $2x+5$
B. $x+5$
C. $4x^2-10x+25$
D. $4x^2+10x+25$

GO ON TO THE NEXT PAGE.

DO YOUR FIGURING HERE.

18. Which of the following is equivalent to the expression $\frac{2}{\sqrt{-8}}$ where $i^2 = -1$?

F. $\frac{\sqrt{2}}{2}i$

G. $-\frac{\sqrt{2}}{2}i$

H. $\frac{\sqrt{2}}{4}i$

J. $-\frac{\sqrt{2}}{4}i$

19. What is the 10th term in the sequence $\{3, 4, 7, 11, 18, \ldots\}$?

A. 33
B. 123
C. 199
D. 4374

20. If $\Delta JKL \simeq \Delta JKM$, the perimeter of $JLKM = 394\,cm$, and $JK = 56\,cm$, find the perimeter of ΔJKL.

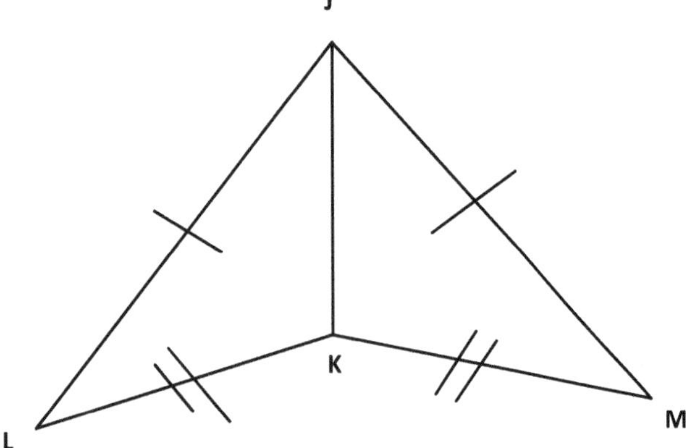

F. 216
G. 253
H. 309
J. 394

GO ON TO THE NEXT PAGE.

DO YOUR FIGURING HERE.

21.

In the figure below, a circle is inscribed in a square. Find the area of the shaded region if the circumference of the circle is 8π.

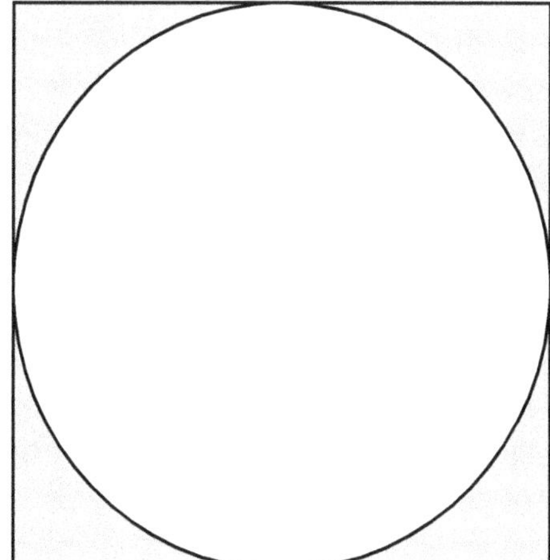

A. 9.75
B. 11.25
C. 13.73
D. 15.85

22. Which of the following is a graph for the values of x defined by the inequality stated below?

$|2x-8| \leq 4$

F. −10 −9 −8 −7 −6 −5 −4 −3 −2 −1 0 1 2 3 4 5 6 7 8 9 10

G. −10 −9 −8 −7 −6 −5 −4 −3 −2 −1 0 1 2 3 4 5 6 7 8 9 10

H. −10 −9 −8 −7 −6 −5 −4 −3 −2 −1 0 1 2 3 4 5 6 7 8 9 10

J. −10 −9 −8 −7 −6 −5 −4 −3 −2 −1 0 1 2 3 4 5 6 7 8 9 10

23. An initial investment of \$2500 that earns 6% annually is modeled by $A = 2500(1+0.06)^t$ where A is the amount of the investment, in dollars, after t years. What is the amount of the investment after 20 years?

A. \$4000
B. \$8018
C. \$25,000
D. \$26,500

GO ON TO THE NEXT PAGE.

DO YOUR FIGURING HERE.

24. What is the measure of $\angle CAE$ if A is the intersection of $\overline{CD}$ and $\overline{BE}$ for the figure shown below?

F. 25
G. 31
H. 124
J. 149

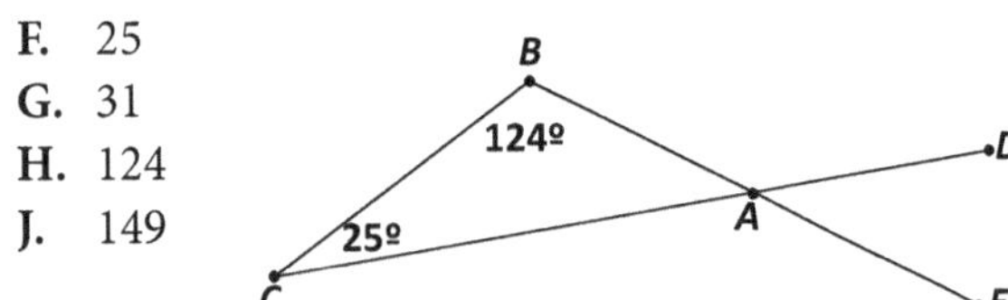

25. Which statement is true about graphs of the functions $10x - 2y = 16$ and $y = 5x + 3$?

A. They intersect at the point (1, –8).
B. They intersect at the point (2, 13).
C. They intersect at infinitely many points since they are the same line.
D. They do not intersect since they are parallel and have different y-intercepts.

26. Which expression is equivalent to $\dfrac{42x - 3x^2}{6x}$?

F. $\dfrac{42 - x}{3}$

G. $\dfrac{14 - x^2}{2x}$

H. $7 - \dfrac{x}{2}$

J. $\dfrac{42 - 3x}{6}$

27. The central angle of sector S is 72°. What is the probability that the spinner lands on S?

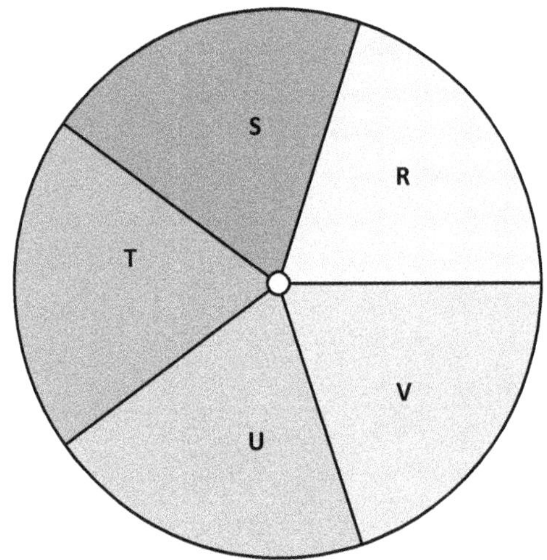

A. 1/288
B. 1/72
C. 1/5
D. 1/3

GO ON TO THE NEXT PAGE.

DO YOUR FIGURING HERE.

28. What is the equation of the circle graph below in the standard (x, y) coordinate system?

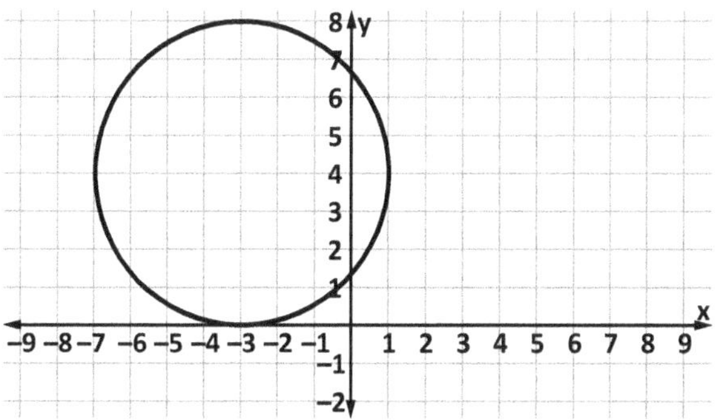

F. $(x+3)^2+(y-4)^2=4$
G. $(x-3)^2+(y+4)^2=4$
H. $(x-3)^2+(y+4)^2=16$
J. $(x+3)^2+(y-4)^2=16$

29. Match list 1 with list 2. Choose the correct answer from the options below.

List 1 (Number)	List 2 (Scientific Notation)
A. 0.00004	I. $4.0 \times^{-10}$
B. 0.00000004	II. $4.0 \times^{-5}$
C. 0.0004	III. $4.0 \times^{-4}$
D. 0.0000000004	IV. $4.0 \times^{-8}$

A. A - II, B - IV, C - III, D - I
B. A - II, B - III, C - IV, D - I
C. A - III, B - IV, C - II, D - I
D. A - III, B - I, C - IV, D - II

30. One of the sides of a square, measuring 8 units, is adjacent to one of the sides of an equilateral triangle. What is the area of the polygon, in square units, formed by the square and the equilateral triangle?

F. $64 + 4\sqrt{3}$
G. $64 + 16\sqrt{3}$
H. 96
J. 108

GO ON TO THE NEXT PAGE.

DO YOUR FIGURING HERE.

31. Which of the following represents the area, A of an equilateral triangle having sides s, in terms of its perimeter?

A. $A = \frac{\sqrt{3}}{2}s^2$

B. $A = \frac{\sqrt{3}}{4}s^2$

C. $P = \frac{\sqrt{3}}{18}A^2$

D. $A = \frac{\sqrt{3}}{18}P^2$

32. A shipping company ships packages locally for \$0.55 per kilogram. How much does the shipping company charge to ship a package locally that weighs 103 pounds, given that 1 pound is 0.454 kilograms?

F. \$25.71
G. \$46.71
H. \$56.56
J. \$84.93

33. If one of the interior angles in a decagon measures 55 degrees, what is the sum of the rest of the interior angles in degrees?

A. 1025
B. 1385
C. 1440
D. 1745

34. If the first and second terms in a geometric sequence are 2 and $\frac{3}{4}$ respectively, which expression represents the 10th term in the sequence?

F. $\frac{3}{8}(2)^{10}$

G. $2\left(\frac{3}{8}\right)^{10}$

H. $2\left(\frac{3}{8}\right)^{9}$

J. $2+\frac{5}{4}(10-1)$

GO ON TO THE NEXT PAGE.

DO YOUR FIGURING HERE.

35. The sum of three numbers is 348. The first number is 4 more than the second, while the third number is the average of the first two numbers. Which of the following is the set of numbers?

A. 120, 116, 118
B. 126, 106, 116
C. 118, 114, 116
D. 115, 111, 113

36. Find the expected value or mean value of the variable X from the given table below.

$X = x_i$	1	2	3
$P(X = x_i)$	0.3	0.5	0.2

F. 0.8
G. 1.4
H. 1.9
J. 2.7

37. The product of some number and the sum of the number and 7 is 60. Which of the following could be the number?

A. –12
B. –5
C. 3
D. 12

38. Albert's car averages 25 miles per gallon of gasoline. Gas cost \$2.45 per gallon. From an empty gas tank, Albert spends \$36.75 to fill the tank. How far can Albert drive in his car before it runs out of gas?

F. 345 miles
G. 375 miles
H. 500 miles
J. 735 miles

GO ON TO THE NEXT PAGE.

39. The table shows the number of students in three different degree programs and whether they are graduate or undergraduate students. Take note that each student can only be in one degree program. If we know that the selected student is an undergraduate, which of the following probability shows that /she is from the nursing department?

	Graduate	**Undergraduate**
Accounting	32	31
Engineering	26	17
Nursing	18	12

A. $\frac{1}{7}$

B. $\frac{2}{3}$

C. $\frac{1}{5}$

D. $\frac{12}{30}$

40. Twelve more than the square of some number is eight times the number. Which of the following could be the number?

F. −6
G. −2
H. 4
J. 6

41. Which of the following statements is always true about real numbers x and y?

A. If $x > 0 > y$ then, $y - x > 0$.
B. If $x > y$ then, $x - y > 0$.
C. If $x > y > 0$ then, $\frac{y}{x} > 1$.
D. If $x > 0 > y$ then, $x \cdot y < 0$.

42. The mean for a set of 7 numbers is 24. What must be the value of an eighth number added to the set that changes the mean to 27?

F. 3
G. 24
H. 27
J. 48

DO YOUR FIGURING HERE.

GO ON TO THE NEXT PAGE.

DO YOUR FIGURING HERE.

43. Two rectangular prisms are shown below with its dimensions. The volume of the larger prism is the same as how many small rectangular prism?

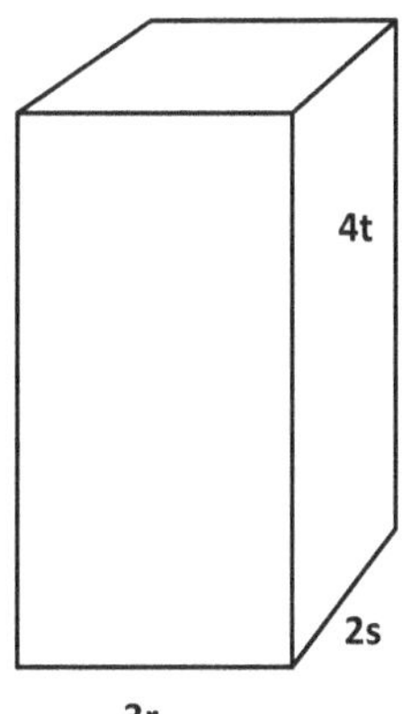

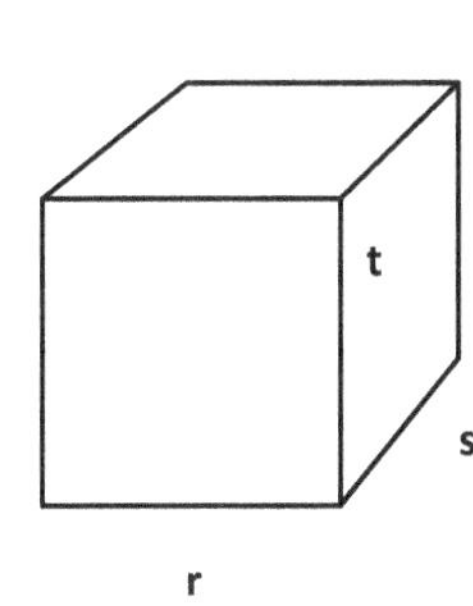

A. 12
B. 18
C. 24
D. 36

44. An initial investment of \$1200 grows at a rate of 8% annually. The amount, A, of the investment after t years is modeled by the function $A = 1200(1 + 0.08)^t$. Approximately how long will it take, in years, for the investment to have a value of \$24,000?

F. 19
G. 20
H. 25
J. 39

45. A pouch contains 12 red marbles, 5 yellow marbles, and 15 green marbles. How many additional red marbles must be added to the 32 marbles already in the bag so that the probability of randomly drawing a red marble is $\frac{3}{5}$?

A. 15
B. 16
C. 18
D. 20

GO ON TO THE NEXT PAGE.

Answer Key

Question	Correct	Make your correct answers
1	B	
2	J	
3	C	
4	J	
5	D	
6	G	
7	B	
8	F	
9	B	
10	F	
11	C	
12	F	
13	C	
14	J	
15	B	
16	F	
17	D	
18	G	
19	C	
20	G	
21	C	
22	J	
23	B	

Question	Correct	Make your correct answers
24	J	
25	D	
26	H	
27	C	
28	J	
29	A	
30	G	
31	D	
32	F	
33	B	
34	H	
35	C	
36	H	
37	A	
38	G	
39	C	
40	J	
41	D	
42	J	
43	C	
44	J	
45	C	

1.

Category: IES
Skill: Sets of numbers | **Level:** Easy

Choice B is correct because the obtained answer is 63 and 189

Given: Arithmetic mean of two numbers = 126
Ratio between numbers = 3:1

Let x be the first number and y be the second number.

$$\frac{x+y}{2}=126$$
$$x+y=126(2)$$
$$x+y=252$$

If ratio between number is 3, then $x:y=3:1$.

$$x+y=252$$
$$x+\frac{1}{3}x=252$$
$$\frac{4}{3}x=252$$
$$4x=3(252)$$
$$4x=756$$
$$x=189$$

Find y.

$$y=\frac{1}{3}x$$
$$y=\frac{1}{3}(189)$$
$$y=63$$

Choice A is incorrect because 84 and 168 do not represent the given numbers. **Choice C** is incorrect because 72 and 216 do not represent the given numbers. **Choice D** is incorrect because 85 and 255 do not represent the given numbers.

2.

Category: IES & Modeling
Skill: Sets of numbers | **Level:** Easy

Choice J is correct because I, II , are possible arithmetic mean of the given data.

Set up the data.
There are 7 numbers, 2 and 20 are the least and greatest numbers, the median of the list is 6, and the number 3 occurs most often.

2, 3, 3, 6,__, __, 20

Let x be the first number and y be the second number.

The biggest value of the sum of the missing numbers are 6 + 20 = 26.

Check whether the choices are possible.

I. 7

$$\mu=7=\frac{2+3+3+6+x+y+20}{7}$$
$$7=\frac{34+x+y}{7}.$$
$$34+x+y=49$$
$$x+y=49-34$$
$$x+y=15 \qquad \text{POSSIBLE}$$

II. 8.5

$$8.5=\frac{34+x+y}{7}$$
$$34+x+y=59.5$$
$$x+y=59.5-34$$
$$x+y=25.5 \qquad \text{POSSIBLE}$$

III. 10

$$\mu=10=\frac{2+3+3+6+x+y+20}{7}$$
$$10=\frac{34+x+y}{7}$$
$$34+x+y=70$$
$$x+y=70-34$$
$$x+y=36 \qquad \text{Not Possible}$$

Choice F is incorrect because I only does not include II. **Choice G** is incorrect because II and III only includes III which is not a possible solution. **Choice H** is incorrect because I and III only includes III which is not a possible solution.

3.

Category: PHM & Modeling
Skill: Sets of numbers | **Level:** Medium

Choice C is correct because the obtained average is 1.19.

Find the average of the given data.

From the table, the values of densities are 1.05, 1.11, 1.15, 1.21, 1.29. An additional solution with a density of 1.35 is added to the experiment.

$$n=6$$
$$Average=\frac{1.05+1.11+1.15+1.21+1.29+1.35}{6}$$
$$Average=1.19$$

Choice A is incorrect because 1.16 is less than the obtained value. **Choice B** is incorrect because 1.18 is less than the obtained value. **Choice D** is incorrect because 1.21 is greater than the obtained value.

GO ON TO THE NEXT PAGE.

4.

Category: PHM
Skill: Lines and Angles | **Level:** Medium

Choice J is correct. $\angle ABC = \angle ADB + \angle CBD$. Let $\angle ABD = x$, then $\angle CBD = 3x - 11$ then,

$$137 = x + (3x - 11)$$
$$137 = 4x - 11$$
$$4x = 148$$
$$x = 37$$

So, $\angle CBD = 3 \times 37 - 11 = 100°$.

Choice F is incorrect. This is value of $\angle ABD$. **Choice G** is incorrect. This may result from conceptual error. **Choice H** is incorrect. This may result from conceptual error.

5.

Category: PHM
Skill: Equations | **Level:** Difficult

Choice D is correct. Completing the square, you get,

$$x^2 + 16x + \left(\frac{16}{2}\right)^2 - \left(\frac{16}{2}\right)^2$$
$$= \left(x^2 + 16x + 64\right) - 64$$
$$= (x + 8)^2 - 64$$

Choice A is incorrect. This may result from a wrong calculation in completing the square. **Choice B** is incorrect. This may result from a wrong calculation in completing the square. **Choice C** is incorrect. The square should be $(x+8)^2$ instead of $(x-8)^2$.

6.

Category: PHM
Skill: Matrices | **Level:** Easy

Choice G is correct because the obtained values of k, a, and b respectively are $-12, -4, -6$.

Given: $A = \begin{pmatrix} 0 & 3 \\ 4 & -2 \end{pmatrix}$ and $kA = \begin{pmatrix} 0 & 6b \\ 12a & 24 \end{pmatrix}$.

$$KA = k\begin{pmatrix} 0 & 3 \\ 4 & -2 \end{pmatrix}$$
$$\begin{pmatrix} 0 & 6b \\ 12a & 24 \end{pmatrix} = \begin{pmatrix} 0k & 3k \\ 4k & -2k \end{pmatrix}$$

From the matrix above, we can set up 4 equations.

$$0 = 0k$$
$$6b = 3k$$
$$12a = 4k$$
$$24 = -2k$$

Find the values of k, a, and b respectively.

$$24 = -2k$$
$$\frac{24}{-2} = k$$
$$-12 = k$$

$$12a = 4k$$
$$12a = 4(-12)$$
$$12a = -48$$
$$a = -4$$

$$6b = 3k$$
$$6b = 3(-12)$$
$$6b = -36$$
$$b = -6$$

Choice F is incorrect because the value of b should have been –6. **Choice H** is incorrect because the value of k should have been -12. **Choice J** is incorrect because the values of k, a *and* b should have been negative.

7.

Category: PHM
Skill: Equations | **Level:** Medium

Choice B is correct Let t be the time, in hours, it takes Nick to catch up with Karen. The distance Karen walks is $3t$, and the distance Nick walks is $15(t - \frac{1}{6})$ where 10 minutes is $\frac{1}{6}$ of an hour. Nick catches Karen when their distances are equal so.

$$3t = 15\left(t - \frac{1}{6}\right)$$
$$3t = 15t - \frac{5}{2}$$
$$-12t = -\frac{5}{2}$$
$$t = \frac{5}{24} \text{ hours}$$

Converting to minutes, Nick catches up in $\frac{5}{24} \times 60 = 12.5$ minutes.

Choice A is incorrect. Misinterprets the difference in speed or the head start. **Choice C** is incorrect. May result from solving using a wrong distance or incorrect conversion. **Choice D** is incorrect. This assumes they meet at the store, not before.

GO ON TO THE NEXT PAGE.

8.

Category: IES & Modeling
Skill: Equations | **Level:** Hard

Choice F is correct because the obtained answer is $y = 6x + 1$ and its graph is

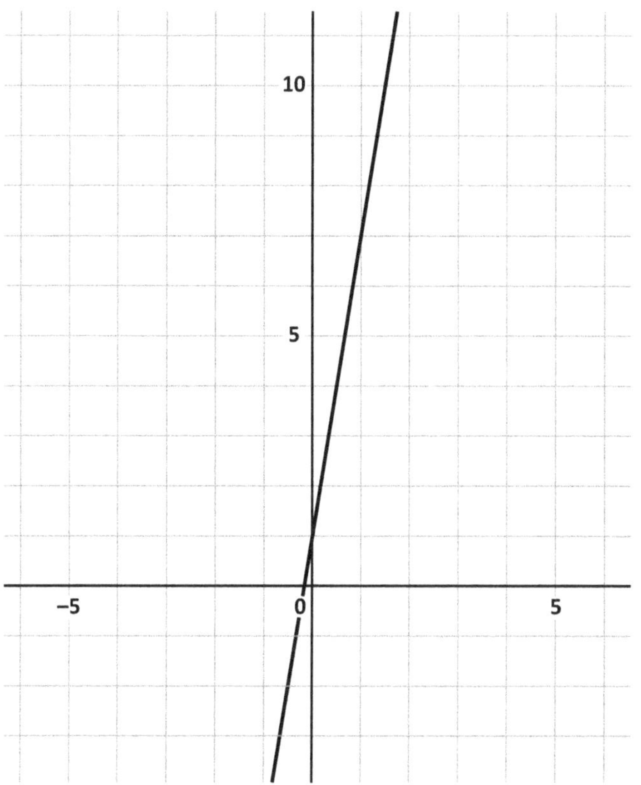

Find the equation of the line by taking two points from the given table.

Use points (1, 7) and (2, 13) to find the slope and the y-intercept.

$$m = \frac{y_2 - y_1}{x_2 - x_1} = \frac{13-7}{2-1} = \frac{6}{1} = 6$$

$$y = mx + b$$

$$7 = 6(1) + b$$

$$7 - 6 = b$$

$$1 = b$$

Hence, the equation of the line is $y = 6x + 1$.
To find the graph, plot the points on the $xy-$ coordinate.

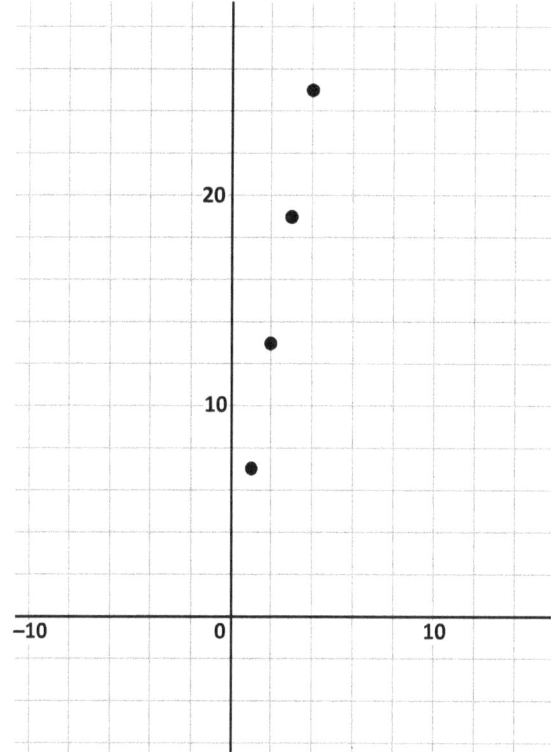

Connect the points.

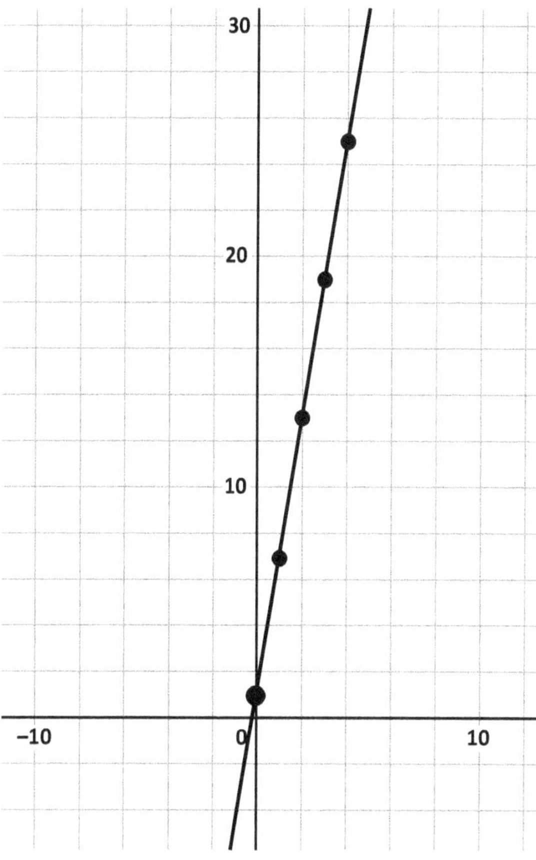

Choice G is incorrect because both the equation and the graph do not represent the given table. **Choice H** is incorrect because both the equation and the graph do not represent the given table. **Choice J** is incorrect because both the equation and the graph do not represent the given table.

9.

Category: PHM
Skill: Equations | **Level:** Difficult

Choice B is correct. Completing the square, you have,

$$y = x^2 + 8x - 5$$
$$y = x^2 + 8x + \left(\frac{8}{2}\right)^2 - 5 - \left(\frac{8}{2}\right)^2$$
$$y = \left(x^2 + 8x + 16\right) - 5 - 16$$
$$y = \left(x^2 + 8x + 16\right) - 21$$
$$y = (x+4)^2 - 21$$

Choice A is incorrect. If expanded, this is equivalent to $y = x^2 - 8x - 5$, which has the wrong sign on the linear term ($-8x$ instead of $+8x$). **Choice C** is incorrect. If expanded, this is equivalent to $y = x^2 + 8x + 27$, which is too large for the constant term. **Choice D** is incorrect. If expanded, this is equivalent to $y = x^2 + 16x + 43$, which has both the wrong linear coefficient and the wrong constant term.

10.

Category: IES
Skill: Scientific notation | **Level:** Medium

Choice F is correct. Let h be the hours each person rakes leaves. Todd rakes $\frac{1}{4}$ of the leaves in the yard each hour, and Patty rakes $\frac{1}{7}$ of the leaves in the yard each hour. In h hours, Todd rakes $\frac{h}{4}$ of the leaves in h hours, and Patty rakes $\frac{h}{7}$. Together they rake $\frac{h}{4} + \frac{h}{7}$ of the leaves in the yard. To complete the entire job together $\frac{h}{4} + \frac{h}{7} = 1$. Solving for h,

$$\frac{h}{4} + \frac{h}{7} = 1$$
$$\frac{7}{28}h + \frac{4}{28}h = 1$$
$$\frac{11}{28}h = 1$$
$$h = \frac{28}{11}$$

So, it takes $\frac{28}{11} = 2.5$ hours.

Choice G is incorrect. This is a guesstimate. **Choice H** is incorrect. Only takes Todd's time to rake the leaves since it is the shorter time. **Choice J** is incorrect. The average of 4 hours and 7 hours.

11.

Category: IES
Skill: Equations | **Level:** Medium

Choice C is correct because the obtained answer is $c = 25w + 11{,}136\ calories$.

Given: every pound equals 25 calories and an additional of 11 calories.

Let c is the total calories the veterinarian recommends the hamster should eat each day
w be the hamster's weight

Equation: $c = 25w + 11$

Find c when $w = 5$.

$$c = 25w + 11$$
$$c = 25(5) + 11$$
$$c = 125 + 11$$
$$c = 136 \text{ calories}$$

Choice A is incorrect because $c = 11w + 25{,}80\ calories$ both the equation and the value are incorrect.
Choice B is incorrect because $c = 25w - 11{,}114\ calories$ does not represent the given problem. **Choice D** is incorrect because $c = 2w + 25{,}35\ calories$ has an incorrect equation and answer.

12.

Category: IES
Skill: Probability | **Level:** Medium

Choice F is correct because the obtained answer is $\frac{1}{49}$.

Given: 54 members
5 members that are officers

Probability of Jane to be chosen where she is a member of the club but not an officer.

$$P = \frac{number\ of\ favoured\ outcome}{total\ number\ of\ possible\ outcomes}$$

$$P = \frac{1}{54 - 5}$$

$$P = \frac{1}{49}$$

GO ON TO THE NEXT PAGE.

Choice G is incorrect because $\frac{1}{54}$ is less than the obtained probability. **Choice H** is incorrect because $\frac{5}{49}$ is greater than the obtained probability. **Choice J** is incorrect because $\frac{5}{54}$ is greater than the obtained probability.

13.

Category: PHM
Skill: Trigonometry | **Level:** Medium

Choice C is correct
$|\sin\theta| \le 1$ is equivalent to $-1 \le \sin\theta \le 1$ which occurs for any value of θ in the first and second quadrant. So, choices A can be eliminated. Choices B and D can also be eliminated since they contain angles in the third and fourth quadrant respectively.
Choice A is incorrect. This contains angles in the first quadrant. **Choice B** is incorrect. This contains angles in the third quadrant. **Choice D** is incorrect. This contains angles in the fourth quadrant.

14.

Category: PHM
Skill: System of equations | **Level:** Medium

Choice J is correct. Writing the equation of the parabola in the form $y = a(x-h)^2 + k$ where (h, k) is the vertex and a is a constant you get, $y = a(x-4)^2 + 3$. Substitute (6, –1) into the equation to find the value for a.

$$-1 = a(6-4)^2 + 3$$
$$-1 = 4a + 3$$
$$-4 = 4a$$
$$a = -1$$
$$\text{So, } y = -(x-4)^2 + 3.$$

Choice F is incorrect. The vertex is (6, –1) not (4, 3).
Choice G is incorrect. The vertex is (–6, –1) not (4, 3).
Choice H is incorrect. The vertex is (6, 1) not (4, 3).

15.

Category: PHM
Skill: System of equations | **Level:** Easy

Choice B is correct. Completing the square you have,

$$x^2 - 18x$$
$$= x^2 - 18x + \left(\frac{-18}{2}\right)^2 - \left(\frac{-18}{2}\right)^2$$
$$= \left(x^2 - 18x + 81\right) - 81$$
$$= \left(x-9\right)^2 - 81$$

Choice A is incorrect. This incorrectly completes the square. **Choice C** is incorrect. This incorrectly completes the square. **Choice D** is incorrect. This incorrectly completes the square.

16.

Category: IES
Skill: Number Line and Absolute Value | **Level:** Medium

Choice F is correct. As seen in the table, the oil is decreasing over the 5-minute interval. Since the difference in the temperatures from one minute to the next is getting larger, we say the rate of change in the difference in the temperatures is increasing so, choices B and C can be eliminated. There is no direct variation in the temperature in terms of time, and the temperature and time are not inversely proportional with each other so, choice D can be eliminated, leaving A as the correct choice.

Choice G is incorrect. As per the explanation above, the rate of change in the difference in temperatures is increasing and not decreasing. **Choice H** is incorrect. As per the explanation above, the rate of change in the difference in temperatures is increasing and not decreasing. **Choice J** is incorrect. As per the explanation above, the temperature and time are not inversely proportional to each other.

17.

Category: PHM
Skill: Equations | **Level:** Medium

Choice D is correct. Use the difference of cubes $(a-b)(a^2 + ab + b^2)$ to factor $8x^3 - 125$ where $a = 2x$ and $b = 5$. Then, $8x^3 - 125 = \left(2x-5\right)\left((2x)^2 + 2x \cdot 5 + 5^2\right) = \left(2x-5\right)\left(4x^2 + 10x + 25\right)$. So, choice D, $4x^2 + 10x + 25$ is the correct choice.

Choice A is incorrect because this use $\left(a-b\right)\left(a^2 + ab + b^2\right)$ to factor the given expression. **Choice B** is incorrect because this should be $2x - 5$ and not $x + 5$. **Choice C** is incorrect because this use $\left(a-b\right)\left(a^2 + ab + b^2\right)$ to factor the given expression.

18.

Category: PHM
Skill: Equations | **Level:** Easy

Choice G is correct. Simplifying you have,

$$\frac{2}{\sqrt{-8}}=\frac{2}{\sqrt{-1\cdot 8}}=\frac{2}{\sqrt{-1}\sqrt{8}}=$$

$$\frac{2}{i\sqrt{8}}\cdot\frac{i\sqrt{8}}{i\sqrt{8}}=\frac{2i\sqrt{8}}{8i^2}=\frac{i\sqrt{8}}{-4}=\frac{2i\sqrt{2}}{-4}=-\frac{\sqrt{2}}{2}i.$$

Choice F is incorrect because it neglects that $i^2 = -1$. **Choice H** is incorrect because it neglects that $i^2 = -1$. **Choice J** is incorrect because it neglects to simplify the denominator.

19.

Category: PHM
Skill: Series, Sequences and Consecutive numbers | **Level:** Medium

Choice C is correct. The sequence is recursive since any term is the sum of its 2 previous terms. The first 5 terms are given so, the 6th term is 11 + 18 = 29, 7th term is 18 + 29 = 47, 8th term is 29 + 47 = 76, 9th term is 47 + 76 = 123, and 10th term is 76 +123 = 199.

Choice A is incorrect. Incorrectly identifies the sequence as arithmetic with a common difference of 3 to determine the 10th term **Choice B** is incorrect. This is the 9th term in the sequence. **Choice D** is incorrect. Incorrectly identifies the sequence as geometric with a common ratio of 3, multiply it to each successive term to the 10th term.

20.

Category: IES & Modeling
Skill: Two-dimensional shapes | **Level:** Hard

Choice G is correct because the obtained answer is 253.

Let x be the length of JL and y be the length of LK

Since perimeter of $JLKM = 2(x+y) = 394\,cm$.

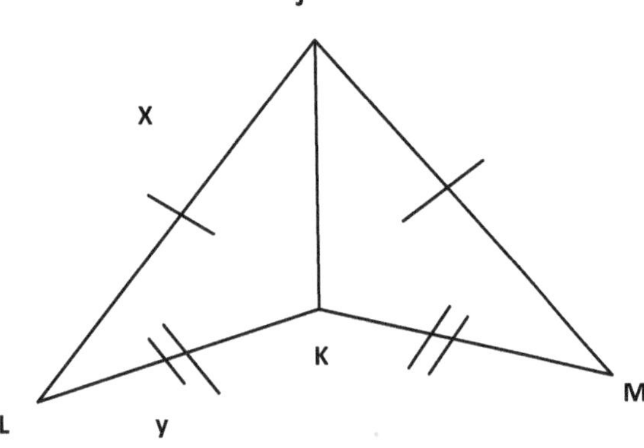

Since $x = JM$ and $y = KM$, then perimeter of ΔJKL is $x+y+56$.

Find $x+y$.

$$2(x+y)=394$$
$$(x+y)=197$$

Hence, perimeter of ΔJKL is $x+y+56=197+56=253$
Choice F is incorrect because 216 is less than the obtained perimeter of ΔJKL. **Choice H** is incorrect because 309 is greater than the obtained perimeter of ΔJKL. **Choice J** is incorrect because 394 is greater than the obtained perimeter of ΔJKL.

21.

Category: IES & Modeling
Skill: Two-dimensional shapes | **Level:** VCMP

Choice C is correct because the obtained answer is 13.73.

Find the radius of the circle using the given circumference.

$$C=2\pi r$$
$$8\pi=2\pi r$$
$$\frac{8\pi}{2\pi}=\frac{2\pi r}{2\pi}$$
$$4=r$$

Find the area of the square. The diameter of the circle is the same as the side of the square.

$$A=s^2$$
$$A=(2*4)^2$$
$$A=8^2$$
$$A=64$$

Find the area of the circle.

$$A=\pi r^2$$
$$A=\pi(4)^2$$
$$A=16\pi$$

Find the area of the of the shaded region.

$$A=A_{square}-A_{circle}$$
$$A=64-16\pi$$
$$A=13.73$$

Choice A is incorrect because 9.75 is less than the obtained answer. **Choice B** is incorrect because 11.25 is less than the obtained answer. **Choice D** is incorrect because 15.85 is greater than the obtained answer.

22.

Category: IES
Skill: Number Line and Absolute Value | **Level:** Hard

GO ON TO THE NEXT PAGE.

Choice J is correct because the graph of the obtained value of x in the number line is

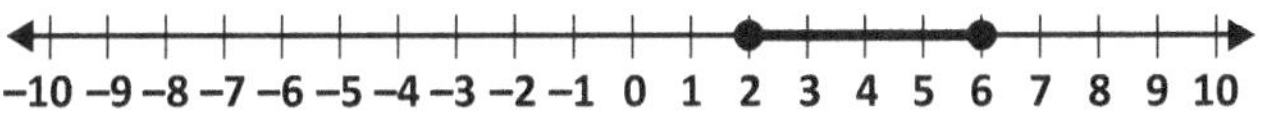

Given:

$$|2x-8| \le 4$$

Find x.

$$2x-8 \le 4 \quad \text{or} \quad 2x-8 \ge -4$$
$$2x \le 4+8 \qquad 2x \ge -4+8$$
$$2x \le 12 \qquad 2x \ge 4$$
$$x \le 6 \qquad x \ge 2$$

Graph the values of x.

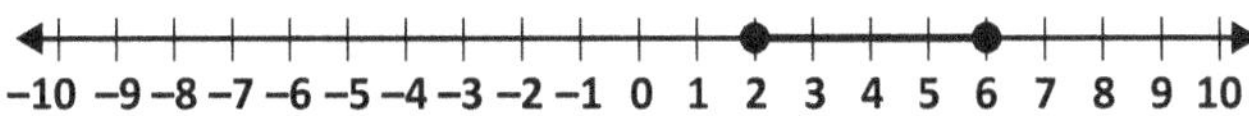

Choice F is incorrect because it does not represent the obtained value of x of the given expression. **Choice G** is incorrect because it does not represent the obtained value of x of the given expression. **Choice H** is incorrect because it does not represent the obtained value of x of the given expression.

23.

Category: PHM
Skill: Function Evaluation | **Level:** Easy

Choice B is correct Substitute $t = 20$ and solve for A.

$$A = 2500(1+0.06)^{20}$$
$$A = 2500(1.06)^{20}$$
$$A = 8017.84$$

Choice A is incorrect. This is the result of 2500 × 1.6.
Choice C is incorrect. This is the result of 2500 × 10.
Choice D is incorrect. This is the result of 2500 × 10.6.

24.

Category: PHM
Skill: Lines and Angles | **Level:** Easy

Choice J is correct. The sum of the angles for ΔABC is 180°. Combining the angles, you get,

$$\angle BAC + 124^\circ + 25^\circ = 180^\circ$$
$$\angle BAC + 149^\circ = 180^\circ$$
$$\angle BAC = 31^\circ$$

$\angle BAC$ and $\angle CAE$ form a linear pair so,

$$\angle BAC + \angle CAE = 180^\circ$$
$$31^\circ + \angle CAE = 180^\circ$$
$$\angle CAE = 149^\circ$$

Choice F is incorrect because this is the measure of $\angle BCA$. **Choice G** is incorrect because this is the measure of the angle at A inside of the triangle. **Choice H** is incorrect because this is the measure of $\angle CBA$.

25.

Category: PHM
Skill: Graphed functions | **Level:** Medium

Choice D is correct. Write $10x - 2y = 16$ in slope-intercept form.

$$10x - 2y = 16$$
$$-2y = -10x + 16$$
$$y = 5x - 8$$

So, the slope is 5.
The slope of $y = 5x + 3$ is also 5 so, the lines are parallel. The lines do not intersect since they have different y-intercepts.
Choice A is incorrect. The lines do not intersect since they have different y-intercepts. **Choice B** is incorrect. The lines do not intersect since they have different y-intercepts. **Choice C** is incorrect. The lines do not intersect since they have different y-intercepts.

26.

Category: PHM
Skill: Equations | **Level:** Easy

Choice H is correct. Dividing each term by the GCF (greatest common denominator) of $3x$ you have,

$$\frac{\frac{42x}{3x} - \frac{3x^2}{3x}}{\frac{6x}{3x}} = \frac{14-x}{2} = \frac{14}{2} - \frac{x}{2} = 7 - \frac{x}{2}.$$

Choice F is incorrect. $42x$ is only divided by x not $3x$. **Choice G** is incorrect. Divided by a common factor of 3 but should be divided by the GCF $3x$ to completely simplify the expression. **Choice J** is incorrect. Divided by a common factor of x but should be divided by the GCF $3x$ to completely simplify the expression.

27.

Category: IES & Modeling
Skill: Probability | **Level:** Hard

Choice C is correct because the obtained answer is ⅕.

The probability of landing on S is

$$Probability = \frac{Area\ of\ sector\ S}{Area\ of\ the\ Circle}$$

GO ON TO THE NEXT PAGE.

The central angle S is 72°. The area of the sector is

$$\frac{72}{360}A.$$

Hence, $Probability = \dfrac{Area\ of\ sector\ S}{Area\ of\ the\ Circle} = \dfrac{\frac{72}{360}A}{A} = \dfrac{72}{360} = \dfrac{1}{5}$

Choice A is incorrect because 1/288 is less than the obtained probability. **Choice B** is incorrect because 1/72 is less than the obtained probability. **Choice D** is incorrect because 1/3 is greater than the obtained probability.

28.

Category: PHM & Modeling
Skill: Two-dimensional shapes | **Level:** Medium

Choice J is correct. A circle in the form $(x-h)^2+(y-k)^2=r^2$ has its center at (*h*, *k*) and a radius of *r* units. The figure shows the center to be at (−3, 4) and the radius can be found by counting horizontally or vertically the number of units from the center to a point on the circle. So, *r* = 4. Substituting you get,

$$(x-(-3))^2+(y-4)^2=4^2$$

$$(x+3)^2+(y-4)^2=16$$

Choice F is incorrect because the radius is not squared. **Choice G** is incorrect because the radius is not squared. **Choice H** is incorrect because it substitutes the center into the equation as (3, −4).

29.

Category: IES
Skill: Scientific notation | **Level:** Hard

Choice A is correct because the obtained answer is A - II, B - IV, C - III, D - I.

Find the scientific notation of the given decimals .

- Move the decimal point to the right of the first nonzero digit
- Count the number of places you moved the decimal point
- Multiply the decimal number by 10 raised to a power of the number of places you moved the decimal point
- Drop all leading or trailing zeroes
- Write the number in scientific notation as the mantissa multiplied by 10 raised to the power

$0.00004 = 4\times10^{-5}$
$0.00000004 = 4\times10^{-8}$
$0.0004 = 4\times10^{-4}$
$0.0000000004 = 4\times10^{-10}$

Choice B is incorrect because the answers for B and C do not match the scientific notation. **Choice C** is incorrect because the answers for A, B and C do not match the scientific notation. **Choice D** is incorrect because the answers for A-D do not match the scientific notation.

30.

Category: PHM
Skill: Coordinate geometry | **Level:** Medium

Choice G is correct. Since the square and triangle are adjacent, the lengths of the sides of the triangle are also 8 units. Combining the area of the square and triangle, the area of the polygon is,

$$8^2 + \frac{\sqrt{3}}{4}(8)^2 = 64 + 16\sqrt{3}.$$

Choice F is incorrect. Use 4 as the length of the side of the equilateral triangle. **Choice H** is incorrect. Uses the base and height of the equilateral triangles as 8 and 8 to determine an area of 32, then combining it with the area of the square. **Choice J** is incorrect. This may result from calculation error.

31.

Category: PHM
Skill: Two-dimensional shapes | **Level:** Medium

Choice D is correct. The perimeter, *P*, of an equilateral triangle is, *P* = 3*s*. Solving the perimeter in terms of *P* you have $s=\dfrac{P}{3}$. The area, *A*, of an equilateral triangle is, $A=\dfrac{\sqrt{3}}{2}s^2$. Substituting for *s* you get,

$$A=\frac{\sqrt{3}}{2}\left(\frac{P}{3}\right)^2=\frac{\sqrt{3}}{2}\left(\frac{P^2}{9}\right)=\frac{\sqrt{3}}{18}P^2.$$

Choice A is incorrect. The area is written in terms of *s*. **Choice B** is incorrect. The area is written in terms of *s*. **Choice C** is incorrect. The equation is incorrectly written for the perimeter.

32.

Category: PHM
Skill: Two-dimensional shapes | **Level:** Medium

Choice F is correct. One pound = 0.454 kilograms so, 103 pounds = 103 × 0.454 = 46.76 kilograms. At $0.55 per kilograms, 103 pounds costs 46.76 × 0.55 = $25.71.

Choice G is incorrect. May result from using the wrong rate or not converting pounds to kilograms correctly. **Choice H** is incorrect. May result from using the wrong

GO ON TO THE NEXT PAGE.

rate or not converting pounds to kilograms correctly. **Choice J** is incorrect. May result from using the wrong rate or not converting pounds to kilograms correctly.

33.

Category: PHM
Skill: Two-dimensional shapes | **Level:** Easy

Choice B is correct. The sum of the measure of the interior angles in a polygon is $(n-2)\times180^\circ$ where n is the number of sides. A decagon is a 10-sided polygon so, the sum measure of the angles is $(10-2)\times180^\circ = 8\times180^\circ = 1440^\circ$. Since one of the angles measures 55 degrees, the sum of the other 9 angles is, 1440 – 55 = 1385º.
Choice A is incorrect. This is the sum for an octagon.
Choice C is incorrect. This is the sum for a decagon.
Choice D is incorrect. This is the sum for a 12-gon.

34.

Category: PHM
Skill: Series, Sequences and Consecutive numbers |
Level: Difficult

Choice H is correct. The common ratio, r, for geometric sequence is the ratio of a term to it preceding term. So, $r=\frac{\frac{3}{4}}{2}=\frac{3}{4}\times\frac{1}{2}=\frac{3}{8}$. The nth term, a_n, in a geometric sequence is $a_n = a_1\cdot r^{n-1}$, where a_1 is the 1st term in the sequence. So, the 10th term is,

$$a_{10} = 2\cdot\left(\frac{3}{8}\right)^{10-1} = 2\cdot\left(\frac{3}{8}\right)^{9}.$$

Choice F is incorrect. This exchanges the value of a_1 and r. **Choice G** is incorrect. This results in an incorrect formula for the geometric sequence. **Choice J** is incorrect. This results in an incorrect formula for the geometric sequence.

35.

Category: PHM
Skill: Real and Complex number systems |
Level: Medium

Choice C is correct. Let x be the 2nd number, then 4 + x is the 1st number, and 2 + x is the 3rd number. The sum is,

$$(4+x)+x+(2+x)=348$$
$$6+3x=348$$
$$3x=342$$
$$x=114$$

So, the 1st number is 118, the 2nd is 114, and the third is 116.
Choice A is incorrect. The sum of the numbers is 348 but the numbers do not meet the given conditions.
Choice B is incorrect. Their sum is not equal to 348.
Choice D is incorrect. Their sum is not equal to 348.

36.

Category: IES
Skill: Probability | **Level:** Easy

Choice H is correct because the obtained answer is 1.9.

Find the expected value.

$$E(X)=\sum\left(x_i\cdot P(x=x_i)\right)$$
$$E(X)=1(0.3)+2(0.5)+3(0.2)$$
$$E(X)=0.3+1+0.6$$
$$E(X)=1.9$$

Choice F is incorrect because 0.8 is less than the obtained expected value. **Choice G** is incorrect because 1.4 is less than the obtained expected value. **Choice J** is incorrect because 2.7 is greater than the obtained expected value.

37.

Category: IES
Skill: Equations | **Level:** Medium

Choice A is correct. Let n be the number, then $n(n + 7) = 60$. Solving for n,

$$n(n+7)=60$$
$$n^2+7n=60$$
$$n^2+7n-60=0$$
$$(n+12)(n-5)=0$$
$$n+12=0 \text{ or } n-5=0$$
$$n=-12 \text{ or } n=5$$

So, n = –12 is the correct answer choice.
Choice B is incorrect. Incorrectly factor $n^2+7n-60$ to (n – 12) and (n + 5). **Choice C** is incorrect. This may be the result of calculation error. **Choice D** is incorrect. Incorrectly factor $n^2+7n-60$ to (n – 12) and (n + 5).

38.

Category: IES & Modeling
Skill: Sets of numbers | **Level:** Easy

Choice G is correct. To find how many gallons of gas the gas tank can hold, divide the cost to fill the tank by the cost per gallon of gas. So, there are $\frac{36.75}{2.45}=15$ gallons of gas in the gas tank when it is filled. Next, to determine how far Albert can travel in the car before running out of gas, multiply the number of gallons in the gas tank by the miles per gallon the car averages to get, $15 \times 25 = 375$ miles.

Choice F is incorrect. This may result if the gas tank can hold 13.8 gallons of gas. **Choice H** is incorrect. This may result if the gas tank can hold 20 gallons of gas. **Choice J** is incorrect. This may result if the gas tank can hold 29.4 gallons of gas.

39.

Category: IES & Modeling
Skill: Sets of numbers | **Level:** Hard

Choice C is correct because the obtained answer is $\frac{1}{5}$.

Find the probability of being a nursing undergraduate student.

$$P = \frac{number\ of\ favoured\ outcome}{total\ number\ of\ possible\ outcomes}$$

$$P = \frac{12}{31+17+12}$$

$$P = \frac{12}{60}$$

$$P = \frac{1}{5}$$

Choice A is incorrect because $\frac{1}{7}$ is less than the obtained answer. **Choice B** is incorrect because $\frac{2}{3}$ is greater than the obtained answer. **Choice D** is incorrect because $\frac{12}{30}$ is greater than the obtained answer.

40.

Category: PHM
Skill: Real and Complex number systems |
Level: Medium

Choice J is correct.

Let n be the number. Then,

$12 + n^2 = 8n$

$n^2 - 8n + 12 = 0$

$(n - 6)(n - 2) = 0$

$n = 6$ or $n = 2$

Choice J is the only correct answer choice.
Choice F is incorrect. Incorrectly uses factors of $(n + 6)(n + 2)$. **Choice G** is incorrect. Incorrectly uses factors of $(n + 6)(n + 2)$. **Choice H** is incorrect.Incorrectly uses factors of $(n - 4)(n - 3)$.

41.

Category: PHM
Skill: Real and Complex number systems | **Level:** Easy

Choice D is correct. If $x > 0$, it must be positive. If $y < 0$, it must be negative. A positive number times a negative number is a negative number.

Choice A is incorrect. You are combining a negative and a negative number which yields a negative number. **Choice B** is incorrect. You are combining a negative and a negative number which yields a negative number. **Choice C** is incorrect. $\frac{y}{x}$ yields a proper fraction since $x > y$.

42.

Category: PHM
Skill: Sets of numbers | **Level:** Difficult

Choice J is correct. The sum of the first 7 numbers in the set is $24 \times 7 = 168$. Adding another number, n, to the set changes the mean to 27 so,

$$\frac{168+x}{8} = 27$$

$$168 + x = 216$$

$$x = 48$$

Choice F is incorrect. This is the difference between the new and original mean. **Choice G** is incorrect. This is the original mean. **Choice H** is incorrect. This is the new mean.

43.

Category: IES & Modeling
Skill: Three-dimensional shapes | **Level:** Hard

Choice C is correct because the obtained is 24.
Find the volume of each rectangular prism.

$$V_{small} = rst$$

$$V_{large} = 3r(2s)(4t)$$

$$V_{large} = 24rst$$

Hence, there are 24 small rectangular prisms in one large rectangular prism.
Choice A is incorrect because 12 is less than the obtained number of small prisms. **Choice B** is incorrect because 18 is less than the obtained number of small prisms. **Choice D** is incorrect because 36 is greater than the obtained number of small prisms.

GO ON TO THE NEXT PAGE.

44.

Category: PHM
Skill: Function Evaluation | **Level:** Medium

Choice J is correct. Substituting A = 24,000 and using logarithms to find the time, t,

$$24,000 = 1200(1+0.08)^t$$
$$20 = (1+0.08)^t$$
$$\ln 20 = \ln 1.08^t$$
$$\ln 20 = t \ln 1.08$$
$$t = \frac{\ln 20}{\ln 1.08}$$
$$t = 38.93$$

So, it takes about 39 years for the investment to have a value of $24,000.

Choice F is incorrect because it results from incorrectly dividing the growth ratio (20) by the growth factor (1.08), which is not a valid method for solving exponential equations. Time in exponential growth must be solved using logarithms. **Choice G** is incorrect because it assumes linear growth instead of exponential growth. While 24000 is 20 times the initial investment, this does not account for the compounding nature of exponential growth over time. **Choice H** is incorrect because it likely comes from dividing the final amount by a miscalculated or irrelevant value (such as 960). This ignores the exponential model and applies incorrect arithmetic reasoning to estimate time.

45.

Category: IES
Skill: Probability | **Level:** Hard

Choice C is correct because an additional of 18 red marbles is needed to have a probability of randomly drawing a red marble is $\frac{3}{5}$.

Find the total number of marbles.

12 red + 5 yellow + 15 green = 32 marbles

Find the additional number of red marbles if the probability of drawing red is $\frac{3}{5}$.

Set up the equation. Let x be the additional red marbles.

$$Probability = \frac{3}{5} = \frac{12\,red\,marbles + x}{32\,marbles + x}$$
$$\frac{3}{5} = \frac{12 + x}{32 + x}$$
$$5(12 + x) = 3(32 + x)$$
$$60 + 5x = 96 + 3x$$
$$5x - 3x = 96 - 60$$
$$2x = 36$$
$$x = 18$$

Choice A is incorrect because 15 is less than the obtained value. **Choice B** is incorrect because 16 is less than the obtained value. **Choice D** is incorrect because 20 is greater than the obtained value.

END OF TEST 2

This page is intentionally left blank

www.ingramcontent.com/pod-product-compliance
Lightning Source LLC
Chambersburg PA
CBHW080129270326
41926CB00021B/4404

* 9 7 8 1 6 3 6 5 1 5 0 5 2 *